*The Religious Roots
of Rebellion*

The Religious Roots of Rebellion

Christians in Central American Revolutions

Phillip Berryman

ORBIS BOOKS
Maryknoll, New York 10545

The Catholic Foreign Mission Society of America (Maryknoll) recruits and trains people for overseas missionary service. Through Orbis Books Maryknoll aims to foster the international dialogue that is essential to mission. The books published, however, reflect the opinions of their authors and are not meant to represent the official position of the society.

Manuscript editor: Lisa McGaw

Library of Congress Cataloging in Publication Data

Berryman, Phillip.
  The religious roots of rebellion

  Bibliography: p.
  Includes index.
  1. Christians—Central America—Political activity.
2. Revolutions—Central America. 3. Central America—
Social conditions. 4. Central America—Economic
conditions—1979-   . 5. Central America—Politics
and government—1979-   . I. Title.
BR620.B47   1984   261.7'098   83-19343
ISBN 0-88344-105-5 (pbk.)

Contents

v

Acronyms

ACLEN	Asociación del Clero Nicaragüense (Nicaraguan Clergy Association)
AFL-CIO	American Federation of Labor-Congress of Industrial Organizations (United States)
A.I.D.	*see* U.S.A.I.D.
AIFLD	American Institute for Free Labor Development (AFL-CIO organizing arm in Latin America)
AMNLAE	Asociación de Mujeres Nicaragüenses Luisa Amanda Espinosa (Luisa Amanda Espinosa Association of Nicaraguan Women)
AMPRONAC	Asociación de Mujeres ante la Problemática Nacional (Association of Women to Deal with National Problems; Nicaragua)
ANACAFE	Asociación Nacional del Café (National Coffee Association; Guatemala)
ANDES	Asociación Nacional de Educadores Salvadoreños (National Association of Educators of El Salvador)
ANEP	Asociación Nacional de la Empresa Privada (National Private Sector Association; El Salvador—private-sector umbrella organization)
ATC	Asociación de Trabajadores del Campo (Association of Rural Workers; Nicaragua)
BPR	Bloque Popular Revolucionario (Revolutionary People's Bloc; El Salvador)
CACIF	Cámara de Agricultura, Comercio, Industria y Finanzas (Chamber of Agriculture, Trade, Industry and Finance; Guatemala—private-sector umbrella organization)
CACM	Central American Common Market
CAN	Central Auténtica Nacionalista (Authentic Nationalist Headquarters; party of General Carlos Arana Osorio, former president of Guatemala)
CAR	*Central America Report*
CAV	Centro Antonio Valdivieso (Antonio Valdivieso Center; Nicaragua—study and reflection center for Christians engaged in the revolutionary process; named for sixteenth-century bishop who was killed for his defense of the Indians)

CDP	Coordinadora de Pobladores (Shantytown Dwellers Coordinating Committee; Guatemala)
CDS	Comités de Defensa Sandinista (Sandinista Defense Committees; Nicargaua)
CEDIAL	Centro de Estudios para el Desarrollo y la Integración de América Latina (Research Center for the Development and Integration of Latin America; headquarters in Bogotá, Colombia)
CEHILA	Centro de Estudios de la Historia de la Iglesia en América Latina (Center for Studies of the History of the Church in Latin America; Mexico City)
CELAM	Consejo Episcopal Latinoamericano (Latin American Episcopal Council; umbrella organization uniting Bishops Conferences of individual countries; headquarters in Bogotá, Colombia)
CEPA	Centro de Educación y Promoción Agrícola (Center for Rural Education and Development; Nicaragua—training center for peasant leaders)
CEPAD	Comité Evangelico Pro-Ayuda y Desarrollo (Protestant Committee for Aid and Development; Nicaragua—ecumenical organization)
CESPROP	Centro de Estudios y Promoción Popular (Center for Research and Popular Development; El Salvador)
CGUP	Comité Guatemalteco de Unidad Popular (Guatemalan Committee for Patriotic Unity)
CIA	Central Intelligence Agency (United States)
CISPES	Committee in Solidarity with the People of El Salvador
CLAR	Confederación Latinoamericana de Religiosos (Latin American Conference of Religious Orders)
CLAT	Confederación Latinoamericana de Trabajadores (Latin American Trade Union Confederation; headquarters in Caracas, Venezuela—international labor organization, originally Christian Democratic)
CNT	Central Nacional de Trabajadores (National Workers Federation; Guatemala)
CNUS	Comité Nacional de Unidad Sindical (National Committee for Labor Unity; Guatemala)
CONDECA	Consejo de Defensa Centroamericano (Central American Defense Council)
CONFER	Confederación de Religiosos (Confederation of Religious; Nicaragua)
CONFREGUA	Conferencia de Religiosos de Guatemala (Conference of Religious of Guatemala)
CONIP	Consejo Nacional de la Iglesia Popular (National Council of the People's Church; El Salvador)

COPEFA	Consejo Permanente de la Fuerza Armada (Permanent Council of the Armed Forces; El Salvador)
COSDEGUA	Confederación de Sacerdotes Diocesanos de Guatemala (National Council of Diocesan Priests of Guatemala)
COSEP	Consejo Superior de la Empresa Privada (Higher Council of Private Enterprise; Nicaragua—private-sector umbrella organization)
CRIE	Centro Regional de Informaciones Ecuménicas (Regional Center for Ecumenical Information; headquarters in Mexico City; publishes bulletin also called *CRIE*)
CRISOL	Cristianos Solidarios (Christians in Solidarity; Nicaragua)
CRM	Coordinadora Revolucionaria de Masas (Revolutionary Coordinating Body of Mass Organizations; El Salvador)
CROS	Comité de Reorganización Obrera de El Salvador (Committee for Labor Reorganization of El Salvador)
CST	Central Sandinista de Trabajadores (Sandinista Labor Federation; Nicaragua)
CTN	Confederación de Trabajadores de Nicaragua (Confederation of Workers of Nicaragua)
CUC	Comité de Unidad Campesina (Committee for Peasant Unity; Guatemala)
DEI	Departamento Ecuménico de Investigaciones (Ecumenical Research Department; headquarters in San José, Costa Rica)
ECA	*Estudios Centroamericanos (Central American Studies*; published by UCA in El Salvador)
EGP	Ejército Guerrillero de los Pobres (Poor People's Guerrilla Army; Guatemala)
ERP	Ejército Revolucionario del Pueblo (People's Revolutionary Army; El Salvador)
ESA	Ejército Secreto Anticomunista (Secret Anticommunist Army; Guatemala)
FAPU	Frente de Acción Popular Unificado (United Popular Action Front; El Salvador)
FAO	Frente Amplio de Oposición (Broad Opposition Front; Nicaragua)
FAR	Fuerzas Armadas Rebeldes (Rebel Armed Forces; Guatemala)
FARN	Fuerzas Armadas de Resistencia Nacional (Armed Forces of National Resistance; El Salvador)
FARO	Frente Agrícola de la Región Oriental (Agricultural Front of the Eastern Region; El Salvador)
FDCR	Frente Democrático Contra la Represión (Democratic Front against Repression; Guatemala)

FDR	Frente Democrático Revolucionario (Revolutionary Democratic Front; El Salvador)
FECCAS*	Federación Cristiana de Campesinos de El Salvador (Christian Federation of Peasants of El Salvador)
FER	Frente Estudiantil Revolucionario (Revolutionary Student Federation; Nicaragua)
FERG	Frente Estudiantil Revolucionario Robin García (Robin García Revolutionary Student Front; Guatemala)
FMLN	Frente Farabundo Martí para la Liberación Nacional (Farabundo Martí National Liberation Front; El Salvador)
FPL	Fuerzas Populares de Liberación (Popular Liberation Forces; El Salvador)
FP-31	Frente Popular 31 de Enero (January 31 Popular Front; Guatemala)
FSLN	Frente Sandinista de Liberación Nacional (Sandinista National Liberation Front; Nicaragua)
FTG	Federación de Trabajadores de Guatemala (Federation of Workers of Guatemala)
FUR	Frente Unido de la Revolución (United Revolutionary Front; Guatemala)
GNP	Gross National Product
IDESAC	Instituto para el Desarrollo Económico y Social de América Central (Institute for Economic and Social Development of Central America; headquarters in Guatemala)
IHCA	Instituto Histórico Centroamericano (Central American Historical Institute; Nicaragua)
INPRUHU	Instituto para la Promoción Humana (Institute for Human Promotion; Nicaragua)
IRD	Institute for Religion and Democracy (Washington, D.C.)
ISAL	Iglesia y Sociedad en América Latina (Church and Society in Latin America)
LP-28	Ligas Populares 28 de Febrero (February 28 Popular Leagues; El Salvador)
MDN	Movimiento Democrático Nicaragüense (Nicaraguan Democratic Movement)
MIPTES	Movimiento Independiente de Profesionales y Técnicos de El Salvador (Independent Movement of Professionals and Technicians of El Salvador)
MLN	Movimiento de Liberación Nacional (National Liberation Movement; Guatemalan political party)
MNR	Movimiento Nacional Revolucionario (National Revolutionary Movement; El Salvador)

*Federated since 1976, FECCAS and UTC often use the combined form: FECCAS-UTC.

NACLA	North American Congress on Latin America (New York)
NOR	Nucleos Obreros Revolucionarios (Revolutionary Workers Cells; Guatemala)
OAS	Organization of American States
ORDEN	Organización Democrática Nacionalista (Democratic Nationalist Organization; El Salvador—paramilitary organization)
ORIT	Organización Regional Interamericana de Trabajadores (Inter-American Regional Workers Organization)
ORPA	Organización Pueblo en Armas (People-in-Arms Organization; Guatemala—guerrilla group)
PCN	Partido de Conciliación Nacional (National Conciliation Party; El Salvador)
PCS	Partido Comunista de El Salvador (Communist Party of El Salvador
PGT	Partido Guatemalteco del Trabajo (Guatemalan Workers Party; communist)
PID	Partido Institucional Democrático (Institutional Democratic Party; Guatemala)
PR	Partido Revolucionario (Revolutionary Party; Guatemala)
PRI	Partido Revolucionario Institucional (Institutional Revolutionary Party; Mexico)
PRUD	Partido Revolucionario de Unificación Democrática (Revolutionary Party of Democratic Unification; El Salvador)
PSD	Partido Social Demócrata (Social Democratic Party; Guatemala)
RIPEN	Retiro Interdenominacional de Pastores Evangélicos de Nicaragua (Interdenominational Retreat for Nicaraguan Protestant Pastors)
UCA	Universidad Centroamericana (Central American University; name of Jesuit-run universities in both Nicaragua and El Salvador; the full name in the latter country is Universidad Centroamericana José Simeón Cañas)
UCS	Unión Comunal Salvadoreña (Communal Union of El Salvador)
UDEL	Unión Democrática de Liberación (Democratic Union for Liberation; Nicaragua)
UDN	Unión Democrática Nacional (National Democratic Union; El Salvador—political party)
UGB	Unión Guerrera Blanca (White Warriors Union; El Salvador—paramilitary group)
UNO	Unión Nacional Opositora (National Opposition Union; El Salvador—political coalition)

URNG   Unidad Revolucionaria Nacional Guatemalteca (Guatema-
            lan National Revolutionary Unity; organization of guer-
            rilla groups)
U.S.A.I.D. United States Agency for International Development
UTC*   Unión de Trabajadores del Campo (Union of Rural
            Workers; El Salvador)

*Federated since 1976, FECCAS and UTC often use the combined form: FECCAS-UTC.

Introduction

There is no need to justify the topic: Christian involvement in revolutionary movements in Nicaragua, El Salvador, and Guatemala is something new and unprecedented. Historically the churches have opposed revolutions and only reluctantly have they submitted to revolutionary governments as de facto realities. While there has been Christian-Marxist dialogue in recent years, and a convergence of Christians and Marxists in Latin America (in the Christians for Socialism Movement, for example), it is in Central America that for the first time Christians have been significant actors in Marxist-led revolutionary movements that have taken power or may well take power.

This book attempts to describe and explain how this process has occurred and to reflect on the issues it raises. Roughly half the book is a fairly detailed chronological account of how Christians became involved in revolutions in Nicaragua, El Salvador, and Guatemala and might be considered as a series of case studies in political science. However, the exercise as a whole might best be considered a species of interdisciplinary practical theology.

This book is being written with several audiences in mind. First are Christians who are concerned about what has been happening in Central America. Many have worked ardently to oppose what they see as mistaken United States intervention there. In addition, it is not too early for those in leadership and opinion-making roles in the church (hierarchy, theologians, media) to begin to see the issues raised in Central America in their complexity, magnitude, and possible further consequences.

There are yet other potential readers who, although they may not regard themselves as believers, may find the topic important, either out of their own involvement in struggles for social change or out of a desire to understand this somewhat surprising phenomenon.

Yet another group of readers would be those clearly and actively opposed to this new phenomenon. In the first place there is a growing "neoconservative" tendency among church people in the United States. All indications are that the 1980s will continue to see major public controversy in and around the churches over capitalism, socialism, revolution, and the proper role of the churches in the political sphere. Additionally, policymakers in the United States government and in the "intelligence community" should diligently study the material assembled here. For all the millions of dollars they spend, they show themselves systematically unintelligent when faced with popular movements, their lack of understanding deriving from a basic bias that impedes them from seeing ordinary peo-

1

ple, the poor, as real social actors. Although such readers will not find much new material here that they could not find by a diligent search of their files—I have screened any information that could lead to the identification of persons—I would hope that reading this book would lead them to understand better the depth of these movements and hence to be more cautious in their attempts to suppress them.

By now it should be evident that I am not a partisan of "value-free" social science. Rather than attempting to bracket my own sympathies I propose to incorporate them into this enterprise. I believe my close involvement with the struggles of church people has put me into a privileged position for understanding them. Although my basic sympathy and commitment is with the poor in Central America and those groups struggling for change, I am under no less obligation to assemble the relevant data (and not to exclude data that may run counter to my position), to arrange them in a coherent order, arrive at plausible explanations, and submit the results to verification or modification in public discussion. In other words, I do not argue for any less rigor than those who advocate a "value-free" approach; rather, I view the relationship between personal involvement and research in a different way.

This book, while it is in no sense autobiographical, represents a summation of much of my work thus far. More remotely, I worked as a priest in Panama City (1965–73) and came to know the Latin American church during the period of Medellín (the Second General Conference of Latin American Bishops, held in Medellín, Colombia in 1968), and the emergence of liberation theology and "basic Christian communities." More recently my wife, Angela, and I served as Central American representatives for the American Friends Service Committee. Arriving in Guatemala in the aftermath of the 1976 earthquake we were witnesses to the intensification of struggles in Nicaragua, El Salvador, and Guatemala during the next four years. Our work included grassroots involvement with Indian peasants, collaboration with social-change groups, and the preparation of reports and audiovisuals on many aspects of events in Central America (for example, I prepared detailed reports on political violence in Guatemala starting in 1977).

Violent death looms large in my recollections of those years: from Bill Woods, the Maryknoll priest whom we saw shortly before he was killed in a mysterious plane crash (probably shot down by the army); to the town of Comalapa, where we assisted in a post-earthquake project and which the army brought under military occupation in 1980, kidnapping and killing the town leaders; to Archbishop Romero, whose last Sunday Mass I attended; to Enrique Alvarez and Juan Chacón, Salvadoran leaders murdered in late 1980. I could easily fill pages with a martyrology.

Yet around each death there was an affirmation of life and each funeral became a defiant act of faith in the resurrection, not only in an afterlife but a conviction that these martyrs would rise in their people, as Archbishop Romero said of himself.

In a modest way this book is a tribute to those martyrs, and although its tone is one of exposition, I intend it as a contribution to the cause for which they died.

I am convinced that important issues are at stake in Central America. Most immediate and obvious for Americans is the role of the United States in its efforts to stop revolutionary movements by bankrolling the Salvadoran military, attempting to destabilize the Nicaraguan revolution, and in general by orchestrating a regionalization of the conflict.

At a somewhat less obvious level, Central America raises questions of wider import. For example, it is sometimes asserted that Nicaragua is heading toward totalitarianism because it has not held national elections. I would submit that to the extent that we pursue the root meaning of "democracy" (Greek *demos* "people," and *kratos* "power" or "rule") we shall be led not only to question a facile identification of elections with democracy—even when, as in El Salvador and Guatemala, they are used precisely to thwart the people's will—but to examine the extent to which the United States's own institutions are really democratic. Similarly, theological themes emerging from Central America—for example, the role of the church in the political sphere, and politico-economic "idolatry"—should bring Americans to confront their own theologies.

Some of the shortcomings of the present account should be mentioned. While it emerges from personal experience, it is largely an exposition of information that is publicly available or was gathered in interviews. It is highly concentrated in the Roman Catholic experience, in part because of the Catholic church's preponderant role. Since the major public protagonists have been largely male, the full importance of women (at grassroots and middle-level leadership positions) is not conveyed. Much of the story will have to wait until it is possible to gather information systematically from many different locales.

The outline is simple. The opening chapter on the Christian community at Solentiname, Nicaragua, gives a sampling in the people's own words of the theological vision underlying the struggle. The next two, brief chapters deal with the Latin American and Central American backgrounds. Thereupon follow accounts in some detail of Christian involvement in the struggles in Nicaragua, El Salvador, and Guatemala and comparisons between the different countries (chapters 4 through 7); similarly there is an account of the first two and a half years of the Sandinista period in Nicaragua (chapter 8). Finally, the emerging issues are systematically outlined under the rubrics of ethics, ecclesiology, and theology proper (chapters 9 through 11). A brief epilogue offers some reflections on the import of these issues for the United States.

Many individuals contributed to this book with their encouragement, helpful criticism, and corrections, and to all of them I express my gratitude. Maryknoll's Walsh-Price Fellowship helped make this project possible. I especially wish to thank my wife, Angela, and our daughters Catherine, Margaret, and Elizabeth for their patience and loving support.

PART ONE

THE BACKGROUND

1

Prelude in Solentiname

Some examples of Christian participation in Central American struggles are dramatic and have been made well known through the media: in El Salvador, Archbishop Romero; and in the same country, four American church women, who were martyred; in Nicaragua, clergy in the Sandinista government. The most important fact of participation, however, is the least documented: the strong grassroots connection between Christianity and revolution. Large numbers of Christians in Central America, especially peasants, have come to reinterpret their lives based on a new understanding of the Christian gospel. They have frequently then joined militant organizations.

This is not a spontaneous process but the result of pastoral work with peasants and the poor. The setting is the *comunidad de base*, the "basic Christian community," in a village or barrio (see pp. 21 ff.). This process is unperceived from the outside, and the worship meetings and Bible discussions go unrecorded. Without some sense of what happens at the grassroots community level, however, it is impossible to have a real understanding of other aspects.

THE SOLENTINAME COMMUNITY

One way of getting a glimpse into such communities is to examine *The Gospel in Solentiname*,[1] the transcription made of Gospel discussions in a fishing and peasant community on an island of the Solentiname archipelago in Lake Nicaragua during the mid-1970s. Solentiname was not a "typical" basic Christian community inasmuch as it was started by Ernesto Cardenal, a priest and poet, and later Nicaragua's minister of culture. However, having participated in many such discussions, this writer can testify that those in Solentiname are surprisingly similar in both style and content to such dialogues in ordinary circumstances.

In January 1966 Ernesto Cardenal and a small group of friends moved to the island of Solentiname in the archipelago toward the southern end of

Lake Nicaragua, near the Costa Rican border. They originally intended to live in a contemplative/artistic community, and only gradually did they change their focus, becoming more involved with the inhabitants of the island.[2]

The project was largely an outgrowth of Cardenal's earlier life. Born in Granada, Nicaragua, in 1925, he became a member of a new generation of young poets in the late 1940s, in a land that produced Rubén Darío, one of the greatest Spanish-language poets. Like many other young Nicaraguans, Cardenal participated in an anti-Somoza uprising in 1954, which failed. Subsequently he joined the Trappists (the order known for its practice of silence) at Gethsemane in Kentucky, where Thomas Merton was his novice master. The germ of the idea of the Solentiname community is said to have come from Merton, who expressed to Cardenal his vision of a new kind of monastic life. Together the two shared the dream of a community in Latin America. When he had to leave Gethsemane for health reasons, Cardenal spent two years in Cuernavaca, Mexico, and then studied theology in Colombia, being ordained a priest in August 1965. By this time the ideas for the community had ripened, although Merton in the end did not participate.

At the core of the new community were Ernesto Cardenal; William Agudelo, a Colombian poet; Agudelo's wife, Teresita, and their children. They chose the island of Solentiname, no doubt because of its beauty and remoteness; it can be reached from Managua only with a journey of several hours by car and boat. The inhabitants at the time numbered about 1,000 people, scattered throughout the islands, engaged in subsistence farming and fishing. The newcomers' original intention was to become self-sufficient themselves through farming and some craftwork.

Only gradually did they enter into deeper contact with the island people. During 1967, in response to them, Cardenal and his friends began a more systematic pastoral work, borrowing for the purpose the course titled "The Family of God," which had been used in a basic Christian community in Managua by Father José de la Jara (who in turn had borrowed it from the work in San Miguelito, Panama city).[3]

With the help of de la Jara and others from his parish, Cardenal organized Family-of-God discussion groups, the great merit of which was their Socratic method, which enabled people to bring out from within themselves feelings and perceptions about basic life-realities such as justice/injustice, work, sex/love/marriage, family, sickness, death, the fulfillment of life and of the universe—and to connect these with portions of the Scripture. While these discussions served to enhance a sense of community among the participants and to affirm their dignity—as "the family of God," brothers and sisters, with Christ their Brother—they tended to see the community as very local and to ignore the larger social and structural aspects of people's lives. "It was all very beautiful," said William Agudelo, looking back on this stage of "catechesis," "but it didn't lead to any commitment." At about this period, roughly 1970, de la Jara's parish was itself undergoing a similar questioning process (see chapter 5).

Gradually the process of dialogue was broadened and more explicitly social and political dimensions were brought in. A group of young men, Laureano, Elvis, Donald, and Alejandro, became members of the community. Some young people began to present sociodramas in the islands in order to raise consciousness of national problems and their root causes. Having begun as an attempt in some ways to repudiate Somocista society and to escape from it, the Solentiname community became a focal point of resistance to it. In 1970 Ernesto went to Cuba and on his return spoke of it and wrote *In Cuba*. He had some contacts with the Frente Sandinista (FSLN), including Carlos Fonseca Amador, who is today venerated as its chief founder and greatest fallen hero.

THE GOSPEL IN SOLENTINAME

What has been preserved of the dialogue process is a series of Gospel discussions recorded during 1971–76, transcribed and lightly edited by Cardenal. They are thus a partial record of what happened at Solentiname. One supposes that the most important dialogue is that which occurred throughout the week as the islanders and the community engaged in their normal work and contact, and that these Sunday discussions are more a celebration of, and meditation on, their life together. Since Cardenal has rearranged the discussions so they do not follow the order in which they occurred, there is little indication of how a growth in awareness took place.

Each dialogue is a commentary on the weekly Gospel. Usually the setting is the chapel on Solentiname, but occasionally it is another island. The presence of the lake, whether calm or stormy, is usually felt. Often enough the Mass takes place after a meal of beans and rice, or fish from the lake, or perhaps roast pig. Someone reads the Gospel selection as a whole and then it is commented on by verses or sections.

Some of the participants stand out: Tomás Peña, the oldest, exudes common sense and wisdom. Olivia, the mother of seven children, "is the most theological." Marcelino has a mystical vision in which he weaves together diverse strands of the biblical symbols and the people's experience. Pancho indignantly resists anything that sounds like a political interpretation. Others have their particular angles from which they view everything: Laureano (revolution), Elvis (the society of the future), Julio Mairena (equality), Óscar (unity).[4] Some of the participants have come from outside to visit the Solentiname community, living there for some time or simply visiting. These vary from young Latin American revolutionaries to poets, journalists, relatives of Ernesto, and members of Nicaragua's elite.

In an easy way the participants find parallels between their lives and what they hear in the Gospel; for example, the fish in the miraculous catch are of the same kinds as those in their lake. Events on the island flow into the discussion in surprising ways. Thus the narrative of Jesus calming the sea is discussed three days after Ivan, Bosco, and their mother capsized in the middle of the lake, where they had to wait two hours to be rescued. Recalling her fright once more, Doña Chalía weeps during the discussion (2:182–83*). It is suggested that John the Baptist's fame is like that of a local *curandero* (folk doctor) named Nando.

On virtually every page parallels are drawn between the Gospels and the political realities of Nicaragua: the manna that perished is like the grains that Somoza gives away (3:55); Old Testament judges were "liberating chieftains," *caudillos* (4:59); the Herods are like the Somozas (1:61; 2:6); Jesus is born in an atmosphere of terror and repression (Herod and the Magi) (1:62); the young Jesus speaking with the scribes and Pharisees is doing *concientización* (1:95–100), and his programmatic announcement in Luke 4:16–30 is called his "first political manifesto" (1:131); Satan tempts Jesus to a "developmentalistic" or imperialistic messianism. Like a dictator (that is, Somoza), the devil "knows how to make propaganda." Jesus has to explain the parables "clandestinely"; for example, the man with the water jug is understood not as a miracle but as a kind of secret signal, and Judas' betrayal consists in revealing the hideout, Gethsemane (4:122). Pilate is like the "gringo ambassador" in Nicaragua, and one of the participants makes him speak with the pigdin Spanish attributed to such an ambassador: "Me not know nothin', . . . Me innocent" (4:229). Jesus before the Sanhedrin is like Tomás Borge, the Sandinista leader, who had been put on trial (4:202); the Roman soldiers are like Somoza's National Guard (4:233) or like Green Berets (2:193).

There is an extensive comparison between the death of Jesus and that of Sandino (murdered by Somoza's National Guard; see chapter 4): both were betrayed and both realized their deaths would lead to liberation (4:186–211). Parallels are drawn with a young revolutionary, David Tejada, who was killed in prison on Good Friday, while Managua celebrated Holy Week (4:244).

Very often Cardenal employs a kind of relaxed demythologization, not to draw attention to itself but, rather, to clear away possible points of distraction from the central focus. For example:

> We can't know the details of what happened on the lake because the stories were modified by the readings of the first communities. Undoubtedly something once happened with Jesus on the lake, in a boat. There are very realistic details that were engraved on the memory of a witness: the fact that Jesus was asleep in the stern with his head on a pillow (maybe just some rope), and the fact that there were other boats crossing. There may have been a squall. He may have calmed their great fright. But this dramatic story of the storm stopped in an instant was created for a frightened little community, and the words of Jesus are meant to take away their fear. They are no less now for us, and this is

---

*References in this section are to volume and page number of *The Gospel in Solentiname* (See n. 1, above).

what is important in this gospel—not what happened once on a stormy lake in Galilee [2:188].

Of Matthew's infancy narrative he says that the magi were like philosophers or scientists, that the star may have been like Kohoutek or even just a figure of speech and that "possibly this whole passage from Matthew is fiction, an imaginary narrative, that he chose to insert here. But it could have happened this way" (referring to Herod's actions) (1:62). When he says the manna may be a white substance that comes from the tamarisk tree and is still eaten by Bedouins, he does so in order to emphasize Jesus' message that there is no such bread come down from heaven: "The only bread that comes from heaven is the word of love" (3:58). Psychologizing approaches are also used, such as hinting that the multiplication of the loaves occurred through sharing what little the disciples had (2:152–53).

There is a generally freewheeling quality about the dialogues:

> NATALIA: "Then they abandoned their belongings. Yes, they left the boats right there and the nets."
>
> RODOLFO: "Probably a rotten boat like the one that belongs to the Cooperative."
>
> NATALIA: "They were poor, but they had their few things. The way poor people do. And they left their things right there and followed Jesus."
>
> DOÑA ÁNGELA: "They let themselves be caught by him." Another of the boys said: "That was the miraculous catch, and not the haddock and shad and mojarras and all the other different fish they caught with the net. And they caught us and that's why we're gathered here. . . ."
>
> MARCELINO: "Because they left their belongings right there, the word of God came to these islands. Perhaps later we can carry the word to the other side of the lake too. To Papaturro, or maybe San Carlos, San Miguelito . . ." [1:147–48].

This passage exemplifies the ease with which the people move from the biblical world to their own. Similarly the following dialogue seems to wander far from its starting point in a discussion on the slaughter of the innocents:

> ELVIS: "The importance of the birth of Christ is that it was the birth of the Revolution, right? There are many people who are afraid of the word as they were afraid of Christ because he was coming to change the world. From then on the Revolution has been growing. It keeps growing little by little . . . and nobody can stop it."
>
> [CARDENAL]: "And it has to grow here also, doesn't it?"
>
> PANCHO: "We have to get rid of selfishness and do what Christ said, and go on with the Revolution, as you socialists say. I'm not a socialist,

I'm not a revolutionary. I like to hear the talk and grasp what I can but really I'm nothing. Although I *would* like to see a change in Nicaragua.''

MANUEL: "But if there's going to be a change you have to cooperate with it. . . .''

PANCHO: "But how do you do it! I'd like somebody to tell me: 'That's the way it's going to be done.' But you can't! When we rise up they kill us.''

ALEJANDRO: "But look, they killed him too.''

PANCHO: "Correct, but he was Christ and we're never going to compare ourselves with him.''

MANUEL: "But I heard there have been other men, like Che, who also have died for freedom.''

PANCHO: "Right. You can die, you, and tomorrow we'll all be dancing and we'll never think that you died for us.''

WILLIAM: "Then you think that those deaths are useless?''

PANCHO: "They're useless. Or they're almost useless!''

YOUNG MYRIAM: "I say that when there's someone who will free our country there will be another Christ.''

[Ernesto's] brother FERNANDO (to Pancho): "When you say 'What can I do? Nothing!' I agree with you. But when you ask another 'What can *we* do?' I would say everything. And that day when you ask each other 'What do we do?' you'll already know what you are going to do. And the people all united are the same Jesus that you see in this manger scene, against whom Herod couldn't do a thing" (Fernando pointed to the clay manger scene, made by Mariíta, that we had put at the foot of the altar during this Christmas season.) [1:77–79].

Through discussion the people move to a more complex view of the Gospel. At first Jesus' statement "I have not come to bring peace but a sword" seems to clash with their previous understanding. Óscar says he is puzzled, because Jesus came to bring union: "Why does it say here that he is a cause of division. He's supposed to be love!" Distinguishing the peace of conformity from true peace, the people conclude that only when oppression is overcome will there be true peace, even for a quiet and happy community like Solentiname. And Óscar says: "Ah, now I understand. What Jesus brought was unity for some but not for all. For some—those who are on the side of love. He's the cause of division because he's the cause of unity" (1:260, 262).

Cardenal is more than a neutral facilitator. Both he and the other outsiders bring their own viewpoint and they leave their imprint. But the dialogue goes both ways and he insists that the peasants' commentaries are deeper than those of many theologians—not surprising, he says, since the Gospel was written for them, the poor, and by people like them. At one point the text on the "sin against the Holy Spirit" comes up. Cardenal's two cousins, Xavier and Silvia, ask what the Holy Spirit is.

There is silence until Marcelino speaks:

I've heard in the Creed that the Holy Spirit proceeds from the Father and the Son. I've also read in a catechism that I have at home that the Holy Spirit is God the same as the Father and the Son. Now, we know that God is love. What is it that proceeds from God and is also God? It has to be love. But if it proceeds it has to go somewhere. Where? To us. Then that is the Spirit of love that comes to us. What for? To stay there? No, to proceed also from us out to others. The Holy Spirit is, then, the same as the Spirit of unity and love among us. Even though people reject Christ, if they love others they are saved. But if they refuse to love others, they won't be saved in this world or in the other.

And Alvaro says: "It's wonderful how you get so many reflections and such wise ones, like those of the fathers of the church" (2:35). Cardenal frequently tells the people they have shed light on texts that scripture scholars could not explain.

Throughout *The Gospel in Solentiname* runs a religious vision with its own characteristic accents. More than a particular doctrinal point, or even a leitmotiv, is the constant reading of the Gospel from the viewpoint of the poor. To take a few from a multitude of examples: Olivia says of Jesus, "The truth is that ever since he was at his mother's breast he had the rich against him" (1:68). And old Tomás Peña says that the angel congratulates Mary "because she's going to be the mother of the Messiah and he congratulates all of us because . . . the savior is not going to be born among the rich but right among us, the poor people" (1:14); the rich do not realize that what they have has come to them through the poor. The poor should organize to confront the rich:

> . . . Because we go right on being like that, with somebody's foot on our neck. And the rich, how do they look at us? They look down on us.
> That's why we've got to get together to win. Or even all be a single revolutionary. Like Christ. He was the greatest revolutionary, because being God he identified with the poor and he came down from heaven to become a member of the lower class and he gave his life for us all.
> The way I see it, we all ought to struggle like that for other people and be like him. . . . And nobody will have to go on being humiliated by the rich [1:48].

Olivia says, "The rich and the poor will be liberated. Us poor people are going to be liberated from the rich. The rich are going to be liberated from themselves, that is, from their wealth. Because they're more slaves than we are" (1:14). This last point is made more than once. A discussion on the Beatitudes touches the familiar theme of inner conversion and outward behavior.

> ALEJANDRO: ". . . And we're sure that the kingdom will have to be estabished with the poor, right?"

PANCHO: "With everybody that shares the love, because if there are rich people that share the love, they too can enter the kingdom."

MARIÍTA: "But a rich person that shares love has to share his goods too. That's how he shows that he shares love. Because if he says he has love and doesn't share his goods, how are we going to believe him?"

REBECA: "But it's all the same. Some of us, even though we're poor, we don't inherit the kingdom of God either. If we're poor and don't have love. . . ."

ÓSCAR: "I think we have to be clear about this. You either love God or you love money. You decide to make money? Well, go love your money, that's your god. Somebody else loves God? He shares his money and is poor . . ." [1:174–75].

While it would be possible to summarize the Solentiname religious vision by arranging texts in a traditional (God-Christ-Spirit-Church-Last Things-Ethics) order, it seems that an order that starts with practice will bring out more clearly the real center of gravity.

Frequently the conventional practice of religion is contrasted with the practice of love. One woman comments:

. . . we can be in a church singing day and night tra-la-la-la, and it doesn't matter to us that there are so many prisoners and that we're surrounded by injustice, with so many afflicted hearts, so many people without education who are like blind people, so much unfairness in the country, so many women whose eyes are filled with tears every day. And if they take somebody else prisoner, what do we lose? "Maybe he did something," they say, and that's the end of the story [1:129].

Similarly Felipe says priests should say, "Here is something greater than the temple" (revolution), but in practice religious worship is seen as more important than people (2:22); Julio says it is more important to be on the side of love and equality than simply to read the Gospel (2:125). Laureano says that doing what Christ says is more important than believing he is God (2:138); and Fernando, Ernesto's brother, says that the great division is not between believers and atheists but "between those who act and those who don't act. . . . those who love and those who don't love" (2:139). Ernesto himself, in the sharpest statement, understands Jesus to mean that "the whole Bible, all it talks about is love for others. Not serving God, not worshiping God, not loving God, but doing unto others what we want them to do unto us. We might almost say he makes an atheistic interpretation of the Bible" (1:241).

Frequently there are extended discussions on the relationship between love of God and love of neighbor.

[CARDENAL]: ". . . It's true that the law said, . . . 'Love the Lord your God with all your heart, . . .' but in the Bible it says that this is because

Yahweh . . . is the only one who does justice to the poor and the oppressed. It's like saying that you don't need to have any God except human love and justice. That's why Jesus somewhere else says that the second commandment is 'like the first.' . . ."

LAUREANO: "In other words, he's saying that there is no God then, that God is your neighbor."

[CARDENAL]: "He's saying that God is love."

LAUREANO: "He's saying that to love others, that's God."

[CARDENAL]: "He's saying that there *is* a God but God is that."

LAUREANO: "God's all of us, then."

[CARDENAL]: "Love. All, but united; not all separated, hating each other or exploiting each other. It's really not all of us, because those two who passed by there [the scribe and Pharisee who passed the man beaten by robbers] they weren't neighbors of the other one. If we have a meeting here in which there are exploiters and murderers, you're not going to say, 'God is all of us.' "

LAUREANO: "God is all of us who love each other. And all of us who don't love each other and are screwing the people, that's the devil."

[CARDENAL]: "Saint Augustine says God is the love with which we love each other" [3:101–3; cf. 4:111–20].

A similar passage ends with Cardenal saying that loving the neighbor as oneself means "Having consideration for others as for yourself, and for the people's cause as for the cause of each one of us. In reality all of us are a single organism, and all together we are a single I. That's why each one of us must love the others as part of our own person (that means 'as oneself'). If we don't, we don't belong to the complete Man, we are cut off from humanity" (1:244).

In the Solentiname vision, Christian love demands the building of a new kind of society, the seeds of which they are sowing.

FELIPE: "The teaching [of the multiplication of the loaves] is also that if we come together to hear the message we're not going to be hungry, because with a united people there are no problems. Maybe I won't have food, but my neighbor will. If we're together something can happen to us like what happened to those people with Jesus Christ. If we're together it doesn't hurt to share. And then we're practicing the message of God."

ALEJANDRO: ". . . Christ not only uses words, . . . but he feeds [the people] through his disciples. . . ."

MANUEL: . . . "He divided them into groups so there'd be organization, so there wouldn't be abuses, also everyone could eat and so there'd be enough for everyone."

FELIPE: "It seems that's a fundamental teaching that he gives us: that that's the way the world ought to be. That that's what his followers ought to do when he has gone, that we ought to organize ourselves in communities."

JULIO MAIRENA: . . . "If the whole country was organized like that in communities, not just fifties but thousands, it would be very different, I tell you" [2:149–50].

When someone says, commenting on the Golden Rule, "Just as the rich want us to work for them, so also they should work for us," Ernesto responds: ". . . this system is called socialism. Everyone works for everyone" (2:118).

Cuba, which Ernesto has seen firsthand, serves as a shorthand reference point for the kind of society that should be built. When Cardenal is referring to people's innate abilities, which can be developed if they have good food and education, Natalia breaks in "Like in Cuba where all the children are healthy. They're all taken care of when they're sick and everything. If you're old they take care of you. They give you everything you need and you're healthy and eager to work. And there the poor can learn a profession . . ." (1:57). William observes that a Holy Year should not mean going to Rome and getting a papal blessing but land reform (as in the Old Testament Jubilee Year) and socializing the means of production, and someone adds: ". . . what's been done in Cuba" (1:130).

It may have been partly the isolation of Solentiname that permitted the participants to discuss "communism" freely:

> LAUREANO: "A perfect communism is what the Gospel wants."
>
> PANCHO, who is very conservative, said angrily: "Does that mean that Jesus was a communist?"
>
> JULIO said: "The communists have preached what the Gospel preached, that people should be equal and that they all should live as brothers and sisters. Laureano is speaking of the communism of Jesus Christ."
>
> And PANCHO, still angry: "The fact is that not even Laureano himself can explain to me what communism is. . . ."
>
> [CARDENAL] said to Pancho: "Your idea of communism comes from the official newspaper [Novedades, Somoza's newspaper] or radio stations, that communism's a bunch of murderers and bandits. But the communists try to achieve a perfect society where each one contributes his labor and receives according to his needs. Laureano finds that in the Gospels they were already teaching that. You can refuse to accept communist ideology but you do have to accept what you have here in the Gospels. And you might be satisfied with this communism of the Gospels."
>
> PANCHO: "Excuse me, but do you mean that if we are guided by the word of God, we are communists?"
>
> [CARDENAL]: "In that sense, yes, because we seek the same perfect society. And also because we are against exploitation, against capitalism."
>
> REBECA: "If we come together as God wishes, yes. Communism is an

equal society. The word 'communist' means community. And so if we all come together as God wishes, we are all communists, all equal.''

WILLIAM: "That's what the first Christians practiced, who had everything in common" [1:178–80].

At the core of Christian faith, in this vision, is a conviction that things can change. Cardenal says that the novelty of Jesus' preaching was that the kingdom was near, and Felipe says, "Anyone who believes society can't change, that it will always be unjust, doesn't believe the kingdom is near" (2:143). Commenting on Matthew 16:13–20, William says that Jesus called Peter "blessed" because he "believed in the changing of the world" and that the Solentiname community should be happy because it also believes that the world can be changed. Cardenal comments that those who see Jesus as simply a prophet and not one who came to carry out a revolution do not believe in him as Messiah. "Saint John calls them the Anti-Christs, the Anti-Messiahs" (2:225).

This notion of faith is discussed at some length in connection with Jesus' calming of the sea (Mark 4:35–41), a discussion made more vivid since it occurs three days after Ivan, Bosco, and Doña Chalía have narrowly escaped drowning when their boat capsized.

ALEJANDRO: ". . . Faith is having faith in the company of Christ, who goes with us on the stormy lake. And that's the same as saying that faith is having faith in your friend.''

FELIPE: ". . . Faith is the faith that many young people have today. It's faith in change, in the revolution. It's faith that the world can be changed by love, that evil can become good, that those angry waves can be calmed. . . .''

Alejandro's mother: "The greatest evils of humanity are due to lack of love, and God doesn't solve them personally. He does it through love among people. . . .''

[CARDENAL]: "We also see many miracles or signs—'miracle' means 'sign'—that Jesus has performed throughout history, the transformations that his word has brought about. And still we often doubt that the world can be transformed, that the winds and the waves of history can be calmed" [2:183–85].

For a long time this revolutionary and subversive power of the Gospel has been kept hidden, a secret (2:168). A visitor named Gigi says that Christ presented the idea of a "society of love" 2,000 years ago: "We now have a social organization, socialism, which certainly didn't create for the first time the idea of love but it does give love a possible form among people. Humanity will have evolved a lot in the next two thousand years and we're going to have a really perfect society but I don't believe it'll take two thousand years; it'll be much sooner" (3:124–25).

Ernesto states elsewhere:

. . . Jesus had to tell his message to a few people and because of the historical conditions of that time, his message could not influence politics. Until now the Gospels have been followed only individually or in small communities (monasteries and convents) but we see that the time is now coming when it should be made *public*—in political life and in social life. Now the historical conditions allow the change of attitude to be a change in society as a whole [1:257].

In a discussion of Matthew 25 (the Last Judgment, "I was hungry and you gave me to eat"), the question of individual versus collective charity comes up. Cardenal says:

. . . Camilo Torres used to say that revolution is *effective* charity. And he explained it by saying that only with it could there be effective carrying out of works of mercy in society as a whole: to feed the hungry, give drink to the thirsty, clothe the naked, teach the ignorant, etc. In the past the saints, when a just society wasn't possible because of the means of production that were then in force (slavery, feudalism, or capitalism), what they did was to practice charity individually or through a small group: a religious society that they founded. But now Camilo Torres' effective charity is possible [4:51–52].

On a number of occasions (for example, 3:35–36, 45, 73–74, 91; 4:199), Cardenal relates this vision to a larger sense of evolution and mentions Teilhard de Chardin and Juan Luis Segundo. It is clear that the members of the community (at least the "outsiders") see the "laws of history" as analogous to the laws of nature. Commenting on the parable of the seed (Mark 4:26–29), Ernesto says it means there is a delay in the kingdom "as in any natural process."

. . . This is what we call evolution, which is slow but it is also certain and goes toward a goal. And it seems to me that in this parable it is not only telling us that the kingdom of heaven is like a natural process but that it is part of that same slow process of the evolution of the whole universe . . . of nature and human beings themselves. That's why we can also say that the kingdom is within us, and within us it is growing and growing. Its development is everything that improves and progresses in the world. And we can also say . . . that this kingdom is inevitable, because the world simply *has* to improve and progress. It's a natural law [2:176; cf. 2:54–55].

While the tone here seems rather Promethean, there are moments when the community considers setback and failure. Óscar says, ". . . if we as a group are opposed to injustice and if we're struggling and can't get what we want, if we can't bring about the change for the time being, well, let his will be done. But we don't lie down! We have to keep moving ahead." Cardenal says that we have to accept failures that are not avoidable and should rebel only against avoidable failure. From failure can come good and this can be God's will. Jesus, facing his own failure, prayed, "*Abba* (Papa), may your will be done" (1:215).

Death and life are major categories for the community (anticipating what will be developed more explicitly later in Central America). William says, "The truth is that in today's world there are two kinds of people: Some are on the side of life and others are on the side of death" (2:108), and "Life and love are the same thing and the person who embraces love is the person who really lives. And the life of the selfish person isn't life. And therefore to save your life selfishly is to be in death and not in life" (2:244–45). Someone else says that "love leads you to die and, after all, dying is living more" (4:217). Felipe says that one who has died serving others "is resurrected among the people," and in the ensuing discussion it is stated that Marxists and Christians are close in their conviction about the resurrection (3:134–35).

There is very little discussion of specific points of ethics, beyond the general orientations cited here. Even the whole question of violence and taking up arms is discussed infrequently, although several times guerrilla groups are pointed to as examples of heroism and love. On the "sharp as serpents but as harmless as doves" saying, Laureano says, ". . . he's telling us that we must be aggressive and peaceful. . . . When you have to use violence, use it, and when you can do things peacefully, do them peacefully. It's only a matter of tactics . . ." (1:246). Although Cardenal at one point seems to see Jesus as personally a pacifist (4:236) and William Agudelo makes a specific application of the "other cheek" to nonviolence (strikes, demonstrations, and factory takeovers) as effective revolutionary tactics (2:113), in general there is a refusal to conclude that the Gospel calls for pacifism, and Ernesto quotes Sergio Ramírez approvingly: "Christ forbade the sword but not the machine gun" (4:196), that is, Jesus' saying was specific to those circumstances.

Rather than focusing on such issues, the people emphasize that even class struggle must be done with love. A Chilean priest is quoted as saying, "Only love is revolutionary. Hatred is always reactionary," and Marcelino reflects, with frequent pauses: "If we hate we are no longer struggling against the enemy. . . . We are the enemy, because we are evil. . . . [Christ] says we must love the enemy but he doesn't say we can't fight them. . . . The question is how are we going to fight them. If they hate, the weapon against them is love. The difference between us and the enemy is that we fight them without wanting to oppress them, only to liberate them" (2:111–12).

Most of this attempt to summarize the religious vision of Solentiname concerns "what is to be done." In view of the tenor of the quotations thus far, it should not be surprising to learn that the Solentiname theology is highly "functional": statements about God and Christ are related to human activity and there is virtually nothing said about their intrinsic nature or inner life. Some statements about God, if taken literally, border on the heterodox (as do some statements by the mystics).

[CARDENAL]: "The fact is that as God became man, now man is God. First God became flesh in a person, Jesus Christ, to become flesh afterwards in all the poor and oppressed in history. The word is now the people. It's the people that do the work of God."

FELIPE: "With no need for God to do it."

[CARDENAL]: "God doesn't have anything to do here any more. The work of creation was begun by him but now he's left it in our hands, so that we can continue the work" [1:10].

MANUEL [commenting on the parable of the sower who went to sleep]: ". . . It seems like Jesus Christ died and doesn't exist now. It's like he's sleeping. But the seed is in us and we have to harvest it."

FELIPE: "It's the earth that has to take charge of that now. And the weather—the sun, the rain."

[CARDENAL]: "Which is like saying people and history" [2:173].

On a number of occasions it is affirmed that the people are God, and Ernesto Cardenal quotes Mao approvingly : ". . . for us, God is the masses" (4:56). Underlying such seemingly exaggerated expressions is a concern to overcome false images of God, for example, as a "dictator" (1:208). Cardenal says: "Yahweh in the Bible appears as the God of Freedom, the God that brought Israel out of Egypt; and he's a God that doesn't force anyone even to worship him since he doesn't want images; he only forces you to be free, and he doesn't tolerate any image that makes people subjects" (3:86; cf. 3:3–4). A Felipe says, "A lot of people think now too that the revolution is against God, because they identify God with the system" (4:210–11).

In one remark, Cardenal points to what will soon become a key point of Latin American theology: "In the Bible the opponent of God isn't atheism; it's the idols" (4:119).

The figure of Jesus is seen first in its human dimension. He is "what we would call a boy (*muchacho*)" (1:117), a young man, and a young rebel (1:97) and frequently a revolutionary. He was poor, maybe even his clothes were dirty, since he was a worker, but he spoke with authority (1:135–36). There is virtually nothing that refers directly to traditional Christological or soteriological themes.

Similarly there is rather little said about the church as such. Although there are occasional critical remarks about the usual manner in which the church operates, there is little preoccupation even about building a "new church"—the kingdom rather than the church is a reference point. Cardenal says that "the church that Christ founded upon the rock of Peter (maybe because Peter, a militant in a national liberation movement [a Zealot] had a firm messianic faith) was intended to create the kingdom, but the kingdom would not be the church. It would overflow it and it would cover the whole earth'' (2:229–30).

Cardenal cites more than once Camilo Torres's statement that there will be a valid Eucharist only with the revolution (1:202; 4:128; cf. 2:23–25), and he is also fond of noting that the early Christians used the same word, *koinonia*, for Eucharist, communion, and the community of goods: ''We have spoken here of community and communion and communication of wealth and commune and communism. . . . a humanity with a unity of people, a society in the image of the Trinity'' (2:157).

We have already noted this Teilhardian eschatology several times. Somewhat speculatively, Cardenal notes that, according to Marxist philosophy, matter is eternal, and he adds that there must be eternal consciousness: ''And when we die we can go to form part of that universal consciousness, depending on the degree of evolution that we have reached; or else we can remain eternally separated. And it seems to me that we can understand the resurrection of our bodies this way: that since we're part of the consciousness of the universe, our bodies will be the whole universe'' (4:58–59).

What is remarkable about the vision of Solentiname is not so much individual ideas as the facility the people have for connecting apparently disparate realities. Two such examples can close this section. First Marcelino, reflecting on what a city is (many people together so that the light from their houses can be seen from a great distance), dreams of the day when electricity will arrive in Solentiname (in an unconscious variation on Lenin's famous dictum): ''. . . And we may even get to be a city, too, because then we won't be in scattered huts the way we are now, and we'll have electric light, and when somebody goes by in a boat he'll see those lights of our union. But the thing that will shine most, and that's what Christ is talking about, is love'' (1:196).

And Laureano says: ''It seems to me that if we were all well organized in a socialist society, or even better, communist, we'd all be sharing the bread and everything else, as we do in the Eucharist. It wouldn't any longer be the Eucharist that we have at Mass but we would celebrate it every day eating in perfect brotherhood and sharing in all the wealth all alike: it would be a Super Eucharist'' (3:65).

SOLENTINAME AND THE BASIC CHRISTIAN COMMUNITY

The intent here has been to convey the central thrust of the religious vision of the Gospel in Solentiname by choosing and arranging texts and ideas, and imposing an order on statements made in Gospel discussions over a period of years.

Some of this vision obviously derives primarily from Cardenal himself. One is struck by his ability to simplify and summarize a great deal of biblical research and use it not to attract attention to itself or for demythologization but in order to center the discussion on the message in the text. Alert readers will have noticed distinct affinities between his viewpoints and the theology of Karl Rahner: the unity of love of God and love of neighbor, the incarnation in an evolutionary context, even his ideas on death are similar to Rahner's speculation on the body becoming "all-cosmic" at death. However unorthodox some statements seen by themselves might seem, they are simply emphatic ways of stating basic Christian doctrine, for example, the doctrine of the body of Christ.

For our present purpose what is more relevant is the similarity between these dialogues and the more typical cases of basic Christian communities. The basic dynamic of these discussions is the same: the pastoral agent (Cardenal) brings a knowledge of the Scripture, and the people bring their experience of life—and both learn from each other. However, it is not simply a Scriptures-and-life division of labor, since the pastoral agents usually have to encourage the people by showing appreciation for their culture and indeed for their ability to think and express themselves. Thus the people themselves often find new pearls in the Scripture texts, despite the fact that they have hitherto usually been led to believe that those "above" (authorities, politicians, priests, teachers, doctors) have *the* word. These Gospel commentaries were first recorded several years after this process began and hence there is already a certain freedom and ease among the people. As was mentioned at the outset, Cardenal and his community themselves evolved from their original intention of living in a contemplative/artistic community.

The greatest difference between what is recorded here and a "typical" basic Christian community is that the latter has lay (peasant) leadership. After an initial period of courses and training, when communities form in villages, they have their own leaders and hence the normal discussion leader is someone in the community. In some cases the pastoral team working with, perhaps a dozen, twenty, fifty, or more such leaders, meets with them prior to each weekend and goes over the Gospel, or distributes a mimeographed discussion guide with questions. In other cases, pastoral teams have preferred to allow discussion leaders to follow their own inclinations.

In the basic-Christian-community process, both members and leaders acquire a "key" to the Scriptures, a basic approach that helps them to understand fundamental concepts and to make connection between the Scriptures and their lives. Underlying it all seems to be a basic change in attitude from one of accepting the world as it is to one aiming at transforming it—becoming active agents or subjects in history, as is frequently said in Spanish. This involves a change in religious vision from one in which God made things the way they are—us poor and others rich—to one in which God calls us to assume responsibility. Certain values become central: human dignity, basic human equality (as an underlying fact and as something to be worked out), unity, struggle, hope.

Certain themes of the Bible take on central importance: *Creation*: human beings made in "God's image"; dignity of work (subdue the earth); the earth made for all (not just landholders). *Adam, Cain*: sin means the disruption of unity, raising the question "Am I my brother's keeper?" *Exodus*: God hears the cry of his people and liberates them from oppression; we are a people on the march. *Jesus*: announcement of liberation (Luke 4); preaching to the poor and challenging the rich and powerful; preaching a kingdom of unity and love; executed by religious and civil authorities, Jesus is resurrected by God: life triumphs over persecution and death, justice over injustice. *Kingdom*: the definitive kingdom will be total unity; working for unity, love, and equality now is part of the process toward the kingdom. *The church* (Acts 2 and 4) should be a community of sharing and a sign of the kingdom.

The foregoing is simply a listing of the biblical motifs that are central to most basic Christian communities. It is obviously selective; for example, there is little evidence of the classic emphasis on the grace of God (characteristic of both Catholic and Protestant churches since the Reformation), in part because this new vision is attempting precisely to overcome a certain fatalistic providentialism that immobilized people and made them accept as God's creation what was the work of human beings. Awareness of gratuitousness would come in other forms, such as collective and spontaneous prayer.

There is very little concern for building up the church as such, virtually no mention of sexual morality or church authority beyond some criticism of church authorities tied to ruling elites or repressive regimes. There is little speculation on the inner life of God.

If this view is selective, so, it must be recognized, is any religious view and indeed any theology. All theologians—from Origen to Aquinas to Calvin to Moltmann—have their focal points, their recurring Scripture texts, and their frames of reference (philosophical or otherwise). Again the efforts of Rahner and others to create a "short creed" explicitly recognize this as part of the human condition.

With the qualification expressed here, this chapter should provide the reader with a quick overview of the kind of dialogue that takes place in basic Christian communities. That this process is at the root of the experiences we are about to describe cannot be overemphasized.

For the people of Solentiname, especially the young people, these discussions were an intellectual and moral rehearsal for the eventual decision to take an active part in the anti-Somoza struggle. Their remoteness has allowed them a certain luxury to discuss for years the need of revolution; Cardenal and some of the others had been in direct contact with the Frente Sandinista (FSLN). In October 1977, moving from its previous defensive posture and intending to begin a major offensive, the FSLN launched a series of attacks on National Guard outposts. One of the garrisons chosen was that of San Carlos near the Costa Rican border and the town nearest to Solentiname.

With relatively little training a number of the young people who had participated in the Christian community (and the Gospel discussions recorded here) took part in the attack. Several things went wrong: the hoped-for synchronization with actions elsewhere in the country did not take place and the leader of the attack force deserted. The original orders were to destroy the garrison, but when Alejandro heard the cries of the wounded soldiers he did not set fire to it. This act of compassion made it easier for Somoza to call the attack a failure.

As the attack force began its retreat, Elvis (Chavarría) and Donald (Guevara) were surrounded and killed by the National Guard. The rest made their way to Costa Rica where they rejoined other FSLN forces. There Cardenal made public his militancy in the FSLN.

The National Guard meanwhile destroyed the community property in Solentiname and killed people suspected of FSLN sympathies. The young people in Costa Rica entered other Sandinista units and continued to struggle: some fell in combat; others are pursuing studies; some are in important leadership positions.

Some of the things the islanders speculated on in another kind of society (medical care, electricity) are becoming realities in Solentiname.

2

Laying the Groundwork: The Latin American Church

Since the 1960s there has been talk of "revolution" in Latin America; it has been commonplace to speak of the "revolutionary church." What is curious is that revolutionary movements should approach taking power, or actually take it, not in the larger countries that saw the earlier ferment—Chile, Brazil, Argentina, Colombia—but in the tiny countries of Central America. Why this should be so is the subject of chapter 3. Here the purpose is not to present one more survey of the "revolutionary church," but in broad strokes to indicate how that earlier experience contributed to what has happened in Central America subsequently.

The decisive and formative period was that framed by the end of Vatican Council II (late 1965) and the military coup in Chile (September 1973). It is well to recall that during that time there seemed to be several ways in which basic change, revolution, could occur. First, of course, were the guerrilla movements in Guatemala, Venezuela, Peru, Colombia, and somewhat later the Tupamaros in Uruguay. Second, in Chile, and to a lesser extent in Uruguay and Venezuela, there seemed to be a possibility that electoral coalitions could lead to meaningful changes that would be nonviolent. A further variation seemed to be populist movements, such as Peronismo in Argentina, which through political education and organization might become vehicles for change. Finally, there were the "progressive military," such as those that came to power through coups in Peru and Panama in 1968 and those that briefly held power in Honduras and Bolivia.

In the event, all of these apparent paths to basic change finally led nowhere, at least during the period in question; there was nevertheless a mood that revolutionary change could come and a great deal of discussion of issues around it. This background must be taken into account as we consider rapid developments in the Catholic church during the same period.

25

VATICAN COUNCIL II AND LATIN AMERICA

Somewhat magisterially John Cobb has said: "The greatest event in twentieth-century church history was the Second Vatican Council. The greatest achievement which this event has made possible is the liberation theology and praxis of Latin America."[1] Perhaps Vatican II has been too quickly assimilated and made routine so that we see it simply as the "opening of the windows" in a number of areas: liturgy, ecumenism, religious freedom, biblical studies, and the taking of a positive stance toward the modern world. However, if we consider for a moment the typical view of the church among clergy, religious, and laity up to the eve of the council, another picture may emerge. At that time it was commonly thought that the business of the church was to get people into the state of grace and keep them there. Humanity on its own was a *massa damnata*, and "Outside the Church . . . [there was] no salvation." Clearly in such a scheme those who administered the "means of grace" had roles of incalculable importance.

The Vatican Council (and the theology surrounding it) turned this view inside out: God's grace was everywhere saving humankind. What good are sacraments, then, and the priests who administer them? What good is the church itself? It is called to be a *sign* of God's universal saving grace, came the answer. More important than the theological answer was the general impact of the council of the church's full-time "troops," religious and clergy: they had to define anew their whole raison d'être. Out of this came a great deal of ferment, comparable only to the Protestant Reformation and in a number of ways analogous to it. In each case a generation of people in the church seeks both to return to the "sources" and to find forms adequate for their world. In both cases there is great creativity in preaching, forms of worship, new forms of ministry, forms of congregation, church governing, and new theologies. Rather than simply opening some windows, Vatican II opened a floodgate of energy and creativity. Perhaps the main difference between Catholic renewal and the Protestant Reformation is that the former occurred within the boundaries of the Roman Catholic church.

This point should be emphasized because its effects are more important than any of the particular issues discussed at Vatican II. With the exception of the document on the Church in the Modern World (*Gaudium et Spes*), Vatican II dealt almost exclusively with internal church concerns, according to an agenda set largely in Europe. Latin Americans had relatively little input into the council.

However, as the impact of the Vatican Council began to be felt, pastoral agents, priests and sisters, national and foreign, began to apply the same kind of energies released elsewhere in issues such as birth control, church authority, and new theologies into examining their pastoral situation with a fresh eye. They questioned traditional models of pastoral work, for example, a priest circuit-riding a parish with 30,000 inhabitants in scattered areas, most of whom he can see only on the occasion of religious celebrations. It was partly on observation of Latin America that Ivan Illich wrote his 1967 essay "The Vanishing Clergyman," which was one of the major catalysts in questioning the existing models of ministry.[2]

More important, when Latin Americans turned to look at the "world" they saw not so much the world of "human progress," affirmed by Vatican II, as a world of poverty and even misery, which the efforts at "development" were proving unable to change. Poverty was not so much the effect of "backwardness" as of exploitation and dependence. In an extraordinarily short time there were a multitude of new efforts, in a pastoral practice of "going to the poor"—priests and sisters going to live in rural areas and barrios—and soon in a series of meetings and documents raising a voice of protest and calling for alternatives. Most dramatic was the example of Camilo Torres, a Colombian priest and sociologist, who became radicalized through experience, attempted to rally the Colombian people in a nation-wide political front, and soon felt forced to join the guerrillas—with whom he died in combat in February 1966.[3] His experience, while perhaps a premature condensation of what had to be a long process, nevertheless served to challenge others. Even official and hierarchical statements of the period echoed some of these concerns (for example, Paul VI's *Populorum Progressio* and the 1967 statement of the Bishops of the Third World).[4]

In August 1968 the Second General Conference of CELAM (Latin American Episcopal Council), known as the Medellín Conference, met to "apply" Vatican II to Latin America. It is not out of place to note that 1968 seemed to be a year of worldwide revolution: the "Paris May," the antiwar movement in the United States, and similar phenomena. The 146 bishops plus some priests, religious, and laity who were also delegates were assisted by about 100 *peritos* (experts) whose influence proved decisive. More important than any particular statement at Medellín was the conference methodology: rather than starting with doctrine and moving to applications, a style that characterized even Vatican II with the partial exception of the document on the Church in the Modern World, the bishops used a threefold structure of reality/reflection/pastoral consequences both in the overall order of the documents (human promotion/evangelization/the church and its structures) and, internally, in each document.[5] This "Medellín method," already in use to some degree, became canonized. It became common at pastoral meetings to discuss the "national reality" in order to establish a basic framework; at a more local level peasants would talk of local problems and relate them to biblical texts.

Some of the individual statements of the Medellín documents contained code words, for example, *concientización*, which implied the whole pedagogy associated with Paulo Freire and in fact a whole political practice. The bishops said that "sweeping, bold, urgent, and profoundly renovating changes" were needed, and they not only used the term "liberation" several times, but in a typology of attitudes "conservative," "developmentalist," and "revolutionary" indicated their sympathy with the last-named. They endorsed pastoral work in basic Christian communities, a term that was just coming into usage. One of the most provocative ideas was the statement that the poor should not simply be integrated into existing structures, which can be oppressive, but should become *autores de su propio progreso,* subjects of their own development.[6]

Even before the Medellín *Conclusions* were duly approved by Rome, they were being feverishly mimeographed and discussed throughout Latin America. People who had been searching for a new kind of pastoral practice felt vindicated and, in a larger sense, Medellín gave the Catholic church in Latin America its own identity, that is, its issues were no longer those emanating from the Vatican Council and its aftermath but those arising out of native soil and as articulated by Latin Americans.

LIBERATION THEOLOGY

One of the clearest expressions of this new Latin American identity was liberation theology, which sprang upon the scene with surprising rapidity. Ever since the early 1960s some Latin American theologians had been discussing the possibility of their own theology and some of its themes were anticipated during the middle of the decade. However, it was largely Gustavo Gutiérrez in an early essay (1970) and then in *A Theology of Liberation* (first published in Spanish in 1971) and Hugo Assmann in *Theology for a Nomad Church* (also first published in Spanish in 1971) who laid out "maps" of the territory and anticipated almost all the major themes to follow.[7] To characterize them roughly, Assmann was more concerned to develop a new methodology, particularly showing how Latin American theology was breaking away from North Atlantic models, while Gutiérrez expressed the basic themes, treating the new practice of the church in its "option for liberation" and showing how traditional themes (salvation, Jesus Christ, the church, Eucharist, and so forth) are seen differently in the light of that practice.

In a very short time the main lines of liberation theology were laid out,[8] among them the following concepts:

1. The notion of a "separation of planes" (spiritual and temporal) was rejected in favor of a concept of a single history of humankind, thereby undercutting the justification for the exclusion of the church from "political" questions.
2. An ideological critique of the church's action (for example, preaching or theology) revealed that it was not "above politics."
3. While the definitive kingdom was seen as beyond history, it was said to be built up by partial realizations within history.

4. Conflict, even class struggle, was seen as a part of history and could not be covered over by appeals to the "unity of the church."

Although its foes have tended to attack liberation theology as "Marxist penetration," one should note that none of its major exponents have devoted systematic attention to Marxism as such, with the exception of José Porfirio Miranda in *Marx and the Bible* (biblical exegesis) and *Marx against the Marxists* (a philosophical polemic); Miranda is a unique case. Rather than dealing directly with Marxism (for example, by showing convergences with Christianity), the theologians for the most part simply assume some of its concepts and terminology when treating social phenomena. They thereby reflect the Latin American ambiance where Marxist terminology is as all pervasive as psychological jargon is in the United States.[9] That the theologians have not devoted themselves to a more direct confrontation with Marxism—or, more appositely, Marxisms—does not mean that the time for such confrontation may not eventually come. Indeed, there is reason to believe that developments in Central America may demand precisely such work. However, it should be emphasized that the "classical" works in liberation theology have concentrated on the pastoral and theological consequences of what Christians were experiencing in their efforts and struggles.

Some themes from liberation theology found their way into the discourse of official church documents, most notably a vocabulary relating injustice to "oppression" in the Synod of Bishops in 1971, and a treatment of "the mutual relationship between evangelization and integral salvation or the complete liberation of man and of peoples" in the 1974 Synod. In fact, as early as 1971 Pope Paul VI in *Octogesima Adveniens* had noted that "Some Christians are today attracted by socialist currents and their various developments." The pope did not issue condemnations but he urged caution and discernment.[10]

He probably had Chile in mind where, under the Popular Unity government of Salvador Allende, a group of "Christians for Socialism" was in formation. In 1972 delegations from all over Latin America met in Santiago, Chile, in a Christians for Socialism conference, whose final document may be seen as representing a further development of issues coming from Medellín. Some statements reflected more the situation in Chile, for example, vigorous rejection of a "third way" between capitalism and socialism (namely, Christian Democracy). Other statements reflected the optimism of the moment—for example, "The revolutionary process in Latin America is in full swing"—or should be taken as referring to a broad historical period. The document noted a "growing consciousness of the need for a *strategic alliance* between revolutionary Christians and Marxists," utilizing the term employed by Fidel Castro on a visit to Chile in late 1971. The delegates insisted that many Christians had discovered a "convergence between the radical nature of their faith and of their political commitment," which led to a fertile interaction. One of the more developed areas of the document was its treatment of the ideological use of Christian elements to reinforce domination, and hence the task of "unmasking" those elements.[11]

As soon became evident, there was no socialist *proyecto* (plan, proposal, project) on the immediate horizon. In fact no delegates from Brazil, Bolivia, or Uruguay could appear openly at that meeting: if they were identified they could be picked up by the authorities upon their return. Similarly Central American delegates caucused and found that their common denominator was repression, for instance, the Salvadoran delegates planned to make several stops on their way back so that their passports would make them plausible as tourists rather than as visitors to a "socialist" country.

The Chilean coup (1973) dashed hopes throughout the continent that electoral politics offered a peaceful path to social transformation. In spite of growing popular support (increasing percentages with each election), Allende's coalition had controlled only a part of the state apparatus and could not affect much of the economy and the media and, most important, the armed forces. Brazil's National Security State, with economic policies of deliberate redistribution toward the wealthy, and torture and death squads for malcontents, seemed to be the model for Latin America.

In the meantime there had been a "coup" in CELAM itself in late 1972, when in a meeting in Sucre, Bolivia, Bishop Alfonso López Trujillo was chosen as secretary-general. He lost no time in closing CELAM training institutes, which had been giving courses to several hundred pastoral agents a year in the spirit of Medellín, and collapsing them down to one located in Colombia where it could be carefully watched. Already, in 1971, the Belgian Jesuit Roger Vekemans had set up an institute in Colombia as a "think-tank" to criticize liberation theology. In its review *Tierra Nueva*, CEDIAL sought to distinguish "true" liberation theology from "one-sided" political interpretations—an approach that emptied the meaning while keeping some of the terminology.[12]

However, these events should be seen less as the result of politicking on the part of López Trujillo, Vekemans, and others, and more as simply a reflection of backlash from the bulk of the Latin American episcopate.

As the meaning of these events sank in, the mood among pastoral agents shifted. It was clear that before "liberation" came there would be a long period of "captivity."[13] One frequently heard remarks like "We may not see it, but we're working for our grandchildren." Characteristic of this new phase was a concentration on quiet, steady work on the local level, especially with basic Christian communities. These had begun in the middle and late 1960s but were initially upstaged by the more dramatic and newsworthy public statements and controversies.

In the long run the most important developments may have been what happened at the grassroots level. Pastoral agents throughout Latin America have followed similar trajectories, so much so that their experience may be generalized in a series of "steps":

1. The first step is simply "going to the people," often by leaving a level of comfort (for example, sisters leaving a convent attached to a middle-class high school) and sharing their conditions: wooden shacks, water shortages, poor bus service, the dust and mud of unpaved streets.
2. The aim is evangelization, understood as two-way dialogue, often systematically organized in evening meetings and courses, but also understood as a wider process of interaction in the community.
3. Participants acquire a critical view of their inherited religiosity and take on a new vision, which emphasizes their dignity as "God's image" and their vocation to shape their own destiny rather than to accept passively things as they are. Local communities with their own leadership emerge and begin to act on their own to some extent.
4. At some point there is conflict, very often as people make the step from *concientización* to organization. The conflict is typically first at the local level (for instance, people demand their rights of a local landholder, who may denounce them as "communists" to the army or police).
5. Conflict brings pastoral agents to recognize the factor of *class*, namely, the problem is not simply the particular landholder but the elites who have economic and political power, which they maintain by force and, if necessary, by violence. From this realization pastoral agents may become convinced that the problem lies in capitalism as a system (the ownership of the main means of production in private hands) and that only through socialism (the socialization of those means of production) will people's basic needs be met and repressive violence stopped.

It is remarkable how often one can trace the steps just sketched in the experience of individual pastoral agents and pastoral teams working with the poor. The process has often taken years. It is *not* a matter of reading liberation theology or Marxist texts and leaping into political action. In almost every case there is a step-by-step process, even in the case of people who are notionally familiar with the ideas of socialism.

After one comes to question capitalism, there are further steps. "Opting for socialism" in itself does not tell one what to do, for example, in a rural area where there is no viable national organization. As pastoral agents have come in contact with existing political organizations they have encountered factional and personal disputes, immaturity, and large, unresolved problems of strategy and tactics and have begun a long process of political apprenticeship.

During the 1970s priests, sisters, and their lay associates came under increasing attack. At first the murder of a priest caused worldwide headlines, but as the numbers mounted into the dozens it lost its novelty. By one account over 800 priests, religious, and laity had been arrested, tortured, killed, or expelled by the late 1970s.[14] In Bolivia in 1975 the CIA (Central Intelligence Agency of the United States) and local government authorities worked out a plan to divide pastoral agents and discredit those considered leftists.

When "human rights" became a rallying point in the mid-1970s and picked up momentum with the Carter presidency in the United States, church people insisted that it should be applied to all, including peasants. The weakness of the conventional human-rights critique is that it simply seeks to curb the "excesses" of repressive governments but offers no real alternative.

Much of the experience of church people came to a head in the preparation for the Third General Conference of Latin American Bishops, to be convened at Puebla, Mexico, in 1979 (for instance, one bibliography prepared prior to the conference listed over a thousand titles).[15] In spite of a control over preparations exercised by Archbishop López Trujillo (and although the conference virtually ignored Central America), premature condemnations were avoided and certain emphases were included in the final document: stronger and more specific language than Medellín's on some issues; repeated emphasis on the "preferential option for the poor."[16]

During the 1960s and the 1970s some Protestants were passing through similar experiences. There was a similar interaction between international meetings of the World Council of Churches and meetings on a national or Latin American level. ISAL (Church and Society in Latin America) served as a network of like-minded Protestants and its review, *Cristianismo y Sociedad* (Christianity and Society), was a forum for the emerging liberation theology. Theologians such as José Míguez Bonino and Rubem Alves were publishing, and some Protestant seminaries (for example, in Costa Rica and Argentina) began to shift their orientation. However, in Latin America the denominations are usually far outnumbered by sect-type churches on whom such tendencies have little effect. Protestants who became radicalized in a process similar to that described above tended to find themselves isolated from their parent churches and would gravitate to ecumenical circles.

While the experience in Latin America did not lead immediately to any viable *proyecto* of liberation, it served as a preparation for what was to happen in Central America in the 1970s and 1980s. Without the benefit of those earlier experiences it is difficult to see how Christians could have taken such an active role in the later struggles.

3

Central America: Why the Crisis?

Although at first glance it may seem ironic that revolutionary movements are occurring in the tiny countries of Central America rather than in the larger nations of South America that may have seemed to be in a prerevolutionary state some years earlier, in reality there are reasons why this is so, as we shall see. It is useful at the outset to have a sense of scale when considering Central American countries. Their smallness, in size, population, and economic output, should be borne in mind throughout this study.

Statistics on Central American Countries[1]

Country	Size (square miles)	Population	Gross Domestic Product
Guatemala	42,042 (size of Tennessee)	6,813,000	$6,966,000,000
El Salvador	8,260 (size of Massachusetts)	4,436,000	3,060,700,000
Honduras	43,277 (size of Tennessee)	3,565,000	1,947,000,000
Nicaragua	45,698 (size of Pennsylvania)	2,463,000	1,545,000,000
Costa Rica	19,653 (size of New Hampshire and Vermont combined)	2,166,000	2,840,000,000
Total		19,443,000	$16,358,700,000

Even a medium-sized Latin American country such as Colombia has roughly one and a half times the population of the five Central American

NOTE: Although part of the same isthmus, historically Panama has never been part of Central America, but was part of Colombia until 1903. Moreover, economically it has served as a trade center and only secondarily an agroexport producer.

countries combined. Total annual trade between the United States and Central America is around $1.7 billion, which is less than 2 percent of American foreign trade.[2]

These countries are similar in their agroexport economics: as recently as 1977, 85 percent of their exports were made up of just five commodities: coffee, sugar, cotton, beef, and bananas.[3] Most of these products are grown on flat plains on the Pacific coast (Guatemala, El Salvador, Nicaragua, Costa Rica). Coffee is grown in the foothills or other hilly regions. The Caribbean coast is largely undeveloped, the north coast of Honduras being a notable exception. Guatemala, Honduras, and Costa Rica offered cooler highlands to the early settlers so that the capitals and main population centers were established there. Individual countries have their own particular exports, such as gold (Nicaragua), timber (Honduras), and shrimp (El Salvador). With the exception of Guatemala, however, which has a major nickel mine and at least modest oil deposits, there are no proven natural resources of great importance.

This relative unimportance of Central America, coupled with its governments' normal subordination to the United States, helps to explain why it has normally received little media attention. For example, Emile McAnany found that Central America occupied less than one-tenth of 1 percent (0.01 percent) of network television news during the 1972–77 period—despite the fact that these five countries are separated from the United States only by Mexico. More revealing, the same study found that during the years 1972–75, there was not a single story on El Salvador on any of the networks, and only ten appeared during the next three years.[4]

As should be apparent from the narratives in this book, Central American countries were in crisis long before the fact was discovered by the American media and policymakers. Even after the crisis was recognized there has been a rather remarkable ignorance of, and even disdain for, the history leading up to the crisis. To quote one example illustrating the point: in a mid-1981 interview the United States ambassador to El Salvador, Deane Hinton, made a reference to "General Whatever-his-name-was" who had ordered the massacre of thousands of peasants in 1932. The name was Maximiliano Hernández Martínez and he ruled El Salvador from 1931 to 1944, roughly the same period that Franklin Delano Roosevelt held the United States presidency; indeed, the general's impact on his own country was of similar importance. If an ambassador to the United States were to refer to Roosevelt as "Whatshisname," Americans would conclude he or she did not know much about American history and had a cavalier disregard for it.

Much of the present book will be history, mainly the history of Christian involvement in the struggles of the 1970s and 1980s in Nicaragua, El Salvador, and Guatemala. However, as a backdrop to modern developments some notes on Central American history indicating factors from the past that are relevant for understanding later events are in order here.[5]

ORIGINS AND CONQUEST

When Europeans "discovered" Central America (Columbus's fourth voyage took him along the coast of Honduras down to Panama), they found a land already settled for millennia, presumably from the time that the peoples who had migrated from Asia through the Bering Straits passed through on their gradual way south. The evidence of archeological artifacts indicates that the Central American isthmus was a meeting place of the cultures of North, Middle, and South America. After 500 B.C. an advanced civilization began to arise in what is today Guatemala and El Salvador, as attested by the ruins of Kaminal Juyu within present-day Guatemala City. From A.D. 300 to 900 the Maya civilization arose and flourished in the northern jungles of Guatemala and part of Honduras, best exemplified in the ruins of Tikal. After A.D. 900 this civilization declined for reasons still unknown; there were other Indian groups with high civilizations, however, partly under the domination of Indians from Mexico. In addition there were other cultures throughout the isthmus, which, while they did not build cities, nevertheless showed well-developed social systems and intricate art, especially in pottery and gold work.

As in the rest of the Americas, the indigenous peoples of Central America, despite their heroic resistance, were conquered by the superior technology (guns and horses) of the Spanish. In Guatemala Pedro de Alvarado allied himself with the Cakchikel Indians in order to defeat the Quiché Indians. Then he turned on the Cakchikels, defeated them, set up his capital on the site of theirs, Iximche, and went on to "pacify" other Indian groups. Meanwhile other conquistadores, while fighting among themselves, had taken Nicaragua and Honduras. Pedro de Alvarado was made governor of the kingdom of Guatemala, which covered present-day Central America as well as Chiapas in southern Mexico.

What we know as Central America is thus based on an act of conquest and domination, with thousands of Indians being killed; the Spaniards at one point burned Indian leaders alive. Although at first the conquerors hoped to find precious metals, they soon realized that the region's natural resources were its land—and the labor supply, the indigenous people. Initially this labor was harnessed through a feudal or even slave system called the *encomienda*. However, the Spanish Crown promulgated the New Laws of the Indies (1542), which allowed the Indians to live in their own towns and villages while obligating them to do a certain amount of work for the landowners (legally one week a month, but in practice often more). In Guatemala, Indians were grouped into towns and obliged to wear clothing of certain patterns (the designs were taken from the Spanish court) to mark where they lived. Hence the colorful clothes today admired by tourists originated in the systems of social control imposed by the colonizers.

In this conquest the church was a key factor. Missionaries were the only force denouncing the cruelties and attempting to moderate the effects of the conquest. Fray Bartolomé de las Casas came to Guatemala in 1536 and the following year attempted an experiment with the Indians in the Verapaz region ("True Peace," the name reflecting his "pacification" of what had been regarded as a hostile area). His experiment failed when the Indians revolted against the friars. De las Casas was the prime influence in instigating the Spanish Crown to promulgate the New Laws. In Nicaragua, Bishop Antonio Valdivieso was murdered by the governor for defending Indians.

Despite heroic exceptions, however, the church normally acted as an integral element of the overall enterprise of conquest and domination. The very teaching of Christianity, as it came from Counter-Reformation Spain, had a domesticating effect on the indigenous peoples. Ralph Woodward, in *Central America: A Nation Divided,* notes a number of parallels between Mayan religion and the form of Christianity brought by the friars, which may have facilitated domination: both had a theocratic vision of society where priests were powerful, emphasized the struggle between good and evil, and believed in an afterlife while fearing death; Mayan myths of the creation were similar to Genesis, and Christian saints appeared to resemble the lesser Mayan gods. In some areas the Mayans even used a cross to symbolize the rain god. Thus Spanish friars could take the place of the Indian religious leaders, many of whom were killed.[6]

Whereas Indians in Honduras, Nicaragua, and Costa Rica were either killed or pushed to sparsely populated lands, and thus have been marginal to those countries' histories, in Guatemala and El Salvador they were integrated into the economy as the basic seasonal labor supply and thus can in no way be considered "marginal," except in the sense that they have not received services such as schooling and health care. Over the centuries there have been periodic Indian uprisings; for example, one document lists five such uprisings in eighteenth-century Guatemala.[7] (In El Salvador almost all the Indians dropped their traditional dress and languages in the aftermath of the 1932 massacre of peasants.) The large-scale incorporation of Indians into the present-day struggle in Guatemala can be better understood in the light of the history of conquest and domination.

During the colonial period Central America was a backwater. Its first important export crop was cacao, followed somewhat later by indigo for dyes. During the three centuries of the colonial period society was stratified: there were small elites of landholders, a few independent farmers and tradespeople, and a large number of people who worked for them, especially Indians. For example, David Browning estimates that in El Salvador some 300 to 400 families owned 400 plantations, averaging 2,000 acres each, which together occupied a third of the territory. (From early times El Salvador seems to have had many settlers, and it is eerie to read on one of Browning's maps of the area around San Salvador the names Opico, Guazapa, Suchitoto, San Pedro Perulapán, Soyapango, Mejicanos—all sites of battles in the early 1980s.)[8]

In colonial times the religious orders, rather than the diocesan clergy, represented the church. By 1600 there were twenty-two Franciscan, fourteen Dominican, and six Mercederian houses in Guatemala. Arriving in the seventeenth century the Jesuits, while not numerous, became important in education and agricultural production, especially in sugar. In fact the wealth of the religious orders and clergy stirred some resentment. As civil authority weakened during the seventeenth century, due to the degeneracy of the Spanish monarchy, the clergy assumed greater authority. New churches, monasteries, and convents were built so that at the end of the century Santiago (present-day Antigua, Guatemala) ranked only behind Mexico City and Lima in size, importance, and grandeur. At the end of the colonial period there were 424 churches in the diocese of Guatemala (including El Salvador), 145 in Honduras, and 88 between Nicaragua and Costa Rica.[9]

While it is an oversimplification to attribute today's crisis to the Spanish conquest, and one which misses the point that precisely the kind of "development" promoted in the 1960s and 1970s has produced the crisis, there is nevertheless significant continuity. Since the conquest Central American society has been organized around the forced expropriation of the best lands and the forced conscription of labor in order to produce export crops that generate fortunes for small local elites. The church's role, noteworthy exceptions notwithstanding, has been one of supplying religious legitimation.

INDEPENDENCE: A CHANGE OF MASTERS, NEW CROPS, AND "PROGRESS"

In the closing years of the colonial period the lines began to be drawn for what would become more than a century of political disputes and local wars in Central America. Those who came to be called "Liberals" saw themselves as bearers of "progress": they propounded the ideas of the Enlightenment (including anticlericalism) and advocated independence from Spain (and later on nation-building and new crops, particularly coffee). Conversely, the "Conservatives" sought to defend older traditions and the church, and were more tied to local power.

Central America received independence along with Mexico; there had been virtually no fighting in the isthmus. Recently many have come to interpret independence as simply the separation of the local dominant elites from the Spanish Crown, a shift that enabled them to trade directly with new emerging economic powers, especially Great Britain, but which meant little for ordinary people, especially the Indians.

Lying unexpressed in such a contention is an intuition that although these countries became nations on a formal level more than a century and a half ago (with constitutions, elections, assemblies, and so forth), in important ways their real nationhood is not yet achieved and still lies ahead. Consequently, today's struggles are aimed not simply at achieving justice but at enabling the countries to become the nations they have been prevented from being.

During the first few, convulsive years after formal independence in 1821, Central America became independent from Mexico and then split over Liberal-Conservative battles. After a Conservative government (1826–29), the Liberals under Francisco Morazán and Mariano Gálvez retaliated. During their period in power they took severe measures against the church, such as taking church funds, suppressing monastic orders, abolishing religious holidays, and so forth. However, the Liberals could not hold Central America together and by 1838 regional and personal rivalries had split it into the present five republics. Some Central Americans regard this "Balkanization" as artificial and hope to see their countries eventually reunited, a point that Woodward makes the underlying thesis of his history cited above. In any case, the postindependence histories of these countries show many parallels.

In broad outline, the Conservatives dominated Central America during the middle decades of the nineteenth century, until the 1870s when the Liberals returned to power and kept it until well into the twentieth century. In Guatemala and El Salvador especially, the Liberals' goal was coffee production and export, and to achieve it they enacted "land reforms," requiring that all land be held as private property, thus eliminating the Indians' communal lands and the properties of religious orders. The Liberals saw coffee as the key to progress, and both the Indians and the religious orders as symbols of backwardness. The elites, who could hire lawyers, were able to acquire the new lands quickly. In some cases the peasants fought back: several thousand Indians were killed in Nicaragua during an uprising in 1881 and there were peasant revolts in El Salvador in 1880, 1885, and 1889.[10] In Guatemala and El Salvador the military was upgraded, and special forces were created just to keep order in the countryside.

Coffee export increased rapidly—twenty times between 1870 and 1890 in Guatemala—and the new elites rode to prosperity on the crest of popularity of the dark tropical beverage among the new European middle classes of the late nineteenth century. In the closing years of the century the banana companies were set up in all Central America except El Salvador. In contrast to coffee, which was grown and exported by local elites, bananas were grown in self-contained American company enclaves, which had very little impact on the rest of the country.

Much of the subsequent history and even present character of the Central American countries can be traced to the varying ways they entered the international market as agroexporters. In Guatemala and El Salvador narrow elites controlled coffee production and export, and so accumulated fortunes, part of which was spent on luxury imports and part of which their descendants were able to invest. Nicaragua entered coffee production in the 1890s, but to a much lesser extent. The coffee boom bypassed Honduras, and the banana enclaves on the isolated northern coast traded directly with New Orleans in the United States, leaving the rest of Honduras largely untouched. Honduras remained a backwater—scarcely a nation at all—until the mid-twentieth century. In sharp contrast to the other countries, Costa Rica began coffee production in the 1830s and 1840s and, although there were some large producers, the coffee prosperity was much more evenly shared and a prosperous middle-level peasantry developed. As the country became urbanized in the twentieth century there was a more egalitarian foundation for the institutions of Costa Rica's electoral democracy and social-welfare programs. Rather than being the product of some "national character," Costa Rica's stability and even conservatism has an economic basis. (By the same token, the severe financial crisis of the early 1980s, unresolved at this writing, may strain those institutions to the breaking point.)

Part of the Liberals' program, for both ideological and economic reasons, was the curtailing of clerical power. Woodward explains:

> Although specific restrictions varied from state to state, all five states confiscated Church lands and nationalized the endowments of religious orders. They removed some orders from the country altogether, forbade clerics to wear clerical garb except in the discharge of their religious functions, banned or restricted religious processions, permitted civil birth registration, first legalized and then made compulsory civil marriage, established religious toleration and welcomed Protestant immigration, abolished compulsory tithe taxes and the clerical fuero, once more removed the Church's monopoly on education, and restrained the moral censorship which the Church had been allowed to impose. In addition, other concerns of the Church, such as hospitals, charity, and care of orphans and the aged, began to be taken over by the state. Reductions in the number of clergy left many rural areas without priests, thereby diminishing the Church's influence over the peasant population.
>
> The Church fought back, particularly in Guatemala, where it was strongest. There it excommunicated President Barrios and other officials. Barrios responded by exiling the Archbishop and Bishops, and in the end the Liberals succeeded in reducing the Church in power and prestige. While it remained the refuge of Conservative upper-class elements, the Church lost the strong authority it had once held over the masses. Although not totally ended even today [1976], the major role the clergy had played in rural Central America became minor. This was one of the most important changes ever to take place in Central America.[11]

Although the Liberals were "modernizers" as exemplified by the secularizing measures listed above, it should be recalled that the normal form of Liberal government was dictatorship: from the 1870s until the 1940s Liberals ruled Central America with an iron hand; for example, the Somozas, in Nicaragua, were Liberals. Hence it is understandable that the poor, particularly the Indians whose lands were expropriated, were not enthusiastic about such "progress."

A wave of Protestant missionaries was encouraged by the Liberals: President Barrios of Guatemala personally invited the Presbyterians to the country and donated land for a church that still stands in the shadow of the National Palace in Guatemala City. The Liberals saw Protestants as bearers of modernity and as a means to weaken Catholic clerical influence. Today some Protestants take a critical view and ask to what extent their inherited version of the Gospel has been a vehicle of values associated with the existing "order" (individualism, respect for the state). Much of the Catholic church's behavior can be seen as a response to the effects of Liberalism. Until Vatican II it seems to have been mostly preoccupied with coping with its institutional weakness and trying to build up a national clergy; in any case it was not a prominent actor on the scene, for the most part.

During the period 1890–1920 the United States, buoyed by its industrial expansion, sought to assert its Manifest Destiny in the Caribbean and Central America with major interventions in Puerto Rico and Cuba (1898), Panama (1903), the Dominican Republic (1904, 1916), Haiti (1915), and Mexico (1914, 1917), and with smaller military actions in Costa Rica, Honduras, and Guatemala. Starting in 1912 the U.S. Marines occupied Nicaragua and ended up fighting a guerrilla war in the late 1920s and early 1930s (see chapter 4). While to American readers these may seem to be the boisterous excesses of a newly adolescent nation, to Central Americans they have decisively shaped (or distorted) their countries.

Coffee prices fell drastically with the Great Depression: from $15.75 a bag in 1928 to $5.97 in 1932,[12] and the tightening economies and growing unrest were undoubtedly a major explanation for the dictatorships of the 1930s and 1940s in all countries but Costa Rica. Maximiliano Hernández Martínez in suppressing a peasant revolt in El Salvador ordered a peasant massacre, whose victims were said to number 30,000 (see chapter 5).

Unlike the larger South American countries, Central America could not take advantage of the 1930–50 period of relative neglect from Europe and the United States to begin industrialization through import substitution. However, during this period the agroexport elites began to expand into cotton and sugar on the flat lands along the Pacific coast.

"DEVELOPMENT" AND CRISIS

By the late 1950s the Central American Common Market (CACM) seemed to be an idea whose time had come. The underlying reasoning was obvious: tiny countries of a million or so people would not attract investors, especially since the market for manufactured goods would be only a fraction of the total population. However, if by dropping tariff barriers the five countries could be made into one market there would be incentives for new investments.

United Nations experts proposed a strategy emphasizing a balanced industrialization, centralized planning, and strong government participation. It was assumed that the new industries would be in the hands of Central Americans and that tariffs would be used to protect them from outside competition during initial phases. Industries would be parceled out among the countries and duplication would be avoided so the new industries could aim at the whole region and achieve economies of scale. In 1958 the five countries signed agreements creating a free market for certain products, the list of which would gradually expand.

The United States objected that such a plan ran counter to the free market. Two State Department experts arrived in 1959 on an "exploratory" mission, urging a more rapid timetable for a complete free movement of goods, people, and capital in the region. They let it be known that the United States would offer $100 million to aid economic integration. Soon the United Nations approach was abandoned. By paying half of the operating costs of the Central American agency that was designing the integration plans, the United States was able to reshape the concept. Further influence came through the United States' strong control over the Central American Economic Integration Bank (for example, forcing it to concentrate on infrastructure and not permitting it to make loans to local industries).[13]

While ostensibly the United States was championing the principles of the free market against excessive state intervention, in practice it made the CACM serve foreign investment rather than aid the growth of autonomous Central American industries. Most of the recent "Central American" industries are really local operations for multinational firms: food processing (Kellogg, Kerns, Log Cabin Syrup, Ritz crackers, and so forth), pharmaceuticals, and clothing, as well as items like tires (Firestone).

The CACM entered into crisis as long ago as the 1969 war between El Salvador and Honduras and its shortcomings, enumerated below, became increasingly clear during the 1970s:

1. Even under the best of conditions the market is limited, a fraction of the 20 million people of the area.
2. Economic strategies centered on the CACM have a built-in tendency to direct production to the elites rather than the whole population and there are, accordingly, tendencies to skew income distribution further in their favor.
3. The CACM has favored those countries that had a head start, Guatemala and El Salvador, rather than fomenting more balanced growth.
4. Rather than setting up new industries, foreign capital often simply bought out local industries.
5. The CACM did not promote national industries so much as terminal operations (even packaging or bottling) for multinational companies.
6. Being capital intensive, the new industries created few jobs.

Despite these serious limitations Central American trade grew from very little in 1960 to $272.7 million in 1971 and to $839 million in 1977.[14]

Accompanying the CACM as part of the Alliance for Progress were development programs ranging from infrastructure (roads, water systems, dams, communications), institution-building (namely, making government institutions more efficient), and, more recently, aid directed at the poorest 40 percent. The following table indicates totals of economic and military aid from the United States economic aid and from international institutions, and also the growth rates of Central American countries (in millions of dollars):[15]

Aid from the U.S. and International Financial Institutions to Central America 1953–79

Country	U.S. Aid (1953–79), Economic	U.S. Aid (1953–79), Military	Aid from International Agencies	Growth Rate of Countries (1960–78)
Guatemala	526.0	41.9	593.0	5.8
El Salvador	218.4	16.8	479.2	5.55
Honduras	305.1	28.4	688.0	4.2
Nicaragua	345.8	32.6	469.5	6.5
Costa Rica	305.2	6.9	682.4	6.25

Direct United States investment in Central America is calculated at over $1 billion.

There were development and impressive growth in Central America until the late 1970s, not stagnation. How, then, can one explain the subsequent crisis? The conventional explanation is that, despite efforts at development, extremes of wealth and poverty still remain. Income distribution shows deep inequalities:

Income Distribution in Central America Annual Per-Capita Income in Dollars (1970)[16]

Country	Bottom 50%	Next 30%	Next 15%	Top 5%
Guatemala	73	228	543	2,023
El Salvador	81	213	568	1,442
Honduras	52	164	401	1,349
Nicaragua	91	148	627	1,643
Costa Rica	152	366	750	2,478
Central America	74	246	568	1,760

The inequities shown here statistically have life-and-death consequences. In Guatemala, for example, half of all deaths are of children under five, in most cases of preventable intestinal and respiratory diseases; and the poorest half of the population consumes only 56 percent of the recommended daily calorie intake. In El Salvador in 1975 a typical family of six needed $533 a year to survive, yet 60 percent earned less than that. Per capita calorie intake there is the lowest in the Western hemisphere.[17]

Poverty by itself does not create prerevolutionary conditions, and indeed by conventional measurements most countries of Asia and Africa are poorer than those in Central America. What has been little noticed in most commentaries is that despite efforts at development—or better, *because* of so-called development—real living conditions for many, perhaps most, people in Central America have deteriorated. One study showed that while nominal wages in Guatemala rose during the 1972–77 period, average wages in real terms declined from $0.39 to $0.33 per hour.[18] Such statistics should be regarded with caution; nevertheless people who worked with the poor during those years were convinced of the economic deterioration.[19]

Two related tendencies explain the crisis: growing rural landlessness and decreasing production of basic foods. In El Salvador the percentage of rural landless families increased from 11.8 percent in 1961 to 29.1 percent in 1971 to 40.9 percent in 1975.[20] More than half the rural families depended on salaried work for over half their income. However, the rapid increase in landless peasants meant there was less work available, and it was calculated that in 1975 the average rural worker could count on only 141 working days a year.

Shelton Davis has shown that in Guatemala, while exports were increasing rapidly, basic food production fell behind population growth. Between 1960 and 1974 Guatemala's five major export crops increased in value from $105.3 to $367.5 million, outperforming twenty-two other Latin American countries in the process. However, between 1950 and 1973, while population grew at about 3 percent a year, corn production increased only 1.6 percent, wheat 2.3 percent, and beans 4.8 percent compared with an annual growth rate of 5 percent for the export crops. The main reason was that new arable land for export crops expanded by 6.5 percent a year, while such land for food production increased by 1.7 to 2 percent a year. By the early 1970s the country was importing record amounts of corn, wheat, and beans.

To describe the situation in somewhat broader terms: the agroexport elites have acquired new lands and expanded their operations, while small peasants find themselves with less land to cultivate. As the population increases, subsistence lands are subdivided and more peasants become dependent on day labor. Such day labor itself, however, becomes increasingly scarce as there are more landless people looking for work (which is seasonal and is concentrated at harvest time, from November to February) and as some operations (cotton and sugar) are mechanized. According to Davis, between 1950 and 1970 in Guatemala the average size of farms decreased from 8.1 to 5.6 hectares and the number of landless peasants increased to about one-fourth of the rural work force.[21] In the Indian highlands the average size of farm units decreased from 1.3 hectares per person in 1950 to less than .85 hectare in 1975.[22]

Some might argue that it would be more rational for these countries to increase the exports of those products in which they have a comparative advantage and to import even their basic grains, such as corn. It is true that the cash return on an acre in coffee tends to be much higher than it would be in corn. However, such an argument misses the question of *power,* the power of the oligarchical elites who own and rule these countries.

Only the landowners reap any such comparative advantage; the landless-ness and hunger of the majority are *functional* insofar as they assure a cheap supply of labor. Since we shall be using the term "oligarchy" with some frequency let us at this point establish its meaning as used here. It is frequently pointed out that in Central American countries 2 percent of the landholders have two-thirds of the land. Or, in Guatemala the top 2 percent receive 25 percent of the income while the bottom 50 percent receive 10 to 15 percent.[23] (Note that this means that the top 2 percent have a 50-to-1 income differential over the lower half of the population.) More specifically, in Guatemala just 322 coffee operations produce 55 percent of the coffee, or, using another set of figures, 79 operations account for one-third of the production.[24] Although some of these operations may be jointly owned, it is also true that some families have more than one operation so that coffee production is concentrated in a very small group of families. In El Salvador one study found that six (extended) families (Guirola, Sol, Dueñas, Daglio, Samayoa, Romero Bosque) among them had 71,923 hectares—an amount equivalent to that held by 300,000 families, 80 percent of the Salvadoran population.[25] The oligarchy in the first place is constituted by the tiny group of large landholders.

On the basis of profits made in agroexport, the same elites have entered business and industry in recent years, often in joint ventures with multinational companies attracted by the CACM. The Central American oligarchies live in the capital cities, leaving their plantations in the hands of administrators (some occasionally fly out in their helicopters). Their children attend the same schools, they see each other in the same clubs, and they intermarry.

To represent their interests, they have a whole structure of organizations. In Guatemala ANACAFE (National Coffee Association) represents coffee producers, and is paralleled by similar organizations of growers of sugar, cotton, and so forth, all of which make up a Chamber of Agriculture. There are also chambers of Industry, Commerce, and Finance, which are united in CACIF (Chamber of Agriculture, Trade, Industry, and Finance), which represents the whole private sector. In El Salvador the similar organization is ANEP (National Private Sector Association) and in Nicaragua it is COSEP (Higher Council of Private Enterprise).[26]

For Americans the notion of such chambers may conjure up a vision of small-town boosterism. While there is undoubtedly a measure of business camraderie, in Central America these organizations are the articulation of the class interests of the narrow oligarchical elites and as such are, along with the military, the most powerful actors in these societies. These organizations will be appearing in the stories of each country.

There have been, of course, variations from country to country. In Nicaragua the Somoza dictatorship used state resources and power for its own aggrandizement, leaving a relatively less powerful bourgeoisie. In Guatemala from the early 1970s the army as an institution, and army officers individually and in groups, sought to move beyond a gendarme function at the service of the oligarchy and share in some of the profits from landholding and business ventures. Somewhat later there was a similar tendency in El Salvador, where, it would seem, the military simply took advantage of the crisis to acquire wealth through corruption and extortion.

Given the degree of concentration of wealth and power, it should come as no surprise that political parties have been essentially a mechanism for legitimizing the status quo with the appearance of democracy, through formal institutions such as elections and assemblies.

The mechanisms of debate and legislation in the national assembly may serve to solve secondary contradictions in the power structure, for example, when coffee growers and their agroexport allies fight the business and industrial groups who propose a higher tax on coffee export. No political parties can legitimately claim to represent the majority. One small example: in Guatemala during 1974–78 there were two Indian deputies (among fifty-two), and from 1978 to 1982 there were none—although Indians are about 55 percent of the population.

These considerations, seemingly an excursus, may bring us back to the underlying question: Why is Central America in crisis and revolution?

To a great extent the kind of "development" pursued during recent years has actually aggravated the crisis. Expanding agroexport and the new industries benefited the oligarchies and a small urban middle class (the 80–95 percentile), but conditions for the rest of the people did not improve and for some, particularly peasants and landless rural workers, they deteriorated.

For a time the pressure on the peasants may have been partially offset by development programs aimed specifically at them, especially through the introduction of chemical fertilizers and the formation of cooperatives; by 1976 there were 510 cooperatives in Guatemala with a combined membership of more than 132,000 people.[27] Yields did increase for some years and perhaps the peasants were less alarmed by their shrinking plots. However, the less land one has the less help is afforded by cooperatives and fertilizers—and they offer no help to the landless.

The increasingly precarious state of the peasantry was affected by external events, such as the fourfold increase in fertilizer prices during the mid-1970s. Peasants who had become dependent on chemical fertilizers and pesticides now found themselves increasingly indebted and forced to do more migratory work simply to be able to plant a new crop. A dramatic illustration came with the Guatemalan earthquake in 1976: while relief and development agencies, seeing the Indian highland towns in rubble, drew up plans for new self-help housing, the Indians were much more concerned about simply getting a few bags of fertilizer for the May planting.

Neither the oligarchies, nor the military, nor the traditional political parties were prepared to deal with the crisis of the majorities, which—as should be clear to readers now—was structural. When electoral coalitions offering mild reform proposals appeared they were defeated by fraud (El Salvador, 1972, 1977; Guatemala, 1974); but for the most part reform proposals were excluded long before they became political proposals.

IN CONCLUSION

We may now sketch the main lines of the Central American crisis as it unfolded in the 1970s:

1. Large groups of people, particularly small peasants and the landless rural poor, suffered real declines in their already desperate conditions (less work, declining food intake, high infant mortality).
2. These conditions had *structural causes:* increasingly land was being used for agro-export crops, food production growing less rapidly than population.
3. Narrow oligarchies felt no need for reform and change, particularly since they were enjoying a boom, and they thought the military and the police would be sufficient to control dissidence.
4. External factors, inflation (particularly the petroleum price rise), and natural disasters (the Guatemalan earthquake) augmented the crisis.

(To these main "objective" tendencies, two other elements could be added):

5. The scale of Central American countries is such that what might be a local or regional crisis in Brazil or Colombia can become a national crisis in a Central American country, and organizers can build up a national movement with relative ease.
6. Until 1978 the United States government paid little attention to developments in Central America.

This chapter has dealt with "objective" factors. The following generalizations about the "subjective" factors may be useful as we proceed:

1. New kinds of revolutionary groups were formed, Marxist in inspiration but pragmatic and independent in their criteria, and willing to learn from experience and to make alliances.
2. Effective political organizing work was carried out.
3. The regimes in power were not able to cow the populations even with torture, murder, and terrorism but have, on the contrary, delegitimized themselves.
4. By the same token, the opposition movements acquired increasing legitimacy, both among their own populations and internationally.

In each country a time came when the oligarchies and foreign investors recognized the crisis and large-scale capital flight began. At a certain point the struggles of opposition groups, the repression unleashed by groups in power, and the economic decline caused mainly by capital flight became mutually reinforcing.

A further new (even unprecedented) "subjective" element was the participation of Christians in these struggles, which this book will consider in detail.

PART TWO

EXPERIENCE

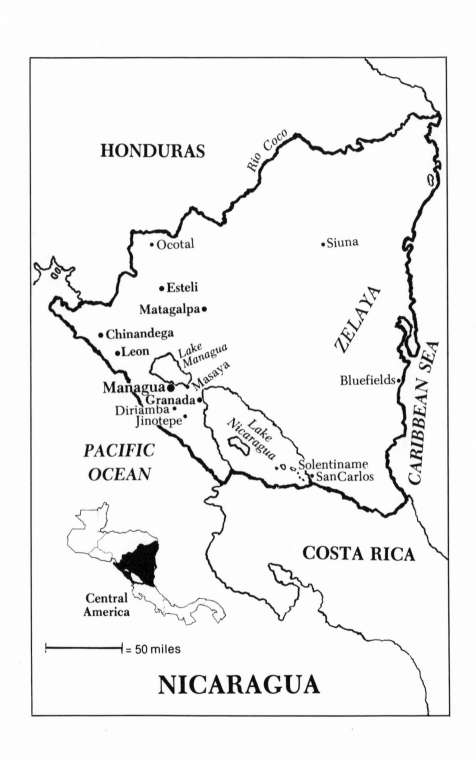

HONDURAS

Rio Coco

•Ocotal

•Siuna

•Esteli

Matagalpa•

•Chinandega

•Leon

Lake
Managua

Masaya

ZELAYA

Managua•

Bluefields•

Granada•

Diriamba•

Jinotepe•

Lake
Nicaragua

Solentiname
•SanCarlos

PACIFIC
OCEAN

CARIBBEAN SEA

COSTA RICA

Central
America

⊢———⊣ = 50 miles

NICARAGUA

4

"Free Country or Death!"

SANDINO, SOMOZA, AND THE CHURCH

Although church involvement in the anti-Somoza struggle began in the late 1960s, some remarks on prior history may serve as useful background, particularly the "Walker affair," United States intervention, and the struggle of Augusto César Sandino.

As elsewhere in Latin America, Nicaraguan politics in the nineteenth century was a Liberal-Conservative seesaw. In the 1850s a Tennessee-born adventurer named William Walker led a group of American mercenaries to Nicaragua at the invitation of Liberals from the city of León. When they took power Walker became commander-in-chief of the army and even became president. At that point, in what he saw as an effort to modernize the country, he sought to attract foreign investment and enacted legislation legalizing slavery (with the idea of making Nicaragua a state in the American south) and making English the official language. Walker was driven out by armies from other Central American countries and was later executed in Honduras after another invasion attempt.

While it may be viewed simply as a bizarre incident, the Walker episode was an expression not only of the Conservative-Liberal struggle of Nicaraguan elites but of international competition over control of the country which was a strategic transit point rivalling Panama as a potential canal site. Walker represented J. P. Morgan, and the opposition that overthrew him was partly financed by Cornelius Vanderbilt, whom Morgan had cheated. In addition, Walker may be seen as a manifestation of United States expansion and the opposition as allied with British resistance to such expansion.[1]

Curiously, the majority of the clergy and hierarchy collaborated with Walker, the "Liberal," and Father Augustín Vigil donated money to Walker and served as a minister in his government. To another priest supporter, Father Herdocia, Walker wrote, "Without the aid of religious sentiments and religious guides, there can be no good government since the fear of God is the basis of all social and political organization."[2] Some clergy, however, did oppose Walker.

51

For Nicaraguans, William Walker (the "filibusterer") is a permanent symbol of imperialism and they call the war in which he was defeated the National War. Disgraced by their alliance with William Walker, the Liberals were out of power until the presidency of José Santos Zelaya (1893–1909), who may be described as an "authoritarian, modernizing nationalist."[3] Zelaya increasingly ran afoul of the United States because of his hopes to build a canal (in conjunction with Germany or Japan) and his cancellation of some American concessions. The United States government also professed concern at his involvement in attacks on neighboring countries. In 1909 the United States showed its backing of a Conservative revolt by landing 400 marines in Bluefields on the Atlantic coast to protect retreating rebel forces. The execution of two American demolition experts contracted by Conservatives gave the United States a pretext to break with the Zelaya regime, and a few months later he felt forced to resign.

Supporting Conservative forces and using gunboats at critical moments, the United States was able to put into the presidency Adolfo Díaz, a former accountant with an American mining company. When Díaz was under threat from rebel Liberal forces, the United States again sent the marines, 2,700 of whom were used to defeat General Benjamin Zeledón. The consequences were decisive for subsequent Nicaraguan history. In Richard Millett's words:

> Following the defeat of Zeledón's force the bulk of American troops in Nicaragua were rapidly withdrawn. A 100-man legation guard, however, remained in Nicaragua until August 1925. Small as this force was, its mere presence exercised a major influence on internal politics. Its retention symbolized to Nicaraguans the United States' determination not to allow a revolution. Combined with the experiences of 1912, this served to keep the minority Conservative Party in power and internal disturbances at a relatively low level from 1912 until 1925.[4]

The United States took a direct part in the administration of the Nicaraguan government, particularly in customs and tax collection, essentially in the interests of New York banks. (During the same period the United States similarly intervened in the Dominican Republic, Haiti, and Cuba.) By the 1914 Bryan-Chamorro Treaty the United States acquired exclusive rights to build an interoceanic canal through Nicaragua.[5]

Rather than focus on the issue of foreign intervention and domination, the Catholic church's view of events during this period was affected more by Liberal anticlericalism and Conservative support of the church. Zelaya had enacted anticlerical legislation intending to secularize the state and to end the clergy's economic privileges, abolishing the *cofradías* (religious associations), thus freeing their land to be taken by coffee producers. Clerics understandably were allied to the Conservatives, and when they came into power, church-state harmony was restored (for example, one cabinet minister ordered pictures of the Sacred Heart put in all government offices), and there was a Catholic renewal, with many religious orders returning.[6]

Although he had also protested the anticlerical measures of the Zelaya government, Bishop Simeón Pereira y Castrellón in 1912 wrote to Cardinal Gibbons of Baltimore protesting that his tiny country was feeling the power of the United States "millions and its men": "Your strong country, with its gunboats and cannons, has dominated our weak country, and the treasuries of the bankers are fortified with its daily and annihilating suctioning of our empty coffers to support heavy debts, unjust treaties and unequal contracts." In this vein, with elaborate parallel sentences, Pereira continued, pleading that American hierarchy take the case to the tribunal of public opinion, warning that behind the material conquest would come "spiritual conquest," a "wave of Protestantism."[7]

Under the umbrella of the U.S. Marines' occupation, the Conservatives remained in power, while the United States sought to achieve some stability by training a Nicaraguan armed force. Although they were withdrawn in 1925, the marines returned in 1926 to help put down a Liberal rebellion on the Atlantic coast. This they accomplished by establishing increasingly wider "neutral" zones, ostensibly to protect American property and citizens. Finally in 1927 Henry Stimson arrived as an emissary of President Calvin Coolidge to give the Liberal leader, José María Moncada, an ultimatum: either lay down arms and take part in the 1928 elections to be supervised by marines, or face military opposition from the marines. Faced with this threat all the Liberal "generals" but one surrendered: Augusto César Sandino.

Born the illegitimate son of a landowner and a peasant woman, Sandino had worked at different jobs in his country and in Honduras, Guatemala, and Mexico (during its revolution). He had arrived back in Nicaragua in the midst of the Liberal-Conservative struggle and, taking his place alongside Moncada, he gathered a group of peasant fighters.

After his lone refusal to surrender, Sandino engaged in a guerrilla war against the National Guard, which was being trained by the U. S. Marines, and against the marines themselves for five and a half years. While he initially saw his struggle as one for the Liberal party, he soon came to see it as essentially against a foreign invader. After suffering severe defeats he switched to guerrilla techniques and was remarkably successful against the marines who, with superior forces and weaponry including airplanes, were not able to defeat Sandino, whom they sought to discredit as a "bandit."

Support for Sandino, together with protest over United States intervention, grew internationally (and in the United States). Sandino was interviewed in the mountains by Carlton Beals for *The Nation* and voices of protest were raised in congressional hearings. The United States moved toward a policy of what might later have been called "Nicaraguanization," by training the National Guard. In 1933 the marines were withdrawn, having failed to defeat Sandino's irregulars.

At this point Sandino entered into truce negotiations with the government. However, when he went to Managua in 1934, Sandino and a number of his close associates were murdered by orders from the head of the National Guard, Anastasio Somoza García.[8] Hundreds of Sandino's followers were then killed and the sporadic guerrilla resistance was defeated as Somoza tightened his grip on Nicaragua.[9]

Today Sandino's cowboy-hatted figure and profile are omnipresent in Nicaragua, and his words are quoted in speeches and on billboards. A few examples may give some idea of why his words still echo:

> Nicaragua does not owe the United States a cent; but they owe us the peace lost in our country since 1909, when Wall Street brought in the weed pest of the dollar.

> [Demanding as a prior condition for any truce the withdrawal of the U.S. Marines]: . . . You do not discuss the sovereignty of a country; you defend it by taking up arms. . . .

> [At the Last Judgment] the oppressed peoples will break the chains of humiliation, with which the imperialists of the earth have wanted to keep them backward.

> [To General Hatfield, who demanded surrender, offering guarantees for his safety]: *Yo quiero patria libre o morir* [I want a free country or death].[10]

All evidence indicates that the church hierarchy did not see Sandino's resistance as a patriotic struggle. Bishop Canuto Reyes y Balladares of Granada blessed the marines' weapons as they set out to pursue Sandino in 1927. In a pastoral letter in October 1930, the bishops of Managua, León, Granada, and Matagalpa spoke of the struggle as one that could only bring misfortune on those fighting, and they exhorted the combatants to "abandon sterile armed struggles, return to the life of home and work and to the fulfillment of religious duties."[11]

Dictatorship was the norm in Central America from the 1930s until the late 1940s (see chapter 3), partly in order to quell potential unrest provoked by the effects of the Great Depression. In Nicaragua, Anastasio Somoza García, who started with virtually no property (and had once sold cars in Philadelphia) began to concentrate his power, using his control over the National Guard and the Liberal party. He made immense profits from war-related products, acquired more and more land, and siphoned payments from organized vice. At the time of his death he was said to have a tenth of the cultivated land, a large percentage of incipient industry, and a fortune estimated at $60 million, a large sum indeed in a poor country the size of Nicaragua.

Throughout this period the church served symbolically to legitimate the

Somoza rule. For example, in 1942 Archbishop Lezcano crowned Somoza's daughter queen of the army in a ceremony in the national stadium, using a crown from the statue of the Virgin of Candelaria.[12] In a 1950 pastoral letter the Nicaraguan bishops expressed the traditional view that "all authority comes from God" and that Catholics should realize that "when they obey the Ruler, they do not abase themselves, but on the contrary, they perform an act which ultimately amounts to obeying God."[13] Hence when Anastasio Somoza García was assassinated in 1956, Pope Pius XII and Cardinal Spellman sent condolences and Archbishop González offered 200 days' indulgence to Catholics assisting at prayers for Somoza, who was buried with the honors of a "Prince of the Church."[14] There was one exception to this general policy of legitimating, at least implicitly, the Somoza rule. Bishop Calderón y Padilla refused to attend Somoza's funeral and instead went out to visit rural missions in his diocese.[15]

Certainly the Nicaraguan hierarchy at the time would not have seen its role as one of legitimating an opprobrious dictatorship. Such a role was largely unconscious and nonproblematic, simply a reflection of the traditional doctrine and practice of respect for constituted authority as long as it allowed the church to act in its own sphere. Reflecting the mentality of the period the hierarchy expressed its preoccupation over the advances of Protestantism and communism.[16]

FROM THE FALL OF SOMOZA GARCÍA (1956) TO THE MANAGUA EARTHQUAKE (1972)

On September 21, 1956, Rigoberto López Pérez, a poet, made his way into a reception for Anastasio Somoza García and shot him five times point blank before being gunned down himself by Somoza's bodyguards. The dictator died a few days later despite the Eisenhower administration's efforts to save him with the best medical treatment at its disposal. Eisenhower referred to López as a "cowardly assassin," a curious designation for one who knew that his act would surely bring his own instantaneous death.[17] As just mentioned, official church figures, for the most part, uncritically echoed the expressions of mourning.

Far from ending the dictatorship, the assassination of Anastasio Somoza García led to its becoming institutionalized into the "Somoza system." Somoza García had sent his sons to the United States for schooling, and Luis, who was president of the Nicaraguan Congress, took over from his father, while Anastasio, a West Point graduate and head of the National Guard, seized and imprisoned civilian politicians. Luis Somoza was "elected" president of Nicaragua in 1957, and, while it seemed he might relax some controls and permit somewhat more "democratic" freedoms, nevertheless he ruled through puppet presidents René Schick Gutiérrez and Lorenzo Guerrero until 1967. At that point by means of blatant fraud Anastasio Somoza Debayle was "elected" president. Although his term ended in

1971 he had the Constitution amended to allow himself an extra year, and with the advice of United States Ambassador Turner Shelton, he made a pact with the head of the Conservative party, Fernando Agüero, whereby he would hand power over to a triumvirate of two Liberals and one Conservative (Agüero) while he continued to hold real power as head of the National Guard until he could be "elected" again in 1974.[18]

This Somoza-Agüero Pact illustrates the false nature of the legal anti-Somoza political parties; for example, one Conservative faction was derisively called *zancudos* ("mosquitos") to indicate how little "bite" they had in reality. Since they were guaranteed a 40 percent participation in Congress and were given a share of positions in government and administration, the Conservatives were always co-opted, but they could never come into power, since elections were rigged. According to Thomas Walker, in his book *Nicaragua: The Land of Sandino*, "On election day, there was multiple voting by the pro-Somoza faithful, tampering with the ballot boxes, and cleverest of all, the use of a translucent secret ballot that, even when folded, could easily be scrutinized by government election officials as it was deposited in the ballot box."[19] Several other parties functioned: the Independent Liberal party, the Nicaraguan Socialist party (both founded in 1944, the latter by communists), and the Nicaraguan Social Christian party, begun in 1957.

When co-optation, bribery, and fraud were not enough, intimidation and repression were used, both against individuals and occasionally against groups; in January 1967 during the electoral campaign, the National Guard attacked an opposition demonstration. According to Millett, the opposition parties hoped to incite the Guard to revolt against Somoza and encouraged demonstrators to arrive with weapons. The Guard attacked, and 40 were killed and at least 100 wounded. (Some say 200 or even 400 were killed.)[20] Today this incident is seen as evidencing the traditional opposition's irresponsibility and ineffectiveness as well as the Somoza regime's brutality.

Throughtout this period the Somozas increased the economic empire begun by their father in the 1940s. They continued to accumulate land and began to assemble dozens of industries and businesses, which they operated as monopolies, among them dairy products, a steamship line, the airline, and a cement factory with many spinoffs such as street-paving blocks and roofing materials. One Somoza tactic was simply to request that investors hand over shares in their enterprises as part of the price of doing business in Nicaragua.[21] Those who profited from the Somoza system included not only family members but also allied Liberal politicians (and even the token opposition) and particularly National Guard officers, who, for example, owned much of the bus and taxi system of the country and could collect from certain taxes and auto fines. Some have likened the whole system to a Mafia operation.

During the 1960s the Somozas adopted the Alliance-for-Progress rhetoric and government technocrats prepared high-sounding development plans.

The funds, however, ended up largely in the hands of the Somozas and their associates. Thomas Walker recounts a revealing anecdote, which he heard directly from Francisco Lainez, who had been the chief of those technocrats.

> One day Luis Somoza, in a pensive mood, asked Lainez to tell him in all frankness what one thing he, Lainez, would do if he were in Luis's shoes, to bring development to Nicaragua. Lainez thought for a moment and then responded that he would take each of the major categories in the national budget—health, education, etc.—and see to it that *at least half* of that money actually went for the purposes for which it was ostensibly destined. According to Lainez, Luis simply smiled sadly and responded, "You're being unrealistic."[22]

Throughout this period the Somozas were unconditional allies of the United States. As his father had allowed Nicaragua to be used for the overthrow of President Arbenz in Guatemala (1954), Luis Somoza allowed it to be used as training and launching site for the Bay of Pigs invasion attempt (Cuba, 1961). Nicaraguan Guardsmen participated in the invasion of the Dominican Republic (1965), and the Somozas offered them for use in Korea and Vietnam. When, with Pentagon urging, CONDECA (Central American Defense Council), a regional military alliance, was established in 1964, Anastasio Somoza was a key figure.

The Sandinista National Liberation Front

Any treatment of Christian participation in the anti-Somoza struggle must take up the question of how opposition to the dictatorship was formed. However, explanations for Anastasio Somoza's fall vary widely. Somoza himself, in *Nicaragua Betrayed*, explained it as largely the infidelity of other countries and in particular the United States under President Jimmy Carter, a view later echoed among American conservatives. Some accounts present the FSLN as essentially one element among several—the implication being that its later hegemony represents a usurpation. On the other hand, some FSLN writings tend to minimize all non-Sandinista opposition.[23]

The point is more than academic: at stake is the nature of the anti-Somoza struggle, and accordingly the postvictory mandate from the people; in other words, who "owns" the revolution? And one's choice of events to highlight or to ignore is qualified by one's reading of the process as a whole. The present writer sees the primary actor as the Nicaraguan people itself, and in particular large numbers of the ordinary people, who were willing to struggle and to die. Through a complex process they came to see the Sandinista Front as the leading edge—the "vanguard"—of the whole struggle. Although the numbers of Sandinistas in any action were never more than a few dozen until the final year, yet they seem to have both grasped the people's aspirations and, through a long apprenticeship, learned to lead the struggle. At the same time, the role of the middle-class opposition, both through the private sector and its organizations, and through opposition political parties, was crucial. Institutionally the Catholic church may be counted as part of the middle-class opposition. One of the fascinating aspects of the Nicaraguan revolution is how the diverse opposition forces eventually came together (under the hegemony of the FSLN). But that is anticipating the story: here the purpose is to indicate this writer's angle of vision and, insofar as humanly possible, do justice to the various groups involved.[24]

From the time of Sandino onward, sporadic resistance to the Somoza regime appeared; one plan to assassinate Somoza in 1954 failed when one of the conspirators turned informer. Between the death of Somoza García (1956) and 1960 there were more than twenty armed movements, typically launched from neighboring countries.[25] As an outgrowth of some of these struggles the FSLN was founded in 1961. John Booth has found interesting similarities among the three men commonly considered to be its founders: Carlos Fonseca Amador, Tomás Borge Martínez, and Silvio Mayorga: "they had all (1) been student activists in the late forties and fifties; (2) come from Matagalpa where they attended the Instituto Nacional del Norte; (3) been victims of imprisonment or torture for their real or suspected political activities; and (4) become Marxists during the 1950s."[26] Borge, however, considers a number of others, who did not participate in the founding meeting, to be nevertheless "founders" of the FSLN.

After spending some time in training (Colonel Santos López, who had fought alongside Sandino, had joined them), the FSLN engaged in its first organized guerrilla actions in 1963, both in a bank "recuperation" and in rural fighting in the area of the Coco and Bocay rivers, near the Honduran border. This experience ended badly and a number of FSLN militants were killed. (Also during this period some 300 peasants in the Chinandega area were said to have been killed in response to their efforts to organize rural unions.)[27]

During the mid-1960s the FSLN devoted itself more to political work (for example, teaching peasants to read and forming trade unions), returning to armed actions in 1966–67. The National Guard caught and destroyed one of the three guerrilla forces in the mountains, at Pancasán. What was then a resounding military defeat was later seen as a political triumph because it brought the FSLN to national attention. A number of others were arrested (including two women, Gladys Baez and Doris Tijerino).

In 1968–69 the FSLN, while continuing its activities, was reorganized and Carlos Fonseca Amador became secretary-general. He and several other FSLN leaders were captured and jailed in Costa Rica. In 1969 there appeared a "Program of the Popular Sandinista Revolution," which was summarized in fifteen points that are the more interesting in the light of later developments:

1. People's guerrilla combat. 2. People's power. 3. A special plan for the Atlantic Coast and abandoned areas. 4. Land for peasants. 5. End to exploitation and misery. 6. Woman's emancipation. 7. Administrative honesty. 8. A patriotic popular army. 9. Revolution in culture and teaching. 10. Respect for religious beliefs. 11. Independent foreign policy. 12. Abolition of the Bryan-Chamorro Treaty [which had given the United States rights to build a canal through Nicaragua]. 13. Popular Central American unity. 14. Solidarity among peoples. 15. Veneration for martyrs [of the revolution].

There were also major protest actions such as a teachers' strike and demands that the bodies of fallen Sandinistas be handed over.

In January 1970 three FSLN militants, including Leonel Rugama, a young poet, were attacked in a private home by 300 troops, helicopters, and tanks. Their defiant fight to the end was yet another symbol to the people. Throughout 1970–72 the level of armed combat stepped up. At the same time there were large nonviolent actions protesting the dictatorship: a teachers' strike in 1970 with parental support; the occupation of churches in 1971 with demands for the release of political prisoners; and in 1972 a hunger strike by political prisoners, supported by their families.

Church Renewal and Clash with the Somocismo

The renewal associated with Vatican II was first seen in middle-class manifestations because those classes were most in contact with the church, and the church in middle-class milieux was most similar to the church of the North Atlantic countries that had, to a great extent, set the Vatican Council's agenda and carried it out. In this connection one may mention the Cursillos de Cristiandad, which in fact antedated the council but profited from the general movement of renewal; the Christian Family Movement; and the foundation of UCA (Central American University), staffed by Jesuits and set up originally to provide an atmosphere academically more serious and freer of leftist influence than the National University.

Also in the early 1960s the Nicaraguan Social Christian party, originally the product of Catholic intellectuals of the 1950s, began to grow. Christian Democratic parties tend to show an inherent tension between the forces of reform and those of anticommunism and the Nicaraguan party was no exception, splitting into two parties, one calling itself the Popular Social Christian party. People of this latter tendency formed INPRUHU (Institute for Human Promotion) in 1964 and set up the CTN (Confederation of Workers of Nicaragua). In the late 1960s INPRUHU undertook various kinds of development projects and literacy training, using the *concientización* methods of Paulo Freire.

Ultimately, however, the most significant kind of church work took place in basic Christian communities. A pioneering effort was that of Father José de la Jara, begun in 1966 in San Pablo parish, in what was then a squatter settlement on the outskirts of Managua, whose conditions varied between the mud of the rainy season and the thick dust clouds of the dry season. De la Jara borrowed the pastoral method of the San Miguelito "experiment" in Panama City, which had begun in 1963 with a pastoral team of priests and sisters led by Father Leo Mahon of Chicago. Mahon's genius was that of grasping basic themes of human life as experienced by the people and linking them with basic scriptural motifs, all brought together into a course called "The Family of God" (see chapter 1). These Socratic dialogues were so much in tune with people's experience and expression that lay people could learn to lead them, with a consequent multiplier effect. Initial formation was deepened in weekend *cursillos*, patterned initially on some aspects of Cursillos de Cristiandad.

Looking back on this experience, one of the priests in the parish noted positive benefits from this Family-of-God phase: its stress on the family and the Christian community (which was a "revolutionary idea" for Nicaragua at that time), the importance given to women, a new way of celebrating the Mass as a meeting of the community, dialogue sermons, and the fact that the parish developed the first Nicaraguan folk Mass (1967). The effects from San Pablo parish began to radiate out to other groups such as in Solentiname.

However, after some time the people began to feel a certain unease about the Family-of-God approach. It all seemed aimed at the internal renovation of individuals and the church but not oriented to the larger society. Gradually emphasis began to shift toward a focus on people's rights. At one point the parish was a major factor in a protest against a busfare hike, in which some 20,000 people protested.[28]

Similar types of work were being undertaken in some rural areas. In 1968 American Capuchins, who were in charge of the Atlantic coast region, held the first course for "Delegates of the Word," leaders who were given training not only to lead worship but also to promote development in health, agriculture, and literacy. Many of the people in these areas were settlers who had migrated from other parts of the country where they had been pushed off their lands by the powerful and were now living in scattered settlements. Such education programs helped them to overcome their isolation, confront their problems, and begin to work as communities.[29]

In early 1969 large numbers of clergy, religious, and lay people met to discuss the Medellín documents, which were just being published. Although the meeting in itself accomplished little, it provided the opportunity for taking a critical look at existing pastoral practice, furthered dialogue among pastoral agents, and legitimated a more radical role for the church in society.[30]

During the mid-1960s a small group of evangelicals, mainly Baptist, which was in contact with developments elsewhere in Latin America, became radicalized. While the immediate effect for most of the individuals was estrangement from their own congregations, some subsequently became important Sandinista leaders, and a few played important roles within their churches during the 1970s.[31]

Although there was no broad-based church opposition to Somoza during this period, individual actors in the church played significant roles. Bishop Calderón y Padilla, who had refused to attend Somoza García's funeral, continued to be opposed to the dictatorship. In 1960 young insurgents who had attacked an army barracks asked that he mediate a settlement, and in 1963 the opposition proposed to him to be president of the National Electoral Council. When Somoza wanted to see Calderón during one of his 1967 electoral-campaign tours, the bishop said he would not receive Somoza while there were so many political prisoners. On the other hand, Bishop Donaldo Chávez Nuñez publicly defended the government after the bloody repression of the opposition demonstration in January 1967.[32]

A decisive factor was the arrival of a number of new priests in the mid-1960s after their studies abroad. In 1968 seven of them, rather in the style characteristic of Latin America during that period, produced a document calling for a ministry of service and human development on the part of the church, and demanding that the government halt repression and torture and free political prisoners.[33]

When 400 National Guardsmen attacked a house where an FSLN militant, Julio Buitrago, held out until the end, two bishops and seven priests protested the government's use of excessive force. Similarly, on January 15, 1970, Father Francisco Mejía intervened personally when the National Guard attacked the house where Leonel Rugama and other Sandinistas were fighting, hoping to reduce the violence. When Mejía was jailed Bishop Borge y Castrillo visited him, later saying Mejía had not been mistreated and noting that he was not in clerical garb. Bishop Barni of Matagalpa contradicted this version, saying the priest had been beaten and had a head wound. The Priests' Council of León protested his treatment and related it to other developments:

> There are many expressions of dissatisfaction which appear every day in our society: strikes repressed with violence; students killed with no efforts to save them; protest theater, student demonstrations at different academic levels, arbitrary arrests, proven repeated torture of political prisoners; calls to the people from the young clergy, and for the first time in Nicaragua, physical and moral torture of a priest, Father Francisco Mejía.[34]

Later in 1970 students at UCA began to question the orientation of the university, and when the authorities refused to dialogue they occupied it. In August a group of students and some priests occupied the cathedral of Managua, protesting human-rights violations.[35] In September José Antonio Sanjinés, a Jesuit who had participated in the occupation, was expelled from the country, and by late that year almost a hundred students associated with the movement had been jailed. There were further occupations of churches in 1971. Out of these experiences emerged the Revolutionary Christian Movement, although it came formally into existence some time later, and in the National University.[36]

Around this period the hierarchy gave signs of moving away from its traditional role of legitimating the Somoza regime. All observers found it highly significant that the new archbishop of Managua, Miguel Obando y Bravo, sold a Mercedes-Benz given him by Somoza (who had the dealership) and gave the money to the poor. Late in the year he issued his first pastoral letter, echoing Medellín and speaking of the church's mission to denounce injustice and commit its members to a peaceful transformation of society so that people may become "free artisans of their own destiny." Obando refused to attend the ceremony celebrating the Somoza-Agüero Pact, which ostensibly ended Liberal-Conservative feuding, but was, as noted earlier, a device to perpetuate Anastasio Somoza in power.[37]

On June 29, 1971, the bishops published a pastoral letter on "The Duty of Witness and Christian Action in the Political Order," which called for the formation of a "civic consciousness since our people have new demands in their soul regarding the distribution of goods, and the organizational structures which make up the framework of communal life."[38]

In order to appreciate the sense of the bishops' next important document—and the reaction it provoked—it is necessary to put it into its political context, the triumvirate formula, which resulted from the Somoza-Agüero Pact. The bishops released a letter "On the Principles of the Church's Political Activity," which opened with a warning that beneath the apparent stability were dangerous tensions. They claimed they were not defending the "rights or aspirations of any political group." Distinguishing party politics from politics understood as the pursuit of the common good, they noted that the church

> has always considered that it had a right to be involved and an obligation to be involved in the political life of peoples. . . .
> As pastors, bishops and priests may be obligated to refrain entering into partisan struggles but never when it is a question of struggling for a more just order. . . .

Noting that Nicaragua's political structures did not measure up to the demands of the age and that although the struggles in Latin America (whether more or less peaceful, or in the form of guerrilla actions or open warfare) might be taken advantage of by political forces, they were

> but the irrepressible cry of a people which is becoming aware of its situation and is seeking ways to break the molds holding it in. What is sought is a whole new order. These efforts being made in many places may be

repressed or delayed by force but the movement is underway and the old systems have many faults.

In an allusive way the bishops said that

Systematically shutting out other groups from access to public activity leads to exacerbating the political tensions among those who are left out, thus endangering peace and depriving the country of a necessary contrast in opposing viewpoints on such activity, clearly harming the public good, which is the only purpose of political activity.[39]

Despite the convoluted prose, the antidictatorial message was clear.

This letter provoked considerable commentary. For example, the poet and Christian intellectual José Coronel Urtecho went so far as to say, "I think the latest pastoral letter of the bishops is the most important document the church has put out since Father Agüero said the first Mass on Nicaraguan territory in 1523."[40] This remark revealed a phenomenon that would continue to recur: although the bishops claimed that they were simply presenting broad principles, the anti-Somoza political parties seized upon such statements as supporting their own positions. Bishop Calderón y Padilla of Matagalpa was honored in a ceremony by the opposition parties as "the bishop of dignity" in June 1970, clearly as contrasted with Bishops Borge y Castrillo, Chávez Nuñez, and García y Suarez, who were considered friends and supporters of the Somozas.[41] In the highly charged atmosphere of Nicaragua, the bishops' statements would inevitably be received as either favoring or opposing the Somoza dictatorship, whatever disingenuous protestations might be made in the text. It was also clear that the bishops were warning that, unless the political system were given greater flexibility, other forces such as the Frente Sandinista would benefit.

In the early 1970s a group of university students who had participated in the cathedral occupations and other actions sensed the need to form a "Christian community" (partly inspired by the examples of Solentiname and San Pablo parish). They approached Father Uriel Molina, pastor of a parish in barrio Rigueiro, with the idea. Launching the community with a midnight ceremony in November 1971 were Molina, three sisters, and several students. Molina later described the experience:

We set up a schedule. Every morning before breakfast we got up for prayer. At night after university classes, we had a session analyzing Nicaragua using Marxism as a method. . . . The community became news. Many young people came to take part in prayer or reflection. It ended up with chats that went far into the night with guitar serenades and protest music. We deepened our faith and our political commitment. Soon there were reactions, as was to be expected. Once when dairy-owners raised milk prices, the young people could explain the problem, since they were linked to the parish council and parish religious organizations. After some reflection, a decision was made to organize a boycott and stop milk trucks by throwing tacks on the road.[42]

This experience in the Rigueiro barrio proved to be very important. A number of those in the community later became prominent Sandinista leaders, including Luis Carrión, one of the members of the FSLN Directorate. For the FSLN the parish was a place to meet young people. Molina describes his reactions: "Many young Sandinistas who were not yet involved in clandestine struggle frequently came to the community to talk with the young people. I confess it was very hard for me to unite the Christian experience with the Sandinista struggle." He felt pressured by his superiors and the hierarchy and did not feel he could accept armed struggle as an "objective fact." "Now after victory I see it clearly. We have not been able to incorporate risk and struggle into our formation. The Sandinista Front gave the young people something I could not: risk and struggle till death for a cause (the cause of the people)."[43]

During this same period, Fernando Cardenal, who was forced out of UCA (run by his own order, the Jesuits) and went to work at the National University, began to have contacts with FSLN people. In one conversation, Oscar Turcios, a Sandinista commander, told him: "It shouldn't concern me if you believe there is something after death, nor should it interest you if I think that after death I'm going to rot here. What should concern us is that we can both work together to build a new Nicaragua."[44] Cardenal also spoke with Carlos Fonseca Amador about similar questions. At least by hindsight he does not seem to have experienced the same difficulties as Molina:

Since I began working with the Sandinista Front I have never—never!— at any moment met anything which contradicts my Christian faith, nor which clashes with my Christian morality. Never. Just the opposite. For me the Sandinista Front has been the channel that has enabled me to live my Christian faith more authentically, that is, with actions.[45]

By late 1972 church people were involved in the initial stages of the anti-Somoza struggle. Important grassroots work had begun in Managua and in the countryside, and there were significant contacts between the FSLN and some people in the church. The clergy and hierarchy had been involved in conflictive situations, particularly in protest over human-rights abuses, and the hierarchy had taken some steps, in both symbolic actions and statements, to move from its traditional posture of legitimation.

Missing, however, was a viable and feasible alternative to the Somoza regime.

INTENSIFYING CONFLICT:
FROM THE EARTHQUAKE (1972)
TO SOMOZA'S HEART ATTACK (1977)

In December 1972 the community of Fatima parish and others were holding a fast outside the cathedral in Managua to protest the consumerism of the Christmas season. Suddenly, on December 23, shortly after midnight, an earthquake jolted Managua. The whole downtown section (mainly adobe structures, but also some reinforced concrete) was destroyed, either by the earthquake itself or by fires. Some 10,000 people were killed, tens of thousands were injured, and hundreds of thousands were homeless. Many were in a state of shock from the terror of the earthquake and grief over the loss of family members.

During the first two or three days there was anarchy: Somoza's Guard disbanded as its members took care of their own family problems, or took part in the massive looting of stores, sometimes with officers directing and using National Guard vehicles. Guatemalan, Salvadoran, and United States troops were used to restore order until the National Guard could be reassembled. During this time the American ambassador, Turner Shelton, calmed Somoza's fears, coached him in how to handle the situation, and encouraged him to take total power. He accordingly made himself head of the National Emergency Committee and shoved the triumvirate aside.[46] Later he amended the Constitution to allow himself another presidential term, which he "won" in the election of 1974.

For Somoza and his associates the earthquake presented an unparalleled opportunity for further aggrandizement, which began with the international aid arriving on planes from countries around the world. National Guard officers siphoned off what they desired. A 600-block area had been destroyed and most of the buildings left partly standing were knocked down and the area was bulldozed and fenced off. Poor families sought out relatives in other cities or erected instant shantytowns around the outskirts of the city. During the next two or three years there was little government-organized reconstruction despite large aid loans for that purpose. Public transportation without a city center became much more difficult and costly. In the meantime Somoza and his cronies began to speculate in land, using their knowledge about potential reconstruction sites to buy and sell. In the most famous example, a Somoza military aide bought 93.6 acres for $71,428 in July 1975 and sold 56.8 acres of it to the government for $1.7 million a little more than two months later. A later audit showed extreme corruption in the use of $76.7 million in United States A.I.D. funds.[47] Much of the profiteering was technically legal inasmuch as Somoza could simply award himself contracts; for example, since he owned the cement industry he had the streets paved with *adoquines* (interlocking blocks), which were also manufactured by the factory he owned.

Somoza at this point had a fortune estimated at perhaps $300 million. The family owned 5 million acres of land—an area approximately as big as El Salvador—although there were 200,000 landless Nicaraguan peasants. Somoza also owned the twenty-six largest businesses in the country.[48] With such vast wealth Somoza became a business associate of Howard Hughes, the contact being made through Ambassador Shelton. (Hughes was occupying a floor of the Intercontinental Hotel the night of the earthquake.) Part of Somoza's undoing was his own voracious greed after the earthquake, which began to exhaust the tolerance of significant segments of the upper class.

Somoza's greed angered other sectors as well, since he imposed new taxes and increased the working week to sixty hours with no increase in pay. There were strikes by workers and teachers. Immediately after the earthquake the FSLN had spread its cadres around the country to work in relief and reconstruction and in political work, and it was able to participate in the strikes. Other FSLN militants began to establish peasant contacts in the mountainous northern regions and to lay the basis for guerrilla forces there.[49]

In May 1974 Amada Pineda, wife of a union activist and herself a member of the Nicaraguan Socialist party, was picked up by the National Guard, beaten, tied up, and repeatedly raped for three days. When she later denounced this in *La Prensa* she was herself formally accused of calumny by the officers she had denounced. Her case was unusual only in that it came to public attention.[50]

Curiously, in their postearthquake message the Nicaraguan bishops were remarkably muted in their criticism. While they stated that "robberies and repression will only increase discontent and hunger," they seemed to emphasize more the embarrassment of Nicaraguans over their "image abroad" and said, "We are all to blame."[51]

At the grassroots level many pastoral agents moved into closer contact with the people. The Sisters of the Assumption saw firsthand the corruption of the Somoza regime, as did the Maryknoll Sisters in OPEN 3, a shantytown now swelling with new families from the destroyed area several kilometers away. The university students in barrio Rigueiro "organized cleanup brigades, passed out food, and took advantage of the moment to raise consciousness and mobilize people."[52] Bayardo Arce, an FSLN commander, speaks of deepening contacts with Christian groups:

With the earthquake they became a little more radicalized, saw that the alternative had to be political, and agreed to enter the FER [Revolutionary Student Federation]. Luis Carrión, Joaquín Cuadra, Alvaro Baltodano, and Roberto Gutiérrez made up the first Christian cell. They were given the task of organizing a progressive Christian movement, which could bring together the Christian people in an organized manner and could do intermediate tasks for the Front.[53]

A similar front was formed in León.

In the eastern and northern part of the country the Capuchins deepened the grassroots work begun earlier, using *concientización* techniques such as sociodramas, discussions of drawings, and pantomimes. One interesting twist was to have discussions around simplified versions of the Nicaraguan Constitution and Labor Code. Discussion leaders invited the people to compare the texts with their actual experience. Even some police and *jueces de mesta* (similar to justices of the peace, but frequently serving as government informers) participated in the discussions. Leonel Espinosa, who was organizing for the FSLN during this period, speaks of having benefited from the "Franciscans" (i.e., Capuchins) who "were speaking of the differences between rich and poor and creating a new consciousness." He himself acted as a Delegate of the Word and worked closely with Father Evaristo Bertrand.[54]

Not all pastoral innovations served to encourage resistance to the dictatorship. In 1974 there appeared the *Catecumenado*, a Bible study program originally from Italy. Deriving its name from the "Catechumenate," the lengthy teaching given to prospective converts from paganism during the early centuries of Christianity, it was structured as a seven-year program with assigned biblical texts for discussion. Critics pointed out that the discussion revolved around texts and not about their relation to events in the surrounding society, so that the net effect was to turn people inward on themselves and on a small church community and thus nullify any wider impact. The Catechumenate, which made inroads not only in middle-class parishes but also in barrios such as OPEN 3, illustrates the contrast between pastoral efforts that take society as a central reference point and those that, even though innovative in some ways, have the effect of turning people inward.

The earthquake's impact on Protestant churches was dramatic and far-reaching. Gustavo Parajón, a Baptist doctor, called Protestant leaders together four days after the earthquake and soon CEPAD (Protestant Committee for Aid and Development) was established and began to administer clinics, refugee centers, and breakfast programs for victims of the earthquake, and subsequently began a housing program. As the emergency period passed, CEPAD moved into longer-term development projects, using its network of Protestant congregations and funds from international church agencies, eventually becoming one of the largest private voluntary agencies in Nicaragua.

Perhaps more important than CEPAD's projects was a process of unification among the churches and group reflection on the purpose of pastoral activity. Among Nicaragua's 70,000 Protestants (3 percent of the population), the largest churches are the Moravian, Baptist, and Assembly of God. However, there are many smaller churches often engaged in sharp rivalry at the local level. CEPAD succeeded in bringing over thirty denominations and churches together, first in order to receive and administer aid, and then to initiate a process of dialogue. A retreat of 300 pastors and church workers gave CEPAD its mandate to continue this work.[55]

One incident may serve to symbolize the increasing conflict between parts of the Catholic church and the Somoza regime.

> On the first anniversary of the earthquake the Church hierarchy held a commemorative mass in the central plaza of Managua. Somoza, who had intended to hold a government-sponsored event, cancelled his plans and invited himself to the Church celebration. Meanwhile, the Christian communities of Managua, particularly from such parishes as San Pablo and Fatima, resolved to make their own presence felt at the celebration. . . . With the assistance of priests, parishioners made hundreds of hand-held placards and carried them secretly into the plaza. As the ceremony unfolded, Somoza and his officials were deeply offended by the statements of the bishops and angered by the display of anti-regime slogans. Abruptly he got up and walked out, while national guardsmen disconnected the loudspeakers carrying the Archbishop's speech to the audience.[56]

The church was increasingly seen by opposition forces as a space for expressing discontent. For example, the traditional New Year's procession, which often displayed slogans adapted from Vatican pronouncements—for example, "If you want peace, work for justice"—would attract notable figures from the middle-class opposition and opposition parties.

In 1974 the bishops produced two statements obviously occasioned by the "election" scheduled for September (which Somoza would clearly "win"). In May they noted that the "military institution" should not serve particular interests—a not-so-veiled recognition that the "National" Guard was Somoza's personal army. They declared that those in public office should be the first to serve public order, and that "disorder" results if freedoms are not served equally. Though the language was somewhat hypothetical they seemed to be denouncing abuses such as house searches by the National Guard, torture, and the injustice of the legal system, noting that their letters to the government on these matters had gone unanswered.

Rather more pointed was the pastoral letter "Man, Church, and Society," dated August 6, 1974, which proposed to "clarify the duty of participation in political activity." Despite its treatise-like appearance, it was for the most part a collection of remarks, some surprising: "Whether we like it or not, we are in revolution. In all orders old and rigid molds are falling apart . . ."; "Peace . . . cannot be established on the basis of repressive force." The bishops insisted on the "right to dissent," which could even become a duty ("Better for us to obey God than man!" Acts. 5:29): "The right to dissent is based on the right of every person not to be alienated by anyone, nor in favor of anyone against that person's conscience. It is invoked especially against totalitarian regimes." The bishops applied their general principles to voting and insisted more than once that people could not be obliged to vote "against their people" or "against their own conscience" and that political parties existed not for themselves nor for the state but for the people.[57] The emphasis on this latter point would seem to be a clear allusion to Somoza's Liberal party, which was in effect a part of the system keeping him in power (along with the National Guard, his economic holdings, and United States backing).

This episcopal statement was made in a highly charged political atmosphere. Twenty-seven prominent leaders, including Pedro Joaquín Chamorro, representing nine political parties and labor organizations, published a document declaring "There's no one to vote for," since both Somoza and his puppet opposition were unconstitutional. Charging that it was they who had violated the Constitution, Somoza arrested and tried these people, sentencing them to the loss of their political rights.[58] Hence despite the bishops' stated intention of simply offering some "principles," the overall thrust of the letter, coming a month before the election, and with its insistence on the "right to dissent" and the right not to be compelled to vote against one's conscience, was taken as an implied criticism of the Liberal party system and a quasi-endorsement of the opposition criticism.

In late 1974 the opposition forces—political parties and unions—who had boycotted the election, formed a broad coalition called UDEL (Democratic Union for Liberation). For the first time these groups had joined together, not in order to participate in elections, which they could never entertain any hope of winning, but rather, to constitute a permanent and public anti-Somoza front. From its inception the most prominent UDEL figure was Pedro Joaquín Chamorro.

THE INCREASING REPRESSION OF THE SOMOZA REGIME

UDEL was soon upstaged by a daring Sandinista action, which caught headlines worldwide. In fact, part of the FSLN's motivation seems to have been to preempt what it saw as a possible attempt of the anti-Somoza bourgeoisie and the United States to find an alternative to Somoza that would stop far short of revolutionary change and would amount simply to terminating an anachronistic dictatorship.

Although a small commando group had been training and planning a hostage-taking action since October 1974, they decided upon the actual scene for it only on December 27 when a radio announcer read an invitation to a reception to be held that evening at the house of José María ("Chema") Castillo, at which the American ambassador would be present. Arriving ten minutes after Ambassador Shelton's departure, they took as hostages a number of prominent Somocistas, including the Nicaraguan ambassador to the United States (Somoza's brother-in-law). According to the FSLN, several of the hostages were notorious for their responsibility for killing and their involvement in graft. After sixty hours of negotiations (in which Archbishop Obando served as mediator) the kidnappers left on a plane with fourteen political prisoners and $5 million in ransom money, having had a communiqué published in the media. Thus did the FSLN help to weaken the myth of the invincibility of the dictatorship and awaken enthusiasm and hope.[59]

However, the most immediate effect was a wave of repression launched by an enraged Somoza, who declared martial law. During the 1975–77 period the National Guard went out in patrols in the mountains seeking the FSLN and intensified an already existing campaign of terror. Hundreds and eventually thousands of peasants were killed.

The Frente Sandinista lost its initiative and was largely reduced simply to evading guard patrols. A number of prominent Sandinistas were killed, including Carlos Fonseca Amador (in 1976), its leading theorist. The FSLN could only occasionally ambush small guard patrols and "execute" government informers. Also at this time the FSLN suffered divisions. Since the FSLN today prefers to minimize their importance, it is difficult to understand the situation fully. However, the divisions seem to have originated in a combination of personal differences and conflicts over tactical conceptions. One group, identified with Jaime Wheelock, felt that primacy should be given to political organizing with salaried workers, and hence was nicknamed the Proletarios (Proletarians); the original group, identified with Tomás Borge and Bayardo Arce, was called the Guerra Popular Prolongada (Prolonged People's War) and concentrated on war in the mountains. A third group, sometimes called Terceristas but more properly Tendencia Insurreccional, thought that conditions for a broad insurrection could be developed. Some felt that this latter group was "less Marxist," more heterodox, more open to alliances with other sectors both among the anti-Somoza bourgeoisie and with international allies, such as social Democratic political parties and governments. While for some years these divisions, combined with the repression, weakened the FSLN, in the longer run they seem to have permitted it to broaden its appeal and base of support. One curious item about the FSLN is that these divisions and the conditions of war were such that it acted in an extremely decentralized way, so much so that the National Directorate never had a meeting with all members present until July 21, 1979, two days after victory.[60]

As the guard went through the countryside looking for the FSLN it tended to pick up peasants it perceived as guerrilla suspects or collaborators, among whom prime candidates would be church leaders, especially the Delegates of the Word. In Zelaya province, for example, the Capuchins had trained 900 Delegates, to help them "respect their own dignity as children of God and to know better their own rights . . . to discover their ability to work out their own destiny . . . especially by working together." This process was "not aimed at moving the peasants to take up arms against the dictatorship" but to develop a critical judgment, "getting beyond fatalism," according to one of the Capuchins, Gregory Smutko.[61]

For some two years the Capuchins had been gathering information in the countryside where they served, drawing up a list of 100 people killed or disappeared. For example, in February 1976 in a village named Sofano the National Guard entered with a list of names "and they moved from one isolated hut to the next, taking the men out, beating and torturing them in front of their families, demanding that they divulge the names of guerrilla collaborators in the area. These men were then marched out into the fields and shot." Women and children were also killed, including an eight-year-old boy who was hanged and decapitated. A guard commander took over the land of those who had been killed.[62] The Capuchins' list grew to 350 names. Bishop Schlaefer had gone privately to Somoza three times with the information. Finally, after lengthy discussions in June 1976, thirty-one American Capuchins released public letters to Somoza and to the Nicaraguan Bishops Conference documenting the repression in the rural areas. The letter to Samoza immediately became a news item and, thus prodded, the bishops in subsequent pronouncements accepted the Capuchins' documentation.

Shortly afterwards Fernando Cardenal furnished similar information in congressional hearings in the United States (as did Miguel D'Escoto, a Maryknoll priest, the following year, 1977).[63] Thus began church involvement in the systematic documentation and denunciation of human rights violations by the Somoza regime.

The repression also hit church-trained leaders in other parts of the country. For some years CEPA (Center for Rural Education and Development), set up by Jesuits and others, had been training Delegates in a number of areas on the Pacific side, from Chinandega to near the Costa Rican border and in the north to Estelí. CEPA training combined a preparation for worship and Christian community leadership with skills in agriculture. In time its leaders constituted a network and the Delegates came under harassment and repression. During 1975 CEPA entered into a period of crisis and eventually the Jesuits severed their connection with it and lay people took it over. By mid-1977 its style of operation had become semiclandestine (with most work done in the field and not in its central offices) and limited. By this time also a number of Delegates were actively collaborating with the FSLN.

In general, grassroots pastoral work became more difficult during this period—like the "catacombs," said one priest in San Pablo parish. While the number of people active in the local communities was around 500 during the heyday of "The Family-of-God" approach in the parish it was now much less, since any kind of meeting was viewed with suspicion.[64] In another parish, as the pastor began to realize the seriousness of the crisis he set up an intensified leadership training "school," which interspersed biblical training with sessions analyzing national problems and events.

Uriel Molina gave some idea of life in barrio Rigueiro during this period (although he seems to have telescoped developments spanning several years):

The taking of churches played an important role during the period of popular agitation. Around the occupied church there were significant popular demonstrations . . . in which the Christian aspect was highlighted in a quasi-liturgical way. Every night there was a bonfire with protest music. A biblical message or a poem was presented; then there was a demonstration through the barrio to call people to become involved in the struggle: "People unite! . . . People unite!"

Initially Somoza's Guard didn't worry about such demonstrations but later the repression increased; the National Guard first tried to dissolve them with tear gas and later with rounds of machine-gun fire. When it was impossible to have demonstrations in the street we had vigils in the church, often staying until dawn. These vigils are evidence of how a believing people can respond at a given moment. When the repression became stronger and the youth of the barrio were persecuted and massacred, the community moved to the church to pray and express its protest in liturgical forms, which were increasingly consonant with what we were living through.

Holy Week was a privileged time. The Stations of the Cross and the Good Friday Liturgical Action were a way of making present the process Jesus went through, and this enabled us to shed light on the sufferings of our people. Reflection went on all through Holy Saturday. During the Vigil the people divided into groups according to the different readings, reflecting on the Hebrew and Christian passovers, interspersing Mejía Godoy songs, renewing baptismal vows and committing themselves to struggle for liberation. At dawn we commemorated the Lord's Resurrection with a procession headed by a cross covered with flowers.[65]

Molina's description may serve to exemplify how people combined the most profound Christian symbols with their aspirations and struggle.

People in the barrio took in underground FSLN militants, hid arms, and served as messengers and message carriers. On one occasion a child gave Molina a note from Tomás Borge: "I want you to know I'm delighted to hear the gospel you preach. We have to enlist more Christians in the struggle." They had many long meetings together.[66]

A priest in a lower-middle-class parish found that, increasingly, young people would come to him asking his advice on whether or not it was morally acceptable to join the FSLN. Parents also came with the "problem" of their children leaving for the guerrillas. He answered in orthodox terminology that it was a legitimate option for Christians. Subsequently it became clear that even the head altar boy in this parish was collaborating with the FSLN.[67]

Since its first pastoral week in 1974 CEPAD had sponsored some twenty pastoral retreats among Protestant church workers. Out of this grew RIPEN I (First Interdenominational Retreat for Nicaraguan Protestant Pastors) held in 1976. Basing themselves on documents from an international meeting in Switzerland the fifty participants made a measured statement about the "social responsibility of the church," church unity, and human rights—which, while short of a specific denunciation of the dictatorship, did represent an advance over the normal theology and practice of the churches. In fact, the very unification of churches in broad ecumenical action and group reflection was somewhat unusual. CEPAD was given a mandate to engage in human-rights work.[68]

On the Catholic side, the bishops in January 1977 published a statement that echoed and validated the Capuchin denunciation of a half-year before. They spoke of a "state of terror" in which peasants had to flee from their homes; they denounced tortures and summary executions, the jailing of people without trial or any legal proceeding; they noted that whole towns had been abandoned. Singling out cases of interference with religious liberty, they noted that in some areas army commanders required special permission for each religious meeting, that troops had used chapels as barracks, and that Delegates of the Word had been pressured, jailed, tortured, and killed. Although they disclaimed any partisan intentions and said they were only seeking a sincere conversion in everyone, the bishops made no attempt at a "balanced" judgment on violence, all of which was attributed to the National Guard and the "authorities." The document therefore was intended as a warning to the Somoza regime. At the same time the bishops, with a few lines, were careful to make it clear that they were not endorsing the FSLN. The government's actions

> put the authorities themselves on the margins of the institutional laws of the nation and of every sane principle of public order just like those other movements which call themselves liberating but which cause passions to overflow and lead to personal revenge, with the sole result that new masters run public affairs with no gain for human freedoms.[69]

In April CONFER (Confederation of Religious), the umbrella organization of religious orders, published a document backing the bishops' statement.

For their part, some Somocistas were becoming angry at the church's abandonment of what they saw as its mission. In May 1977 Martha Cranshaw, the daughter of the director of the police (who was a leader of the Anti-Communist League of Nicaragua), was captured as a guerrilla in the mountains. The regime decided to utilize the incident, publishing photos of the police chief embracing his (apparently repentant) daughter (who in fact soon returned to the FSLN). Police chief Cranshaw attacked Uriel Molina, since his daughter had occasionally attended Mass in Molina's parish, and went on to blame "all the priests in the Red Cassock who . . . send youth into armed struggle'' and particularly to attack Archbishop Obando for supporting "communist revolution with his inflammatory pastoral letters.''[70]

Soon afterward Somoza suffered a heart attack and was rushed to Miami in the United States. While his health was in a state of doubt all Nicaraguans suddenly began to speculate on a Nicaragua *sans* Somoza. Some of his associates began jockeying for position and, when the dictator returned, one of his closest collaborators was banished from public life for such presumption. That the bishops' previous documents did not reflect an utterly coherent stance may be seen in their public messages of concern for Somoza's health sent during this period. The Somocistas had at least 233 Masses celebrated for his recovery.[71]

The new United States human-rights policy under President Carter was taking shape and consequently the United States began to assume a more formal and less intimate relationship with Somoza. This is turn encouraged the opposition political groups to think they might gain United States support for a future government formula.

THE FINAL PHASE: OCTOBER 1977 to VICTORY (1979)

What Kind of Revolution?

As the crisis in Nicaragua deepened, events moved with increasing acceleration, and church people were more and more involved in the struggle. Lest this narrative become simply a dizzying series of events and names, a way of focusing for the reader is to note that at stake was the future direction of Nicaragua, or as Latin Americans would say, the *proyecto* (plan, or proposal) for the country.

Two of the *proyectos* were obvious: the Somoza group intended to stay in power and the FSLN intended not only to overthrow the dictatorship but to initiate revolutionary structural changes. There was, however, another *proyecto*, that of the anti-Somoza bourgeoisie, which was less defined: while they wanted to overthrow Somoza and perhaps acknowledged the need for some changes, they understandably did not want changes that would threaten their own way of life. Their stress was on the need for political reforms: free elections and in general the end of the opprobrious aspects of the dictatorship. This latter *proyecto*, to be called *Somocismo sin Somoza*, became the policy pursued by the United States.

Such a schematic simplification benefits from the clarity of hindsight. There were variations: for example, some people in the Social Christian party and other opposition parties genuinely wanted basic structural changes without having to accept Sandinista hegemony. However, as events unfolded, all variants of the third *proyecto* proved nonviable and the choice came down to one between Somoza and the National Guard on one side and the bulk of the Nicaraguan people and all the opposition organizations on the other side.

Readers will find it helpful to focus on this question of the *proyectos* for two reasons: (1) The mandate of the National Reconstruction government came from this struggle, and (2) church people were not in agreement on the *proyecto* being pursued.

As noted previously, after its hostage-taking action in December 1974, the FSLN had suffered under the repression launched by Somoza and militarily remained in a largely defensive posture. During 1977 it began to consider going on the offensive and intensified plans when Somoza's heart attack made it seem possible that the bourgeoisie and the United States might provide an alternative. Some Sandinista leaders began to change their conception of the struggle from one in which the FSLN, supported by the people, would battle the National Guard to one in which the Nicaraguan people itself, supported and led by the FSLN, would rise in insurrection against the Somoza system. This latter idea was that of the "Insurrectional Tendency" led by the Ortega Saavedra brothers (Humberto, Daniel, Camilo). In early 1977 Sergio Ramírez, a writer and intellectual, explored upper-class support with Managua business leaders.[72]

In October 1977 the FSLN attacked the National Guard in actions near Ocotal (near the Honduran border), Masaya (only a half-hour ride from Managua), and San Carlos (near the Costa Rican border). This last attack is the one in which the Solentiname community participated (see chapter 1). While these attacks did not achieve their original goal (Humberto Ortega Saavedra even thought they might touch off an insurrectionary movement), they showed that the FSLN was still in existence and, indeed, on the offensive.[73]

In Costa Rica, to which the new guerrillas of the Solentiname community had retreated, Ernesto Cardenal announced his militancy in the FSLN, and he became a kind of international ambassador for the Frente. The news of a Christian community joining the guerrillas provoked some commentary and even controversy (such as a public exchange of letters between Daniel Berrigan and Ernesto Cardenal) and served to bring the Nicaraguan war to the attention of church people.

On October 17 a group of prominent Nicaraguans (immediately called "the Twelve") made their first public appearance with a short statement. Two were priests, Fernando Cardenal and Miguel D'Escoto, and several others were active in church lay movements. Intellectuals, professional people, and businessmen, the Twelve (a biblical number) were all people of unquestioned integrity.

In their message they denounced the regime's violence and corruption and its confusing of public interests with those of the Somoza family. What had most impact, however, was their recognition that the FSLN had struggled with generosity for a change, proving themselves by spilling their blood. The Twelve concluded by calling on all "conscientious Nicaraguans to work for a solution, from which the . . . FSLN's participation cannot be excluded if what is wanted is the guarantee of a permanent and effective peace."[74]

Shortly thereafter Archbishop Obando said it was time for the vital forces of the country to enter into a constructive dialogue. UDEL and various private-sector organizations began to call for such a dialogue, and on October 26 the Commission to Promote National Dialogue, which included Bishops Obando, Salazar, and Vega, was formed. When the commission met with Somoza in November, however, it was told that he would be willing to dialogue after municipal elections, scheduled for February 1978. The United States ambassador, Mauricio Solaun, was encouraging Somoza to begin such a dialogue, aimed at democratization.[75] The Twelve, meanwhile, clarified that they did not propose any dialogue with Somoza—his resignation must be a prior condition for dialogue.

This was a period of agitation and protests over human-rights violations. *La Prensa*, which had accumulated extensive files during almost three years of martial law and press censorship, was publishing exposés of the regime. One story, which caught the public imagination, was about a company that exported blood sold by desperate Nicaraguans. Somoza was a prominent stockholder in Plasmaferesis, as it was appropriately called.

A new women's organization, AMPRONAC (Association of Women to Deal with National Problems), Christian Communities for Peace, and the Permanent Commission for Human Rights began a campaign around the 350 peasants whose disappearance the Capuchins had reported a year and a half earlier, as well as other victims. In December priests and sisters of the OPEN 3 barrio were beaten when they tried to intervene to reduce Guard violence against young people. The chancery office supported them and warned that those attacking them incurred ipso-facto excommunication.[76]

As 1977 drew to an end Gaspar García Laviana, a Spanish priest of the Sacred Heart Congregation, announced his decision to "go into the clandestine struggle as a soldier of the Lord and soldier of the Sandinista National Liberation Front," as he put it in a letter dated Christmas day. After working nine years as a priest he was convinced that people in their thirst for justice needed "more than the consolation of words, the consolation of actions." In words echoing the book of Exodus, he stated:

> . . . [A]s a priest I have seen, myself, the wounds of my people. I have seen the vile exploitation of the peasant, smashed under the boots of landowners protected by the National Guard. . . . I have seen how a few obscenely become wealthy under the cover of the Somoza dictatorship. I have been a witness to the filthy traffic in flesh to which poor young women are subjected, forced into prostitution by the powerful, and I have touched with my hands the vileness, the slaughter, the deceit, and the robbery that the Somoza family in power represents.
> . . . Like the best of our youth . . . I have decided to join this war as the humblest soldier of the Sandinista Front, because it is a just war, a war that the Holy Gospels consider good, and which in my conscience as a Christian is good because it is a struggle against a situation that is hateful to the Lord, our Lord.

García pointed out how Medellín had recognized that a revolutionary insurrection might be legitimate. After addressing various groups (business people, guardsmen, peasants and workers and others in the FSLN, but interestingly not any group explicitly in the church), he concluded:

> *Somocismo* is sin, and freeing ourselves from oppression is freeing ourselves from sin. With rifle in hand, full of faith and full of love for my Nicaraguan people I will fight to my last breath for the coming of the kingdom of justice in our country, this kingdom of justice that the Messiah announced under the star of Bethlehem.[77]

Gaspar García's announcement did not scandalize ordinary people and seems to have found much sympathy.[78]

On January 6, 1978, the Nicaraguan Bishops' Conference published a "Message to the People of God," which, while it quoted heavily from papal and conciliar statements, was by far the most pointed denunciation it had made to that date. In their most striking passage the bishops said ". . . we cannot be silent, when . . ." and listed sixteen categories of abuses:

> When the largest part of our population suffers inhuman living conditions as a result of a distribution of wealth that is unjust by any standard, . . .
> When the death and disappearance of many citizens (in city and country) remains a mystery, . . .
> When a precious portion of our people—part of the youth in classrooms and countryside—can only visualize patriotic solutions which involve taking up arms to fight, . . .
> When public servants backed up by [public] power, insolently enrich themselves, forgetting their mission of service to the people, whom they claim to represent, . . .
> When the citizens' right to choose their authorities is falsified in the game of political parties, . . .
> When there is disproportionate repression, . . .
> When vice (gambling, alcohol, drugs, prostitution) is protected and exploited, sometimes by those whose duty it is to combat it. . . .

Other abuses listed in the same section included lack of civil rights, lack of freedom to unionize and of expression, accusations against the church and physical harm to its leaders, administrative corruption, arbitrary extortion of taxes, an unjust court system, a budget that does not serve the poor, and a situation in which decent housing, public health, and adequate food, education, and employment are out of reach for half the population.[79]

The Outrage Explodes

On January 10, 1978, a hit squad ambushed Pedro Joaquín Chamorro, the editor of *La Prensa*, as he was driving to work. He was killed almost instantly as buckshot made more than thirty wounds in his body. While there was some logic in the murder of the regime's chief critic, one who had opposed the dictatorship since he had participated in one of the frustrated insurrections of the 1950s, the initial public reaction was one of astonishment and then outrage.

In contrast to dictatorships elsewhere, the Somozas had normally permitted a certain amount of public opposition. This policy had in fact proved intelligent, since it offered opponents an escape valve. The freedom allowed *La Prensa*, which circulated among the relatively privileged (literate urban people who could afford it), was not granted to radio stations.

Chamorro himself, who had been the most prominent figure in UDEL (the umbrella opposition organization) was moving toward the FSLN when he was killed. He had recently met with Miguel D'Escoto and was scheduled to meet with a representative of the Twelve during the second half of January.[80] As editor of *La Prensa* and as the most prestigious figure in the anti-Somoza bourgeoisie, Chamorro seemed destined to play a pivotal role in the future of Nicaragua.

All indications are, however, that it was not Anastasio Somoza Debayle himself who arranged the murder, but rather, his son, Anastasio Somoza Portocarrero. The motive was anger at *La Prensa*'s exposés of the operations of Plasmaferesis, the blood export company. One of the cars used in the killing was rammed by Chamorro's car and had to be left at the murder site, thus permitting its owner to be traced. Under interrogation the car owner mentioned a Cuban named Pedro Ramos, the owner of Plasmaferesis (although it seems clear that the Somozas were also stockholders). Four of those involved in carrying out the killing were jailed; neither Ramos nor any of those who gave the orders or paid for the killing were ever brought to justice.[81]

This event provoked the first mass outpouring of anti-Somoza sentiment: Chamorro's body was carried from the hospital to his house in a procession that lasted seven hours and in which 50,000 people were said to have participated. The wake took place in *La Prensa*'s building. Thousands attended the funeral and some were attacked by the National Guard with tear gas in the cemetery. In spontaneous actions mourners attacked Somoza-related businesses and started fires in some, in particular, Plasmaferesis. For the most part the guard avoided direct contact with the large angry crowds. For the first time people's indignation seemed to get the better of their fears.[82]

Also, the murder of Chamorro suddenly catapulted Nicaragua and indeed Central America onto the media stage in the United States. From 1972 through 1977 the region had occupied an infinitesimal portion of media attention, less than one-tenth of 1 percent of the nightly news on all three networks. In one year this coverage increased almost 500 percent, an attention provoked initially by this killing.[83] Nicaragua in the eyes of the media was becoming a country in crisis.

Chamorro's murder ended any talk of "national dialogue" for the moment. The chambers of commerce and industry called for a work stoppage, which construction workers and others joined and which soon spread across the country. At its height the stoppage was 80 to 90 percent successful. The FSLN meanwhile maintained silence and took no action, apparently intending to show that nonviolent actions by themselves would be insufficient to topple the dictatorship.

A group of women organized by AMPRONAC occupied the United Nations office in Managua, initially to protest the killing of Chamorro. After several days there was a demonstration of 600 women, some of whom came from lower-class barrios, especially from basic Christian communities, and they began to add to the original middle-class concerns a protest over the disappeared and murdered peasants. When elite troops led by Somoza's son broke up the demonstration with tear gas, some of the women threw the gas cannisters back at the troops.[84]

A number of radio stations, including Radio Católica, were prevented from transmitting material that was considered contributory to unrest. Media workers then went on strike and began to use the churches to transmit information at regular daily hours. This "catacombs journalism" was at first supported by the Managua archdiocese but some days later the Nicaraguan Bishops Conference stated that there had been disrespect for the churches when they were used for protest or strictly journalistic purposes. The bishops did, however, defend Radio Católica against the government's accusations.[85]

On January 28, 1978, the bishops made a general statement referring to the "latest events" and assuring the people that the bishops were "at their side," stressing that Christians cannot be uninvolved in the solution of urgent problems and have a tranquil conscience in the face of "sinful structures . . . which harm the common good."[86]

The following day representatives of religious orders released a statement with seventy signatures largely based on the bishops' January 6 document and quoting in full the "We cannot be silent when . . ." section. However, where the bishops had spoken vaguely about examining the "signs of the times" the religious mentioned the "killing of peasants" as just such a sign and saw the murder of Chamorro as simply the "last straw" for the people's wrath. Pointing to people's reaction, "Christian nonviolence," as another such sign, they supported the work stoppage.[87]

In their own brief statement the priests of the Managua archdiocese also supported the stoppage, emphasizing the use of nonviolence and commenting that it would be regrettable if the stoppage ended in being a "game between the powerful," thus mocking the majority of the people.[88] They here anticipated the "mediation" efforts, which would attempt to secure Somoza's resignation while maintaining the National Guard in place and not threatening upper-class privileges.

When it was clear that the work stoppage organized by business was not going to topple Somoza—some Latin American dictators had been overthrown by such actions—its effectiveness began to wane. Actions in popular sections meanwhile continued strong. There were numerous demonstrations, often with Masses celebrated for Chamorro. One form of protest was to bang on pots and pans at agreed-upon times. Barricades were put up to impede National Guard vehicles.[89]

On the night of February 2 the FSLN, in its most serious military action thus far, occupied the cities of Rivas and Granada, inflicting many casualties on the National Guard,[90] apparently to underscore the point that Somoza could not be overthrown without armed struggle. (It is worth noting that subsequently the Frente Sandinista sees the final phase as having begun with the October 1977 attacks, while anti-Sandinista forces see Chamorro's killing and the popular indignation it provoked as being the critical detonator.)[91]

Municipal elections, held on February 5, 1978, with the opposition abstaining, were so clumsily managed that *La Prensa* was able to show the same people voting in more than one polling place, using photos from *Novedades*, Somoza's paper.

In early February, Archbishop Obando declared that, while he favored nonviolent means, some theologians and moralists hold that collective armed resistance is permitted when there is grave injustice and all possible peaceful means have failed, because armed struggle creates fewer problems than the injustice that causes it.[92]

When Bishop Carranza of Estelí died and Somoza announced national mourning, saying that high dignitaries, including the whole cabinet, would attend the funeral, the clergy rejected the proposal, saying that the bishop wanted a "poor burial." Ribbons on floral wreaths indicating that they came from the government were removed.[93]

On the night of February 21 the barrio of Monimbó, in the town of Masaya (a half-hour drive from Managua), initiated a spontaneous uprising. María Chavarría describes it:

> We were celebrating a Mass at Don Bosco [school] demanding justice in the case of Doctor Pedro Joaquín Chamorro, who had been killed a little over a month before, and when we were leaving the National Guard came and began to drop tear-gas bombs from a helicopter. They didn't care if children were asphyxiated. . . .

She narrates how her son came to the house looking for a mask used in folklore festival of Tata Chombito (so he would not be recognized). They began to use homemade bombs against the guard, and FSLN militants arrived on the scene.

> It was only then we realized that *we* were the Frente Sandinista; that they would give guidance but that it was us, alongside them, who had to fight. That day the red-and-black bandannas came out. . . .

... We all helped. We kept bombs, medicine, and everything needed for war in our houses.

One night we swept the barrio of informers. . . . That day the young people put on masks so the informers wouldn't recognize them. . . . That night the Guard shot up the church and the next day they came to arrest Father Pacheco and put weapons in his room to justify his expulsion from the country. We all went to protest; we went to the killers' garrison to ask that Father Pacheco be released. From February 24 on we stopped being afraid of the Guard.

She added some remarks relevant to the issue of whose revolution it was:

Our struggle was the people's struggle. . . . We never saw any of these bourgeois, who say they helped, fighting. We never saw any of those who say they're for human rights. We didn't see anyone but our children; we were, and are, of the Frente. . . . So they can't tell us anything, if it was us who put up the corpses.[94]

It took the National Guard a week (with 600 troops, 2 tanks, 2 helicopters, and 2 light planes) to subdue the rebellion of the people of Monimbó with their .22 caliber rifles and homemade bombs. This struggle caught the national imagination, since these people are considered to be the most authentic representatives of Nicaragua's "Indian" tradition. There were protests in several areas of the country. During the fighting the Red Cross had not been allowed to assist victims.[95]

Humanitarian relief for the victims of Monimbó furnished a concrete point around which people could unite and in so doing take an anti-Somoza stand. One ecumenical effort was called Cristianos Solidarios (Christians in Solidarity), or CRISOL.

Moved by the killing of Chamorro and the repression in Monimbó, Protestants associated with CEPAD began to take a stance against the Somoza dictatorship. One such expression was a new monthly paper called *Orientación*, which in mildly worded, biblically phrased language, reflected such a posture.

In early March the public was jolted by the news that a notorious torturer had been killed by a middle-class woman—who in addition announced she had joined the Sandinistas. Nora Astorga had grown up in comfortable circumstances, gone to Catholic schools, and been sent abroad to study. Later she studied law at the National University and became involved with the FSLN. In 1978, as head of personnel of a construction company, she had business contacts with General Reynaldo Pérez Vega who wanted to sell some land. When he noted that she was divorced, he tried to seduce her. Together with other FSLN members she invited him into her house on the night of March 8, with the intention of kidnapping him and then using him to obtain the release of political prisoners, but due to his resistance, they ended by killing him. They left his body with a Sandinista flag and an explanation of their "execution." The public reaction was one of amazement that such a notorious Somocista could be killed—and by a middle-class professional woman, who at the same time left a photo of herself in an FSLN uniform and announced she was going underground and into combat.[96]

Terrence Todman, the United States under-secretary of state for Latin American affairs, expressed condolences on the death of Pérez Vega, either ignorant of, or indifferent to, his reputation as a torturer. He expressed a hope that Somoza and the opposition could find a peaceful solution and even mentioned some measures taken by Somoza to improve human rights. Three days later United States Ambassador Solaun, similarly urging the opposition to work for dialogue, was said to have called opposition leaders "hysterical," "intransigent," and "emotional." They for their part said the main obstacle to dialogue was Somoza himself.[97]

Signs of economic crisis began to appear. Government tax collection declined 38 percent during the first three months of 1978, coffee prices were declining, and the United States embassy's economic report declared that the year would probably bring zero growth. Most serious was the beginning of large-scale capital flight.[98]

The calm after the Monimbó uprising was only relative. Peasants connected with CEPA were occupying lands. When students went on strike, the government ended the school year. A grassroots organization with strong FSLN ties, called the People United Movement, was spreading around the country, uniting a vast array of organizations, mainly from organized labor and students. The FSLN was making major efforts in grassroots political organizing. Often their starting points in a new area were the basic Christian communities.

During this period people deepened their commitment to the struggle and recognized what it might mean. For many Holy Week 1978 was the moment for a definitive commitment. In their areas of Zelaya department, where the brutal persecution of peasants continued, the Capuchins organized courses around the books of Maccabees (which tell of the resistance of the Jews to their oppressors) and the book of Revelation ("subversive" literature against the Roman empire, the Beast, proclaiming the ultimate victory of Christ).[99]

The Nicaraguan Permanent Human Rights Commission was publishing a detailed documentation of cases of repression and providing legal aid for the victims' families. Although the Human Rights Commission was a spinoff of the conservative faction of the Social Christian party and not directly related to the church, there were priests and prominent lay people on its board and it maintained close relations with the church.

In July the Twelve returned from exile, thus openly defying Somoza. The

FAO (Broad Opposition Front), an umbrella organization of opposition parties, business organizations, and unions, called a one-day strike, which was 90 percent successful in Managua and 70 percent successful elsewhere.[100]

Early August saw two more noteworthy church pronouncements. The Nicaraguan Bishops Conference in effect repeated its earlier appeals for a "new sociopolitical order," saying thàt Nicaragua was calling for "radical (not extremist) proposals . . . not personalistic selfishness . . . in order to avoid an unnecessary loss of life and goods." Although they said it would be an illusion to try to stop the violence of those who, "tired of asking for justice, turn to other means," they nevertheless, in a seemingly oblique reference to the FSLN, stated that hopes of true liberation cannot come "from systems that ignore God and respect for other sacred values of the human person."[101]

The very next day (August 3, 1978) the Priests' Council of the Managua archdiocese produced a more pointed document, also signed by Obando. Its reading of the "spiral of violence" was similar, but it noted that, since large sectors of the population did not believe there could be "democracy" under those currently in power, any kind of "electoral solution" would be out of the question. Hence the priests proposed a transition period with a "national government, which both in those who make it up and in its acts and measures . . . would return credibility and confidence to Nicaraguans." Their most important proposal was delicately worded:

> As an option within this policy of mutual concession, the Ruler, by resigning, could promote the formation of this national government, which by obtaining the support of the majority [of the people] would keep Nicaragua from falling into the kind of power vacuum and anarchy that are always a danger in processes of change.[102]

This second document could be read as making more specific what the bishops had said implicitly. In plainer language the priests were saying that for the good of the nation and in order to avoid greater bloodshed, Somoza should step down and allow a transition to electoral democracy with a substantial reform component. Some evidently hoped such a move would help to avert a more radical outcome, namely, a Sandinista victory.

The Palace Operation and "Mediation"

On August 22, 1978, some two dozen Sandinistas in National Guard uniforms drove to the National Palace and hurried past the guards, saying, "The Chief's coming," as if they were Somoza's advance guard. Within minutes they had taken the building and held almost 2,000 people hostage, including most of the country's congressional deputies and many regime figures, and even a cousin and a nephew of Somoza. Members of the Insurrectional Tendency had decided on this operation (which they dubbed "Operation Pigpen"), partly because they perceived that a new transition formula for persuading Somoza to step down while leaving the National Guard in place was in the making.

The FSLN's demands included the release of political prisoners, the publication of a communiqué, and a sum of ransom money. Negotiations were tense and at one point when Somoza resisted, Eden Pastora ("Commander Zero") told Archbishop Obando, who was mediating, that in thirty minutes they would begin to execute deputies. Obando hurried to meet with Somoza. When twenty-five minutes had passed, Pastora told Luis Manuel Martínez, "You're going to die; you've got five minutes." At that point the telephone rang. Pastora narrates:

> I picked it up: "National Palace, free territory of Nicaragua. This is the Sandinista National Liberation Front," I answered.
> I heard the voice of Archbishop Obando y Bravo, who told me, "Commander, General Somoza accepted the conditions and it's just a question of spelling them out."
> "Good," I answered, "Come down here and we'll spell them out."
> I turned to the rest: "You've been saved, you sons of bitches. Somoza gave in."[103]

The FSLN had fifty-nine political prisoners released (including Tomás Borge) and a half-million dollars paid in ransom. More important, with unimaginable audacity they had forced a humiliating defeat on Somoza.[104]

Another phase of protest and incipient insurrection followed. The FAO called for another national work stoppage or strike, demanding Somoza's resignation. The strike lasted for almost a month. Meanwhile, in Matagalpa there was an uprising, with barricades, and a few days later the National Guard bombarded the city with rockets. Soon there were similar actions in Chinandega, León, Masaya, and Estelí. These uprisings were largely spontaneous—the FSLN's role was to help the people defend themselves.

Somoza sent elite troops, led by his son, to put down the uprisings one by one, first bombing them to "soften them up" and then attacking with troops. Although in some towns the people held out for a week or more, all uprisings were put down. The FSLN fighters managed to escape, usually taking with them young people who feared they would be in danger when the National Guard entered. An estimated 3,000 to 5,000 people were killed during these uprisings, mainly noncombatants killed in the bombing or "suspects" summarily executed during the guard's mop-up operations. The net effect was to drive people into the FSLN. Humberto Ortega later said, "We came to Estelí with fifty people; when we left there were thousands who wanted to take up arms."[105]

On September 15 the priests of the Managua archdiocese and CONFER sent a public letter to President Jimmy Carter analyzing the inability of the Somoza regime to solve the country's problems and calling on the United States not to aid it.[106]

People were scandalized the following day when they saw in *Novedades* a photograph of the papal nuncio drinking a toast with Somoza—at the very time Somoza's planes were bombarding Estelí. That it was a routine function of the nuncio's as dean of the diplomatic corps was not considered an excuse.[107]

The United States embassy and government had never taken the anti-Somoza groups seriously, and particularly underestimated the degree of opposition among the popular masses. In fact, President Carter in early August had even sent Somoza a letter congratulating him on improvements in human-rights observance.[108] Convinced by the August-September uprisings that the Sandinistas were indeed a serious threat, the United States began actively to pursue a "mediated" solution, dispatching William Bowdler, an experienced senior diplomat, as special ambassador. He was joined by representatives from Guatemala and the Dominican Republic, acolytes presumed sympathetic to Somoza and the opposition, respectively. From the United States point of view the goal was clearly to remove Somoza as a focal point for opposition and yet to avoid a Sandinista takeover. It was accordingly viewed as essential that the National Guard remain in some form, purged of those officers viewed as most involved in corruption and repression—a proposal understandably viewed as *Somocismo sin Somoza*.

Within the legal opposition (political parties, unions, the Twelve) there was a basic division between those who would accept such an agreement, and would therefore stress political reform and "free elections," and those who were convinced that the guard had to be dismantled, that some serious economic reforms had to be made, and that the FSLN could not be excluded from any real solution. For its part the FSLN deliberately reduced its activities to allow the mediation effort to reveal its contradictions and to fail.

Some of the opposition groups, headed by the Twelve, split from the FAO, but others, led by Alfonso Robelo, remained, while the United States urged a "plebiscite" on the Somoza regime. One idea proposed was that special elections be held, with Somoza out of the country. Finally, in January 1979, Somoza showed his stubbornness, refusing even this attenuated type of process.

After the September 1978 uprising, church people worked both in caring for the victims of Somoza's bombing and in helping in the reconstruction in the hardest-hit areas, such as Estelí, where many whole blocks were destroyed. Even institutions normally considered to serve middle and upper classes, such as Catholic schools, offered their resources. International agencies arrived with some aid. People began to plan for what they felt was an inevitable insurrection, and food and medicine were stockpiled in schools and parishes.

While the Protestant churches as such had not been public protagonists during these months of struggle, many individual Protestants and pastors were increasingly working in collaboration with the opposition and with the FSLN. Violence against Protestant families, and events such as a rocket hitting a Baptist church in Estelí in September 1978, contributed to radicalizing Protestants.

Church people continued to prepare human-rights documentation and helped visiting journalists and delegations interpret the situation and contact opposition figures. As the final offensive drew near it became more clear that there were close contacts between the FSLN and many pastoral agents.

The Final Offensive

In part spurred by the recognition that the people themselves were anxious to resolve the crisis once and for all, the three "tendencies" of the FSLN entered into discussions and solved their differences, announcing their unity in April 1979. In a way, all three "tendencies" were partly correct in their strategies: the Prolonged People's War, for having developed peasant bases; the Proletarians, for their political work; and the Insurrectional Tendency, for giving full importance to the mass uprising of the people and for being willing to work with the middle and upper classes. More than any correct strategy, however, it was their unity itself which provided the decisive element.[109]

Militarily during this period the FSLN sought to bog down and disperse the National Guard, presenting it with the problem of whether to chase the FSLN in the countryside and thus leave the towns free for organizing or to allow free rein in rural areas. The strategy was at times costly; for example, of a column of 120 who entered the region of Nueva Guinea only 20 survived.[110] There were several important battles in different parts of the country and Estelí was once more occupied by the FSLN and then attacked by the guard in April.

Somoza meanwhile was increasingly under pressure. After he had rejected even a minimal electoral procedure in January, the Carter administration for some months followed an apparent hands-off policy, suspended military and economic aid, recalled the Peace Corps, and reduced United States personnel in Nicaragua, even recalling military attachés. Somoza traveled to the United States in April, and the FSLN expressed its suspicion that some sort of "coup" might be underway. When opposition leaders Robelo and Córdoba Rivas were jailed, the United States protested, saying that strangling the moderate opposition would only benefit the extremists.

Searching for allies, Somoza could count on only the regimes in Guatemala and El Salvador, who eventually did send small numbers of soldiers unofficially but were unable or unwilling to offer substantial aid. The Mexican government took an increasingly anti-Somoza stand and broke off diplomatic relations, and Costa Rica, although professing neutrality, looked the other way while the Sandinistas used its territory for training and arms supply. Economic decline continued and Somoza was forced to devalue the córdoba.

On May 29 the FSLN launched a series of attacks, which began the final offensive. Entering from Costa Rica, FSLN troops engaged in conventional warfare with the elite troops of the National Guard. In the north and in most of the cities a combination of regular FSLN troops and large numbers of ordinary people attacked the guard, which found its forces dispersed. The FAO, now allied with the FSLN, once more called for a work stoppage.

During the first few days of the offensive the Nicaraguan Bishops Conference issued a statement reaffirming the traditional doctrine of a just insurrection when all other means have failed. The government prohibited publication of the decree. Archbishop Obando urged the combatants to "humanize the struggle" and the FSLN promised to do so.

The FSLN now had several thousand combatants as compared to approximately 14,000 in the National Guard (a figure that was diminished by desertions). The Frente saw its role as one of largely supporting and coordinating what was a popular uprising. Around the country the people took over cities and towns, set up barricades, and organized committees for defense, medical care, and food distribution. Typically, most of the town would be occupied and the guard would be surrounded in its garrison. Soon cities and towns like León, Chinandega, Masaya, Granada, Jinotepe, Diriamba, Matagalpa, and Ocotal were in the hands of the people and the FSLN, although they could always be bombed or shelled by the guard. Thousands of refugees fled to Honduras and Costa Rica.

In Managua the FSLN at first occupied the poor barrios of the eastern side, which they had organized. Some operations failed, such as an uprising attempt in OPEN 3 in early June: because of poor coordination, weapons failed to arrive and the FSLN militants had to withdraw; thousands of people became refugees in a nearby area.

It seemed clear that Somoza's troops by themselves could not defeat the guerrillas, nor were the FSLN guerrillas by themselves going to defeat the guard in a strictly military fashion. However, the nearly unanimous support of the people, as shown in the strike and support activities for the FSLN, added to the support of the business community (which gave the revolt "respectability") and the international repudiation of the Somoza regime, made eventual victory seem very probable.

By the period of combat it seemed that the church had little public role (for instance, there were no longer many documents issued). However, pastoral agents and the basic Christian communities worked full time.

Churches were opened to serve people, FSLN combatants were welcomed into people's homes. As one priest said later, "Everyone was Christian and everyone was a Sandinista."

There are many stories of how pastoral agents helped Sandinistas. At one point a Capuchin priest took Henry Ruiz ("Modesto"), today a commander of the revolution, to Bluefields and Managua disguised as a Costa Rican seminarian. The missionary Sisters of Christ in Siuna received medicines and ammunition by air and sent them to the Sandinistas.[111]

Recognizing the seriousness of the situation, the Carter administration made renewed efforts to find a solution short of a Sandinista victory, sending William Bowdler once more to negotiate. When the opposition, now including all sectors, announced the formation of a provisional Junta and its government program, the United States pressured it to expand the Junta and include two more "moderates" (an army officer and a representative of the Liberal party), but to no avail.

The United States suffered a severe defeat in the OAS (Organization of American States) when Secretary of State Cyrus Vance (against his own judgment) proposed the formation of a "peacekeeping force," which was interpreted as an attempt to impose a "solution" that would impede a Sandinista victory. A majority of nations, led by Mexico, rejected such an intervention.

It seems clear that Somoza offered his resignation to the United States some two weeks or so before he in fact left. During this period the FSLN and the other opposition groups were working out the basic agreements for the shape of a new government and its policies. Even at such a late date there were proposals under which some elements of the National Guard (those not directly responsible for repression) might be incorporated into a new armed forces. The Sandinistas were evidently flexible and ready to make some compromises in order to halt the bloodshed. However, any such plan unraveled when Francisco Urcuyo, chosen to be a twenty-four hour transition president between Somoza and the new Junta, for unexplained reasons announced his intention to remain in office until 1981. At this point the National Guard fell apart: officers panicked and hijacked planes while troops threw down their weapons and ran away in their underwear. Urcuyo left the day after his defiant stand and the way was prepared for a triumphant Sandinista entry into Managua.

The victory had been costly. Some 50,000 people were dead (2.5 percent of the population), mainly noncombatants. Tens of thousands more were wounded. Homes and factories were in ruins and the country was bankrupt.

Church people had come a great distance since the days when they unquestioningly supported the dictatorial regime. From participating in the sporadic movements of the late 1960s and early 1970s, through the grassroots training in the countryside and barrios, through particular experiences such as Solentiname and the university community of barrio Rigueiro, through militancy as FSLN combatants, and finally through an increasingly antidictatorial stand by the Catholic church hierarchy itself, as well as important participation by Protestants, church people had been an integral part of the first revolutionary victory in Latin America in twenty years.

As Catholics celebrated Masses in recognition of the victory, and Protestants praised God that the war was over and the dictator gone, all looked toward the future with expectation.

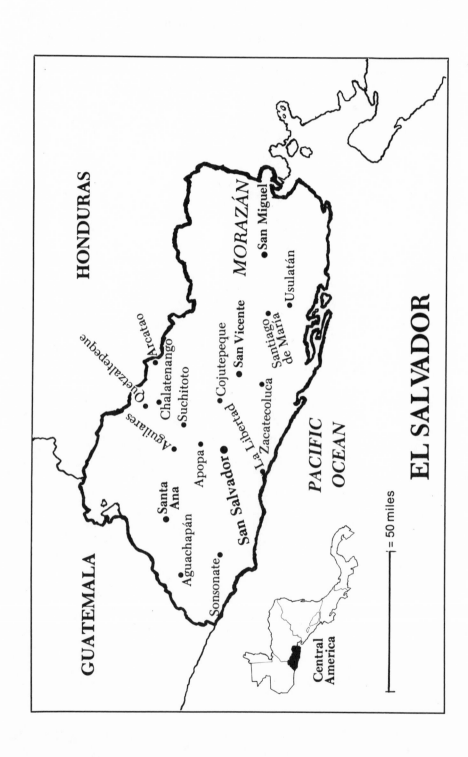

HONDURAS

GUATEMALA

MORAZÁN

Arcatao
Quezaltepeque
Chalatenango
Aguilares •Suchitoto
Cojutepeque •San Miguel
Apopa •Usulatán
Santa •San Vicente •Santiago
Ana San Salvador• de María
Aguachapán La Libertad•
Sonsonate •Zacatecoluca

PACIFIC
OCEAN

EL SALVADOR

= 50 miles

Central
America

5

"No Law Higher Than God's: Thou Shalt Not Kill!"

As we turn to El Salvador, certain differences from the case of Nicaragua come to mind. First and most obvious, the struggle is far from over as this is being written. Only after a resolution is reached will it be possible to find the "untold story." Second, the Nicaraguan struggle was essentially one to overthrow a dictator who had alienated the support of the upper classes and the United States; in El Salvador people are struggling against an oligarchy and military strongly backed and financed by the United States.

Before turning to a detailed account of the Salvadoran struggle, some introductory remarks may be useful.

The country's small size has become a cliché ("Massachusetts-sized"). To express it another way: from San Salvador, the capital, it is a half-hour drive south to the ocean, an hour and a half north to the Honduran border, an hour and fifteen minutes west to Guatemala, and about two and a half hours (on a slow highway) to Honduras on the east. Virtually the entire country is settled and any potentially useful land is under cultivation or used for pasture. There are no real jungles (although some creative news-magazine rewrite people have put them there for the guerrillas to lurk in). The country has no known mineral resources of any importance and its population density is the highest in the Western hemisphere (550 per square mile), seven times that of neighboring Honduras. Such pressures have made Salvadorans hard working and entrepreneurial, and many have had to emigrate.

El Salvador's history followed the general contours laid down in chapter 3 while having a few characteristics of its own as well. Its first export crops were balsam and cacao (of which it was the largest producer in the Americas). These products later gave way to indigo, which in turn was succeeded by coffee during the latter part of the nineteenth century. The transition to coffee was facilitated by a decisive victory of the Liberals in El Salvador. The consequence of the Liberal domination was that El Salvador was

91

laicized earlier and the church had little influence on the political sphere. The coffee oligarchy presided over decades of prosperity (for itself), often appointing its own members to the presidency (for example, the so-called Meléndez-Quiñonez Dynasty, 1913–27).

Two particular characteristics of the traditional Salvadoran economy should be mentioned. First, the coffee oligarchy was made up either of Salvadorans (with last names like Dueñas, Alfaro, Palomo, Regalado, Menéndez) or of nineteenth-century immigrants who became Salvadorans (Hill, DeSola, Wright, Dalton, Sol). In other words, El Salvador did not have foreign enclaves (American banana companies), and its own oligarchy was truly in charge of the national economy. Second, the agricultural system became thoroughly capitalist more rapidly than in neighboring countries, since the oligarchy quickly seized control of all potential export lands and the rest of the population became wage laborers (even those who had small parcels of land). There were no people really "marginal" to the labor market and very few in a feudal arrangement (such as receiving land-use on haciendas in return for labor).[1]

LA MATANZA: THE 1932 UPRISING AND MASSACRE

All commentators see the 1932 *Matanza* ("slaughter") as a pivotal event. It is just as much a part of the prehistory of today's conflict as was Sandino's struggle in Nicaragua during the same period.

In the century since independence there had been peasant revolts in El Salvador, beginning with that of the Indian leader Anastasio Aquino in 1833, a rebellion which in the confusion of early independence amounted to a revolt against white domination.[2] In the 1870s and 1880s there were other revolts, this time fundamentally against the abolition of the Indians' communal lands and their usurpation for coffee.

In 1918 the first labor union was formed, and in 1920 railroad workers went on strike. The 1920s were a time of increasing agitation, partly inspired by news of revolutions in Mexico, Russia, and China. By 1932 the Regional Federation of Workers of El Salvador (called *La Regional*), begun in 1924, had organized over 10 percent of the work force.

Emerging from this process was the figure of Agustín Farabundo Martí, who was born in 1893 and was a revolutionary from his days as a law student. Arrested for the first time in 1920, he went to Guatemala where he and others founded the Central American Socialist party in 1925. One writer sees interesting parallels to Ho Chi Minh: both worked and traveled in foreign lands (Martí in Mexico, Central America, and the United States), both were primarily practitioners rather than theoreticians, and both were jailed during similar periods. Martí returned to El Salvador and worked underground with *La Regional* between 1925 and 1928, when he announced that he was joining Sandino's struggle in Nicaragua. After fifteen months together, during which Martí came to be Sandino's personal secretary, the two split in Mexico. Martí was a convinced Marxist while Sandino was fighting against foreign domination.[3] Martí later underlined the difference while paying tribute to Sandino: "His flag was only that of national independence . . . not that of social revolution. I solemnly declare that General Sandino is the greatest patriot in the world."[4]

After some months in Mexico City, Martí returned to El Salvador, where a communist party had been founded. He soon became a principal leader and was again arrested and deported, this time to San Pedro, California, but Martí insisted on his right to be in El Salvador, and after two months he reentered the country. Throughout 1931 Martí was resisting the authorities, being arrested, going on hunger strike, being freed (even being offered a government post if he would leave the Communist party).[5]

In conventional views the 1932 uprising is referred to as "the first communist revolt in the hemisphere" and with some justification. However, there was another root to the conflict, more difficult to assess and less open to documentation: that of Indian resistance. The Indians could still recall their communal lands and resented their expropriation by the oligarchy, whom they were forced to serve as a labor force. The social base of their organization was the *cofradías*, or religious societies. According to Thomas Anderson these organizations facilitated the penetration of the "advanced ideas" of communism. He quotes a Santa Ana landowner writing in a newspaper after the uprising: ". . . there was not an Indian who was not afflicted with devastating communism. . . . We committed a grave error in making them citizens."[6] The leader of the most powerful *cofradía*, that of the Holy Spirit, was Feliciano Ama. To what degree the 1932 uprising was a product of the efforts of leftists such as Martí and their organizations, and to what degree it was a spontaneous rebellion arising out of peasant and Indian resentment for the mistreatment of decades and centuries remains an open question. Clearly both flowed together but the proportion is unclear, and it is this writer's impresssion that the latter factor has been underestimated.

In any case, the immediate context of 1932 was the Great Depression and the resulting economic and political crisis in El Salvador. Coffee prices fell so low that the beans were often left to rot on the plants (in Brazil they were used to fuel locomotives). Many peasants who depended on coffee-picking simply could not find work.

In the meantime El Salvador experienced its only reasonably free election, in 1931. With the traditional oligarchy split and running three candidates, and the military running two generals, a reforming sixth candidate, Arturo Araujo, supported by workers, peasants, students, and intellectuals (and communists) was able to win a plurality and assume the presidency. However, some of his associates were corrupt, and his administration was unable to meet the challenges it faced. Even though he used some repression against peasants and workers, Araujo was overthrown by a military coup in December 1931.

In the meantime the Communist party and others had been planning an insurrectionary strike, counting on help from dissident ranks in the military. The date was fixed for January 22. However, the plot was discovered and the barracks revolt did not materialize. Martí, who was to be the military leader of the revolt, was arrested along with others on January 19, and the following day the government declared a state of siege.[7]

However, the people went ahead with their revolt on the night of January 22—when, according to legend, volcanoes in the region erupted. The largest town attacked was Sonsonate, where the peasants with their machetes drove soldiers armed with rifles and machine guns into retreat. The peasants withdrew, led by a woman called "Red Julia." Writes González Janzen:

> With no leadership, means of communication, or concrete plan, the rebels took some towns, especially in the departments of Sonsonate, Ahuachapan, La Libertad, Santa Ana, Chalatenango, and San Salvador, without knowing what to do after their first "victories."
>
> In Juayua, Nahuizalco, Colón, and other towns the Indians took government offices and warehouses, pillaged the stockpiles and burned some buildings, killed some local inhabitants—the list does not go over fifty victims—mainly the most exploitive and repressive storeowners and officials. That was all: a march with shouts, machetes held up in indignation, and joy over the *victory*. They did not meet any resistance. But for the government it was enough: Military circles denounced "massive crimes," profanation of churches (which did not occur), "killing of religious," and "rape of women, girls, and little children" (there was never proof of any case of rape). The troops were given orders to "smash the communists," taking no prisoners.[8]

The rebellion as such was over in about forty-eight hours. The army lost about twenty men in combat, the rebels four hundred. After the combat was over, General Hernández Martínez ordered the killing to continue, undoubtedly carrying out the desires of the coffee oligarchy. Troops systematically went through the country killing large numbers by firing squad. One survivor, Miguel Marmol, communicates something of the cold-blooded sadism:

> General Ochoa . . . made everyone who had been captured crawl on their knees to where he was seated in a chair in the courtyard of the fort and he said to them: "Come here and smell my gun." The prisoners pleaded with him in the name of God and their children, having heard the sound of intermittent shots before entering the courtyard.
>
> But the general insisted: "If you don't smell my pistol then you are a communist and afraid. He who is without sin knows no fear."
>
> The campesino smelled the barrel of the gun, and in that instant, the general would put a bullet in his face.
>
> "Bring the next one in," he said.[9]

Electoral rolls were used to locate and kill members of the Communist party.

There is no reliable way to know how many were killed in *La Matanza*. Anderson puts the figure at 10,000, which he says would represent a retaliation of 100 to 1, since he estimates that the rebels killed no more than 100. Others make higher estimates and it has become common to put the number at 30,000, which, if true, would amount to 2 percent of the entire population.[10] When the bodies became too numerous to bury they were heaped up, sprinkled with gasoline, and burned.

Martí was taken before a firing squad early on the morning of February 1, 1932. He refused the last rites and defiantly shouted "Viva el socialismo!" just before being shot. Feliciano Ama was captured and jailed, but landholders took him out, beat him, and lynched him in the plaza. Photos of Ama's dangling body were later sold in San Salvador.[11]

The massacre of 1932 permanently scarred the memory of Salvadorans. Because it had been considered an "Indian" revolt and people were killed as Indians, the survivors put away traditional clothes and customs; there are virtually no "Indians" in El Salvador today. Many of the areas of the rebellion, particularly around Sonsonate, have been precisely those areas where the popular and revolutionary organizations have had least success, largely, it would seem, because that slaughter of many years ago is still a living nightmare.

For the oligarchy 1932 has signified what peasants can do when control is lost. Essential to them is a myth of rape, pillage, and murder. In the late 1970s some of the oligarchy's paid political statements in newspapers hinted that something like 1932 might be necessary again.[12]

While there are some analogies and parallels to the struggle of Sandino, the differences are greater. Sandino waged what was a partially successful struggle—the U.S. Marines did not defeat him and eventually withdrew—against a foreign invader, whereas Martí took part in preparing a disastrous attempt at insurrection, wherein the peasants with their machetes were no match for soldiers armed with machine guns.

Church participation seems to have been even more marginal than in the Nicaraguan case. None of the accounts seen by this writer make any allusion to statements of the hierarchy. On the other hand, some observers today see Feliciano Ama and the *cofradías* as the manifestation of an *iglesia popular*, a people's church, which, kept suppressed for centuries, is only now in the process of achieving its own identity.

THE FALL OF HERNÁNDEZ MARTÍNEZ AND THE BEGINNINGS OF "MODERNIZATION"

Hernández Martínez ruled for some twelve years, having himself elected (as the only candidate) in 1935, partly to gain diplomatic recognition from the United States. After introducing some reforms in banking and even setting up a government agency to aid peasants and dividing up some large haciendas, Hernández Martínez contented himself with consolidating his hold over a police state and spending increasing amounts of time with spiritism and the occult. Gabriel García Márquez used him as a primary model for the archetypal Latin American dictator in *Autumn of the Patriach*.[13] During a measles epidemic, for example, he ordered that street lights be covered with colored cellophane so that the colored light would purify the air. Two examples may serve to illustrate his bizarre "wisdom":

> It is good that children go barefoot. That way they can better receive the beneficial effluvia of the planet, the vibration of the earth. Plants and animals don't use shoes.

> It is a greater crime to kill an ant than a man, because a man who dies is reincarnated while an ant dies forever.[14]

Hernández Martínez eventually became an anachronism. Economically he had represented the coffee growers and had even had legislation impeding industrialization enacted. In 1944 there was a complex opposition movement (actually two movements, one more popular and another more elite). When the archbishop urged Hernández Martínez to stop the execution of people in the early phase of the movement, he answered, "In El Salvador, I am God."[15] Nevertheless in May 1944 he was overthrown; after a brief liberal period, however, hardliners representing the coffee oligarchy reasserted control.

It was only when another coup in 1948 brought to power Major Óscar Osorio that a systematic attempt at "modernization" in agriculture and industry, and liberalization in politics, was begun. One sector of the oligarchy recognized the need for diversification away from extreme dependence on coffee export and allied itself with a new breed of technocratic military officer. Armstrong and Shenk summarize the formula in three words: developmentalism, reformism, and repression.

Economic modernization first meant expanding into other crops, especially cotton. The existing landholders acquired lands on the flat Pacific coast and, since cotton requires relatively large amounts of capital expenditure, it was the domain of the wealthy from the beginning. The Osorio government repealed Hernández Martínez's anti-industrial legislation and during the 1950s industry grew more than 5 percent a year.

Even during the later 1940s, after the Hernández Martínez dictatorship, there had been a resurgence of labor organizing, in particular through CROS (Committee for Labor Reorganization of El Salvador). When attempts to co-opt CROS failed it was outlawed in 1952. Two of its leaders who suffered repression would reemerge: Salvador Cayetano Carpio, a baker, later founded the FPL (Popular Liberation Forces), and Mario Cardona later became a leader of the UTC (Union of Rural Workers). Under the legal umbrella of a "Law for the Defense of Democratic and Constitutional Order," repression was unleashed against union organizations. In the latter 1950s the government encouraged "bread-and-butter" (as opposed to "political") unionism, imported from the United States through the AFL-CIO organization ORIT (Inter-American Regional Workers Organization).

Osorio, who had lived in Mexico and admired the efficiency of the PRI's one-party rule, aspired to do something similar in El Salvador, establishing for that purpose an "official" party, the PRUD (Revolutionary Party of Democratic Unification). Behind the idea was an attempt to institutionalize army rule through smoothly run elections, and thus Colonel José María Lemus was elected in 1956. However, at the end of the decade Lemus reacted to growing protest (over government corruption, among other things) with widespread jailings and repression—for example, stopping demonstrations with bullets. In October 1960 junior officers, fearing the results of a popular revolt—the impact of Cuba was sinking in—staged a coup and set up a government of military and professionals, promising elections and reforms. The United States embassy, afraid of the consequences, balked. Fabio Castillo, a doctor and Junta member, later recalled a meeting with the American chargé d'affaires:

> Accompanied by Mr. Ricardo Quiñónez, a well-known financier of conservative views, he said that the U.S. embassy did not agree with the holding of free elections and that he supposed that we were not talking seriously. He . . . added that the embassy would agree to a "free election" held with two candidates previously approved by them. Of course, I rejected the proposal. Thereupon, the two visitors immediately got up and Mr. Quiñónez, unable to control his anger, turned to the chargé d'affaires and said, "You see, they are Communists; we have to go ahead."[16]

After only three months a new group of officers overthrew the Junta, ending the brief promise of reform.[17]

In the Catholic church during the 1940s and 1950s the dominant figure was Archbishop Luis Chávez y González, who occupied the see of San Salvador from February 1939 until February 1977. During the 1944 uprisings against Hernández Martínez he is said to have sheltered opposition figures and enabled them to escape, sometimes in his own automobile, and to have been influential in persuading Hernández Martínez to resign, even though the theosophical dictator had had little use for the church.

Archbishop Chávez devoted himself to encouraging Salvadoran priestly vocations. He had the present seminary built and sent a number of priests to study in Europe. Perhaps as a consequence of Chávez's concern, El Salvador has a relatively high proportion of national priests, and they are well trained. However, they are mainly from rural families (though not from the most destitute), rather than from the urban middle classes; hence they have been close to the peasantry.

Even in the early 1950s Chávez encouraged the cooperative movement, particularly for peasants who felt the pressure of expanding population and diminishing land (as the oligarchy expanded export crops). Priests were sent to Canada to study cooperatives and the Pius XII Institute was set up to teach cooperativism and the church's social doctrine.[18]

THE FAILURE OF MODERNIZATION
AND THE BEGINNING OF CHURCH RENEWAL (1960–72)

By some readings the 1960s were years of progress for El Salvador. A September 1981 U.S. State Department White Paper, for example, mentions that the economic growth of 5 percent was greater than the population growth (3 percent) and that agroexport and small manufacturing boomed, while conceding that most of the population still lived at subsistence levels. The same report saw the success of Christian Democrats as a sign of growing democracy.[19]

El Salvador in the early 1960s was indeed regarded as a "testing ground for U.S. policies," in the words of the *Wall Street Journal*. Such a small country seemed to be an ideal place for producing results with industrialization, development projects, and democracy. President John F. Kennedy revealed something of the underlying motivation, however, when he said, "Governments of the civil-military type of El Salvador are the most effective in containing communist penetration in Latin America."[20]

Under the impulse of the Central American Common Market, El Salvador's manufacturing sector grew by 24 percent between 1961 and 1971, but the new capital-intensive plants forced the small artisan shops out of business without absorbing the displaced labor; consequently industrial employment grew only 6 percent during the same period. Such statistics went unnoticed in the first flush of enthusiasm as forty-four multinational corporations set up operations in El Salvador during the 1960s, and regional trade in Central America increased at an annual rate of 32 percent during the 1961–68 period.[21] Having a head start on infrastructure, the Salvadoran and Guatemalan oligarchies were able to entice the multinationals into joint ventures.

However, the oligarchy adamantly refused any kind of land reform, which in the United States conception was to have been an integral part of the Alliance for Progress model of development. As a result, development aid went into a mixture of ad hoc projects ranging from schools and clinics to basketball courts (with Peace Corps coaches) but did nothing to address fundamental issues.

Politically the overall tendency was toward the consolidation of army rule. A new party, the PCN National Conciliation party, was created to be the "official" party and won the legislative election of 1961 and the presidential election of 1962—running unopposed both times. It then went on to "win" presidential elections in 1967, 1972, and 1977 as well as most municipal and legislative elections in other years. It is true that the Christian Democratic party, started by a group of Catholic intellectuals in 1960, began to gain some ground, and José Napoleón Duarte was elected mayor of San Salvador in 1964 and reelected in 1966 and 1968.[22] He was able to improve city services for the middle classes (street lighting, for instance) and promote development projects in the shantytowns. Two smaller parties (one Social Democratic and the other Communist-influenced) also participated in elections.

Nevertheless the presence of opposition parties should not obscure the fact that the main political development between 1944 and the 1970s was a transition from personal dictatorship (Hernández Martínez) to institutionalized military rule with only a veneer of electoral democracy.

In the later 1960s, as the economy tightened in response to a drop in prices for exported products, urban unions grew in numbers and militancy. In 1967 there were strikes, and in 1968 a teachers' strike was organized by ANDES (National Association of Educators of El Salvador), and the teachers camped outside the Ministry of Education building. Repression began to increase during this period: thirty teachers were arrested and there was a case in which two industrial workers "disappeared" after being arrested by the National Guard in 1968. According to one Salvadoran leader "at least 30 union leaders were captured and disappeared."[23]

In 1967 General José Alberto Medrano, the director of the National Guard and coordinating chief of the various intelligence services, together with President Fidel Sánchez Hernández, set up a paramilitary organization called ORDEN ("order," also acronym for "Democratic Nationalist Organization"). ORDEN was consciously patterned on models of counterinsurgency in the Philippines, Malaysia, Vietnam, and elsewhere, and it soon set up a national network of informers serving under the military. Although members received no pay, they could carry weapons and would have "pull" with local authorities (for example, for getting jobs).[24]

The United States showed its concern about possible problems with the Salvadoran peasantry in another way, by setting up a peasant organization. Normally the American Institute for Free Labor Development (AIFLD), sponsored by the AFL-CIO, with strong support from the United States government and business, concentrates on training urban workers in Latin America, encouraging them to adopt "bread-and-butter" (as opposed to "political") unionism. However, in El Salvador, AIFLD worked to organize the peasants into the UCS (Communal Union of El Salvador) in collaboration with the Salvadoran government. The UCS was never a militant organization but worked with governments. It became a major actor only when the government sought a conduit for its land-reform proposals (1976 and 1980).[25]

Renewal Movements

Later developments in the Catholic church, and especially the radicalization of important sectors, are the outgrowth of a renewal movement going back to the late 1950s and early 1960s. As has been mentioned, Archbishop Chávez devoted a great deal of attention to the training of the diocesan priests. For instance, he hosted a monthly meeting at which topics were presented and discussed. While initially these might have been of a moralistic nature, as Vatican II began to unfold the priests were discussing the liturgy, the church and its role in the modern world, and the other council themes.

The Christian Democratic party and its various spinoffs were another focal point of renewal. In the late 1950s a group of young Catholic intellectuals had shifted from a more "Italian" (conservative) kind of Catholic Action to a "French-Belgian" line emphasizing "temporal commitment." Some of these people went into the nascent Christian Democratic party. While the party was essentially a lay initiative, there were clearly close ties between Archbishop Chávez, and later Bishop Rivera y Damas, and Christian Democratic leaders and intellectuals during the 1960s. As happened elsewhere the party seems to have attracted people both with its anticommunism and with its proposals of reform—and these two aspects would become the source of tension and finally cause a split.

One Christian Democratic spinoff was FECCAS (Christian Federation of Peasants of El Salvador), which operated as a peasant league and was especially strong in the areas around and to the north of San Salvador—the very areas that more recently have been strongholds of the opposition and have become battlegrounds. Another by-product was CESPROP (Center for Research and Popular Development), a group of young professional people who researched the country's problems, prepared position papers on them, and served as advisers to FECCAS, as well as to other groups and local development projects. It is noteworthy that many of the people associated with CESPROP became radicalized: some joined the guerrillas in the early 1970s and others ended up in the united opposition at the end of the decade.[26] Apparently "consciousness-raising" worked in both directions.

During this period many groups were studying the social doctrine of the church; several retreat centers, such as Domus Mariae in San Salvador, were set up and were used for courses by pastoral agents and grassroots groups. Young people took part in Cursillos de Capacitación Social (intensive courses in the church's social doctrine).

One example of how linked the church was with what would later pejoratively be called "developmentalism" may be seen in its collaboration in the creation of the UCS (the United States-sponsored peasant organization mentioned above). In 1965 and 1967 parish Caritas Clubs, the Christian Democratic party, and local Alliance for Progress committees all proposed candidates for seminars to train peasant leaders. In mid-1968 leaders from twenty cooperatives were brought together by AIFLD (AFL-CIO training institute) to form the UCS.[27] Noteworthy in this case is the convergence of United States government programs, Catholic church institutions, and the Christian Democratic party, all in apparent harmony with the Salvadoran government, the common denominator apparently being agreement that "development" and its concomitant organization were necessary as an antidote to "communist" movements. If church people later came to repudiate "developmentalism" it could not be said they had not given it a try.

The signs of crisis already affecting peasants and labor began to appear in sectors of the church working with them. For example, in 1966 several peasants were jailed for having "subversive literature"—which turned out to be copies of Pope John XXIII's encyclical *Pacem in Terris* distributed by Christian Democrats.[28]

In 1969 Father José Inocencio Alas had been giving two months of intensive training to a group of nineteen peasant leaders of the area of Suchitoto, following the lines of the recently published Medellín documents. The peasants decided to apply what they were studying to a concrete local case involving what they saw as injustices practiced by landholders who were buying and reselling land. When the peasants organized a demonstration, the case became national news and Alas was denounced by representatives in the assembly and in the newspapers. Twice Suchitoto was occupied by troops under the command of General Medrano, the founder of ORDEN, and President Sánchez Hernández himself even showed up at the occupation. On the other hand, Archbishop Chávez allowed a discussion of the situation at a meeting of the clergy and was supportive when a number of priests backed the peasants.[29]

War and the Deepening Crisis

In July 1969 the world press reported what it called a "Soccer War" between El Salvador and Honduras, which, when examined, was neither as comic nor as incomprehensible as it was presented in the media.

The conflict had several roots. First, and most obviously, many thousands of Salvadorans had gone to find land and work in Honduras for more than a generation. Initially such immigration was even encouraged by governments in Honduras, whose population density is only about one-seventh that of El Salvador. However, the better lands are also owned by small elites, and during the 1960s militant peasant organizations, often supported by the church, were demanding land reform. The military government began to move in that direction and found it easier to expel those who were not "born Hondurans" than to expropriate large landholders. For its part the Salvadoran oligarchy feared the return of 100,000 or more landless peasants.

Another cause was the negative impact of the Common Market on Honduras. Salvadoran light manufactured goods (for example, toothpaste) had replaced similar United States goods, even though they were often both more expensive and inferior. Honduran industry with its later start could not compete with El Salvador and, although it could sell some agricultural products, Honduras suffered a trade deficit. Hence another element in the conflict was the resentment of Honduran elites.

The war was also useful to the ruling elites—particularly the military—since it could be used to make scapegoats of others and to distract attention from internal problems. It should be emphasized that ordinary Hondurans and Salvadorans did not regard each other as enemies; and in the border areas there was a good deal of common trade, friendly contact, and inter-marriage. However, in early 1969 there were border clashes, which when added to some incidents revolving around soccer playoffs were whipped up to a war frenzy. On July 14 Salvadoran planes bombed the Honduran airport in Tegucigalpa and the Salvadoran army invaded Honduras, which retaliated by bombing the Salvadoran airport. In the five-day war 2,000 people were killed and 4,000 wounded (many being Honduran peasants who met the invading army with only their machetes). Both armies had been equipped and trained by the United States. The OAS (Organization of American States) arranged a ceasefire and then a truce.[30]

However, the two countries did not renew relations for more than ten years (when the United States engineered a solution as part of the larger effort to enlist the Honduran army against the Salvadoran opposition). The solution was impeded by the interests of those who gained by the war. With El Salvador out of the picture the nascent Honduran industries could "take off" more easily (for example, Hondurans could buy toothpaste and plastic products made in their own country). Salvadoran manufactures, moreover, could not be shipped by land to Nicaragua and Costa Rica (and the ferry to Nicaragua was cumbersome and expensive) so other manfacturers in the region had reasons for not wanting the rift healed, since they could replace Salvadoran manfacturers.

Inside El Salvador the political effects were most noticeable. The army and the official party could bask in the sun of patriotism and their "heroic" courage proved in battle. However, the economic effects were soon felt as the price for corn and beans (now unavailable from Honduras) increased, and efforts to stimulate their production through credit to small and medium producers were of no avail. Losing Honduras and (for the most part) Nicaragua and Costa Rica as markets for its exports was a jolt to Salvadoran manufacturing. However, it should be noted that Guatemala, with its larger population, was always the largest single customer, and that Salvadoran exports to the region managed to grow after some initial readjustment. Nevertheless, the 1969 war precipitated a general crisis in the CACM, and it was no longer seen as the economic salvation of the region.[31]

It is not clear exactly how many Salvadorans did return to their country, nor exactly what happened to them (despite the government's demagogic talk of taking care of them). It is quite possible that many simply emigrated elsewhere (Guatemala, Belize, Mexico, or the United States). Those who stayed, however, undoubtedly added to peasant and worker militancy, especially those who had participated in the banana-company strikes in Honduras.

The economic effects of the war aggravated the already declining living conditions of many people, perhaps even a majority of the population. Thus between 1965 and 1970 the average *real income* of 62.2 percent of rural families (the landless and those with less than one hectare) actually declined from about $330 to $323 per family per year in 1962 dollars, while the increase of income among those who owned up to ten hectares was insignificant.[32] By 1971 rural unemployment was estimated at 54.4 percent, and during the mid-1970s it was estimated that the average rural worker could get only 141 days of work a year. While some figures may be open to question and modification (methods of gathering statistics may vary and may not always be reliable), it seems clear enough that in the early 1970s the majority of people in El Salvador were not benefiting from "development"; moreover, their condition would not improve simply through policy adjustments or more growth but, rather, their poverty was itself a by-product of the kind of development being pursued: further "development" along the same line would simply aggravate their condition.

In a remarkable coincidence just as Catholics were striking out in the directions pointed to by Medellín, some Marxists were both questioning existing orthodoxies and forming independent organizations. In April 1970, after what must have been a long period of discussion, a baker and long-time militant labor organizer, Salvador Cayetano Carpio, secretary-general of the PCS (Communist party of El Salvador), broke with the party over its policy of rejecting armed struggle and participating in electoral contests, in subservience to existing directives from Moscow. Another element was the party's support for the military in the war with Honduras. Together with some union leaders, Carpio and others formed the FPL (Popular Liberation Forces). "There were not more than ten of us. We didn't have even a pistol; not even a *colón*."[33]

The origins of the ERP (People's Revolutionary Army) are still somewhat obscure. It arose in 1971 partly out of disaffected Christian Democrats who had been involved with CESPROP and had been radicalized by the frustrations and limits of working for change. At first it was called simply "the Group." The 1971 kidnapping of Ernesto Regalado Dueñas, one of El Salvador's wealthiest people, has sometimes been attributed to the ERP, but this is not completely clear.

Neither the FPL nor the ERP made much impact during the first half of the decade and some observers even doubted their existence, considering them a fabrication of the military to justify repression. Some day these groups will tell their story; until then one is left to speculate that they must have undergone a long apprenticeship of working with people and a maturing process. It seems plausible that some time in the early 1970s the FPL made a decision to devote itself to political work, particularly in the countryside, while the ERP maintained a militaristic approach until the late 1970s. In a curious inversion, the group that began with more direct "Christian" involvement, the ERP, had relatively little to do with church groups, whereas the group with directly "secular" origins, the FPL, was linked to the popular group most directly related to church groups, the BPR (Revolutionary People's Bloc).

Church people had not been swept away by the militaristic fervor of the war; in fact on July 8, 1969, less than a week before Salvadoran troops invaded Honduras, the bishops from the two countries met in the border area, urging peace and in particular reminding the media of their responsibility.[34] Their warning was little heeded. By 1970 the country's real problems once more assumed center stage. When church people from both UCA (the Jesuit-run Central American University) and the chancery office participated in a conference on land reform held at the National University in early January, one of the participants, Father "Chencho" Alas, pastor of Suchitoto, was kidnapped from a parking lot by security agents and driven off. Vigorous protest by Archbishop Chávez and Bishop Rivera y Damas and candles lit in churches all night in protest may have helped to save his life. His captors drugged Alas and left him naked on a mountain top.

There had been meetings to discuss the Medellín documents in 1969. However, it was in June 1970 that some 200 bishops, priests, sisters, and lay people met for a Pastoral Week, which, by all accounts, furnished a platform for new directions in pastoral work. The final document was forthright in its critique of existing work: for example, "There is no proper evangelization." The church had not worked to advance liberation, partly out of a faulty understanding of its mission and partly out of "fear of losing privileges or suffering persecutions." Yet, "people still look to the church as the force that can help to liberate them." Most of the document was a list of "pastoral decisions": to form basic communities, to end clericalism, "to form leaders who will be not only catechists but responsible individuals dedicated to the integral development of the human person and the formation of communities"; to work for conscientization so people will see themselves as children of God and equal to each other; to struggle against obstacles to peasant unionization. There is stress put on having a minister personally identified with the community and representing the church there. His functions will be to preach the Word, baptize, distribute the Eucharist, and assist at weddings. (Whether in 1970 women were envisioned in such a role is not clear.)

The document reflects some of the optimism of the time. There is a stress on coordination and training, study and reflection, rethinking, the development of teams and institutes, and the reexamination of existing movements. While a conflictive analysis of society is implied, the remedies still appear mild (spreading cooperatives is one), and there is little anticipation of the forces that will be unleashed against the church people who take these decisions seriously or of the problems of unity they will provoke within the church itself.

The nuncio and some of the bishops found some of the conclusions to be "in violation of sound doctrine" and Bishop Rivera y Damas, who as president of the Pastoral Commission was largely responsible for the Pastoral Week, was chastised. However, there was some confusion when the Pontifical Commission for Justice and Peace in Rome sent Rivera y Damas a congratulatory telegram. An institutional solution was to commission a group to water down the conclusions before publishing an official version.[35] One of the participating bishops was Oscar Arnulfo Romero.

Armed with the conclusions of the Pastoral Week and encouraged by the contact with one another, pastoral agents intensified the grassroots work already begun. There was a loosely knit group of priests, largely Salvadoran (the Alas brothers, David Rodríguez, Rutilio Sánchez) and some foreign, such as Bernando Boulang, working in parishes around San Salvador, and around Chalatenango in the north and San Vicente in the east. Under Archbishop Chávez's urging a number of religious orders sent sisters to these areas. Those parishes were later to become battle sites: Aguilares, Suchitoto, Rosario Mora, Guazapa, Quetzaltepeque, Zacatecoluca, Tecoluca, Arcatao, Cojutepeque.

One participant, Father Benito Tobar, later described the effects of the Pastoral Week:

> From that moment pastoral agents began widespread Bible distribution, not just for people to get to know it but to have it in their communities and to use it like a machete as the working tool every Christian ought to have. . . .
>
> . . . It was during the first half of the 1970s that lay people took charge of the work of the church . . . bringing people together . . . planning courses . . . meeting to study and see how to solve community problems. It is interesting to see the changes brought about. . . . There are *cantónes* in Chalatenango, San Vicente, Morozán, Cuscatlán . . . where . . . peasants just got together to get drunk, celebrating the weekend, getting "happy." Starting with the Word of God . . . with the work of catechists and communities, everything changes. . . . They feel that they are not just the catechist . . . but the priest in the community, they bring the community together, prepare an agenda, celebrate the liturgy in their own way, starting with God's Word, asking questions about what the reading says, then discussing the commitment they are going to make.
>
> We would see how they would go out of the celebration of the Word to destroy a clandestine liquor still that someone might have that was doing damage to the community. Or they would go to help Don Pedro who was sick, giving him a little gift, some money, a pound of corn or beans, whatever they could. Or they would go to help Doña María, whose house was sagging because she was a widow and had no one to help her.

This summary gives some idea of what the basic Christian communities represented. One of the most outstanding of the priests who participated in this movement was David Rodríguez, whom one of his colleagues called "a great theologian although he has no academic degree, a prophet . . . a joyful peasant priest, the one most persecuted . . . the 'Che' of the Bible. . . ."[36]

PASTORAL WORK AND THE BIRTH
OF THE POPULAR ORGANIZATIONS (1972-75)

As the 1972 election drew near it seemed that UNO (National Opposition Union), a coalition of Christian Democrats, the MNR (National Renewal Movement, a Social Democratic party), and the UDN (National Democratic Union, a party with communist influence) might actually win. Its presidential candidate, José Napoleón Duarte, the popular former mayor of San Salvador, faced a divided power structure, which was proposing two candidates, Colonel Molina of the official PCN party and General Medrano, a hard-line favorite and founder of ORDEN. The vote-count itself was clumsily handled as it first favored Molina, and then Duarte—and then election news was suspended from Tuesday to Friday when a doctored vote-count had Molina winning once again. A month later a portion of the military attempted a revolt in the name of the Constitution, but they were put down—with the aid of bombing from the dictatorships of Guatemala and Nicaragua.[37]

After the 1972 experience many began to lose their faith that elections could serve as vehicles for meaningful change. The disenchantment would eventually serve to swell the ranks of the popular organizations.

The Aguilares Experience

The most significant church activity took place at the grassroots. Because normally there is no written record of the basic Christian communities, they tend to be overshadowed by the public controversies. However, one case is known in some detail, that of Aguilares, partly because it was the parish of Father Rutilio Grande, the first priest killed in the present struggle.[38] Since the experience of Aguilares has been well documented,[39] we shall review it at some length. When the full story of the role of the church in the Salvadoran struggle is told, it will undoubtedly be seen as only one example among many.

Pastoral work in Aguilares was atypical in several ways, starting with its initiator, Rutilio Grande. He had studied and received his Jesuit training in several Latin American countries and finally did his theology in Spain. He went to Belgium for further study around the time of Vatican II, and after returning to El Salvador was prefect of discipline in the seminary and one of the key figures in pastoral renewal in the archdiocese. In 1971 he took a course at the Instituto Pastoral Latinamericano in Quito, Ecuador, in order to make contact with current thinking among Latin American theologians and pastoralists. While in Ecuador he spent some time in the diocese of Riobamba, of Bishop Leonidas Proaño, where the basic method he would use in Aguilares fell into place for him.

Grande was somewhat reluctant to accept the parish of Aguilares, since he had been born in El Paisnal, a smaller town in the parish, and he still had relatives there, but such was the decision of Archbishop Chávez. Aguilares is about twenty-seven miles north of San Salvador just off one of the country's main highways, situated in a flat plain in the midst of sugarcane fields. There are about thirty-five large haciendas and three sugar mills. Of the 30,000 or so inhabitants, 10,000 live in Aguilares, 2,000 in El Paisnal, and the rest in villages or on the haciendas.

Economically Aguilares is a microcosm of El Salvador. The best land is that of the cane plantations, most of whose owners are absentees. For their subsistence the peasants work the hard stony ground, which they own in small plots, or rent, and supplement their own work with wage labor. The town is relatively new, however, having been set up in the 1930s.

Grande and the Jesuit team with him took a methodical approach from the outset. While he was studying in Ecuador a fellow Jesuit had been working with the Alas brothers in Suchitoto (the parish bordering on Aguilares), studying their work with basic Christian communities. In addition they were able to draw on a large pool of people to form the team, which was made up of four Jesuit priests and a number of students preparing to be Jesuits, as well as others, mainly university students, who came from the capital to help with specific tasks. As a consequence the team was able to move much faster than would be the more normal case where a priest would be working largely alone in his parish.

From September 1972, when they entered the parish, until January 1973, they worked systematically in the town of Aguilares itself and from then until June they worked in the countryside. Borrowing a traditional term, they gave two-week "missions" area by area, centering the work, however, not on otherworldly salvation and the conferral of sacraments but on evangelization. The town was divided into ten districts and the rural area similarly divided. Even as the team was invited to give a mission it began gathering data on the district by talking to people and putting the data into a card file. During the mission the team would live in the area, each member deliberately eating each meal at a different house and making the utmost effort to meet all the people and to gather further information, adding it to the card file. As a matter of principle, they had decided not to accept hospitality from landowners so as not to be compromised in any way.

During the evening session, to which the whole community was invited, a Scripture passage was read, part by part, at least twice and by different readers, and interspersed with questions or comments. It was here that the information on the community gathered by the team was fed into the process, since it had been studied and "codified" (in Freirean terminology) into basic images or words. That is, what the people had expressed was being returned to them in a kind of feedback. The team had made a clear option to work within the framework of people's religious vision, however. In other words, the idea was certainly not to turn them from religiosity to activism but to deepen the traditional religious vision and to transform it from an attitude of passivity (accepting things the way they are as the "will of God") to one of active struggle for change.

After the initial presentation the larger group (around sixty persons) broke up into discussion groups of eight or ten people. At the end they returned for a plenary session and presented their conclusions, after which a priest or other leader would make a summary or point out common themes, using the people's own words.

During this two-week period a number of natural leaders would begin to emerge. Toward the end there was a process of selection of Delegates of the Word chosen by the whole community present. The process was so set up as to avoid the emergence of traditional *cacique*-type leaders, who could dominate and aspire to the role of intermediary between the community and the powers-that-be. Rather, the emphasis was on a spirit of service and on a collective leadership, and in fact there was an average of one Delegate for every four or five participants. As the mission closed the new Delegates were presented to the community in a formal manner, and baptisms were celebrated in a way to emphasize commitment. The next day, Sunday, there were first communions and a large number of Bibles were distributed.

This first phase ended on Pentecost (June 10) 1973 with a Mass for all those who had participated in the missions. Townspeople were surprised to see so many from the surrounding hills. In his sermon Grande mentioned the criticisms of the work: that it was "Protestantism" (presumably because of the use of the Bible), or "communism," or "politics," that it dealt with the material rather than the spiritual, or simply that it would attract the National Guard, who would carry people off. He went into the principles guiding the work: the team would administer no sacraments without evangelization; it would have nothing to do with political groups of any kind; its only politics was to be announcers of the gospel; all injustices would be denounced whatever their source; the goal was "a community of brothers and sisters, committed to building a new world, with no oppressors or oppressed, according to God's plan."[40]

As a result of this first phase, there were now 10 urban communities and 27 rural ones with about 300 leaders. In their own evaluation, however, the team estimated that of the 30,000 inhabitants of the area, no more than 5,000 had an inkling of the gospel, for 2,000 it meant something, and about 400 could be said to be committed.

A second phase then began, extending until August 1976. Essentially it was a series of short courses of many kinds designed to help the communities and their leaders grow in their responsibilities. They were structured

around the Word of God. Some dealt with specific areas such as cooperatives. At one point there was a "community vaccination" against the effects
of a coming electoral campaign (that is, to help people approach elections
with a critical awareness and to reduce the manipulation practiced by politicians), and leaders studied the Salvadoran Constitution. Delegates were
helped to prepare for baptism and marriage, do youth work, and lead meetings, as well as lead the weekly worship. Average attendance at the celebration of the Word was 673 people.

While the starting point was people's religious tradition and stress was on
the Word of God, the Aguilares team made a conscious effort not to define
the Christian community over against the larger community by drawing
precise lines of who was inside and who was not. The church was to be one
of service, and the work was defined as being in a "mass line."

To terminate the second phase the team organized a "Corn Festival," a
newly created harvest liturgy. The people themselves chose the date and
brought their best ears of corn, as well as corn to make *atol,* a thick peasant
beverage. Each community was to choose a *madrina,* a patroness from
among the women and girls, but not on the basis of conventional beauty
standards—it was explicitly made clear she could be of any age—but on the
basis of her service to the community. This may have been a conscious
counterallusion to the Miss Universe Pageant, held in El Salvador in 1975 as
part of an attempt on the part of the oligarchy and the Molina government
to put their country "on the map" for tourism and investment. The patroness and a similar male figure presented the corn, local handicrafts, and
songs composed for the occasion in a contest that avoided the negative connotations of competition.

By this time Grande had less than seven months to live.

Growing Conflict

In the early 1970s there had been isolated instances of worker and peasant
militancy and repression or intimidation from the power structure, some of
which affected the church. Thus, for example, when the Externado San
José, a very large and prestigious Jesuit grammar and high school, sought
to introduce some aspects of Medellín into the classroom, parents became
irate and many of the wealthiest ended by taking their children elsewhere.
One Jesuit, Father José María Cabello, was expelled from the country for
his work with marginal people of the capital.[41]

Conflict became more organized and direct, however, when FECCAS,
the peasant league that had begun in 1964 and then had passed through a
period of internal problems, reemerged with new militant leadership. When
the government announced the construction of a giant dam at Cerrón
Grande to provide electricity for the cities, it became clear that some 15,000
peasants, largely around Suchitoto, were going to be displaced. Their cause
became a rallying point. A series of meetings and planning sessions began

among organizers, university people, teachers, some members of political parties, and some church pastoral agents with the idea of forming a new common front. Undoubtedly a part of the conviction came from the March 1974 legislative elections when the Central Election Board declared that the PCN had defeated the UNO coalition, without even posting election results.

Out of these discussions emerged a new type of organization uniting these various sectors into one front, called FAPU (United Popular Action Front). This "first FAPU" ultimately proved to be short-lived. Some organizations, such as the Communist party, did not join; other organizations, such as FECCAS, were not fully committed;[42] and within FAPU there was not sufficient agreement on how to proceed. The new umbrella organization did, however, presage what would become the most important political force of the decade, the popular organizations. Events themselves provoked new kinds of unity.

On November 23, 1974, National Guard troops with tanks and bazookas attacked a group of peasants in La Cayetana, San Vicente, killing six and arresting twenty-six (later thirteen were found to have disappeared). These peasants had occupied sixty *manzanas* of idle land belonging to an absentee owner, after repeated attempts to rent the land had failed. They had even deposited rent money with a local judge. By some accounts, the military met in Zacatecoluca and decided that to allow the land occupation would be setting a dangerous precedent, and so they decided to attack the area.

These peasants occupying land had not been members of any peasant organization but of a basic Christian community. After the repression they formed such an organization, which they called the UTC (Union of Rural Workers).[43]

Possibly as a result of this incident, in early 1975 the FPL wrote a letter to "progressive Christians" attempting to allay reservations, questions, and concerns about their organization. They insisted that religious beliefs and practices did not constitute an obstacle to joining the FPL and expressed their confidence that the "advanced sectors" of clergy, who were defending justice and equality against great odds, would always take their stand with the working classes. For them the incorporation of the peasants, "who are basically Christians," was "strategic work," and they were engaged in this both where organizations existed and where they did not, and whether priests were progressive or conservative.

Read from hindsight, the letter seems to indicate that the FPL was devoting a good part of its energies to political, as opposed to military, activity, and that this work would soon feed into the formation of the BPR (Revolutionary People's Bloc). While the FPL in no way intended to undermine or belittle anyone's religious beliefs, it insisted that people needed a "scientific focus on objective reality."

To the objection that they might be taking advantage of work done by others—it is easy to imagine that priests might feel this way about their basic Christian communities—they replied that it is the people who take advantage of revolutionary work and that behind such an objection might be a desire to maintain an exclusive influence over people, whose consciences, on the contrary, should be respected.

After noting the example of priests elsewhere in Latin America, the FPL warned Salvadoran priests that they would have to overcome the effects of their own class extraction (generally well-off peasantry or urban petite bourgeoisie) and that given the fundamental class contradiction, which appears even in the church, it was unrealistic to expect backing from the hierarchy.

This letter gives a rare glimpse into the kind of thinking going on within a revolutionary organization, a product, it would seem, of an intense debate about what stance to take toward "progressive Christians" and a rejection of more traditional and orthodox Marxist positions. Although the letter was signed by the central command of the FPL, a priest was involved in writing it.[44] This would seem to be the earliest formal statement from a revolutionary organization in Central America on the question of the participation of Christians.

Two further instances of armed repression brought events to a head. On June 21, 1975, National Guard troops broke into two homes in Tres Calles, a hamlet in the eastern part of the country, killing the two fathers and their sons. Then on July 30 university students organized a demonstration to protest the military intervention in the campus in Santa Ana. As they passed a bridge on 25th Avenue they found themselves caught in a crossfire with troops at either end. Some were killed on the spot, some jumped from the bridge, some were picked up by ambulances and never seen again. At least twenty died.

A group of priests and sisters were in a "reflection meeting" on the outskirts of town when a sister brought news of the attack. They had been reflecting on prophetism and in particular on Isaiah, and they felt that they had to act. They decided to hold a funeral for one of the victims in the cathedral and then occupy it. Over seventy protesters remained inside the cathedral while others gathered outside (including some Christian Democrats).

The cathedral interior soon became the scene of furious ideological debate as the participants in FAPU considered the next step. When the occupation ended with a Mass on August 6 (Feast of the Transfiguration and a national feast in El Salvador) the most militant groups, including FECCAS, UTC, and ANDES, had split from FAPU, and had decided to form their own front, the Revolutionary People's Bloc (BPR), which then became the largest of the popular organizations.[45] FAPU, for the moment, seemed to have been left largely as a shell but it soon reappeared with new vigor, particularly among urban labor unions.

EXPANSION OF THE POPULAR ORGANIZATIONS (1975–79)

Thus far we have mentioned the guerrilla organizations only briefly, noting their origins in 1970–71 and the FPL letter to Christians in 1975. In fact, little is known about their early years and one can only speculate. However, something must be said about the "Roque Dalton case."

Roque Dalton was born into a middle-class family and was educated at the Jesuit Externado San José. He became both a poet and a political activist and narrowly missed death by execution twice in 1960 (the second time he was saved by an earthquake, which split the jail walls). He spent years of exile in Mexico, Western Europe, Cuba, and Czechoslovakia, writing both poetry of a rather direct, "proletarian," if ironic, sort, as well as some basic historical and sociological overviews of El Salvador.

Returning to El Salvador in 1973 he joined the ERP and worked underground, not as a major organizer but as a writer. Within the ERP divisions were appearing, some members questioning a focus on military action and insisting that there must be political organizing. Dalton was of this group. In circumstances that are still obscure, he was "tried" and "executed" on May 10, 1975, along with another member of the organization. By some accounts he was accused of being an agent both for Cuba and for the CIA.[46]

Some commentators have seen the killing of Dalton as revealing the inner nature of the guerrilla groups: organizations that can kill their own members must be pathological.[47] It should be pointed out that leftist commentators subsequently saw this action as an "error" and as reflecting the immaturity of some of the revolutionaries at that time. However, when they join guerrilla organizations people do accept the need for a high degree of discipline (including the extreme sanction of "trial" and "execution") as a necessary condition of revolutionary action, and there have been occasional similar cases in Central American revolutionary organizations.

What seems more remarkable is how these organizations, which at mid-decade must have been very small and obviously immature and militaristic, made up largely of radicalized university graduates, became in the space of a few short years the genuine leading edge, or "vanguard," of a vast popular opposition movement in El Salvador. This process of growth and maturation must have occurred largely through the involvement of some members in the popular organizations. That is, it was contact with the ordinary people, the peasants, in their struggle for their rights that transformed these organizations from small conspiratorial bands into genuine mass-based revolutionary organizations.

The most important development in the 1975–79 period, spanning government changes, violence, persecution of the church, and so forth, was the growth of the popular organizations. What made the peasantry ripe for organizers' efforts were the worsening conditions of life. By the Salvadoran government's own estimate a minimum diet (corn, beans, rice, less than two pounds of meat a month) cost a family of six around $533 a year in the mid-1970s. Sixty percent of Salvadorans had a *total* income of less than $533 a year. A simple minimum diet was beyond the reach of the vast majority. Although the peasants could grow some of their own food, 96.3 percent of the rural population in 1975 had less than five hectares, whereas it was estimated that seven hectares were necessary to make a family self-sufficient.[48]

Not only was there poverty in El Salvador in the mid-1970s—it was increasing. Average real earnings actually declined between 1970 and 1975. The most direct cause was the growing landlessness. In 1961, 11.8 percent of rural families were landless, a figure that grew to 29.1 percent in 1971 and 40.9 percent in 1975.[49] Landless peasants are totally dependent on day labor on the plantations. However, work days tend to decrease as more landless peasants look for work. A further blow was the fourfold increase in petroleum prices in the mid-1970s, which affected peasants who had small plots and had become dependent on chemical fertilizers.

What led to the rise of the popular organizations, then, was an increasing pauperization and proletarization of large numbers of rural people. The kind of development taking place displaced them from land but could not absorb them into the labor force. As the decade went on they became increasingly desperate and many came to feel there was little to lose: "Better to die of a bullet than die of hunger" was a common refrain.

Not all were affected in the same way, however: El Salvador had its own "geography of hunger." Sugar and cotton are grown on the Pacific coastal plains and in some valleys of the interior. Cattle are raised in these same areas. Coffee is a hillside crop and much of the production is centered around Santa Ana, the second-largest town, located in the west. The hilly and mountainous area in the north, leading to Honduras, is not useful for agroexport crops and is inhabited by peasants.

The condition of peasant families will vary according to their place in this land-tenure pattern. The most secure, even in their poverty, will be those who have enough land to make themselves self-sufficient in corn and beans and to provide cash for minimum necessities. Relatively secure, also, are the permanent employees of the plantations, although the price is obviously subservience to the managers and owners. However, very few—less than 10 percent, probably—fall into either of these categories. The largest number are those who have too little land to support themselves and must supplement their own production with cash income during harvest time, and those who have no land at all and are entirely dependent on the work they can find. A further variation is those who rent small parcels of land. Rental lands are not of prime quality and their owners are not themselves wealthy. Plantation owners find agroexport production more profitable than renting land to peasants for subsistence crops. Geography is therefore a differentiating factor. In the coastal areas and central valleys a few are permanent employees of the plantations and the rest are landless day laborers, engaged in an unending search for a few days' work. In the hills around the valleys and in the northern mountains, some families have almost enough land for subsistence, but most do not and must either find work in the valleys or migrate to the coast.

In a situation of precarious dependence some people will seek to have good relations with higher-ups, whether plantation administrators, local public officials, or military and police. Thus there is a built-in tendency for some to seek their security through collaborating with the power structure, for example, members of ORDEN. Others may join "safe" peasant organizations such as the UCS, which claimed it was a means whereby peasants could get land, but at the same time was government-sponsored.

Because of these varying conditions some areas of the country were more "ripe" for organization than others. In this sense the most responsive areas turned out to be those areas of landless or near landless peasants in the hills around the central valleys and in the northern mountains (Chalatenango, San Salvador, Cuscatlán, Cabañas, San Vicente). Moreover it would seem that those most disposed to becoming organized were those who had a small piece of land or could recall owning land. While it would seem that those who most needed the power of organization would be the utterly landless in the coastal plains, it would also seem that the domination of the plantation owners was a strong deterrent so that in fact the popular organizations did not develop there initially.

As the newly formed BPR began to grow rapidly among peasants, questions were raised about the relation between political organizing and grassroots church work, especially in Aguilares. It would seem that in some areas priests and other pastoral workers saw it as self-evident that they should "accompany" their people in their search for effective instruments for organization. At Aguilares itself, some of the students who were working with the pastoral team were themselves involved in working with FECCAS and therefore with the BPR.

Rutilio Grande and the other Jesuits, however, were doubtful. They had not participated in the cathedral occupation. He seems to have maintained the official church teaching that political options are for the laity and that the priest as a representative and unifier of the community should not take partisan options. This position was in constant tension with the people's need to be supported in pursuing their rights. The issue came to a head in December 1975 when FECCAS was preparing its first public demonstration, and some leaders, who were also Delegates of the Word, asked Grande to celebrate a special Mass for the organization. After some discussion the team refused the request but arrived at a compromise solution: a "Peasant Christmas" could be celebrated in the church at Mass time and the organization could hold its demonstration outside afterward, but they should not carry placards or shout slogans while in the church. During the sermon Grande said: "We cannot get married to political groups of any sort but we cannot remain indifferent to the politics of the common good of the vast majority, the people. . . . we cannot ignore this today or ever."[50]

The question would continue to recur: How far should pastoral agents go with people as they moved toward political commitment? Should they simply help at the stage of *concientización*/evangelization, after which each individual would make his or her own decision, for example, joining FECCAS (or eventually, even an armed group)? Or did the notion of pastorally "staying with the people" mean that priests and sisters could and should become "collaborators" or even members of the organizations?

Grande clearly tried to maintain a distance, although he believed that "as a result of the dynamism of conversion and growth in faith" Christians "would normally become agents of change, as the church itself wants," working for "unionization and the defense of labor rights."[51] This whole question became a crisis for the team and for Grande personally—he called it his "Galilean crisis."[52]

His own efforts to maintain the distinction did Grande and the team little good. He was repeatedly under accusation from right-wing groups, and even the office of the presidency, and had to explain his position to the nuncio and Archbishop Chávez (who, however, supported him).

The Oligarchy Rejects the "Insurance Policy"

In 1976 the Molina government proposed a very mild beginning of land reform, which mobilized the whole oligarchy to defeat it. The controversy is important for what it reveals about power in El Salvador.

For some years a small group among Salvadoran elites—and a group of foreign "experts"—had become convinced that El Salvador was becoming increasingly nonviable as an agroexport country. With demographic growth stretching it to the limit, not even aggressive population-control programs would provide a solution.

What was needed, then, was a new model of economic development. Some called it the "Taiwan model": develop free-zone-type export industries (electronics assembly, clothing, and the like). Just as Taiwan had undergone a land reform, so should El Salvador, and indeed landowners could be encouraged to disinvest in land and reinvest in export industry, presumably in joint ventures with foreign capital and know-how. In fact, other countries of the region, encouraged in part by United Nations agencies, were beginning to set up their own free zones.

Looked at with cold rationality, such a plan would be in the best interests of the oligarchy. The Molina government was to call the land reform a "life insurance policy for our grandchildren," meaning, one assumes, that it would save them from losing all in a peasant revolt. However, in order to succeed, a radical modernization, even if thoroughly capitalist, would need to convince a sector of the oligarchy sufficient to prevail over the rest (backed up by the government and the military). In some countries there is an "industrial bourgeoisie" distinct from the landholding bourgeoisie, and some people thought they could discern such a group around the figure of Francisco De Sola, whose main investment was in industry and coffee processing and export. The existing evidence, however, is that while individual families may have investments that are predominantly agroexport or industrial or commercial/financial, in fact almost all have a mixture in their possession.[53] In other words, there was no significant sector of the Salvadoran oligarchy that could be "objective" enough to tolerate its own lands being taken for land reform, even in order to defend its own long-range interests.

While the idea of a "Taiwan model" with its antecedent land reform had been in the air for some time (for instance, the military studied land reform in seminars during 1973), a formal "Agrarian Transformation" plan ("agrarian reform" was considered a Marxist term) was announced in mid-1976. It was more a pilot project to begin in two departments of the country, San Miguel and Usulatán, and would benefit 12,000 peasants (only two-thirds of those in the area and a miniscule 3 percent of the peasants of the country). Owners could keep up to thirty-five hectares. They would be reimbursed at market value, partly in cash and partly in bonds, with incentives to reinvest in industry. It would take from three to five years to finish and, if carried at the same pace to the rest of the country, would take decades to complete.

This Agrarian Transformation came under immediate attack. The popular organizations denounced it simply as a plan made by "Yankee experts" in order to modernize capitalism in El Salvador, while the Christian Democrats, possibly seeing part of the plan's motivation as undercutting their own appeal in the 1977 elections, criticized it and called for a true land reform.

The most virulent attacks came from the landowners themselves, who formed a new organization, FARO (Agricultural Front of the Eastern Region), to fight back, using newspaper ads to call Molina "a communist in uniform." FARO was joined by ANEP (National Private Sector Association), the oligarchy's umbrella organization, which seemed most interested in defending the inviolability of private property.

While the United States government supported the plan and was planning to release large amounts of A.I.D. money (some say $50 million) for the project, few groups inside the country gave public support. One that did was the UCS, whose members would have had priority in entering the plan and administering it at lower levels. The only other groups to do so were the Communist party and the UCA (Catholic University); the latter devoted extensive coverage to land reform in all its aspects in its publication *ECA* (*Central American Studies*).[54] The UCA's position might be summarized as follows: although the land reform is slow, entirely capitalist, and aimed at modernizing the economy and reducing social discontent, it may be seen as a positive step toward needed changes and it should be supported with the proposal of deepening the process of change through popular participation. This position, of course, is similar to orthodox Marxism's tendency to view the appearance of a "national industrial bourgeoisie" as a transitional step toward the maturation of conditions for revolution. At the official level the church said little or nothing about the land reform.

By October FARO and ANEP had prevailed, finding allies among the military, the most important of whom was the defense minister, General Carlos Humberto Romero, soon to be the PCN candidate for the presidency. Threatened by a possible coup, Molina backed down and the Agrarian Transformation was watered down to simply a mechanism by which landowners could subdivide and sell marginal land. The whole process revealed the oligarchy's unity and tenacity when it felt its interests threatened. It also manifested a confidence that its domination of El Salvador was secure.[55]

In the meantime BPR organizers had been working seriously. At its first major demonstration on July 30, 1976 (first anniversary of the attack on the student demonstration), it attracted 3,000 peasants from FECCAS and UTC, 250 from ANDES, and smaller numbers from slumdwellers and student groups. In November it organized four demonstrations to demand that the agricultural daily wage be raised to nine colónes ($3.60) plus one colón ($0.40) for a meal.

One of these demonstrations took place on November 14 in front of the mayor's office in Quetzaltepeque. When police arrested a demonstrator the others appointed a commission to deal with the authorities and said they would not withdraw until their member was released. A policeman then shot into the crowd of about 2,500 people. Enraged, the people attacked the town hall, breaking windows, and some firing weapons. This was the first use of violence by the popular organizations. In their later evaluation, they concluded that their actions had shown a lack of discipline.[56]

Assault on the Church

What took place during the first half of 1977, the intensity of the confrontation, seems astounding even when seen in the light of later events. In a few months the government began to arrest, torture, and expel priests, two priests were murdered, two top government officials were kidnapped and killed by guerrillas, the official party won elections through widespread fraud and a massacre, Oscar Romero became archbishop, troops launched a military attack on Aguilares, and a terrorist organization threatened to assassinate all Jesuits in El Salvador. This period was a watershed and will be narrated here in some detail.[57]

An incident in Aguilares on December 5, 1976, may be taken as setting off the chain reaction. By this time the Cerrón Grande dam project was underway, the water was beginning to rise, and peasants were going to be displaced. Some peasant families on the property of Francisco Orellana had been there for fifty years and thought the owner, whom the government had paid for his land, should help them to acquire land elsewhere. Accompanied by other peasants from FECCAS, about 250 in all, they marched to the hacienda and were met by the Orellana brothers, Francisco and Eduardo. There was some confusion, shots were fired, and Eduardo Orellana was killed. The most likely explanation was that Francisco had killed his brother accidentally (and rural police after interrogation made no arrest).[58]

FARO and other landholder organizations, however, decided to make

Orellana a "martyr" at the hands of the "murderous hordes" and began to publish advertisements in the newspapers denouncing FECCAS, the Jesuits, and other priests, even invoking anticlerical arguments from the nineteenth century.

Part of the oligarchy's motivation may have been a feeling of power after defeating the Agrarian Transformation and at the same time a conviction that the popular movements should be stopped before they spread. Another source of their feeling of power may have come from the coffee boom just beginning to be felt as a result of a frost in Brazil.

Both the government and right-wing groups began an attack on church people. In January 1977 two Jesuit students who had worked in Aguilares were expelled from the country, a bomb was set off in the house of Father Alfonso Navarro in Miramonte, a middle-class area of the capital, and accusations were made against two UCA Jesuits, Ignacio Ellacuría, a theologian and editor of *ECA*, and Luis de Sebastián, an economist. Finally, Roberto Poma, head of the government tourist agency (and considered a leader of the modernizing sector of the bourgeoisie), was kidnapped on January 28.

Since late 1976 the electoral campaign had been underway. General Romero, clearly representing the landholding oligarchy, whose side he had championed during the Agrarian Transformation controversy, led a lackluster campaign with no real content, relying on posters showing him as balding and smiling benevolently. The UNO (opposition) once more fielded candidates, this time choosing Ernesto Claramount, a retired general, as its presidential candidate, in the hope that his presence might be able to reassure the military that they could live with UNO government. The popular organizations were calling for abstention. There was a strong feeling that this was a last chance for an electoral formula that might open the way to peaceful change—and at the same time there was strong anticipation of impending fraud. The campaign itself aroused little public interest.[59]

The fury of the oligarchy was further aroused on February 10 when Roberto Poma's body was found. The government had agreed to the ERP's demands and had released two political prisoners, one being Ana Guadalupe Martínez, a top ERP leader. Poma, however, had died in captivity as a result of wounds received during the kidnapping. (In their account of the kidnapping, ERP members related how they had got medical treatment for the wounds and that Poma seemed to be in a stable condition, so much so that they were carrying on lengthy discussions with him about business and politics. His death came in the midst of what seemed to be a fairly normal conversation. Deciding that revealing his death might jeopardize the political prisoners, they decided to go ahead with negotiations in the hope of freeing their colleagues. These details emerged only much later—at the moment when Poma's body was found there was much speculation and wild rumor.[60])

On February 8, 1977, it had been announced that Archbishop Chávez

would be retiring after thirty-nine years of administering the archdiocese
and that he would be replaced by Bishop Oscar Romero, of the diocese of
Santiago de María. Initially it was assumed that Romero had been chosen
because he was "safe" as opposed to the auxiliary bishop, Arturo Rivera y
Damas, who had shown support for progressive clergy since the early 1960s
and was a friend of the founders of the Christian Democratic party. Both
Chávez and Rivera found themselves defending priests, and particularly the
Jesuits, against increasingly aggressive advertisements placed by the landholder organizations. FARO made insulting attacks on Chávez himself in at
least one advertisement.

Romero was considered conservative, timid, "spiritual," and in poor
health. In the past he had had conflicts with priests (he had participated in
"correcting" the conclusions of the 1970 Pastoral Week and had disagreed
with the priests when they had protested the occupation of the National
University by troops). His appearance was clerical. Romero had risen in the
approved fashion, being secretary of the Salvadoran Bishops Conference in
the 1960s and then auxiliary bishop of San Salvador, where he had been
assigned secondary tasks. However, he had certain personal qualities and
experiences that would serve him as he changed in response to crisis and
conflict. His study of theology in Rome and his reading had given him a
penchant for logical frameworks, while, on the other hand, his experience
in a rural diocese gave him a sense of the peasants' plight. Many who knew
him have commented on his basic personal honesty and his plain Christian
faith.[61]

In late January Father Mario Bernal, a Colombian, was picked up by
security forces, kidnapped, and appeared a few days later in Guatemala.
Hence on February 13 all the priests of the vicariate, with many people from
other parishes, particularly FECCAS members, celebrated a Mass at
Bernal's parish in Apopa. During the hot dusty procession to the church
government informers were out with tape recorders. Rutilio Grande
preached the sermon, which is quoted below at some length because it gives
a sense of the level of conflict and also of Grande's characteristic style of
relating events in El Salvador to biblical themes.

As Grande began the sermon he noted that some of the flyers passsed out
during the procession (presumably by FECCAS) were not official and
should be judged on their own merits. Grande said that Jesus' message is
utterly clear:

> We all have a common Father. . . . So we are obviously all brothers and
> sisters. All of us alike, one to another. But Cain is an abortion of God's
> plan; and there are groups of Cains. . . . Here in this country there are
> groups of Cains who invoke God, which is worse.
> God the Lord in his plan gave us a material world . . . for everyone
> without limits. That's what Genesis says, not what I say.
> [Imitating another voice]: "I bought half of El Salvador so I have a

right to it! No objections! It's a bought right, because I have a right to buy half of El Salvador!''

That's a denial of God! There is no right over the majority of the people!

So the material world is for all without limits. It's a common table with a large tablecloth like this Eucharist. With a spot for everyone. And so everyone will come up to it, a tablecloth and food for all. Christ had a reason for making a supper the sign of his kingdom. . . . And he celebrated it the eve of his total commitment.

. . . We are not here out of hatred. In fact, we love these Cains. . . . The Christian does not have enemies. Even those who are Cains are not enemies. They are brother Cains.

He went on to say that love is conflictive and demands moral violence, and noted that the procession and Mass were under surveillance.

Along the way I saw tape recorders, which don't belong to Father Mario's parishioners but belong to those who betray God's Word [applause].

. . . The violence is in God's Word, which does violence to us . . . and . . . to society.

Continuing to range over various themes, Grande said it was a false pretext to expel Bernal because he was a ''foreigner.''

It is practically illegal to be a true Christian . . . in our country. Because . . . the world around us is radically based on an established disorder, before which the mere proclamation of the gospel is subversive.

Touching on living conditions in El Salvador and its ''false nominal democracy'' (a week before elections), Grande continued:

I'm very afraid that soon the Bible and the gospel won't be able to enter our borders. We'll just get the bindings because all the pages are subversive—against sin, of course.

He said that the government was encouraging an avalanche of sects with the slogan ''Freedom of Worship''

for those who bring a false God, in the clouds, sitting on a hammock. . . .

I'm afraid that if Jesus of Nazareth came back, coming down from Galilee to Judea, that is from Chalatenango to San Salvador, I daresay he would not get as far as Apopa, with his preaching and actions. They would stop him in Guazapa and jail him there.

. . . They would accuse him of being a rabble-rouser, a foreign Jew, one confusing people with strange and exotic ideas, against democracy, that is, against the minority. Ideas against God, because they are a clan of Cains. They would undoubtedly crucify him again.

In Christianity today you have to be ready to give up your own life to serve a just order . . . to save others, for the values of the gospel.[62]

Some later felt that this sermon sealed Grande's fate.

Between February 17 and 21 a Belgian priest, Willibrord Denaux, was tortured and expelled; an American Maryknoller, Bernard Survil, was also expelled; and Rafael Barahona, a Salvadoran priest of San Vicente, was picked up and savagely tortured. Archbishop Chávez in tears begged to be relieved.[63]

In the meantime, on Sunday, February 20, the election took place. Amateur radio operators picked up (and recorded) strange messages: "The level is low. There is too much sugar" (The vote count is low. There are too many opposition votes). "Buy some tamales and get the little birds out of there" (Stuff more fake ballots and remove the opposition observers [who had a legal right to be there]).[64] Seeing the fraud, many thousands of opposition supporters began a permanent vigil in Plaza Libertad, camping out, with the candidates present.

In these circumstances it was felt the government might see Archbishop Chávez as a "lame duck," and it was decided to speed up Bishop Romero's assumption of the archdiocese. A private ceremony was accordingly held on February 23 without the usual presence of government representatives. That same day the Salvadoran Bishops Conference met with President Molina and there were accusations on both sides.

The government officially announced the election results (with the PCN winning by a 2 to 1 margin). There was clearly massive fraud in the vote count; what is less clear is the extent to which people abstained from voting because they were already convinced that elections were meaningless. In any case, although the president declared that the election was over and the communists had lost, the UNO continued its vigil all week. On Sunday Father Alfonso Navarro was asked to celebrate Mass in the plaza and did so, remarking afterward with some foreboding that he might be killed.

In the early morning hours of February 28 occurred the "Monday morning massacre." At around 1:00 A.M. trucks with members of the army, the National Guard, national police, customs police, and treasury police arrived (El Salvador is prolific in "security forces"). Sealing off all entrances but one, they turned on high-powered hoses. The crowd huddled under a statue and sang the national anthem. After troops opened fire, wounding about four people, an officer announced with a megaphone that the people had ten minutes to leave the plaza. Some of the people, including Claramount and UNO leaders, fled into nearby Rosario Church, which was then tear-gassed. The rest fled up the remaining street, which seemed open, but found it to be a trap and were made to run the gauntlet of soldiers in groups of five. All were beaten and some were shot.

At 4 A.M. a truce was arranged through Archbishop Chávez and the Red Cross. Bishop Rivera y Damas accompanied General Claramount, José Morales Ehrlich, and other UNO leaders out of the church and to the airport, whence they flew to Costa Rica. An American reporter, Georgie Anne Geyer, later expressed her shock:

> I was kept out of the plaza, so I could hear only the screaming and the shooting. Then, when it was over, I got in and found it literally covered with blood, although the bodies had been removed. But perhaps the most horrible thing was when I returned again an hour after *that* to find they had hosed down the plaza and there was a chill as though nothing had happened at all.

It was estimated that 100 had been killed, 200 wounded, and 500 arrested. A state of siege was declared.[65]

In the midst of this national crisis, with the morning papers telling of the bloody happenings, the clergy of the San Salvador archdiocese met for the first time with the new archbishop in what had been originally planned as a three-day study session. After opening words from Rutilio Grande, the group decided to drop the study topic and hear reports on events in the plaza, especially from Father Octavio Ortiz. Romero listened and asked questions and finally, to the surprise of the priests, suggested the meeting be suspended and that each return to his parish, ready to open the door to those who felt in danger. For his part he would be in his office waiting for their reports and for further information in order to plan what to do. This attitude of putting the church—starting with the chancery office—at the disposition of the people in times of crisis would be a characteristic of Romero.

On March 5 the Salvadoran Bishops Conference published a letter "on the moment the country is living through." According to some, Romero prepared the initial draft just as he became archbishop. In any case it was the most forthright statement of the hierarchy, which would soon be clearly divided.

The bishops began by listing a series of facts including repression of peasants and those working with them, the increase of uninvestigated murders, intimidation, the expulsion of priests, and the campaign of FARO and ANEP (mentioned by name) against the church. They quoted and alluded to Medellín in their analysis and used a vigorous language that they would not repeat:

> As injustice is concrete, the promotion of justice has to be also concrete. . . .
> . . . the church cannot but raise its voice when injustice takes over society. It cannot remain silent when human rights are trampled.

Denunciation, in our case . . . comes from fidelity to Him who un-
masked sin wherever He found it: in Pharisees, priests, the rich, Herod,
or Pilate.

. . . the church should give clear signs that it is with the dispossessed,
with those for whom no one normally cares or takes any interest. This
will produce, as in the case of Jesus, persecution, and lack of understanding from the powerful, surprised perhaps that the church should
become involved in the things of this world, and annoyed, seeing this
mission as a threat.[66]

The bishops' letter seems to have provoked little public reaction.

During this period Felipe Salinas, leader of a Christian community, was
dragged out of his house in his underwear by National Guard agents and
interrogated about his activities. He was then dressed in a cape and crown,
beaten, and made to carry a cross for three miles. Several days later the
same troops interrogated and tortured him, threatening him with death.[67]

Late in the afternoon of Saturday, March 12, 1977, Rutilio Grande was
driving through canefields on his way to say Mass in El Paisnal. Accompanying him were Manuel Solórzano, an old peasant, and Nelson Rutilio
Lemus, a teenager, and some children to whom Grande was giving a lift in
his Safari jeep. Ambushers opened fire killing Grande instantly along with
Solórzano and Lemus, while the children were allowed to escape from the
car, which had pitched on its side.[68]

Although President Molina called Archbishop Romero at 7 P.M. to express his condolences (an hour and a half after the killing) all indications are
that from the beginning there was never any serious effort to investigate the
killing even though a man named Benito Estrada was soon indicated as
involved in the killing. Some would see the killing as an "eye for an eye"
after the killing of Roberto Poma. However, it should be noted that the
ERP did not operate in Grande's area (where the FPL was active). It is unclear whether the assassination was ordered at the local or the national level.

That evening Grande's Jesuit superior, César Jerez, many priest colleagues, and Archbishop Romero arrived. There was a Mass and then an
autopsy. All night long the peasants came by the church and passed silently
by the three bodies. The following Monday morning the funeral was celebrated in the cathedral with the participation of the nuncio, 4 bishops, 200
priests, and a very large crowd, which extended into the adjoining streets.
Then a motorcade left for Aguilares and El Paisnal where the three bodies
were buried to applause and the guitar-accompanied singing of a song newly
composed to honor Rutilio Grande.

Meeting the following day the priests of the archdiocese and the two
bishops made several important decisions. Catholic schools were to be
closed for three days (students were given materials for themselves and their
families to reflect on). All Masses for the following Sunday would be suspended except for one to be celebrated at the cathedral. The archbishop
would attend no more government ceremonies until Grande's murder was

cleared up. A permanent committee was to be set up to monitor events.

During this time YSAX, the archdiocesan radio station, began to broadcast a combination of Scripture readings, religious and protest songs, official church statements, and its own reflections. In addition, the chancery office began to issue bulletins, which became in effect an alternate form of news, since the existing media were closed to whatever might be considered critical of the government.

Representatives of the oligarchy were incensed at what was happening. FARO said the Jesuits had taken control of the hierarchy and the church was struggling to take power. Some were scandalized by the suppression of all Sunday Masses except one, ostensibly because it would cause people to "miss Mass." An estimated 100,000 people attended the one Sunday Mass at the cathedral.

On March 26 Archbishop Romero left for Rome to confer with Pope Paul VI. One commentator saw the decisions and actions made around the death of Grande as constituting basic changes in Romero and the church itself: a break with existing legality (burying him without waiting for the legal permission and holding public gatherings in defiance of the state of siege), a departure from the Christendom form of church-state relations (refusing to attend official functions), as well as a new liturgy, a new focal point of church unity, a new kind of service to the people, even allowing large religious gatherings to be used by popular organizations, and beginning to speak in the name of the poor.[69]

Grande's murder has frequently been presented as a turning point, or moment of conversion, for Archbishop Romero. Grande, after all, was forty-nine years old, not at all a young firebrand, and was one of the most respected priests in the country and a friend of Romero's. However, Romero's conversion dated back to experiences he had had as bishop of the rural diocese of Santiago de María. In mid-1975 he found that Father David Rodríguez was coming to speak to some members of his clergy. Having been told by Bishop Aparicio that Rodríguez was a communist, Romero decided to listen secretly to what Rodríguez told the priests. After hearing three talks he concluded that Rodríguez was simply applying the gospel to El Salvador (and said so to Bishop Aparicio). He later said, "David opened my eyes and evangelized me from behind that door."[70] Grande's murder deepened and radicalized a process already under way.

There was no respite during April and May. Archbishop Romero returned from Rome encouraged by his consultation with the pope and was quoted as saying that in Holy Week (then underway) "liturgical acts are not unincarnated but set in the midst of real life. . . ."[71] In many places the celebration took on a prophetic character. The oligarchy continued its attacks; for example, a group called for the formation of a "National Committee for the Defense of Catholic Education" and Sacred Heart High School, run by sisters, was mentioned by name.[72]

On April 30 the Salvadoran bishops and the nuncio met with President

Molina, who was accompanied by his cabinet ministers and President-elect Carlos Humberto Romero. Molina began by saying that the object was to deal with the "deterioration in the relations between church and state" and accused priests of being involved in political activities (the elections and the postelectoral vigil), and of using Holy Week ceremonies subtly to accuse the government of responsibility for Grande's murder. Catholic schools, he said, were teaching things that confused parents, and he blamed "international communism" for Grande's death. His conclusion was that the bishops should advise the clergy, especially foreigners, to obey the law strictly.

Archbishop Romero in his reply first insisted that he wanted dialogue and that the government should not confuse the church's post-Vatican II and post-Medellín evangelization with Marxism-Leninism and that accusations against the clergy should be specific and with proofs. Bishop Aparicio of San Vicente, president of the Salvadoran Bishops Conference, expressed similar ideas and said that in the case of land occupations by peasants, the owners themselves had committed injustices and he proposed that a mediating commission be formed. He further urged that the status of ORDEN be clarified, since it was not clear why a civic organization should be directed by local military commanders. He also said that FARO's tendentious statements should be curbed.[73]

This meeting illustrated the fact that what was happening at every level in the church was being regarded as a national problem (for instance, the president of the country being concerned about what was being taught in Catholic classrooms). It further showed that the later division among the bishops had not yet become manifest.

There was at this moment, however, a more immediate crisis. Mauricio Borgonovo, the foreign minister, had been kidnapped by the FPL, who were demanding the release of thirty-seven political prisoners. Romero, after consulting with the Priests' Senate, published an appeal for serenity, asking both the government and the FPL for restraint. At the request of Borgonovo's family he made an appeal on television but the government allowed it to appear only once. That same day, April 23, there appeared a communiqué from the UGB (White Warriors Union) opposing negotiation, blaming the Jesuits and "communist priests" for the situation, and stating that if the foreign minister were killed or the government negotiated they would kill "an eye for an eye." Molina a few days later appeared on television saying that negotiations were impossible. Although the Borgonovo family was willing to pay a ransom fee it seems that no more than six of the prisoners were still alive.

Events continued to heighten the crisis. On May 1 a demonstration was broken up by troops and at least eight were killed. Another priest, a Panamanian, was deported, and a few days later the UGB set off a bomb in the archdiocesan print shop. Rubén Zamora, a member of the Justice and Peace Commission, and Eduardo Colindres were arrested and held incommunicado. Both were prominent Christian Democrats and UCA professors. On May 5 the clergy and the archbishop produced yet one more communiqué, this time seeking to put all these events into a broader context, by not just focusing on the Borgonovo kidnapping but starting with the problem of land tenure, political prisoners, and an underlying "state of permanent injustice in which most Salvadorans live."[74]

Having concluded that the government would not negotiate, the FPL carried through its threat and killed Borgonovo. His body was found on May 10, and the following day Alfonso Navarro was gunned down in the parish house in Miramonte. When first ordained Navarro had served in a rural parish but he had been forced out, after being (absurdly) accused of involvement in the 1971 kidnapping of Ernesto Regalado Dueñas (see p. 103 above). In Miramonte, a new middle-class area, he had felt out of his element but had decided to work with youth. Long under surveillance (government agents taped his classes with high school students), he had received increasing threats and a bomb had destroyed his car and garage. In his last weeks Navarro spoke several times of death and at Grande's funeral was heard to say, "What a prize . . . there are few who receive the honor of being martyrs." It seems that Navarro had been in the presidential palace the day he was killed, but it is not clear for what.[75]

In a communiqué the White Warriors Union took credit for Navarro's killing, claiming it was retaliation for the murder of Borgonovo. Throughout this period advertisements continued to appear from phantom groups such as the Association for Catholic Improvement and the Salvadoran Christian Society, with headlines like, "Mothers! Terrorism Threatens Your Children. Unite to Defend Them!" There began to circulate printed handbills reading, "Be a Patriot! Kill a Priest!"[76]

Preaching at Navarro's funeral, Oscar Romero expressed a new eloquence, using as a leitmotiv for the young priest's life the figure of a Bedouin, pointing ahead toward the future. He emphasized that every human life is sacred, whether it be that of a foreign minister, a peasant, or a priest. "Violence is produced not only by those who kill, but by all those who impel toward killing," having in mind, it would seem, the hate propaganda appearing in such proliferation. In the next sentence he challenged President Molina to carry out his promises of investigations into the killings of Grande and Navarro. In a variation on the normal notion from canon law, he said the "excommunion" for this killing would come from the people of God. Standing before Navarro's body, he reiterated an "oath of fidelity," citing the apostle Peter in Acts 5:29: "Better for us to obey God than men!"[77]

In mid-May government troops carried out a military sweep of the Aguilares area, the first such action to take place. The initial justification for "Operation Rutilio," as it was called, was to end a land occupation by FECCAS members, who had taken lands after their efforts to renew their rental contracts were repeatedly rejected by the owner. Arriving with helicopters and armored troop carriers, the army swept through the entire region, El Paisnal and all the villages, finally surrounding the town of Aguilares before dawn on May 19.

Some peasants were sleeping at the church, and when the sacristan and another peasant sought to alert the town by ringing the church bell they were shot and killed from below by G-3 fire. The troops surrounded the church and knocked the door down. They stripped and blindfolded the Jesuits and threw them and peasants onto the ground. Windows were smashed, pews were overturned, the tabernacle was shot open, and hosts were strewn on the floor. That day the troops made a house-to-house search, "beating and carrying off all the people who had Rutilio Grande's picture."

According to the government bulletin, only seven were killed in this police action. People in Aguilares said fifty had been killed, hundreds had been arrested, and the fate of hundreds of others was unknown. Foreign reporters who tried to pass through the roadblock to the town were told at gunpoint that they had two minutes to leave or they would be arrested.[78]

In order to show his support for the people of Aguilares and the Jesuits, Archbishop Romero celebrated Mass in the town and preached there in early June, beginning by saying, "It's been my lot to go around picking up bodies and victims of persecution. . . ." Persecution, he said, was the sign of the Lord's predilection, and he admitted that "we have mutilated the gospel a great deal, we have tried to live a very comfortable gospel." At the same time he clearly warned against "class struggle, which is the false force of other liberations, which do not lead to any liberation." He urged the people of Aguilares, which he said was a "torch lifted up," to be firm in defending their rights but not to harbor any resentments.[79]

One final event closed this intense period. On June 21, with a few days left in the Molina presidency, the White Warriors Union said that all Jesuits had to leave the country within thirty days; if they did not, they would be systematically eliminated. The UGB would not consider itself responsible if third persons (such as students in Jesuit schools) were harmed, since sufficient warning was being given. The attack was not against the church, they said, but against "Jesuit guerrillaism."

The Jesuits replied that they would stay: "Christian power is far stronger than a two-edged sword because it is based on the teachings of Jesus Christ. It is a power neither money nor guns can destroy."[80]

It was the bizarre nature of this threat—the suspense of a thirty-day countdown—and the fact that Jesuits are an international order that for the first time put El Salvador on the map of countries with human rights violations. News reports, however, showed little sense of the context out of which it arose.

The full significance of these conflicts would become clear only considerably later. One fact that merits mention is the behavior of the oligarchy and the military. Although the Agrarian Transformation had indicated a momentary split between the modernizers and the hardline conservatives, throughtout this period (the first half of 1977) there was a remarkable similarity in expressions by the government, the oligarchy (as represented in FARO, ANEP, and other organizations), and right-wing groups such as the White Warriors Union. It should be noted that Major Roberto D'Aubuisson, who at the time was in army intelligence, was reputed to be a founder of this paramilitary organization. (He was to play an increasingly visible role after 1979, finally emerging as speaker of the assembly after the United States-sponsored elections of 1982.)

Judging from what happened during 1977 it seemed quite clear that the oligarchy was newly unified (or had silenced the dissident modernizers) and that the government, military, and right-wing groups were best seen as parallel expressions of the oligarchy, each to be employed in its own way. This should not be taken to mean that all members of the Salvadoran elites were involved in violence—nor even that they personally agreed with how violence was used—but simply that the organized expression of the oligarchy was orchestrating an overall approach to what it saw as a threat from the popular organizations and the church.

A New President—and Little Change

In the five months prior to General Carlos Humberto Romero's inauguration as president on July 1, 1977, two priests had been killed, two tortured, one beaten, two jailed, four threatened with death, seven refused reentry to the country, and eight expelled.[81] Since Romero was the choice of the landholding oligarchy, made president through fraud, it was understandable that people connected with the church were apprehensive.

They were therefore somewhat surprised when his inaugural address proved to be serene, carried no threats, and was replete with references to democracy, dialogue, peace, justice, equality, dignity, solidarity, order, and freedom of expression. In the middle of the month a government-church commission was formed to deal with existing problems. *ECA,* taking the new president's speech at face value, urged a new climate of respect for human rights, which would permit a subsequent phase of needed structural changes to begin.[82]

President Romero's apparent olive branch may have been partly motivated by a recognition that the government's image had been seriously affected by news of recent events, and that the Carter administration was serious about making human rights a factor in its foreign relations. In fact it was Ambassador Ignacio Lozano, a Gerald Ford appointee, who had begun to raise human rights concerns. Rather than subject itself to human rights scrutiny, El Salvador in February 1977 had rejected United States military aid, along with three other Latin American countries. Lozano and a political officer in the embassy had made themselves unwelcome over human rights, particularly in the case of James Earl Richardson, an American black who died in a Salvadoran jail, probably murdered by order of a Salvadoran official. They left the country just before General Romero's inauguration, and the Carter government, as a sign of displeasure, did not fill the vacancy for about three months. For further leverage the United States voted against a $90 million Inter-American Development Bank loan for a hydroelectric project.[83]

Hence it was ultimately not so surprising that as the UGB deadline approached, the Jesuits were given police protection: President Romero had apparently been able to prevail over the White Warriors Union. Not all were as visible as the Jesuits, however. In August Felipe de Jesús Chacón, a Delegate of the Word, was arrested by the National Guard and tortured, by cutting off his scalp and stripping the flesh from his face. He was then drawn and quartered, and when found was being eaten by dogs. Archbishop Romero went to the customary ninth-day Mass and began his sermon, "These days I have to go around picking up bodies of loved ones, listening to widows and orphans, and spreading hope." The experience of being in the Chacón family house, sharing tamales and homemade fruit juice, and hearing Chacón's wife, Evangelina, tell of the condition they found Chacón in, made an impact on Romero and he continued to discuss the situation of peasants, their organizations, and their struggles with his priest-colleagues. Chacón's son Juan was already a BPR leader and would eventually become the most prominent leader of popular organizations.

The national feast day of El Salvador is August 6, the Transfiguration, and on this day Romero released his second pastoral letter, "The Church, the Body of Christ in History." In a rather doctrinal style, which would characterize Romero's letters and formal sermons, this letter dealt with changes in the church, the accusations that it was Marxist or political, and the fact of persecution. Most of the letter was dedicated to a statement of principles, with very little specific reference to recent events.[84]

For several months in mid-1977 the earlier crisis atmosphere seemed to have abated. ANEP had been able to dictate the key cabinet posts in the new government, but it became clear that the oligarchy's main objective was preventing further initiatives like the previous year's Agrarian Transformation rather than making any positive proposals. Only after many months did the new government come up with its five-year plan, titled "Welfare for All," which, far from being a comprehensive plan, was simply a list of conventional construction and development projects.

President Romero lifted the postelectoral state of siege in October, and Washington named as ambassador Frank Devine, a career officer, for whom El Salvador was his first ambassadorship. Although there was extensive material on record about El Salvador (as this chapter should amply attest), Devine arrived insisting that he was going to spend a great deal of time listening and observing before making up his mind on human rights. When the Carter government gave its approval on the $90 million dam project, Washington-watchers in El Salvador must have concluded that the "human rights problem" was solved.

In the meantime the popular organizations had begun to do serious organization among labor unions. FAPU, in particular, after the cathedral occupation in 1975, had concentrated more on working with existing labor unions. The BPR took a somewhat different approach, working to set up new parallel organizations where existing unions were considered insufficiently militant. At the same time it continued to organize among the peasants.

In early November the BPR occupied the Ministry of Labor to put pressure on it on behalf of workers from two striking unions. Some of the occupants were peasants: the BPR was putting into practice its concept of a "worker-peasant alliance." While the ministry occupation was in effect, an industrialist, Raúl Molina Cañas, was killed under mysterious circumstances. It is unlikely he would have been killed by the left, since such an action might put in danger those occupying the ministry, and the circumstances indicated either a robbery or personal revenge (this latter version prevailed in the capital's rumor mills). However, Molina's death offered a suitable pretext for another barrage of propaganda against the popular organizations and subversives in general, and once more the papers were filled with paid advertisements.

The campaign found its fulfillment with the promulgation of a "Law for the Defense and Guarantee of Public Order" on November 24, 1977. In extremely vague and arbitrary language it listed eighteen categories of activities that could be considered crimes and for which detention without charges was allowed by the law. One article made it a crime even to furnish what might be considered "false or tendentious news or information destined to disturb the constitutional legal order, the tranquility and security of the country," and so forth, a provision seemingly aimed at those supplying the outside world with information about repression. Legal critics said the law added nothing useful to the Constitution and existing Penal Code. What it did set up, however, was a quasi-legal framework for repression. Ambassador Devine seemed little disturbed by its implications: "We believe that any government has the full right and obligation to use all legal means at its disposal to combat terrorism," he told the American Chamber of Commerce in El Salvador the day after the law was approved.[85]

How much the power structure feared outside scrutiny may be gleaned from headlines on one of the dailies on the occasion of the visit of a human rights delegation made up of Father Robert Drinan, John McAward of the Unitarian Universalist Service Committee, and Thomas Anderson, a historian: "Foreign Priests in El Salvador with Contacts to the International Terrorist Mafia"; "Members of the Society of Jesus, Orchestrators of the Campaign to Shame Our Country"; "The Priest Drinan Brings Instructions from the Marxists to Archbishop Romero."[86]

For months the repression remained at routine levels but flared up again during Holy Week (1978) in San Pedro Perulapán, a rural area not far from San Salvador. During February the BPR had proposed legislation to lower land-rent fees and prices for fertilizer and other agricultural inputs. The minister of agriculture had refused to see them, but the president of the Agriculture Development Bank had told them to return on March 17. When a hundred peasants arrived they found the bank closed; they started a march through the city until they were attacked by police, leaving four dead and thirty wounded.

Prior to these events, in San Pedro Perulapán itself some fourteen people had disappeared after being picked up by security forces. There was an atmosphere of tension between FECCAS-UTC and ORDEN. On Palm Sunday ORDEN members attacked one family and two days later attacked a group meeting for worship, hauling off Tránsito Vásquez, whose tortured and beheaded body was later found, with his head impaled on a tree above it. At one point FECCAS militants captured five members of ORDEN, took them to Vásquez's body, and forced them to "ask forgiveness" and dig a grave.

Then ORDEN and the National Guard working together began to attack FECCAS members. (ORDEN families had been brought to the town hall for protection and to further the idea that FECCAS was the aggressor and ORDEN the victim.) FECCAS seems to have taken an essentially defensive posture. In its report the Commission of Solidarity of the archdiocese said six were known to have been killed (all FECCAS), fourteen were wounded, and sixty-eight had disappeared. The conclusion stated that ORDEN had provoked the violence, admitting that FECCAS had allowed itself to be provoked. The commission said the government was using the event to discredit FECCAS, making false accusations, and rounding up ORDEN members in order to make them appear to be the victims in need of protection so as to justify to public opinion "a repressive military operation in which they have intimidated, tortured, and killed an undetermined number of people."

The picture painted in San Salvador dailies was entirely at variance with the archdiocese's report. FECCAS was entirely to blame and the security forces were seen as simply restoring order at the request of the citizenry. Once again there were references to "religious terrorism," the "leaders of these religious groups of peasants and the BPR who do not hesitate to send peasants to the slaughter," and a "mob inflamed by the catechists of the left."

In protest the BPR peacefully occupied the cathedral, and the embassies of Costa Rica, Panama, Venezuela, and Switzerland.

The Secretariat of Social Communications of the archdiocese prepared a minute and lengthy description of the events in San Pedro Perulapán with an analysis of how the media had reported them. For some months the archdiocese had been preparing to do a systematic analysis of human rights violations and this was the first major case. In effect, church people were beginning their apprenticeship in what was to become an increasingly important activity. Soon journalists and human rights groups were coming to the chancery office, located in the huge battleship-gray seminary complex built under Archbishop Chávez, in order to receive data and interpretation of events.

Motivated, it seems, by the incidents in San Pedro Perulapán, a group of lawyers and other professional people gathered to form the Salvadoran Human Rights Commission. From the outset some of its members seem to have had sympathies with the popular organizations, while others were Christian Democrats, and some were simply concerned about the increasing violence and the fact that existing channels, such as the press, were not making known human rights violations. The commission worked independently of the archdiocese but maintained contacts.[87]

On March 31, an archdiocesan bulletin suggested to the government that there be a general amnesty and an *ECA* editorial fleshed out the idea, saying that such a move could constitute the new beginning President Romero had promised in his inaugural address almost a year previously: by showing respect for human rights, the government could establish a new relationship with the church, mend its international image and, more important, begin the reconciliation with its own people that would be a precondition to addressing the nation's problems.[88]

This suggestion occasioned yet another public conflict when Archbishop Romero in a sermon at the end of April supported the call for amnesty, mentioning in passing "judges who sell out . . ." as he stated that a good part of the country's problems derived from injustices in the legal system. A few days later the Supreme Court wrote him a short note asking for the names of the "venal judges," perhaps attempting to put Romero into some kind of legal trap.

In his reply, given in a Sunday sermon on May 14, Archbishop Romero adroitly sidestepped the trap, himself using the overblown language characteristic of legal documents, noting that the court's note could hardly be considered a formal accusation, and pointing out that he had not used the term "venal." Insisting on his own "theological" perspective, he said that the mothers and families of the disappeared had indeed made accusations of venality, and showed how the rights of Salvadorans, guaranteed by the Constitution, the Universal Declaration of Human Rights, and other documents, were being denied in practice; for example, rejection of habeas corpus, and eighty cases of people disappeared after arrest. There had been no hearing given to a request of amnesty for the people arrested after the events of San Pedro Perulapán, nor to a group of lawyers charging that the Law for the Defense and Guarantee of Public Order was unconstitutional. Workers' rights to organize and strike were ignored. He ended by asking where the Judicial Power had been while rights were being trampled.[89]

While such a reply might seem semijuridical fencing, irrelevant to the overall course of events, it may also be seen as Romero's way of taking advantage of a malicious attempt to entangle him, in order to raise the larger issue of the use of state power to nullify people's basic rights.

As was becoming his custom, the archbishop published a major pastoral letter on August 6, the Feast of the Transfiguration, this time on "The Church and the Popular Organizations." Its content, which was innovative not only for El Salvador but for Latin America, will be dealt with in greater detail in chapter 10. Here we shall consider its pastoral significance at the time of publication.

First it would be well to situate the pastoral problem itself. As should have become clear in the course of this narrative, the process which led to the formation of the popular organizations was intimately involved with church pastoral work: remotely, from the Christian Democratic party and church involvement with rural cooperatives as far back as the 1950s, and more recently with the basic Christian communities, beginning around 1969 in Suchitoto and taking root in a number of parishes in San Salvador, Cuscatlán, Chalatenango, San Vicente, and so forth. Crucial events in 1974–75 (land invasion and massacre at La Cayetana, organizing in Aguilares, cathedral occupation) gave origin to the BPR. The government/oligarchy attacks on the church in 1976–77 were evidence of how the links were perceived.

In the peasants' minds the connections were undoubtedly close. For them evangelization had led to a sense of their dignity and then to a need to organize. It will be recalled that Felipe de Jesús Chacón, father of BPR leader Juan Chacón, was a Delegate of the Word, and that Tránsito Vásquez, the FECCAS leader whose head was cut off and impaled on a tree in San Pedro Perulpán, had been dragged out of a Sunday worship meeting. If at the village or *cantón* level the same people made up the basic Christian community and the peasant organization—and they met under the same thatched or adobe roof—it would be understandable that they might see little or no difference between the two.

Thus, to put it most sharply: what some people saw as Marxist or "terrorist" organizations, others saw as practically synonymous with the church.

Pastorally, there were more generic questions such as the relationship of faith and politics and more specific ones such as the possible role of pastoral agents, especially priests, vis-à-vis these organizations as well as the issue of violence.

In preparing the pastoral letter Romero made a wide consultation, seeking to find out what happened in practice. Along with the letter were published three accompanying documents, one a statistical analysis of El Salvador and its problems, and the others collections of relevant biblical texts and quotations from official church documents.

Romero made no effort to situate himself in some "neutral" position from which, for example, joining ORDEN or FECCAS would be options equally acceptable to Christians. In order to appreciate the letter it is worth pointing out that in El Salvador unionization of agricultural workers is illegal. While affirming in general the legitimacy of popular organizations and even viewing a relationship between evangelization and the organizations as "possible and natural," Romero emphasized that faith and politics, while united, were not to be identified. Specifically, there were two errors that should be avoided: (a) replacing what is of faith with the content of an organization; (b) holding that people can express Christian faith only by joining a particular organization. While sympathizing with people's situations, the archbishop emphasized that a Christian's ultimate loyalty could never be to an organization. That he should have to make such pointed statements implicitly confirms how symbiotic the relationship was in practice.

On the case of priests, Archbishop Romero found it normal that they should have sympathies with particular organizations and be asked to collaborate with them, and he conceded that in exceptional cases, in consultation with the bishop, a priest might engage in collaboration. This hesitating, tentative admission of an "exception" would, one year later, in the next (and last) pastoral letter become a recognized pastoral option. He reminded lay leaders of Christian communities that if their militancy in an organization undermined their effectiveness—their unifying role, for instance—they should choose between their leaderships, after "serious discernment before the Lord."[90]

Romero recognized the action of the Spirit in the popular organizations and their efforts at liberation. This direct application of a common postconciliar theological notion (that the Spirit is at work in the "world") to the organizations contrasted sharply with the attitude of the other bishops, who toward the end of the month published their own "Declaration" on the organizations. While they recognized the people's "right of association," the other bishops emphasized that these organizations were seeking to take power, were inspired by Marxist-Leninist ideology, and had infiltrated the church. Insisting that they were not church organizations (referring to FECCAS, which still had the term "Christian" in its title), the bishops said that the organizations should not use the church and that priests and religious should not collaborate, directly or indirectly, with FECCAS, UTC, or any such organizations.[91]

Such direct confrontation on the same issue between Catholic bishops—in this case Romero and Rivera y Damas, who had signed the letter, on one side, and bishops Aparicio (San Vicente), Barrera y Reyes (Santa Ana), Álvarez (San Miguel and Military Vicar), and Revelo (auxiliary bishop in San Salvador), on the other—is virtually unheard of in the Catholic church and may be taken as a measure of how polarized the situation was.

Violence was taken up in the last part of Romero's letter. During this period violence had been increasing. Guerrilla groups had kidnapped a number of businessmen, both Salvadoran and foreign, and they now seemed to be offering armed protection to the popular organizations and sometimes "executing" notorious government collaborators and informers or taking retaliation for actions against the organizations. El Salvador's wealthy began to move to Guatemala or to Miami, Florida, commuting for business purposes and removing money from the country. Foreign investment slowed and companies began to look for ways to close and move elsewhere. Government violence was also on the rise.

In taking up the topic, Archbishop Romero made distinctions between various kinds of violence: institutionalized violence, repressive state violence, seditious or terrorist violence ("which some call revolutionary"), spontaneous violence, violence of legitimate defense, and the violence of nonviolence.[92] The immediate pastoral effect of making such a distinction, fairly common since Medellín, was to undercut the influence of the position that would theoretically oppose any use of violence but would find normal its use by existing powers. Again the following year's pastoral letter would bring a significant shift of emphasis.

When Father Ernesto ("Neto") Barrera was killed on November 28, 1978, Romero had to deal more directly with the issue of violence. The government called the incident a shootout. Meeting with priests about what to do, Romero heard some urge that the body simply be handed over to the family, while others pointed to Barrera's character and said whatever he had done was done out of "faith in the Lord and great love for the people." Romero simply asked, "Don't you think Neto's mother will be at his side, without asking about his practices or methods? So I, as his bishop, should be there too." He met with some labor leaders close to Barrera and said another priest would be appointed to take his place and insisted that he, as archbishop, wanted to meet with them for an afternoon in a retreat center at the Mass commemorating the one month anniversary of Barrera's death.

Although at first he saw the government's claim that Barerra died in a shootout as one more fabrication, Romero subsequently received a letter from the FPL, confirming that the priest had indeed died in combat as one of their militants. While he said nothing public at the time, the incident undoubtedly forced him to meditate on how sincere Christians could feel obliged to take up armed struggle.[93]

During 1978, according to church sources, 1,063 people had been arrested for political reasons, 147 were killed by security forces, and another 23 had disappeared.[94] *ECA* sought to summarize the situation at the year's end, pointing out that repression had been concentrated on the popular organizations and "had diminished or taken less virulent forms against politicians, intellectuals, and church people." Inflation of at least 15 percent had annulled any nominal rise in wages. Groups on the left, both popular and guerrilla, were divided among themselves. The church had become perhaps the most credible institution in the country. *ECA* editors wrote:

Archbishop Romero is not only the most important religious leader in the country, but also someone in whom those who most need social change believe. Nevertheless he is not a political leader seeking political power for himself or for the church, although by carrying out his intention of being on the side of the people he has ended up not on the side of the government. His nomination for the Nobel Peace Prize by 118 members of the British parliament for being against injustice and against violence has meant a great support for his position, which has been fiercely fought by those whose interests are threatened.

This editorial continued to urge a process of democratization, and explicitly warned that the popular organizations should not think of taking political power at short range (insisting, rather, that they should be legalized), and stating that their role could be "energizing" but not "hegemonic." In veiled terms it suggested that they cut their ties with guerrilla groups, and elsewhere expressed the opinion that neither the church nor its most notable members, such as priests or religious, should become exclusively tied to one political approach.[95]

This posture, of seeking some way of addressing El Salvador's deep-seated problems without adopting the approach of the guerrilla organizations, would continue to be characteristic of UCA and other forces in the church until after the first experience of the October 1979 military coup. For months and even years people and groups were seeking a "middle way"—which they would not have called "middle" but, rather, "rational." Part of the story is how they reluctantly concluded they had no choice but to ally themselves with the armed opposition.

A new embarrassment to Carlos Humberto Romero's regime was the leaking of an OAS (Organization of American States) Human Rights Commission report on El Salvador. The investigation had taken place a year earlier but the results had been held up (the OAS is slow to act in any way that will embarrass a member government). In this case the investigating delegation had received information from a former prisoner on the site of a clandestine torture cell actually in National Guard headquarters. Making an unannounced visit there they were able to verify the report even to the prisoners' names carved in the doorway. One of the cells measured just one meter in all directions. President Romero, in Mexico hoping to get oil on good terms, was forced to improvise answers as journalists grilled him on the leaked report. What gave the report weight was the fact that it emanated from the normally cautious OAS.[96]

Signs of intensifying conflict and crisis multiplied in January 1979. The National Guard attacked a retreat center in the parish of San Antonio Abad, on the outskirts of San Salvador, killing Father Octavio Ortiz and four adolescents, and jailing a nun, a teacher, and thirty-three young people. Although the National Guard called the meeting being held there subversive, all indications are that it was in fact a weekend religious retreat.

The tone of Romero's preaching the next day as he prepared to leave for the Puebla Conference in Mexico (Third General Conference of Latin American Bishops) was sharp. In part it was a recital of the life and ministry of Ortiz as well as a lengthy eyewitness account of the attack and commentary on the general fact of "persecution" of the church. President Romero, in Mexico, had just attacked the archbishop as "political" and motivated by a desire for the Nobel Prize. In response to the president's claim that there was no persecution of the church, the archbishop said the bodies in the cathedral were enough to show "how great a liar he is."[97]

Other incidents served to underscore the gravity of the moment. A coffee grower, Ernesto Liebes, had been kidnapped by a leftist group and was in bad health. Archbishop Romero remonstrated: "Keep it in mind, you who are violent with kidnappings. Kidnapping is not civilized, any more than making people disappear. . . . it is savagery, that's all."[98] Two Englishmen and a Japanese were also being held by guerrilla groups.

Seeking to dramatize the law of public order and to gain a general amnesty, FAPU had occupied the Red Cross building, the Mexican embassy, and the OAS offices in San Salvador. In response to an OAS request from Washington for the church to intervene, Archbishop Romero had sent a delegation of priests to the occupation sites, but when they arrived government forces took away their passports and documents. Romero summarized the overall situation: "The conflict is not between church and government, it is between government and people. The church is with the people and the people are with the church, thank God."[99]

A few days later a large number of priests and sisters marched in silence through the capital with crosses and signs reading simply "Enough." This type of protest—its silence more telling than the normal shouted and echoed slogans—was important in giving a sense of how many of the clergy and religious were supportive in general of Romero's witness, even though they were not all doing basic-Christian-community work with peasants. While exact figures are unavailable it seems that a majority of the priests of the country were present and a large proportion of sisters.[100]

Romero in the meantime had gone to Puebla for the January 1979 conference—he had not been chosen as a delegate by his fellow bishops but was nominated by the Vatican. In the archdiocese of San Salvador systematic efforts had been made to get grassroots input into the Puebla process. While at Puebla Romero was solicited for his views by journalists and was applauded enthusiastically by the many observers who had come to lobby the conference from "outside the walls"; also, he received a letter of support from over forty bishops, although the situation in El Salvador (as well as Nicaragua) was largely ignored in the official business at Puebla.

Also in January the United States ambassador, Frank Devine, after more than a year of virtual silence (presumably while he "made up his own mind" about what was happening) gave a programmatic speech at a joint session of the American and Salvadoran Chambers of Commerce. In very general terms he stated that reforms should be made in El Salvador, presumably to head off more radical solutions. It was, one observer noted, a "proconsul's speech."[101]

One brief, hopeful sign was the repeal of the Law for the Defense and Guarantee of Public Order, which in fact had served largely to discredit the Carlos Humberto Romero government internationally. Archbishop Oscar Romero publicly acknowledged and welcomed this move. However, as the year went on a sense of crisis deepened. The wealthy and foreigners continued to leave. For example, the Japanese colony (Japan had been leading in new industries) declined from 2,400 to 200 people. Some embassies closed and others reduced their staffs.

Events in May were one more evidence of crisis. When five BPR leaders were jailed, the organization occupied the cathedral, as well as the embassies of France and Costa Rica. On May 8 official forces opened fire on a demonstration as it arrived at the cathedral and at least twenty-five were killed and several hundred were wounded. It happened that international television film crews and magazine photographers were present and filmed the attack directly, which, while in itself little different from similar incidents reported in this chapter, suddenly served to make El Salvador a recognized "crisis" country for the international media. The occupations continued and extended to other churches around the country and to the Venezuelan embassy, where on May 22 there was a similar ambush with many more wounded.[102] In early June, after negotiation, the occupiers left by plane for Cuba.

In his Sunday sermons during these occupations, Archbishop Romero recognized the reasonableness of the BPR's demands, saying that the remaining three leaders (two had been let go) should either be released or formally accused (in fact, it is reasonable to assume they had already been killed).

In retaliation for those killed in the attacks the FPL killed Carlos Herrera Rebollo, the minister of education, and the government then declared a state of siege. One of the victims of the counterretaliation may have been Father Rafael Palacios, assassinated in June (by some accounts he was murdered in retaliation for the killing of a major). Palacios had been one of the priests associated with a national movement of Christian communities. When he found a white hand with the initials UGB painted on his car, he had ignored the warning.[103] Alirio Macías, a priest of the diocese of San Vicente, was killed in early August; Archbishop Romero attended the funeral and mentioned Macías in his sermons.

Repression was reaching higher and higher levels. During June around 30 teachers were killed, and during July, 123 people were killed, 47 were arrested, and 18 disappeared (presumably some were killed by the left).[104]

Undoubtedly the specter of Nicaragua hung over El Salvador. Until Somoza's downfall the Romero government had consulted with him, given diplomatic support, and sent at least some soldiers unofficially to fight the

Sandinistas. The spectacle of Somoza's officers hijacking planes to escape made its impression, especially since some stopped in El Salvador. For their part many ordinary Salvadorans sympathized with the Sandinistas. The FPL and the ERP publicly claimed to have had members fighting with the FSLN, some of whom fell in combat.[105]

In a belated gesture of "dialogue," the Romero government announced a National Forum to deal with the country's problems. However, the government ended up talking to itself, since in the first months no political parties except the PCN showed up, nor did union groups, the universities, or other social forces. Somewhat later, opposition parties and labor unions not tied to the armed opposition created what they called a "Popular Forum."

The U.S. State Department also began to take a serious interest in Central America. There were visits from diplomats such as Undersecretary of State for Latin America Viron Vaky, and special ambassador William Bowdler, as well as programmatic speeches in the United States Congress, all with the clear message that El Salvador, Guatemala, and Honduras were unavoidably caught in a movement for change and would have to make internal reforms. In their initial reactions Salvadoran elites did not appreciate the message.

The foregoing may indicate the aptness of the title chosen by Archbishop Romero for his fourth (and last) pastoral letter: "The Church in the Midst of the Country's Crisis." Part of the preparation was a questionnaire sent to priests and basic Christian communities. In its general approach the letter was an application of the Puebla documents to El Salvador. On many points Romero was explicit: "Growers of coffee, sugar, cotton, and others in the agroexport sector find it necessary that the peasants be unemployed and unorganized so they can use this abundant and cheap labor supply to produce, harvest, and export their crops." A good part of the letter applied Puebla to the church (for example, unity vs. division in the church). Romero did not refrain from criticizing the popular organizations (warning them against "absolutizing" themselves).

Archbishop Romero's treatment of violence will be taken up in detail in chapter 9. Here it should be noted that his view was more nuanced than that of the previous year and he even recognized that insurrection might be legitimate. What he seemed to be saying was that if the people, after presenting their just demands for a long time nonviolently, were met continually with violence, their efforts to resist and struggle, using violence, could be seen as legitimate self-defense even when it came to insurrection (one assumes that the Nicaraguan case was fresh in his mind).[106]

Romero's remarks on Marxism, taken in the context of El Salvador, were, at a minimum, a refusal to issue condemnations. He distinguished between various meanings of the term (atheistic and materialistic ideology, method of analysis, and political strategy) and urged that there be more study to help guide people "on this topic, which today absorbs many people's minds and disturbs many Christians. . . . The best way to win the field from Marxism is to take seriously the preferential option for the poor." In taking up the topic of "national dialogue," Romero emphasized that all social forces should be involved—or at least all those that had not gone underground. He insisted that the main topic of such a dialogue should be structural change to get at the roots of the problems.[107]

Possibly the greatest innovation in this letter was his recognition of what he called *pastoral de acompañamiento*, "pastoral practice of accompanying" (people). It was a carefully worded recognition of the legitimacy of doing pastoral work with the popular organizations—and in some cases, one assumes (although it is not stated), from within them as members, after "prayer and discernment."[108] This topic will be developed more in chapter 10.

As 1979 went on the government's hold on El Salvador weakened. There were major strikes and occupations of factories. At one point workers cut off electricity for twenty-three hours. After Somoza's fall the popular organizations at demonstrations chanted, "Romero y Somoza, son la misma cosa" (Romero and Somoza are the same thing). Despite the increasing level of repression—by mid-October 460 people had been arrested for political reasons, and 580 had been killed—there was a feeling in the air that an insurrection in El Salvador was no longer unthinkable and, indeed, had to come.[109]

COUP, JUNTA, AND CIVIL WAR (OCTOBER 1979 TO 1982)

It must be obvious to readers by now that the history of events leading up to the October 1979 coup is indeed relevant to subsequent events—despite the fact that the authors of the State Department's February 1981 White Paper mentioned only one date prior to 1979, although the statement was long enough to fill a page of the *New York Times*.[110] These events are certainly not obscure to Salvadorans, and especially to church people. In the following period the story became concentrated to an extraordinary degree around the figure of Archbishop Romero, and at his death the church for a time almost ceased to be a public protagonist in the struggle, precisely when there was a seemingly inexorable drift toward civil war and then, thanks to increasing United States intervention, toward a regionalization of the conflict.

The October Coup: Hopes Raised and Dashed

On the morning of October 15, 1979, some 400 officers of the Salvadoran army carried out a coordinated action, arresting all commanders and carrying out a coup without firing a single shot. In their initial proclamation the armed forces accused the government of President Romero of violation of human rights, corruption, and mismanagement, and promised a wide range of reforms, including the disbanding of ORDEN and amnesty for political prisoners. The statement went out of its way to mention a desire for close relations with Nicaragua (this was less than three months after the Sandinista victory), in what could be interpreted as a signal of "revolutionary" intentions.[111]

In its first moves the armed forces purged their own ranks, retiring or sending into exile about fifty officers who were most identified with Romero, and assembled a group of prestigious and competent civilians as cabinet ministers and heads of important government agencies. Two of the three civilian members of the Junta were from the UCA: Román Mayorga, the rector, and Guillermo Ungo, a law professor, who represented the Popular Forum. The third, Mario Andino, was a businessman not representing any political group. Although the civilians represented a relatively wide spectrum ideologically—from communists to moderate businesspeople—they were united in a concern that the coup represented perhaps the last opportunity for a peaceful solution to El Salvador's problems.

That the civilians sincerely desired basic changes there was no doubt. What was in doubt was the sincerity of the military, and its political will to stop human-rights violations and make basic reforms. According to some observers the reform-minded officers began to be outmaneuvered by hardliners even on the day of the coup. Others see a complex unfolding of events, in which in fact there were initially three groups involved in the coup: reform-minded young officers headed by Colonel Adolfo Majano; hardliners, linked to the landholding oligarchy; and a group more directly linked to Pentagon contacts. According to this "three-coup hypothesis" the hardliners and those with United States links allowed some people to proclaim reforms, while they quietly consolidated their control over posts with troop commands.[112] Nevertheless, while the eventual outcome seemed clear within a few days, the process of marginalization of the "reformers" stretched out for many months. Whatever the process within the military ranks, hopes for a peaceful solution were soon dashed by events, as the level of repression increased under the "revolutionary" government.

Was the coup "made in Washington"? This has frequently been assumed, and one source says the United States embassy was informed the night before. According to other sources, however, it was the United States preference that President Romero resign early and call elections, which the Christian Democrats might be permitted to win and then usher in the kind of reforms judged needed.[113] Nothing would prohibit there being a "two-track" policy, that is, the State Department encouraging Romero to resign and Pentagon/CIA personnel engaged in contacts with potential coup-makers.

Initial reactions from the United States embassy in San Salvador and from the State Department were of hope bordering on enthusiasm. United States officials began to resurrect hopes for changes in El Salvador, including the "Taiwan model" of development.[114]

While the left had for some time been speculating on a possible military coup (these groups, especially FARN-FAPU, had their sources inside the military), they were nevertheless caught off guard to some extent. ERP/LP-28 (Peoples' Revolutionary Army/February 28 Popular Leagues) called the people to insurrection, possibly hoping for something like the spontaneity of Nicaragua or simply expecting the military's reaction to reveal that nothing had changed. When they occupied the suburbs of Mejicanos and Cuscatancingo the area was surrounded with tanks and troops and strafed with helicopters, leaving at least twenty-three dead. ERP/LP-28 subsequently changed its position sharply, and then changed again, the zigs and zags making other sectors of the left brand them as immature.

While to some extent the popular organizations put pressure on the new government, in fact the armed forces used repression where there was no provocation. On October 16, the day after the coup, combined security forces and army troops attacked five factories that had been occupied by the BPR, killing eighteen and arresting seventy-eight, some of whom were tortured. On October 22, a FAPU demonstration—itself a funeral for two militants surrounded and killed while distributing literature—was attacked from behind by uniformed troops and at least three were killed. In all, more than 100 people were killed by official forces during the first week, and on October 29, an LP-28 demonstration was attacked and some eighty people were killed.[115]

Those who believed the new government might succeed insisted that the repressive actions were the work of military units not sufficiently under central control. Armed leftist groups engaged in some actions such as an ambush of a Guard patrol near Zacotecoluca in which six were killed, the "execution" of a Lieutenant Castillo, considered to be one of the main torturers, and the setting off of a number of bombs.[116]

In the church initial reactions to the coup were mixed. One group associated with UCA was clearly involved with the civilians in the government—roughly a half-dozen UCA professors were in the government. UCA people had supported the 1976 Agrarian Transformation and since then had continued to insist that the country's problems could be solved through "rational" approaches; they had maintained a clear distance from the popular organizations. Another sector, particularly pastors working with basic Christian communities in the countryside and closely identified with the popular organizations, reflected these latter in their thinking and from the outset saw the coup as a product of "Yankee imperialism."

Archbishop Romero in consultation with his close collaborators took a nuanced position, which some read as an endorsement of the Junta. Preaching during the Junta's first week and recognizing that the armed forces' proclamation reflected the people's aspirations, Romero said that not promises but actions were needed. He mentioned the brutality of the security forces. One point he mentioned with special insistence was the fate of 176 people who had "disappeared" after being arrested during previous governments. The people should be freed or, if they were dead, those responsible should be brought to justice according to existing laws. (This point seemed to be a litmus test: if the new government could not do anything about the "disappeared" it evidently had insufficient control over the forces of repression. On October 22 at a meeting of the Family Members of the Disappeared sponsored by the Archdiocesan Legal Aid Office, Romero repeated this challenge.)

Archbishop Romero issued a further challenge to the media, especially the newspapers, for their complicity with violence under the previous government, and for attacks on the church and in particular the archdiocese; he singled out newspapers for printing attacks on the church and the archdiocese, especially those from fictitious groups. He also criticized ERP and LP-28 for their "irresponsible and hasty" call to insurrection, "giving arms to people. . . . thus bringing about death for at least thirty-one people and wounding 80 more."[117]

Two weeks later Romero seemed to be insisting that the Junta should be given a chance, although he explicitly stated "this is not a blessing to any coup d'état." He urged that there be an investigation into the killing of over eighty people in demonstrations on October 29 and 31, saying that most "impartial" witnesses put the blame on the security forces.[118] He criticized the people's organizations, saying that some fell into the temptation to politicize the church and that the sectarianism of the organizations was impeding dialogue even among themselves.[119]

Archbishop Romero noted that some were saying that the church no longer had anything to say, and that it had "betrayed" the people—presumably he had in mind the more radical sectors of the popular movements who did not wish to give the junta formula a chance. His reply was that this was a calumny and he insisted that it was up to the people to decide what kind of society they wanted: "democratic, socialist, communist. It's up to you, the people. So what I'm doing is issuing a challenge to the political creativity of the people." However, he was evidently distinguishing the popular organizations from the guerrilla groups:

> What I am doing here is a challenge to the political creativity of the people. I am telling the organizations they should know how to speak in political terms, they should know how to exert pressure rationally and intelligently. A language of violence provokes repression . . . this is not the time for guerrillas. Today guerrilla struggle and everything that sows violence and clandestine activity is out of place, since you are being called to open dialogue. The church has had a supplementary role, it has been the voice of the voiceless. But when you can speak, it is you who have to speak. The church remains silent. . . .[120]

Romero's stance accepting the government's reform intentions at face value seemed too weak to some who saw him as influenced by his friendship with many of the civilians in the government and UCA priests and professors.[121]

During November the popular organizations deliberately sought to reduce the pressure of their activities and allow the Junta formula to reveal its contradictions. The government seemed to take some positive steps. Agricultural wages were raised to $4.50 a day. ORDEN was abolished—but the decree had no effect. A commission was appointed to look into the fate of the "disappeared" but it predictably came up with nothing. Major Roberto D'Aubuisson, who had resigned from the army at the time of the coup, announced the formation of a new right-wing organization, the Broad National Front.[122]

Not only were the civilians unable to take effective steps toward a reform policy, they were not even consulted on what the military regarded as the most important items. Hence in December when the United States sent a Defense Survey Team to study the needs of the armed forces, neither Ungo nor Mayorga was consulted. Throughout the period of the first and second Juntas, Colonel Eldon Cummings, the United States military attaché, was in daily contact with the Salvadoran high command. It seems reasonable to suppose that while attention was focused on the "reform" government there was a parallel process of working with the Salvadoran military in preparation for the insurrection that seemed predictable. Modest ("nonlethal") military aid and training was restored at this time. Archbishop Romero said such aid should be conditioned on a reform of the security forces and a solution to the problem of the disappeared with sanctions for those responsible. Otherwise, such aid would "only be reinforcing the oppressors of the people" and allowing them to "repress the people more confidently."[123]

In addition to the fate of the disappeared, and the continuing repression, the third most pressing question was what the new government and especially the military could do vis-à-vis the popular organizations. They were without doubt the most powerful political force in the country and any genuine political solution would involve coming to terms with them. What is obvious is that such did not happen. It is doubtful that there was any sincere desire to do so on the part of the military, and while it must be admitted there is little information available, it seems that the BPR, always mistrustful of the military, was not receptive to offers of alliance.

For its part it seems that the United States, after some initial enthusiasm, was less encouraged by the civilian makeup of the government. State Department spokespersons would subsequently describe the first Junta as so ideologically mixed that it could not operate, in contrast to the coherence of Christian Democratic juntas. Armstrong and Shenk claim to see signs that the United States supported the hardliners in their maneuvering during the early weeks and in fact see a three-sided bargaining process beginning in November 1979 involving the United States, the Salvadoran military, and the Christian Democratic party, José Napoleón Duarte now having returned from his seven-year exile.[124]

It is open to question to what extent United States embassy personnel were actively shaping events and to what extent they were clumsily following events they only partly understood. What was undeniable was that by December official violence was on the rise again. According to figures given the Archdiocesan Legal Aid Office, after 159 were killed by security forces during the latter half of October, the figure dropped to 10 during November but shot up to 281 during December. In one incident on December 18, hundreds of troops attacked two haciendas and a slaughterhouse where workers were on strike, killing at least 35 people.[125]

On December 28 virtually all the cabinet-level civilians presented an ultimatum to the military. Pointing out that there had been a "rightward shift" since the original coup and that in fact the defense minister, Guillermo García, and some regional commanders were running the country, they proposed that COPEFA (Permanent Council of the Armed Forces), an organization recently formed by reform-minded officers, show that it was clearly in charge.[126] Choose between them and García, they said to the armed forces. Their statement was ignored, and they resigned en masse on January 3, 1980.

Five of these officials carried the analysis further in another document, saying that the democratic sectors of the country had been "used" and that they as government officials had suffered "humiliation" from officers who told them in effect that they had been put in their posts by the military but were not really needed "to do what had to be done in the country." Although they now saw that "this whole political project was a maneuver against the people from the start" they did not regret having tried to make it work: "But we would have to regret it our whole lives if we continued to collaborate now that everything is clear. Perhaps some of us—military and civilians—were naïve at the start but we are not going to be dishonest at the end." For them the most positive result was the strengthening of the popular movement. "Now the people will undoubtedly know what they have to do."[127] Salvador Samayoa, the minister of education, made a public appearance to announce his resignation and, before television cameras, took up a gun and announced he was joining the FPL guerrillas.

While the new government was still being formed, Archbishop Romero discussed these resignations at some length in a Sunday sermon. First he recalled how he had been asked to intervene and had met with those resigning on January 2, urging them not to act emotionally or to follow the crowd, but to obey their consciences. He pointed out that some had resigned out of protest and some (Christian Democrats) in order to permit the formation of a new government. All of them he praised for their honesty and witness (distinguishing himself from those, like the BPR, who were now praising those whom they had previously denounced as "traitors").

Twice he adverted to the fact that the only minister who had not resigned was Defense Minister García, who he said should resign, because he gave a "bad image" outside and could be a "real block for the government." His advice to the government was to make a choice: to build unity either around the armed forces or around the common good of the people.[128]

A New Junta and the Murder of an Archbishop

A new Junta, with Christian Democrats Héctor Dada and José Morales Ehrlich and independent Ramón Avalos Navarrete joining Colonels Majano and Gutiérrez, was formed. Ostensibly the armed forces had committed itself to a "popular and anti-oligarchic *proyecto.*" Archbishop Romero expressed skepticism, asking why it was willing to accept now what it had not accepted with the previous civilian government. He repeated his insistence on stopping repression and clarifying what had happened with the disappeared.[129]

Of more permanent significance was the movement of unification that was taking place on the left. On January 8 the FPL, the FARN, and the Communist party held a secret press conference to announce their unification into a Coordinadora Politico-Militar (Coordinating Politico-Military Body). The ERP was still not involved. Three days later the popular organizations, in what was clearly a parallel development, announced the formation of the Revolutionary Coordinating Body of Mass Organizations (CRM). The ceremony took place before hundreds of cheering supporters in the law school auditorium of the National University as representatives of FAPU, the BPR, LP-28, and the UDN raised clenched left fists when their names and organizations were announced, and later joined their hands and raised them together.

Some 300 churches were occupied on January 20 and twenty-six radio stations were briefly taken over on January 21 for the transmission of a message. On January 22, the anniversary date of the 1932 uprising, the CRM staged a huge march to celebrate and to demonstrate its unification.

Lining up at a main intersection, columns stretched in all directions, filling a total of approximately forty blocks. In order to participate people had faced intimidation and threats (for example Major D'Aubuisson publicly encouraged "patriots" to impede the demonstration). The popular organizations' offices had been shot at and bombs had been set off in them. Anticipating a transit stoppage and roadblocks on highways to the capital— which in fact occurred on the day of the march—most of the rural demonstrators came in during previous days, some sleeping in churches. As the crowd waited to begin the march, a helicopter and a plane flew overhead, and there was a smell of insecticide, which some later said had been sprayed on the demonstrators.

Shortly after 11 A.M. the march began, with 25,000 people under the

UDN banner followed by 40,000 FAPU people and 15,000 from the LP-28 (plus 22 commandeered buses). Two smaller groups followed and the BPR with 55,000 was waiting, its lines stretching sixteen blocks to the statue of Christ the Savior ("El Salvador") of the World. Before the BPR had begun to move, the first marchers had reached downtown, where they were ambushed by snipers, both plainclothes and security forces, from the tops of about a dozen government and commercial buildings. Some in the demonstration shot back but there was little to shoot at. Partly in protest and to help the evacuation, they set some cars on fire. The BPR and smaller organizations began a retreat toward the university.

In all some 21 people were killed and around 120 wounded. People who had taken refuge in El Rosario Church downtown and in the university were shot at by security forces and it was only through the efforts of the chancery office, the Red Cross, the Human Rights Commission, and journalists that they were allowed to leave. Those in the university were surrounded until the next day. In its various communiqués the Junta insisted that the armed forces had been kept in their barracks and, although it first said that demonstrators had begun shooting, it later said the demonstration had been orderly until "unknown persons" had opened fire.

This demonstration, probably the largest and arguably the most important in the history of El Salvador, prompted very divergent estimates of its strength (as tends to be the case with demonstrations everywhere but especially in Latin America). The organizations subsequently claimed 350,000 people had demonstrated (this estimate was later supported by an American photojournalist who was present). Privately the United States embassy personnel put the number at 50,000 to 100,000. Francisco Andrés Escobar, in a carefully prepared account,[130] calculated 140,000 marchers. Adding those lining the streets cheering the demonstration, 200,000 seems to this writer to be a reasonably accurate estimate of those who took a stand with the popular organizations, against obstacles and at considerable risk. (Curiously, later when it wished to demonstrate that the popular organizations were losing their support, the United States State Department used the figure of 200,000 for the January demonstration.)[131]

If this figure of 200,000 is correct, 4 percent of the population of the country participated in that demonstration, which would seem to indicate that the popular organizations were indeed the most important political force in El Salvador.

During this period Archbishop Romero's commentaries began to take on a new sharpness. For example, when asked about the decision of the former education minister, Salvador Samayoa, to join the FPL, Romero said that Samayoa's conscience should be respected and that the decision served to show "that those who are really responsible for the violence in our country are the families of the oligarchy, and that those who close off peaceful solutions to problems are idolizers of wealth."[132]

Two days before the unity demonstration Romero made a lengthy commentary on what he called the three *proyectos,* or three alternatives, facing the country, one proposed by the oligarchy, one by the armed forces/Christian Democrats, and one by the popular and politico-military organizations. Prefacing his remarks by saying that it is not the church's place to "identify itself with any particular project, nor to be a political leader," he went on to offer a pastoral vision. First, he rejected the oligarchical *proyecto,* which meant in effect maintaining present structures and privileges. Turning to the Christian Democratic/military *proyecto*, he criticized once more the violence and repression. When he read a letter from a group of soldiers who asked, among other things, that they "not be sent out to repress the people," he was interrupted by applause. Arriving at the "popular *proyecto"* he saw the efforts at coordination as hopeful, especially since the organizations were extending their invitation to democratic sectors (political parties, professional associations, and so forth) to join them. At the same time he expressed his concern at some actions such as kidnappings and at the manner in which some churches had been occupied. Although he did not "identify" the church with any *proyecto,* his sympathy with the popular *proyecto* was obvious; he closed the same sermon urging the "non-organized sector . . . to act according to the recommendations of Medellín and act in favor of justice . . . and not remain passive for fear of the sacrifices and personal risks that every bold and really efficacious action implies."[133]

On February 12 a group of students who were marching in the street to celebrate a successful negotiation with the education minister (after occupying the ministry's building) were attacked by official forces and six were killed and many wounded. Shortly afterward official forces attacked the Christian Democratic headquarters, which was being occupied by the LP-28. When two prominent women Christian Democrats protested and said that negotiations were underway, they were insulted. (One, who said she was a cabinet minister's wife, was told it didn't matter: she could be the wife of three ministers.) At least four were killed, many were wounded, and a large number were arrested. This killing, commented the archbishop, showed that neither the Junta nor the Christian Democrats were ruling the country but "the most repressive sector of the armed forces and the security forces." If the Christian Democrats did not want to be accomplices they should punish those responsible. Otherwise they would simply be lending their presence to create a favorable international image. They should examine not only their intentions but the effects of their presence.[134]

Romero also sent a public letter to President Carter, urging him out of his religious feelings and respect for human rights not to send military aid, which would simply increase the repression. Even the gas masks and protective vests had served only to allow the security forces to repress the people with greater violence. Insisting that it was the people who were more and more aware and organized, he said it would be unjust if the people's will was frustrated by foreign intervention, quoting Puebla in favor of the "free self-determination of peoples."[135]

Major Roberto D'Aubuisson, who was becoming increasingly visible as the charismatic figure of the "far right" (obviously enjoying very good ties inside the military), appeared on television denouncing a series of people as "communists." One of them, Mario Zamora, attorney general in the Christian Democratic government, was shot down in his house on February 23. The Christian Democrats accused D'Aubuisson and threatened to resign if the killers were not brought to justice, but in fact nothing happened.[136]

As a party the Christian Democrats remained in the government, but during the next two months the majority of the leaders most respected for their intelligence and honesty left the party; the ones who remained were considered "politicians" in the pejorative sense. Observers in a position to know claim that the grassroots strength of the party had long since evaporated, many of the members going into the popular organizations. What was left was largely a hollow shell. On March 3 Héctor Dada resigned from the Junta and soon left the country. He was replaced by José Napoleón Duarte.

In this context as the "center" seemed to be dissolving, and the government had produced no tangible basis for its claim to be "revolutionary," it suddenly announced a "land reform" and reforms in banking and export marketing. All indications are that the major impulse came from the United States, which sorely felt the need for reforms (some United States officials, knowing little of the real context, may have genuinely felt that such reforms could address El Salvador's problems). How the land reform functioned will be discussed below. Its most immediate effect was a widespread military action in the countryside. A state of siege was declared as troops moved out to take over the 250 largest estates in the country. Simultaneously, however, they moved against peasant organizations, often in areas such as Chalatenango where there were few large holdings to expropriate. Significantly it was the land reform that precipitated the exodus of the first peasant families who became refugees. Within days there were 2,000 in the capital, most of them seeking shelter and protection from the church.[137]

On March 23 Archbishop Romero again gave the customary hour-and-a-half sermon, beginning with a leisurely meditation on the biblical texts of the day, which was structured around the dimensions of liberation (personal community, transcendent). He then commented on events in the church, including the security forces' search of a parish in the capital, and on national events. Once more he praised the Revolutionary Coordinating Body, admitting that it had faults and needed to mature but clearly distinguishing himself from those who called the popular organizations subversive. "They are persecuted, massacred . . . and this will lead to their radicalization." He saw the country in a "prerevolutionary" state. "The basic question is how to take the least violent way out in this critical stage." He described many acts of violence, including a police attack in the UCA in which a student had been killed. Finally he addressed the ordinary soldiers and police (his voice was being transmitted throughout the country in what was easily the most listened-to radio program of the week):

> Brothers, you belong to our people. You are killing your own brothers and sisters in the peasants. God's law, which says, "Thou shalt not kill," should prevail over any order given by a man [applause]. No soldier is obliged to obey an order against God's law [applause]. No one has to carry out an immoral law [applause]. It is time to recover your conscience and obey it rather than orders given in sin [applause].
>
> The church, defender of God's rights, God's law, of human dignity, of the human person, cannot be silent in the face of such abomination.
>
> We want the government to recognize seriously that reforms stained with so much blood are worth nothing [applause].
>
> In the name of God, and in the name of this long-suffering people whose cries rise ever more thunderously to heaven, I beg you, I implore you, I order you, in the name of God: stop the repression [prolonged applause].[138]

In effect, Romero had encouraged the troops to refuse to obey orders if those orders were to shoot (unarmed) peasants. And since that was the normal case in the kind of repression taking place—the number killed by official forces in March was in fact 488—it was tantamount to challenging what is most sacred to the military, the discipline and the chain of command.

This was not an improvisation of the moment. The whole sermon had been prepared the day before with a team of priests, sisters, and lay people who normally met for this purpose. It was a calculated risk the moment seemed to demand.

The next day—March 24, 1980—as he was celebrating an anniversary Mass for the mother of Jorge Pinto (editor of *El Independiente*) just after a sermon reflecting on the connection between earthly work and its fulfillment, the archbishop prayed that the Eucharist would "feed us so that we may give our body and our blood to suffering and pain, as Christ did, not for himself but to give ideas of justice and peace to our people." At that moment, a sharpshooter stepped into the entrance of the small hospital chapel, took aim down the middle isle, and shot Romero through the heart. Efforts to save him were unavailing and he died soon afterward.

Who shot Romero—and why? The judge appointed to investigate the charge, Atilio Ramírez Amaya, within a few days left the country after escaping an assassination attempt. In Costa Rica he said his preliminary investigations had pointed to Major D'Aubuisson and General Medrano (founder of ORDEN). Much later former United States Ambassador Robert White stated that he had delivered documentation to the State Department strongly implicating D'Aubuisson.

However, it would be wrong to see D'Aubuisson (or whoever was responsible) as simply a fanatic. A *New York Times* writer studied the Salvadoran oligarchy and quoted one of his main informants, an oligarch he called "Francisco," speaking of Archbishop Romero: "How could the army tolerate a man in his position telling the soldiers not to obey orders; lay down their guns, rather than shoot?"[139] If D'Aubuisson ordered the murder he was only putting into effect the desires of the power structure.

Some at first expected an uprising such as followed the killing of Pedro Joaquín Chamorro in Nicaragua (this seemed to be the expectation inside the United States embassy). However, the popular organizations immediately concluded that the killing was intended as a "provocation" perhaps to precipitate a premature uprising that would justify a bloodbath—and they gave orders for people not to react. In fact, for the next several days there was a relative calm as many thousands came into San Salvador to pay their respects, filing by the casket.

In this writer's opinion, the assassination of the archbishop was a calculated move. Those who planned and ordered it knew that the benefits would outweigh the risks taken, at least at short range. In looking over the other bishops, they could calculate that the Vatican would choose as his successor either one of the four bishops clearly with the government, or Bishop Rivera y Damas, who would not be as vigorous as Romero. Should there be a spontaneous uprising, a *chamorrazo* (after Chamorro, in Nicaragua), the army would be ready.[140]

In the days following the assassination there was a mixture of shock, sadness, and disbelief—along with the feeling that in El Salvador this killing was entirely to be expected. Throughout the week the popular organizations called on their members not to succumb to the "provocation." Plans were made for a large public funeral on Sunday. (The more "ecclesiastical" ceremony was held on Thursday—neither the other bishops, except Rivera y Damas, nor the nuncio would appear at the "popular" ceremony to be held on Sunday.)

By Sunday it seemed that the funeral would be uneventful. A disturbance with world media focused on El Salvador did not seem to serve the interests of the government, the oligarchy, or the popular organizations. The popular organizations began a march toward the plaza, but noting what looked like snipers on roofs, they made some detours. At the same time an official church procession, with many visiting dignitaries, began. Meanwhile tens of thousands of people had gathered in the plaza, in the full heat of the noon sun. Shortly after the Mass began the popular organizations marched around the plaza in silence and took a wreath up to the casket. There was applause from the people in the plaza, virtually all of them poor. The liturgy proceeded. Cardinal Corripio of Mexico continued a sermon, not in the spirit of the martyred archbishop, but full of Vatican-style qualifications. Suddenly a bomb exploded from behind the National Palace, which lined one side of the plaza. The people murmured but did not move. Then there came another bomb and more murmuring. When automatic rifle fire crackled the crowd began to move. Since people could exit from only one corner of the plaza there was considerable anxiety and confusion, as well as a great deal of discipline (people raising their hands and insisting "Don't run!"). Most made their way to safety several blocks away but some 5,000 went into the cathedral and were pressed together, sweating, sharing the anxiety of hearing the sound of shots and explosions magnified and echoed. After an hour and a half they were allowed to leave. The death toll was at least twenty-six, mainly people crushed against a fence or inside the cathedral.

In its first communiqués the government insisted that all troops had been in their barracks and that leftist groups had set off the bombs and started the shooting. (In fact, numerous troops were seen in the downtown area.) Ambassador Robert White of the United States, in his post about a month, took a similar position (although he had blamed the assassination on the right), his theory being that the left intended to capitalize on a Chamorro-style uprising. In view of the left's repeated warnings to its networks not to be provoked, this position seems untenable. Only two explanations seem tenable to this writer: (1) the funeral was indeed attacked (by "right-wing groups") or (2) a bomb in the possession of someone in a left group went off accidentally. What makes this latter improbable is the fact that another bomb went off soon afterward. It is conceivable that if a bomb went off accidentally, and armed members of popular organizations shot, for example, at the National Palace and fire was returned, the rest could follow. However, eyewitness accounts and the government's own overstated case (its communiqués said the left groups had tried to steal the casket) make it highly probable that the funeral was indeed attacked by government-connected groups.

An assessment of Archbishop Romero will appear in chapter 10. Here suffice it to say that from the moment he took office (in the midst of the 1977 postelection protest vigil, which ended in a massacre and an attack on the church that would soon include the first assassinated priest) until his own martyrdom, the archbishop in a most extraordinary way took into his own person the suffering and struggle, the new issues and challenges, the risks and dangers of Christians involved in the struggle of the poor. Those who disapproved said he was being led by his advisers; in fact, he was working collegially and giving voice to a whole series of communities so that it is impossible to say what was his personal contribution and what was collective. It will be a long time before the church has absorbed the impact of Oscar Romero. After his death many Salvadorans recalled his words, "As a Christian I do not believe in death without resurrection: if they kill me I will arise in the Salvadoran people."[141]

After Romero

It is not excessive to say that after Romero's murder the church ceased to be a major public protagonist in the struggle. Individual Christians and pastoral agents became more involved, but the church as institution largely withdrew from the stage—so much so that the remainder of this chapter will almost constitute an epilogue. Rather than chronicle events and the participation of Christians in them, we shall review this more recent period in general terms.

When it designated Bishop Arturo Rivera y Damas interim archbishop, the Vatican surprised many by choosing the man least unlike Romero to be his successor. The choice was no doubt shrewd, since he was clearly the most intelligent and competent of the bishops. However, whether it was the original intention or not, Rivera became "permanently interim," that is, he was not confirmed as archbishop for almost three years. The inevitable consequence was that any move he made had to involve a calculation of whether the Vatican would approve; he was placed in an unending probation period.

In addition, Rivera soon found himself in isolation—at least in comparison to Romero, who had surrounded himself with advisers and colleagues. Rivera himself dismissed some of his predecessor's close collaborators, and in the wake of the killing, most of the pastoral agents doing direct grassroots work had to become very discreet (or even go underground) or leave the country. It is estimated that some fifty priests did indeed leave and at least one-third of the parishes (mainly rural) of the archdiocese were without priests. The chancery office and the church institution ceased to be a rallying point for priests and others committed to the popular cause.

This situation became clear when CONIP (National Council of the People's Church) announced its existence after the killing of Romero. CONIP was a network of basic Christian communities, which, while not seeing itself as an "alternative church," nevertheless by its very existence reflected a feeling that the existing church structure did not fulfill its needs. It should be added that not all elements of the church that supported the popular organizations were affiliated to CONIP.

One other focal point of the church was UCA, which after its involvement—and almost immediate disillusionment—with the first Junta put some of its resources at the disposal of the popular movements. In particular its review, *ECA*—which inexplicably continued to appear—served to gather both analytical articles and documentation, and in fact was the only serious opposition periodical that continued to be published despite occasional bombings of its offices and press. UCA social scientists continued to do research and publish the results in bulletins.

Not only was Rivera y Damas on "permanent probation" and relatively isolated; his own views and temperament were different from Romero's. While he frequently denounced the brutality of the official forces—and sometimes with indignation—he was clearly less open than Romero to the possibility of a government dominated by revolutionary forces. In other words, he seemed to be more clearly opposed to—and perhaps afraid of—Marxism. In this he would be similar to those Christian Democrats who, while they may have a desire for reform, have a fundamental aversion to

Marxism so that in concrete contexts such as El Salvador's their desire for change becomes a velleity. Rivera not only shared this mentality but had maintained Christian Democratic friendships since the foundation of the party in 1960. Finally, by temperament Rivera was reserved and cautious, and had always found it difficult to assume a position that would be conflictive.

As a consequence of all these factors, both personal and circumstantial, Rivera's posture in the archdiocese and the country shifted away from that of Romero. He sought to take a stance "above" the conflict, equidistant from both sides, opposing outside intervention (whether from the United States or Marxist countries) and encouraging a negotiated end to the conflict.

Two days after Romero's funeral, the Carter administration's move to restore large-scale military aid to El Salvador passed a significant vote in the House Appropriations Subcommittee on Foreign Operations, and thus $5.7 million was freed for "reprogramming" (that is, using immediately monies not spent elsewhere as opposed to waiting for the next fiscal year). The aid was called "non-lethal": vehicles, communication equipment, and so forth. For many months the administration, echoed by the media, portrayed the Duarte government as centrist, albeit besieged by extremes on right and left—and precisely for that reason deserving of United States aid. It was not noticed that no one on the right was ever brought to justice, or that there was no sign that Duarte or the other civilians had the slightest quota of power—even though Romero had raised these issues clearly.

A crucial figure in the drama was the new United States ambassador, Robert White, whose credentials included having infuriated the Stroessner dictatorship in Paraguay with his championing of human rights. What most observers failed to notice was the basic difference between the two countries: in Paraguay there was no movement seriously threatening Stroessner's hold, and hence he could be pressured to "clean up his act"; in El Salvador, however, any pressure over human rights violation could serve to weaken the regime and thereby would aid the increasingly viable alternative. This is a key factor for explaining the gulf between rhetoric and practice in human rights on the part of the Carter administration.

From the United States viewpoint, land reform was a critical part of the strategy: some United States officials perhaps genuinely felt that it could solve real problems and thus offer an alternative to civil war; at a minimum it should serve to undercut the left inside El Salvador and help the international image of the Salvadoran regime. In conception the land reform had three stages: the expropriation of large estates (over 1,250 acres), of medium estates (500–1,250 acres), and a "land-to-the-tiller" program, by which sharecroppers or renters would become owners of the land they were working. This last phase was imposed by decree (without even consulting the Ministry of Agriculture), clearly with United States pressure and modeled after a similar program in Vietnam. In fact, although it was decreed, only a token number of peasants got title to land. Phase 2 (medium-sized farms), which would have affected the bulk of the coffee production, was postponed and eventually ended.

Thus the only part significantly put into effect was Phase 1, by which approximately 250 large estates were passed over to peasants who could become organized into cooperatives. Initially the greatest problems were violence (many peasant leaders were killed by the army as it carried out land reform) and corruption (army commanders were making money on land and even collecting "protection money" from the cooperatives). Understandably perhaps, a large number of the beneficiaries were peasants favorable to the government and military, either members of ORDEN or of the UCS, the government-favored peasant organization. Often the owners had removed equipment or livestock and the government was unable to supply needed capital. In any case, far from the extravagant claims made for the reform, fewer than 10 percent of peasant families (and the figure is probably under 5 percent) benefited from the land reform. Since the large plantations are concentrated along the coastal plains and inland valleys, the reform did nothing for the areas of the north and east—precisely where the landless and impoverished peasantry lives. Politically it may have limited the appeal of the guerrillas in the agroexport areas, but it neither made substantial contribution toward structural change nor undercut the appeal of the opposition in the bulk of the peasantry. "The oligarchy," wrote Paul Heath Hoeffel, "has for the most part been able to find its way around the reforms it so bitterly opposes."[142]

The year 1980 can be seen as one of the unification of the opposition. The formation of the FDR (Revolutionary Democratic Front) in April was a very important step, since the five popular organizations were now joined by all major labor unions, the universities, and MIPTES (Independent Movement of Professionals and Technicians). Although MIPTES included at most only a few hundred people, they could be the core of administrators of a new government and their presence helped to assure the middle class that it could have a role after a revolutionary victory. Enrique Álvarez Córdova, an American-educated oligarchical dairy farmer who had three times been minister of agriculture (and frustrated in his efforts at land reform), was named president of the FDR. Archbishop Romero had encouraged precisely this kind of broadening of the opposition in his final weeks.

It seems clear that key figures from UCA were prominent in establishing the FDR and working out its positions. Some of its most prominent people were UCA professors (among them, Guillermo Ungo and Rubén Zamora). A whole double issue of *ECA* was dedicated to "the search for a new national *proyecto*." A long and thoughtful editorial took stock of the overall situation of struggle and the FDR's proposal, recognizing the clear decision to move toward an insurrection, which would combine both military action and a strike and passive resistance. It suggested that 10,000 lives might be lost by year's end if violence continued on its course, a prediction that proved accurate. A major article dealt with the economy implicit in the Programmatic Platform for a Revolutionary Democratic Government, first put forward by the popular organizations and in effect adopted by the FDR. Thus by this time UCA had taken a definite option to support the FDR and the popular organizations, putting its resources (research and analysis) at their disposal.[143]

Events in May (1980) revealed much about what was really happening in El Salvador. Major D'Aubuisson was caught attempting a right-wing coup. (To clarify, the use of the term "right wing" is conventional: what distinguished Colonel Guillermo García, the defense minister, and others from people like D'Aubuisson was their willingness to tolerate some token reforms as the price of maintaining United States support, while D'Aubuisson preferred to be straightforward in making the annihilation of the opposition the sole preoccupation.) Immediately after the major's arrest all 700 officers of the Salvadoran army met and voted to have D'Aubuisson released and Colonel Majano, who had ordered him jailed, demoted from being head of the Junta (and army commander in chief). The Christian Democrats, who had threatened to resign, retracted their threat.[144] D'Aubuisson, who had lost his visa to the United States because of his ties to death squads, sneaked into the United States to speak to right-wing groups. So firmly set was the "centrist-government" image that practically no one in the American media noticed that the supposed reformers such as Majano and the Christian Democrats had no power.

On May 14 Salvadoran peasants fleeing an army "clean-up operation" were trapped at the Sumpul River, between Salvadoran and Honduran forces. At least 300 were massacred (possibly many more) in the first of numerous such massacres—yet it remained merely an "alleged" massacre for almost a year until the *Sunday Times* of London gave it some prominence.

In June the popular forces organized a two-day strike, which was reported as 90 percent effective. One day later (June 27), in retaliation, it seems, the army attacked the university with 600 troops; sixteen students were killed. It was alleged that people were using the university's traditional autonomy to hide arms on its premises, and much media attention was given to "tunnels"—which were in fact simply the sewer pipes. What was more likely the object of the attack were the offices of the popular organizations, which for some time had been rather like an ideological bazaar, an area of barracks-like buildings where the various organizations hawked their documents and, more important, where they could meet, exchange ideas and analyses, and make plans. The attack on the university forced the popular organizations to go completely underground.

A strike in August was not so successful as the one in June, since the government had had time to prepare. New decrees forbade participation by public-sector unions and made occupation of churches a "terrorist crime." Many leaders were arrested, bus lines were militarized, union headquarters were raided, and, most important, army, police, and security forces were mobilized to make sure people opened shops and workers showed up.[145] The government was learning and a tendency was beginning that would become more and more marked, for the government forces to assert their strength in the cities and towns and consolidate their hold there.

One of the unanswered questions was the loyalty of the Salvadoran army. Since the troops were themselves usually of peasant origin and conscripted by force, was it possible they might rebel, particularly if there were a sector of the army, presumably connected with Colonel Majano, willing to come to an understanding with the popular and revolutionary forces? Armies operate by chains of command, however, and since the coup the hardliners had worked to assure that their people held the key posts. Nevertheless, some opposition sectors—especially those of FARN (Armed Forces of National Resistance) and FAPU—thought a split in the army feasible and worth working for in order to diminish the social cost of victory. There were rumors of defections. Finally, in early September, there was a showdown when Defense Minister García in the normal announcement of assignment changes further marginalized some Majano supporters. These at first refused to be moved, but subsequently they accepted the orders. Some believe that, had the revolutionary organizations been willing, at that moment they could have made a move and split the army; others see the officers' acquiescence as simply the consequence of Majano's indecisiveness from the beginning. In any case, the moves were consummated and there was no longer any sector of "reform-minded" officers with power. United States government spokespersons downplayed the significance, out of either ignorance or lack of real concern for reform.

Following the example of the broad support movement that had arisen in the United States during the anti-Somoza struggle, groups meeting in Washington and Los Angeles in October formed CISPES (Committee in Solidarity with the People of El Salvador). From the beginning church people and voices were prominent. The United States Catholic Conference (bishops) had already gone on record against military aid to El Salvador and would continue to maintain this position, and almost all major Protestant denominations took similar stances.

Ronald Reagan's election to the United States presidency was to set in motion a whole new phase. One of the first results was a "Dissent Memo," ostensibly a leaked document from discontented staff members of various United States government agencies. Briefly, in their analysis United States policy was wrong: rather than support a repressive government, calling itself reformist, it should seek a "Zimbabwe option," namely, a negotiated solution (the hope was that the Reagan administration would prove to be pragmatic rather than ideological). However, it would be over a year before "negotiations" became part of the lexicon about El Salvador.

The year's end was marked by multiple murders. First, on November 27, 200 soldiers and police surrounded the Externado San José, a Jesuit high school, while 20 went in to pick up 5 leading FDR leaders, including Enrique Álvarez Córdova and Juan Chacón. All five bodies were found the next day. Then on December 2, Sisters Ita Ford and Maura Clarke of Maryknoll, Sister Dorothy Kazel, an Ursuline, and Jean Donovan, a lay worker, were stopped by National Guardsmen; at least two were raped and all four were murdered. At the end of the month Michael Hammer and Mark Pearlman, who had been sent by the AFL-CIO to work with the land-reform program, were killed along with its director, Rodolfo Viera.

These murders, when seen from El Salvador, were simply further instances of what had been occurring for months, years, decades. However, they were a jolt to the American public and a jarring cognitive dissonance to the claims of a moderate government, since in all three situations the participation or connivance of official forces was clear.

The rape/killing of American church women came at the end of many acts of violence against the church. The Archdiocesan Legal Aid Office had tabulated 180 such acts between January and early October 1980: murders of priests and lay people; arrests; violent searches, bombings, and shooting at church buildings; desecration of the Eucharist. Archbishop Rivera published a statement blaming the security forces for the killing of the church women and others and rejecting the government's picture of "extremes" in battle:

> . . . in the almost four years of persecution suffered by the church, it has been clear that most acts of persecution have been carried out by members of security forces and paramilitary groups.
>
> Hence we blame . . . the security forces and the ultra-right bands . . . and also the government Junta.
>
> Their statements have no credibility and we cannot accept their excuses.
>
> . . . We also want to say a word of encouragement and hope. . . . Persecution is a sign of the authenticity of the church because it makes it resemble its Divine Founder, Jesus Christ, who was also persecuted for speaking the truth and opting for the poor.
>
> By our faith we know that this cross leads to a glorious resurrection with Jesus Christ and to a liberation in history, which will issue in a more just and brotherly society where there will be true peace, and where fear and terror will give way to equality and joy.[146]

Reagan Administration and Insurrection in El Salvador

The die was cast sometime in early 1980, whether with the resignation of the first Junta or the killing of the archbishop. With the Nicaraguan insurrection fresh in the memories of all—the opposition, the Salvadoran military and power structure, and the Carter administration—it seemed only a question of time until full scale war broke out. By one count 2,780 civilians were killed between June and August. During that same period the armed opposition carried out 2,170 actions, many of a propagandistic nature, but several hundred involved direct conflict with official forces; one instance

occurred on August 2 when guerrilla groups broke through an army encir-
clement of 3,500 troops, inflicted 68 casualties, and suffered 17.[147] The army
and security forces for their part were trying "clean-up" operations.

As Reagan's inauguration (January 20, 1981) drew near the Salvadoran
opposition, now formally united into one command—the FMLN (Farabundo Martí National Liberation Front)—prepared for an insurrection
attempt in the waning days of 1980, hoping to present the new United States
administration with a fait accompli. What resulted was neither the "failed
offensive," as claimed by the Carter administration, nor the uprising some
of the opposition leaders apparently hoped for. Once again in the cities, and
especially in the capital, results were much less than expected, while the
FMLN managed to extend its control in the countryside.

One result was a quick escalation of the level of United States involvement. President Carter renewed military shipments (suspended in the furor
over the church women's killing), increased the amount, and approved the
sending of United States advisers.

The Reagan administration brought changes. From even before the
nomination, Reagan-related people had been studying Central America and
attempting to alert the public to its dangers. Its differences with the Carter
administration might be summarized as follows: (1) the solution was seen as
fundamentally military: defeating the guerrillas; (2) the conflict was seen as
regional, involving all Central America; and (3) it was put into the context
of East-West confrontation and indeed seen as a "textbook case of communist interference" and a "test case" of United States resolve. However,
there is rather more continuity than difference between the approaches of
the two administrations. Both agreed that the opposition must be stopped;
each differed only on the most effective ways to do so. While it undoubtedly
felt more affinity with the D'Aubuisson types, the Reagan administration
had to push for at least the appearance of reforms and to support Duarte.

This writer sees the Salvadoran conflict since the advent of the Reagan
administration as falling into three periods when viewed from a United
States perspective. The *first period* was marked by an attempt to make the
conflict in El Salvador a proof of what the new Reagan administration
would do. All indications are that it was regarded as an "easy win," which
would send signals all the way to the Kremlin. Internally in the United
States two things caused it to unravel: (1) public indignation over the killing
of the church women and Archbishop Romero (the first anniversary of
Romero's death occurred soon after Reagan's inauguration) and (2) the
clumsiness of the administration's first White Paper, which turned out to be
a highly suspect mixture of extrapolation, false reading, and probably fabrication of documents by the CIA, although it took the media months to
recognize the criticisms made initially by the left.[148]

By the middle of 1981 (and the beginning of the *second period*), there was
an apparent lull—not in El Salvador, of course, but in public attention in
the United States—broken only by Assistant Secretary of State Thomas
Enders's July speech proposing elections in El Salvador as a step toward the

solution of the country's problems. The opposition was to lay down its arms and compete at the polls—while the official forces kept and used their arms.

Mexico and France, followed by several other nations, nevertheless offered another approach: negotiations between the sides in conflict. Washington gradually recognized that the FMLN, far from having "failed," had now asserted something like control over about 30 percent of El Salvador and was having increasing military success, while the army, plagued by morale problems, was killing very few guerrillas, although security forces and right-wing paramilitary groups were killing about a thousand civilians a month. The answer from the United States was to step up accusations aimed at Nicaragua and Cuba (and implicitly at the Soviet Union) and to make almost daily threats of action. Indeed, during this period Reagan authorized covert action against Nicaragua. This period closed with the announcement that 1,600 Salvadoran officers and troops would go to the United States for training (almost 10 percent of the total uniformed troops)—and then Central America was upstaged by events in Poland.

The *third period* centered around the 1982 elections for a constituent assembly in El Salvador. In fact it seemed more like a plebiscite than an election, its purpose being to show citizen support for the group in power. Although apparently the idea was at first a United States imposition, serving no real function for the Salvadoran populace, at a given point Salvadoran right-wing groups began to see their chance to marginalize the Christian Democrats and nullify the annoying aspects of the reforms enacted under United States pressure. What happened on election day is unclear. In many parts of El Salvador a large number of people turned up. There is reason to believe, nevertheless, that the high final figures were considerably inflated.[149] However, the election also indicated that where the government was able to assert its control through violence and intimidation, people did not feel free to defy it. One commentator saw evidence that the policy of widespread killing had had its effect: in urban areas the leadership that had been built up through labor unions, neighborhood associations, and the like had either been eliminated or gone underground.[150] In large parts of the country the opposition did not have enough military strength to protect people, and most people, whatever might be their preferences, had to adapt in order to survive.

With the legitimacy granted by elections, the consolidation of right-wing groups headed by Major D'Aubuisson, and an unofficial geographical division of the country into areas held by the government, held by the opposition, and disputed, negotiations seemed further away than ever. It seemed that the conflict would be decided militarily.

As has been stated, with the murder of Archbishop Romero the church ceased to be a protagonist in the struggle in the same manner as before. To a degree the same could be said of the popular organizations: after the huge January 22, 1980, demonstration such actions became impossible, and as the country drifted toward open combat through 1980, the popular organizations more and more tended to become support structures for the armed organizations.

Similarly, those elements of the church committed to the popular cause found themselves moving into closer collaboration with the overall opposition structure, coordinated by the politico-military groups, and then unified into the FMLN. In areas under government control (mainly the cities), those publicly identified with the opposition could only go underground or leave the country.

Basic Christian communities continued to meet for Bible study, reflection, and mutual support. There was a renewed interest in traditional feasts, which gave an opportunity for people to express their religious conviction in large public acts. Implicit in such acts was an expression of solidarity and a yearning for a new kind of church and even a basic change in society.

In areas under opposition control, lay people continued to lead basic Christian communities. In some cases pastoral agents took up their work permanently in occupied territory. In early 1981 Sister Silvia Maribel Arriola was killed when the National Guard overran an FPL camp, where she was tending the sick, and killed all in the camp. By some reports she was killed as a combatant.[151] Similarly Father Rogelio Poncelle took up permanent pastoral work in the area of Morazán, controlled by the ERP.

Pastoral agents, priests, and sisters in this kind of work saw themselves as carrying out the "pastoral work of *acompañamiento* ('accompanying'),'' that is, the "conscious and explicit Christian presence within the politico-social organizations.''[152] While information is scarce, it seems that a number of priests and religious have joined the organizations. When they do so they must make a radical new commitment and submit to a whole new discipline and new "values,'' such as austerity and concern for others (the mutual relying on one another necessitated by conditions of war and repression).

It seems almost certain that a new experience of the church is occurring in El Salvador and that (unless the army, backed and bankrolled by the United States, can somehow "win'' through massive killing) today's communities are pioneers of a new kind of "people's church'' living in the midst of a revolution.[153] The pastoral consequences are impossible to predict. One imagines that lay people formed through such a struggle will have a great deal of autonomy, that is, that clericalism (and even more, "hierarchalism'') will be greatly reduced.

The positions of the bishops have varied from outright support for the government (for example, Bishop Revelo blessing United States military equipment and Bishop Alvarez wearing his uniform as military chaplain, and especially their backing of the United States-sponsored election) to Archbishop Rivera y Damas's studied efforts to be "neutral'' and to call on all sides for a nonmilitary resolution of the conflict. Should there be a revolutionary victory, with a "people's church'' clearly identified with the revolution, the hierarchy's stance will turn out to have been shortsighted to say the very least.

MEXICO

BELIZE

PETEN

GULF OF HONDURAS

QUICHE   ALTA VERAPAZ

Chajul• •Cotzal •Coban   El Estor•
Nebaj•   •Uspantán   Panzós•
IXCAN   • Huehuetenango   Morales•

San Marcos•   Santa Cruz   BAJA
               del Quiché VERAPAZ
Quetzaltenango• Sololá•   Zacapa•
           •Tecpán   Chiquimula•
Santiago Atitlán• •Chimaltenango
           Antigua •Guatemala
Tiquisate• Escuintla•   City   ORIENTE •Esquipulas
              •Santa Lucía   HONDURAS
              Cotzumalguapa

EL SALVADOR

Central
America   PACIFIC OCEAN

|——————| = 50 miles

GUATEMALA

6

"The Color of Blood
Is Never Forgotten!"

Both the struggle in Guatemala and Christian involvement in that struggle were slow to come to public awareness in the United States, partly because there was no Archbishop Romero-like figure to personify it and even more because there had been no recent deep United States involvement. Yet the struggle in Guatemala has shown levels of cruelty and repression equal to, or greater than, those in El Salvador at comparable stages of struggle; and, given United States perceptions of its hemispheric role, there is every reason to believe that the struggle will continue to be costly.

What most distinguishes the Guatemalan movement today from similar movements in Nicaragua and El Salvador is the involvement of the native people—the Indians—descendants of the Mayas, who make up over half the Guatemalan population.

As was noted in chapter 3, Guatemala's native people after their conquest were regimented into their towns and were used as a standing labor supply. In fact, the Indians were never totally pacified and there were local rebellions in 1708, 1743, 1760, 1764, 1770, 1803, 1817, 1818, 1820, 1838, 1839, 1898, 1905, and even in 1944 and 1968.[1] The legal framework for utilizing Indian labor has varied from the sixteenth to the twentieth centuries, but all methods were means of "legally" coercing Indians to work the lands that small non-Indian elites had acquired.

Guatemala came to be organized geographically and demographically around its agroexport function. Today the prime agroexport region is the south coast, a flat plain running along the Pacific Ocean, which is used for sugar, cotton, and cattle-raising. Where the plain gives way to the foothills of the highlands, coffee production begins. Other agroexport areas include coffee farms in Alta Verapaz, cattle ranches along the Motagua River in Izabal, and in recent years, cardamom production in the northern colonization areas. Since there is not enough labor supply on the south coast at harvest time, crews of Indians are brought down from the highlands. It happens that the fallow time for corn and beans coincides with the harvest period for coffee, sugar, and cotton (October–February) and large numbers of Indians are chronically in need of cash—in fact, in debt, and usually to the labor contractor—so that there is guaranteed a seasonal labor supply. As a system it dovetails neatly: the different growing cycles for the highlands and the coast, and the Indians' need for cash vis-à-vis the plantations' need for cheap seasonal labor.

One sometimes hears such an economy referred to as "feudal," meaning, in the speaker's mind one assumes, "backward." However, properly speaking, under feudalism the "lord" has some obligations in return for the services given by the "fief." There are still places in Guatemala where plantation workers are allowed to use small plots of land for their own crops in return for which they must supply labor, but these have been disappearing; most work is done on a cash basis, with no obligation on the part of the plantation owners; in other words, the plantations are truly capitalist enterprises and the workers are more and more "proletarized," meaning they have nothing but their labor power to sell.

Guatemala's Indians, accordingly, are anything but "marginal," since they are essential to the functioning of agroexport production, the backbone of the economy. In that sense they are different from the Indians of Nicaragua's Atlantic coast. They have been marginalized, however, from schooling, health care, and other services.

Along with the south coast and the highlands, which may be seen as forming the basic economic axis of the country, there are other zones: the Oriente ("east") a large part of the country, bordering on El Salvador and Honduras, somewhat arid, with small and medium producers and cattle ranching; the northeast, mainly Alta Verapaz, which produces coffee and now oil and minerals; and finally the sparsely inhabited regions to the north (Petén, Northern Transversal Strip), which are colonization regions. Except for the Kekchi Indians in Alta Verapaz, the inhabitants of these areas are mainly ladinos (non-Indians culturally, although they are of mixed blood by ancestry).

These considerations are relevant to the story of the struggle in Guatemala inasmuch as they point to differences and even divisions between people. First, and most obvious, is the split between Indians and ladinos. Guatemala's Indians are a majority; estimates range from just over, to well over, half the population.[2] Since they are the reserve labor force for the plantations, and since there has been direct racial discrimination, some have said that the basic conflict in Guatemala is racial, the exploitation of the Indian by the ladino. Others, particularly those of an orthodox Marxist orientation, have stressed class conflict, tending to ignore the specifically racial dimension. What seems to have happened in the 1970s is that while the controversy still simmered among theoreticians, revolutionary organizations solved it, at least for practical purposes; that is, Indians in large numbers became involved with revolutionary organizations.

The Spanish conquerors found the Indians divided and even at war with one another—and one element in the technique of domination was to maintain them in isolation, partly, as has been mentioned, by assigning them to their own areas and obliging each group to wear distinctive dress. Indians are further divided by language—there are twenty or so languages, although about 90 percent of the people speak one of six major languages. Until the present, different language groups have not had strong links among themselves, but such unity as exists has come through their integration into the nation.

In addition to the Indian/ladino split and divisions among the Indians along language and township lines, people have been further divided as a result of differing roles in production. Thus agricultural laborers on the south coast, highlands Indians with their small plots of corn and beans (who migrate seasonally to earn enough to survive), dirt farmers in the Oriente (who may be sharecroppers), employees of the banana company, colonizers of the northern jungle, along with urban workers in factories or government—or those without steady work—all relate in different manners to the economy. While these people are all part of one agroexport system, run by and for a narrow elite, their experiences are different because they have been divided from one another by historical, linguistic, and ecological factors. The story to be told is largely one of their convergence both in the overall revolutionary process and in the specific instance of the church.

FROM 1944 REVOLUTION TO 1954 COUNTERREVOLUTION

As Nicaraguans refer to the United States intervention/Sandino-Somoza dictatorship complex, and Salvadorans to the 1932 uprising/massacre, Guatemalans take the 1944–54 experience as their reference point. Some specifically Guatemalan characteristics to the Central American history outlined in chapter 3 need to be briefly mentioned here as background to the 1944–54 experience.

First, in Guatemala the Liberal period in the nineteenth century led to a repression, which, one writer says, is "perhaps the longest and most severe restriction that the Catholic church has suffered in Latin America."[3] Many priests left Guatemala and those remaining numbered not much over 100 for the better part of a century. Consequently the church was institutionally weak and never developed a strong Guatemalan clergy.

Politically, dictatorship was the norm. Justo Rufino Barrios, the initiator of the Liberal period, was succeeded by two presidents, and then in 1898 began the twenty-two-year dictatorship of Manuel Estrada Cabrera. During this time the United Fruit Company began banana production in both Atlantic and Pacific areas, and through a nominally independent company built the country's railroad system. Under one of Estrada Cabrera's successors (he was declared insane and deposed by a revolt in 1920), the United Fruit Company was exempted from taxes for twenty-five years.

General Jorge Ubico became president in 1931 and ruled dictatorially for thirteen years. During Ubico's rule the interests of landholders were maintained, in part through enforced low wages. Ubico generally favored American interests: he allowed the United States to build an air base in Guatemala during World War II and expropriated lands from Germans (and Guatemalans of German ancestry), who were sent to internment camps in the United States.

Gradually, however, opposition to Ubico formed, and in June 1944 a student demonstration, joined by army officers, and a general strike forced him out of office shortly after a similar movement overthrew Hernández Martínez in El Salvador. When his replacement made little concession to the people's aspiration for democratic reform, a definitive revolution took place, led by armed students and workers and dissident army officers, on October 20—a date subsequently made into a national holiday more meaningful than the September 15 Independence Day. In March 1945 Juan José Arévalo was elected president with 85 percent of the vote.[4]

Interpretations of what happened during the 1944-54 period tend to be almost polar opposites and are largely a reflection of people's basic understanding of Guatemala—there is no "objective" reading possible, it would seem. Briefly, one version is that during Arévalo's presidency a small group of communists began consolidating their power in labor and student groups and in the government, and under Arbenz (1950-54) they came more and more to control policy, until a rebellion, led by Colonel Carlos Castillo Armas, with great popular support, led to "liberation." The opposing version is that under both Arévalo and Arbenz there was a gradual process of capitalist modernization, but that the Eisenhower administration, disturbed because there were some communists in the Guatemalan government (this was at the height of the cold war) and because Guatemala pursued an independent foreign policy and undertook a vigorous land reform that affected United Fruit, engineered a coup through the CIA. As a result, a democratically elected government was overthrown, and the landholding oligarchy consolidated its grip over Guatemala and so was able to block gradual routes to reform.[5] The present author not unexpectedly shares this latter view. In this brief survey the role of the church in events and their influence on subsequent developments will be pointed out.

Under Arévalo, who liked to speak of his programs as "spiritual socialism," a number of reforms were rapidly enacted. Voting rights were extended to women and the illiterate, political parties could be organized (except those that were foreign, that is, communist), freedom of speech and assembly was permitted, and unionization grew rapidly. Social security programs were begun, and there were new expenditures on schooling and health services. That the government was viewed favorably is evidenced in a 1950 World Bank study on Guatemala.[6]

When he took power in 1951 (after winning 63 percent of the vote), Colonel Jacobo Arbenz declared his government's intention to transform Guatemala into a "modern capitalist country."[7] When the 1952 land reform law was decreed there had already been some conflict with both the United States and foreign companies. Beginning in January 1953 the land reform expropriated over 1,000 haciendas and by a year and a half later they had been distributed to over 100,000 peasant families—an extraordinary pace when compared to other land reforms. Peasants were to pay for the land and owners were to receive compensation according to the value declared for tax purposes. United Fruit found the government expropriating 400,000 of its 550,000 acres (no more than 15 percent of which was cultivated), and was offered less than $1.2 million (based on its own declared value) rather than the nearly $16 million it now claimed the land and installations to be worth.[8]

While the land reform would seem to have been enough to guarantee broad support for the Arbenz government from the population, it is not clear to what extent that was the case. The revolution had been initiated by urban middle-class elites, and although unionization increased, there are indications that feelings among the Indian peasants were mixed. It seems that the Indians would not benefit proportionately from the land reform, possibly because there was much less land to expropriate in the highlands. Furthermore, the government did not seem to be able to communicate well with the Indians. People who have first-hand recollections recall feelings of fear and uncertainty.[9]

The United States was later to justify its intervention on the grounds that the Arbenz government was communist-dominated. The PGT (Guatemalan Workers party) was legalized in 1951; there were four PGT members in the Guatemalan Congress (out of a total of fifty-six seats), and PGT members held several important posts and were strong in labor and peasant organizations. However, the charge that communists controlled the government must rest on an assumption that they had power far out of proportion to their numbers and that they were able to control Arbenz as a puppet. One participant, the writer Luis Cardoza y Aragón, later said that the PGT was one of the parties that influenced Arbenz. He continued: "I do not think there was a fixed strategy or political analysis on the part of Arbenz or the PGT. Had there been real influential communists, things would have been oriented differently and there would have been intense struggle."[10]

Whatever may have been the overall influence of the PGT it seems that some government functionaries alienated the clergy, which had initially welcomed the 1944 revolution and the reforms begun under Arévalo. Observers reported incidents where officials ridiculed the people's religious practices and insulted or humiliated the clergy: for example, after local officials in Huehuetenango, including army officers, attended a special military Mass, they all lost their jobs or were transferred, including the governor, who was ordered to report to Arbenz and then made to sit waiting for days outside his office.[11] It is not clear whether this was a pervasive attitude or simply reflected the viewpoint of a certain group of government officials.

Archbishop Mariano Rossell and the clergy began to organize against the government. Thus the First Eucharistic Congress (1951), which drew an estimated 200,000 for the closing ceremony, was seen as a demonstration of the church's power vis-à-vis the government. Starting in 1953, Rossell organized nationwide tours with the revered "Black Christ" of Esquipulas. The opposition of the clergy and its influence with the Indian population was undoubtedly one of the main internal factors undermining support for the Arbenz government.

Meanwhile, almost from the beginning of Arbenz's presidency the United States had become increasingly displeased, and the first moves against it were made even under the Truman administration. To recount fully the United States intervention would require a book in itself. However, it may be summarized as follows: the United States secured the cooperation of other Central American countries, which allowed their territory to be used (Anastasio Somoza was intimately involved); diplomatic action by the United States isolated the Guatemalan regime internationally; the CIA trained and equipped a mercenary army and promoted psychological warfare inside Guatemala (rumors, leaflets, radio programs); and military officers were convinced (or bribed) to desert Arbenz. Although the actual "invasion force" led by Colonel Carlos Castillo Armas (seemingly chosen by the CIA) was only 160 to 200 men and stopped just inside the Honduran border, the desertion of the military officers and the bombardment of Guatemala City by CIA planes led Arbenz, who had been unwilling to give arms to the people, to resign on June 27, 1954. Castillo Armas was flown into Guatemala City on the United States embassy plane on July 3.[12]

To many observers the 1954 CIA coup is a "classic," following on the heels of the 1953 overthrow of Mossadegh in Iran and indeed a pattern for future actions, such as that in Chile in 1973. Although these perceptions may be correct, they may be tempered by some reports from the time stating that the "liberation" was welcomed or at least passively accepted, since Arbenz had alienated much of the population—otherwise how can one explain the successful "invasion" by fewer than 200 "invaders"?

Archbishop Rossell played a highly useful role in the overthrow of Arbenz. He had already organized the pilgrimages of the "Black Christ" and, it seems, had a representative at the formulation of the Pact of Tegucigalpa (a meeting in late 1953 where opposition leaders agreed on guidelines for a new government) where he secured guarantees for the church. The CIA asked Cardinal Spellman of New York to arrange a clandestine contact between Rossell and a CIA agent "so we could coordinate our parallel efforts." Hence when Rossell wrote a pastoral letter in April 1954 "On the Advance of Communism in Guatemala," the CIA had thousands of copies dropped by plane on remote towns and villages.

During the days of the actual invasion Rossell was in direct contact with the United States ambassador, John Peurifoy, and followed events closely. At one point, losing confidence in Castillo Armas, he told the ambassador that the United States might have to intervene directly. The papal nuncio

Monsignor Gennaro Verrolino was also involved; at one point Peurifoy brought him in to end a dispute among the "liberation" leadership. After Arbenz's fall Rossell sent Castillo Armas a congratulatory telegram:

> I send you warm greetings and fervent congratulations in the name of the nation which awaits you with open arms, recognizing and admiring your sincere patriotism. May our Lord God guide you and your heroic companions in your liberating campaign against atheistic communism. You all have my pastoral benediction.

He once referred to Castillo Armas as a "legitimate saint." To be fair, however, in later years he criticized some of the abuses of subsequent governments.[13]

Castillo Armas lost no time in undoing the work of the Arévalo-Arbenz period under "communist" influence. Scores of peasant and union leaders were killed, and it is estimated that 9,000 were arrested and many tortured. The United States embassy helped the government hunt "communists" by supplying lists. A total of 533 unions had their registration canceled and the labor-movement membership dropped from 100,000 to 27,000 during the first year of the "liberation." Over 99 percent of expropriated lands were returned to their former owners. Literacy programs were ended and hundreds of rural teachers were fired.

The original United States intention had been to make Guatemala a "showcase of democracy." "This is the first instance in history where a communist government has been replaced by a free one" said Vice-President Richard Nixon (using both adjectives loosely). "The whole world is watching to see which does the better job." To help with the job the United States pumped $80 or $90 million into Guatemala for development, but it bore little immediate fruit, given the ineptitude and corruption of Castillo Armas's and succeeding governments.[14] Castillo Armas was assassinated in 1957—not by the left, but by agents of Rafael Trujillo, dictator of the Dominican Republic.

For the Catholic church, institutionally at least, there were immediate benefits from the "liberation." Archbishop Rossell was awarded the Order of Liberation and several priests served in the National Assembly that was called to write a new Constitution. Restrictions on the church's holding property were removed, priests were allowed to perform civil weddings, and the teaching of religion was allowed in public schools. A First Central American Eucharistic Congress held in 1959 with multitudes in attendance was seen as a sign of triumph over atheistic communism.[15]

REPRESSION AND RESISTANCE (1960–1976)

Throughout the many developments since 1954, perhaps the clearest and most persistent tendency in Guatemala has been the increasing control by the army over Guatemalan life, a control exercised not as a personal dictatorship but as the rule of the army institution. The later 1950s may be seen as a period of transition. After Castillo Armas's assassination, General Miguel Ydígoras Fuentes became president and ruled until he was overthrown by a military coup in 1963. Politically what set the tone for all of Guatemala during the 1960s was a struggle between a small band of guerrillas and the army.

During the 1950s and 1960s export agriculture diversified and expanded, particularly as landholding elites acquired new lands. Thus cotton acreage on the south coast increased almost tenfold between 1952 and 1962, and crop value increased from $3 million to over $30 million. During the 1960–74 period the total value of the five main agroexport products increased from $105.3 to $367.5 million,[16] one of the fastest agroexport growth rates in Latin America. As was already pointed out, the fact that this growth was accompanied by very slow rates in production of subsistence crops—and in fact took place at the expense of subsistence—is the major structural reason for the later crisis.

Manufacturing also boomed during the 1960s, since Guatemala, along with El Salvador, had a headstart on industrialization. By 1970 some forty-six of the "Fortune 500" companies had operations in Guatemala. Twenty of these had begun with the United States company buying an existing Guatemalan operation. In the most general terms it may be said that the Common Market spurred industrialization, provided some new products, and increased the country's exports, but provided relatively few jobs; its production was aimed at the privileged rather than at the poor majority.[17]

What dominated Guatemalan life throughout the 1960s was a guerrilla movement and the mobilization of the army to defeat it. The movement was launched in November 1960 when young army officers, disgusted with Ydígoras's cooperation with the United States in allowing Guatemala to be used in preparation for the Bay of Pigs invasion, led one-third of the army into a revolt that failed. Its leaders, Luis Turcios Lima and Marco Antonio Yon Sosa, became heads of guerrilla movements. During 1962 there were protest movements of university and high school students, government employees of various kinds, and some professionals—and again an attempt at an uprising, this time led by the air force.

Out of these initial uprisings—which were essentially barracks revolts—there gradually developed a guerrilla movement, which moved toward a broader understanding of the nature of the problem, although it seems never to have worked out a clear and effective strategy combining political with military elements. In part it was inspired by the Cuban model of revolution, which came to be called the *foco* theory, namely, that by operating out of small zones the guerrillas could eventually extend their influence. Such *focos* were established in parts of Izabal, Zacapa, and Baja Verapaz, in the north and east of Guatemala. Some smaller groups operated in the capital, along the south coast, and in the Quetzaltenango-San Marcos area.

By hindsight it is clear that although they succeeded in surviving militarily for several years during the mid-1960s, these guerrilla groups did not develop a solid base in the peasant population, and particularly among the Indians of the western highlands.

In 1963 the army, urged by the oligarchy (which feared an electoral victory by ex-president Arévalo), toppled the Ydígoras government and installed Colonel Enrique Peralta Azurdia as president. The United States, which had been training the Guatemalan military in counterinsurgency at a secret base since May 1962, found Peralta to be stubborn and insufficiently aggressive with the guerrillas. For the 1966 election Mario Méndez Montenegro, a civilian of the PR (Revolutionary Party), promised to carry out the ideals of the 1944–54 period; but in fact, as a condition for receiving the presidency, he had to agree to allow the army and the United States a free hand in counterinsurgency, which became the real priority of his government period.

The United States played a key role in training and advising the Guatemalan army, paying for its equipment, and upgrading the police. There were many similarities to techniques used in Vietnam and some twenty-five State Department people in the United States embassy in Guatemala during the 1960s had previously seen service in Vietnam.

Repression increased dramatically. Even on the eve of Méndez Montenegro's election, twenty-eight top PGT leaders were kidnapped, interrogated with torture, and reportedly dropped from helicopters into the sea. In the Oriente, Colonel Carlos Arana went after the guerrilla *focos*, using a combination of infiltration, informers, terrorism, and military attacks. Bases were bombed and napalmed sometimes by planes piloted by Americans and flown from the Panama Canal Zone. Between 1966 and 1968 Arana succeeded in putting down the guerrillas at a cost of an estimated 6,000 to 8,000 lives, even though the guerrilla fighters themselves never numbered more than 300.

This period saw the rise of the right-wing death squads such as the Mano Blanca ("White Hand"), which Mario Sandoval Alarcón, the leader of the MLN (National Liberation Movement—referring to the 1954 overthrow of Arbenz), all but admitted to have founded. Kidnapping became common, with the tortured bodies later found by roadsides. These were similar to "assassination squads" used in Vietnam.

In the late 1960s there were attempts at urban guerrilla activities in the capital. The head of the United States military mission was killed, and United States Ambassador John Gorden Mein was killed in a kidnap attempt, as was later the German ambassador, Karl von Spretti. However, despite sporadic guerrilla activities, the main movement was ended by 1970 and its leaders were dead.[18] Colonel Arana was elected president in 1970 and launched a new wave of repression, this time aimed at students, labor leaders, professionals, and intellectuals. Gabriel Aguilera, who has studied violence in Guatemala, distinguished this as the "second wave of terror."

Throughout most of Arana's presidency, fear dominated public consciousness.

During the Arana period major changes in the kind of economic development and in the role of the army took place, although they were only discerned clearly some years later. Since the 1950s it was known that there were nickel deposits near Lake Izabal. During the 1960s EXMIBAL (a joint Canadian-United States firm) was seeking from the Guatemalan government favorable terms for nickel mining through, for example, drafting the government's mining code. In 1970–71 two vocal critics of government concessions were assassinated. During the mid-1970s EXMIBAL built the mining installation at El Estor on Lake Izabal and began operations late in the decade. At the time this was the largest single investment in Central America ($120 million, although figures varied somewhat).

Similarly, oil companies had been considering operations in Guatemala since the 1950s and became more serious in the mid-1970s. In addition there was a great deal of unused land, inaccessible to vehicles. For some time there were proposals that these lands be used for colonization. Some colonization took place in the 1960s in the Petén in the far north. The government designated for colonization a strip of land about forty kilometers wide, the Franja Transversal del Norte (Northern Transversal Strip) running from Huehuetenango to Lake Izabal. From the beginning, although the government publicly claimed that the colonization lands were for peasants to settle with "family-sized plots" (ten hectares), in fact the general tendency was for them to be acquired by military officers and existing large landholders. According to an AID study, the Northern Transversal Strip could have provided 500,000 hectares of good farmland, or enough for 50,000 peasant families. Had such a course been taken it would have reduced the pressure of landlessness. In fact the bulk of the lands were soon taken by the colonels and generals.[19]

These new kinds of development (large infrastructure projects, oil and nickel, colonization projects) were a sign of the emerging role of the army, which, under Arana, began to move beyond its gendarme function and enter directly into the economy. This happened in two ways: (1) individual army officers and groups of officers increasingly took advantage of their power for their own aggrandizement (getting kickbacks on government contracts and becoming large landholders); (2) the army institutionally played a larger role, for example, through opening its own bank (Banco del Ejército), which competed with other banks, in receiving deposits and making loans.

Internally in Guatemala these developments produced divisions in the oligarchy between a traditional elite, more identified with coffee production and export, and other groups with new wealth made through association with the army and the new development projects. The new groups, called the "bureaucratic bourgeoisie" by some analysts, were clearly linked to foreign corporations. Some of this development took place with the aid of loans from the international lending agencies.

During the Arana period political violence became routine to the point where it was no longer newsworthy. At least 2,000 were said to have been killed from November 1970 to June 1971. A count made from newspaper sources showed 400 people killed or disappeared during the first five months of 1974 (period of the elections) and another 142 wounded; the Committee of the Relatives of the Disappeared listed 15,325 cases of "disappearance" between 1970 and 1975 and attributed 75 percent of the cases to official forces. Where bodies were found there were usually signs of torture or mutilation.

As the 1974 election approached some groups took advantage of the government's relative reluctance to use violence (so as not to lose votes) in order to press their demands, notably in a teachers' strike in June 1973 and other public-employee strikes. The main contenders in the election were a coalition of the MLN (representing the landholding oligarchy) and the PID (Institutional Democratic Party—military and some business sectors) and another coalition around the Christian Democrats and lesser parties, with General Efraín Ríos Montt as its candidate. With a clumsy fraud (the vote count was suspended until it could come out right) General Kjell Eugenio Laugerud was declared the winner. Ríos Montt showed his military loyalty by quietly accepting an ambassadorship. This election was one step in the rapid disenchantment that forced more people to conclude that elections could bring no real change.[20]

FIRST STIRRINGS IN THE CHURCH

Perhaps the most immediate effects of the post-1954 lifting of restrictions on the church was an influx of foreign personnel and the strengthening of Catholic institutions. Priests, who numbered only 132 in 1950, increased to 483 by 1965. The number of sisters increased from 96 to 354 during the same period. Hence in fifteen years the number of priests and religious registered an extraordinary 266 percent increase.[21] In the late 1950s and early 1960s the Maryknoll Fathers arrived (from China via Ecuador) and accepted the area of Huehuetenango, the Sacred Heart Fathers from Spain went to Quiché, the Belgian Sacred Heart of Mary Congregation went to the south coast, and American Benedictines went to Alta Verapaz. Initially they adopted a more or less traditional style of "missionary" apostolate, living in central towns and circuit-riding the outlying areas. The Maryknoll Fathers brought the experience of training "catechists" from China and the Andes. In the early and mid-1960s other, younger generations of priests arrived, bringing the new ideas and questions emerging from Vatican II. The arrival of many priests from other countries perhaps accentuated a chronic problem, the lack of Guatemalan vocations to the priesthood. Only 15 or 20 percent of the clergy is Guatemalan.

A measure of the growth of Catholic institutions was the burgeoning of Catholic schools, which by 1968 numbered 160 with an enrollment of over 41,000 students. Over half of these were in the capital city. By this time over

20 percent of high school students were in Catholic schools. In general these institutions were serving urban elites, but an important exception was those schools aimed at developing leadership among Indians, such as those started by Maryknoll in Huehuetenango.[22]

As in neighboring countries, apostolic movements such as the Cursillos de Cristiandad, the Christian Family Movement, and, it is reported, Opus Dei were strong among the middle classes. Emerging from a group of young people who first knew each other as members of the Central American University Youth, an apostolic movement in the National University (San Carlos), the Christian Democratic Party was formed in the early 1960s. While some priests had sympathies with Christian Democratic ideas and the leaders knew some of the bishops personally, the lines between the party and the church were kept distinct. Part of the reason may have been that conservative parties such as the MLN also made overtures to the hierarchy. In the early 1960s IDESAC (Institute for Economic and Social Development of Central America) was born as a Christian Democratic spinoff, and served to some extent as its training center, gradually developing more autonomy, however. As elsewhere, Guatemalan Christian Democracy showed tensions between those who favored more radical reforms and those whose orientation was primarily anticommunist.

Social concern continued to grow even before there was a "liberation theology" to provide a theoretical basis. In the late 1950s and early 1960s the Young Christian Workers were giving leadership training to labor and peasant leaders, some of whom became militants in the CNT (National Workers Federation), which, initiated as another Christian Democratic institution in 1962, was eventually to emerge as a leading force in labor struggles.

What was to prove the most important work of the church in the 1960s and 1970s was the grassroots activity, both pastoral and social, with peasant and Indian communities in the countryside. In a number of areas foreign missionary orders began the formation of small communities with local leaders, using a variety of formulas. In Huehuetenango, as already mentioned, they were called "catechists"; on the south coast for some years Belgian priests used the "Family-of-God" method, borrowed from Panama; in Quiché, Spanish Sacred Heart priests used the name of Catholic Action. In this latter case, priests arriving from Spain in the early 1960s changed the earlier more sacramentalist notions to an approach more in line with the theology emerging from Vatican II.

By all accounts the council itself did not have a major impact on Guatemala until the period of Medellín, which in effect applied its spirit to Latin America. To take one example, the vernacular liturgy would be of only limited value to the Indian highlands if the vernacular was considered to be Spanish rather than the native languages.

During the 1960s these same foreign clergy began to be concerned about the obvious poverty of the peasants, and for some years the approach to development was through cooperatives. Again the impulse came from the Maryknoll priests, the Sacred Heart priests in Quiché, Belgian and Canadian priests in the Oriente, as well as American Benedictines in Alta Verapaz and American diocesan priests in different parishes in the area of Sololá (one of the latter started what became the cooperative with the largest investment in the country).

Cooperatives had been begun under Arbenz, and during the succeeding counterrevolutionary period it was the tactic of the government to seek to control them. Catholic priests were major factors in their promotion during the 1960s, along with Peace Corps volunteers and Christian Democrat-related organizations. By 1967 there were 145 cooperatives with a membership of over 27,000 people. The movement continued to grow, and by 1976 there were 510 cooperatives, in eight large federations, with more than 132,000 members.[23]

For most of this period the cooperative movement was viewed with suspicion by the power structure, since to some of the more ideologically fanatical it reeked of "communism." On the local level, a cooperative could be a threat to local merchants; for example, if members could get fertilizer cheaper by buying in bulk and bypassing the store altogether.

However, cooperatives had serious inherent problems. A marketing cooperative can do nothing for the landless, and not much for those who have so little land that they have little produce to sell. In fact, peasants could benefit in proportion to the land they owned, and thus cooperatives tended to favor the formation of a slightly more prosperous peasantry and to separate it from those who were poorer. In some cases, due to poor management, dishonesty, or bad luck (crop failure), cooperatives could serve to drive people further into debt. One way or another, sincere development workers, including church people, sooner or later reached the limits of cooperatives—the limits of "developmentalism."

An early case of reaching these limits (taking action prematurely, it is clear by hindsight) was the "Melville case." Sister Marian Peter had come to Guatemala in the late 1950s as a Maryknoller and through a period of several years began to move away from her original assignments in an upper-class Catholic high school, Monte María, and to become involved with the urban poor and in organizing vacation work for high school students with the rural poor. She then came into increasing contact with university students, some of whom in the mid-1960s were also in contact with the guerrillas fighting in the east.

At the same time Father Thomas Melville was working with Indians in the highlands, at first in part of Huehuetenango and then in Cabricán near Quetzaltenango. He helped to set up a local cooperative and then was part of the effort to create a national federation. As he began to see the depth of the land problem he organized a colonization project for his people in the isolated tropical lowlands of the Petén region in the north.

At the same time that Tom Melville (and his brother Art) ran into the limitations of cooperatives for solving the peasants' real problems, and as the leaders they had trained were murdered or intimidated by the power structure, Sister Marian Peter met some students connected with the guerrillas, and then the guerrilla leader Luis Turcios Lima. In 1967 the Melvilles and Sister Marian Peter concluded they should join with the guerrillas.

Events conspired to prevent these plans from being realized. In late 1967, after a meeting with some trusted church people to discuss possible ways of collaborating, word somehow got out through Maryknoll to Cardinal Casariego, who lost no time in informing the government. Their Maryknoll superiors ordered the two Melville brothers and Sister Marian Peter out of the country along with some other Maryknollers. For a short period they continued in Mexico, with some of the university students associated with them, but soon returned to the United States. There Tom and Marjorie (Sister Marian Peter) were married, became active in the anti-Vietnam War protests, and eventually went to jail for an action of pouring blood on draft files.[24]

Inevitably this episode is viewed differently from our later perspective than it was at the time. It is not clear what the Melvilles would have done had they joined with the guerrillas. Turcios Lima seems to have been interested in the possibilities of alliance with church people. One writer found another guerrilla leader, César Montes, carrying around a copy of Pope Paul VI's encyclical *Populorum Progressio*.[25] The Melvilles and Sister Marian Peter undoubtedly had in mind the example of Camilo Torres, killed in combat just a year and a half before. Part of their motivation seems to have been the desire to have a Christian presence in the guerrilla movement.

Actually, however, by 1967 the guerrillas had passed their peak. They were soon to be almost annihilated militarily. Most important, their rural presence was concentrated in a few areas of the east, and was virtually nil in the Indian highlands. In other words, there was almost no connection between the grassroots work being done under church auspices and the guerrilla movement. Hence, while the Melvilles in their analysis and motivations were similar to those who have become radicalized in recent years, the circumstances were entirely different. Their action may be viewed as either "ahead of its time" or "premature."

For years afterward the "Melville case" signified to both the government and the oligarchy the dangers in the church. For example, at one cabinet meeting the expulsion of all Maryknollers was discussed. Inevitably, all church people engaged in social action came under suspicion.

One further incident, shortly after the expulsion of the Melvilles, may be briefly mentioned here. In March 1968 Archbishop Mario Casariego was "kidnapped" in an operation that at first was made to seem the work of leftist guerrillas. Subsequently it was generally seen to be a clumsy attempt on the part of the right to provoke some kind of uprising, similar to the public reactions when Archbishop Rossell had been threatened during the 1950s. However, there was no public reaction, since Casariego inspired no affection from most people. Vice-President Clemente Marroquín Rojas called it a "self-kidnapping" in his newspaper. Although the incident always remained somewhat obscure, it seems to have been partly a reflection of factional disputes within the government and political parties.[26]

In the late 1960s a great deal of creative pastoral activity was taking place. One sign was the existence of many training centers around the country, such as the Center for Integral Development in Huehuetenango, retreat houses in Escuintla and Lake Panajachel, and radio stations with educational programs. However, pastoral agents were becoming increasingly concerned about a number of recurring problems: (1) the lack of communication and coordination between these efforts; (2) the almost total lack of response to the repression and violence; and (3) the preponderance of foreign clergy.

For a period of time there were meetings to work out a *pastoral de conjunto* (coordinated pastoral work) with workshops given by outside experts such as Canon Boulard and Father Edgard Beltrán of CELAM. In one of these meetings 1,200 people participated, yet Cardinal Casariego sought to ignore its conclusions and told a representative from the meeting, "Only God and the pope can give me orders." Such an attitude from the cardinal eventually frustrated those who were striving to bring together the clergy and religious (who were widely dispersed geographically and separated by nationality, training, and experience). People continued to work largely in isolation.

Similarly it seems clear that the machinations of Cardinal Casariego prevented the Guatemalan Bishops Conference, which was just beginning to function as such, from taking any clear stand vis-à-vis the violence unleashed in the name of "counterinsurgency."[27] In May 1969 the bishops published a pastoral letter urging Catholics to vote and even saying that abstaining can be a grave transgression. Although the bishops criticized some of the abuses of elections (pressuring people to vote for a particular party), they did not question the legitimacy of the electoral process in the specific context of Guatemala, so that in the concrete they were seen as supporting the process that elected General Arana to the presidency.[28]

Routinely the deliberations of the Guatemalan Bishops Conference were reported to the government by Casariego and other bishops; hence those who might want to voice criticism would scarcely dare to do so. On one occasion, when a pastoral letter made some mention of violence, President Arana remarked that it was not as strong as the draft version—which he had seen shortly after the bishops themselves saw it.

In February 1971 the bishops wrote a message whose title conveys its general tone: "We Reject Violence in All Its Forms."[29] With no elements of analysis that might indicate causes, the bishops lamented "the blood spilt in this senseless struggle" (even though by this time there was little violence from the guerrillas). It was a plea for constructive action toward development, but scarcely a clear denunciation of the Arana-directed repression then in full swing. Moreover, the bishops made no major statement on social problems for several years thereafter.

Toward the end of 1971 a group of Catholics and Protestants—priests, pastors, and bishops—made a statement urging an end to the state of siege. Accusing the signatories of being involved in politics the government expelled the foreigners (including Episcopal Bishop William Frey), threatened and warned Guatemalans (Catholic Bishop Gerardo Flores left the country for a period), and told the Bishops Conference to watch over priests.[30]

In 1969 a group of priests, indignant over the elevation of Casariego to the cardinalate, had formed COSDEGUA (National Council of Priests of Guatemala). While this group initially seemed to be a vehicle for rallying Guatemalan priests and resembled priests groups springing up elsewhere in Latin America, it soon became embroiled in what was more a personal battle between José María Ruiz Furlán ("Padre Chemita"), its flamboyant leader, and the cardinal. COSDEGUA rapidly became more a personal vehicle of Ruiz Furlán than an expression of a voice within the church.

In these three problem areas—the lack of national pastoral communication and coordination, the lack of a strong voice of denunciation, and the lack of a strong Guatemalan clergy—much of the responsibility was seen to rest with Cardinal Casariego. Regarding the latter point, for example, it was his consistent policy not to send priests for study abroad, except perhaps to study canon law.

Scarcely noticed during this time, but ultimately of great importance, were some instances of pastoral work in the northern colonization areas of Quiché and Huehuetenango and in the part of Quiché around Nebaj. In the early 1970s Father William Woods of Maryknoll organized a colonization project for some 2,000 families in Ixcán Grande, and at the same time a Sacred Heart priest, Luis Gurriarán, who spurred the cooperative movement, was helping to organize a similar project in an adjoining area to the east. This was a tropical lowland area, three or four days by foot from the nearest roads, and at first the colonists simply had to fight the normal problems of isolation and the government bureaucracy. Woods was a pilot and was able to fly in essential supplies and fly out people with medical or other emergencies, and also some of their products. However, the lands were in the Northern Transversal Strip, near the site of oil exploration, and the colonizers would soon become the object of army suspicion, harassment, and then attack.

The Ixil people living around the towns of Nebaj, Chajul, and San Juan Cotzal in the department of Quiché seem somewhat different from other Indian groups. They have a very independent spirit, and, in fact, there were three Ixil uprisings, two during the time of the dictator Ubico and one in 1971. In this last incident 18 were left wounded and the uprising was put down with the arrival of 2,000 soldiers. Contrary to what happened elsewhere, in Quiché the Ixil participated in the Arbenz land reform, and as a punishment some 500 were sent to the Petén and others were jailed or disappeared under Castillo Armas. The local power structure was made up of the descendants of a group of Spaniards who arrived in the late nineteenth and early twentieth centuries and built up their fortunes as contractors for Indian labor. Some families having acquired the original wealth in this way went elsewhere, for instance, the Botrán family, the leading manufacturer of rum. Others have remained and not only have economic power as landholders, storeowners, and loan sharks, but also wield political power.

Like Indians elsewhere, the Ixil people felt increasing pressures as the available land shrank. At first they thought the lands to the north in Quiché (which they regarded as ancestrally theirs) and even the Petén would be available, but as the government asserted control with its own colonization plans, they felt increasing desperation.

Into this context stepped one of the Sacred Heart priests, Javier Gurriarán (cousin of Luis), in the early 1970s. Until this point the Ixils had not been very receptive to overtures from pastoral workers. Gurriarán, perhaps able to profit from analyzing previous experiences, entered the area with a disposition first to learn from the people their experience and viewpoints. Gradually, working with Catholic Action and also with the traditional *cofradías*, he built up a program of local communities that used a "celebration of the Word." He found the people so reluctant to allow anyone to accumulate power that the leadership of the communities had to be rotated every six months. Another peculiarity of the Ixil was the relatively strong position of women, who had some economic power and who participated fully in community decisions (at least after they had children). Hence women entered into ministerial roles, such as carrying out the ministry to the sick, including anointing.

A measure of the seriousness of this kind of work may be the fact that leaders spent a whole day each month planning the next month's work and a week each year evaluating and planning. Eventually there were some 400 coordinators of 68 communities in the parish of Nebaj. Similar work was done in the neighboring parishes of the Ixil area.

In 1973 this work began to run up against the local power structures when the people sought to organize themselves so they would not be economically forced to supply migratory labor for the contractors. At first it seems the people saw their object as simply defending themselves from the local power structure and perhaps getting some revenge for the accumulated wrongs, but gradually they acquired a broader vision of the structural roots of their plight and the kind of struggle that would be necessary to overcome it.[31]

During this period Protestants tended to be concerned primarily with their own growth and development. As has been mentioned, President Justo Rufino Barrios invited the Presbyterians to Guatemala and the first missionary arrived in 1882, and indeed the church was given property on which a church building was erected in the shadow of the National Palace. Barrios sent his own children to a school set up by Presbyterians and urged his cabinet ministers to do the same. More generally, the Liberal reforms and their effects on the Catholic church paved the way for Protestant missionaries. In succeeding decades there arrived the Central American Mission, the California Yearly Meeting of Friends (a conservative, almost fundamentalist, yearly meeting, unlike "silent" Quakers), the Primitive Methodist Church, and the Nazarenes, all of whom reached an agreement to work in separate areas of the country, an agreement subsequently abolished by mutual consent.

Protestant growth has been extraordinary in Latin America. There were over 40,000 members in the late 1930s and 300,000 by the mid-1960s. By the end of the 1970s there were sixty-seven denominations in Guatemala, thirty-eight of which arrived during that decade, and it was calculated that 10 to 15 percent of the population was Protestant.

Protestants set up schools, and the first full hospital in Guatemala was the American Hospital, set up by the Presbyterian church. Some churches sponsored development efforts, one such being the Presbyterians' Agape program.

During the period we have been considering (until 1976) it would seem that very few Protestants were involved in social struggles. Exceptions may be mentioned: "Pascual" (nom de guerre), a Cakchikel Indian who became one of the main leaders of the Edgar Ibarra guerrilla front, was a Protestant pastor; and William Frey, expelled after the ecumenical protest over the first wave of Arana's repression, was an Episcopal bishop. For the most part, however, the Protestant sects in Guatemala tended toward an otherworldly theology that led members to see "salvation" as the only important goal, and this vision was centered on the church, rather than on the larger community. Typically, those Protestants who were radicalized by their experience ended up being estranged from their congregations.[32]

EARTHQUAKE—AND TREMORS
IN THE SOCIAL STRUCTURE (1976–78)

In the early morning hours of February 4, 1976, a series of earthquakes rocked Guatemala, and adobe structures came tumbling down, killing 22,000 people, injuring 77,000 more, and making about one million people (about one-sixth of the country) homeless. This earthquake today may be seen as the detonator of what evolved into a strong revolutionary movement.

While the area of greatest destruction and death was centered in a section of the highlands between Antigua and Tecpán, in fact there was severe destruction in a.a arc-like path that passed through the highlands, Guatemala City, and along the highway toward the Atlantic coast. More than one commentator noted that the earthquake tore back the veil to reveal the truth about Guatemala, for, despite the official rhetoric that all had suffered alike, the victims were almost exclusively the poor—killed by falling adobe and tiles. The privileged suffered at most a temporary inconvenience such as interrupted electricity or water service; the poor saw the equivalent of years of savings destroyed in a house, with no prospects for replacing it.

Early in the emergency period the Laugerud government, perhaps recognizing the damage done to Somoza by his earthquake profiteering, decided to utilize the reconstruction in order to improve its own image, tarnished by electoral fraud and routine political violence. Rather than centralize the distribution of aid from foreign governments and international agencies, it decided to serve more as a broker linking outside aid to communities. A National Reconstruction Committee, under General Ricardo Peralta Méndez, was set up and attracted well-intentioned and honest civilian administrators, so that it came to be seen as a center of reformists in a governmental structure distinguished mainly for its repression. In addition to being honest, the earthquake aid was administered with relative efficiency.

However, the problems created (or accentuated) by the earthquake went beyond good intentions. At first the international agencies assumed that the most pressing need for the victims was housing. However, the Indian peasants, seeing the May planting season coming, saw their most urgent need as fertilizer and, after erecting a temporary shelter, sought to see how they could acquire it. As the agencies began to propose various kinds of self-help housing, usually highly subsidized, but typically costing the participants around $300, the poorer peasants usually felt they could not honestly take on such a debt. The end result was that the beneficiaries of the housing programs tended to be those victims who were somewhat better off (that is, owned more land).

Some in the power structure seemed to take advantage of the post-earthquake confusion. For example, a textile factory laid off 120 workers on February 13, and on February 20, Rolando Andrade Peña, a city official in the capital, was machine-gunned to death apparently for having encouraged homeless families to squat on unused private land. In all some fifty people were killed in death-squad operations during the first month after the earthquake.[33]

Nevertheless, whether by conscious decision or not, the Laugerud government also seemed to allow for a slight political opening, and the unions in particular moved to take advantage. During the first days of the Castillo Armas government the labor movement had been largely dismantled, and ever since then it had suffered harassment and violence, especially during the Arana period. By some figures only 2 percent of the labor force was unionized in the mid-1970s, while other sources put the figure at 5 to 6 percent.

It was the Coca-Cola strike of March 1976 that proved to be the opening wedge of what became a broad opposition movement. When the management fired 154 workers to break the union, the workers decided to occupy the plant. Arriving around midnight, the police entered the plant and forcibly ejected the workers, injuring some and jailing fourteen. On March 31 representatives of the major unions and federations met and decided to form a common front, called CNUS (National Committee for Labor

Unity), deliberately taking the name of a front formed during the Arévalo period. In fact, preliminary steps had been underway since 1973. President Laugerud met with a CNUS delegation, thus in fact recognizing it, although legal recognition was never given. On April 7 the government ordered the company to rehire the workers and recognize the union. However, from that point on the union suffered direct violence from the company. Both sides (management/government and labor) saw the Coca-Cola case as being not so much over specific worker demands as over unionization itself.

On June 25 the police attacked the headquarters of the CNT, which was becoming the spearhead of the renewed labor movement. Knocking down the door with a jeep, they came in shooting and arrested some leaders. Miguel Ángel Albizúrez, the secretary-general, was able to escape over neighboring rooftops and later turned himself in accompanied by a large labor delegation and with a number of reporters on hand to record his arrest. All the labor leaders were eventually released, since the charges against them had been absurd. During 1976 there were at least twenty-five major labor conflicts involving workers in food processing, textiles, transportation, banking, and government. When hospital workers went on strike, Mario Sandoval Alarcón, the vice-president (and head of the MLN party), proposed a state of siege to deal with it. Sensing that such drastic action could hurt business, representatives of the industrial sector contacted the union leaders and urged them to accept mediation to resolve the crisis. That a simple strike should involve the vice-president and the representatives of the oligarchy indicated the underlying volatility in Guatemala.[34]

These events formed the backdrop for a pastoral letter of the Guatemalan Bishops Conference titled "United in Hope," which was in fact the most forthright hierarchical statement made up to that time. While its reference point was the earthquake and reconstruction, it was a wide-ranging statement. Early in the letter there was a commentary on social classes, which mixed moralistic and analytical notions: the "so-called upper classes" were seen as "giving in to immorality, the immoderate desire for profit, and the insatiable search for pleasure" and as having become insensitive to the poor.

Much of the vocabulary was taken from Medellín (for example, "situation of sin"). Particularly pointed was the commentary on land tenure:

> Most of the arable land is in the hands of an insignificant minority of the population, while the bulk of the peasants lack even a bit of land of their own for their crops. . . .
>
> The oligarchy, which has insistently tried to maintain its privileged situation at the expense of a whole population being marginalized, has been upset even over the few labor reforms in our laws. . . .
>
> Present legislation seems to be designed above all to defend the untouchability of private property, impeding a better distribution of land, which, we should not forget, God has given to all his children and not just to a few privileged ones.

They mentioned areas, including Nebaj, where "peasants often die for the crime of defending lands they have held peacefully for a long time." They denounced the abuse of power by officials, armed groups that kidnap and kill, government corruption, unequal application of the law, and the use of torture. They pointed to the rise of voter abstention as an indication that people no longer believed in "politics." Moving to the area of values, the bishops stated that "the humblest Guatemalan, the most exploited and marginalized, the sickest and most unlearned, is worth more than all the country's riches and his or her life is sacred and untouchable." The disregard for life was alluded to several times and was what attracted most attention. At one point the bishops noted that human life was attacked so easily and

> killing becomes a business. In fact, some think that with this crime they are doing a . . . service to their country, and even acting to defend Western Christian civilization.
> We acknowledge that God is the only Master and Lord of life.[35]

Significantly the bishops did not condemn equally the "violence of left and right," and the letter was perceived as an indictment of both the government and right-wing paramilitary groups. Appearing after years of silence on the part of the bishops, it had an immediate impact on national public opinion. Cardinal Casariego had not signed the letter—in fact, the other bishops took advantage of his absence to write it—and when he returned he gave long, rambling press conferences, which served to dilute the effect of the statement.

Pastoral agents in particular were encouraged. In some groups the text itself was studied and several groups prepared simplified, comic-book versions for use with lay groups.

It was in 1976 that the first news of conflict in the Ixcán region and in northern Quiché became public. In 1972 a small band of guerrillas, some of them survivors from one of the guerrilla fronts of the 1960s, had quietly entered the jungle region from Mexico and had begun a long apprenticeship, simply learning how to survive. Gradually they established contact with some of the very isolated Indian settlers. By mid-1975 they were ready for their first action. Luis Arenas, a landholder known in the region as the "Tiger of Ixcán," was hated because he kept Indians in virtual slavery to work his lands. On June 7 they caught him while he was paying workers and shot him. They explained this "execution" to the Indian workers present, who themselves added accounts of his cruelty from their own experience. In a neighboring village there was a celebration with two days of marimba music.[36]

Arriving in planes and helicopters the following day, the army made sweeps through the whole area. Paratroopers dropped on the communities of colonizers organized by Luis Gurriarán and Bill Woods. Thirty-seven cooperative leaders and catechists were kidnapped, apparently on the supposition that the leaders might be linked to the guerrillas. One group of twenty-eight was forced to dig its own grave. A chance survivor later said the army sought to force them to state that Gurriarán and Woods were telling the people to join the guerrillas.

The army's motives, in addition to the killing of Arenas, seem to have been a mixture of counterinsurgency (against a very small band of guerrillas, fewer than ten in 1975), protection of the oil exploration area, and protection of lands that its own officers were in the process of acquiring.

In 1976 the army began kidnapping in the area of Nebaj, Chajul, and Cotzal (in the highlands about a three-day walk south of Ixcán) and began bombing. Permanent military detachments were set up in the region, sometimes cordoning off areas the army would enter in its search for guerrilla leaders. Again the catechists were prime suspects.[37]

It is in this context that the fatal plane crash of Maryknoll Father Bill Woods should be viewed. He was clearly not a revolutionary: his whole approach had been that of the American "roll-up-your-sleeves" missionary, and he disagreed with the Melvilles' action in the 1960s. Even his colonization project in the Ixcán was considered "developmentalistic" by people with a leftist analysis.

After the earthquake Woods spent time mainly in Guatemala City, partly because he had had his pilot's license removed, clearly as a sign of the army's displeasure. One reason for this displeasure may have been his support for Ixcán peasants who had sent a protest to President Laugerud over the disappearance of their leaders. In mid-1976 the United States ambassador privately told Woods that he should leave the country, since four generals, including Romeo Lucas García, the defense minister (and next president), wanted to get rid of him. After thinking matters over and (to his surprise) being licensed to fly again, Woods decided to continue his work.

In late November he was taking four other Americans out to the cooperatives when he crashed on a hillside near the pass that leads out of the mountains toward the Ixcán lowlands. Although at the time the crash was viewed simply as an unfortunate accident, a closer look revealed numerous indications that he had been shot down. Woods himself had written to his mother that this pass would be the logical place for such an attack. The army and the Civil Aeronautics Board seemed to be engaged in a coverup, not informing Maryknoll until that night even though they knew of the crash—and the army had been at the site—since the morning. Government reports were contradictory, at first blaming the crash on the weather, even though it was a clear day. Neither the United States embassy nor the Guatemalan government was helpful to an independent American investigator. While some other explanations are conceivable—a sudden heart attack, or the explosion of a tank of compressed gas that Woods was carrying—all signs indicate that Woods was the first of a string of priest-martyrs, and his passengers the unfortunate victims.[38]

HUMAN RIGHTS AND SIGNS OF STRUGGLE

When the new Carter administration made "human rights" one of its key points, Guatemala, along with El Salvador and other Latin American governments, rejected United States military aid rather than subject itself to human rights scrutiny. (However, the Guatemalan government had about $15 million in unused credits it could draw on.) Relations between the State Department and the Guatemalan military cooled.

The Guatemalan power structure felt quite confident in 1977 as coffee prices shot up due to the frost in Brazil. While some of the profits went to higher taxes and some to speculators (exporters who deal in futures) the 300 families who own half the coffee production contemplated the prospects of many extra millions of dollars. Another source of optimism was the earthquake itself, which had drawn hundreds of millions of dollars for construction, infrastructure, and development projects. Construction boomed, and even helped ease unemployment.

However, accompanying the boom came inflation, and workers' real salaries were dropping. In fact one study showed that the average real industrial wage from 1972 to 1977 dropped from $0.39 to $0.33 an hour in real terms despite its increase in nominal terms.[39]

This was the underlying reason for increasing pressure from unions, and the growth of unions, as well as a growing coordination among them. In February workers occupied a plastics factory and were supported by other workers who came to the occupation site. During May unions denounced what they saw as a systematic plan from management and government to repress the union movement. Shortly thereafter Mario López Larrave, a leading labor lawyer, was machine-gunned to death while driving to his office. He had been instrumental in setting up CNUS and had led negotiations in many major cases, including one involving the Pantaleón sugar mill, property of the wealthy Herrera Ibargüen family. Fifteen thousand people attended López Larrave's funeral. Similarly when student leaders Robin García and Efraín Leonel Caballeros were brutally tortured and killed in August, many thousands marched in silence through downtown Guatemala City carrying red carnations.

Peasant struggles were less visible than those of the unions and student groups. In northern Quiché around the area of Chajul and Cotzal, army actions were making the people more receptive to the guerrillas, now calling themselves the EGP (Poor People's Guerrilla Army). The EGP "executed" some well-known government informers. In August a group of women came from Cotzal to the capital to protest the kidnapping of their husbands. Locally people began to organize vigilance patrols to protect against kidnapping, and by the year's end the guerrillas were no longer seen to be a small group of outsiders but to be a growing group, now composed of Ixil people themselves.

Peasants around the country were beginning to raise their voices protesting the abuses against them, such as the dangerously rickety trucks used to haul them to the coastal plantations and the exposure of cotton pickers to pesticides which produced well over a thousand cases of intoxication a year and an undeterminable number of deaths (landholders pressured doctors to give other reasons for deaths). The guerrilla groups sometimes dramatized these abuses; in November 1976 the EGP had burned some twenty crop-duster planes in one action.

In many places peasants were asserting their rights to lands, sometimes plots that they had held in their family for generations (for instance, in Santa María Xalapan in the Oriente) and sometimes they even invaded lands such as a case in Santo Domingo Suchitepequez, where they had sought in vain, for eight years, to acquire lands legally; all the government had offered was to send them to one of the colonization areas in the north. Peasants began to take de facto actions such as burning sugar-cane fields on the south coast. In one incident in San Marcos a group of 300 peasants over-powered treasury guards who were carrying off a peasant. It is significant that, although unarmed, the peasants were spontaneously fighting back against established authority.[40]

Many of these struggles converged late in the year around the march of the miners of Ixtahuacán who were working under very dangerous condi-tions with very low wages, while the owners of the mine, an oligarchical family (Abularach), were making a fortune. In order to dramatize their plight they determined to march from Ixtahuacán, Huehuetenango, near the Mexican border to the capital. A leader of the march was CNT organi-zer Mario (Wiwi) Mujía, who for years had worked at the Maryknoll Center for Integral Development in Huehuetenango.

At first the government sought to stop the march with threats, but the imagination of the country had been ignited. Peasants and others came to the roadside to cheer the miners on and give them food. They stayed at churches and received other voluntary hospitality during the nine days of the march. In the meantime, workers who had been fired from the Panta-león sugar mill had marched from the south coast and joined the Indian miners on the outskirts of the capital. Together with student and labor groups they entered the capital and were greeted by an estimated 100,000 people. Such a reaction was to some extent simply a spontaneous feeling for the underdog. At the same time it showed that, given a chance, ordinary people would repudiate violence and injustice.

On the last day of the year the EGP kidnapped Roberto Herrera Ibar-güen, the most prominent member of the Herrera family, the wealthiest in Guatemala (and owners of the Pantaleón sugar mill). Through January 1978 they held him captive and forced the government to publish lengthy communiqués detailing both Herrera's involvement in violence (thus un-dercutting sympathy for an "innocent" victim) and the EGP's analysis of Guatemalan society and proposal for popular struggle. After these com-muniqués and a ransom payment, Herrera was released unharmed. By comparison the actions of other guerrilla groups at this time seemed to be limited to small actions such as setting off propaganda bombs, which scattered leaflets and served to establish a certain presence.

As Laugerud's presidency neared its end the problem of succession appeared again. The question was whether, given Lauguerud's attempt at a relative "opening," a moderate reform candidate might be allowed to win. General Ricardo Peralta Méndez, the candidate for the Christian Democrats, bearing in mind what had happened to Ríos Montt in 1974, was very cautious and sought to assure the military that he could be trusted. The official candidate was General Romeo Lucas García, a landholder and defense minister, who chose as his running mate Francisco Villagrán Kramer, an intellectual, to give some substance to the claim that his candidacy was "center-left." Because voters were either apathetic or opposed to the election—63 percent of the electorate abstained—it seems the MLN party candidate may have received the largest number of votes (not necessarily out of agreement with its right-wing ideology but simply because the party is well organized around the country). Only after a clumsily engineered fraud and the threatened use of troops was the army able to assure a Lucas victory. Apprehensive as they were, people could not imagine the terror that the next four years would bring.

Church participation in these events was not highly visible. In early 1977 Cardinal Casariego sent a private letter to all the priests of his archdiocese warning them not to become involved in politics, lest there happen in Guatemala what was happening in El Salvador.

There was in fact an almost total lack of coordination and mutual help among pastoral agents. The Guatemalan Bishops Conference said nothing of consequence, and there was no organized way in which people from different areas could come in contact. There were, however, informal contacts such as through religious orders. One example was a small community of Jesuits (called the "Zone 5 community" from the working-class neighborhood they lived in) who were in contact with different people in the church from bishops to sisters and priests, to lay peasants and union leaders, journalists, and intellectuals. Another informal means of contact was the magazine *Diálogo* edited by Julia Esquivel, who had received biblical training at a Protestant seminary and worked with church groups. However, there was neither a way for church people from different areas to meet nor any voice of the church in the country, capable, for example, of raising human rights concerns.

One more illustration of the hierarchy's contradictions came prior to the election of March 1978. For almost a year the bishops had wanted to prepare a letter on the topic of faith and politics as a follow-up to "United in Hope." The text had been prepared and approved in the cardinal's absence; when he returned, he made numerous textual changes through an auxiliary bishop. Bishop Manresa of Quetzaltanango, chagrined at the changes (the Bishops Conference required unanimity), decided that the text should not be published because the emendations changed the overall meaning of the text, from one of raising critical questions about the election, to one supporting the "civic duty of voting responsibly and freely"—and thus in fact supporting the process by which the army would transfer power.

On his own authority the cardinal then had the text with emendations published in a Sunday newspaper as the "catechesis" of the bishops. Seven of the bishops were furious with this manipulation and change of meaning of a document they had worked on, but their only response was to read the original version in their dioceses.[41] From that point on, these bishops began to make representation to the Vatican about Cardinal Casariego's actions, but to little avail.

OPEN CONFLICT (1978–82)

At this point, coinciding with the election and inauguration of General Romeo Lucas to the presidency, events in Guatemala began to move with a rapidity and intensity similar to periods of greatest conflict in Nicaragua and El Salvador. The army, the real arbiter of events, had decided that Laugerud's relative "opening" had failed and that a stronger hand in dealing with the opposition, particularly from labor unions and restless peasants, as well as the guerrilla movements, was needed. It is unclear to what extent the way this decision was carried out was due to the particular influence of Lucas and his circle in the army and to what extent it was the action of the army as an institution. That Lucas did not enjoy unanimous support became evident when some officers began to complain of corruption and eventually overthrew him in March 1982.

Three developments in the early months of 1978, before the watershed event of the Panzos massacre, deserve mention here. First, in March the CNT broke with CLAT (Latin American Trade Union Confederation), the continental umbrella organization of those unions with a Christian Democratic orientation. What precipitated the break was CLAT's criticism of CNT's alliances with other unions, especially those with Marxist orientation. CLAT has consistently stood ostensibly for a "Third Way" between capitalism and communism; its critics charge that in a capitalist system such a stand inevitably weakens overall labor unity and amounts to supporting existing capitalism. In the Guatemalan case it signified that a labor movement that began with Christian Democrats, and many of whose leaders had originally emerged from Catholic Action, in a crisis took its stand with larger union solidarity.

A second development was the emergence of CUC (Committee for Peasant Unity), which soon became the largest peasant organization in Guatemala and a major protagonist in the struggle. From its inception CUC, owing to the conditions of repression in Guatemala, operated in a semiclandestine manner; for example, its leadership was collective and decentralized, and its leaders did not appear openly in public, nor were their names listed. CUC represented the outgrowth of several years of work in the countryside (especially Quiché and Chimaltenango) done by a group of young people during their university days in the early and mid-1970s. Most of these were active Christians, and from the beginning CUC had close ties to pastoral agents and found in church-related groups its normal starting point.

As its name implies the Committee for Peasant Unity began not as a new organization to rival or supplant others, but as an attempt to unify existing peasant organizations in a more militant way. One may speculate that to some extent the CUC organizers took into account the experience in El Salvador (FECCAS-UTC, leading to the formation of the BPR) and the role of Delegates of the Word there. CUC's first public appearance was in the May 1, 1978, demonstration wherein for the first time a large group of peasants (almost 1,000) marched along with other sectors. In that demonstration CUC marchers drew attention to the plight of 40,000 peasant families whose water supply was endangered by a private company, Aguas, S.A., which proposed to divert water from ten rivers to supply the capital.[42]

A third and somewhat parallel development was the appearance of the Committee for Justice and Peace. Throughout 1977 groups of lay people and pastoral agents, increasingly frustrated with the hierarchy's virtual silence, had been discussing alternate forms of giving voice to the church. In the course of these discussions a group of people in the capital, mainly lay, began to emerge as an incipient human rights commission. Formal meetings began in January 1978, and a group of roughly a dozen members laid down guidelines for the activity of the committee, which would include denouncing human rights violations, aiding Christian communities to link to those who might supply needed services (such as union or peasant-league organizing, legal advice, or even medical aid), and elaborating an ongoing theological reflection. While it regarded itself as supplying what the hierarchy had not been able to do, the group wished to be at the disposal of at least some of the bishops and would have been open to becoming recognized as a Pontifical Justice and Peace Commission. Events were soon to close off the possibility of any official relation to the hierarchy and to propel it far beyond the original human rights-commission model of organization and activity.

In late 1977 CELAM had released what came to be called the "Green Document," intended as the background material for the coming CELAM conference at Puebla (at that point still scheduled to be held in 1978). As its first activity the Pro-Justice and Peace Committee (as it called itself reflecting its provisional status) arranged a conference of pastoral agents and representatives of Christian communities to supply grassroots input into Puebla.

On Monday, May 29, 1978, however, there occurred the Panzos massacre, which was the real starting point for many further developments. Initially a brief army communiqué indicated that thirty-four Indians had died when a crowd had attacked an army garrison. Because of the relative isolation of Panzos it was several days before the full story began to arrive at the capital.

The root problem in Panzos was the encroachment of local landowners on lands traditionally held and worked by Kekchi Indians. Tensions had been building, a fact noted in the newspaper three weeks previously. Two days before the massacre, employees from Agrobón, the farming subsidiary of EXMIBAL, the nickel operation that was further down the road, shot from a pickup truck and wounded seven peasants in the area near Panzos. On Monday morning, May 29, a group of several hundred peasants assembled, having been summoned by the mayor. The local army detachment had been reinforced and some landholders were on hand, heavily armed. What provoked the outbreak is not clear, but at a certain moment the soldiers (and landholders) began shooting and the Indians, including men and women, fled, some drowning in the river. Subsequent investigations revealed that over 100 people died.

As details came in, Panzos became the subject of much commentary—although reporters were not allowed on the scene for several days and then only on government-arranged trips. Newspapers were careful not to contradict the army's version, but they did allow protest statements from dozens of groups to be placed as paid advertisements.

Participants in the Justice and Peace meeting, convened originally to discuss Puebla issues, listened as a priest from the diocese of Cobán presented one of the early accounts of what had really occurred. Justice and Peace then made its own protest statement. In response a government spokesman called it a "phantom group." Several days after the massacre CNUS organized a protest march in which tens of thousands participated. In the march was a delegation about a half-block long from Justice and Peace: sisters, priests, students, parish groups, and individuals who felt more comfortable marching under the church's banner than under that of a militant organization. Although two bishops had made an appearance at the meeting and its conclusions seem to have influenced a pre-Puebla document prepared by Guatemalan Bishops Conference, by participating in the protest march Justice and Peace became further removed from the bishops. During the furor over Panzos, the government expelled Sor Alonso Queralt, a Spanish nun doing pastoral work in the same diocese, for involvement in politics, although it offered no evidence for the charge.[43]

On the day before Lucas's inauguration, Father Hermógenes López, a fifty-year old Guatemalan priest, was machine-gunned to death in the town of San José Pinula, where he was pastor. López had supported the efforts of the people in their struggle against the company that was seeking to divert their water supply and had protested the army's forced recruitment of peasant youth. In what seemed an extraordinary display of naiveté, two days before the inauguration he had taken out a small advertisement in a newspaper, praising President Laugerud for what he had done and urging him to disband the army—since that was what the people really wished. Christian groups, and particularly Justice and Peace, protested López's murder—in contrast to Cardinal Casariego, who made no public protest.

In July Mario Mujía, a CNT labor organizer and a main force in the march of the Indian miners in Ixtahuacán the previous November, was machine-gunned in Heuheutenango and died after three days of agony. "Wiwi," as he was known to friends, had had close ties to many pastoral agents and church-related organizations, particularly through the Center for Integral Development in Huehuetenango, where he had been a development worker for several years. He was another martyr, less than a month after the killing of López. It began to seem as though the main occasions for Christian liturgy would be murders and massacres.

In early August CNUS sought to have a demonstration honoring Mujía and also the anniversary of the murder of labor lawyer Mario López Larrave. The government demanded that the organizers apply for a permit. Arguing that peaceful demonstration was a constitutionally guaranteed right and fearing the establishment of a precedent, the organizers did not ask for a permit. Riot police attacked the demonstration, throwing tear gas and swinging clubs; 31 people were hospitalized and the Red Cross treated over 200. This attack signaled the end of the regime's tolerance for demonstrations except those traditionally held on May 1 and October 20.

The new regime's main lines soon became clear. Lucas himself had large landholdings, owning some 79,000 acres near the Northern Transversal Strip, which area, not surprisingly, was soon declared the government's "number-one priority." He was surrounded by other officers intent on quick wealth.

To the extent the government developed a plan, it tended to be centered on infrastructure projects, which undoubtedly offered opportunities for kickbacks, rather than on projects aimed at meeting the basic needs of the poor. Four of the cabinet ministers were military officers (Defense, Education, Finance, and Foreign Affairs), and the founder of the Chamber of Agriculture was made minister of agriculture and could accordingly have little sympathy for subsistence peasants. As head of the police, Lucas appointed Colonel Germán Chupina, who had been Arana's chief assistant during the 1966–68 "pacification" and had close ties with the agroexport and business elites. Police, including the *judiciales* (plainsclothesmen) were brought under much closer control by the army.

People in government and the power structure were undoubtedly becoming nervous over what had been happening in Nicaragua (the killing of Chamorro and its aftermath, and then the August taking of the National Palace and the September uprisings) and El Salvador. Their fears were realized in October with the spontaneous resistance in the capital when busfares were raised from five to ten cents—a 100 percent increase, which would severely affect families with children who had a daily bus ride to school and whose budgets were tight. Protesters blocked car traffic and used barricades to stop buses. High school students piled school desks as barricades and factory workers, women market vendors, and even bank employees lent support. Police attacked with tear gas, and armed men in unlicensed pickups (presumed to be plainsclothes police) shot at random into crowds. At one point crowds set fire to restaurants belonging to a fried-chicken chain because they believed Somoza was one of the main owners.

At the end of the week of violence, at least 30 people were dead, 300 wounded, and 800 jailed; the loss to business was estimated to be about $4 million. The busfare was held at five cents. The busfare unrest revealed that people were ready to protest and were kept from doing so only by repressive force.

Not all the violence during the controversy was random. Two union leaders were gunned down during this period and the police seemed particularly intent on breaking a public-employee union, which had organized a series of strikes around election time. When a city councilman changed his position on the busfare, there was an attempt on his life, and when René de León, the Christian Democratic leader, said the president and the minister of defense were responsible for repression, an attempt was made on his life.

Before the controversy had subsided the ESA (Secret Anticommunist Army) published its first death list, which included thirty-eight names (largely union leaders, but also university professors, journalists, and others). Subsequent information supported the initial suspicion that the ESA was in no sense an organization outside the government but simply a tactic of the police. Two days after the first list, Oliverio Castañeda, a student leader whose name was on the list, addressed a rally in downtown Guatemala City, at the end of the traditional October 20 demonstration. As he was leaving, he was gunned down by a hit squad, about 100 yards from the presidential palace, with hundreds of onlookers. This style of assassination—which flaunted the perpetrators' assurance that no police or army forces would interefere—soon became a characteristic of the Lucas regime. The killers' cars had been seen driving around the square during the demonstration. When another student leader, Antonio Ciani, "disappeared" after being picked up by the police, Lucas accused the university students themselves, saying they wanted martyrs.

This whole period was characterized by an assault on labor-union leadership, particularly of the CNT, for example, the assassination of Pedro Quevedo y Quevedo of the Coca-Cola union. In addition students, teachers, and journalists were all killed or intimidated. A statistical study showed that the numbers of political killings and/or kidnappings went up from 374 to 505 from the first half to the second half of 1978 (that is, from Laugerud to Lucas), an increase of 33 percent. However, if the Panzos massacre were to be excluded as atypical, the increase in "everyday" violence went up a striking 84 percent. Kidnappings increased 72 percent and torture and/or mutilation increased 152 percent.[44] These figures seemed to evidence a policy decision, coincident with the Lucas regime.

Guerrilla actions during this period were still at a low level, consisting mainly of propaganda actions, a few "executions" of government informers, and ambushes of army patrols. The most notable action was the EGP's killing of the Nicaraguan ambassador, who was also an ex-police chief of Managua.[45]

There was little specific participation of church people during these months, but rather, Justice and Peace took its position along with other organizations. After the August 4 demonstration, when Justice and Peace defended the constitutional right to demonstrate, the government threatened to investigate the group.

In December Father Carlos Stetter, a German priest who was serving the peasant cooperatives in the Ixcán, was expelled from the country. By all accounts Stetter was not in any sense politicized. The army apparently considered any priest in the Ixcán to be undesirable, because he might be a witness to repression there.

Fear of Revolutionary Contagion

All the elements present during the beginning of the Lucas period continued during 1979. In public discourse the dominant topic during 1979 was Nicaragua, which was seen as more important than any domestic Guatemalan issue. During Somoza's final months he and his representatives met with Lucas and other representatives of the Guatemalan government, and it seemed that Guatemala might intervene (it did so unofficially and with a small number of troops). After Somoza's fall government and business representatives insisted that Guatemala was different since it had a strong economy and elected governments. Clearly, however, such assurances were motivated by the growing feeling that revolution in Guatemala was not unthinkable.

The numbers of victims of repression grew, and it became increasingly clear that terrorism was a routine instrument of the army and the police. A study of political violence based on information from newspapers showed the following rate of increase:

January–June 1978 (Laugerud)	62 victims per month
July–December 1978 (Lucas)	84 victims per month
January–December 1979 (Lucas)	114 victims per month

The overwhelming majority of these victims were the poor: only about a dozen were categorized as "large landowners, industrialists, or big businessmen." Twenty soldiers, 27 police, 11 bodyguards, and 23 *comisionados militares* (local reservists who serve as informers) were killed, out of a total of 1,371 victims. In 201 cases victims were kidnapped, in 434 cases there was mention of torture and/or mutilation, and in 483 cases the bodies were reported as "unidentified." Often these killings were attributed to a "death squad,'' frequently with the indication that the victims were criminals, but this seems to have been partly a way of covering the more directly political reason for killing.[46]

As revealing as the increase in numbers was the kind of people killed. In January Alberto Fuentes Mohr, the head of the Social Democratic party and a distinguished Guatemalan intellectual, diplomat, and congressman, was assassinated. Two months later Manuel Colóm Argueta, easily Guatemala's most popular politician, was gunned down in a similar manner by a hit squad on a busy thoroughfare early in the afternoon. (The EGP later claimed that General Cancinos directed this operation from a helicopter.) The cynicism in these killings appeared in that both men's parties were in the process of becoming legalized to run in elections. The message was clear: not even immense popularity and international contacts would afford protection, and no serious proposals for change could take place through electoral mechanisms. Subsequently members of both these men's parties (PSD—Social Democratic Party; FUR—United Revolutionary Front) were under threat and dozens of them were murdered during the next two years.

The assault on labor continued as a number of labor leaders were killed and others were intimidated with further death lists or assassination attempts. In fact, by mid-1979 ordinary strikes became almost impossible to carry out, and legal union activity became less and less relevant. Students, both university and high school, came under attack. Journalists were assassinated; others had to leave the country; one newspaper, *Nuevo Diario*, which in a mild way had sought to maintain certain standards of journalism, was forced to sell to an ex-government official. As always the largest number of victims were the peasants.

Despite the Carter administration's profession of concern for human rights, little was done by the United States government. Relations between the two countries lapsed into a cool formality, as United States attention, to the extent it turned to Central America, was fixed on Nicaragua.

In February 1979 a large number of organizations—labor unions, student groups, shantytown-dweller associations, peasant organizations, with some professional organizations (and soon to be joined by FUR and PSD)—all spearheaded by CNUS, formed the FDCR (Democratic Front against Repression). Although it was not a political front offering to be the basis of a new government, the FDCR expressed an aspiration for unity and pointed toward such a political front. Its main activities were the organization of such demonstrations as were permitted and statements protesting acts of repression.

The most important new development during 1979 was the emergence of the guerrilla organizations as a mass-based challenge to the regime. In January the EGP occupied the town of Nebaj for a whole Sunday morning. Most of the occupiers were not university-trained outsiders but Indians, men and women, from the region itself; the Indians wore the distinctive dress of the locale. In subsequent weeks and months the EGP made dozens of such occupations. It became clear that it had a large base of support from the people of the region. On one occasion a group of Kaibiles (Guatemala's "special forces") arrived one day in Nebaj. An officer spotted two Indians sitting down and asked them to help carry the Kaibiles gear into the military base and bragged about how the government had sent them out since they were specialists and were going to get the guerrillas in a certain place. After complying, the Indians went back to sitting down as though they had nothing better to do. Then they slowly walked off—to tell the EGP.

In mid-1979 ORPA (People-in-Arms Organization) made its first announced attacks and soon was operating in the Indian highlands. This group's core seems to have been made up of survivors of the 1960s, guerrillas from what had been called the Regional del Occidente. These people seem to have spent years reflecting on the experience of the 1960s and silently rebuilding. When they reemerged, they had strong roots in the Indian highlands. The guerrilla groups continued to carry out propaganda actions and "executions," the most noteworthy of which was the EGP's killing of General Cancinos. The kidnapping of a member of the wealthy García Granados family (closely connected with Lucas) gave the EGP the opportunity to disclose its thinking to the public with a long communiqué. What is most important is that toward the end of 1979, the guerrillas were moving from purely defensive actions to increasing military engagement with the Guatemalan army.

There were few open controversies involving the church as such during 1979. A post-Puebla statement by the Guatemalan bishops on violence was scarcely noticed. Father Gregorio Barreales was expelled from the country for alleged subversive activities, and Bishop Flores warned that people should stay calm because "we're in a country where nothing is respected and it seems everything is solved with arms."

At midyear Bishop Luis Manresa of Quezaltenango resigned his diocese. It was widely rumored that in fact he had presented the Vatican with an ultimatum—either remove Cardinal Casariego or accept my resignation—and that he was backed by six other bishops. (The same group had protested Casariego's changes in the pastoral letter prior to the 1978 elections.) Somewhat to their chagrin the Vatican accepted Manresa's resignation. (Other versions saw the resignation as due to death threats, although in fact Manresa had not been outspoken.)

In October when a group of peasant laborers on a coffee plantation occupied a church to dramatize their situation, they were expelled by police and one of their leaders was later found dead. It seems quite clear the pastor had called the police. While Cardinal Casariego criticized the occupation and insisted that the church was a "house of prayer where people should ask for the grace they need to save their souls," CONFREGUA (Conference of Religious of Guatemala) made a statement condemning the "sacrilegious profanation" of the church by security forces and the profanation of the "living temples," which all Guatemalans are. The police action—and the cardinal's statement—were probably intended to discourge any further occupations of churches as had occurred frequently by this time in El Salvador. A number of pastoral agents and religious orders, particularly the Jesuits, were regularly receiving public accusations and private threats.[47]

Throughout 1979 the Justice and Peace Committee was expanding its activity. Early in the year it held a retreat-and-reflection session wherein it was clear that the group was more a network of pastoral agents and Christian communities than a human rights commission. There was a concerted effort to set up local committees in the major departments, and to decentralize work away from the capital city. At times the commission provided help to some bishops. Increasingly Justice and Peace participants were asking themselves just what the organization was. In many respects it operated like a popular organization: it analyzed events, produced communiqués denouncing injustice, helped to involve people in the struggle for justice, had marched in demonstrations, was a member of the FDCR, and had to utilize the same kinds of security measures used by popular organizations (care with phone calls, meeting in different places, constant checking for surveillance). Yet Christians were not a "sector" (like peasants, workers, or students). Moreover, it could be asked whether, as the conflict deepened, Justice and Peace would come to make alliances with one or other revolutionary organizations, or whether it was not simply a place where Christians could meet for support and prayer with each person carrying out his or her options as seemed best. In other words, what was the specific characteristic that would distinguish Justice and Peace from the popular organizations and what should be the practical consequences?

Such questions were put aside for some time during a crisis in early 1980, which, in retrospect, seems to have marked the point of no return.

The Spanish Embassy Occupation and Attack

Since 1976 the area of Quiché had been under increasing army repression, and by 1979 dozens of leaders had been kidnapped or killed. In September 1979 a delegation of Indians went to the capital, attempting to bring their protest to public attention, and were rudely treated in Congress (but managed to have a message read there). Around this time the areas of Chajul, Cotzal, Nebaj, and Uspantán came under virtual army occupation. Even the amount of corn women brought to the local mill was counted (to make sure no families were consuming unusual amounts—which might be going to guerrillas) and women were tortured if they could not say exactly where their husbands were. Guerrilla intelligence detected a major army campaign coming and warned the people.[48]

In mid-January 1980 a large group of Ixil people again came from Quiché to the capital and, camping at the university, contacted media and schools in order to present their case to the public. At one point they attended a session of Justice and Peace and at another a Mass of solidarity was celebrated with them. They spent a few minutes at the Colegio Belga, a Catholic girls school, until the sisters, despite their sympathy for their cause, asked the peasants to leave. Nevertheless, on television that night the head of the plainclothes police accused the sisters of hosting a communist meeting.

Finally, on January 31, some twenty-three peasants, with five labor and university leaders, entered the Spanish embassy and occupied it. Among the occupiers were many who had been involved with the church, for example, catechists such as Vicente Menchú, who was over sixty years old. Máximo Cajal, the ambassador, who was meeting with a former vice-president and a former foreign minister of Guatemala, said he would meet with the occupiers. (In fact, he had some sympathy with them, since he had recently been visiting Spanish priests in Quiché and had heard their story.) The occupiers' demand was that a commission of respected people, not identified with any political group, go to Quiché to investigate their claims.

Meanwhile several hundred police arrived and surrounded the embassy, which was located in an upper-middle-class district. Cajal and the two Guatemalan former officials used a megaphone to warn the police that the embassy enjoyed diplomatic immunity and that they should not intervene. However, at around 2 P.M. the police broke in downstairs, at which point the occupiers took the two Guatemalans and the embassy employees as hostages to a room on the second floor. The ambassador continued to protest. Finally, at around 3 P.M., the police attacked the room from balconies and from a skylight overhead. There were shots and soon an explosion, and the room with the occupiers and hostages was ablaze. Police stood by as onlookers shouted, "Break down the door! They're burning alive!" Within minutes twenty-seven occupiers and twelve others were dead.

What caused the fire was never completely clear: the official version was that it was caused by Molotov cocktails, thrown by the demonstrators, which bounced back (the communiqué called it "self-immolation"); one newspaper report gave the impression that shots from police caused the explosion; and a third idea, that the police had incendiary bombs, gradually gained some credence. What is clear is that the attack was over the repeated protests of the ambassador, who had insisted that the embassy was Spanish territory and that progress was being made in talks with the occupiers.

The ambassador in fact proved to be a serious embarrassment, since he had escaped in a moment of confusion just before the police attack (police held him over his protests, "I'm the ambassador!" until they were persuaded by a United States embassy official on the scene to let him go). Spain broke relations and the international reaction began to pour in.

It took the government about seven hours to prepare its version of events for the public. Far from feeling chastened, however, it went on the offensive, denouncing the "terrorist" occupation on television. One peasant who had survived under the pile of bodies, Gregorio Yujá, was kidnapped from his hospital bed early the next morning; among the kidnappers hospital employees recognized two plainclothes police. That same day the two

Guatemalan dignitaries were buried with full honors, Cardinal Casariego presiding. The government insisted that the occupiers were not peasants but "terrorists" from the university, and this version gained favor in the upper classes—even though the victims' names, listed in all the newspapers, clearly showed they were Indian.

The following day labor, peasant, and student organizations prepared a funeral for some of the victims. Heavily armed police, both uniformed and plainclothes, lined the streets leading to the starting point of the procession and made threatening remarks. Just before the funeral marchers set out, two university leaders were gunned down in full sight of hundreds of on-lookers, evidently by a government hit squad. Nevertheless, the funeral march began, with tens of thousands marching and shouting, "The color of blood is never forgotten!" and other slogans. Some marchers carried red carnations.

Ambassador Cajal, meanwhile, seemed to be in danger even in the hospital with a police guard. When the United States ambassador inquired whether it might be a good idea to take him into the embassy residence, the foreign minister agreed. Members of the diplomatic corps, incensed over the original attack, indignantly refused the offer of police protection during the transfer. Subsequently Cajal left for Spain.[49] The "Spanish embassy massacre," as it was immediately called, was a watershed: from that point on it was commonly recognized that Guatemala was at war and that the struggle must go to its conclusion.

Among the many statements condemning the police attack, one was especially significant. On February 14 a group of some 200 people met secretly at the ruins of Iximché, the ancient capital of the Cakchikel Indians, near the town of Tecpán. Most were representatives from some fifteen Indian language-groups, but some came from non-Indian organizations. The "Declaration of Iximché" began with a description of events leading up to and including the embassy attack. It then pointed out that this was "not an isolated case but part of a chain of massacres" (which it listed) going back to 1524, whose explanation was simply the greed of the original invaders and their descendants. Faced with this aggression, "the Indian has never stopped struggling," and again the document listed Indian uprisings from the beginning to the present.

The declaration noted that four of the victims were Indian women who confirmed their

> courage, commitment, willingness, and heroism in the struggle for the liberation of our life, disregarding the fact that they might have to leave their parents, their husbands, and their children forever. This is not by chance, since the Indian woman always was, and is, a part of our struggle because she has always been exploited in cotton fields, sugar-cane fields, and coffee orchards, and because her dress, her language, her customs, and her very condition as a woman cause her to be discriminated against

and abused, as happens in the rapes of both married and single women, made pregnant by the army and the rich . . . all over Guatemala.

In what may subsequently be viewed as a very important statement, the signers said they had to struggle

in alliance with workers, peasants, students, shantytown dwellers, and other popular and democratic sectors and strengthen the bond of union and solidarity between Indians and ladinos, since the solidarity of the popular movement with the Indian struggle has been sealed with its life in the Spanish embassy. The sacrifice of these lives brings us closer than ever to a new society, to the dawn of the Indian.

This was the strongest and most emphatic recognition of the convergence of Indians and non-Indians made up to this point.[50]

In Uspantán, Quiché, which was occupied by 600 soldiers, the EGP in February attacked and killed 11 plainclothes police and then had a two-hour shootout with the army. At that point the army surrounded the parish compound and threw four bombs into the patio parking lot. A week later the army again surrounded the compound and machine-gunned it and threw fragmentation grenades into the patio. The next day the pastoral agents left for Guatemala city, where they continued to receive death threats. The priests left for Spain in March.

Prior to the Spanish-embassy attack, CUC had been preparing a campaign on the south coast to raise plantation wages. The legal minimum was $1.12 a day and the actual rate somewhere around $1.75 to $2.00. CUC was demanding that the basic daily wage be raised to $5.00, the amount that it calculated a minimum tortilla-and-bean diet would cost a family of five.

In mid-February CUC began its organizing on one plantation near Tiquisate, and the workers then organized commissions to go to neighboring plantations, about a half-dozen of which went on strike. At that point the workers became enthusiastic and began forming commissions on their own, commandeering plantation vehicles to extend the strike. Within days harvesting had ground to a halt on a vast portion of the agroexport belt; estimates of how many persons went on strike varied widely from 15,000 to 60,000. A group of several thousand workers gathered at one point on the highway, with an army detachment nearby and ready to shoot.

Coming in the wake of the government's hardline reaction to the Spanish-embassy occupation, this strike seemed likely to provoke more repression. In fact some leaders were killed, including one catechist. However, partly through the persuasion of some business sectors and the United States embassy, the government, out of concern for its "image," negotiated a pay raise to $3.20 per day. (In practice many plantations refused to pay the new wage.) And in order to forestall strikes in industry it posted a series of raises, making the new average daily wage $4.00. The success of the strike was a spur to further organizing and efforts at unification despite the repression.

On Sunday, March 2, 1980, the army surrounded the town of Nebaj, after people had come to the market, and forced the men to form a line to receive identification cards. The soldier assigned could not type and an estimated 3,000 people were forced to stand in line all day, in the cold and rain, hungry and frightened. The next morning the process continued. When a group of women from neighboring villages came down it was first reported that guerrillas were coming and soldiers began to prepare for combat. Two women who could not find their husbands tried to pass the army lines and tempers flared. After women threw rocks the army opened fire and an undetermined number of people were killed. The army would not let the local doctor take care of the wounded and flew the bodies off in a helicopter. When the Quiché diocese made a pronouncement the army blamed Father José María Gran, who had been a witness.[51]

It was during this period that the first signs of economic crisis began to appear in Guatemala, after strenuous efforts on the part of the oligarchy to make it appear that events in Nicaragua and El Salvador would have no effect. Some of the factors were external: the end of the post-earthquake construction boom and lower world prices for agroexports; but most were related to the regional crisis: lower demand for exports to other Central American countries, sharply reduced tourism (especially after the Spanish-embassy attack and as a result of an organized tourism boycott), and a lowered business confidence. Exchange controls were imposed in March and April, since it was estimated that over $100 million had been taken out, partly because the wealthy were nervous and partly because they could receive higher interest elsewhere, since Guatemalan interest rates were held down for political purposes.

The Assault on the Church

During the next several months repression reached a new level of intensity in the numbers of people killed and in the openness with which repression was carried out. While the attack was directed at all sectors of society, for the first time there was a systematic and virtually indiscriminate attack on church pastoral agents.

Although one of the first acts of the Lucas government was to make it clear that most demonstrations would be stopped, it had continued to tolerate the traditional May 1 and October 20 marches. Initially it seemed that the May 1, 1980, demonstration had taken place without violence—but then numerous reports of people being abducted or killed in its aftermath began to appear (for instance, two youths painting graffiti were summarily shot). The number of victims was never satisfactorily determined but it seemed to approach thirty, and some estimates were much higher.

Two of them were Father Conrado de la Cruz, a Filipino and member of the Immaculate Heart of Mary Order working in the cotton area of Tiquisate, and Herlindo Cifuentes, who was with him. Both were picked up on the streets of Guatemala City after the demonstration, which they had simply observed. Less than two weeks later, Walter Voordeckers, a Belgian of the same congregation in the neighboring parish of Santa Lucía Cotzumalguapa, was gunned down in mid-morning as he was walking between the parish house and the nearby post office.

Neither of these priests was active in any leftist organization but both were supportive of people's efforts to organize (and specifically of CUC). Their parishes were in the heart of the cotton and sugar plantation areas where the massive strike in February had paralyzed the harvest of agroexport crops. In view of what followed it must be concluded that these actions were the beginning of a direct attack on the church or on any sectors of it capable of raising any voice of protest. In comparison to El Salvador, the assault moved quickly from words to actions, and was more indiscriminate. It is conceivable that the group in power in Guatemala, again reflecting on the Salvadoran example, concluded that it would be preferable to deal vigorously with the church all at once—this was in the aftermath of the killing of Archbishop Romero.

Voices were raised in protest of these killings. The Immaculate Heart of Mary Congregation released a statement speaking of Conrado and Walter as "friends of the people, messengers of life and truth" and, speaking of their resurrection, promised that the congregation would not abandon Guatemala. For their part the Guatemalan bishops issued a statement denouncing the fact that "bands of hired assassins . . . function all over the republic . . . with impunity . . . in broad daylight." However, they were careful to denounce the violence of both "extremes."[52]

On June 4 Father José María Gran, a Spanish Sacred Heart priest in Chajul, Quiché, was returning from parish visits. He was being followed by an army helicopter (he had been accused of providing details for the Quiché diocese's denunciation of the killing in Nebaj in March). On a stretch of road leading to Chajul he was ambushed and shot in the back, along with Domingo Bats, a lay assistant. In a terse communiqué the army announced that two subversives had been killed in combat.

This time the bishops reacted vigorously with no compensatory speaking of violence on the left and the right. In the opening sentence they spoke of a "profound crisis of humanism" and immediately listed "murders, kidnappings, tortures, and even vicious desecrations of the victims' bodies." As examples of "persecution" of the church they stated:

—As we have denounced on previous occasions, there have already been numerous catechists, prayer leaders, and other Christians kidnapped, tortured, and murdered.

—We pastoral agents are continually watched, our sermons are taped, and our every activity is checked.

—In a basically Catholic country, three priests have recently been murdered and another kidnapped. Several other priests and religious are threatened with death, and others have been expelled from the country.

—For us there is special significance in the circumstances surrounding the violent death of Fr. José María Gran Cirera, S.H.M., pastor of Chajul . . . who was shot in the back as he returned home by horseback after having gone to minister to the numerous members of his parish in the remote villages accompanied only by his sacristan, Mr. Domingo Bats, also murdered.

—A part of this religious persecution is the campaign to discredit and slander certain bishops, priests, and religious, a campaign that tends to create a climate of distrust in the body of the faithful towards the legitimate pastors. This campaign has also seen the abusive manipulation of the pope's words and church documents.

—The very priests who have offered their lives as martyrs for Christ, in preaching the Gospel, have been afterwards the objects of insidious calumnies meant to blacken their obvious Christian witness.

This last note was clearly a reference to the army's claim that Gran was killed as a guerrilla in combat. The bishops stated that some "wrongly think that by encouraging and financing the persecution against Christians they are defending the integrity of the faith and driving away the dangers of communism," but warned that those who "plan and execute" murders of priests are excommunicated and that those who encourage hate campaigns could not be considered Catholics.[53]

A reflective document from Justice and Peace in this period speaks of the "blood of these martyrs" as a "seed of liberation, which will happen soon for all, due to the effort of all." However, it urges a reevaluation of methods and especially "measures of security and prevention; there is no point in being martyrs before our time; the people need servants who are living." Evangelization is seen as implying, in some cases, actually joining the people's organizations—whether both people's and armed organizations is not made clear. Several times the document urges the unity of all sectors, which would lead to the creation of a "government which . . . will give the popular and democratic sectors fundamental social and political freedoms and rights so that a process of economic transformation may be developed that will bring to an end the great misery of the people. . . ."[54]

This was a clear reference to a further evolution in the Democratic Front against Repression and the organizations making it up, which, starting with the May 1 demonstration, had been calling for the formation of a "revolutionary, popular, and democratic government." Although the language was similar to that used by the FDR, formed in El Salvador shortly before, Guatemala's FDCR was not a political front prepared to form an alternate government; nevertheless, there was a feeling in the air that such a front might soon be announced. In May FDCR representatives, including Carlos

Gallardo, a Social Democratic deputy in Congress, and Miguel Ángel Albi-zúrez and other union leaders, met with representatives from many Social Democratic parties and labor unions in Costa Rica in an international solidarity conference, and from there a delegation traveled to Latin American and European countries making known the FDCR's position and seeking support.[55] During the tour internal disagreements broke out and the aim of announcing a political front was indefinitely postponed.

Meanwhile repression reached new and unsuspected levels. On June 13 in the coastal area of Tiquisate more than 100 peasants were kidnapped by the treasury police, who arrived throwing bombs, and burst into houses claiming they were looking for arms. When they loaded the men onto trucks, the families at first believed it was simply a normal army "recruiting" operation but none was ever seen again.[56]

Then on Saturday afternoon, June 21, armed men stopping traffic broke into a meeting at the CNT headquarters and abducted twenty-seven union leaders (nine of them women, at least one pregnant). This action took place a block and a half from the headquarters of the plainclothes police (which always had guards posted at nearby intersections), two blocks from another police station, and four blocks from the presidential palace itself. It was clearly the work of government forces. None of the leaders was ever seen again.[57] The CNT closed the union headquarters a short while later. Many were now arguing that normal union activities were impossible and that other means of struggle were imperative; nevertheless the union leadership itself resisted such a conclusion, and several months of crisis ensued.

On July 14 a group of about twenty-five armed men entered the university grounds and began shooting at random at passersby and passing vehicles. Some eight students were killed and twenty-five wounded. This was the most open violation yet of traditional university "autonomy." (The previous month two government secret agents had begun shooting in the university but were overpowered by groups of students who killed one and stripped and beat the other.)

The July attack was rumored to have been made in revenge for the killing of a police chief the same morning. Not all the killing was being done by the government: guerrilla actions were increasing in the mountains and "executions" were taking place with increasing frequency in Guatemala City itself. For example, on June 20 Francisco Javier Rodas, a reserve army lieutenant and head of personnel at the Coca-Cola plant, and considered responsible for the repression of the union, was killed by the FAR (Rebel Armed Forces). The same day Edgar René Aldana, a union officer, was killed inside the plant.[58]

To attempt at this point to indicate in any detail the increase of repression would require far too much space: we are here mainly concerned with providing a background for events in the church. There was a concerted attack on peasants, union leaders, university and high school students and leaders, and journalists (an attack that will be summarized below).

In the midst of the growing violence CONFREGUA held its Second National Congress, in preparation for which it had circulated a questionnaire among all religious. The process of the meeting was largely one of reporting on the context of pastoral work in different parts of the country. The conclusion was that official violence was the most common pastoral problem, and the publicly released final statement was a short summary of the state of violence and a renewal of the dedication of the religious. They spoke of a commitment

> to make our communities, our apostolic institutions, and our parishes instruments of service for the people, homes which welcome the poor and Christian groups and which, by means of a process of conversion and in the midst of the dangers and risks of today, we are beginning to live the fraternal style of the new society which we wish to build.[59]

On the night of July 10 two men came into the parish house of another priest in Quiché, Faustino Villanueva, shot him twice in the head, and then rode off on a yellow motorcycle. Villanueva was described by those who knew him as a "typical traditional priest, humble, simple, loved, a good companion, but . . . not a man of initiatives or an organizer of people." People in the town of Santa Cruz saw the same men on the motorcycle go into a treasury police barracks an hour and a half after the killing. The next day these same two went looking for Donald McKenna, an Irish priest, and in the days following were looking for two sisters in a Dominican school.[60]

All these events came to a head in Quiché when Bishop Juan Gerardi himself was nearly ambushed. On Saturday, July 18, he called from the capital to ask a priest to say the Mass he normally said in a nearby hamlet. The priest left in a jeep:

> Five kilometers before arriving, a boy on bicycle moved out onto the road and signaled them to stop. And he told them, "Look, Father, don't go to say the Mass because my father and the directors of the Christian community sent me because they have seen armed people who have been going around asking when the Bishop arrives to say mass and after that they went down to the bridge and now they are about a kilometer from there waiting to kill you."
> Then Father Fernando returned with the two priests who accompanied him and found that the bishop had already returned and he told him what had happened. Father Fernando was telling the bishop when an agent of the police of El Quiché came and asked, "Listen, Father, what's happening today that you are not going to say Mass in San Antonio?" The priest replied that he would not be able to this day. And the police insisted, "You have to go to say Mass in San Antonio. If you are afraid, we can take you in the police car. We'll take you." The thing was so crude that the bishop decided to get out of there and went to sleep at

Chichicastenango. The same individuals, on the same yellow motorcycle, arrived in Quiché to look for him.

The next day, the nineteenth of June, the bishop called the priests and all the pastoral agents who worked in El Quiché and told us: "I have decided to leave the diocese and I ask you to study my decision and I ask solidarity with this decision. It is not possible to work here anymore. They will kill all of us."[61]

For some of the pastoral agents the decision to leave was clearly not easy: they felt they were abandoning their catechists and the people for whom leaving the area or the country was not a possibility. Yet the very fact that the assassins traveled about so openly and undisguised was in itself a signal. Moreover, by killing Villanueva and looking for the bishop, the army had made it clear that the object was not simply to rid the area of priests considered "subversive" but, rather, that it was determined to drive all pastoral agents out. Even those considered conservative might still be in a position to witness or hear about the kinds of atrocities the army might feel obliged to commit in the pursuit of the guerrillas.

While the departure of priests and sisters was presented as a protest, it may also be seen as the result of a calculated move on the part of the army, rather like the decision to kill Archbishop Romero in El Salvador. In both cases the church was weakened institutionally and lay Christians were left on their own.

By comparison with its strong and pointed denunciation in June, the statement made by the bishops about the decision to leave the Quiché diocese was extraordinarily calm, avoided even hinting at who might be responsible, and expressed a desire for "dialogue with the authorities" "to solve this most serious problem as soon as possible."[62]

In August there was another mass kidnapping of union leaders, this time from Emaus, a church retreat center in the diocese of Escuintla. When Bishop Mario Ríos Montt protested, he was informed he was on a death list, and thereafter had to live in semihiding.

At first church people wondered if attacks like that in Quiché would continue systematically throughout the country, particularly when grenades were thrown at a convent of Canadian sisters in Morales, Izabal (near the banana areas).

After leaving Guatemala, Bishop Gerardi had gone to Rome to present the case of Guatemala to the pope and Vatican authorities. Pope John Paul II sent a letter to the Guatemalan bishops, and its contents was revealed in mid-November. The pope's language was more direct than usual. He spoke of the dramatic "scale of suffering and death that presses down, giving no sign of letting up, upon so many families and church communities, deprived not only of many catechists, but also of priests who have died in obscure circumstances, at times in vile and treacherous ways," and mentioned Quiché by name. He said he joined them in exhorting "those responsible in your country to spare no effort at remedying this tidal wave of discord and hatred," and repeated his insistence that "the Church must inspire those responsible for the common good to undertake . . . reforms opportunely, decisively, and courageously. . . ."[63]

Bishop Gerardi arrived back in Guatemala shortly after this letter had become known and was immediately put into custody in the airport and subjected to two hours of interrogation. He was not permitted to see the priests and a bishop who had come to receive him. He was then put on a plane to El Salvador, which refused to receive him, and then went to Costa Rica, where he went into exile. After numerous protests the government sought to pass the incident off as a mistake, but several days later the foreign minister was quoted as saying that it should serve to remind people to examine their conduct. (He even made the extraordinary observation that priests like Bartolomé de las Casas had not had problems with authorities.)[64]

In October several hundred army troops systematically occupied the town of Santiago Atitlán, a favorite site for tourists who would cross Lake Atitlán to see it and buy Indian weavings and clothes. The army began kidnapping several people, including Gaspar Culán, the manager of the radio station Voice of Atitlán, which had begun under church auspices and continued programming in literacy and development. Soldiers went through the area looking for leaders of any sort: cooperative leaders, literacy trainers, basic Christian community leaders, and Protestant pastors. Although the number of people who disappeared was relatively small—around seven—a group of several hundred people gathered in the church and slept there for their own security.[65]

From the army's point of view the immediate motivation may have been the fact that some time previously a group of ORPA guerrillas had come into the town and held a meeting. Some said Culán had spoken favorably of what the guerrillas said. In a more general sense this army occupation seemed to mark a new stage in which whole towns could come under siege and in which the prior presence the guerrilla organizations could be the pretext for retaliatory actions against people in towns and villages. Such had been the situation in Quiché for years, and it now became characteristic of large parts of the Indian highlands.

Image and Reality

During much of this period the Guatemalan power structure, and in particular the government, seemed to feel misunderstood and in need of communicating its side of the struggle to counteract what it saw as international communist propaganda. In April 1980 a delegation from the American Chamber of Commerce in Guatemala had gone to the United States, and Edward Carrette (a Guatemalan) had given congressional testimony and a press briefing in Washington, while the chamber's president, Thomas Mooney, spoke to corporation leaders in New York. After saying something about government development projects, Mooney described a difference of opinion between the State Department and Guatemalan authorities on the "cause and effect and the appropriate method of resisting" a communist effort. Although the State Department opposed privately supported "death squads" because they "only serve to incite the people," Mooney said:

> There is another point of view that contends that the only feasible way to stop communism is to destroy it quickly. Argentina and Chile are demonstrated as nations which used this approach with considerable effectiveness and have gone on to become Latin America's most stable and successful countries. In spite of the fact that they do not enjoy U.S. support on human rights grounds, there is increasing skepticism in Guatemala respecting the intensity of the U.S. resolve to combat communist insurgency in Central America. . . . There is a very evident concern among Guatemalans that they have been stereotyped by the U.S. Government and the U.S. press. This concern is justified. The truth is that the great majority of people in Guatemala are neither leftist nor rightist. They are ordinary persons who are tired of terrorism and incensed by a foreign press, which is normally uninformed and often totally fictitious in its reporting.
>
> In fact no solution can be really satisfactory. The U.S. Government tends to opt in favor of the more idealistic one presumably aware of its impotence, while increasingly greater numbers of Guatemalans are leaning toward a pragmatic solution, without much enthusiasm for all of its ramifications.

Carrette in his congressional testimony said that violence was not used "as a matter of government policy."[66]

Within Guatemala the Lucas government sought to blame the subversives and orchestrated a nationwide series of anticommunist demonstrations culminating in one in front of the presidential palace in September. However, events were undermining the government's efforts to improve its image. In early September, Francisco Villagrán Kramer, the vice-president, safely in Washington, announced that he was "left with no option but to resign, after all efforts to ensure the respect of human rights in the country had failed." After lending his prestige to Lucas's ticket in 1978, Villagrán had been totally ignored, and had spent months without even talking to the president. At certain moments he had been able to register a mild dissent from the policy of violence, but in general he had been so totally unemployed in the administration that he had a great deal of time to talk to visiting journalists.[67]

At around this same time Elías Barahona, a press secretary for the minister of the interior, fled to Costa Rica, where he held a press conference stating that he was a member of the EGP and had served as an infiltrator in the government for several years. He gave many details of how the repression was carried out: that the "Secret Anticommunist Army" had been invented by the interior minister himself (Barahona's boss); that death lists were made within the government and the repression was coordinated from within an annex to the presidential palace; that Lucas himself gave the order to attack the Spanish embassy; and so forth. By its own contradictory reactions to Barahona's report, the government served to lend them credence (and in fact, Amnesty International in its report a few months later used some of his information).[68]

In one case international attention had some effect. The Coca-Cola conflict, which in some sense had been the beginning of the whole cycle of labor and popular organizing, had never been resolved. Several union members had been murdered. When European unions organized a boycott and workers in Sweden threatened a work stoppage at a Coca-Cola plant, the parent company in Atlanta, Georgia, moved to solve the problem by forcing John Trotter, the owner of the Guatemalan franchise, to sell. In September 1980, after several months during which more workers were killed and at least two managers were killed by guerrilla groups, an agreement was reached; it was signed in December. Church groups in the United States (the Eighth Day Center in Chicago and the Inter-faith Center for Corporate Responsibility) had played major roles in support of the workers.[69]

If the Guatemalan government and business sector were disappointed with the Carter government (as indicated by statements of Mooney, above) they were hopeful that a Reagan victory would mean renewed support. In fact, Barahona indicated that Roger Fontaine, a Latin American expert in right-wing circles (subsequently in the National Security Council), visited Guatemala in April 1980 (before Reagan's nomination) and assured the government it would have a Reagan administration's support.[70]

Alan Nairn, an investigative reporter, found a series of links between the Guatemalan government and the Reagan circle. A number of American new-right figures were taking trips to Guatemala in 1980. The Amigos del País, a business club, was spending a reputed half-million dollars to repair the country's image, much of it with public relations firms in the United States. One of these, Deaver and Hannaford, was partly owned by Michael Deaver, who became one of Reagan's three main White House aides. The most interesting links were the repeated rumors that wealthy Guatemalans had contributed to the Reagan campaign. While Nairn found this to be something widely assumed in Guatemala, there was never any proof; such contributions would have been illegal. The impression created by all these contacts was that a Reagan administration would renew military training and aid, cut back criticism, be more understanding of the tactics of the government and, if necessary, back up the Guatemalan government with United States troops.[71]

Finally in January 1981 Amnesty International released its study called "A Government Program of Political Murder," the title itself being unusual for an organization that strives for balance and objectivity. What prompted the title was largely the increasing evidence that the repression was in no sense the work of private right-wing groups "tolerated" by the government but was clearly directed largely by the army, from the communications center in the annex to the presidential palace. By Amnesty International's estimate, between January and November 1980 "some 3,000 people described by government representatives as 'subversives' and 'criminals' were either shot on the spot in political assassinations or seized and murdered later; at least 364 others seized in this period have not yet been accounted for." In addition to numerous examples the report cited two interviews, one of a man who described being interrogated under torture, and the other of a former soldier who described surveillance, abduction, and murder carried out by the army.[72]

For their part the armed opposition movements were stepping up their activities. Until some time in mid-1979 it could be said that the guerrilla actions were defensive or for propaganda; the guerrillas were not interested in direct military confrontation with the army. However, late that year there were increasing attacks on the army in larger and larger units, and gradually the groups moved into an offensive posture. Throughout 1980 both EGP and ORPA occupied towns, plantations, and villages, and serious guerrilla activity began to extend to large parts of Guatemala; in fact, the only areas without much guerrilla activity were in the Oriente, long an MLN stronghold. During the first three months of 1981 it was estimated that the army suffered 1,000 casualties in over 200 confrontations with the guerrilla organizations.[73]

The army's response was more violence—not against the guerrillas, who were difficult to locate and who could defend themselves, but against those identified as part of the opposition, at all levels from the capital to the villages. Some might justify this policy on counterinsurgency grounds: that the leaders were the contact point between the masses and the guerrilla organizations. Hence there was an intensified all-out attack on any kind of leadership in unions, student groups, and the church, on journalists and political party leaders, as well as on whole villages and towns in the Indian highlands and other peasant areas. Not all the victims were utterly "innocent" in that most, one assumes, were clearly opposed to the government (although there were a goodly number of people killed by "mistake"); some would be members of organizations that at some level might be in contact with guerrilla organizations; and a few might be clandestine members of the guerrilla organizations themselves. However, the normal case was that unarmed people, themselves not responsible for armed activity, were being systematically abducted, tortured, and killed.

Ethical discussion on the issue of violence will be taken up in chapter 9. Here it might be useful simply to note that there were clear differences in the way violence was used by the army and by the guerrilla groups. In a word, the army practiced systematic torture and terrorism (that is, killing or threatening to kill noncombatants as a political technique) and was largely indiscriminate in its violence, while guerrilla violence was targeted. The army's deliberate policy of leaving tortured and mutilated bodies by roadsides was intended to have an intimidating effect. The army, moreover, made little distinction between people actively serving as combatants with guerrilla organizations and ordinary people considered to be in opposition or even simply suspected of being so. People were kidnapped, interrogated under torture, and killed; even when torture failed to uncover evidence of subversive activity, the suspects were still killed, possibly because, if set free, they could say who had kidnapped and tortured them. In contrast, torture was not practiced by guerrillas, and they made every effort not to endanger innocent bystanders (occasionally there were civilian casualties and deaths, however). Besides engaging in combat, guerrilla groups sometimes sought to kill (or "execute") informers, people who on the local level had "fingered" their neighbors to the police or army and were hence responsible for the death of innocent people.

It would seem that the Guatemalan army entered a new phase in its repressive tactics some time in early 1981 when systematic attacks on peasant villages, which had occurred occasionally, especially in Quiché, became routine. Hence, for example, on February 4 some 300 soldiers came to the village of Sacalá las Lomas (San Martín, Chimaltenango), and attacked with machine guns, grenade launchers, and helicopter fire. Seventeen bodies were thrown into a ravine, eighteen were carried away, and fifteen people were carried off alive. The next day the soldiers returned to a nearby village, Pachay las Lomas, where they found the peasants ready to resist and so they did not attack directly, although they killed an estimated ten people and kidnapped two. This area is close to the capital, an hour's drive on paved road and another hour on unpaved road. In a similar action on April 9, sixty heavily armed men entered another village in the same area and carried off twenty-four peasants, tortured them, and dumped their bodies. In the village of Coyá, San Miguel Acatán, Huehuetenango, on July 19 troops attacked and the people fought with rocks against hand grenades, bazookas, and aircraft. The number killed was estimated at between 150 and 300, largely women and children.[74] As the year went on such direct attacks on villages, almost always Indian villages, became more and more frequent.

In May 475 peasants in the Petén region fled from army bombardment and were enabled to escape by FAR guerrillas, who escorted them across the border into Mexico. However, after a few days Mexican authorities returned them to Guatemala where their ultimate fate was never clear. Then in June soldiers in civilian clothes took members of cooperatives out of seven villages and interrogated them, with torture, about the guerrillas. Upon returning to their villages they found their homes sacked and their equipment destroyed. Some 4,000 peasants decided to cross the Usumacinta River into Mexico. This time, due to public pressure, the refugees were allowed to stay and the presence of Guatemalan refugees became an ongoing fact in Mexico. Predictably, President Lucas said it was all a maneuver to discredit his government.[75]

For a long time, especially after the mass kidnappings of union leaders in June and August 1980, there had been discussion among the groups making up the Democratic Front against Repression about what kind of response should be made to the increased repression. Increasingly some were convinced that the struggle was entering a new phase and that the era of strikes and demonstrations and legal opposition was over: new methods of organization and struggle were needed. Others were convinced that the general populace was not ready and that a premature advance could alienate those who were uncommitted.

Emerging from such discussions in early 1981 was the FP-31 (January 31 Popular Front) which was made up of the CUC, two student organizations (high school and university FERG), the CDP (Shantytown Dwellers Coordinating Committee), the NOR (Revolutionary Workers Nucleus), and Revolutionary Christians.[76] In the first four cases whole organizations had simply joined to form FP-31; but the Revolutionary workers and the Revolutionary Christians represented some union members and some members of church groups belonging to Justice and Peace who had decided to join FP-31. It is not clear how many and what kinds of people joined the Revolutionary Christians, but it would seem to have been mainly young people rather than, for example, pastoral agents.

Typical of the FP-31's methods were acts of sabotage such as stopping traffic by spreading homemade tacks on roads, setting off propaganda bombs, setting up barricades of burning tires, and similar acts, which, while short of engaging in combat, were a step beyond their previous legal activities.

During 1981 the attack on the church and pastoral agents increased. After Bishop Gerardi and the priests and sisters left Quiché, Cardinal Casariego and others sought to find some way to have priests return to the area. The ostensible reason was to have the people's spiritual needs attended to. However, to the extent they could, the existing basic Christian communities were still functioning with catechists, who on occasion would spend several days traveling to another part of the country either for counsel or, in some cases, to carry the Eucharist. In any case, Casariego's real motive seems to have been to cover up the scandal of a diocese with no priests or bishop because of government violence.

In early 1981 it seemed that some kind of solution was underway and a bishop was appointed to oversee the situation. Christian groups such as Justice and Peace in Guatemala and the Church in Exile (priests who had served in Quiché) were angry. Father Juan Alonso Fernández, a Sacred Heart priest of conservative views, was chosen to go. But he was killed on February 15—just ten days after his arrival—as he rode his motorbike to say Sunday Mass. Efforts to restore the diocese to an appearance of normality stopped.

Not all the church victims were Catholics. Marco Antonio Cacao Muñoz, a journalist and union leader killed in July 1980, was also a Protestant pastor. Other Protestant pastors killed included Roberto Ortiz Morales (July 8, 1980), Apoliciano Albeno López and Raúl Albeno Martínez, Protestant preachers ambushed and killed returning from a church service in Jutiapa in November 1980, and Santos Jiménez Martínez, a pastor of the Brotherhood of Evangelical Churches of the People, who was shot on November 19, 1980, after celebrating a service.[77] He had worked for many years in the cotton area of Santo Domingo Suchitepequez.

In April 1981 about fifteen foreign development organizations, including Church World Service, and some others with church relationships such as Heifer Project International, received death threats. The director of one of these projects, using family connections to inquire of army officials whether this threat was serious, was assured that it was. These organizations were doing conventional village-level development work, that is, they were not helping revolutionary, or even popular, organizations. Since most of the development work was taking place in the Indian highlands, now increasingly the site of direct undisguised attacks on villages, those passing the death threat had perhaps concluded that foreign agencies could be a source of problems if their personnel were simply present as witnesses.[78]

In June Luis Pellecer, a Jesuit, was kidnapped, badly beaten, and driven off in a car. His case, to be recounted below, became a crucial one in Guatemala. An Italian priest, Marcelo Maruzzo, who had worked in Izabal region for twenty-one years, was killed on July 2, and Carlos Pérez Alonso, a Spanish Jesuit, was kidnapped on August 3.

The murder of Father Stanley Rother of Okalahoma City briefly brought the situation of repression to public attention in the United States. Rother, who had been in Guatemala since 1968, was (like Maryknoller Bill Woods) clearly not a leftist, but one who sought to help the people in practical ways. For example, Rother had made it clear he did not want CUC people to use the parish facilities. However, Santiago Atitlán, where he was pastor, had come under army occupation in 1980, and in December of that year he saw Diego Quic, one of his main catechists, kidnapped while he watched helplessly from the bacony of the parish house. Shortly afterward, under death threat he and his Guatemalan assistant left the country. However, after some time he received word that it seemed safe for him to return and he did so for Holy Week, 1981.

On the night of July 28 three armed men, with ski masks, came for him and shot him. Twenty-five hundred people attended the funeral, including two bishops and thirty-five priests. The government, apparently sensing pressure and perhaps wishing to avoid prolonged international attention such as that given to the murdered church women in El Salvador, found three men who "confessed" to killing Rother in a robbery attempt. No serious person who had any knowledge of Guatemala could believe such a story.

Rother's death was inopportune for the Reagan administration, which at this time was seeking to renew military aid to the Lucas regime. One of the witnesses at hearings on Guatemala was Mrs. Frankie Williams of Wichita, Kansas, who for several years had done volunteer work at Santiago on her vacations and who had also witnessed the kidnapping of Rother's catechist. Congress was apprehensive about renewing aid, but the administration was able, nevertheless, to lift restrictions on the sale of fifty trucks and one hundred jeeps to the Guatemalan army.[79]

Beginning in July the Guatemalan army, which in its combat with guerrillas in the mountains had enjoyed little success, made a series of raids on guerrilla "safe houses" in Guatemala City. It seems that one discovery led to another and the guerrilla organizations, especially ORPA, suffered serious losses. Many observers saw this success as the work of Argentine and Israeli advisers, who had experience in breaking urban revolutionary networks. There was also some suspicion that when the government and army saw its prestige among the nervous upper classes increase with these successes, it added some further theatrics and in some cases made up further incidents.

One of these raids was featured prominently in the Guatemalan press, which announced that two "priest guerrillas" had died in combat and it named them as "Commander Pedro," allegedly a Spanish priest named Angel Martínez, and "Commander Miguel," said to be a Canadian priest named Raoul Leger. At the same time the government pointed to the publication of interviews with Father Donald McKenna, a priest from Belfast, Northern Ireland, who had served in Quiché and was now an EGP guerrilla fighter. Colonel Clementino Castillo, the education minister, said that all priests and religious would be investigated to see whether or not they belonged to extremist groups.[80]

In their commentary dated August 6, the Guatemalan bishops seem to have been at pains to separate themselves from any connection with people who might feel forced to join revolutionary organizations. Although they recognized that the church was "suffering persecution as an historical verification of its fidelity," they clarified that Raoul Leger and Ángel Martínez were lay volunteers who had not been associated with pastoral work "for some time" and that, in regard to McKenna,

> if a priest or religious chooses the option—denying our wisdom—to join whatever political faction or subversive group he no longer belongs to the pastoral body of the Church and therefore the hierarchy cannot be held responsible for his later actions.
>
> . . . As bishops we are profoundly saddened that persons in one way or another connected with the pastoral activity of the Church have opted for the path of armed struggle in order to resolve the enormous social, economic, and political problems that afflict our country. Any terrorist action merits our condemnation and we never will be able to endorse with our moral support those who commit it, as we are also unable to

propose actions that lead to the implantation of communism in our country.

They insisted that their efforts at dialogue with the government had not met with success and said they did not fear the investigation of priests and religious but found it "highly offensive."[81]

While recognizing that it was the product of extreme pressures, many Christians found this letter discouraging for its weak stand toward the government. Although they were not directly part of guerrilla organizations they felt increasingly vulnerable as they saw the army with its improved intelligence capacity breaking all kinds of networks. Many lay people associated with church groups were kidnapped, such as Emeterio Toj, one of the main CUC leaders.

In a televised press conference on September 30 the government triumphantly produced Father Luis Pellecer, who had been presumed dead after his kidnapping in June. He "confessed" that he had been a member of the EGP until he had decided to leave it by way of a "self-kidnapping." Now repentant, he said he was appearing to warn people of what church people were doing. He began by describing the three basic "weapons" used: liberation theology, Marxist-Leninist analysis, and the option for the poor. He went on to describe his own experience as a Jesuit in El Salvador (Aguilares) and Nicaragua, as well as Guatemala, and wove a vast web linking Delegates of the Word, CUC and other people's organizations, Operation Uspantán (a summer program whereby the Holy Family sisters had their students spend part of their summers doing catechetical work in the Quiché), CONFREGUA, literacy training programs, and European funding agencies (whose monies, he said, the revolutionary organizations would use for their work among the people); at the center of this web were Jesuits, and some former Jesuits, now in the EGP. Pellecer announced that he was repentant and asked for pardon; he hoped to continue to serve as a priest, although he was leaving the Jesuits.[82]

There were many indications that Pellecer's statements were the product of coercion and/or brainwashing, beginning with the fact that he was kept in tight control by government authorities and simply brought out for a few press conferences and for very brief, and observed, contacts with the bishops and with his Jesuit provincial. Moreover, to those who knew him his speech was an uncharacteristic monotone and his attitudes were totally changed from his normal personality. An attentive reading of the text gives the impression that his captors' categories have been amalgamated into his own; for example, his description of liberation theology is a caricature that not even the most nondiscriminating enthusiast could endorse. Experts in Mexico and Canada who saw videotapes of the press conferences saw evidence that he had been drugged. A further sign was that his statements were frequently almost verbatim repetitions. Also, more than once in his several press conferences, when confused he began again: "My name is Luis

Eduardo Pellecer Faena. I am thirty-five years old. . . ." It was said that even the upper class in Guatemala did not believe the self-kidnapping story and recognized the brainwashing but nevertheless thought his testimony important for showing the links of church people with the guerrillas.

Much of Pellecer's testimony was in fact true: that is, he had been an EGP collaborator (recognized by the organization in a bulletin wherein they emphasized the distinction between "collaborators" and "members"), and the popular organizations did connect with church people at various points. However, it should be clear from this whole narrative that in general people were radicalized by suffering the effects of official violence and feeling that they had no other option except to become organized. In other words, what had happened was not the result of a conspiracy organized by tiny radical groups, with the Jesuits at the center of the web but, rather, a large popular movement with its own dynamic, in which many different elements had participated, one of which was the presence of church pastoral agents.

Part of the government's feeling of triumph was punctured when Emeterio Toj, the CUC leader who had been captured and had also been presented in press conferences and had spoken over the radio, was freed from prison—through a combination of infiltration in the army and an EGP attack. He then recorded a message, which was broadcast over a number of radio stations that were simultaneously taken over. In it he described the tortures and coercion he had been subjected to, namely, that people in his family and village would be killed if he did not cooperate.

The latter part of 1981 saw the revolutionary organizations attempting to reorganize themselves after the blows inflicted in midyear. One measure of their effect was the increasing frequency of actions in Guatemala City, including a very large bomb explosion outside the heavily guarded plainclothes-police headquarters in December. At the same time the army escalated its tactics by moving from attacks on towns and villages to coordinated search-and-destroy actions in large areas, one example being in the department of Chimaltenango in November.

Elections, a Coup, and Intensified Violence

For the elections of March 1982 the key question from the beginning had nothing to do with the possibility of genuine change—since the army would continue to be the real arbiter of the country—but whether the Lucas group would continue to hold power or whether there might be a minor shift in power. As far back as April 1981 the Reagan administration had dispatched (retired) General Vernon Walters to attempt to persuade the Lucas group and the army that a civilian president would be desirable. Walters was reportedly rebuffed by Lucas and as the year went on it seemed probable that General Aníbal Guevara, the defense minister and Lucas-group candidate, would become president.

In January 1982 Guatemala's four guerrilla groups (EGP, FAR, ORPA, and PGT) announced that they had joined together in the URNG (Guatemalan National Revolutionary Unity). Its proclamation was soon followed by the formation of CGUP (Guatemalan Committee for Patriotic Unity), a group of over forty respected Guatemalans who began to operate as something of a proto-political front. The purpose of these moves seems to have been to make clear before the election that there did exist a real alternative in Guatemala. The opposition felt that a new president, even hand-chosen and imposed by Lucas, would for a time enjoy the legitimacy conveyed by elections.

At the same time the URNG issued the clearest manifesto yet of its proposals for a new government, summarized in the following five points:

1. The revolution will end repression against the people and will guarantee to citizens life and peace, the supreme rights of the human being.
2. The revolution will lay the groundwork for satisfying the basic needs of the great majorities of the people by ending the economic and political domination of the repressive national and foreign wealthy who govern Guatemala.
3. The revolution will guarantee equality between Indians and Ladinos, ending cultural oppression and discrimination.
4. The revolution will guarantee the creation of a new society where all the patriotic, popular, and democratic sectors will be represented in the government.
5. The revolution will guarantee the policy of nonalignment and of international cooperation, which poor countries need in order to become developed in the world today, on the foundation of the self-determination of peoples.

These points were elaborated on in the text itself, which evidenced an overall pragmatic stance: among other things, it recognized the roles of the private sector and of foreign investment. Regarding Christians, the URNG document said that they would be one of the "pillars of the new society" because many Christians had proved themselves by their commitment to the struggle.[83]

Opposing Guevara in the elections were three civilian candidates, the former vice-president Mario Sandoval Alarcón (MLN party head and identified with death squads since the mid-1960s), Alejandro Maldonado Aguirre, representing a small "moderate" party splintered from the MLN and allied with the Christian Democrats, and Gustavo Anzueto Vielman, candidate of the former president Arana's party (CAN). If designations of "right" or "left" have any meaning for such an election, all four candidates would have to be called "right wing."

As in 1978 there was widespread voter abstention—65 percent by some estimates—and fraud so clumsy that it could not be hidden. The three civilian candidates joined forces to protest, and their street demonstration was tear-gassed in full view of the international press. As it began to seem that the army would support Guevara, the United States State Department began to prepare public opinion for seeing his presidency as a change.

However, on March 23 there was a coup: with very few shots fired, Lucas and his main army commanders were dismissed. Exactly what happened is unclear. By some accounts the original intention of the young officers was simply to take power briefly, supervise "clean" elections, and have a civilian president, essentially with the purpose of doing away with the bad image created by Lucas and to facilitate the obtaining of aid and support from the United States. That these officers were "young" does not argue they were any more "progressive" or "social-minded" than those in power but, rather, that they resented the gross corruption of the Lucas group and saw it as undermining support needed for the battle against the guerrillas.

Their plans were foiled when General Efraín Ríos Montt assumed the presidency of the new Junta. By one story Ríos Montt was contacted where he was teaching Sunday school in the church where he had been "born again" some years previously. Lucas had refused to surrender to anyone less than a general, and Ríos Montt seemed to be the handiest general. Subsequent reports indicated that Ríos Montt had met with some of the conspirators ten days before the coup.

Whatever be the truth of the anecdote Ríos Montt did not see his role as that of a caretaker preparing for elections, and in fact he began to make elections sound more and more distant. Taking his words at face value, one concludes that he saw his role as being one of correcting the "corruption" of Guatemala. He spoke like a preacher, knelt down to pray with army commanders and visiting journalists, and seemed to see himself as God's instrument. Jokes began to circulate about the "Ayatollah" and "*Dios Montt.*"

Repression in Guatemala City and some of the larger towns dropped off overnight. It seemed that some steps were being taken to control some of the repressive forces. However, a closer look would reveal that there was simply a shuffle in command posts. The notorious police chief Colonel Germán Chupina was dismissed, but the man who replaced him had had the same position during the Arana repression (1970–74). Ríos Montt's two associates on the Junta, Colonels Horacio Maldonado Schaad and Francisco Gordillo, both had backgrounds in torture (both were dismissed, however, a few weeks later when Ríos Montt had himself made president). Even Lucas and his group were simply put under "house arrest," and reports indicated that it was a very free house arrest.

Comparisons with El Salvador came to mind. To some Ríos Montt was "Duarte with a pistol." Like Duarte, Ríos Montt had run for president under the Chrisitan Democratic banner and had been defrauded (1974). However, it was pointed out that Ríos Montt, as a military man, should be able to work better with the army than Duarte, a civilian politician. A quite clear difference, moreover, was the fact that Ríos Montt did not even offer the pretense of structural reforms in Guatemala. He presented himself as battling "corruption," a broad term in his use, which could be applied to graft within the government and to violence whether by the government or by the opposition. At one point he gave "Fourteen Points" for his government, none of which hinted at any kind of structural reform.

During May he announced that June would be a month of amnesty for both the opposition groups and those security forces that had committed abuses. Since virtually no guerrillas turned themselves in (as could have been predicted), the main result of the amnesty was to make clear that none of the perpetrators of the thousands of abductions, tortures, and killings on the part of the army and the police would ever be brought to justice.

Although there had been a lull in the repression in the capital, the violence in the countryside intensified. It seemed, in fact, that the idea was precisely to circumscribe war zones in the Indian highlands and in the colonization lands to the north. This was evident as lists of new massacres began to appear. At first even the press in Guatemala City gave some reports on massacres (without, however, directly stating they were carried out by the army). After one of them, *Gráfico* editor Jorge Carpio said that if such actions did not cease, Guatemala was not "worthy" of aid—thus manifesting an underlying concern.

The Justice and Peace Committee in Guatemala drew up lists of these actions and found that in April more than 559 people were killed by official or death-squad violence (the figure was undoubtedly low). To take one example, in the villages of Jua, Amachel, and Chel, in Chajul, Quiché, during April 3–5, the army "raped the women, cut off the men's heads, and dashed the children against rocks along the river," and in other villages, on April 15, they tied twenty peasants to posts in their houses and burned them alive.[84]

Since these massacres were occurring in relatively isolated areas the image of an improvement in Guatemala, bolstered by Ríos Montt's bizarre public evangelizing, served to create a certain confusion, which the Reagan administration sought to utilize. The United States Congress, nevertheless, seemed loathe to make a large commitment to Guatemala.

Ríos Montt declared that after the June "amnesty" period there would be a state of siege, and it began on July 1. One of the government's techniques was to force the peasants to take sides by calling out all males and putting them into "civilian militias," ostensibly to protect the towns and villages. Villagers were thereby forced to join the government side—not to do so would be taken to mean that they were with the guerrillas. While out on patrol the militias were supposed to find guerrillas, sometimes simply by killing as suspect whomever they came across. They also served as "cannon fodder" for the army, since they could be sent out to draw guerrilla fire, while the army waited in the town or village.

A *New York Times* article in July 1982 caught the flavor of the strange mix of evangelism and repression characteristic of Ríos Montt. In the town of Cunén the people had been assembled for a pageant complete with a "Miss Cunén," a nineteen-year-old Indian woman in traditional dress. "He who resists the authorities is resisting the will of God," said a preacher of the Church of God. "With the help of the people and with the help of God we will soon eliminate the guerrilla," said a second lieutenant. The reporter pointed out that Ríos Montt's approach was being called *fusiles y frijoles* ("bullets and beans"). The Christian Church of the Word, to which Ríos Montt belonged, was helping in Cunén as part of a larger program directed by the Gospel Outreach of Eureka, California, which hoped to raise $20 million for Guatemala. The report ended with one officer's version of the army's message: "If you are with us, we'll feed you; if not, we'll kill you."[85]

In Catholic Church circles the Ríos Montt presidency seemed to change little. During the first few days there were contacts between the hierarchy and the army. Cardinal Casariego was quoted in the press as saying, "What God sends should be respected. But there's no reason to fear, they're all good people. If I had not been a priest, I would have been a soldier."[86]

However, in April the bishops spoke of their concern for refugees, estimating that some 200,000 had fled the country and as many as one million had had to flee their homes within Guatemala. On May 27 (more than two months after Ríos Montt's assumption of the presidency) they made a statement about the massacre of peasants: "Never in our national history have we come to such grave extremes. These murders are being committed in the rural area and are genocide. We have to recognize that these deeds are the greatest contradiction to the divine commandment: 'Thou shalt not kill.' " They quoted Pope John Paul II: "Murder has to be called by its proper name."

However, the bishops also spoke of "sectors of the extreme right and left, who pretend to justify murder" and did not indicate that the army was directly responsible for most of the killing. CONFREGUA produced a similar document, adding that it wished to "say to our people of God who are suffering that we walk with them and that they are not alone." By likening the present to the Israelites' forty years in the desert, they hinted that the present suffering would lead to a "promised land."[87]

7

Christians in Struggle:
Parallels and Contrasts

An attentive reader will have sensed numerous parallels in the manner in which Christians increasingly became involved in revolutionary struggles in Nicaragua, El Salvador, and Guatemala. At this point a systematic (even schematic) comparison between the processes themselves and Christian involvement in them would be useful.

In chapter 3 some of the "objective" conditions for revolution were delineated through a treatment of the history of the region and developments during recent decades. "Subjective" factors, that is, the people's response in organization and struggle were treated in chapters 4 to 6. Some of the most obvious parallels may be noted as follows.

BASIC REVOLUTIONARY DEVELOPMENTS
SEEN COMPARATIVELY

1. In each country there was an "original sin," an event or a period that reflected both the people's resistance and the use of force to maintain in power a dominant elite, which thereafter resisted even minimal reforms:

Nicaragua: domination of U.S. Marines, struggle of Sandino, departure of the marines, murder of Sandino, establishment of the Somoza dictatorship

El Salvador: 1932 massacre of peasants and the institutionalization of de facto army rule (with "official" parties, which always won elections)

Guatemala: 1944 overthrow of Ubico dictatorship, ten years of reforms cut short by 1954 United States-organized coup, and installation of governments representing the landholding oligarchy and, increasingly, the army itself.

2. Modernization and development, spurred by the Central American Common Market and Alliance for Progress programs brought growth but no improvement for most and deteriorating conditions for many. While

220

landholders expanded acreage, peasants had less and less land and the number of the landless increased dramatically, especially in El Salvador.

3. People became increasingly disenchanted with existing political mechanisms, particularly as the regimes employed blatant fraud and violence:

Nicaragua: Somoza's massacre of the opposition demonstration in January 1967 and electoral fraud later that year; later his "pact" with the opposition, assumption of control after the earthquake, and tinkering with the Constitution to permit his reelection in 1974

El Salvador: fraud against the UNO reform coalition in 1972 and 1977, along with other fraud in nonpresidential elections

Guatemala: electoral frauds in 1974 and 1978 and the de facto system of succession whereby ministers of defense became presidents.

4. External events and developments compounded the crisis: the war with Honduras, for El Salvador (1969); earthquakes, for Nicaragua (1972) and Guatemala (1976); quadrupled petroleum prices and inflation, for all.

5. The people sought new channels for pressing their demands:

Nicaragua: the anti-Somoza movement was largely spontaneous (for example, the Monimbó and September uprisings of 1978) and was broader than the FSLN, which sought to organize and channel it

El Salvador: the popular organizations grew out of conflicts during 1974–75 (especially BPR and FAPU) and both made immediate demands (for example, increase in pay for agricultural day labor) and challenged the government and oligarchy

Guatemala: the spearhead was an increasingly militant labor movement starting in 1976, joined by students, organized peasants (CUC), and other sectors.

Such popular movements eventually came to have clear links to specific politico-military organizations, but in their earlier stages they acted autonomously and represented the people's own desperation and courage.

6. New Marxist-inspired revolutionary movements, either independent of, or splitting from, the traditional communist parties had been formed, and through many years of struggle, sometimes with rivalries and factional fighting, they came to head up a broad opposition movement posing a real threat to existing regimes:

Nicaragua: the Sandinista National Liberation Front was formed in the early 1960s; Carlos Fonseca Amador had been a member of the Nicaraguan Socialist party (communist) and had traveled to the Soviet Union; others came in through different paths; in the mid-1970s until 1979 it was split into three "tendencies," which were reunited in early 1979

El Salvador: around 1970 Salvador Cayetano Carpio split from the Communist party and formed what became the FPL; others independently formed what became the ERP (from which FARN split)

Guatemala: a guerrilla movement originating with discontented army officers went through a complex history during the 1960s until being almost wiped out at the end of the decade; survivors began the EGP (1972) and

ORPA (early 1970s, appeared publicly first in 1979); FAR and PGT (communist) had continued from the 1960s, although their level of activity and radius of action was less than that of the other two.

In all cases the official communist parties remained on the sidelines until around 1978-79 and hence were regarded as very late arrivals and had relatively little influence.

7. The ideology of these groups was Marxist, but it was a "homegrown" Marxism. They showed little evidence of having elaborate Marxist theories and indeed seemed to have put their emphasis on studying their own countries rather than on examining fine points of Marxism. Similarly, their internal splits and conflicts were a product of different strategic conceptions—and to some extent personal rivalries—rather than different international "lines." In Nicaragua a focus on Sandino helped the FSLN to maintain a very flexible Marxism.

8. A large number of non-Marxist, opposition groups found themselves increasingly forced into de facto alliance with Marxist organizations:

Nicaragua: the "strategic class alliance" of the FSLN and the anti-Somoza bourgeoisie

El Salvador: Revolutionary Democratic Front, including political parties, labor unions, universities, church sectors, professionals, and so on

Guatemala: the Democratic Front against Repression (1979) united labor, students, political parties, and so forth, and later the Guatemalan Committee for Patriotic Unity (1982) was founded. These broad fronts enjoyed growing legitimacy both internally and internationally.

9. In response the state resorted increasingly to terror, thereby delegitimizing itself and weakening international support:

Nicaragua: National Guard counterinsurgency campaign of 1975-77; summary execution of youths as suspects during the war; bombing of civilian population

El Salvador: military attacks against villages in rebel territory; large-scale use of death squads; massacres

Guatemala: death squads; mass kidnappings; attacks on all sectors of society, especially Indian peasants.

On this latter point it should be observed that there was a progression in cruelty and lack of scruples. Somoza, for example, permitted the middle-class opposition to function until the end; although they were harassed, virtually no middle-class people were killed unless they had taken part in guerrilla actions. In El Salvador, also, for a period some nonviolent opposition was tolerated; for example, the Salvadoran Human Rights Commission, whose offices were bombed but which continued to function openly until early 1981, and then operated using church-related facilities. In Guatemala, on the other hand, no such activity was ever permitted and the broad-daylight assassinations of very popular and respected politicians such as Alberto Fuentes Mohr and Manuel Colóm Argueta (1979) were evidence of a greater ruthlessness. In 1981 and 1982 repeated massacres of Indian villages reflected a genocidal logic to the government's action.

10. In their proposals the opposition movements were similar: all put an end of repression (and of repressive army and policy) as their first proposal, and proposed broad economic reforms, especially land reform, but at the same time advocated some kind of a "mixed economy," and while they did not emphasize elections they hoped to form broad coalition governments, led, however, by their recognized "vanguards."

The main differences between the revolutionary movements have already been mentioned:

Nicaragua: the struggle was conceived as one to overthrow a dictator and a dynasty

El Salvador: organized peasants were the leading edge of what was clearly a class confrontation

Guatemala: the main distinguishing characteristic was the large-scale involvement of Indians for whom struggle seemed essential for survival; ORPA as an organization seemed to be built around Indians and saw itself struggling for Indian affirmation; the EGP was largely made up of Indians.

One obvious question is to what extent there were organizational links in these revolutionary movements from one country to another. While definitive information at present would be extremely difficult to obtain, it would seem that the splits within each country were indigenous. Although there might be an apparent affinity in style and conception between, for example, the EGP in Guatemala and the FPL in El Salvador, there was no ground for seeing any strong organizational links. One assumes that the top leadership of the FSLN, FMLN, and the URNG maintained minimal contact.

THE ROLE OF THE CHURCH SEEN COMPARATIVELY

1. Until the 1960s the Catholic church in Central America tended to be institutionally weak (for example, over 80 percent of the clergy in Guatemala and Nicaragua was foreign) and raised no objections to oligarchical/military rule.

2. In the early and mid-1960s there arrived new groups of priests and sisters, both foreign and national (from study abroad), who began to reflect the spirit of Vatican II (and later, Medellín).

3. The first phase of "going to the people" was often aimed at "development" (for instance, cooperatives in El Salvador and in Guatemala) and was sometimes related to Christian Democratic initiatives. Such development eventually showed its limits.

4. A second type of "going to the people" emerged from the Medellín period, now with a stress on *concientización* and basic Christian communities:

Nicaragua: Solentiname, San Pablo parish, and barrio Rigueiro; Capuchins in the countryside (all in late 1960s)

El Salvador: basic Christian communities started in Suchitoto (1969) and in many parishes in rural areas of the archdiocese of San Salvador (early 1970s)

Guatemala: *Acción Católica* in Quiché, work of Belgian priests on south coast (1960s).

5. In the late 1960s and early 1970s there were sporadic examples of church people being involved in conflicts with representatives of the power structures:

Nicaragua: ferment during 1968–72: letter of seven priests; participation in occupation of Catholic university and cathedral; priests beaten or thrown in jail

El Salvador: kidnapping of Father José Inocencio Alas (1970) and accusations of involvement in kidnapping against Father Alfonso Navarro

Guatemala: Melville incident (priests and sister beginning to work with guerrillas discovered, forced to leave), expulsion of clergy after letter in 1971.

6. Grassroots pastoral experience and new ideas and methods coming from Medellín were discussed and debated in pastoral study weeks and meetings in different countries. While they did not bring unity, these meetings clarified issues and helped some pastoral agents to come together. In some cases informal working groups were formed to share work and experiences. Many retreat and conference centers were set up and became important centers of information and training.

7. In some cases there were direct contacts between pastoral agents and leaders of guerrilla movements, especially in Nicaragua where Uriel Molina, Fernando Cardenal, and Ernesto Cardenal all met with Sandinista leaders. Some similar contact seems to have occurred between guerrilla leaders and some rural pastors in El Salvador by the mid-1970s.

8. As the crisis deepened, the church and church people became major public protagonists:

Nicaragua: pastoral letters criticizing govenment; Archbishop Obando as mediator after Sandinista hostage-taking actions (1974 and 1978); Solentiname participation in attacks on San Carlos (1977); priests and prominent laymen in the Twelve

El Salvador: oligarchy/government, linking church to popular organizations, unleashing attack on church in 1977; Archbishop Romero, the "voice of the voiceless" for the whole country, dramatizing in his person the conflict with the power structure; role of UCA; occupation of churches

Guatemala: higher level of repression, less public "space" for the conflict; hierarchy largely neutralized by Cardinal Casariego.

9. Other functions under the church included documentation of human rights violation and interpretation of events in these countries (through publications, contact with media people), and humanitarian work, especially with people displaced by the war within El Salvador.

10. Because either the church institutionally or individuals within it were seen as involved in the opposition, pastoral agents and catechists came under persecution and in some cases martyrdom. Frequently the victims were not involved in revolutionary organizations:

El Salvador: starting in 1977 killings of priests, expulsions, harassment, threats, and finally the killing of Archbishop Romero and the rape/killing of the American church women

Guatemala: killing of priests; persecution and killing of catechists; closing of Quiché diocese; dozens of priests and sisters forced to flee

Nicaragua: killing of catechists during 1975–77 "counterinsurgency."

11. Some church pastoral agents became either collaborators or members, and occasionally combatants, in revolutionary movements. In Guatemala and El Salvador, especially, there was a concern to "accompany" the people pastorally; eventually some pastoral agents and the whole structure of lay leaders were functioning under war conditions.

12. The clearest differences in the manner of Christian involvement in the struggle emerged from the stance of the hierarchies:

Nicaragua: virtual unanimity in the anti-Somoza struggle, the hierarchy aligned with the bourgeois opposition—tensions and divisions only after the FSLN victory

El Salvador: four bishops supporting government; Archbishop Romero (supported by Bishop Rivera y Damas) a rallying point for committed Christians; and the archdiocese's resources (radio station, publications, buildings) utilized for de facto opposition purposes, for example, to protest official violence

Guatemala: hierarchy largely neutralized; Justice and Peace Committee (most of whose activities in El Salvador would have taken place in the seminary/chancery office under Romero) established independently.

13. Throughout most of the period there was no systematic contact between like-minded Christian groups and, despite the small size of the countries (from Guatemala City to Managua, Nicaragua, is about a fourteen-hour drive), many church people had little contact with neighboring countries. Since the provinces of most religious orders covered all Central America, their members had some informal opportunities for contact and exchange of information. It was only in 1980 that the first organized meetings of basic Christian communities on a regional level took place.

8

Christians in Sandinista Nicaragua

Somoza's fall did not mean the end of struggle in Nicaragua. The task was now to consolidate the revolution and set in motion basic changes in the face of growing international and internal opposition and counter-revolution. This struggle inevitably affected the church.

In simplest terms the struggle was over what kind of revolution this was to be. Since Somoza had been overthrown by a "strategic class alliance" rather than by a sharp class struggle, to some extent certain points had been put in brackets or had been expressed in general language during the insurrectionary phase. Before long their opponents would accuse the Sandinistas of having "betrayed" the revolution by attempting to monopolize a victory won by the Nicaraguan people as a whole; the Sandinistas would reply that they were the vanguard recognized by the Nicaraguan people, which was itself "Sandinista."

From a different angle, the issue was whether this revolution would evolve along its own lines, seeking to learn from other experiences including the Cuban revolution, but creative and original in its responses to new situations (and, in particular, keeping a mixed economy and a nonaligned foreign policy) or whether it would end up closer to previous revolutions than its leaders would prefer to be.

For the church also, the Sandinista revolution presented a new situation, and perhaps a new opportunity. Twenty years previously in the Cuban revolution the churches had quickly become the refuge of those resentful of the revolution, because church people were prominent neither in the struggle to overthrow Batista nor in efforts at structural transformation.[1] Christians were indeed active in and around the Popular Unity government of Allende in Chile—but that government never really took power: blocked economically by national business and international corporations, thwarted in the legislature by an alliance of opposition parties, tied by a government bureaucracy filled with Christian Democrats, "destabilized" by the CIA, the Allende government was finally overthrown by the military and its sympathizers were brutally wiped out, sent into exile, or terrorized.

226

What was new in Nicaragua was the significant participation of church people in a revolution actively consolidating itself in power. As chapter 4, above, made clear, the church itself institutionally had a role in the overthrow of Somoza; for example, the bishops had publicly legitimated insurrection the very week the final insurrection began, and in a multiplicity of ways both Catholics and Protestants had been active in the insurrection. What should the position of the church be now: one of active support? or possibly of opposition (since the Marxist-influenced Sandinistas had emerged with virtually total political control)? or should the church seek to be apolitical, leaving it to each individual to decide whether to support or oppose the revolution? And, if there was no agreement on these matters, how could the church settle the disagreement or learn to live with it? This chapter will be focused largely on the public controversies over these issues.

RECONSTRUCTION: FIRST STEPS

Doubts and questions about what the Sandinista revolution would bring were initially submerged in a general euphoria throughout Nicaragua, particularly in those areas most affected by the bloodshed and destruction. Church bells rang, families were reunited, jubilant citizens and guerrillas paraded and celebrated in the streets, Radio Sandino ceased being clandestine, and Sandinista television programs appeared on screens.

On July 20 the largest crowd in Nicaraguan history gathered to receive the new National Reconstruction Government Junta and the nine-man Sandinista Directorate and heard Tomás Borge say, "We won the war against Somocismo. Now we face the war against ignorance and backwardness: the war to reconstruct our country."[2]

Most immediate were simply the tasks of restoring order and beginning to move the economy—particularly in agriculture where the normal planting had been disrupted by the war. During the final phase of the insurrection the Sandinista ranks had swelled, and thousands of *muchachos* (teenage guerrillas) had joined the fighting with little opportunity for political instruction or training in discipline. During the rest of 1979 there was a gradual effort to restrict the possession of arms and to form a regular Sandinista police and Sandinista popular army out of these irregulars and return the rest to their homes and schools.

The wealthiest Somocistas had fled, but many who had collaborated with the regime remained, especially several thousand troops. True to its slogan, "Implacable in the Struggle, Generous in Victory," the Frente Sandinista (FSLN) showed great discipline and was able to reduce spontaneous "executions" to a minimum. Seven thousand guardsmen and suspected Somoza collaborators were jailed, partly to put them on trial for crimes they might have committed during the dictatorship and to halt terrorist nighttime actions, which had continued during the immediate aftermath of the victory.[3]

Food distribution continued to be a problem. International agencies sent emergency food shipments which were handled through the Red Cross and agencies such as CEPAD, which claimed to be aiding over 10 percent of the population. Since Somoza and his entourage had taken almost all Nicaragua's liquid assets (leaving a bare $3.5 million in the national treasury), government offices had to begin from scratch. Fernando Cardenal, the Jesuit appointed to direct the Literacy Crusade, spent his first week in an office without a typewriter and wrote in a school notebook the names of people who appeared offering to work. Those in charge of municipal trash collection in Managua found a few broken-down trucks and several brooms with which to carry out their duties.

The first official decree of the new government was the expropriation of the properties of Somoza and the Somocistas (having fled along with the dictator defined one as a Somocista). Thus at the stroke of a pen the government became the owner of 20 percent of the arable land (initial estimates showed a much higher figure) and some 154 major businesses and industries.[4] For government planners and economists, the challenge was to reactivate the economy as quickly as possible and at the same time to lay the foundations for a process of gradual but real transformation. Such goals were beset with thorny problems: to simply "reactivate" the previous economy would amount to "Somocismo without Somoza," that is, an economy dominated by the interests of agroexporters and business elites. On the other hand, a hasty socialization would frighten and alienate the private sector, which was needed and which, the Sandinistas insisted, had earned a right to participate in the revolution. The aim was to maintain the "strategic alliance" with "patriotic" businesspeople.

A further challenge was the foreign debt. Somoza had left a public foreign debt of $1.6 billion (equivalent to almost a year's gross domestic product) and much of this money had gone to the dictator and his associates rather than to projects benefiting the people. Given the need for economic reactivation and development, it would be tempting for the new government to contract further debt, but such a course could subject the revolution to controls imposed by the international lending institutions. Initially the Sandinistas declared their intention to meet the obligations incurred (except for the bills to Argentina and Israel for several million dollars' worth of military equipment); they sought to renegotiate the loans and accepted money for the short-term emergency. With this money, they could renew essential government services and begin some public-works projects that would bring immediate social benefits (such as playgrounds and recreation facilities) and generate employment.

In its foreign policy, which it called nonaligned, the National Reconstruction Government sought a delicate balance: as a revolutionary government it did not hide its sympathies with other revolutions and it sought to overcome Nicaragua's decades-long situation as a client state of the United States; yet it did not wish to repeat the history of the Cuban revolution and become isolated in the hemisphere and suffer the hostility of the United States. The Carter government helped with some emergency cash and with continued food shipments (although it insisted on disbursing the food through the Red Cross rather than through the Sandinista government). At one point the Nicaraguan government even expressed an interest in acquiring arms from the United States.

Less than one week after the victory celebration a delegation was in Cuba taking part in the July 26 celebration there. An indication of the initial euphoria is seen in the statement of Alfonso Robelo (soon to emerge as a leading opposition spokesperson): "Cuba and Nicaragua together will triumph."[5]

Many questions remained unanswered during this period: To what extent would this revolution go in the direction of Cuba? (Those who were worried pointed to the presence of Cuban doctors.) How far would expropriation of property go? Did the Sandinistas really intend to have a "mixed economy," or were their statements simply a tactic to gain time while they consolidated themselves in power? Would there be "pluralism" or was the country headed toward one-party rule? The eventual outcome was, of course, only partly dependent on the intentions of the Sandinistas (who had divergent ideas on some issues): much would depend on the Nicaraguan bourgeoisie and on other countries, especially the United States.

To the extent these questions were raised in public there seemed to be general agreement. Robelo, as a member of the Junta, found himself defending the government's actions and intentions when faced with the doubts and hostility of the elites, even in his own party, the MDN (Nicaraguan Democratic Movement).[6]

The Frente Sandinista for its part was less interested in defining the answers than in engaging in an intensive effort to set up, extend, or consolidate the "mass organizations." Hence, the CDSs (Sandinista Defense Committees), became an elaborate neighborhood structure, involving people in dealing with local problems, from vigilance to clean-up; the CST (Sandinista Labor Federation) burgeoned, as did the ATC (Association of Rural Workers); AMNLAE (Luisa Amanda Espinosa Association of Nicaraguan Women) evolved out of AMPRONAC; and other organizations for youth and for children (many of whom had fought in the insurrection) were set up. For the Frente Sandinista these organizations were the means whereby people could begin to participate in the revolution, come to understand its purposes, and, if necessary, defend it.

Misgivings and Enthusiasm

Church pastoral agents were immediately involved in the tasks of reconstruction, as they had been in humanitarian tasks during the insurrection (for instance, a Jesuit managed the logistics of Red Cross food distribution for the whole country). At the local level many pastoral agents and members of Christian communities were active in Sandinista Defense Committees and in starting new ones.

Some priests found themselves celebrating Mass several times a day for the *caídos* (those who had fallen), since it was Nicaraguan tradition to celebrate not only a funeral Mass but one on the ninth-day, the month, and the year anniversaries of death. These were occasions for the gathering of family and community and an opportunity for evangelization—not only about the significance of these deaths but about the revolution they had made possible.

Discussion of what the revolution was to mean for the church was intense. In some areas there were courses for catechists and pastoral agents. Those most committed to the revolution began to think of how to carry out the kind of ongoing education that would be necessary if the church were to remain part of the revolutionary process.

On July 31, 1979, a week and a half after the installation of a new Junta, the Nicaraguan Bishops Conference issued a document expressing "anguishes and fears in this transition period." Claiming that they had been advocating "substantial changes" all along, the bishops made a number of statements, which in the context were a warning to the FSLN.

> As the church, we ought to remain free . . . vis-à-vis any system to opt always for people.
>
> It would be neither just nor sensible, after so many sacrifices imposed on our people, to forget the primary sense of life, and of human values involved in true liberation.
>
> We realize there are serious confusions both in ideological aspects and in the organization of new state structures.
>
> But not putting into practice an immediate respect for personal guarantees and basic human rights, not speeding up juridical proceedings, freedom of expression, of work, and of action, would erect a powerful barrier to the trust in the revolutionary projects that everyone wants. . . . Consciousness-raising does not mean imposing something from outside [*ajeno*, which also means "foreign"].[7]

The bishops at this first moment were already expressing a concern over Marxism (a "system"), human rights, and, it would seem, the presence of Cubans (in their remarks about consciousness-raising).

This statement provoked reactions. Daniel Ortega, who was both a member of the Junta and on the FSLN Directorate, said the bishops should speak clearly: "There is no need to use the ambiguous language they used during the Somoza period." Ernesto Cardenal indignantly pointed out that none of the bishops had been jailed, executed, or persecuted and said that the letter should have expressed the enthusiasm of the Nicaraguan people for the victory and its confidence in the government, rather than doubts and fears. Many Christians and pastoral agents seem to have had a similar reaction, and CONFER soon issued a letter which, while it did not criticize the bishops, sought to express the people's rejoicing.

Archbishop Obando, stung by Ernesto Cardenal's criticism, replied: "We incited to rebellion, we justified armed struggle, and the only thing we did not do was take up a rifle and kill National Guardsmen. Doing that would have meant breaking with the gospel." He said that Somoza had twice ordered him killed.

Fernando Cardenal around this same time published an article in *La Prensa* pointing out that some of the clergy, rather than express "the paschal joy of the people, which is being resurrected after fifty years of exploitation and despotism," were criticizing the revolution. The people of the barrios, factories, and fields, he said, knew "that the ideal of the revolution in Nicaragua is not bourgeois democracy with freedoms selected by those with economic privilege."[8]

These exchanges during the first few weeks revealed serious tensions—in fact, basic disagreements—between the hierarchy and that group of pastoral agents committed to the Sandinista revolution. While the disagreement would not become permanent and public until after the "honeymoon" of national unity had passed, several groups of Christians from the outset recognized that when the inevitable counterrevolution came (from the United States and from the anti-Somoza bourgeoisie), it would affect the church, and accordingly they began to lay the groundwork for "ideological struggle" within the church. Two institutions from the anti-Somoza period, CEPA, the center for training peasant leadership, and the IHCA (Central American Historical Institute) were joined by a new one, the Centro Antonio Valdivieso (CAV), named after the sixteenth-century Nicaraguan bishop killed by a conquistador for defending the Indians. Each of these small "think tanks" took on its own specialization: CEPA, training peasant leaders and preparing didactic materials for them (some in comic-book form); the IHCA, systematic documentation of the revolutionary process and publications such as discussion guides on the aims of the Sandinista revolution and Christianity; the CAV, the elaboration of an appropriate theology and training courses for pastoral agents and leaders of basic Christian communities. There was a certain amount of overlap and collaboration.

In September 1979 the IHCA held a conference on "Christian Faith and Sandinista Revolution in Nicaragua." The organizers' concerns at this early date were indicated by some of the topics: Jesus Christ in the revolutionary process, socialism and Christianity, and the experiences of Cuba and Chile.

Alvaro Argüello, S.J., speaking of the stances Christians take vis-à-vis the revolution, said that the indignation of the middle classes against Somoza, while commendable, would no longer be enough: they would have to take on "the cause of the poor" in order to stay with the revolution. Argüello did not focus on the role of the basic Christian communities, presumably because in numbers they were a very small minority; he pointed to the

Nicaraguan people as a whole, *el pueblo de los pobres*, as Christian, and saw their participation in the struggle to overthrow Somoza as Christian. He was thus taking a "mass line" and, as he closed, he wondered whether the churches would have the lucidity to value the justice of the new order more than the formal liberties of the old regime and "the courage to become masses with the . . . poor so that their joys and hopes and not the fears of the exploiting and dominating classes"[9] would beat in the hearts of the churches.

A panel discussion between Christians and Sandinista leaders dealt with two questions: what do Christians expect of the FSLN, and what does the FSLN expect of Christians? Juan Hernandez Pico, S.J., put his finger on "the great problem . . . of all revolutions . . . the relation between party and masses, between vanguard and people." His hope was that by being close to the people, the FSLN would achieve "the true democracy of the people." Miguel Ernesto Vigil, a layman and minister of housing, who came from a privileged background said that the revolution meant equality: "We all cost the blood of Jesus Christ and hence we are all equal." The revolution was offering an opportunity "to make real what we've said we believed for a long time."[10]

Commander Luis Carrión at one point made a reference to the "strategic alliance" between revolutionary Christians and revolutionary nonbelievers. The phrase went back to Fidel Castro, who created enthusiasm by his usage of it in Chile in 1971. According to Carrión, alliances are made with those who may not make the whole journey: those who are going the whole distance should be called *compañeros* (the favorite Sandinista term).[11] Christians should not see themselves as something added on; they had a full right to be Sandinistas, and "revolutionaries should fuse together into one embrace . . . in one huge Sandinista unity." Carrión was thus saying that the FSLN saw Christians in a more positive manner than previous revolutionary movements had. In time this position would become more explicit.[12]

A few days later 500 evangelical pastors and leaders met in RIPEN II (Second Interdenominational Retreat for Nicaraguan Protestant Pastors; the first, held in 1976, had been an important impulse among Protestants). The "Declaration of the 500," as the final document was called, rather more terse and less given to theologizing than comparable Catholic statements, nevertheless was a clear affirmation of the "victory of the Nicaraguan People and its instrument of liberation, the Sandinista National Liberation Front," for which God was thanked. "As we remember our heroes and martyrs, we recognize that the evangelical churches had their political, military, moral, and spiritual part in the struggle for the liberation of our Nicaragua."

Recognizing the government and the FSLN (the vanguard) as the legitimate authorities of the nation (with the proviso that "every human project is relative to . . . fidelity to . . . Jesus Christ"), they promised their cooperation in development and specifically urged participation in the Sandinista Defense committees "as places of Christian witness and service in concrete instances, such as literacy, health, liberating education." The Protestant leaders condemned the twenty-year blockade against Cuba and called for the "immediate lifting of this criminal . . . measure of North American imperialism," asking the backing of North American churches. Some Cuban Protestants participated in the retreat, and this statement may reflect a spontaneous reaction on the part of Nicaraguan pastors suddenly in contact with the Cuban experience, which had been utterly closed to them during the Somoza period. In closing the pastors made some particular suggestions for the Atlantic coast region, where there was a high proportion of Protestants. RIPEN II had been organized by CEPAD, which began to take on ambitious development projects in cooperation with the government, with financing from European and North American churches.[13]

Pastoral Letter

Of all the statements made during the initial period the most significant by far was that of the Nicaraguan Bishops Conference (November 17, 1979), which was in sharp contrast to its initially expressed fears and indeed to the opposition posture it was soon to assume, so that it stands unique. Christians sympathetic to the revolution took it as a Magna Carta for their own involvement.

Even the introduction was somewhat unusual in that the bishops included "basic Christian communities" and "Delegates of the Word," in the salutation. They recognized that "we have not always measured up to what the needs of the people demanded," and saw their contribution as one in dialogue in order that all together might "discern . . . options and commitments."

With a Medellín-like approach the bishops discussed the accomplishments of the revolution and of the issue of socialism, laid out a compendium of relevant biblical and theological concepts, and concluded with remarks on the challenges of the moment. Possibly made sensitive by criticism of their first statement, the bishops made a positive assessment of the accomplishments of the "revolutionary process." (Even in using the term "process"—the word most favored by the Sandinistas—they were showing their sensitivity.) The people's experience both of suffering and of struggle now offered a basis for liberating action. There were new forces at work, especially youth and women ("left behind for centuries"), a new originality from Sandino's thought, and a new creativity in the joy of a poor people in charge of its country for the first time. Significantly the bishops admitted that the struggle against an unjust system continued even after the overthrow of Somoza, and they recognized the existence of conflicts among opposing interests (over expropriations, for example). They welcomed the revolution's legal guarantees such as freedom of information and the freedom to organize political parties, and noted the "first steps in agrarian reform," which seemed to be a recognition that it would go further than the initial expropriation of the Somocista properties.

In the section on "tasks," positive-sounding statements were interspersed with warnings and allusions to abuses. Thus, while they believed "the present revolutionary moment" was "a propitious occasion to make real the church's option for the poor," they emphasized that "no historical revolutionary realization can exhaust the infinite possibilities . . . of the Kingdom of God" and warned that commitment could not mean "naiveté or blind enthusiasm and much less the creation of a new idol. . . ." Noting the official policy against summary executions, they said there had been abuses by local leaders. At one point they said, ". . . let us remember that the work of reconstruction belongs to the whole people and not just to certain sectors." That they had in mind the FSLN was evident from the next paragraph:

> With regard to the freedom of organization in party politics we think the conscious and active participation of the Nicaraguan majorities in the revolutionary process . . . is very necessary; this should take place through bodies of direct popular democracy that already exist and through those that may be created through national dialogue. Different forces have contributed generously to the historical process and no one should block their contribution. Heading up these forces, it is obvious that the Sandinista National Liberation Front has earned a place in history. To consolidate this position, its main work, in our judgment, is to continue to convoke the whole people to go on forging its own history through a pluralistic and decisive participation in national life. This demands of the present leaders an absolute fidelity to the people of the poor that will not contradict the principles of justice and the name of "Sandinista," won in the struggle for liberation.

Since it pointed to what would be the crux of the debate over the political forms of the revolution, this paragraph calls for some exegesis. There seemed to be something for all sides: the bishops in speaking of "bodies of direct popular democracy" seemed to be referring to the mass organizations (CST, ATC, AMNLAE, CDS, and so forth); they recognized a special place for the FSLN and they made no mention of elections, thus seemingly opening the way for a different method of exercising democracy (etymologically, of course, the word "democracy" makes no reference to elections). On the other hand, they warned against excluding other forces and urged a pluralistic participation, which seemed to envision a multiparty system. Less clear was whether the bishops thought the FSLN, having headed the struggle to the present, should simply become one party among several, or whether it should continue to "head" a pluralistic process—that is, pluralism embracing those who supported, and did not seek to overthrow, the revolutionary process.

Perhaps what provoked most commentary was the bishops' treatment of socialism. They made a distinction between a "spurious" socialism, seen as arbitrary power to be obeyed blindly, antireligious, and violating human rights, and a socialism that would aim at satisfying the needs of the majority of Nicaraguans, would have a nationally planned economy, be increasingly participative, and diminish the injustices and inequities between city and country, and between intellectual and manual work, and would increase the participation of the worker in the fruits of his or her labor, and so lead to a "true transferring of power toward the popular classes."[14]

To those fearful of "socialism" in Nicaragua, these counterposed distinctions must have seemed to be contrived argumentation, as did the following:

> Regarding class struggle, we think the dynamic fact of class struggle that should lead to a just transformation of structures is one thing, and something else again is class hatred, which is directed at people and radically contradicts the Christian duty to be ruled by love.

They closed this section by affirming:

> We are confident . . . that the revolutionary process will be something original, creative, deeply national, and in no way imitative, because along with the majority of Nicaraguans, what we want is a process that strides firmly toward a society that is fully and authentically Nicaraguan, neither capitalistic, nor dependent, nor totalitarian.

(When the bishops and many other clergy later took a negative view of the revolution, they would point to warnings and allusions in these paragraphs to show that their position was one of continuity and not a reversal of the pastoral letter.)

In the middle section the bishops presented a compendium of themes from liberation theology. These quotations may serve to exemplify the thrust:

> The heart of Jesus' message is the announcing of the kingdom of God. Jesus makes explicit that the kingdom means liberation and justice (cf. Luke 4:16–20) because it is a kingdom of life; the necessity of building it is the basis for our taking on, and collaborating with, the present process, which aims at assuring that all Nicaraguans really have life. Faith in this God moves us to insist again on what we have always preached but which now takes on exceptional concreteness and urgency. Believing in this God means giving life to others, really loving them, practicing justice. . . .
>
> Announcing the kingdom involves making it present in history so that it comes to us. . . .
>
> Today in our country we experience an exceptional opportunity for

giving witness to, and announcing, God's kingdom. It would be a grave infidelity to the gospel to let pass this demanding moment for making concrete the preferential option for the poor, out of fears and resentments, out of the insecurity that every radical social-change process creates in some people, or out of a defense of individual interests, whether large or small. . . .

The poor of whom Jesus speaks are the real and authentic poor, hungry and afflicted, oppressed; they are all those who are not taken into account in the organization of society and are rejected by it. . . .

Nicaraguan brothers and sisters, here is how our faith in Jesus and in the God of life, now incarnate in an effort directed by reason, should illuminate the commitment of Christians in the present revolutionary process.

The final section noted how the "eyes of Latin America" and of the Latin American church were fixed on Nicaragua. The revolution, the bishops repeated, demanded a conversion, which meant austerity of life so that it would not be the majority who would have to suffer the consequences of the war and the resulting economic emergency. They called for an end to capital flight, for reinvestment in Nicaragua, and for just conditions for a renegotiation of the national debt.[15]

Obviously the letter's thrust, both in its judgments on the "process" and in the invocation of gospel themes appropriate to the moment, was supportive of the Sandinista revolution in a manner perhaps unprecedented in an official public stand by any Bishops Conference. Doubtless there were coincidental factors at work—one wonders who had a hand in helping the bishops think through and write the text. In addition the letter reflected the "honeymoon" period during which different groups, using the same language, could retain different ideas about where the "process" was headed.

For the church the situation was to become more problematic as it became increasingly clear that the option offered was not some revolutionary process with ideal characteristics, but *this* revolution—Sandinista, led by the FSLN—and that the choice would come down to supporting it or opposing it. Support of course did not have to be uncritical, but criticism without an underlying position of support would inevitably serve to undermine the revolution itself and would aid the opposition (or counter-revolutionary) forces.

The foregoing has dealt almost exclusively with ideological considerations, mainly with considerations on the direction of the revolution. Brief references to some other events in the church will round out this section.

When Somoza fell, the previous nuncio, Gabriel Montalvo, had been declared persona non grata by Miguel D'Escoto because of his close association with Somoza. After some delay the Vatican appointed Pietro Sambi, who had previously served in Algeria and Cuba and was therefore more suited to a country in revolution.

The bishops met periodically with government representatives, sometimes to bring up problems such as the condition of political prisoners. Government officials admitted the bad conditions, inherited from Somoza, but when they asked whether the church would care to take responsibility for the prisoners' food and medicine, the bishops backed off.

On some occasions there were reports that CDSs participated directly in popular religious festivals such as the novena of *La Purísima*.[16] Questions were raised about the place of popular religiosity in the new Nicaragua, and whether or not it was appropriate for revolutionary organizations to participate. Others rephrased the question: Do these celebrations belong to the church or to the people?

CONSOLIDATION AND CONFLICT

During 1980 the Sandinista revolution became increasingly well defined and consolidated in power and began to face organized opposition and counter-revolution. During the same period signals from the United States passed from the Carter administration's attempts to "moderate" the revolution through aid (delayed for many months in Congress) to the election of Ronald Reagan and the signs of impending direct confrontation.

When the Literacy Crusade was formally launched in March, the "honeymoon" was still in effect. From then until August an estimated 120,000 people, mainly students (the schools were closed), went out to the countryside to "battle" illiteracy. Several purposes were served by the campaign: illiteracy was reduced dramatically from 52 to 13 percent; the poorest and most marginal received a concrete and dramatic benefit from the revolution; people were prepared to enter more directly into political participation; job skills were upgraded (reading, for instance, would be useful to peasants learning to operate farm machinery); basic issues of history, politics, culture, and development were discussed; groundwork was laid for further mass mobilizations, for educational follow-up, and for future health campaigns, among other things; and not least, the relatively privileged students were brought into sustained contact with the "real Nicaragua," experiencing, for example, the feeling of a gnawing stomach when they had to share the standard diet of the peasants. By the time the crusade finished in August, the political "honeymoon" was over and the opposition was viewing it as Sandinista indoctrination.

The litmus test of a revolution must be its economic policy—and performance. Innumerable tensions and dilemmas had to be dealt with: how to achieve both a more just distribution and increased production; how to obtain needed aid and at the same time make the enormous foreign debt manageable; how to meet basic needs in the short term while laying the basis for a new kind of economy in the future.

Some of these issues were dealt with in the economic plan for 1980 called "The Program for Economic Reactivation for the Benefit of the People," a title suggesting the Frente Sandinista's belief that the key question was not so much the *ownership* of the means of production in itself as the overall "logic" of the economy. At longer range the idea was to work toward a "Sandinista economy"—for the most part they avoided the term "socialism," although in another context one leader spoke of a "creative application of Marxism"—where, through planning and the control of key sectors of the economy (banking and finances, foreign trade and some domestic marketing, natural resources, and the former Somoza holdings), the "logic of the majorities" would prevail.[17]

In other words, the FSLN seemed genuinely to believe that a "mixed economy" could be revolutionary. Fidel Castro himself counseled the Sandinistas not to eliminate all the private sector, and one assumes they must have arrived at similar conclusions based on their own observations.

Small and medium businesses were given encouragement and incentives. Even some of the large businesses were able to function reasonably well under the Sandinistas—cotton growers, for example. In many cases the problems faced by business were external: declining world market prices and political instability in Central America, which diminished demand for exports to neighboring countries. In some cases factory- and business-owners chose to continue to operate not simply for economic reasons but because their children were working with the revolution or had died in combat. Nevertheless there was a strong, and perhaps dominant, apprehension among business people that their days might be numbered. Certainly the elite would see its privileges eroded if the Sandinista government were to carry out a thorough revolution.

Yet the steps actually taken were modest: among them, an income tax varying from 6 percent to a maximum of 50 percent (for incomes of $20,000 and above, which only a very small number received);[18] a top limit on government salaries of $1,000 a month for cabinet ministers; middle-ranking administrators and technicians would receive several hundred dollars, which put them far above peasants making $2 a day, but still represented a "sacrifice" vis-à-vis what they could earn in the private sector.

Policies regarding peasants and workers were rather conservative. The government resisted pressures for increases in wages, convinced that such increases would be inflationary, and sought, rather, to increase and emphasize the "social wage": health care, literacy campaign, new parks and recreational facilities. Unemployment was attacked through public-works projects.

Land reform was also approached in a conservative and pragmatic fashion. Former Somoza estates were left as large enterprises rather than divided up, and the effort was toward efficient management and production. Workers were encouraged to see them as belonging to the Area of People's Property (rather than the state) and were given a larger role in management, but they did not directly share the profits. In other cases cooperatives were formed, and in still others the effort was simply to help existing small farmers.

In order to undertake its long-range plans the Sandinista government had to arrive at a satisfactory settlement of the foreign debt, which at $1.6 billion amounted to several hundred dollars per person. It astutely decided to renegotiate the easiest debts first—those with foreign governments—and then to pass to the international lending institutions, and finally to settle with the private banks, which would be the hardest. (Of the $600 million in this category, $56 million was owed to Citibank and $30 million to Bank of America.) The debts were renegotiated on terms that were concessionary to Nicaragua—allowing a grace period of several years and lower interest rates—while preserving the principle that debts should be honored. Through the process the Sandinista government successfully avoided having to subject itself to International Monetary Fund conditions, which could have been used to block structural changes.[19]

Nicaragua was also successful in obtaining aid both from such international agencies as the Inter-American Development Bank and the World Bank, and from individual countries. Although it delayed the process for many months and attempted to place conditions on its loan, the United States contributed $87.5 million; West Germany loaned $22.9 million and Mexico $20 million. East Germany loaned $20 million, but aid from socialist-bloc countries was initially not large. Venezuela contributed with concessionary prices on oil and an offer that some of the payment could be turned into a development fund for Nicaragua.[20]

Almost since the fall of Somoza there had been rumblings of discontent, particularly from COSEP, the umbrella organization of the private sector. In April 1980 open opposition was formed around Alfonso Robelo's resignation from the Junta and a crisis in *La Prensa*.

Robelo's resignation was provoked by the Sandinista decision to expand the Council of State, a quasi-legislative body then being formed with representatives from organizations representing various sectors—from thirty-three to forty-seven delegates—most of the new organizations represented being connected with the FSLN. To Robelo this was a violation of agreements made in Costa Rica just before victory; the Sandinistas saw the change as a reflection of changes since their victory, especially the growth of the popular organizations.

This controversy was but a reflection of the larger issue of the role of the FSLN. The private sector saw Nicaragua as headed toward a classical one-party rule and expressed its demands for "pluralism" and "elections." It saw the FSLN as a political party among others and accused it of using its power to secure an unfair advantage. The FSLN, on the other hand, argued that all Nicaraguans were "Sandinista" and that the FSLN was the recognized vanguard leading the revolutionary process.

The crisis at *La Prensa* occurred at about the same time. The Chamorro family was divided over the revolution. Violeta de Chamorro, widow of the owner of *La Prensa,* whose murder had fanned the anti-Somoza flames, had resigned from the Junta, ostensibly for health reasons, but in fact largely because the controversy over the revolution was dividing the Chamorro family itself. When *La Prensa's* board of directors fired Xavier Chamorro, Violeta's brother-in-law, most of the workers (160) went on strike demanding his reinstatement. After some time, Xavier Chamorro took his 25 percent interest in the paper and the employees took their severance pay and started a new paper, *El Nuevo Diario,* which took an independent but pro-revolutionary position. From this point onward *La Prensa* became the organ of the anti-Sandinista forces.[21]

Those seeking to form an opposition faced severe problems: the FSLN had total military control, control of the government, and the ability to lay down the guidelines for the economy and for political processes, although the private sector had considerable economic bargaining power. Hence it was in the ideological arena that the anti-FSLN forces had to operate. However, the opposition could scarcely offer a clear alternative to the Sandinista *proyecto,* since its basic goal would be to retain its own (privileged) way of life. Its only recourse, then, was to criticize the "errors" of the Sandinistas, to warn of the dangers of Marxism, to defend the "values" of freedom, and so forth. In this context, religion came to offer a privileged terrain for ideological struggle.

As the year 1980 went on isolated instances of counter-revolutionary activities were discovered, and increasing uneasiness was felt over the presence of ex-Somoza Guardsmen in Honduras, sometimes reputed to be several thousand in number. In November, Jorge Salazar, vice-president of COSEP, was killed as Sandinista police attempted to seize arms he was transporting. According to the FSLN, people accompanying Salazar opened fire. The incident served to deepen the crisis; for some, the Sandinistas appeared as repressive, while for others there was clear proof that the bourgeois opposition was actively engaged in counter-revolution.

Relations with the United States deteriorated during this period. Initially the Carter administration thought the best way to "moderate" the outcome in Nicaragua was through aid, but its proposed $75 million package ($45 million of which would go to the private sector) became bogged down in the United States Congress as conditions on the aid offer were debated endlessly; the aid was finally approved in June, almost a year after the fall of Somoza. Even after approval, the disbursal dragged on almost until the end of the Carter presidency. The amount of money was important, but equally important was its effect in encouraging the international lending institutions to continue to help Nicaragua.[22]

Throughout this period the government had pursued what it regarded as a nonaligned foreign policy; its most friendly contacts were with Western European countries and it was regarded favorably by the Socialist International. Nevertheless, the United States government and public opinion began to perceive Nicaragua as increasingly aligned with the socialist bloc. For example, in the United Nations vote on the Soviet invasion of Afghanistan, Nicaragua abstained, stating that it opposed all intervention—feeling that the vote was mainly for United States purposes. The presence of Cuban teachers in the Literacy Crusade and some Cuban advisers with the army furthered that impression.

In any case, in the United States the Republican party, whose platform had deplored the Sandinista victory, won the November 1980 election and Ronald Reagan, whose advisers had openly speculated about how to overthrow the Nicaraguan revolution, prepared to become president.

Seeing Christ in Literacy

Events in the church in 1980 to a great extent were a reflection of, or a response to, the developments just described, especially as voices of opposition began to be heard.

At the beginning of 1980, however, voices were still more or less in harmony. On January 1, for example, Archbishop Obando celebrated the traditional Mass for peace, which during the final Somoza years had served as a rallying point for the opposition. Behind the altar were large portraits of Sandino and Carlos Fonseca and present were Daniel Ortega, Sergio Ramírez, and Tomás Borge. In February Obando told the press in Washington that church-state relations were "not tense at the moment," although he said that the church was following the process "without any naïveté." The bishops' Lenten message expressed misgivings about "materialistic and atheistic propaganda" and about political prisoners. But Archbishop Obando, visiting Cuba, said, "We are sure the Sandinista revolution is seeking the good of the majority," and during his visit he stopped at the Isle of Youth, where 550 Nicaraguan young people were studying. Junta members Violeta de Chamorro and Daniel Ortega visited Pope John Paul II, who expressed his wishes for Nicaragua and especially for the Literacy Crusade. Archbishop Romero's assassination provoked an unusually strong statement from the FSLN Directorate. Besides praising Romero's "defense of the humble," it blamed the Salvadoran Junta for genocide and denounced the efforts of the United States government to aid the Junta. Thousands of people filled the Plaza of the Revolution to attend a Mass celebrated for Archbishop Romero.[23]

More than 300 religious participated in the Literacy Crusade, which was launched in March. In January the bishops had issued a statement likening the campaign to the work of "Christ the Teacher" and urging parents to encourage their children to participate. Since there was a great deal of resistance on the part of some middle-class parents to allow their children (especially daughters) to go "to the wilds" in a project directed by (Marxist) revolutionaries, the bishops' support was not idle. The bishops' statement urged the literacy trainers to become "students of the peasants and

workers." CEPAD also issued a statement encouraging people to participate in the crusade and recommending that local congregations offer their
buildings and other resources.[24] Religious, especially sisters, were usually
middle-level cadres in the Literacy Crusade, supervising the young people
who were teaching at the village level.

By the time the campaign ended it had become the subject of controversy,
criticized as being Marxist indoctrination, and defended as being a necessary means whereby the people could become real actors in society. Even
Masses celebrated around the closing became occasions for clashes. In
August at one such Mass for literacy workers celebrated by Archbishop
Obando, groups of Sandinista sympathizers gathered outside were shouting, "Sandino yesterday, Sandino today, Sandino forever" and "We want
a church on the side of the poor." When the people came out from the Mass
they began to shout, "Christ yesterday, Christ today, Christ forever."

Under the title of "The New Face of Christ in Literacy," CONFER organized a seminar to evaluate the experience. Those who participated said
the experience had brought the religious closer to the reality of peasants and
the poor and caused them to question some of their activities, such as
Catholic high schools, which one of them called a "classist, alienating education." Carlos Tunnermann, the minister of education, said, "This crusade has been Christian, revolutionary, and Sandinista," and he was echoed
by Sister Elsa Ruth Ugarte, who said that teaching was an act of justice and
love: "The revolution is Christian."[25] Such sentiments, however, were coming to be seen as shared by only a minority of the church's pastoral agents.

Signs of Opposition

As pointed out above, the first organized, public opposition to the Sandinista government appeared around the formation of the Council of State
and Alfonso Robelo's resignation from it. Monsignor Felix Quintañilla,
president of ACLEN (priests' association), who had been chosen to represent the clergy in the Council of State, made public his decision not to participate shortly after Robelo's resignation, giving as his reason that he had
too much work to do. He was supported by Archbishop Obando. However,
Alvaro Argüello, ACLEN vice-president, replaced Quintañilla, insisting
that it was important for the church's evangelization that there be dialogue
and that a presence in the Council of State was a service to the people.
Around this time a group of priests and sisters denounced the maneuvers of
a "certain sector of private enterprise and imperialism," which was seeking
to destabilize the revolution. They saw participation in the Council of State
as a concrete way of expressing the option for the poor, that is, through
supporting that "historical project" that would benefit the poor.[26]

On May 13, 1980, while Robelo's resignation was still in the air, the
bishops issued a communiqué, stating that, since the "exceptional circumstances" had passed, lay people could now fill the government positions

presently held by priests. They had in mind Miguel D'Escoto (foreign minister), Ernesto Cardenal (minister of culture), Edgard Parrales (minister of social welfare), and Fernando Cardenal (director of the Literacy Crusade), as well as several other priests in middle-level positions. At the same time they stated that the ACLEN representative in the Council of State was there in the name of the clergy and not of the church. The bishops gave several reasons for their decision and rejected any "political or partisan instrumentalization" that might be made of their decision (presumably having in mind the obvious connection to the Robelo resignation). Their only interest, they said, was "the strengthening of unity and effectiveness in ecclesial service."

In a short communiqué on May 20, ten priests and religious in the government said they understood the bishops' concerns, rejected attempts to divide the church, and concluded: "Our fidelity to the church and our fidelity to the poor cannot be in contradiction. On any point humanly open to discussion we are in dialogue, in accordance with the Christian style of our Nicaraguan church."

Moisés Hassán, a Junta member speaking for the FSLN, said the presence of priests and religious in important government posts was due to their role in the struggle for liberation. Ernesto Cardenal said he had been assured by Cardinal Casaroli, the Vatican secretary of state, that while in general priests should not participate in politics, Nicaragua was an exceptional case. In Cardenal's telling, it seemed that Casaroli had urged him *not* to resign (and return to Solentiname).[27] For the moment the issue was postponed: the priests remained at their posts, but the problem continued to simmer for over a year until it boiled up again in mid-1981.

It was less than a month after significant sectors of what had been the anti-Somoza bourgeoisie chose to break with the revolutionary process and go into public opposition that the bishops expressed a similar break with the Sandinista revolution. From this point on the bishops found little to praise and much to criticize. There is a clear parallel: just as the bishops' positions during the 1970s bore a sharp resemblance to those of the bourgeois opposition, and they accepted a de facto alliance with a movement headed by the FSLN only when the bourgeoisie itself had done so (see chapter 4), they found themselves symbolically breaking with the revolutionary process precisely when the bourgeoisie did so.

Mixed Signals

While the controversy over the Council of State and the priests in government was still fresh, Archbishop Obando in a recorded radio message warned against "hatred," in a sense that seemed to serve the anti-Sandinistas. While most of the text of the discourse, printed in *La Prensa*, dealt with hatred on a personal or family level, the archbishop said hatred was easy to stir up where there was resentment or envy: "So political agitators take advantage of this fact to stir up envy and resentment and discontent among their followers and take them to the extreme of hatred whether it be toward a social class or against another country." *La Prensa*'s headline, "The Most Negative Thing: Preaching Hatred," clearly gave an anti-Sandinista cast to Obando's words, no matter what his original intention.[28]

It would seem that, whatever the differences at the level of local congregations, the Protestant churches as institutions did not find themselves in such tension over the Sandinista revolution. CEPAD was carrying out a training program for pastors and other church leaders. Interviewed by *Barricada* (the official FSLN newspaper) at a seminar for 150 leaders, Benjamín Cortés, a minister and CEPAD administrator, said that Protestants felt they should participate directly in the revolutionary process, working in the mass organizations. He said "Marxist philosophy" had made a "positive contribution" to revolutions in history. After a similar seminar some weeks later the participants made a statement reaffirming their commitment to the poor, following the "example of Jesus Christ who, as a poor person himself, was committed to the struggle for the oppressed and exploited of his time and so opened the way to liberation, peace, and social equality." They pointed to how the revolution's values were being translated into the economic plan, the popular organizations, a new legal framework, the Literacy Crusade, the agrarian reform and health programs, and they congratulated the government and the FSLN for their direction of the process.[29] These statements were all the more interesting in that normally CEPAD was not given to making public statements or elaborating any theology of participation in the process.

The citing of these statements is not meant to imply that Protestants were more supportive of the Sandinista revolution than Catholics—in fact, there is probably no basis for accurately measuring such support on either side. It would seem to be that the relative absence of conflict on the Protestant side would reflect three factors: (1) the Catholic church as an institution was willy-nilly an actor in public life; Protestant churches, by comparison, were more "private" in nature and did not have to take an institutional stand on the revolution; (2) among many Protestants it was customary to accept established authority; hence just as they tended to recognize the Somoza government until close to the end, even some conservative Protestant churches were able to accept the Sandinista authority, as long as it permitted them to operate; (3) at the level of the local congregation a pastor might prefer to avoid all references to the revolution—pro or con—since that could divide the congregation. (Explicit stands by pastors could be more problematic among Protestants than among Catholics, where parishes are seen more as entities prior to, and independent of, the individual who at a given time might be the pastor.)

One group of Protestants, belonging to the Eje Ecuménico (Ecumenical Axis), whose chief spokesperson was José Miguel Torres, a Baptist pastor, did seek to elaborate a theological/pastoral position of support for the revolution and engaged in public controversy alongside the IHCA, CEPA, and the Valdivieso Center (where its offices were located for some time). Its position seemed to be that the circumstances demanded open support of the revolution and it found itself in tension with the mainstream Protestant majority as represented in CEPAD. The exact strength of those associated with the Ecumenical Axis was unclear.[30]

An example of how religion, culture, and politics tended to become intertwined in bizarre ways was the dinner of International Brotherhood of Christian Businessmen, which took place at the Intercontinental Hotel with several high government officials in attendance. *La Prensa's* headline was "A Supper with Christ and the *Comandantes.*" In the midst of testimonies about finding peace with Christ, the American astronaut Charles Duke presented Tomás Borge with a flag that had been taken to the moon. Several speakers referred to the revolution in positive terms, although they insisted that the peace of Christ must be found in one's heart. One speaker said the Nicaraguan revolution could be the most important in the world if it put Christ at its center, and pointed out that the Cuban revolution, with all its achievements, could not give the peace of Christ.[31]

Controversy flared in August when the government, intending to end a consumer-oriented celebration of Christmas and recover "its true popular and Christian meaning," published a law prohibiting advertising that would use Christmas to sell goods or services. "Chepe Pavón Pushes Santa Claus Aside" read headlines in *El Nuevo Diario* (Chepe Pavón is the Joseph-figure in Mejía Godoy's song "Christ Is Born in Palacaguina"). Uriel Molina said that from 1976 on, his parish had not even been able to celebrate midnight Mass because of the repression, but that in 1979 they had celebrated Christmas with Joseph and Mary in Nicaraguan traditional dress: "Which is more Christian? Celebrating Christmas like that or going to a supermarket to buy foreign-made toys which are part of a campaign that is not only capitalist but pagan. . . ."

Nevertheless, the opposition seized on the decree as a sign of the FSLN's hostility to the church. The Social Christian party delegate to the Council of State dramatically produced a confidential FSLN document from the previous December, which spoke of giving a "different, fundamentally political content" to Christmas, warning, at the same time, that such a deep-seated tradition should not be attacked head-on; religion was still strong in the Soviet Union after sixty-two years of governmental opposition to it. To FSLN opponents the document, published in *La Prensa,* was a clear indication that the ultimate aim was to end religion in Nicaragua. However, the internal FSLN document could be read another way: evidently written by and for nonbelievers within the Sandinista leadership, it would seem to be a warning not to make doctrinaire and militant atheism a part of the official Sandinista ideology.[32]

A three-day meeting of Delegates of the Word from rural basic Christian communities may exemplify the flavor of pastoral work during this period. One discussion group was devoted to what these communities had done during the insurrection. The fact that more than a year later they were reliving those memories was a testament to how strong they were and how they formed the basis for the continuing revolution. The other two groups, dealing with the present and the future, noted pastoral problems such as the shortage of Delegates: many had become leaders of the people's organizations and some had moved to other parts of the country. Opinion was divided on whether people could be Delegates and popular-organization leaders at the same time. One group worked on delineating the qualities of the "new man" (sic): "oriented to service, honest, responsible, community-oriented, Christian, generous, committed . . . ," and spoke of how to do "Christian and political consciousness-raising at the same time. . . ." All presented their conclusions not simply in words but in songs, skits, and drawings; one drawing contrasted the "old man" (with liquor, money, a bloodstained dead dove, and a black cross) and the "new man" (young, with the machete and hammer of reconstruction, the literacy workbook, a large sun, and the cross painted red, a symbol of liberty). An improvised song provided a slogan for the meeting: "Del rancho surge la unión/ Fe Cristiana y Revolución" ("From the peasant hut comes the fusion/ Of Christian faith and Revolution").[33]

Throughout a good part of 1980 the involvement of CELAM in Nicaragua was a topic of debate. In February CELAM proposed a plan to the Nicaraguan bishops, which was to include several conferences intended to communicate the Puebla conclusions, one for bishops and others for priests, religious, and lay people. In addition, CELAM experts would arrive to give courses on catechesis, 25,000 Bibles would be distributed, and concrete help would be given, including personnel to reopen and staff the seminary. A collection would be taken up in Latin America for Nicaragua. Total cost of the programs was estimated at $300,000. On the official level it was not made explicit why Nicaragua required special attention at this point, when it had not under Somoza, although Archbishop Quarracino, CELAM general secretary, spoke of the danger of Nicaragua becoming a "Marxist and communist state."

Criticism about CELAM's "intervention" appeared quickly. It was pointed out that at the 1979 CELAM conference in Puebla no attention was paid to Nicaragua: a priest sent by the Nicaraguan clergy was not allowed to speak of the situation under Somoza, and Archbishop Obando entered only toward the end of the conference (as a substitute for Bishop Salazar who was sick). In view of the earlier lack of interest, the present interest was considered "suspicious." A group of basic Christian communities warned CELAM not to be used by "great capitalist interests" and pointed out that some of the funding was coming from the right-wing DeRance Foundation in the United States. The suspicion was that the new interest in Nicaragua was to weaken the revolutionary process. When Sergio Ramírez and Miguel

Ernesto Vigil, the minister of housing and a well-known Catholic layman, criticized CELAM, *La Prensa* suggested that there were people who wanted to cause division in the church and insisted on "the strictest respect" for church authorities.

The proposed CELAM materials seem to have aimed not so much at attacking the revolution as at offering a spiritualistic version of Puebla, which would largely ignore what was happening in Nicaragua rather than seek to discern God's will and action within the revolution. The CELAM plans for pastoral formation did not materialize on any large scale. CELAM's main role in Nicaragua seems to have been in frequent contact between Archbishop López Trujillo and the Nicaraguan bishops and to have consisted more in advice on how to proceed both within Nicaragua and vis-à-vis the Vatican.[34]

Questions and Dilemmas

While Christians involved in the Sandinista revolution found themselves putting much of their energies into such public controversies, there were other issues of more long-range importance. In September 1980 the CAV and the IHCA organized a conference to deal with theological and pastoral issues. Among the participants were a number of theologians from Latin America. The summary of the meeting presented here is based largely on a document called "Problems that the Revolutionary Process Poses for Ecclesial Faith." This document was essentially a systematic grouping of dozens of questions that revolutionaries doing pastoral work were sensing; it could well serve as the framework for an extended commentary.

The first series of questions dealt with the new forms of power in Nicaragua (FSLN, government, mass organizations). How balance the need for a strong state and strong vanguard (especially given the opposition, both internal and international) with the "autonomy" of the popular organizations to press for their own demands? Is there a distinction between "totalitarianism" (the accusation of the opposition) and Sandinista "hegemony" of the process? Should Christians support all-embracing unity, or should there be a class alliance even on the international level (meaning, it would seem, aligning with the socialist bloc if necessary to protect the revolution) with the cause of the poor as its criterion? Should not the church support the "revolutionary project" on its own merits, without attempting to baptize it or work for a "new Christendom," yet at the same time criticize errors—but always from a position of support?

Regarding economics, there seemed to be a series of dilemmas: attempt to satisfy real and immediate needs or work toward long-term structural change, even at the cost of immediate needs? Accumulate capital at the expense of the privileged and risk the brain drain, capital flight, and international opposition (whose results the people themselves would suffer) or go slow on needed structural reforms and thus maintain injustice? Accept large new loans in order to finance development (and thereby make the revolution more dependent) or accept greater austerity as the price of independence?

An underlying question was whether or not there were Christian criteria for approaching such problems. Pastoral agents should be given more training in such questions, and some should specialize in them, so these issues could enter into evangelization and preaching.

In order to understand what was being discussed, it might help to imagine how these issues could affect grassroots pastoral practice. Let us suppose that in the local ATC (Association of Rural Workers) some are dissatisfied, since they see their real earnings declining and salaries are frozen. Should the issue be discussed in basic Christian communities? Should the government's technical explanation be made available to people (that higher wages would be inflationary and that the government is increasing the "social wage")? Or should the emphasis be on trusting the people's instincts? Several of the questions mentioned above, both economic and political, would be involved in approaching such a situation on the local level.

The conference dealt with a second series of questions called "pastoral-political," revolving around the notion of the "popular [or people's] church" and its relation both to the people's organizations and to the "established traditional church." Defining the popular church as "the church that the Spirit raises up among the people of the poor, reviving the memory of Jesus and the convocation to follow him," they went on to ask who made it up, who represented it, and how it was defined theologically and sociopolitically. Can the church continue with its same pastoral work after a victorious revolution? How does the revolution question the internal structures of the church? What is the role of the people in creating a new kind of pastoral work?

What is the relationship between political consciousness and religious consciousness, particularly the autonomy of religious consciousness and its influence on political consciousness? What is the relationship between the popular movement and the basic Christian communities? What do the basic Christian communities contribute to building up popular power? How can the popular church deal with political sectarianism or dogmatism?

Does the popular church have the same relation to popular power as the traditional church had with bourgeois power? Should it legitimate popular power? Can it keep a critical consciousness within the process? Does the FSLN have any legitimate influence on the popular church? What is the specific character of the contradiction between the popular church and the traditional church in relation to class struggle? What is the fundamental contradiction that defines the popular church? How should the popular church confront the bourgeoisie? How does it carry out the church's universal mission? How to overcome problems with the hierarchy and CELAM?

ACLEN, the clergy organization, presented a list of pastoral problems, which in a less systematic way was focused essentially on the problems of division in the church (between bishops, between dioceses, between CELAM and CLAR [Latin American Conference of Religious Orders], and between the hierarchical church and the popular church) and the lack of an overall planned pastoral activity. Other items mentioned were a resurgence of clericalism, fear among the bishops, the problem of symbolic competition between the FSLN and the church ("Sandino yesterday, Sandino today, Sandino forever"), and the shortage of grassroots Christian leaders (many of whom were doing political work). This list is perhaps closer to the problems experienced consciously by pastoral agents, while the first series of questions attempts to express underlying issues.

The conclusions reached were not presented systematically and so are not easy to summarize. After an initial statement that the Nicaraguan revolution had been for many a "tremendous experience of God in history," the documents made a statement which could be regarded as their key: "The Nicaraguan people is Christian and revolutionary," using here the word *pueblo* (people) in its fullness. Many Christians live out a synthesis of faith and revolution, with no theological framework, and in fact there is a lack of the means of expressing this unity, especially in the existing liturgy. Popular religiosity is a fundamental element in the history of the Nicaraguan people.

Regarding pastoral tasks and strategies, the conclusions insisted that Christians should opt for the "historical project," which would benefit the poor, but that the church did not have to legitimate the revolution, which already had its own legitimacy. There was much insistence on the need for training, courses, theological reflection, basic Christian communities, and the like.[35]

One aspect worth pointing out is what this writer sees as a "mass line" in these conclusions: that is, the starting point was that the "Nicaraguan people" (*pueblo*) are Christian and revolutionary. Thus the question would not be whether the bishops and clergy on one side or the basic Christian communities on the other were the most legitimate representatives of the church (which "side" could turn out more people for a rally or an outdoor Mass, for instance). The question instead would be: What is the adequate response to the fact of large-scale Christian involvement (even though not consciously formulated) in the revolution?

Ideological Conflict and the FSLN Position on Religion

As has already been remarked, the anti-Sandinista forces turned to ideological struggle because the FSLN had total military control and could set the rules in the economy and the political sphere. Moreover it was impossible to offer an alternate *proyecto* in clear terms, since such a *proyecto* would inevitably be seen as aimed primarily at preserving the privileges of the elites, whatever concessions to the need for reforms it might make.

In the political sphere, opposition parties (Conservative, Social Democratic, Social Christian, MDN) and business groups called for elections and political pluralism. They sought to portray the FSLN as a political party that was abusing its power and leading the country toward totalitarianism. On the other hand, five non-Sandinista political parties formed a National Patriotic Front, supporting the FSLN and seconding it on most issues, including the postponement of elections.

However, for most Nicaraguans political parties meant little, and the call for pluralism had relatively little effect. All the more important, then, became those ideological questions relating to the church and religion. It is here that the extraordinary debate over religion in Nicaragua finds its explanation: what at first glance seemed to be a level of public theological disputation scarcely equaled in the twentieth century—literally hundreds of articles, attacks, and counterattacks in *La Prensa*, *El Nuevo Diario*, and *Barricada*—was to a great extent an ideological manifestation of a class struggle; that is, there was a displacement from politics to "theology."

At issue, in part, was the use of Christian symbols. Thus, for example, some were indignant at the slogan "Sandino yesterday, Sandino today, Sandino forever," and at Tomás Borge's description of archeologists finding Sandino's supposed tomb "empty": "Sandino had arisen!"[36] On the opposite side were the many billboards put up in Managua by fundamentalist and charismatic groups urging people to do "all out of love," presumably to counter "class hatred," and their insistence that there is only "one Lord," again presumably aimed at Sandinista pretensions.

More formal argumentation was carried on in the daily papers. *La Prensa*, which during the "honeymoon" had run pro-FSLN material, now became the opposition mouthpiece. *Barricada*, the official FSLN paper, and *El Nuevo Diario*, an independent pro-revolution paper, responded fiercely.[37] The opposition's polemic was directed at both the FSLN and those Christians committed to the revolution.

Often enough the argument was simply that "a large part of the leadership of this revolution is Marxist-Leninist." Marxism and Christianity were said to be at opposite poles: Marxism was "scientism" and materialism, class struggle and even class hatred, and the use of violence to change things, while Christianity was "faith in God and divine science, peace, love, and pardon. To be a Christian . . . one must root out hatred, revenge, and selfishness." Marxists were cited to show that they were the first to claim they are atheists. Christians see structural changes as radically insufficient due to original sin and believe a new humankind is possible only in Christ. Not money (or capitalism) but power is the root of evil: "Money could be abolished from the face of the earth but men would always have ambitions for power to impose their selfish desires on others," an affirmation that could be read as an indictment of Sandinista ambition veiled in theological terms. Arguments were buttressed by references to existing Marxism in Cuba, the Soviet Union, and elsewhere.[38]

Humberto Belli spoke of Marxist tactics regarding religion, particularly that of dividing the church and counteracting religious beliefs. This they would do by secularizing religious events, giving them a new (political) content, by creating a separation between "progressive" Christians (those with the Marxist authorities) and "reactionary" Christians (those who remain independent), and by "attacking the hierarchy at first subtly, later openly, setting it in opposition to a 'popular' church." As examples Belli cited the FSLN decree on Christmas and statements by FSLN leaders to the effect that the "true Christians" were those with the revolution.

Belli's article was occasioned by a reappearance of the controversy over the slogan "Sandino yesterday, Sandino today, Sandino forever," which Belli saw as the misuse of a "Christian liturgical phrase." He was replying to his sister, Giaconda Belli, who had asked whether Christ, if he were to come today, would be writing in *La Prensa* or organizing workers and peasants. Humberto replied to her that Christ would probably surprise everyone, perhaps going to the jails and being with Somocistas.

Implicit in Belli's argument—and often made explicit in *La Prensa*—is a view of the church centered on the hierarchy. When a visiting Brazilian Dominican, Frei Betto, said the Nicaraguan revolution meant that the church must question things, Roberto Cardenal of *La Prensa* accused him of wanting to "leave us without any guide or a reference point. The revolution would dictate to the church what it must be." When Frei Betto said that the basic Christian communities could not substitute for the mass organizations and that Christians should make a synthesis between the "dialectical rationality of history and the life of faith" and be concerned not for what will happen to the church but for the people, Cardenal sarcastically concluded, "God the Father made a mistake in sending Christ to save the world two thousand years ago. He should have sent Marx and Lenin."[39]

The foregoing is simply a sample of the ideological polemic that was raging and in which religion occupied a prominent place. In October 1980 the Frente Sandinista published its "Official Statement on Religion," seeking to answer what it saw as a campaign by the "enemies of our people." Since this document, while occasioned by particular circumstances, broke with traditional Marxist positions on religion, it (and reactions to it) must be treated in some detail here.

The FSLN recognized that

> Christian patriots and revolutionaries are an integral part of the Sandinista Popular Revolution, not starting from now but many years ago. . . .
>
> A large number of FSLN combatants and militants found in the interpretation of their faith reasons for joining the revolutionary struggle and consequently the FSLN.

A number of these, for example Gaspar García, were mentioned by name; there was a recognition of the dozens of Delegates of the Word killed and an acknowledgment that many non-Sandinista Christians had been combatants, that the Catholic hierarchy had denounced the Somoza regime, and that indeed, as institutions, the Catholic church and some Protestant churches shared in the victory. Christians were said to have participated

> to a degree unprecedented in any other revolutionary movement in Latin America and perhaps in the world. This fact opens new and interesting possibilities for the participation of Christians in revolutions elsewhere, not only in the phase of struggle for power but afterward in the phase of building a new society.

It is this writer's opinion that this statement may at some future date be seen as marking a turning point in relations between Marxist revolutionaries and Christians.

In nine points the FSLN then expressed its position on religion, which may be summarized as follows:

1. The FSLN guarantees the "inalienable right" to freedom of religious faith.
2. Although "some authors" see religion as a "mechanism of alienation"—understandably given the conditions of their age—the FSLN's experience is that people can be Christians and revolutionaries. (This statement was a clear rejection of militant atheism, breaking a tradition going back to Marx himself.)
3. All who agree with FSLN objectives and principles may participate in it, whatever their religious beliefs.
4. Within the party limits of the FSLN there is no room for proselytizing, but elsewhere Christian militants may express publicly their convictions. (Points 3 and 4 were a clear divergence from Marxist practice—in Cuba, for example.)
5. The FSLN "has a deep respect for all the religious celebrations of our people and is making efforts to save their true meaning, attacking the vice and corruption imposed on them in the past." They should not be used for commerical or politicking purposes.
6. Religious discussions are proper to the church; no Sandinista speaking for the FSLN should participate in them.
7. Contrary to reactionary ideologues, the FSLN is not trying to divide the church. "If there is division it is independent of the will and action of the FSLN." (At this point there are several paragraphs devoted to divisions in the church from colonial times to Somoza.) While the immense majority of Christians support the revolution, there is a minority against: Sandinistas are friends of good revolutionary Christians, not of counter-revolutionaries. Nevertheless, the FSLN maintains contact with all the churches and would like the churches to seek dialogue and participation, maturely and responsibly. The churches should look for the causes of division within themselves.

8. The priests and religious in the government are exercising their rights as citizens and have carried out an "extraordinary labor." Should they decide to withdraw for personal reasons, that would be their right.
9. The origin, purposes, and spheres of action of the revolution and the state are different from those of religion, which is a personal matter, proper to individuals, churches, and religious associations. Like every modern state, the revolutionary state is a lay state and cannot adopt any religion, since it is the representative of the whole people, believers and nonbelievers.[40]

The document strove to maintain three basic reference points: first, that Christians de facto had played and continued to play important roles in the revolution; second, that the revolution had its own justification and did not need a religious justification (the Sandinista revolution did not seek to return to some kind of "Christendom model" of church-state relations); third, and perhaps less explicit, political use of religion would be considered political and treated accordingly.

Ten days after the FSLN document, the Nicaraguan Bishops Conference issued a reply, which, despite its initial statement that the FSLN had provided a "basis for dialogue," could only be seen as a sharp attack on the revolution. Its rambling style gave the impression of having been written by one fast-typing individual not inhibited by the editing process inherent in genuinely collective statements; nevertheless, since it was approved by the bishops it provided a view of what was troubling them at that time.

The tone was one of accusation: "Nicaragua has set out to search for its historic liberation, not to search for a new Pharaoh." While the document was ostensibly organized into a framework of principles, historical situations, and errors, one would be hard pressed to find a real structure; it was, rather, a recurring commentary around certain basic themes, which could be summarized as follows:

1. There was a frequent hint—stopping short of outright accusation—that Nicaragua was falling into a new domination in which people are "instrumentalized." A people is not changed by changing its "master" but by making the people lord and master. Quoting the FSLN on the citizens' right to participation, the bishops said, "the less it is carried out in practice the more necessary we feel it is." Weapons without the people easily degenerate into "occupation forces" (a reference to the Sandinista army and police).
2. The FSLN document was seen as restricting the church's role to the personal sphere, a position described as more "liberal" than "socialist" and an injustice against the church's revolutionary action.
3. Yet the church, and specifically priests and religious feasts, were being "instrumentalized," as in "totalitarian systems," which seek to incorporate priests into a system in order to justify it. It was clearly

insinuated that the FSLN was causing divisions in the church (to "wound the shepherd and scatter the flocks") and that priests were being bought to serve the FSLN through "flattery and pay."[41] The FSLN's position on religious celebrations was an open door to intervention.

4. More specifically, there were accusations of atheistic proselytizing and a reference to "new invasions, which endanger the originality of our Process," may be seen as aimed at Cuban health workers and teachers.

5. The overall thrust of the bishops' reply was that the church stood for freedom and dignity against a revolution that was becoming a new force of domination. The church served the people but was not at the service of Power.[42]

Much of the document was expressed in a hypothetical manner and seemed to be a warning of dangers; however, in context, the style, at once allusive and sarcastic, was a form of accusation.

While the content spoke for itself, two brief critical comments may be in order. First, the bishops gave no explicit analysis of what the struggle for freedom was about: no reference to the economic situation of Nicaragua, to the overall thrust of reconstruction, and so forth. The struggle for freedom was seen as against the "totalitarian" tendencies or dangers of the FSLN itself. Second, the "church" seemed rather identified with the hierarchy, and the basic Christian communities were not even taken into account. Christian-Sandinista collaboration was seen as the product of a manipulation of priests by the FSLN.

In response to the bishops a group of religious in various institutions sought to find some positive elements in the bishops' response but objected to the "excessively polemic and cutting" tone, in contrast to the FSLN's serene offer of dialogue. They were particularly incensed that the priests in government service were accused of being there for their own gain, that international aid from Cuba was seen as comparable to United States intervention, and that Christian martyrs had died "to win glory and power over the rest."[43]

In less than a year the bishops' public position had changed from one of extraordinarily positive support to one verging on open opposition, and one that certainly fueled the growing opposition to the Sandinistas.

COUNTER-REVOLUTION AND CRISIS

The accession of Ronald Reagan to the presidency in 1981 serves as a convenient point to mark a new stage: it was now evident that the Sandinista revolution would be facing a multifaceted destabilization effort (anti-Sandinista training camps in the United States, economic and diplomatic pressures, threats, covert action). To what extent this was already underway during the Carter administration is an open question. For example, since the fall of Somoza several thousand ex-guardsmen had been in Honduras, occasionally attacking within Nicaragua. Some source had to be paying for their support and assuring the acceptance of the Honduran government. CIA involvement seems a reasonable hypothesis. Similarly, although the organized opposition within Nicaragua did not publicly support the ex-Somocista troops in Honduras and said it disagreed with pressures and threats from the United States, it is reasonable to ask to what extent these groups maintained contact with avowed counter-revolutionary movements. It is even more apposite to point out that whatever be the subjective intentions of individuals and groups, the FSLN would inevitably see them in the context of an increasingly clear international counter-revolutionary effort.

In order to situate well a discussion of events within the church, we need first to review briefly the political and economic developments of 1981 and early 1982.

Even before Ronald Reagan was elected, his party, in its platform, had deplored the Sandinista victory, and various right-wing groups were seeing the Nicaraguan revolution as the spearhead of an "Attack on the Americas." Secretary of State Alexander Haig saw it as the first country on a Soviet "hit list." The Sandinistas were accused—with no serious proof—of sending large shipments of arms to El Salvador and were in effect blamed for rebel success there.

Initially the Reagan administration suspended the last $15 million of the $75 million aid package to Nicaragua approved during the Carter administration and cut off wheat sales. This latter step, intended to disrupt the economy and provoke discontent (since Nicaragua imports all its wheat) was nullified when a number of other nations offered to sell or donate wheat (including the Soviet Union, which did so precisely as the United States grain embargo was lifted). Ex-Somocista guardsmen training in camps within the United States seem to have received encouragement from the administration, and attacks from across the Honduran border increased. The Atlantic coast region was particularly promising for counter-revolutionary efforts, since its people, especially the Miskito Indians, had not been heavily involved in the anti-Somoza struggle and mistrusted all those who came from the Pacific side (calling them "Spaniards"), including the Sandinistas, who for their part made some errors from both lack of knowledge and insensitivity. Steadman Fagoth, the leader of Misurasata, an Indian movement, was arrested in February 1981 for attempting to lead an uprising; released from jail in order to go to the coast and help calm things, he instead went to Honduras and was joined by some 3,000 Miskitos, who were then prepared to be part of a larger movement (a reminder of how the CIA used ethnic minorities in Southeast Asia). Within the United States, however, the new administration's Central America policy was raising the specter of another Vietnam, and so by mid-spring it sought to downplay the crisis and took no further initiatives for some time.[44]

Within Nicaragua there was an increasing mobilization for defense: the army was gradually expanded, as was the civilian militia (people who received some training on weekends). These efforts, in response to threats from the United States, along with reports that Nicaragua would be getting Soviet tanks, served to fuel efforts to portray Nicaragua as a danger to the other countries of the region—and so justify the Reagan administration's stance.

Relations between the FSLN and the internal opposition continued to be tense, with some periods of relative accommodation. In November 1980 several opposition parties and COSEP, the private-sector organization, had withdrawn from participation in the Council of State because they had consistently been outvoted by the pro-Sandinista majority. While recognizing some achievements of the government (Literacy Crusade, renegotiation of the public debt, honesty in administration, and so forth) the opposition groups continued to criticize what they saw as the abuse of power, postponement of elections, and fostering of class hatred. However, opposition leaders such as Alfonso Robelo criticized pressures from the United States (such as the suspension of aid). During the middle of the year the government organized the Popular Forum, an open debate on public issues, with different tendencies represented, and transmitted live on television and radio. While it did not resolve issues it was one way to encourage open public discussion. Several incidents, such as the suspension of an MDN rally, attacks on radio stations (allegedly by Sandinista youth, although this was denied by Fernando Cardenal), and brief closings of *La Prensa*, increased the climate of mistrust.[45]

From the FSLN viewpoint, the recurring question must have been: What is the dividing line between legitimate opposition and organized counter-revolution?

In a climate of increasing adversity, the Sandinista government managed a number of successes. It maintained strong support from Mexico and several European countries and good trade relations with others. Several countries provided large amounts of aid (West Germany $50 million, Libya $100 million) and the international banks continued to be favorable. Businesses confiscated from Somoza were doing well, production in rice and beans was approaching the point of self-sufficiency, the inflation rate was cut to around 27 percent. On the second anniversary of the revolution, further steps in land reform were announced (expropriation of idle or underused lands). At one point in the year tens of thousands of young people set out to the countryside to eliminate malaria in a campaign modeled on the Literacy Crusade. The Organization of American States Human Rights Commission issued a favorable report on Nicaragua, dismissing some allegations that had been made, although it had some criticisms and offered some recommendations.[46]

During the latter part of 1981 and in early 1982 the Reagan administration, recognizing that the insurgency was gaining territory in El Salvador, turned its attention once more to Central America, this time not only accusing Nicaragua of sending arms but hinting at various kinds of actions (such as a blockade) and pointedly not excluding military action. The armed groups along the Honduran border increased their attacks; in the two months of December 1981 and January 1982 some sixty Nicaraguans were killed. Around ninety United States military advisers were now in Honduras, some along the Nicaraguan border. It was revealed that the Reagan administration had approved $19 million for covert action against the Sandinista government, and the subsequent refusal of comment only served to confirm the impression of an increasingly aggressive attitude. Two incidents revealed the connections of the destabilization efforts: Steadman Fagoth, the Miskito leader, was in a Honduran air-force plane that crashed while carrying ex-Somoza guardsmen; and a plot to blow up the Esso (Exxon) refinery in Nicaragua was uncovered, which implicated many people: members of counter-revolutionary armed groups, José Esteban González (president of the Human Rights Commission, whose "documentation" had often been cited against the government), military attachés of Venezuelan, Salvadoran, and Honduran military officers—all orchestrated, according to Tomás Borge, by the CIA.[47]

Finally in February 1982 the Nicaraguan government ordered the forcible removal of the Miskito Indians living along the Honduran border, saying it could not protect them, and it proceeded to destroy villages in order to make them uninhabitable—in effect the area was militarized. This transfer—which the Sandinistas saw as regrettable but necessary—was then used as an example of the violation of human rights in Nicaragua. In March the government declared a state of emergency and the country went into a further state of preparedness for war.

One effect of the increasing external hostility was greater internal unity. The private-sector groups, which had withdrawn from the Council of State, returned, and the Sandinistas were approaching agreements on the participation of political parties and on incentives for foreign investment. Most Western countries resisted the Reagan administration's policies in Central America.

United States policy objectives were not entirely clear. That an outside invasion could overturn the revolution seemed improbable given the readiness of the Sandinista army and militia to defend their country. Yet the United States was obviously not interested in negotiating with Nicaragua. The most likely result of intensified pressure would be an increasing radicalization and perhaps a more "orthodox" and heavily militarized model of revolution. This could be a goal of the Reagan policy: if the revolution could not be turned around, at least it could be forced to abandon its attempts to find new approaches and become "another Cuba," weakened and hardly attractive to others.

All the foregoing may seem only distantly relevant to the main topic here, the situation of the church. However, only an adequate grasp of the context permits an understanding of what was at issue.

Two Visions

Having briefly reviewed the increasing atmosphere of threats and dangers surrounding the Sandinista revolution, let us now pause to consider two documents—one from the bishops and the other from a largely lay group, "Christians for the Revolution"—each of which in its own way sought to express a broader vision, somewhat removed from immediate controversies.

In October 1980 the Nicaraguan bishops produced a pastoral letter, "Jesus Christ and the Unity of His Church in Nicaragua." Its motivation was stated in the title. What the letter omitted or scarcely alluded to was as significant as what it said. Consisting largely of quotations from, and allusions to, church documents, the letter made little specific reference to actual events, so much so that if the word "Nicaragua" were deleted a reader would be hard pressed to identify the country. Issues facing the church were said to be a "siege of materialistic ideologies," doctrinal confusion, a disregard of the magisterium of the pope and bishops, and family problems. Concern was expressed over what the bishops saw as attempts to pit the hierarchy against the rest of the people of God, and they noted that, regrettably, "those who are opposed to the magisterium are those who obey most readily what is dictated by the mass media or political slogans." In a somewhat more positive sense they spoke of being "committed to the political and socioeconomic transformation of Nicaragua" and of analyzing ideologies to see their convergences toward, and differences from, Christianity. The "preferential love" for the poor "should not be used as a banner with which to foment hatred, nor as a strategy to stimulate the eternal dispute for the domination of one social group over another." Disciplinary matters were of some concern and the bishops insisted that priests must have the approval of the bishop to do pastoral work, evidently with the purpose of limiting priests who might be attracted to come to Nicaragua to work within the revolution.[48]

It is useful to contrast this document with one produced a few months later, in March 1981, by Christians for the Revolution, an informal group of around fifty people, largely of middle-class extraction, who had been meeting for reflection and mutual support. The writers seem to have wanted to discern the main lines of the revolutionary process from a Christian point of view and to offer both support and criticism. To do so they chose as a framework a series of "challenges" inherent in the process, and highlighted each one with quotes from Archbishop Oscar Romero, the anniversary of whose death was the occasion of the document.

The first challenge was that of "national unity" and was focused on the problem of the bourgeois classes: they should be helped to recognize and accept the sacrifices necessary to build a new economy. Surpluses should go to lay the foundations of that economy, and the earnings of the bourgeois class should be simply "high salaries for those who, rather than exclusive owners, should be considered administrators. . . ." The next challenge was seen as the "revolutionary state," which conscious Christians should support "in its efforts to organize national activity rationally for the good of the majority." They pointed to a tendency toward bureaucratization (twenty-one government ministeries, some competing) and they declared that the state is meant to serve, and that even politically conscious technicians cannot substitute for the participation of the poor in achieving real democracy, so often frustrated by the mechanisms of "formal bourgeois democracy."

The next challenge was seen as the Frente Sandinista. The group concluded (not directly from the gospel but from political analysis) that "only a political force like the FSLN" could guarantee the road to a new society; not to support the FSLN was equivalent to choosing a political *proyecto* that would not make the radical changes needed to end domination and exploitation. For the FSLN the danger was that it might fall into pride and so lose the necessary openness to criticism from the poor and cease to engage in a "mutual political education" with the popular classes. (Specific mention was made of the problems on the Atlantic coast.) In similar fashion the mass organizations offered a challenge in that, while they were channels for increasing popular power, they should avoid excesses, and particularly they should not fall into the trap of responding to provocations. This would seem to be a reference to some incidents in which FSLN demonstrations against the bourgeois opposition had gotten out of control and property had been destroyed. The "anger" of the poor was seen as essentially legitimate, however, especially in defense of the revolution, which nourished hopes for a better life.

A fifth challenge was that of maintaining fidelity to the hope of the poor and so overcoming temptations to discouragement or fear. "The revolution is a spiritual problem because it is a problem of solidarity." For the churches, Catholic and Protestant, the challenge was to judge the process, using as a criterion not their own welfare as institutions but the hope of the poor.

A final challenge was seen as the "threat of intervention in El Salvador": the United States, worried about its "backyard," was seeking to involve Nicaragua in the war in El Salvador, threatening it with economic boycott, speculating with its hunger (referring to the wheat-sales cutoff), and practicing "international terrorism."

Although the overall thrust of the document was one of support, there were clear criticisms of tendencies in the government and the FSLN to act in bureaucratic or authoritarian ways and to lose contact with the people. Grassroots groups used this document as the basis for discussion and then met in a conference at the UCA, where each of the "challenges" was commented on by speakers from Christian groups and the FSLN and government.[49] The language of the "challenges" emerged afterward in speeches by FSLN leaders such as Tomás Borge. In other words, criticism by Christians from within the process had a clear impact upon the Sandinista leadership.

The bishops and Christians for the Revolution, admittedly speaking at different moments and to somewhat different audiences, differed sharply in their method and focus: while the bishops were focused on the church (with stress on the hierarchy) and dangers to its "unity," Christians for the Revolution took as their criterion the welfare of the poor, embodied in the FSLN's revolutionary *proyecto* and endangered by growing threats from the United States.

The Priests-in-Government Conflict

Since May 1980 the issue of priests in the Sandinista government had remained unresolved, although more than once there had been public exchanges over the matter. Undoubtedly the fact that priests were ministers of foreign affairs, culture, and of social welfare, and occupied other government posts, helped the Sandinistas to resist an easy dismissal of the government as "Marxist."

In early June 1981 the bishops issued a formal declaration, stating that if the priests "occupying public positions and exercising partisan functions" did not leave them to return to priestly activity, "we will consider them to be in an attitude of open rebellion and formal disobedience to the legitimate ecclesiastical authority, and exposed to the sanctions provided in the laws of the church."[50] The language is undeniably harsh: the bishops were invoking the sanctions of canon law.

Their reasons were several: more than a year earlier they had stated that the "emergency" originally justifying the priests' presence was over; the participation of priests in politics divided the faithful; the priest should be a figure of unity; the church should maintain its own identity.[51] All of these seemed to be on the level of "principle." However, it is revealing that in the paragraph immediately after the passage quoted above, the bishops stated that the IHCA, the CAV, and CEPA were not officially approved or recommended by the Bishops Conference. There was no logical connection between the disciplinary decree and the "de-authorization" of such institutions, but the sequence indicates that the bishops not only were concerned about preserving the "principle" of priestly noninvolvement in partisan politics but intended to make it clear that the church, in their view, did not in any sense support the Sandinista revolution.

In private statements, made while the controversy was in full tilt, Archbishop Obando sharply criticized the revolution: it was falling into a "Cuban model," the Cubans were in predominant positions, and the government was organizing a very large army. The "popular church" was "tied to Sandinista ideology and married to the revolution." "The sharpest thorn

. . . within the Nicaraguan church are those priests who allow themselves to be manipulated by Sandinismo, which is in power." There was risk of a split in the church because the priests in government remained deaf to the call of the Vatican Council, "which explicitly urged them to assume a politically neutral attitude."[52]

Such remarks stirred up considerable reaction against Obando. (It should be said that these remarks were quoted from wire-service stories of interviews made outside the country, and upon his return to Nicaragua the archbishop said there were some interviews that he could not recall. At a minimum, however, it would seem he did not completely refrain from political comments.) Indeed, much of the conflict seemed to swirl around the person of Obando. At one point the Sandinista television network proposed dropping the archbishop's Sunday Mass and sermon in order to cover other Masses as well (retaining for the archbishop one Sunday a month). While there may have been other reasons (to show more variety, with live congregations rather than a studio Mass), the purpose was plainly to eliminate a platform for the expression of what the FSLN saw as political opposition. The clergy protested and the chancery office prohibited all televised Masses.[53]

There were movements to honor Obando—"Comandante Miguel" as he was called (originally by Somoza)—to make up for the insults he was suffering. La Prensa gave a great deal of attention to the Venezuelan government's conferral of high honor on him. "Women for Peace and Democracy" organized a Mass for Obando, which received the most diverse interpretations: La Prensa reported that a "mob" arrived shouting provocative slogans and beating people while the police stood by and at the end Obando took the microphone to report that a priest had been arrested but that all should remain calm; Barricada, on the other hand, described how the Mass was organized by the wives of MDN leaders, and that elegantly dressed opposition figures arrived in chauffeur-driven cars—and that the priest had been arrested while riding in a taxi whose driver had shouted insults at a policeman who mistakenly thought the priest was responsible.[54] (An American remarked that such Masses, which were organized frequently, really functioned as "love-ins for the bourgeoisie.") This incident serves to illustrate that the differences did not unfold in an atmosphere of serene rationality.

Immediately after the bishops' decree a great deal of commentary began to appear, much of it supportive of the priests in government posts. One paper published thirty-four documents from parishes, youth groups, and so forth. It seems that from the outset these groups agreed to show respect and obedience, while criticizing the bishops' position, and especially to avoid an "extreme left" trap of "sharpening the internal contradictions of the church."[55]

Most of these commentaries criticized the way the bishops had handled the matter, without consulting the church and the basic Christian communities. Although the declaration had the seal of the Bishops Conference, no bishops had signed it and several, including Obando, were out of the country when it was made public. At least one of them, Bishop Rubén López Ardon of Estelí did not agree with the decision. *El Nuevo Diario* noted that the bishops were asking the government for a broad, pluralistic, and sincere national dialogue when they themselves refused to do the same thing in the church. Obando gave the impression that the ultimate decision came from Rome, while the priests' supporters insisted that Rome had not taken a position and that the bishops should not shift the responsibility to the Vatican.[56]

While the bishops chose as their framework canon law, their critics insisted that the "most crucial value at stake is the committed presence of Christians in the revolutionary process . . ." for the first time in history. Christians for the Revolution saw a "difference of perception": the bishops having seen some actions against religion from some revolutionaries had decided the FSLN position on religion was merely "tactical" and would change; hence they wanted to withdraw any appearance of approval to a process that would in time become totalitarian and anti-Christian.[57]

Ricardo Zúñiga, director of CEPA, said that while it was impossible to judge the bishops' intentions, the effects of their decisions could be seen: some of the legitimacy would be withdrawn from the revolution; confidence in the revolution, due to the honesty and capability of people like Miguel D'Escoto and Ernesto Cardenal, would be impaired; withdrawing the priests, a symbol of harmony between a popular revolution and Christianity, was a veiled way of saying the revolution was heading toward atheism. The priests were not at the service of a party (the FSLN) but of the majority of the people.[58]

Popular groups were less measured in their expression. "Christ worked for the poor," said one peasant leader, "and these priests are following his message, helping the poor from within the government." The people should be consulted. "This process is Christian and the priests ought not to have their right to work for the poor in the revolution cut off." Many similar expressions were quoted in the pro-revolutionary press. One critic said that the bishops' statement made the problem seem religious, whereas in fact it was political; others noted that it was inopportune, appearing during a period of increased hostility from the Reagan administration. Government officials occasionally referred to the controversy—for example, Borge referred to "two churches," one of the rich and one of the poor—while church people sought to avoid such confrontational language.[59]

Early in the controversy CEPA published a reflection insisting that the question could not be judged in the abstract: there was a deep difference between working in the Nicaraguan revolution in a moment of crisis and holding a government post during Somoza's time, "legitimating a situation of sin." The official Catholic position of neutrality toward political positions was "practically impossible": the power of religion was used "either to defend the people and their interests or to unite, support, and protect the privileged minorities."[60]

One of the strongest themes was what could be called the selective vision of the bishops. A document from basic Christian communities said that the bishops

> have been silent when they tried to take away our wheat, and our bread, when the United States withdrew economic aid, when ex-National Guardsmen have attacked us from Honduras and murdered our brothers and sisters and even some catechists and Delegates of the Word. It has pained us when our bishops have not spoken of the massacre of our brothers and sisters, the poor of Guatemala; that they have said nothing to support adult education, to condemn capital flight, to support the effort for national defense and campaigns for people's health.[61]

Finally some of these groups turned their criticisms of the bishops' position into recommendations for a new approach. Christians for the Revolution suggested that the grace of Christ is not simply interior:

> As there is a sin that is structural and not simply personal, so also there are times, processes, and situations of grace that affect the structures of society.
> For some time we have wondered whether the present process . . . is not one of these historic opportunities for grace. . . .
> Is it not a sign of the times, the breaking-through into history, something new, which the church, and therefore the hierarchy, should discern in a climate of careful dialogue and fertile listening to the Spirit? Is not a part of this historic newness the presence of some priests in services that many Christians see as the service of the Samaritan?[62]

The representatives of the basic Christian communities asked the bishops to fulfill the hope they had created with their earlier pastoral letter (and to write a new one in dialogue with the people). They insisted that political neutrality in a situation of class struggle was not compatible with the gospel and urged that the church further the unification of the people to lessen "selfish individualism," form new values, and help to raise production. They further asked the bishops to denounce the counter-revolutionary bands, not to dissuade people from contributing to defense, and suggested that contacts with Christian communities in Honduras might lessen the chance that they be used by the counter-revolution.[63]

To an extent difficult to decipher, forces both in the Vatican and in CELAM had some role in this controversy. It was widely believed that in the Vatican there were two approaches, one identified with Cardinal Baggio (and influenced by Archbishop López Trujillo of CELAM), favoring a clear position against the participation of Christians in revolutionary movements, and another, identified with Cardinal Casaroli, which in the case of Nicaragua, at least, favored a more cautious wait-and-see attitude (reflecting the Vatican's normal respect for existing governments rather than any adhesion to revolution as such). In mid-June 1981 a consultation of Central American bishops and religious superiors and Vatican officials was held in Rome. The fact that there was no official statement or conclusion probably indicated that there was not a sufficient consensus on what should be done. In any case, the Nicaraguan bishops had to accept direct responsibility for any decision about the immediate controversy of the priests in government service.[64]

At the end of June the bishops declared that, although they had already engaged in a great deal of dialogue with the priests, they would be willing to meet with them again to clarify the situation. At a meeting on July 14 there was an agreement that the priests would not exercise their priestly functions either publicly or privately while holding government positions. To some extent this was a face-saving compromise in which the bishops could be seen as safeguarding "principles." Those Christians committed to the revolution felt it was a satisfactory conclusion and evidence of the possibility of dialogue in the church.

Unresolved Conflicts and an Uncertain Future

Despite the apparent solution to the issue of priests in the government, similar tensions and conflicts continued to recur. Several priests and a sister sympathetic to the revolution were transferred, all after requests from bishops to their religious superiors. These actions were understood as part of an overall effort against basic Christian communities. On one of these occasions, what *El Nuevo Diario* called a "perfumed mob" (in reaction to *La Prensa's* tendency to call FSLN demonstrations "mobs") used force to prevent a group representing the basic Christian communities of San Judas from delivering to Archbishop Obando a letter presenting their frustration with the new pastor who had completely reversed the earlier kind of pastoral work. A few weeks later, while Obando was saying Mass at a parish in Monseñor Lezcano barrio, where a similar transfer had taken place, unidentified people slashed his tires and threw a rock through the windshield of his car. While the basic Christian communities repudiated this action, it was seized upon by *La Prensa*: "Mob Attacks Archbishop" (in fact, there was no attack on Obando), and the MDN and other opposition groups hastened to express their support for the archbishop. At one point the government claimed to have uncovered a plot (directed by the CIA) to kill Obando and cast the blame on the Sandinistas.

Archbishop Obando thus continued to play a leading role. *La Prensa*, at the end of 1981, said he had been named "Man of the Year" in Nicaragua by "independent journalists." In January 1982 Obando traveled to the United States at the invitation of Cardinal Krol of Philadelphia and also gave an address at the Institute for Religion and Democracy and spoke with Assistant Secretary of State for Latin American Affairs Thomas Enders.

Obando was undoubtedly a highly useful figure to the anti-Sandinistas since he could express their sentiments and at the same time maintain a certain immunity and insist he was simply exercising the church's "prophetic ministry." In a sense he was becoming the leading figure of the opposition, more prominent than any politician or business leader.

In February 1982 the bishops issued a statement protesting the forced transfer of the Miskito Indians, stating that their human rights had been violated and even (indirectly) comparing the action to what was happening in El Salvador and Guatemala (without naming those countries). Since they had not visited the border area or the relocation camps, the bishops were particularly vulnerable to criticism. A number of religious delegations to the area contradicted the bishops' conclusion. The government reacted with a vigorous refutation, stating that those who were killing people in those areas could not be called simply the Sandinistas' "political adversaries" (as the bishops had termed them), for they were the "enemies of our whole people." The government pointed out the similarity in language and content between what the bishops said and statements by the Somocista radio station in Honduras and the United States embassy in Managua, and noted that those statements did not condemn the activities of counter-revolutionary bands, which were killing people and preventing food from arriving. Until this moment the government had avoided head-on confrontation with the hierarchy.

Summary and Prospects

Among Catholics there was a basic split over how to respond to the Sandinista revolution: one group, consisting in a part of the clergy, basic Christian communities, and reflection centers such as the CAV, and symbolized by the prominent presence of priests in the Sandinista government, engaged in, and argued for, active support of the revolution as the specific way to embody the option for the poor. The opposed group, made up of the hierarchy, most of the clergy and religious, and middle-class church movements, feared Marxism, expressed concern over certain values, and increasingly resisted the thrust of the revolution. Whether by intention or not, this sector of the church became an important ideological tool of the counter-revolution. The FSLN sought to avoid an open break with the institutional church, and the "revolutionary Christians" sought at least a position of tolerance within the church.

(In general it would seem that Protestant churches as institutions accepted the FSLN as the de facto government but were less inclined to make either support or opposition an issue. Evangelical revival campaigns with their spiritualistic world view were seen as at least indirectly part of the ideological strategy of counter-revolution.)

A critical reader has probably been wondering about the relative strength of these groups and in particular of those committed to the revolution. Unfortunately, it has not been possible to obtain any firm data. All observers interviewed by this writer tended to see somewhere between 15 and 25 percent of the Catholic clergy and religious as supportive of the revolution; the rest were seen as being "with the bishops." One observer gave a more "bell-shaped" picture, with 25 percent or so of the clergy at either end as supporting or opposed and the bulk in the middle as "supportive of the good and critical of the bad"; other observers, however, concurred that in the polarized context of Nicaragua such a position was tantamount to being in opposition.

The basic Christian communities, while very important, are a minority phenomenon; for example, at the meeting in June 1981 in which a document on the priests-in-government controversy was written, some 270 communities were represented from perhaps 20 areas. For the immediate future, the basic Christian communities are not the dominant expression of Nicaraguan Catholicism, and by themselves they will not decide the future of the church.

One could perhaps surmise that the roughly 20 percent of religious and clergy who are supportive of the revolution will have an effect larger than their numbers because they work closer to the poor (for example, many religious still teach in middle-class schools). However, this tendency is counterweighed by the fact that many of them are in tasks not directly connected to grassroots pastoral activity.

Yet it should not be assumed that the anti-Sandinista forces in the church will command the allegiance of the bulk of the people. Popular Catholicism in Nicaragua, as elsewhere in Latin America, is not dependent on the church structure; and the official statements of the hierarchy, whether doctrinal, ethical, or disciplinary, by themselves have little resonance among most people (one example: in Latin America the official church position on birth control arouses little controversy because ordinary people are hardly aware of it, and when they are they feel free to ignore it).

It seems that the bulk of the Nicaraguan people will not necessarily follow either the bishops or the "popular church." This writer's impression, speculative to be sure, is that much will depend on the direction of the revolution. If the people become more committed to the Sandinista revolution, accepting its principles, they will come to see resistance by the hierarchy and other sectors in the church as "counter-revolutionary"; at that point they would be open either to a new understanding of Christianity as proposed by Christians for the Revolution, or to reject the church altogether. The question would be to what extent revolutionary Christians would be able to communicate this alternate understanding and what opportunities there would be to express it in liturgy. On the other hand, to the extent that the Sandinista revolution were perceived to fail the people's expectations of a better life—whether in basic needs such as work, food, schooling, health care, and security or by bringing undesirable by-products such as bureaucracy and extreme ideological control—the church could be an important rallying point of resistance.

However, the success of the Sandinista revolution is to a great extent conditioned on external factors. Thus, for example, if revolutionary regimes take power in El Salvador and/or Guatemala, the long-range success of the Nicaraguan revolution will be more assured. One can even imagine that church authorities, starting with the Vatican, would recognize that the revolutionary regimes were likely to endure, and act accordingly. If, however, those movements are stopped, and Nicaragua is isolated and surrounded, the chances of its both meeting basic human needs and evolving an innovative, attractive model of revolution are reduced, and the likelihood of its becoming hardened and stereotyped increases (through internal militarization and radicalization, and Eastern-bloc alignment as the price of survival).

The church itself not only will be affected by what happens but will be one of the determining factors. Thus, if larger numbers of Nicaraguans come to see revolutionary involvement not only as compatible with Christianity but an expression of it, the Sandinistas' task of consolidation will be facilitated. Hence the counter-revolution's efforts to portray the revolution as inimical to religion.

In sum, the future of Christian involvement—like the future of the revolution—is as yet undetermined and will be resolved only through struggle.

Update

This book was undertaken in the spring of 1981, when the Reagan administration's escalation in Central America was still primarily rhetorical. The manuscript was completed in August 1982 before most Americans were aware that their government was financing and directing a "covert war" against Nicaragua. As it goes to press in late 1983 the early intuitions that Central America might be the site of an Indochina-type war seem more and more probable—the U.S. invasion of Grenada has all the earmarks of a dress rehearsal.

In this addendum, I would like to briefly take into account the main developments between the completion of the manuscript and its publication.

The most obvious development has been the steady movement toward a deeper United States intervention and, quite possibly, toward a region-wide war. The Carter administration had paved the way for a military approach (see pp. 144, 148–149, 154, 159). In early 1981 the incoming Reagan administration seemed to regard Central America, and specifically El Salvador, as a "test case" it could win easily. Later that year, however, the administration realized that the FMLN was strong and at least by April 1982, according to an internal White House memo later leaked, U.S. strategists were foreseeing a struggle perhaps lasting several years. With its military aid and training the U.S. gradually came to take over the prosecution of the war in El Salvador; one sign was the replacement of Defense Minister José Guillermo García in 1983, which allowed U.S. advisors to move the Salvadoran armed forces toward its own version of tactics (small patrols rather than large company actions) and to begin a Vietnam-style pacification program in rural areas. The Reagan administration tried to downplay its military aid by insisting that economic aid was three times as large. However, in 1982 U.S. economic and military aid equaled approximately 80 percent of El Salvador's commodity exports and seemed likely to exceed 100 percent in 1983. Since those commodity exports are the mainspring of the economy, aid from Washington was now propping up not only the government but the economy itself.

In 1981 the CIA began to finance anti-Sandinista exiles (mainly ex-Somoza Guardsmen) ostensibly to interdict the putative arms flow to Salvadoran insurgents. By 1983 this force was an army of 10,000 men and was on its way to 15,000. At the same time the U.S. sought to prevent Nicaragua from receiving international loans and aid, and to isolate it diplomatically. The administration's itch to become more involved in Guatemala was continually frustrated by the violence and repeated coups of the Guatemalan regimes.

Honduras became a key element in U.S. strategy. The U.S. increased military aid and backed Colonel Gustavo Álvarez, who had himself made general and became the de facto ruler of the country, institutionalizing repressive practices and vitiating any effect of the return to ostensibly civilian rule. From its military exercises in late 1981 to those involving thousands of U.S. troops in 1983, the U.S. gradually transformed Honduras into an outpost of U.S. military projection, rather like South Korea. The large U.S. presence made it possible to ship modern weapons and equipment to the anti-Sandinista *contras*.

The inexorability of deepening U.S. military involvement was evident from simple logic: the aims of U.S. policy (the defeat of the left in El Salvador and the overturn- ing of the Sandinista revolution) would not be achieved with the existing means. No combination of funding, training, and advice would alter the fact that the Salva- doran government and military de-legitimized themselves with their corruption and their continual practice of murdering civilians (at a rate of well over 400 a month during 1983). Salvadoran soldiers and officers could not be blamed if they were unwilling to die—ultimately for U.S. hegemony in the region. In Nicaragua the *contras* could do a great deal of damage but the Nicaraguan people saw them as CIA mercenaries rather than as "liberators." If the administration intended to achieve its aims it would have to escalate. One possibility was to unite the armies of El Salva- dor, Guatemala, and Honduras into one coordinated fighting force. This had long been rumored and seemed to be underway in late 1983. Although this might provide more troops for El Salvador or for attacking Nicaragua, it might provoke a parallel unification of revolutionary forces and so lead to a region-wide war. The other alternative was further direct U.S. involvement through an air war or with ground troops (in either El Salvador or Nicaragua).

What I am pointing to is the *logic* of U.S. policy: a military definition of the prob- lem implies a military solution. It was their alarm over the direction of events that led the "Contadora" countries (Mexico, Venezuela, Colombia, and Panama) to urge negotiated approaches. The U.S. at first ignored these efforts, pursuing its own diplomatic policy of working through the bloc of El Salvador, Honduras, Costa Rica, and Guatemala (quaintly called the "Central American Democratic Commu- nity"). When the calls for negotiation could no longer be avoided, the administra- tion sought to defuse them by using the language of political solutions and appoint- ing ex-Senator Richard Stone as a presidential envoy to the region. In July the White House announced the formation of a bipartisan commission chaired by Henry Kis- singer and charged with the task of drawing up guidelines for long-range U.S. policy in the region. All indications are that the Kissinger Commission paid virtually no attention to the dynamics that have led to the crisis, such as are laid out in this book, but instead focused narrowly on definitions of U.S. interest. Most telling was the fact that just as the Commission was being announced, President Reagan dispatched U.S. warships to both shores of Nicaragua and announced exercises in Honduras involving over 5,000 U.S. troops.

This deepening U.S. military involvement was clearly the most important develop- ment from mid-1982 to late 1983. As noted in chapters 4 to 6, the public role of the church, which had been important during the period of consciousness-raising, or- ganization, and political struggle during the 1970s, was diminished to the extent outcomes were being determined on the battlefield. In El Salvador and Guatemala many pastoral agents had to flee; those remaining who were committed to the poor could work discreetly in humanitarian aid and simply stand by their people pas- torally. There were still muted voices from the hierarchy calling for an end to violence.

In the United States, church people have been at the forefront of opposition to their government's policies, both at the national level with repeated public state- ments from the United States Catholic Conference and from over twenty major Protestant denominations opposing U.S. military aid and calling for political solu- tions, and at the local level, where committed lay people, sisters, priests, and minis- ters often play important roles in solidarity groups. It was estimated that some 5,000 congregations across the country had participated in a national campaign for Peace with Justice in Central America (fall 1982–spring 1983). This involvement of the churches stems not from doctrinaire leftist activism, as some would like to believe, but from direct contact with Christians in Central America. Thus, for example, the Protestant churches in Nicaragua, and in particular the Baptists, have made numer- ous appeals to sister churches in the U.S. to prevent American intervention. Church- to-church appeals, transcending national boundaries, are as old as the Pauline epistles. Finally, a major restraining factor on U.S. policy makers has no doubt been a stubborn feeling in the U.S. public that it is wrong for the U.S. to support a government that is unable or unwilling to bring to justice its own troops and officers when they rape and murder American church women.

This book, however, deals with the role of Central American Christians. We will now turn to particular countries, simply highlighting major developments or trends, and then treat Pope John Paul II's trip through Central America in March 1983 and subsequent events.

In *Nicaragua* tensions and conflicts continued along the lines described in chapter 8. In several cases priests or sisters considered sympathetic to the revolution were transferred by bishops or superiors, often over the protests of parishioners who saw the moves as politically motivated. Some of these cases became public, for example, that of Monsignor Arias Caldera, an older priest who had not attracted attention during the anti-Somoza struggle but had quietly aided and hidden Sandinistas.

In August 1982 there were a series of public conflicts. Concerned that fundamentalist sects might be used by the CIA (some pastors in the north were ex-Guardsmen), Sandinista mass organizations occupied the churches of the Mormons, the Adventists, and the Jehovah's Witnesses. *La Prensa* and those unsympathetic to the Sandinistas call these organizations "mobs," claiming that their actions come directly from the Sandinistas. They are no doubt a Sandinista organizing tool, but actions such as the church takeovers might well reflect grassroots rage and frustration at attacks from "imperialism" and a need to do something to deal with concrete "enemies." In this particular case, the move no doubt hurt the Sandinistas by alienating thousands of poor members of these sects, simply because of the suspected activities of some "pastors." CEPAD stepped in to mediate and most of the churches were in fact returned.

At this same time a series of public controversies swirled around the Catholic church. The pope had sent a letter exhorting Nicaraguan Catholics to take the bishops as their point of unity. Given the bishops' de facto role as a voice of the bourgeois opposition, the Sandinistas saw the letter as an attack on the revolution and prohibited its publication. It would undoubtedly have been wiser to allow its publication since the Vatican prose would have been unintelligible to most ordinary Nicaraguans. The censorship made the letter a kind of prized samidzat and the upper-class elements who circulated copies could cast themselves in the role of heroic dissidents. After some time the FSLN allowed it to be published. There immediately followed the incident of the "naked priest": Father Bismarck Carvallo, press secretary for Archbishop Obando, was caught by TV cameras and news photographers being chased from a tryst by an angry husband. Thoughtful observers in Managua thought that while there was probably an amorous liaison, there was also an element of entrapment: both the church and the Sandinistas suffered discredit. Carvallo was the butt of jokes among pro-Sandinistas and a martyr-figure for the opposition. Masses were celebrated to repair the dishonor to him, and street fights broke out between those who attended and Sandinista mass organizations. Several days later counterrevolutionaries entered a Salesian school in Masaya and shot at a pro-Sandinista demonstration. In late 1982 when the Centro Valdivieso published its own version of the Marian novena of La Purísima, a popular devotion celebrated in December, the bishops criticized it as unorthodox. The Centro responded by pointing to Vatican II's teaching on Mary. Karl Rahner gave the Centro welcome support when he sent a letter supporting the orthodoxy of their position and praising them for the "ecclesian manner" in which they had responded to the bishops.

Running through these cases was a common thread: what would normally have been minor internal church matters became major national conflicts in the highly charged atmosphere of Nicaragua. Partisans would see them as instances of Sandinista suppression of religious freedom, or as pro-Sandinista use of religion. One cause of festering discontent was the willingness of the episcopal conference to criticize Sandinista policies, while maintaining utter silence about the CIA-sponsored bands who were killing hundreds of poor Nicaraguan civilians.

As noted in chapter 5 the public role of the church in *El Salvador* was considerably diminished after the murder of Archbishop Romero. Some pastoral agents left the country, some went underground, and some took up pastoral roles in the "liberated" territories (an option which Archbishop Rivera defended as legitimate). Someday their story will be made known. Here we will simply make some observations on the public role of the church.

Archbishop Rivera, while maintaining a relatively cautious position, nevertheless frequently denounced the activities of paramilitary groups, the practice of torture by government troops, Decree No. 506, the state-of-siege law which made arbitrary arrest and detention legal, and attacks on refugee camps. Although he condemned all use of violence, he explicitly pointed out that the violence of the right and the government (torture and murder of civilians) was not to be equated with the normal violence of the left, such as destroying power stations.

Even prior to the March 1982 election he had expressed doubts that it would solve the country's problems, and he soon came to advocate a negotiated solution. In June 1983 Archbishop Rivera traveled to Rome to discuss the situation with the pope. On July 15 the bishops produced a letter urging that a solution be sought "along rational paths and not along the sterile way of violence." They urged all parties to set aside any absolute positions and open the way to a "sincere, clear, loyal, dialogue, one that is inspired by good will and in a spirit of authentic patriotism, putting the unity of the Salvadoran family above individual or group interests." "Dialogue" was here serving as a kind of code word for negotiations, since that term could not be pronounced publicly. The bishops pledged the willingness of the church to work for reconciliation. Pope John Paul II sent the bishops a letter dated August 6, 1982 (the national feast day of El Salvador and the date of Archbishop Romero's four major pastoral letters), in which he used the word "war" to describe the condition in the country and stated that the conflicts and violence "find their true and deep root in situations of social injustice," urging them to continue working for reconciliation.

The significance of this exchange becomes clear in the light of the context: it was clear that the U.S.-sponsored elections held less than six months previously were in no way addressing the country's problems. Right-wing parties controlled the new Constituent Assembly and were busy seeking to stop even the token land reform, while Christian Democrats were being murdered by death squads. Somewhat spontaneously and amorphously there began to take shape a new sort of political "middle ground" made up of non-left labor and peasant organizations, small business people, and some moderate politicians who were alienated from the government and were recognizing that there was no solution for El Salvador's problems without the participation of the organized left. The emergence of this new "center" was somewhat ironic given the U.S. government's contention that it was supporting (or alternately, "creating") the center. However, these groups were not organized and could not even publicly call for "dialogue." The bishops' and the pope's statements may be seen as reflecting this sentiment.

In the meantime the FMLN continued to grow stronger. In October 1982, as they launched a major military offensive, all five FMLN commanders prepared a statement calling for "dialogue without preconditions." The document was sent to the hierarchy, and Archbishop Rivera personally handed it to the armed forces high command. The appeal was noisily rejected by Roberto D'Aubuisson, but there was evidence that some sectors of the government and even the military thought it should not be refused out of hand.

"Dialogue" became a major theme in Archbishop Rivera's public statements, and he received some death threats. In January 1983 the archdiocese of San Salvador held a seminar on dialogue for catechists and others, utilizing words from the pope for protection. Archbishop Rivera continued to insist that war and violence were no solution and he pointed to the danger of a "Vietnamization" of El Salvador.

The official archdiocesan legal aid office (Tutela Legal) monitored human rights violations. For example during the first six months of 1983 it documented 2,527 murders at the hands of official forces and right-wing death squads (about 433 a month); by contrast it found only 43 civilian murders committed by the left. Similarly, it had records of 541 people captured by official forces of whom seven were murdered and 326 disappeared; left-wing groups had kidnapped 22. This simple but courageous service of keeping track of violence may be seen as a ministry of speaking the truth in an atmosphere of falsehood, and of rendering a small tribute to the thousands whose cruel deaths were anonymous.

In *Guatemala* the counterinsurgency campaign coinciding with the advent to power of General Ríos Montt (see pp. 217–19) continued through 1982. The army began in Chimaltenango and moved north through Quiché to Huehuetenango and then to San Marcos and the coastal region. This arc only describes the general direction; in fact the program was simultaneous wherever guerrilla sympathies were suspected. It could be seen as a textbook case of counterinsurgency: cutting off support from the civilian population through massacres of large groups of people including whole villages, almost all Indians. Estimates of the number killed in 1982 vary from 3,000–5,000 (Alan Riding in *Foreign Affairs*) to 8,000–10,000 (Guatemalan opposition organizations). Indians were forced to join "civilian patrols" and sent out to patrol for guerrillas and to kill "suspects." Large groups of Indians, sometimes numbering in the thousands, became internal refugees, wandering from place to place, the weaker members dying of starvation. Perhaps as many as 100,000 fled into Mexico, some into refugee camps and others seeking work where they might.

As in the case of El Salvador, pastoral agents who remained sought to stand by their people. Some church people served as conduits for humanitarian aid for the many displaced people. This activity was virtually clandestine, since any public supply of food or medicine would be dangerous.

Having consolidated himself as president, Ríos Montt made his own "born-again" Protestant identity a national issue. In his Sunday night TV "fireside" chats he became a national moralizer, weaving together themes of political problems and family life (e.g., admonishing irresponsible husbands) as though all were a matter of personal morality. Members of the California-based Church of the Word were his close advisors and one was the head of the State Council. At first Ríos Montt seemed an asset to the Reagan administration: fundamentalist and electronic gospel organizations in the U.S. raised funds and preachers went on speaking tours showing how God was at work in Guatemala and urging support for "Brother Ephraim." The Church of the Word created a spinoff foundation to serve as a major channel of aid for the crucial Nebaj area in Quiché.

In November 1982 Protestants in Guatemala celebrated the hundredth anniversary of their arrival in Guatemala with an outdoor meeting with Luis Palau, a famous evangelist; Ríos Montt was also on the platform. The crowd, variously estimated at between 400,000 and 700,000 people, was a kind of show of force and a sign that Protestants had arrived socially. Not all Protestants were enthusiastic over this kind of public role, particularly in view of government policies. Some Protestants at the grassroots level were identified with the poor and suffered the same fate as committed Catholics. In June 1983 the Guatemalan Human Rights Commission stated that "at least 50 Protestant pastors have disappeared, 35 have been murdered, and 10 are arrested, while others have had to seek exile." These pastors were mainly not seminary trained pastors, but village level church leaders, analogous to Catholic "delegates of the Word."

Ríos Montt's religious identity eventually became a liability, along with continuing divisions in the army, a declining economy, and the fact that the guerrilla organizations continued to carry out attacks even though they had been weakened by the army's counterinsurgency strategy. After surviving several coup attempts, he was deposed by the Defense Minister, General Oscar Mejía Víctores. Whether the United States was involved in the planning (as Mejía's trip to a U.S. warship the previous day seemed to indicate) or not, the coup seemed likely to bring Guatemala more intimately into U.S. regional strategy.

This book has not dealt with *Honduras* and *Costa Rica* because serious revolutionary movements did not arise there. Honduras is as poor as Guatemala and El Salvador but there had not developed a coffee bourgeoisie, and bananas were produced in self-contained American enclaves. The Honduran agroexport elite developed only after World War II. Moreover the relative availability of land attenuated potential sources of conflict, and in fact even under military rule Honduras did not suffer the degree of repression practiced in neighboring countries. Costa Rica's relatively high standard of living and democratic tradition were rooted in its history: coffee was not monopolized by a small class but rather there grew up a broad sector of coffee-growing peasantry; in addition a series of social reforms in the 1940s made Costa Rica a kind of miniwelfare state. The world recession, declining prices for their exports, and the regional crisis put both Honduras and Costa Rica in serious trouble in the early 1980s, however.

In principle, both these countries should be able to seek their own evolutionary paths to development. However, the ultimate effect of U.S. strategy may be to create the preconditions for revolutionary movements in them also. That is, a narrow focus on utilizing them to defeat the left in other countries may prevent them from dealing with their own internal problems. A short-range policy of dealing with protest through repression may convince Hondurans, and even Costa Ricans, that existing institutions will never solve their problems.

The Central American war came to the Honduran church as early as 1980 when the first Salvadoran refugees appeared. Church pastoral agents were involved in humanitarian aid and thus were the object of intimidation by the Honduran (and Salvadoran) armed forces. Some priests were expelled from the country.

In Costa Rica, where the Catholic church has tended to mirror the rather complacent self-image of the country, the hierarchy has generally reflected the viewpoint of Costa Rican elites that the danger to their country came from without. For example, Archbishop Román Arrieta Villalobos has said that some clerics want to "Marxicize Central America." In May 1982 when President Luis Alberto Monge made his first public appearance in the cathedral, Arrieta Villalobos said, "We Costa Ricans would be foolish if we did not close ranks around our leader and his associates, if we did not aid and defend him, if we did not help him to preserve what has cost so many of our compatriots so much blood, tears, and sacrifice." On the other hand, some pastoral agents working at the grassroots were supportive of Central American refugees and of the struggles in El Salvador and Guatemala.

That the pope should even undertake a trip to Central America, given the unpredictability of events (e.g., Archbishop Romero's funeral), was in itself amazing. For about ten days in early March 1983 his visits to each of the countries of Central America, Panama, Belize, and Haiti focused world attention on the role of religion there.

Expectations were no doubt exaggerated, nevertheless. Where the issues are deep-seated it is difficult to imagine how even a papal visit can do much to resolve them. It should have been enough to reflect on the same pope's 1979 trip to the United States: there is no indication that anyone's mind was changed by his stated positions on sexual morality or the role of women in the church.

One way to treat the papal visit would be to search through the over forty addresses and talks which in careful Vatican manner were addressed not only to the particular countries but to classes of audiences: bishops, religious, priests, seminarians, educators, workers, peasants, Indians, families, children, etc. One could then pull out the dominant themes and particular accents. In fact, Ignacio Ellacuría prepared a 10,000 word article on "The Ethico-Political Message of John Paul II to the Central American People" bringing together the elements of the pope's analysis of the roots of the conflicts and the possible lines of solution. Susana Jiménez prepared a similar study on his "Theological disclosure." These efforts, reminiscent of what the "uninvited" theologians did at Puebla for a group of bishop delegates, are valid, since they pick up elements really present in the pope's message. However, the real weight of the papal tour was felt through what was actually perceived in the individual countries, and particularly Nicaragua, and that is what we will treat here.

It was in Nicaragua that the previsit tensions were highest. The anti-Sandinista bourgeoisie saw the event as an opportunity to show mass support for "the church"—as opposed to the "Marxist" government. They complained that the Sandinistas were seeking to prevent them from attending the pope's appearances. In fact the government allocated scarce resources (e.g., two months supply of gasoline) for the welcome. Since 700,000 people (proportionately the largest in the whole trip) turned out for the pope, it is hard to see any grounds for the accusation.

When the pope arrived at the airport, Junta Coordinator Daniel Ortega greeted him with a speech that was called a "tirade" in the U.S. press. However, about 40 per cent of it was a quotation from the letter of Bishop Simeon Pereira y Castrellón to Cardinal Gibbons in 1921 (see p. 53), denouncing the Marine occupation of Nicaragua. It was there also that the pope remonstrated with Ernesto Cardenal.

The pope was then flown to León, where he gave an address on Catholic education, whose content was rather unintelligible to the largely peasant audience. Since the discourse seemed to presume that the normal site for Catholic education was Catholic schools, and since these in Nicaragua largely serve the privileged sectors, his address seemed to favor the elites. That is, it might have been more appropriate to address the leaders of the grassroots communities and parents, who provide a Catholic education for the poor majority.

The pope then flew back to Managua where a crowd of hundreds of thousands awaited him for mass in the late afternoon. Many people hoped for some word of encouragement, some recognition of the accomplishments of the revolution, a condemnation of the attacks from Honduras, or at least a word of consolation. (The previous day in the same plaza there had been a funeral for seventeen young people killed by the CIA-funded *contras*.) None of this was forthcoming. The pope had chosen to speak on the bishops as the focal point of unity for the church. Since the Nicaraguan bishops collectively were clearly identified with the anti-Sandinista bourgeoisie (despite the more moderate attitude of some bishops within their own dioceses), the pope's speech seemed to be fueling the counterrevolution.

At some point people began to become impatient. The mothers of those who had "fallen" pushed forward with pictures of their children urging the pope to say something. People began to chant "We want peace!" In so doing they were probably reflecting the style of their revolution rather than intending an insult. Pope John Paul II, however, gradually became angry and three times interrupted his speech to shout, "Silence!" The encounter became increasingly ugly. Daniel Ortega's speech in the airport as the pope was departing was a plea for understanding.

The reaction among those Christians involved in the revolution was one of frustration, anger, and discouragement—they felt the pope had undone in a day what they had sought to accomplish in almost four years. By the same token it was a boon to the Nicaraguan bourgeoisie and to the Reagan administration, proof positive of Sandinista "hostility" to religion. They lost no time in claiming that the Sandinistas had organized mobs to insult the pope.

That claim must rest on an assumption that the Sandinistas were bent on political suicide, for they were surely the losers. On the contrary, the error of the Sandinistas and Christians involved in the revolution seems to have been that they expected too much: that the pope could cut through his own experience and ideology and the circles in CELAM and the Vatican who briefed him so as to concede some legitimacy to the Nicaraguan experiment and some encouragement to those involved in it.

In El Salvador the pope's gestures counted as much as his words. On the eve of the trip Archbishop Rivera y Damas was made archbishop permanently (ending almost three years of interim status). The pope also interrupted his official schedule to visit Archbishop Romero's tomb. Previously the nunciature together with upper class groups involved in preparing the pope's visit had prohibited a poster showing the pope and Romero on his last trip to Rome (the prohibition was too late to stop all the posters). Yet as the pope was leaving Rome, *Osservatore Romano* carried an article praising Romero as a "prophet and martyr."

In his talk the pope used the word "dialogue" and advocated "reconciliation" but not an "artificial peace that hides problems and ignores worn-out mechanisms that must be repaired. It must be a peace that really is so, one in justice and in complete recognition of the rights of the human person." The official text stated "No one should be excluded from the dialogue for peace." These words seemed to refer to the FMLN. Perhaps out of delicacy to the government they were omitted in the spoken version but remained in the official text.

In Guatemala it was again a gesture that was most significant—the pope embraced representatives of the country's Indians. Bishop Oscar García Urízar greeted the pope on his arrival in Quetzaltenango, noting how the Indians had been treated:

> tens of thousands have suffered mass murder, they have seen their villages destroyed, and been forced to go away to seek refuge; they have been subjected to systematic aggression against their Catholic faith.

The pope responded with a speech to catechists, emphasizing that all human beings have the same dignity and worth before God. He insisted on the value of Indian traditions and recognized that the Indians had suffered injustice regarding their land and violations of their human rights. He declared that "No one should confuse evangelization with subversion," thus pointing to the persecution of church workers.

In short, in contrast to the impact in Nicaragua, church people on the side of the popular organizations in Guatemala and El Salvador saw the pope's visit in their countries as positive.

To this observer one curious note stands out: where there was the least possibility of change on the horizon—Haiti—the Pope said emphatically: "Things must change here!" And where he was staring change in the face—Nicaragua—he was unable to accept it.

After the papal visit events continued on their course. In Nicaragua the bishops continued to take an essentially anti-Sandinista line. Archbishop Obando was even capable of stating in May 1983 when pressed by reporters that he did not know whether the United States was fomenting aggression against the Sandinistas "since all the information comes from only one side." Six months previously the CIA's "covert war" had been widely covered in the U.S., e.g., with a *Newsweek* cover story. Obando's remark was seen as highly cynical, especially by those who knew personally the people being killed. When the Sandinistas produced a new conscription law in order to prepare for what they regarded as an inevitable U.S. invasion, the bishops condemned it.

Archbishop Rivera y Damas continued to urge "dialogue" taking advantage of the papal visit, but the voice of the Salvadoran church was increasingly muted.

In Honduras the bishops, recognizing the danger that their country might be thrust into a war with Nicaragua, issued a strong warning in a pastoral letter. However it had little effect. It would no doubt have been much strengthened if it had been a joint statement along with the Nicaraguan hierarchy but such was evidently impossible.

In May 1983 the Guatemalan bishops issued a major pastoral letter "Confirmed in the Faith." In a rather doctrinal style they made a number of important criticisms: that "massacres" were still taking place and people were disappearing; that a "gradual militarization of the country" was underway at the same time as social services were being neglected; that the "civilian patrols" were being imposed by force; that economic decline was leading to hunger at the same time as the national treasury was being "sacked" and capital was being sent out of the country; the Protestant sects were being fomented for non-religious reasons. They closed reminding Catholics that the pope had called on all Catholics to be "artisans of peace."

Just as other Latin American nations found the prospect of a regional war even more alarming than the spread of Marxism and had begun the Contadora process, CELAM became similarly concerned. In July it issued a statement favoring "dialogue and . . . negotiation. . . ." The Latin American bishops said:

> With the majorities of those peoples, we desire that neither the governments nor opposition groups invite foreign powers to intervene in this conflict, and that those foreign powers, if already present, leave, and if not yet present, refrain from planning to do so.

The following month the bishops of Central America and Panama issued an even more pointed document wherein they spoke of the "meddling of foreign powers," and of the danger of an "open war covering the whole subregion with sorrow and destruction." They urged an "honorable and civilized dialogue."

That dialogue would require a reversal of U.S. policy, which in fact continued its seemingly inexorable march toward a regional war.

—November 1983

PART THREE

ISSUES IN ETHICS, CHURCH PRACTICE, AND THEOLOGY

Although its subtitle promised to deal with the issues raised by church involvement in Central American revolutions, the present work has thus far consisted largely of an account of what has happened. In beginning some systematic reflection on what I regard as the issues, I would point out that the earlier chapters are not entirely pretheological, a preparatory stage, as it were, or merely raw material for reflection. Rather, I would see them as in fact theological, and not simply in the sense that they describe people living a "theology-in-action" or a "theology-of-the-deed" as opposed to "mere" theological reflection. Much of the foregoing has summarized meetings, statements, documents, articles—all of which are themselves the product of some degree of explicit theological reflection, and events have been chosen and described with an eye to their theological relevance.

What remains, then, is to present in a systematic way the issues that have arisen in Central America, to formulate the questions people have raised, and to examine the answers if such have been found. To some extent I shall be simply reporting what church people in Central America have said and to some extent I shall offer my own judgment; often what I say will be a blend of both.

"Issues for whom?" one might reasonably ask. Certainly perspectives differ: the issues are felt in one way by those most immediately involved, grassroots Christians, especially peasants, and the pastoral agents who serve them. At a different level, they challenge those with oversight in the church, the hierarchy. Yet again they are of some importance for the universal

277

church to the extent that Christians elsewhere (for example, in the Philippines and in South Africa) may find themselves in similar situations. Some questions, such as the relationship of the church to politics, appear in a particular form in Central America but are of concern in widely differing circumstances. That United States policy in the region makes the role of the churches of special concern needs no elaboration.

With all that in mind, I would insist that my intent here is modest: to clarify for an English-reading public the issues as they have been articulated in Central America for that situation. Where I intend a wider application I will make it clear. To put it another way: I do not intend this part as a theology for general application but, rather, as the examination of theology in the particular situations of Central America.

For convenience the matter is divided into chapters on ethics, on church practice and ecclesiology, and on theology proper (especially the question of God). However, this is an order that I have imposed rather than one that is characteristic of Latin American theological thought, which tends to integrate these dimensions. Liberation theology has not developed its own ethics. There may be circumstantial reasons, such as the fact that almost all Latin American theology (at least in Central America) is a response to urgent, even burning, pastoral questions and so does not aim at a *Summa*-like completeness. However, there may be a deeper reason in that this theology continually returns to a certain underlying core-experience even as it may deal with practical issues. It may not be too farfetched to invoke comparison with Karl Rahner, who, although he has said much of ethical relevance, has not developed an ethics. As Rahner continually returns to his originating insights (the human being in the world, capable of hearing the Word, living within the horizon of mystery, and so forth), Latin American theology continually returns to its core insights. As an example, almost at random, I would cite this passage from Archbishop Romero:

> Incarnation in the sociopolitical realm
> is where faith in God and his Christ is deepening.
> We believe in Jesus
> who came to give life in abundance
> and we believe in a living God
> who gives life to human beings
> and wants them to truly live.
> These radical truths of faith
> become really truths
> and radical truths
> when the church involves itself
> in the life and death of its people.
> So the church,
> like every person
> is faced with the most basic option for its faith,
> being for life or death.

It is very clear to us
that on this point there is no possible neutrality.
We either serve the life of Salvadorans
or we are accomplices in their death.
And here is where the most basic aspect of faith finds its
historical mediation.
We either believe in a God of life
or we serve the idols of death.[1]

These words, uttered a month before Romero was murdered, express the
unity underlying the diverse issues I shall be examining.

9

Ethics of the Revolutionary Proyecto

> . . . there is no possible neutrality.
> We either serve the life of Salvadorans
> or we are accomplices in their death.
> Archbishop Romero

Christians in Nicaragua, El Salvador, and Guatemala have found themselves participating in movements aimed at taking political power in order to carry out revolutionary programs. This chapter is an attempt to go to the heart of the "revolutionary *proyecto*" and to examine its ethical basis and legitimacy. The three main focal points are economic transformation, the political order (the question of "democracy"), and violence (the means). A brief discussion on human rights will examine these points from another angle.

These issues are in a broad sense ethical in that they raise the question of what should be, as opposed to what now exists. They are among those that most immediately come to the mind of Americans when they think of Central America, especially the question of violence. Yet they are among the questions that have been least developed theoretically in Central America. For example, none of the theologians has written a major essay on violence out of the experience of recent years.[1] Moreover, while they have insisted on criteria for church action—the church should make an option not merely "for the poor" but for the "cause of the poor" and for the "historical *proyecto*" that will serve it—they have not spent a great deal of time proving the need for basic changes. One must assume that these issues are regarded as obvious.

However, some things are not so immediately obvious to American readers. Hence, in this chapter I shall seek to make explicit what is often implicit or assumed in Central America. Even for Americans who are already convinced of the legitimacy of the aims of those struggling for change, the exercise may not prove entirely superfluous.

STARTING POINT—BASIC STRUCTURAL CHANGE

Although the clarity of "first principles" may be illusory, it is important to establish self-critically a starting point, a fundamental criterion or series of criteria for judging and acting. In brief, I would here propose to establish the basic ethical legitimacy of what the revolutionary groups propose in Central America, basic changes in the economy to make it serve the needs of the poor majorities.

Certainly people's conscious "first principles" have an influence on their judgments and actions. Thus "principles" such as "Marxism and Christianity are intrinsically incompatible" or "The right to private property is fundamental and inviolable" have consequences, as do formulations such as "The church does not have the answers to the vexing political and economic questions of our day" or "Above all, the church must maintain its own identity and not take part in partisan positions." That such "principles" are normally not the product of the mind's "pure, disinterested desire to know" should be obvious; nor would I claim that the argument I shall advance is a product solely of detached reasoning.

In practice Christians have become involved in revolutionary struggles not as a result of reasoning but through a radicalization process, which often started with simple efforts to organize (cooperatives, labor unions) or even to save their lives (for example, people in danger of being killed as "suspected guerrillas," who abandon their fields and homes and flee to join the "mountain people"). In other words, their starting point in experience is not a clearly stated program of political and economic transformation as such; nevertheless, it is implicit and they gradually recognize the need for such a program from within their own experience and struggle.

In a similar but somewhat different sense it may be said that the Latin American church itself is going through a process of becoming aware of the changes that should be made. As long ago as 1968 the Latin American bishops at Medellín spoke of the need for changes that would be "deep, rapid, bold and profoundly renovating" (Peace, no. 16).

Over the years the discussion about the "change of structures" and "conversion of the heart" itself became a cliché. Central America has renewed the whole discussion, inasmuch as there are now specific groups proposing definite programs with a real possibility of putting them into effect—and hence challenging the church.

Here, then, I am seeking a starting point for understanding and evaluating the overall revolutionary *proyecto* in Central America and the response of Christians and the church to it. In order to approach this question I would like to start the inquiry with an examination of what may at first seem to be simply an example, but which I believe will lead to the heart of the question: the functioning of a *finca*, or agroexport plantation.

Let us picture a coffee plantation in the foothills of the mountains of

Guatemala (the example could equally well be a sugar or cotton plantation and be in El Salvador or Nicaragua). Coffee production requires considerable expertise and skill for best results: seedlings and plants do not begin to produce until after four years and then attention must be paid to pruning the shade trees carefully, weeding, spraying, vigilance for disease. The day-to-day management is under the care of an administrator and supervisors. Labor is done on a piecework basis. For much of the year little labor is needed and is performed by a small permanent crew and additional, hired day laborers. During harvest time (August–December, varying by altitude) large labor gangs are contracted.

The owner does not live on the plantation but in the capital city because of its better climate, schools for his children, amenities, and social contacts. Moreover, by leaving daily management to the administrator the owner can engage in other businesses, investing profits from the plantation. Basic decisions about the plantation (new investment, financing) and particularly about selling (futures) can best be made from the capital.

Let us examine the profitability of such a plantation, using rounded figures (duly making some qualifications). If annual production is 5,000 one-hundred-pound sacks, production costs are $50 per sack, market price is $200 per sack, and the government taxes sales above $50 per sack at 45 percent, the result is the following:

Production cost (labor and inputs) ($50 x 5,000)	$250,000
Export tax (.45 x 750,000)	337,500
Post-tax profit	412,500
Total	$1,000,000

These simplified figures will require some nuancing, but first I would point to the relative rewards to labor and capital in coffee production. The largest single amount of labor per unit is the hand-picking done during harvest time by Indians, who come down from the highlands. Prior to the 1980 raise in the minimum wage, people would get perhaps $1.75 for picking 100 pounds of coffee beans (roughly a day's work, although some could pick more). Since it would take two-and-a-half bags of picked beans to make 100 pounds of processed and dried beans ready for export, the harvest labor in our example would be $4.37 per bag. This means that the two-and-a-half days of bean-by-bean picking amounted to less than one-tenth of the total production cost and received less than 2.5 percent of the price paid for the coffee on the international market. There were, of course, other labor costs including the care given the seedling and young plant before it became productive, spraying, weeding, and so forth, as well as the processing (which, except for sorting the beans, is largely done by machines).

A plantation producing 5,000 bags of coffee in Guatemala is large, but not the largest: one-third of the coffee comes from fewer than 80 plantations that produce 6,000 bags or more.

As noted, these figures are simplified and demand some qualification. Coffee prices fluctuated considerably during the 1970s, from a low of $62 in 1974 to a high of over $350 a bag during 1977, due to a frost that destroyed much of the crop in Brazil, the world's largest producer. The figure of $200 chosen here is perhaps slightly higher than the average during the second half of the 1970s. During 1981 Guatemalan coffee growers were demanding that the government lower the tax rate, claiming they were not even meeting expenses. For most of the same period sugar profits were quite low. Hence I am not suggesting that plantation owners always make the kind of profit exemplified above; a fair assessment of the relative shares of capital and labor would have to be arrived at through an examination of earnings over a period of time.[2]

With all necessary qualification made, it nevertheless seems clear that a small group of people, the plantation owners, receive great profits while those who do the actual work receive a pittance. Certainly the owners assume the risks of bad weather, insects, and disease (minimized through insurance) and fluctuating prices (which can be passed on to commodities traders or exporters). Plantation owners like to speak of themselves as "producers," meaning that they bring together the "factors of production" (labor, inputs, and management), but they are rewarded in a manner far disproportionate to their real contribution.

Let us take this case from the local level, the plantation, to the country as a whole. In Guatemala 55 percent of the coffee production is in the hands of some 300 enterprises. It is reasonable to assume that these represent approximately 300 families (although some plantations are jointly owned, some families own or have shares in more than one plantation). Taking into account the extreme fluctuations of coffee prices, it is safe to say that each of these families receives hundreds of thousands of dollars—and some receive millions—a year. For the most part this same group is dominant in other kinds of plantations (cotton, sugar, beef, and some new crops) and in business and industry.

This ownership leads to extreme disparity of income: according to the United States embassy in Guatemala, the top 2 percent of the population receives 25 percent of the income, while the bottom 50 percent receives from 10 to 15 percent.[3] If we average the last figure at 12.5 percent, the top 2 percent then receives as a group double the total income of the bottom half. In other words, individuals and families of the *upper 2 percent* enjoy *fifty times* the income of the *bottom half* of the population.

In some regions of the world such disparities might reflect a "dual economy": "backward" peoples living alongside "advanced" groups.

However, the whole point of what we have been saying is that it is the *labor* of that bottom half (largely Indians) that produces the *wealth*, which is then divided unevenly. The *poverty* of Indians in the highlands with too little land is *functional*: it makes them available as a cheap, seasonal labor supply in the agroexport areas. The human results are well known: children are continually undernourished, many die in their first year or early years, families are chronically in debt, children have little schooling and few opportunities, there is little health care.

In addition, there is another effect somewhat more abstract, but important to consider. Not only do the profits accrue to a small class of people; the economy as a whole functions not to meet the basic needs of its people but to supply a series of tropical products to the world market. A clear indication is that while land for export crops in Guatemala increased dramatically after World War II, that devoted to basic foods did not keep up with the population. Thus the economy is distorted by its agroexport function.

At a most generic level—that utter extremes of wealth and poverty are wrong—Catholic church teaching has been insistent. Rutilio Grande, invoking the Genesis teaching that the material world is "without borders," said it was a "denial of God" to claim a right to "buy half of El Salvador. There is no right above the majority of the people." Echoing Puebla, Archbishop Romero spoke of "structural violence," which he called

land tenure and more generally those economic and political structures taken together, that totality of economic and political structures through which some become even richer and more powerful while the rest become ever poorer and weaker.

More forthrightly he declared:

The cause of our problems is the oligarchy, that tiny group of families which has no concern for the hunger of the people, but in fact needs it in order to have cheap and abundant labor power to harvest and export its crops.

From a different angle the Guatemalan bishops stated that "the most humble Guatemalan . . . is worth more than all the country's riches and his or her life is sacred and untouchable."

At Puebla the Latin American bishops called the growing gap between rich and poor a "scandal and contradiction to Christian existence," saying that it was "the product of economic, social, and political situations and structures" and calling for "personal conversion and profound structural changes." Puebla was simply repeating and summarizing what had been stated repeatedly by individual conferences and bishops.[4]

Disagreement begins, however, as soon as the question is raised of how this structural change is to take place. The conventional answer is "development": premature efforts to redistribute wealth in a poor society would simply inhibit growth and make everyone poorer. However, as discussed in chapter 3, Central America has experienced two or three decades of "development": infrastructures (roads, energy, and water systems) have been built, new industries have been created through the incentives of the Central American Common Market, governments have made development plans, technology and managerial expertise has been transferred. In the late 1960s and early 1970s when it was clear that not enough was "trickling down" to give the poor any substantial benefits, international agencies and some governments began to "target" the "bottom 40 percent" with programs directly aimed at improving their welfare (cooperatives, improved agricultural techniques, marketing, health and education services). These programs, in Central America at least, have shipwrecked on the hard rock of economic reality: Central American economies require a cheap labor supply of people who are landless or nearly landless; no "development" threatening that requirement can be permitted, and yet such a group of people can never constitute a market that will stimulate investment to serve its needs. Thus there is an inbuilt structural tendency toward extreme disparities of wealth and poverty, and indeed, pauperization.

Some people, sensing an anticapitalist thrust to the present argument, might say, "The problem in Central America is not capitalism but feudalism. The kind of economy you are describing is backward. What you need is not less capitalism but more, the kind that will develop the daring, creativity, dynamism, and ingenuity of entrepreneurs and enkindle hope in a people who see a chance for their betterment."

This, however, is a loose use of the term "feudal," making it more or less synonymous with "backwardness." Central American economies are not feudal, since the landowner, unlike the medieval lord, has no obligation to the workers (to provide protection, or food in times of famine). Their relationship is thoroughly capitalist in that the owner of the means of production (the plantation) buys the labor power of the workers, who are economically forced to sell it. The overall tendency is proletarization: more and more people are without the least means of production (small plots of land). While this may be "underdeveloped capitalism," it is capitalism nevertheless.

Moreover, there is no built-in tendency for it to evolve in a direction in which the basic contradictions will be resolved. The reason is simple and obvious: the oligarchies, in league with the military, manage the political process and have been willing to support a high degree of repression to maintain their privilege. El Salvador's frustrated "land reforms" (see chapter 5) are eloquent proof.

For our present purposes, the question is not "capitalism" as a whole but the Central American economies, which are capitalist. It is evident, however, that capitalism itself (and not simply "abuses" associated with it) are being increasingly questioned—the very efforts of corporations and the

United States government to "sell" capitalism through advertising is indication of such questioning. While I have no intention of contributing any real substance to the debate, I would simply note that it often tends to be unhistorical and static, that is, the question is stated as "capitalism vs. socialism." However, capitalism is not an eternal essence but a phenomenon in history: as a system it began during the eighteenth century, although elements of it had appeared before. As a phenomenon in history it is either some kind of definitive achievement of the human race, destined to remain forever or—more likely—it is a stage destined to give way to something else. It is the contention of many that the seeds of this "something else" are already present and can be seen in the "contradictions" of capitalism, and that the new form will be called "socialism," since the main means of production will be socially owned and managed. Its convinced defenders might argue that whereas in principle capitalism may eventually be superseded by new forms, they are as yet unforseeable and the question is irrelevant. However, a growing number see the question as indeed relevant and critical for understanding what is happening in our age. This historical angle on the question helps illuminate the objection that "socialism" has failed: socialism has a much shorter history and existing examples may be seen as initial efforts, partial successes, or even false starts toward the "something else" to which capitalism will give way.

What I mean to say with the preceding excursus is that the present discussion on Central America may be seen in two ways. For some it is simply a manifestation of a larger crisis of the capitalist system; for others it may be viewed as a special and extreme case, which may call for extraordinary responses. I would hope that even those who see no need to question capitalism in principle will give some consideration to my present argument.

To return to the basic question of "what is to be done," I would assert that the "structural changes" needed involve changing the functioning of the economy so that the main means of production (plantations, factories) serve the people in such a way that:

1. the workers receive a fair share of the wealth they produce
2. profits are reinvested for true development rather than serving the further aggrandizement or luxury consumption of elites
3. production is aimed at the basic needs of the majority: (*a*) food self-sufficiency, and (*b*) basic consumer items for all (clothing, shoes, household items, and so forth)
4. essential social services (schooling and health care) are provided
5. workers are involved in management rather than simply being factors of production

Such a course would necessitate a considerable amount of direct expropriation. While expropriation might strike some as unjust—to the degree that they hold property rights to be absolute (or a kind of "first principle")

—I would argue that in the case of Central American oligarchies *justice demands expropriation*, and I wish to state this proposition in its most direct and possibly offensive form before considering possible qualifications.

First, the real development of the poor is incompatible with such extreme division not only of wealth, but of income and power. There simply will be no development for the poor in Guatemala, for example, as long as the top 2 percent as a group receives double the income of the lower half of the population.

Second, the wealth of the oligarchy is not primarily the result of entrepreneurial genius, but, rather, the product of an original expropriation (lands taken from the Indians and the church in the 1870s) and continuing exploitation (for example, in Nebaj, Guatemala, all the local landholding elites began their fortunes as labor contractors). Not all are subjectively guilty, of course. Today's families have often simply inherited wealth and consider it "natural" that they should enjoy privilege. Some people of middle-class origins studied, became professionals, saved, and bought agroexport property. However, the agroexport system remains objectively exploitive, independent of the intentions of the owners.

Third, Central American oligarchies have already taken vast sums of their wealth out of their countries. While Swiss bank accounts were traditional, the movement in recent years is astounding. Somoza and his associates took an amount equivalent to 96 percent of one year's GNP (gross national product); figures for El Salvador are imprecise, but it seems that a similar amount may have been removed.[5] That a tiny elite should be able to remove in dollars an amount equivalent to the value of a whole year's production of goods and services in the entire country is another striking example of their economic power. It also lessens concern for their fate in the case of expropriation.

To repeat: in my view, a broad expropriation of the means of production from the hands of the oligarchies in order to restructure the economy to serve the needs of the poor would not only *not* be unjust, but would, on the contrary, be an act of justice.

PAPAL VISION

Further light may be shed on the question of the revolutionary *proyecto* by a source that at first glance might seem surprising, Pope John Paul II's encyclical *Laborem Exercens* (On the Dignity of Work). That this major statement, made in September 1981, was almost unnoticed in American Catholicism is a revealing example of selective vision. At the outset I would make it clear that I do not believe my position stated above follows necessarily from the pope's position, but that it is compatible with the encyclical and indeed has a certain harmony with the pope's essential message.

In this encyclical marking the ninetieth anniversary of *Rerum Novarum*, the first major papal statement on the "social question," Pope John Paul II shows a sensitivity to work as it is today and attempts to outline a philosophy, and even more a theology and spirituality, of work, drawing conclusions and offering guidelines, while at the same time refraining from proposing clear models for the realization of the ideals that he states in general terms.

In words quite plainly applicable to Central America the pope speaks of *"objectively unjust situations"* (emphasis in original) in agriculture:

In certain developing countries, millions of people are forced to cultivate the land belonging to others and are exploited by the big landowners, without any hope of ever being able to gain possession of even a small piece of land on their own. There is a lack of forms of legal protection for the agricultural workers themselves and for their families in case of old age, sickness or unemployment. Long days of hard physical work are paid miserably. Land which could be cultivated is left abandoned by the owners. Legal titles to possession of a small portion of land that someone has personally cultivated for years are disregarded or left defenseless against the "land hunger" of more powerful individuals or groups. . . .

In many situations radical and urgent changes are therefore needed in order to restore to agriculture—and to rural people—their just value *as the basis for a healthy economy* [p. 24].*

At the core of the encyclical there is a conviction, based on both revelation and personalist philosophy, that the human being is the "image and likeness" of God, "called to work," to subdue the earth. "Human work is *a key* probably the *essential key* to the whole social question . . ." (p. 11, emphasis in original).

. . . *the primary basis of the value of work is man* [6] *himself*, who is its subject. This leads immediately to a very important conclusion of an ethical nature: however true it may be that man is destined for work and called to it, in the first place work is "for man" and not man "for work." Through this conclusion one rightly comes to recognize the preeminence of the subjective meaning of work over the objective one [p. 12, emphasis in original].

The pope insists that the human being is the "measure" of the dignity of work and is the purpose for which it is carried out. The implication is that people, even poor peasants, are ends and not means.

From the beginning of the modern age, according to John Paul II, the church has had to uphold these principles against various trends of "mate-

---

*All citations for *Laborem Exercens* are to the translation in *National Catholic Reporter*, September 11, 1981.

rialistic and economistic thought." According to some, work was a sort of "merchandise" that "the worker . . . sells to the employer, who at the same time is the possessor of the capital, that is to say, of all the working tools and means that make production possible" (p. 12). When the human being is "treated as an instrument of production" there is a reversal of the order laid down in Genesis. This "error of early capitalism"

> can be repeated wherever man is in a way treated on the same level as the whole complex of the material means of production, as an instrument and not in accordance with the true dignity of his work—that is to say where he is not treated as subject and maker, and for this very reason as the true purpose of the whole process of production.
>
> This explains why the analysis of human work in the light of the words concerning man's "dominion" over the earth goes to the very heart of the ethical and social question. This concept should also find a central place in the whole sphere of social and economic policy, both within individual countries and in the wider field of international and intercontinental relationships . . . [p. 12].

After noting many changes since *Rerum Novarum*, especially gains made by workers (although flagrant abuses exist and new ones have arisen), the pope turns to the conflict between capital (a "small but highly influential group of entrepreneurs, owners or holders of the means of production") and labor ("the broad multitude of people who lacked these means and who shared in the process of production solely by their labor"). Following the principle of maximum profit, the entrepreneurs sought to pay the lowest possible wages and in addition did not provide for worker health and safety.

He then in somewhat neutral language describes the Marxist approach, transforming the conflict between labor and capital into "systematic class struggle" leading to the "collectivization of the means of production." In order to carry out this program, Marxists aim at winning a "monopoly of power in each society," and finally establishing "the communist system throughout the world" (p. 13). The pope, however, says he does not wish to go into details.

Returning to what most interests him, he insists on the "principle of the priority of labor over capital": (labor is the efficient cause while capital is an instrumental cause). Capital is either God's gift (natural resources) or *"the result of the historical heritage of human labor."* "Thus, *everything that is at the service of work . . . is the result of work"* (pp. 13–14, emphasis in original).

These last statements and the whole philosophical-theological background of the encyclical I find to be extraordinary. The pope's reservations toward Marxism notwithstanding, his position seems to have a definite affinity to the "labor theory of value." His position is not simply an endorsement of that theory and in fact his aim is different. Marxist economic theory is intended primarily to be explanatory, and to this day heated debates continue about the labor theory of value in this respect. The pope's purpose is to sketch a basic humanist and Christian understanding of work. Nevertheless, his position obviously has more affinity with Marxist theory than with the conventional economic analysis coming out of capitalist circles.

So much for Pope John Paul II's starting point. What does he prescribe? Does he have any model of society in mind? More specifically, does he have anything relevant to say to our original question here, namely, the economic reordering of Central American countries, including the expropriation of the wealth of the oligarchies?

On the level of principle he declares:

A labor system can be right . . . if in its very basis it overcomes the opposition between labor and capital through an effort at being shaped in accordance with . . . the principle of the substantial and real priority of labor, of the subjectivity of human labor and its effective participation in the whole production process, independently of the services provided by the worker [p. 14].

The question of capital and labor is clearly linked to that of the ownership of the means of production. Church teaching "diverges radically" from Marxist collectivism, and also differs from the program of capitalism. Referring to the traditional teaching that *"the right to private property is subordinated to the right to common use,"* the pope holds "rigid" capitalism, which sees the "exclusive right to private ownership of the means of production" as an untouchable "dogma," to be unacceptable. He insists, however, that

these many deeply desired reforms cannot be achieved by any *a priori elimination of private ownership of the means of production*. For it must be noted that merely taking these means of production (capital) out of the hands of their private owners is not enough to ensure their satisfactory socialization. They cease to be the property of a certain social group, namely the private owners and become the property of organized society, coming under the administration and direct control of another group of people, namely those who, though not owning them, from the fact of exercising power in society, *manage* them on the level of the whole national or the local economy.

This group in authority may carry out its task satisfactorily from the point of view of the priority of labor; but it may also carry it out badly by claiming for itself *a monopoly of the administration and disposal* of the means of production and not refraining even from offending basic human rights. Thus merely converting the means of production into state property in the collectivist system is by no means equivalent to "socializing" that property. We can speak of socializing only when the subject character of society is ensured, that is to say, when on the basis of his work each person is fully entitled to consider himself a part-owner of the great workbench at which he is working with everyone else [p. 14, emphasis in original].

It should be noted that the pope is not arguing against ending private ownership of the means of production; he is warning that ending private ownership does not by itself "socialize" property, socialization for him being what is desired. In other words, expropriation would be acceptable *if* it led to a labor system in which the worker is "subject."

While neither Marxist collectivism nor capitalism in its pure state meets the criteria he sets down, the pope seems to accept that they may be met where these systems have been modified; for example, in another context he speaks of just remuneration "in a system of private ownership of the means of production or in a system where ownership has undergone a certain socialization" (p. 23). However, at other points he comes close to describing an anarchist model; for example, he says that a way toward the goal of making people subjects of their work

could be found by associating labor with the ownership of capital, as far as possible and by producing a wide range of intermediate bodies with economic, social and cultural purposes; they would be bodies enjoying real autonomy with regard to the public powers, pursuing their specific aims in honest collaboration with each other and in subordination to the demands of the common good, and they would be living communities both in form and in substance, in the sense that the members of each body would be looked upon and treated as persons and encouraged to take an active part in the life of the body [p. 14].

Given the overall direction of the letter, the pope's vision seems to incline toward the anarchist tradition (from Kropotkin to Schumacher, Illich, and the like), without clearly prescribing any model or system.

Summarizing, then, there are several points in *Laborem Exercens* that have a bearing on the revolutionary *proyecto* as we are considering it.

1. More than with specific models (capitalist, socialist, or anarchist), the pope is concerned to lay down a humanist and Christian foundation for understanding work, namely, that human beings are its subject, the measure of its value, and its end.
2. Existing economies in Central America directly violate the encyclical's principles by treating human labor simply as a means for accumulating wealth.
3. The notion of an exclusive right to private property of the means of production is rejected.

4. State ownership and management in itself does not solve the problem; the key question is whether the workers themselves become subjects and whether they have real autonomy.

My purpose in such extensive treatment is not to use *Laborem Exercens* as the basis for my position. What makes the encyclical valuable is not only the pope's authority (which today is scarcely heeded on many subjects, particularly those related to critical issues within the church), but the fact that it expresses admirably the Catholic tradition and moves it forward by a clearer focus on the nature of work. The pope's serene discussion of expropriation and frequent use of Marxist-originated language should serve to indicate that what I have been discussing in this chapter, the ethics of revolutionary structural change, far from being an exotic tropical import, involves issues of fundamental concern for the Christian conscience.

What is being attempted today in Nicaragua (and possibly later in El Salvador and Guatemala) is precisely the reordering of the economy so that human beings (including the poor) will be the subjects of the economy and its end. Hence, in elaborating its economic plans the Nicaraguan Planning Ministry has spoken of pursuing the "logic of the majorities." This does not mean an a priori collectivization; on the contrary, the Sandinistas have sought to set up a "mixed economy," in which privately owned businesses are to fit into an overall design reversing the priorities of the Somoza economy. Similarly the mass, or popular, organizations, such as the CST and ATC, which their opponents might see simply as Sandinista vehicles, are intended to make people protagonists, or "subjects," of the revolutionary transformation.

In a similar sense the "Programmatic Platform" prepared by El Salvador's Revolutionary Democratic Front in 1980 listed among the tasks and objectives of the revolution:

. . . 2. Ending the political, economic, and social power and domination of the great lords of capital and land. . . .
. . . 5. Transferring to the people, through nationalization and the creation of collective and associated enterprises, the basic means of production and distribution, now taken over by the oligarchy and United States monopolies.

Although it says that its measures will include the "expropriation, as it might serve the nation, of monopolistic enterprises in industry, commerce, and services," and a "profound Agrarian Reform," the FDR insists that its measures would not affect the lands of small- and medium-sized land and property holders, who on the contrary would be helped.[7] While less programmatically developed, the aims of the Guatemalan revolutionary movement are along similar lines.

The present chapter has had thus far essentially but one concern: to establish the legitimacy of the basic reordering of the economy in order for it to serve human needs—the revolutionary *proyecto*. I would urge that this must be the starting point for an understanding of, and a responsible judgment on, what has happened in Central America. For many Central Americans this concern would be superfluous: to them it is utterly obvious that basic change is necessary and that the dominant elites have left them no choice but to struggle. Elsewhere, however, the word "revolution" tends to be seen essentially in terms of violence; hence the effort here to emphasize that in essence it is not violence but structural change.

Not only Central Americans find the point obvious. In an essay written some years ago ("On the Theology of Revolution") Karl Rahner emphasized that revolution was not to be defined in terms of "force"; he defined it essentially as the recognition of injustice, the conception of new and more just structures, and strategy and methods for change on the part of a group that was outside the power structure in society. What I find interesting is his serene affirmation that revolution "is necessary if the underdeveloped world is really to obtain a share in the benefits they justifiably demand," and "On any just and unprejudiced view of the present day state of the world, we must say that a global revolutionary situation does exist."[8] Rahner made these statements as if they needed no justification. I hope that my labored effort to state clearly a starting point at least provides greater depth for what many feel is obvious.

It would be well to point out that, although a radical elimination of that kind of privilege that causes the misery of the majorities is justifiable, prudence might dictate a gradual and pragmatic approach.

In Nicaragua, as noted in chapter 8, privileges are only slowly being eroded, more as a result of constraints being put on the economy than by decrees. A too-rapid policy of lessening income differentials, for example, might end in driving out all those with technical and administrative skills. A pragmatic attitude even on the question of ownership may be called for insofar as the critical point is not the ownership as such of the means of production, but the control of their orientation. Privately owned industries, efficiently run, producing needed basic consumer goods, in which the workers share the benefits and the administration, could fit into an economic design according to the "logic of the majorities" (Nicaraguan economic planners) and serve the "subject character" of work (Pope John Paul II).

"DEMOCRACY" IN THE REVOLUTION?

A frequent concern about revolutionary movements is that as a remedy they may be as bad or worse than the disease; for example, someone might say: "Granting that Somoza and these regimes are repressive, is there not a danger of naively supporting Marxist-Leninist groups, which even if they end extremes of wealth and poverty will do so at the expense of something priceless—freedom?''

One reply to such a formulation (which has more than one assumption and bias) is: ''Well, those people have never had 'freedom.' And you need a strong state for development. Hence there may be a kind of tradeoff between democratic freedoms as we know them and the exigencies of development. If that's the case, development—structural change—must come first even if led by an authoritarian party.''

The question to be taken up here is, in a word, that of the political forms of the revolutionary *proyecto*, and in particular the question of democracy. It should be noted at the outset that the issue is clouded. The notion of democracy is a rallying cry and a symbol of legitimacy. Hence the United States engaged in strenuous efforts to pressure the Salvadoran government into holding the 1982 elections, to convince world public opinion that they were valid, and to hold together the artificial government that emerged as a result—all the while pursuing its real goal, the elimination of the leftist opposition. On the other hand, the political arm of the Salvadoran opposition called itself the Revolutionary *Democratic* Front.

That the issue is a live one may be seen in the appearance in 1981 of the Institute for Religion and Democracy (IRD), a neo-conservative religious think-tank, whose purpose seems to be to combat what it considers the churches' dalliance with the Marxist left, especially in liberation movements. Two of its first pamphlets dealt with El Salvador and Nicaragua.

In this section I would like to deal with some notions of what democracy is (and in particular bring some critical focus to bear on conventional views), the previous political experience of Central America, and what the revolutionary movements propose; and then I will examine the position of the Institute for Religion and Democracy (which performs the service of formulating important issues for discussion in the churches). I here alert the reader that my aim is more one of questioning facile assumptions than of arguing a definitive position: I am convinced that the last word has not been said about democracy in either theory or practice.

Part of the difficulty of dealing with the notion of democracy is the spontaneous tendency to identify it with the political forms known in the United States; that is, in the first place, regular elections and an orderly transfer of power, and the freedoms of speech, assembly, and press. At a certain level people understand ''democracy'' by these institutions and by contrast with what the United States is not: monarchies and totalitarianisms. Many even assume that the United States is ''Number One'' in democracy—a counterpart to its preeminence in economic power, military might, technological dominance, and so forth. Yet these same ''civics-book'' ideas can exist side by side with cynicism about how actual politics take place (''politicians are all out for themselves'') and a feeling of impotence about basic problems (for example, the decay of the older industrial cities). Even basic notions in the political lexicon become utterly vulgarized, as when ''America Loves the

Freedom'' (which seems to invoke the myths of the Founders) is used to advertise the Seven-Eleven chain of stores.

Etymologically, of course, the word "democracy" means "rule by the people" (Greek *demos* "people," and *kratos* "power" or "rule"). The experience of the Greek city-states, whose "democracy" did not extend to women or slaves, was rather a historical oddity permitted in part by their small size, although it introduced at least the idea of democracy into subsequent political discourse. Historically modern Western democracy arose in a struggle against the pretensions of monarchies to absolute rule, and was rooted in the restraints put on them by divine law, natural law, and custom. The rise of parliamentary government, and for the United States the whole elaborate system of separation of functions, may be seen as a striving for *limited* government: limited in its power over the individual citizen and in the ability of any person or group to maintain political power indefinitely (the citizens can "throw the rascals out"). Two of the main ingredients of Western democracy are the Constitution (a law above particular individuals and groups holding office) and political parties (seen as instruments for channeling conflicts and achieving orderly compromise and consensus).

In political science itself there is a lack of consensus on what democracy means, at least in practice. Western democracy is often presented as the achievement of (implicitly) superior peoples who have emerged, due mainly to their ethical qualities, from the normal conditions of authoritarian rule characteristic of the mass of humanity. Democracy is a "fragile" acquisition of the human race. There is always a clear qualitative difference between democracy and totalitarianism, whether left- or right-wing.

Many critics, especially Marxists, see such conventional views as "ideological" and particularly naive in that they tend to ignore the relations between economic developments and political forms. Democracy, they would argue, arose not so much from particular moral qualities in certain nations but from a rising class, the "bourgeoisie," and is aptly called "bourgeois democracy." The pluralism of political parties, free press, and other institutions of democracy are functional to capitalism: they permit struggle between competing factions of the bourgeoisie over secondary issues, while maintaining an illusion of equal participation of all; when the interests of the bourgeoisie as a whole are threatened, however, coercion and repression may be used with no compunction.

Theories of politics seeking to deal with the actual power of elites within a political framework ostensibly "representative" of the people vary widely. One investigator has classified dozens of approaches to political science under the main headings of systems (structural functionalism), culture, development/underdevelopment, and class.[9] I would emphasize simply that there is no real consensus on how the "democratic" political system functions. The humble recognition of ignorance is a first step toward insight and knowledge.

It would not be amiss to look briefly at one recent experience of American politics, the 1980 election of Ronald Reagan to the presidency and the subsequent enactment of parts of the Reagan program, with a view to examining to what extent it was "democratic." In that election the most common reaction among ordinary people was either frustration over the choice between a personally sincere but apparently ineffective incumbent (symbolized in the year-long "hostage ordeal") and an engaging former actor, who tempered his well-known right-wing views to appear moderate and responsible. Propelled by right-wing zeal and Moral Majority fervor, and aided by the apathy of others and an anti-Carter feeling, Reagan was elected.

At that point the conservative advisers came out of the closet (for instance, the Heritage Foundation with 3,000 pages of recommendations presented to the "transition team" ten days after the election), and the Reagan circle prepared to "hit the ground running," with an attempt to reverse the trend of fifty years of socially progressive legislation and programs and with a military buildup that would attempt an *increase* in four years equal to the *total* military budget of 1961—the year when outgoing President Dwight D. Eisenhower warned of the military-industrial complex. The new administration cut social spending; made a massive tax redistribution in favor of the rich; sought to reduce the government role in enforcing civil rights, occupational health and safety, consumer protection, and environmental protection; and sought to apply a simplistic anticommunist formula to all international questions (not the least being its intervention in Central America).

At issue here is not so much the Reagan administration programs (the import of which is only summarily indicated) but a question of process: To what extent did the American people *democratically* decide on these programs? Had Reagan clearly stated what he intended to do, would he have been elected? (Would pensioners, parents of college-age children, wilderness lovers have voted for him had the issues that concerned them been debated fully?) More important, how can a process in which so much depends on "packaging" of candidates for media presentation be called "democratic"? Is not the process of elections every two and four years largely a national ritual, which gives a sensation of participation and then allows people to see politics as largely a spectator sport?

Certainly United States democracy is not limited to voting. A small but important portion of the citizenry is actively seeking to promote its causes (pro-life or pro-choice, civil liberties, deregulation or mining safety) through organizations (Sierra Club, National Association of Manufacturers, National Rifle Club), media discussion, and appeals to elected representatives. Polls continually take the temperature of the population, and trends sooner or later show up in voting and thereby in the makeup of Congress and an administration. Even if it is indirect and slow in having an effect, public opinion including that of people-in-the-street has weight and influences policy; one example is the surprising burgeoning of the antinuclear-war movement in 1981–82 forcing all practicing politicians, including Reagan, to take it into account.

There are, nevertheless, large areas in American life that are outside the control of the electoral process. Until recently, for example, the overall thrust of United States "defense" policy was never really questioned and even today public debate is largely a question of trimming or adding a few billion dollars of the Pentagon budget.

Another example in the United States is the impotence of eastern and midwestern cities when large corporations move to the Sunbelt or overseas, not only suddenly leaving many employees jobless but devastating the local economy. Increasingly people are calling for a major expansion in the notion of democracy toward "economic democracy," wherein the people would have power over major economic institutions and, in particular, the large corporations.

That there is much "unfinished business" in the notion of democracy may be exemplified from yet another angle. Amid all the cheers for Solidarity, the Polish labor movement, it was little noticed that one of its demands was that workers be able to hire and fire supervisors. Certainly no United States corporation would consider such a demand, yet it seems to be a logical development of the notion of democracy.

The upshot of all this, to my mind, is simple: neither in theory nor in our experience is it self-evident what "democracy" is. That many fundamental decisions are made with only an apparent and ritual participation by the people, that many areas of life lie outside democratic processes, and that much of what passes for democracy is pageantry should make us humble about our understanding of it and open to the possibility that there is more to learn, that the forms of democracy we know do not exhaust it, and that democracy itself will reveal further potentialities.

Democracy in Central America—Form vs. Substance

Central American countries have had many of the procedures of Western democracy: they have presidents and assemblies, political parties with their ideologies, elections, and the drama of accusations, scandals, and intrigues. Nevertheless the stereotype of fraud and political violence and ever impending military coups is perhaps more correct than not. A common attitude from the United States might be expressed, "Well, of course we can't expect people down there to have full democracy—they're not ready for it yet." The United States ambassador to El Salvador, Deane Hinton, seeking to explain the aftermath of the March 1982 election, told Congress that it "would take a generation" to restore order to El Salvador's politics[10]—an attitude not too distant from the "white man's burden" of a previous era.

A more critical attitude might raise questions both about how these countries are viewed and about the appropriateness of their existing political institutions. Thus many people look at third-world countries with a culture-bound vision, as though "Western civilization" and, in this case, its political institutions were the unquestionable high point of all the previous strivings of humankind and other peoples should be judged by the degree to which they approximated these achievements. More particularly there is a tendency to isolate "violence" and "instability" as though they were aspects of "national character" rather than the products mainly of economic exploitation with its concomitant political and social domination. When I say this I am thinking not only of "people in the street" but of political scientists, media people, and members of the United States diplomatic service.

In looking at Central American political questions, then, I would first urge an effort to be critically aware of such cultural baggage. In addition, I think there is a key distinction to be made between the essence of democracy, rule by the people, and the forms it may take. In the form of a question: Are "democratic" forms, elections, parties, and so forth, an expression of some kind of democracy—or possibly a frustration of it?

Chapter 3 gave some characterization of the political history of Central America. The nineteenth- and early twentieth-century Liberal-Conservative seesaw was a struggle among the elites: neither side represented the bulk of the people; it was the Liberals who, in the name of "progress" (that is, coffee) despoiled the Indians of their communal lands. Governments during the present century have been imposed, whether those of the personal dictatorships of the 1930s and 1940s (and the Somozas until 1979) or the increasingly institutionalized army rule in Guatemala and El Salvador from the 1960s onward.

That there have been blatant electoral frauds (El Salvador, 1972 and 1977; Guatemala, 1974, 1978, 1982) is well known; what is less apparent is that the army is the ultimate arbiter: along with the oligarchy, it can establish clear, if unwritten, parameters, the most elementary being that no political party or coalition would be permitted to propose and carry out measures that would threaten the power and wealth of the elites. The fraud against Christian Democratic candidate General Efraín Ríos Montt in Guatemala in 1974 reflected the army's and the oligarchy's fear of reform. In 1978, accordingly, General Ricardo Peralta Méndez, also a Christian Democrat, avoided any hint at substantial reform and sought to reassure his military colleagues he was trustworthy—and wound up in a distant third place (partly due to fraud but also because voters saw no possibility of change through elections). The following year Deputy Alberto Fuentes Mohr and the former mayor of Guatemala City, Manuel Colóm Argueta, both highly respected and popular leaders of Social Democratic parties, were gunned down in the street by hit squads directed by the military. The cynicism was more evident in that their parties were in the process of being legally recognized. In the 1982 election no candidates offered any sort of reform: the issue was whether the dominant Lucas clique would impose its candidate or allow a civilian to win, a concession that would facilitate the renewal of military aid from the United States. Its shortsighted imposition of General Guevara prompted the military coup, in which General Ríos Montt (now "born again") emerged as at least the apparent leader, advocating no structural reforms that would address the causes of violence in Guatemala but, rather, reducing the most blatant manifestations of official violence in the cities, while increasing it in the countryside.

A brief allusion to the March 1982 election in El Salvador may suffice at this point. Initially the media conveyed the impression that the "large voter turnout" was a repudiation of the leftist opposition. Much less noticed was the subsequent revelation that the government had possibly invented a new kind of fraud: it increased the total count of the votes (as much as doubling it), while maintaining the actual proportions of the vote count: thus the main objective of the election was achieved, the appearance of a large turnout for United States public opinion, and individual parties were prevented from making accusations of fraud.[11] In Honduras the army permitted Roberto Suazo Córdova to win the November 1981 presidential election only after he gave assurances that it (the army) would retain authority over matters of national security, which it intended to interpret in a broad manner.

Some observers would explain such phenomena on the basis of a "weak democratic tradition." Such a phrase tends to place the blame on national traits of some sort and minimizes the de facto rule of the military and the oligarchy. The mere existence of electoral mechanisms, parties, and assemblies is regarded as positive even if they can be nullified at any moment with a coup. The task is seen as making them more functional—even minimal "democracy" is considered preferable to none at all. Such an attitude has been characteristic of Christian Democratic parties, ever waiting in the wings as a "third force" (between existing military/oligarchy combinations and Marxist revolutionaries), and of the United States government, ever willing to find signs of "progress."

Such a position should be questioned. I would submit that the forms of Western governments in Central America, far from being incipient democracy, are a frustration of democracy. However, they are functional to existing dominant groups in three ways: (1) these forms (elections, parties, congresses) serve to mask the de facto rule of the military and oligarchy by giving the illusion of participation and thereby legitimacy; (2) the mechanisms of assemblies, parties, newspapers, serve as a forum for the debate and resolution of secondary issues; for example, one party may represent traditional landholders while another may represent industrialists, and there may be heated debate and conflict over such issues as increasing (or lowering) coffee export taxes; (3) party structures serve as patronage mechanisms at the local level; in a local township, for example, rival groups will vie for the post of mayor and the concomitant job appointments and opportunities.

In several ways, then, the mechanisms and forms of Western democracy are functional to the kinds of regimes that have existed in Central America. The issue of "clean elections" (that is, correct vote-counting), while revealing about the level of corruption and coercion, is superficial—the real fraud has taken place long before election day in that these mechanisms in no sense permit the bulk of the people to effect peaceful change. *Democratic forms are used to thwart democracy.*

Although it is beyond the purview of this study, I would simply assert that by and large there is no "democracy," if the term is taken to mean "rule by the people" (including the poor majority), in all of Latin America. From the gross absurdities of elections and frauds and coups by Bolivia's cocaine-trafficking military, to the murderous dictatorships of Argentina and Chile, to the more apparently democratic countries (Venezuela, Colombia, and Costa Rica), existing political forms tend to legitimize the economic domination of privileged elites. The closest approach to democracy would seem to be the occasional skillful populism of regimes (Mexico and Peru during the early phase [1968–75] of military rule) or charismatic leaders; no regime allows grassroots organization to reach the point where it might threaten basic elite control.[12]

In seeking to understand what revolutionary groups propose as a new political framework, it is important to appreciate what the historical experience of "democracy" in their countries has been. From their viewpoint the problem of "bourgeois democracy" is that it is not really democratic, at least in their countries. Citizen involvement in the best of cases is that of going to the polls on periodic occasions to choose between preselected candidates, who as soon as they are elected will largely forget their constituency until the next election. More to the point, it serves to mask oligarchical/military rule.

The key to democracy, in their mind, is not elections as such but *participation,* in an ongoing way, at different levels, in the tasks of building a new order. Elections are one element in a larger whole.

El Salvador's Revolutionary Democratic Front mentions among the tasks and objectives of the revolution:

> . . . 4. To assure for the whole population rights and democratic freedoms, especially for the working masses, who have least enjoyed them.
> . . . 8. To encourage popular organization at all levels, in all sectors, and in all ways, to guarantee the people's active, creative, and democratic incorporation in the revolutionary process and to achieve the closest identification between the People and its Government.[13]

When it speaks of the political measures it intends to undertake, the FDR stresses the end of repression, the investigation of the fate of political prisoners and the disappeared since 1972, the end of the repressive forces, both official and paramilitary, the strengthening of the People's Army, the writing of a new Constitution, liberating educational programs, and nonalignment. The emphasis is on the elimination of the odious aspects of previous regimes. There is no mention of electoral procedures, although in other statements the FDR has spoken of elections as part of a negotiated solution to the conflict.

Although the Nicaraguan revolution is criticized by its own internal opposition and critics outside as "totalitarian-tending," the Frente Sandinista claims that it is advancing democracy. The kind of democracy it is seeking to build starts at the local level, in the workplace and in the neighborhood. It is claimed that, in those enterprises that are part of the Area of People's Property (publicly-owned former Somoza properties), the "relations of production" have been changed: workers share in the decision-making process and themselves come to appreciate the need for efficient production and are motivated to improve both quality and quantity. Similarly, in the neighborhood, the Sandinista Defense Committees are the means whereby people can meet to discuss and work on local problems and cooperate on local clean-up days, making improvements, organizing community activities, and, where necessary, defending the revolution. In theory at least, workplace and community structures make up the foundation for participation in higher-level decision-making. For example, there were efforts to involve the mass organizations in both the drawing up and the implementation of the economic plans of 1980 and 1981.

When asked about democracy in the revolution, a Sandinista sympathizer will point to the mass organizations (CST, ATC, AMNLAE, CDSs, and so forth), the Literacy Crusade and subsequent adult-education programs, the massive mobilization of volunteers in the antimalaria campaign of 1981, the vastly increased unionization, the volunteers who picked cotton and coffee, and particularly to the Popular Militias and the Popular Sandinista Army: the fact that many citizens are given weapons is cited as proof that the revolution has vast support and the army is viewed as an armed extension of the people rather than as a force above it. An overall term for this concept of democracy is *poder popular*, "people's power."

In the United States it is considered axiomatic that Cuba is simply government by the Communist party in a totalitarian manner. Yet there are some who see in the mechanisms of people's power, introduced in the mid-1970s, a significant implementation of the kind of "democracy" I have been describing in outline. Marta Harnecker, for example, has compiled a book of interviews of people in factory discussions, popular tribunals, neighborhood committees, and in the process of electing representatives for regional and national assemblies. Those interviewed compare favorably the new model of politics with previous kinds. I do not intend to pass judgment either on "popular power" in Cuba or Harnecker's work—simply to say that I do not see why it must be rejected out of hand. On the contrary, I would think it would be worth more observation to see if, indeed, and to what extent, some aspects of democracy might be realized there.[14]

To approach the point negatively: let us suppose that after the fall of Somoza the Frente Sandinista had simply sought to reintroduce electoral politics in Nicaragua declaring a six-month campaign period. What would have been the issues? How relevant would a "pluralism" of several anti-Somoza bourgeois parties be to the essential tasks of consolidating and carrying out a revolution (that is, changing basic structures)? If debate over changes were dependent upon such an assembly, would it not facilitate the bourgeoisie's efforts to assert control of the economy? In what sense would the grassroots be involved in such a "democratic" process?

Thus far my argument has had a modest aim: to suggest that existing forms of "democracy" may be incomplete and that the efforts of revolutionary regimes should not automatically be discounted as antidemocratic.

Religion and Democracy: Pros, Cons, and Qualifications

Just as basic economic questions (capitalism/socialism) may become topics of debate in the churches in the United States in the 1980s, so may political questions such as "democracy." In fact, economic and political systems as a whole may become "disputed questions."

One manifestation of the impending debate is the formation of the Institute for Religion and Democracy (IRD), with headquarters in Washington, D.C., and with the active participation of people like Peter Berger, Richard John Neuhaus, and Michael Novak. Because it is largely at odds with the position I have been arguing, I would like to summarize and discuss in some detail a document titled "Christianity and Democracy" (1981), which may be taken to be the institute's "manifesto":

1. "Jesus Christ is Lord." Equating any political, economic, or social order with the kingdom of God is a betrayal of the Lord. "The first political task of the Church is to be the Church." Communal allegiance to Christ is a "check upon the pretensions of the modern state."
2. The church should be open, encourage diversity, make decisions by the light of day; its leaders should engage in full consultation with members. (This whole train of thought reflects the institute's conviction that the church bureaucracies have been taken over by doctrinaire leftists who, behind the backs of ordinary church members, are using these positions to advance their ideas.)
3. "In this century . . . the most urgent truth to be told about secular politics is the threat of totalitarianism," which means "thoroughgoing monism, political, social, juridical, religious": the party-state becomes the supreme authority. The religious term for totalitarianism is idolatry.
4. Although there can be rightist totalitarianism, today the only global ideology "committed to the monistic denial of freedom is Marxism-Leninism." Marxist-Leninist regimes may vary, but "every such regime and every such revolutionary movement subscribes to this totalitarian

intent.'' Millions have died, millions have been imprisoned and cruelly repressed.

5. "It is both politically and theologically imperative to assert that Marxism-Leninism promulgates a doctrine that is imcompatible with a Christian understanding of humanity and historical destiny. Thus a Christian must be unapologetically anti-communist. . . . Those who do not understand this . . . can contribute little toward the establishment of a more humane world.''

6. The alternative is democracy, which is "limited government" and understands itself to be accountable to values and truth that transcend any regime or party. There is a clear distinction between the state and society. Democratic governance is pluralistic, "contingent, modest in its claims, and open-ended.''

7. There are admittedly tensions and contradictions within democracy, both in theory and in practice, especially regarding relations "between individual and community, formal process and substantive purpose, and between popular participation and power elites.''

8. It is a fact that democracy has existed only where free markets are important; both the market and democracy emphasize the production of wealth rather than redistribution. "Experience in America and the world suggests that when a market economy is open to the participation of all, it works to the benefit of all, and especially the poor.'' Totalitarian regimes have been disastrous for all but the new political elite.

9. A market economy may be a necessary condition but it is obviously not a sufficient condition for democracy: there are capitalist societies with repressive regimes.

10. Formal structures typical of democracy include the rule of law; division of powers within government; freedom to assemble, to speak out, and to publish; and orderly transfer of authority to govern, usually through free and regular elections.

11. Human rights are prior rights; they are not established by the state.

12. Repressive regimes of right and left frequently "pit social and economic rights against the rights of freedom" but "As a matter of empirical fact, those societies which give priority to freedom generally secure social and economic rights more successfully than do those societies which attempt social and economic advance at the cost of freedom.''

13. The most fundamental human right is freedom of religious faith and practice.

14. In their witness the churches should reflect an unwavering adherence to a single standard in the judgment of human rights.

15. In our imperfect world, choices must be made. While no nation embodies these ideals, some aspire to the democratic ideal while others condemn both the ideal and the fact. "The United States of America is the primary bearer of the democratic possibility in the world today. The

Soviet Union is the primary bearer of the totalitarian alternative."
"More profound than the conflict of military and political forces is the
conflict over the dignity and destiny of the human person, and the so-
cietal order appropriate to that dignity and destiny." Although America
is not God's chosen nation, "America has a peculiar place in God's
promises and purposes."

16. As America falls short of the ideal, so some nations aligned with it fall
    short. While Chrisitan citizens have a responsibility to make judgments
    about the wisdom and morality of their country's foreign policy, the
    church, as the body of Christ, "has neither competence nor responsibil-
    ity to design or control the foreign policy of the United States."

17. Not all agree with these positions, especially "some leadership circles in
    the churches, and most especially . . . many who are professionally
    involved in shaping the social witness of the churches." "Arguments
    for oppression are pervasive in our several churches" made out of "bu-
    reaucratic and intellectual habit," reflecting a "selective compassion
    for human suffering and indifference to the meaning of democracy in
    our kind of world." In favor of oppression it is argued that revolution-
    ary changes, especialy through Marxism-Leninism, are inevitable, or
    that we have no right to impose our values on others.

18. "The debate is not between liberals and conservatives, between left and
    right. The debate is between those who do believe and those who do not
    believe that there is a necessary linkage between Christian faith and
    human freedom . . . that in this moment of history democracy is the
    necessary product and protector of freedom . . . and between those who
    do and those who do not believe that freedom, an end in itself, is also
    the surest way to a greater measure of that peace and justice which we
    are to seek."[15]

In my commentary I shall begin with some general observations and proceed to deal with specific issues raised by the IRD, and then make some
references to Central America.

First, if the IRD did not exist, it would have to be invented. The originating impulse is clearly reflected in some words from an IRD brochure: "Religion and Politics—is there a problem in your domination? . . ." "How are
your church dollars spent?" (for "dubious political causes" such as guerrilla movements in Africa, and so forth?). "Can the Churches be rescued?"[16]

Right-wing religio-political organizations and lobbies are not new. What
is distinctive about the IRD is that it is a religious expression of "neo-
conservatism": its leading figures were once liberals (and perhaps still see
themselves as such) who are now convinced that vigorously confronting
the Soviet Union must be a cornerstone of United States policy. A similar
"secular" organization in the United States is the Committee for the Free

World, which in 1981 published a full-page statement in the *New York Times* in support of United States policy in El Salvador, which was signed by some people associated with the IRD. The tone of the IRD remains "liberal," that is, nuanced, "balanced," and it is aimed primarily at influencing the mainstream (liberal) denominations and churches.

It may not be idle to note that in 1971 the Dutch Jesuit Roger Vekemans and Bishop Alfonso López Trujillo set up in Bogotá, Colombia, a center whose purpose seems clearly to have been aimed at countering the influence of liberation theologians by elaborating an alternate position. Part of the early success of the works of theologians such as Gustavo Gutiérrez was the fact that those bishops and others who knew they did not agree with the new theology were at a loss to reply. Concomitant with the "housecleaning" of CELAM pastoral training institutes, López Trujillo and Vekemans, through a magazine, *Tierra Nueva*, and a series of books, were able to articulate something of a theological position (for instance, by insisting there was a variety of liberation theologies, of which Gutiérrez et al. were only one). Although the circumstances are vastly different, the purposes of the IRD would seem to be quite similar: to elaborate a position on United States foreign policy different from that common in many church leaders. This is not to disparage the IRD or its founders. By formulating their position, to which many church members would subscribe, they do the churches a favor.

Profound as my disagreement with the IRD is, it is not total. For example, I agree that the church should reflect diversity and pluralism, and I emphatically agree that there should be a single standard for human rights. However, even these statements are not as simple as they may seem at first glance. The concern over diversity seems to reflect the IRD's impression that church leadership has moved too far left. However, I submit that in many cases people in the church bureaucracies have been directly and professionally exposed to what is happening, as, for example, a National Council of Churches delegation that went to Guatemala in the spring of 1981 and upon return wrote an "Epistle to Believing Communities in the United States."[17] While they may be influenced by ideas picked up in reading— possibly even a book on Marxism—their main influence comes from hearing from the victims of repressive regimes and from sister churches.

Likewise, to affirm that there should be no double standard for human rights does not answer all questions. For example, how does one weigh the restrictions put on freedom of expression in Cuba against large-scale massacre of the civilian population in Guatemala and El Salvador? To what extent should the church denounce human rights violations by communist countries—well known through media coverage and United States government propaganda—and to what extent should it concentrate on those countries where United States influence and responsibility are much greater?

To me the IRD statement is static and unhistorical. There is little sense that democracy has a history and that Western democratic institutions are the products of a particular history. Even less is there a sense of history for existing Marxist regimes. There is no effort to understand what has happened in the Soviet Union and its satellite nations as a story with a past, especially Stalinism, and with a future, possibly even one of change and reform. I find this to be similar to American attitudes toward the Polish struggle, which was cheered as a repudiation of the Soviet system, but little interest is shown in what the Polish people actually want; they did not want to invite the Fortune 500 to take over their economy, nor did they simply want a Western-style parliament. Although their aims were not completely defined, it would seem that the Poles wanted both democracy and socialism—and at different levels, including the workplace. That the majority of the Communist party supported Solidarity would seem to indicate some capacity for reform from within.

Repeatedly the notion of "freedom" is invoked in the IRD document, but it is nowhere defined or clearly described. By default one is left with a concept of freedom as linked to Western culture, since "democracy" (meaning Western institutions) is taken to be its product and protector. Democracy is presented (implicitly at least) as the moral achievement of those peoples who value freedom and avoid the "monistic temptation."

To the extent that connections between economic systems and political forms are noticed, it is to allege a positive correlation between the market economy and democracy. While the authors have undoubtedly heard the third-world critique that a good deal of early Western industrialism was made possible by a plunder of colonies and that the present international "division of labor" makes autonomous development impossible, they clearly feel no need even to take note of such a critique. Capitalism is always described as being characterized by the free market: from the document one could never deduce that there existed transnational corporations with annual operations much larger than most countries, and that repressive third-world regimes backed by the United States tended to be hospitable to them. These are simply "more or less capitalist societies with repressive regimes quite unlike the democratic governance we affirm"—no thought that these regimes might give "freedom" to the corporations at the cost of the freedom of their people.

It is here that I find the core of my disagreement with the IRD position: it shows little real understanding of the experience of the poor majority in the world, nor does it seem to be aware of how the poor have articulated their experience and aspirations. The IRD's assertion that a "market economy open . . . to all" is the key to development is simply unhistorical and irrelevant—at least to Central America. (That "market mechanisms" within an overall planned economy might be very useful is another question.) In brief the IRD is more concerned to make a polemical case for its position than to expose itself to the real struggles of the poor.

Much of the statement revolves around contrasting Marxism, especially as embodied in the Soviet Union, and democracy as expressed in the United States. An adequate reply would require direct experience in those countries and a great deal of space. I simply note here that as much as one must repudiate the killing of millions of people under Stalin, forced labor camps, official suppression of dissidents and minorities, and actions such as the invasion of Afghanistan, and as much as the internal life of the Soviet Union seems not to be an attractive model, nevertheless, few people outside the Soviet Union and the United States would see those two countries as simply embodying totalitarianism and freedom, respectively, in the world. Observers in the third world see them both as superpowers, and acting as superpowers. On balance, if one had to choose, it would seem that the foreign policy of the Soviet Union (for its own, often cynical, purposes) is more apt to support the poor in liberation movements, while the United States (government and corporations) is more apt to be allied with dominant elites and military regimes (Indonesia, the Philippines, South Africa, and Latin America come to mind).

In the next chapter, I shall deal directly with the use of Marxist analysis by Christians. Here I would note only the IRD's homogenizing treatment of all Marxism.

It may not be out of place to observe that the IRD's basic framework of democracy (United States, capitalism) versus totalitarianism (Soviet Union, socialism) is quite at variance with present-day Catholic social teaching. In *Octogesima Adveniens*, for example, Pope Paul VI spoke of "two aspirations, to equality and to participation," which "seek to promote a democratic type of society. Various models are proposed, some are tried out, none of them gives complete satisfaction and the search goes on between ideological and pragmatic tendencies."[18] He ranged over various possibilities, including the use of Marxism by Christians, only warning that there are links between its various kinds of uses. For the pope both Marxism and "liberal ideology" called for "careful discernment." He was rather far from seeing Christians as "unapologetically anti-Communist"—and if he saw the United States as the great standard bearer of freedom he was entirely discreet about this insight. More recently the Puebla Conference saw both liberal capitalism and Marxist collectivism as atheistic and idolatrous (nos. 542–50; 495).

I have devoted considerable space to the IRD statement both because it signals what may become a major issue for debate and because it offers an opportunity for clarifying, although in a largely negative way, the issue of democracy for Central America.

To close this section, I would repeat that my aim here has been modest: to suggest that democracy is not to be identified simply with Western forms, that countries such as those in Central America have to find their own forms, which may begin much more at the local level and with "economic democracy," and that indeed there is much to be learned about democracy in both theory and practice.

THE ETHICS OF MEANS: THE USE OF VIOLENCE

Spontaneously, when considering the ethics of revolution, most people raise the issue of violence. Here I have deliberately chosen to deal first with the end, the revolutionary *proyecto* in both economic and political dimensions, before coming to the means, the use of violence to take power in order to achieve that end.

My purpose here is not to "solve" the question of violence, about which a great deal has been written during the last fifteen or twenty years,[19] but rather, to present systematically how the issue has been dealt with in Central America. In fact, there is very little written on violence in Central America (no major theological essay) and this subject (often the major preoccupation of people outside the region) has not been a main focus of debate within Central America. The reason, I would hold, is that Central Americans did not "choose" violence: rather, after suffering violence for a long time, and seeking to exert pressure for their rights through nonviolent means, they still suffered violence repeatedly; eventually they came to a point where they were collaborating with armed groups (perhaps simply for self-defense) and many eventually engaged in combat. Throughout this process they were not moved by arguments about the use of violence but by a feeling that they had little choice. In other words, for people in the middle of the violence of Central America (from kidnapping, torture, and murder to massed army attacks and aerial bombardment) the question is entirely too obvious to require any theoretical elaboration.

Nevertheless, it may not be so obvious to some readers. In this section, then, I would like to interpret for English-speaking readers the issue of violence, using particularly the statements of Central American hierarchies, but also offering some of my own reflections on what is perhaps only implicitly stated and articulated by Central Americans.

Before taking up particular aspects of the question, I would state two premises, which to my mind must form the background to any serious and sincere discussion of violence in Central America. These statements are amply demonstrated by the material in chapters 4 through 6, above:

1. The aim of the groups in power is essentially unjust, that is, the maintenance of privilege, or of United States hegemony in the region, while the aims of the popular and revolutionary forces is just, the establishment of a new order built around the satisfaction of basic needs and participation by all.
2. The use of violence by those in power is utterly disproportionate. The great majority of those killed are unarmed civilians killed by official forces or officially sponsored death squads.

Nonviolence

Prominent in the opposition to United States intervention in Central America have been pacifists and peace organizations. Yet some people are troubled by, or plainly opposed to, the use of violence by the revolutionary organizations, even as they oppose their own government's support for violence.

It is important to distinguish objections made by people personally involved in nonviolent resistance from another kind of objection, which might bear some superficial resemblance; namely, objections from those who simply invoke the Christian language of turning the other cheek, reconciliation, and so forth, to disqualify revolutionary use of violence. I would assert that people who have not actively opposed the violence of the powerful against the poor, at some cost to themselves, have no moral authority to question the violence used by the poor.

More serious and certainly worthy of consideration are the doubts or objections from those who themselves practice active nonviolence. Their pacifism may be principled or pragmatic, or both. Some argue that "Thou shalt not kill" is an absolute principle, whether derived from a reading of the gospel or simply from deep moral conviction. Others point to a number of reasons why nonviolence is ultimately superior to violence as a means of struggle:

1. Violence hardens the enemy and makes him or her ready to resist to the end; nonviolent resistance may break enemy morale and will to hold power.
2. Violence leads to more violence: revolutions have often brought only new oppression or further upheaval.
3. Contrariwise, a vast nonviolent movement is itself a school of discipline and moral qualities, and so a preparation for a new society.
4. All members of a society, including children and old people, may take part in nonviolent actions and may even be more effective than armed combatants.
5. Nonviolence is the wave of the future: there have been 10,000 years of war and only a few of organized nonviolence. As nonviolence becomes better understood and further experience is accumulated it will increasingly be used to settle conflicts.

Many advocates of nonviolence point to the nearly two hundred types of tactics systematically catalogued by Gene Sharp in *The Politics of Nonviolent Action* as examples of its flexibility and effectiveness.[20]

Does the New Testament require "absolute" pacifism? The question requires more space than I can give it here, but essentially I think the answer is that there is no way to "apply" the New Testament directly across twenty centuries to present-day social contexts. Any such application involves both exegesis and hermeneutics of the texts themselves and some analysis of the conditions to which they will be applied, whether it be done through common sense or scholarship. To say, for example, that the New Testament categorically prohibits any use of violence against others implies earlier judgments about the texts themselves: their origins and purpose (were they meant to communicate categorical judgments, or were they meant to communicate the good news of Jesus and call to a new life?) and about the realities to which such judgments might be applied (What about the case of self-defense?). These considerations are not meant as sophistry; rather, simply to point out that however much an individual might find the Bible leading him or her to a pacifist position, a direct argument from biblical texts is short circuit. In other words some theology, some extra-biblical reasoning, is involved in any application of the scriptural message today.

While very few Latin Americans are "principled" proponents of nonviolence, since the 1960s there have been efforts to study and practice it as a means of social change. Through meetings held in Costa Rica (1971) and Colombia (1974), a continental network called *Paz y Justicia* was set up. Adolfo Pérez Esquivel, who subsequently won the Nobel Peace Prize for his resistance to the Argentine military government, was made its coordinator. It should be pointed out, however, that Latin Americans tend to take positions different from that of those whose starting point is nonviolence. Their primary commitment is to liberation: they hope to be able to develop a genuine and effective Latin American form of nonviolence. Very few Latin Americans—even in the Paz y Justicia network—would take nonviolence as an irreducible starting point.

Chapters 4 through 6 mention numerous instances of de facto nonviolence in Central America: strikes, demonstrations, marches, vigils, published statements. For example, in Guatemala in November 1977 the Indian miners of Ixtahuacán marched over 300 kilometers to the capital rallying public support, and in 1980, less than a month after the Spanish embassy massacre, CUC organized the largest strike in Guatemalan history in the coastal agroexport region and succeeded in getting the agricultural wage raised. During the mid-1970s the popular organizations in El Salvador repeatedly organized large mass demonstrations in the streets of the capital. The basic Christian communities have themselves been a focal point of nonviolent action for change, and in Nicaragua church buildings were used for "catacombs journalism" (getting out the news when the press was censored).[21] It should be recognized, however, that this use of nonviolence was regarded by many as tactical: they were convinced that ultimately the regimes in power would be overthrown only by armed struggle.

The critical question, then, is whether nonviolent means could have been sufficient to overthrow Somoza and the other ruling groups and to initiate a process of basic change. Ultimately such a question is an unanswerable could-have-been, but I would still point to two reasons for doubting the viability of nonviolence in these particular cases.

First, in the classical cases of victorious nonviolent struggle the oppressor side has held itself accountable to some higher tribunal. This is most clear in the case of the struggle for civil rights in the American south, where the movement headed by Dr. Martin Luther King, Jr., could dramatize the lack of constitutional rights and invoke federal intervention with the broad support of public opinion in the rest of the country (despite its own institutionalized racism). Similarly, Gandhi could show world public opinion that the British empire was violating its own principles in violently resisting the Indian independence movement. However, in Central America it is clear that the regimes hold themselves accountable to no higher law.

Second—and here we come to the crux of the matter—the classic examples of nonviolent struggle did not involve revolutionary demands in any strict sense. Indian independence was one more episode in the gradual decline of European empires. The American civil-rights movement, while it made some demands, was not a threat to the existing economic system or political order. Its demands could be absorbed with relative ease.

In Central America, on the other hand, the demands of the poor are not absorbable—at this point they demand a restructuring of the economy, which at the very least will end the existence of a true oligarchy and severely curtail the style of life of the privileged, as well as including a new political order, starting with the dismantling (or thorough restructuring) of the present armies, police, and paramilitary groups. It should come as no surprise, then, that existing power structures are willing to go to such lengths (massive killing tending toward genocide) to defend their privileges and status. From their viewpoint, the reaction is appropriate.

There would seem to be no historical precedent for true revolutions achieved through nonviolence: many of the instances cited by Sharp, for example, took place in an overall context of war; for example, resistance to the Nazi occupation. When governments have been overthrown by nonviolence (Guatemala and El Salvador in 1944), it has not led to true social revolution.

For my part, then, I doubt that in the present circumstances nonviolent means would be sufficient for bringing about the kind of revolution needed in Central America. I would like to believe that increasingly in Latin America nonviolence will prove viable for bringing about basic change, somewhat like the increasingly nonviolent spread to other countries of bourgeois reforms during the nineteenth century.

Official Church Teaching on Violence

There has been a clear tension in Catholic church teaching in Latin America since the mid-1960s: with equal insistence the bishops have mentioned the need for basic structural changes and yet they have clearly opposed the use of violence, which many people were convinced would be necessary for making any significant changes. Since for most of the period there were no revolutionary groups with massive popular support, the question itself remained somewhat theoretical.

During the 1960s a great deal of ink was spilled on one paragraph of Pope Paul VI's encyclical *Populorum Progressio* (On the Development of Peoples):

> We know . . . that a revolutionary uprising—save where there is a manifest, long-standing tyranny which would do great damage to fundamental personal rights and dangerous harm to the common good of the country—produces new injustices, throws more elements out of balance and brings on new disasters. A real evil should not be fought against at the cost of greater misery.[22]

The pope further warned against violent revolution when he visited Colombia in 1968, where two and a half years earlier Camilo Torres had died in combat.

By speaking of "institutionalized violence," the Latin American bishops at Medellín introduced an element that relativized simple condemnations of revolutionary violence. Nevertheless at the Puebla Conference in February 1979 (about four months before the Sandinista final offensive in Nicaragua began), the bishops, after mentioning violence perpetrated by governments, stated:

> The Church is just as decisive in rejecting terrorist and guerrilla violence, which becomes cruel and uncontrollable when it is unleashed. Criminal acts can in no way be justified as the way to liberaton. Violence inexorably engenders new forms of oppression and bondage, which usually prove to be more serious than the ones people are allegedly being liberated from. But most importantly violence is an attack on life, which depends on the Creator alone. And we must also stress that when an ideology appeals to violence, it thereby admits its own weakness and inadequacy.[23]

This paragraph, which is a summary of the arguments against guerrilla groups (made equivalent to terrorism), coupled with the deliberate policy of keeping Nicaragua from being discussed at Puebla, make it all the more interesting that the Nicaraguan bishops soon afterward found themselves repeating the traditional teaching on a just insurrection at the time that the Sandinista final offensive began. What was innovative was not the phrasing (which was in fact traditional) but the timing: they were endorsing the insurrection.

For the most part Central American bishops conferences continued to disavow the use of revolutionary violence and to state explicitly that revolutionary groups would not solve problems. Only four months after the Sandinista victory did the Nicaraguan bishops acknowledge explicitly the special role of the FSLN. Innovation and development in the question of violence came only from Archbishop Romero, especially in his third and fourth pastoral letters. Although formally his authority was limited to his archdiocese, in real terms his magisterium extended to all of El Salvador and even to nearby countries.

The third letter, published in August 1978, was devoted to the popular organizations. Romero found it "natural" that the organizations might have recourse to violence to demand their rights. He began his treatment by taking up Medellín's teaching and distinguishing even further kinds of violence: institutionalized violence, repressive state violence, seditious or terrorist violence ("which some call 'revolutionary' "), spontaneous violence (when people are attacked for demanding their rights), the violence of legitimate self-defense, the violence of nonviolence. After that break-down, he noted that the church gives a different judgment on each type of violence, permitting self-defense under certain conditions, and condemning institutionalized, repressive, and terrorist forms of violence. He repeated the teaching of Paul VI and Medellín, exhorted all to work for justice, and warned the organizations, "not to put all their confidence in violence." In the context of El Salvador, where such organizations were simply branded as terrorist, Romero's letter reflected a striking equanimity; however, his treatment of violence was largely a repetition of existing official texts.

One year later (1979), in his last pastoral letter, "The Church in the Midst of the Country's Crisis," Archbishop Romero returned to the theme of violence. There was no doubt that the conflict was becoming more serious: President Carlos Humberto Romero's administration was increasingly incapable of running the country, it was becoming clear that the popular organizations were indeed linked to the armed groups, and the Sandinista victory in Nicaragua prompted a "We're next" feeling on all sides. The archbishop took as his framework the application of Puebla to the arch-diocese. Stating that he wished to deepen his earlier teaching on violence, he in fact gave it quite another accent, beginning by saying that, since peace is the work of justice, the church "cannot simplistically say it condemns any kind of violence." He then condemned structural violence, arbitrary state violence, and the violence of right-wing terrorists. In El Salvador, he said, repression falls on

> any dissidence against the present form of capitalism and its institutional political forms, inspired by the theory of national security. We also know how the great numbers of peasants, workers, slum dwellers, and so forth, who have organized themselves to defend their rights and promote legitmate structural changes, are simply judged to be "terrorists" and "subversives" and so are arrested, tortured, made to disappear, or are murdered, with no law or judicial institution to protect them or to give them a chance to defend themselves and prove their innocence. Faced

with these uneven and unjust odds, they have often felt forced to defend themselves, even with violence, and again they have encountered the state's arbitrary violence.

He also stated:

The church also condemns the violence of politico-military groups or persons, when they intentionally carry out actions that leave innocent victims or when their actions are disproportionate to the effect they want at short or medium range.[24]

This nuanced statement is very different from the almost total condemnation of the previous year. The logic of the statement would imply a possible recognition of the actions of revolutionary groups except where they intentionally kill innocent people.

Archbishop Romero next repeated the classic teaching on the right to insurrection (adding that the Salvadoran constitution recognized it) and in the same context referred to "legitimate defense," apparently having in mind cases when members of organizations were attacked by the military or the police. While the overall emphasis was on seeking peaceful solutions, the change was remarkable in just one year.[25]

Romero never again had the opportunity to express his thinking on the question of violence in a systematic and formal manner. It should be noted that up to his murder and for some time afterward, government and paramilitary forces did not often clash directly with guerrilla forces but, rather, with the popular organizations: the country was still not clearly at war. In some interviews given during the archbishop's final weeks there were strong hints of further radicalization, or perhaps a recognition that avenues to reform and peaceful change were more definitely blocked and that all-out confrontation was almost certain.

When an interviewer asked about the left, the archbishop said, "I don't call them forces of the left but 'forces of the people' and their anger may be a product of social injustice." And when the same interviewer asked what support the guerrillas might receive from the church, Romero said that Christian moral teaching includes the right to legitimate defense, a right that could be invoked if the defense is proportionate to the attack. During this same period he said:

When a dictatorship seriously attacks human rights and the common good of the nation, when it becomes unbearable and channels for dialogue, understanding, and rationality are closed, when that happens the church speaks of the legitimate right of defense. To define the moment of insurrection, to indicate the moment when all the channels for dialogue are closed, that is not the church's task.

> I'm shouting to this oligarchy to warn them: Open your hands, give up your rings, because the day will come when they'll cut your hands off.

When asked about Salvador Samayoa, who had resigned as minister of education and gone to the FPL (announcing his decison on television), Archbishop Romero said that the decision should be respected, and that while he could not advise anyone to "choose the road of violence," Samayoa's action was a denunciation of the fact that those really responsible for the violence were the families of the oligarchy ("those who chose peaceful ways to the solution of problems are those who idolize wealth").[26]

Since Romero tended to come closer to the popular organizations—a few weeks before his death he said, "I believe more than ever in the mass organizations"[27]—it seems reasonable to assume that he would have defended the people's right to insurrection even during some such event as the January 1981 "general offensive." His successor, Bishop Rivera y Damas, however, judged that not all the conditions for a just insurrection were present: namely, all other means were not yet closed and there was not an assurance that a greater evil would not ensue (this latter reservation seeming to reflect a fear of Marxism).

Hierarchical teaching on violence during this period may be summarized as follows:

1. The bishops have normally quoted existing documents (for example, *Populorum Progressio*) and occasionally reiterated the "just insurrection" theory.
2. What was novel in Nicaragua was the timing: the bishops spoke of a "just insurrection" precisely as the Sandinista-led "final offensive" began.
3. Archbishop Romero (*a*) advanced Medellín's tendency to distinguish different kinds of violence; (*b*) condemned right-wing violence outright, but spoke with nuances of violence from revolutionary and popular organizations; (*c*) increasingly spoke of the right to self-defense and insurrection; and (*d*) most important, showed his support for the popular organizations.

Romero's position is simply an articulation of what many people felt by common sense. It seems to me, in fact, that unless one takes a position of absolute and principled nonviolence, the general legitimacy of the use of violence by opposition groups in Nicaragua, El Salvador, and Guatemala must be conceded.

There are actually two forms of justification for the use of violence in Archbishop Romero's position. The more clearly articulated is the right of insurrection (against a "long-standing tyranny"). His idea of "legitimate defense" is only mentioned and perhaps needs some development.

It would seem obvious that he does not mean "defense" simply as in the case of an individual who legitimately uses proportionate force to repel one or more attackers. The case is more like that of a nation which, when attacked by an aggressor, may legitimately use force. The "nation" being attacked, however, is the poor, or more accurately, that part of the population that is "organized" or is perceived to be so or potentially so. When the Guatamalan Indians became, first, guerrilla sympathizers, then supporters, and finally combatants, they did so because they were under attack as a group from the army. Their defense could not be entirely passive—that is, they could not simply wait until they were attacked in a village and then repel the attack with "proportionate" means. Proportionate means, in this case, must signify keeping the army from annihilating them.

I would say that the moral legitimation of the use of violence by opposition groups is grounded in the right of self-defense as much, or even more, than in the traditional "just-insurrection" theory. By referring to the narratives of chapters 4, 5, and 6, readers may form their own opinion of such a legitimation.

Particular Kinds of Violence

So far I have been speaking of "violence" in generic terms. At this point I would like to make some ethical assessment of specific kinds of violence carried out by the armed opposition groups, that is, those groups opposed to the governments in power and their military forces.

First, however, I would like to make clear the difference between this violence and that practiced by the official forces and their paramilitary adjuncts. There is absolutely no ground for the impression, fostered by the United States government and carried in some superficial media coverage, that both sides are "terrorist" and that the "poor people are trapped in the middle." In Nicaragua, El Salvador, and Guatemala, the official troops as de facto policy have engaged in massive kidnapping, torture, rape, murder, and mutilation of individuals, and indiscriminate large-scale military attacks on whole towns and villages. The vast majority of the victims have been unarmed civilians, noncombatants, although it would be too much to present them as utterly uninvolved and "innocent": many were indeed "guilty" of opposition. But it must be emphasized that these opposition groups have not practiced rape or torture and make every effort to target their violence precisely at the "enemy": the official and paramilitary forces, and those who direct them. Most human rights organizations monitoring El Salvador, for example, have concluded that well over 80 percent of the killing is done by government and government-linked forces. For 1982 Tutela Legal, the official legal aid service of the Archdiocese of San Salvador, documented the cases of 5,399 civilians killed or "disappeared" by official and right-wing organizations as opposed to 46 civilians killed by the left.

Violence used by armed opposition groups may be classified along the following lines: (a) propaganda actions involving violence; (b) damage to property, robbery ("recuperation"); (c) combat, attacks on government forces; (d) killings ("executions"); (e) kidnapping. While the object here is to reflect, in a cursory way at least, on the ethical quality of such acts, I urge caution and humility. Reflecting on such actions from a great distance and never having experienced the violence to which these actions are a response, we may have an insufficient sensitivity to essential aspects. In addition history is written by those who triumph: the Sandinista victory turned the 1974 hostage-taking action of the FSLN from an act of "terrorism" into a heroic exploit.[28]

Propaganda actions are of various sorts. Some examples are painting political graffiti, setting up barricades of burning tires or other materials, laying homemade tacks on the road to give army vehicles flat tires. Another kind of action is the occupation of a village or town in order to speak to the people, or occupation of a radio station in order to broadcast a message. These are called "propaganda actions" because their purpose is to demonstrate strength to the people and to show the weakness of the official forces, and thereby encourage the people themselves to resist. In themselves, these actions do not directly involve violence to people and may be carried out with no violence whatsoever (as when, upon taking over a town, the guerrillas were numerous enough simply to disarm the few police or soldiers who might be on duty; if the police resisted, however, there might be a gun battle). In the extreme situations of Central America, propaganda actions seem to raise no ethical objections in themselves; armed clashes with official forces are treated below.

The next category refers to *property*. The opposition's need for money is obvious enough, and robbing banks or payroll agents on the plantation or charging the wealthy a "war tax" are obvious ways of getting it. Where the right to private property is absolute, such action is seen as gangsterism, more heinous, for example, than the bribes, payoffs, kickbacks, and "protection" that may be endemic among the military and parts of the oligarchy. However, those who see such oligarchical wealth as largely taken from the people in an unjust manner are more inclined to see these actions as a "recuperation" for the people of what was lawfully theirs, not in a Robin-Hood gesture, but in the sense that it is to be used for the liberation of the people. Contrary to the case of professional thieves, the guerrillas make no fortune from these actions and indeed live in utter frugality. Moreover, there is reason to believe that large numbers of the poor would approve of these actions.

The case of property destruction is similar. In Guatemala, for example, the EGP in 1977 set fire to over twenty planes used to spray pesticides on cotton fields. The owners and the oligarchy in general were undoubtedly outraged, but these were among the planes that every year cause thousands of cases of toxic poisoning and an untold number of deaths (since workers have to pick cotton near the spraying planes). The workers (and potential victims) must have seen the action as an eloquent protest that human lives were more important than profits.

Another kind of property destruction is that aimed at disrupting and weakening the economy (destroying bridges, damaging power lines, and so forth) or tying down the official forces, obliging them to spread out to defend potential targets. Such actions presuppose a condition of war and are military tactics. At one level the same limitation of the right to private property mentioned above would be valid. It is sometimes alleged that those who suffer most are "the people" who will be put out of work, and such considerations must influence decisions made (for example, in some cases the guerrillas have waited until crops were harvested—and the workers paid—before burning the harvest). Occasional reports to the contrary notwithstanding, one has the impression that these groups have chosen targets with some care.

In taking up issues of violence per se, that is, *combat* and *killings* (or hurting human beings or threatening to do so), I would lay down some clear principles: (*a*) torture is never justified; (*b*) rape is never justified; and (*c*) the direct killing of civilians or of those not responsible for the death of others is never justified. Since torture and rape are explicitly forbidden by guerrilla discipline, the key issue at question is: Who does, and who does not, constitute a legitimate target? Most obviously, official government troops and other "security forces," including the police who normally are integral to the repression, are legitimate targets.

In Guatemala and El Salvador civilian paramilitary groups have been responsible for repression, either themselves killing "subversives" or designating them to the army or other bodies for killing. Hence, when the guerrillas kill these people, they do not see it as murder but as *ajusticiamiento* ("doing justice") or "execution." In such actions there are several assumptions: (*a*) that the person is guilty of the death of others; (*b*) that the community so judges; and (*c*) that capital punishment is fitting. In addition to the quasi-legal aspect, killing a village informer is an act of collective self-defense, which may indeed save the lives of others. As a safeguard against mob rule, there would have to be extreme discipline in ascertaining facts and, where possible, offering the person a chance to reform.

Lest my matter-of-fact reflection on "terrorism" seem too extreme, I would quote Archbishop Romero again:

> The sin of violence among us is that there is a great disproportion between attack and defense. . . . We are not going to justify the abuse of this armed forces of the people. I found it very disturbing that in Guazapa—a town close by—they publicly shot a man by firing squad; and somewhere else they flogged someone in public. I think these are abuses of defense.[29]

It might have been simpler if Romero had simply denounced the people's taking of the law into their own hands. However, he limited himself to criticizing the abuse, thus admitting in principle the possibility of legitimate defense by a "people's army."

A last case—and by far the most difficult—is that of political *kidnapping* and hostage-taking, examples of which occurred in all three countries under consideration. While the desired outcome is that the demands be met (release of political prisoners, publication of statements, ransom money), it seems essential that the kidnappers or hostage-takers be willing to use violence. If the person taken is "guilty" of the death of other people, the action seems to be morally similar to the "executions" spoken of above. Thus, for example, in March 1978 Nora Astorga and other FSLN members attempted to kidnap Reynaldo Pérez Vega, a well-known torturer in the National Guard. Had the operation gone as planned, using him for political purposes would seem acceptable (in fact, he resisted and was killed in the attempt). Similarly, when the EGP made its demands after kidnapping Roberto Herrera Ibargüen (one of Guatemala's wealthiest people), it published information about his involvement in the killing of numerous people. In their minds Herrera was not "innocent" and killing him would have been a kind of extra-judicial "execution." (In the event the conditions were met and he was released.)

Most prominent victims, however, have not been "guilty" in such a sense, that is, personally responsible for the death of other people (for example, in El Salvador: Roberto Poma, head of the tourist agency; Mauricio Borgonovo, foreign minister; and foreign businessmen and diplomats). Some might want to see such people as "guilty," since they are accomplices or beneficiaries of a system of injustice, but such a notion stretches the meaning of guilt and responsibility too much. I find no grounds for justifying the kidnapping of people who themselves are not guilty of personally shedding the blood of others.

However, I insist that precisely on ethical grounds some proportionality should be kept. In conventional terms today it is "terrorism" to hijack an airplane, and indeed such an act threatens the lives of numerous innocent people. But the same newspapers that give coverage to such an act show little preoccupation for the massacres (not simply threats) of Indians in Guatemala. In El Salvador massacres have generally remained "alleged" and have been considered the "abuses" of troops not fully under control.

Thus far in this chapter I have sought to make some needed distinctions on the subject of violence approached from an ethical viewpoint. Now I turn to the Central American experience of "human rights," which, rather than being a new topic in this chapter, is a reprise from a somewhat different angle.

Human Rights: The Rights of the Poor and the Right to Life

Upon examination the whole question of human rights turns out to be more vexing and less self-evident than it might seem at first glance. Definitions of human rights and attempts at human rights policies often turn out to be refractory. To anticipate with one example: United States Ambassador Robert White arrived in El Salvador in early 1980, having gained a reputation as a human rights activist in Paraguay. However, he had no success in convincing the Salvadoran military that it should reduce its human rights abuses. There was a basic difference between the two cases: in Paraguay there was no movement posing a serious threat to the Stroessner dictatorship; White could therefore use the leverage of United States support to press for curbs on abuses. In El Salvador, however, there was a real alternative from the left, which the United States found to be unacceptable, and so the United States stood by the Salvadoran military; moreover, the systematic killing of civilians (many of whom did support the opposition), far from being an "abuse" or the product of insufficient discipline, was the government's basic approach to defeating the left.

What makes human rights a topic of discussion is mainly their violation. Just as a good part of the impetus behind the 1948 United Nations Universal Declaration of Human Rights came from revulsion over the atrocities committed under Hitler and Stalin, so the fervor in the 1970s over human rights in Latin America came from revelations of the use of torture and death squads in Brazil, Chile, Uruguay, Argentina, and several other countries— and United States connections with those responsible through its police and military training. In the general disillusionment over the war in Indochina, human rights seemed to offer a focus around which the United States could again assume a moral posture in the world. The movement was already well underway (it was enshrined in legislation conditioning United States aid to human rights observance) when Jimmy Carter made it a major theme of his election campaign and the early part of his term in office.

The mid-1970s, particularly after the Chilean coup, were years in which the church in Latin America became involved in the defense of human rights, as documented extensively by Penny Lernoux in *Cry of the People*.[30] (Specific examples of such human rights work in Central America appear here in chapters 4 through 6.) While much of the church's work was a response to very urgent and immediate situations (political prisoners, kidnappings, death squads), the general topic of human rights, and the policies adopted in its name, provoked critiques from Latin America.[31]

For many Latin Americans it seemed clear that the human rights vogue of the mid-1970s was largely the ideological component of a new, more sophisticated kind of domination, after the more direct and crude forms exercised during the Nixon years, and was best exemplified in the voluminous studies produced by the Trilateral Commission.

Such a policy was seen as hypocrisy and, in a way, "blaming the victim." For example, Juan Luis Segundo pointed to the contradiction of blaming the government of his country, Uruguay, for the extreme measures it took, when, ultimately, it was simply controlling the forces of opposition to policies that were themselves a direct consequence of Uruguay's assigned role in the international economic system.[32] Frequently, representatives of the United States made it seem as though human rights abuses derived from something in the "Latin character" rather than from policies that had their own, admittedly barbarous, rationality. For example, in mid-1982 Elliott

Abrams, assistant secretary of state for human rights and humanitarian affairs, was saying that the object of the United States was "to change the political culture of El Salvador," which traditionally relied on violence to solve differences.[33] That during much of its own history the United States had also "relied on violence," that never in previous history had the rate of killing in El Salvador been even a fraction of the several hundred people a month killed by official forces, and that the Salvadoran government was by this point utterly dependent on United States aid seemed beyond Mr. Abrams's purview.

A further kind of criticism found that the notion of human rights was either not clear or was distorted. Putting political rights on an equal plane with, or even prior to, economic rights was seen to reflect a "bourgeois" bias; at most the idea would be that dictatorships (or authoritarian regimes) of the left and the right all violate human rights, with no serious attempt to differentiate human rights and establish priorities among them.

Such a confusion had its effects in the kinds of policies attempted. If the problem was defined as the abuses of an authoritarian regime, typically military, the remedy might logically be seen as a "restoration" of "democratic" (that is, civilian) rule. While such a conception might seem reasonable to United States public opinion—and particularly to elected officials—it concealed a number of unexamined assumptions. First was the assumption that the roots of the abuses were to be found in the ambitions of individuals or a group, rather than in the exploitive economic structures of society, among whose beneficiaries were not only the local oligarchies but foreign corporations who found a congenial "labor climate." Second was an assumption that the Western forms of democracy (competing parties, elections, assemblies) of themselves were some kind of goal toward which all polities should strive, irrespective of history and present conditions, and that they were somehow synonymous with progress.

In practice, to a great extent United States policy became one of nudging military regimes toward civilian rule and supporting honest vote-counts. Civilian regimes returned in Ecuador and Peru, partly at least from United States encouragement, and the semi-dictator Joaquín Balaguer allowed the opposition candidate to win in the Dominican Republic, with public pressure from the Carter administration. Washington's pressure on Bolivia only threw a spotlight on successive clumsy coups and countercoups by cliques of cocaine traffickers until civilian rule was restored in 1982.

Critics picked up the notion of "restricted democracy" to denote the limitations of such an approach to human rights. When brutal military regimes are replaced by civilian governments, some of the worst "abuses" (kidnappings, torture, death squads) may be brought partially into check, but for peasants working on the haciendas it often makes little difference whether the president wears a uniform or a business suit and whether he came in by a coup or by an election. The most immediate beneficiaries are those elements of the middle classes who take part in the political "game": politicians, party cadres, newspaper editors.

From early in the human rights campaign there were people in the church who pointed out that it could be a "trap" in the sense that an uncritical support for human rights could simply lead to such a "restoration of democracy." They accordingly insisted that there should be a priority in defending the rights of those who were most abused, the poor and the oppressed. They thus preferred to speak of the "rights of the poor," or the "rights of the majorities," as opposed to "human rights." This perspective had already been present when Medellín spoke of "defending the rights of the poor and the oppressed, following the gospel mandate" and to some degree was present in many of the bishops' statements.[34] Furthermore, there was a sense that the subject of these rights was not simply each separate individual but the "people" taken collectively. Such questions have had the effect of provoking a more serious effort at understanding human rights.[35]

There is, to begin with, the now classic (and perhaps stalemated) debate over the relationship between economic and political rights. A brief *status quaestionis* might be as follows. Political rights (called "bourgeois" by Marxists) emerged from the British tradition and from the American and French revolutions, and were associated with the rise of capitalism as the dominant mode of production. These rights are those of the individual and are aimed at protecting the individual's autonomy and freedom to pursue his or her chosen goals in life. Arising in opposition to the pretensions of absolute authorities, these rights are meant to limit the state's rights over individuals and are largely negative. To socialists, the bourgeois revolution, like capitalism itself, is but a step toward fuller emancipation. Although it may seem "self-evident, that all men are created equal," in a class society freedom is largely an illusion. Human emancipation must take another starting point, that of production, the right to work, and recognition of basic human needs. Adherents of the liberal tradition (used here in the classical sense, rather than as understood in American politics) would reply that the greatest refutation of any socialist criticism is the actual performance of Marxist regimes both in their callousness toward human life and in their economic failures. Furthermore, they often argue that any rights should be clearly definable in their content and in who is bound to observe them; otherwise they are unenforceable and would more properly be called "ideals" than "rights": for instance, who is to be held accountable to an individual's "right" to employment (or to food, shelter, or even education and health care)? This debate, while it may serve to indicate some of the complexities and tensions inherent in the quest for human rights, is a reflection of differing views on human nature.

To my mind it is useful to recognize that "declarations" of human rights, as "universal" as they might sound, are always the product of particular historical movements. Even the 1948 United Nations Declaration, according to Adamantia Pollis and Peter Schwab, "is predicated on the assumption that Western values are paramount and ought to be extended to the non-Western world." Their study, which is an introduction to a collection of essays on various views of human rights (Western, socialist, Islamic,

African, and Latin American) points out that in many societies the group is seen as antecedent to the individual. Thus assumptions in the 1948 Declaration, such as the right of the individual to hold property or the nuclear family as the basis of society, are culturally conditioned. To them human rights is a "Western concept of limited applicability." In surveying many societies they summarize:

> It is evident that in most states in the world, human rights as defined by the West are rejected or, more accurately, are meaningless. Most states do not have a cultural heritage of individualism, and the doctrines of inalienable human rights have been neither disseminated nor assimilated. More significantly the state—as a substitute for the traditional communal group—has become the embodiment of the people, and the individual has no rights or freedoms that are natural and outside the purview of the state.

They further state that efforts to impose the 1948 Declaration as it stands "not only reflect a moral chauvinism and ethnocentric bias but are also bound to fail" and insist that the "conceptualization of human rights is in need of rethinking." They do not wish to neutralize the notion of human rights totally and in fact find some "commonalities" in all societies, such as limitations on the use of force or violence by their members; their concern is, rather, to move away from simplistic reductionism, such as that in the debate over economic vs. political rights, and to see human rights in a broader historical context.[36] (If I seem to have overstressed this point, I need only point to the Institute for Religion and Democracy as an example of the ethnocentric vision of human rights expressed as though it were self-evident; cf. earlier in this chapter.)

Previously, when considering the ethical legitimacy of the overall revolutionary *proyecto*, I found a certain amount of resonance in a papal encyclical. Likewise on the question of human rights I find it instructive to review Pope John XXIII's views as found in part 1 of *Pacem in Terris* (Peace on Earth):

> . . . every man has the right to life, to bodily integrity, and to the means which are necessary and suitable for the proper development of life. These means are primarily food, clothing, shelter, rest, medical care, and finally the necessary social services. Therefore, a human being also has the right to security in cases of sickness, inability to work, widowhood, old age, unemployment, or in any other case in which he is deprived of the means of subsistence through no fault of his own.
> . . . every human being has the right to respect for his person, . . . to freedom in searching for truth and—within the limits laid down by the moral order and the common good—in expressing and communicating his opinions. . . .

[People have] the right to share in the benefits of culture, and therefore the right to a basic education . . . in keeping with the stage of educational development reached by [their] country. . . .

Every human being has the right to honor God . . . , and the right to
profess . . . religion privately and publicly. . . .

Human beings have . . . the right to choose freely the state of life
which they prefer. They therefore have the right to set up a family, with
equal rights and duties for man and woman. . . .

[In] the economic sphere, it is clear that human beings have the natural
right to free initiative . . . and the right to work. . . .

Women have the right to working conditions in accordance with their
requirements and their duties as wives and mothers.

From the dignity of the human person there also arises the right to
carry on economic activities according to the degree of responsibility of
which one is capable. Furthermore . . . there is the worker's right to a
wage . . . sufficient, in proportion to the available resources, to give the
worker and his family a standard of living in keeping with human dignity. . . .

The right to private property, even of productive goods, also derives
from the nature of [human beings]. . . .

However, it is opportune to point out that there is a social duty inherent in the right of private property.

From the fact that human beings are by nature social, there arises the
right of assembly and association. They also have the right to give the
societies of which they are members the form they consider most suitable
for the aim they have in view, and to act within such societies on their
own initiative and responsibility in order to achieve their desired objectives.

Every human being must also have the right to freedom of movement
and of residence within the confines of [his or her] own country, and . . .
the right to emigrate. . . .

The dignity of the human person involves . . . the right to take an
active part in public affairs and to contribute one's part to the common
good of the citizens. . . .

The human person is also entitled to a juridical protection of [his or
her] rights, a protection that should be efficacious, impartial and in conformity with true norms of justice.[37]

This document is the most direct and programmatic declaration of human
rights in official Catholic teaching. Subsequent documents, such as
Gaudium et Spes (The Church in the Modern World), tend to restate a concept of human dignity that underlies human rights.

The structure of John XXIII's catalogue of rights is more subtle than the
structure of the United Nations Universal Declaration, which emphasizes
largely the rights of the individual vis-à-vis the pretensions of the state and

simply puts economic rights in articles 22 to 25. *Pacem in Terris* exhibits a spiral form, starting with the right to life—and the means to sustain it—and proceeding through various rights of the person toward rights associated with economic and political life. If one were to ask which rights are prior, the answer would have to be "economic rights"; however, the whole point of the pope's structure seems to be to overcome the antinomy implied in the division of such rights.

I do not mean to imply that this vision is without its problems. First is the question of whether there is really a "Catholic tradition" at all. By contrast with Marxist and capitalist visions, which are embodied in particular countries, the whole Catholic tradition from Leo XIII onward seems to be kibitzing from the sidelines, that is, popes and bishops have proposed grand-sounding ideals in generic terms but they have not had the responsibility for running a state. Catholic social teaching proposes no clear economic model. Historically Catholicism resisted capitalism, but this was a reflection of the church's attachment to various "old regimes" (indeed, to the Middle Ages) and its slowness to accept modern values, including democracy, rather than to any clear-sighted, principled critique. Catholic social teaching often seemed to reflect nostalgia for some ancient "organic" type of society and hence could be interpreted as supporting corporative models (such as Italian fascism or Franco's Spain). Where Christian Democratic parties professed to be following the lead of the encyclicals, the result was an attempt at a "third way" between capitalism and socialism—which in no way changed the fundamentally capitalist nature of any society. Thus Catholic social teaching seems to be untested and untestable.

Despite the questions that might be raised, the Catholic tradition offers important resources for understanding and acting on human rights. In refusing to accept one side or the other of the economic/political-rights debate and in stressing the interconnectedness of rights, this teaching is reflecting a conception of humankind that sees both the dignity of each person and the community/nation/human race as all of a piece. Ultimately this vision has religious roots in the doctrines of creation, redemption, and the body of Christ.

In this connection Max Stackhouse, writing from a Protestant perspective, in the anthology *Human Rights in the Americas*, strongly urges that neither liberal individualism nor Marxist collectivism offers an adequate basis for human rights: "Neither provides us with a satisfactory sense of the inviolability of *persons in relationship and community*. . . ." He finds such a basis in the biblical motifs of "covenant," which he sees as the real basis for a tradition of human rights rather than from "conservative Catholicism, liberalism, the French Revolution, or Marxism." Commenting on Stackhouse, Monika Hellwig agrees that the covenant may supply such a basis, but she says that such a focus is not necessarily incompatible with a natural-law approach (thus presumably more open to dialogue with other traditions), and she points to a broader image of covenant in the Bible itself.[38]

In the same collection of essays, Philip Rossi seeks to compare the liberal, Marxist, and Catholic traditions in their views of commonality (What makes you like me?) and community (How are we to live together?), and consistently sees the Marxist and Catholic traditions as having a stronger basis for human living together, a clearer recognition of the role of society, and a sense of freedom that is broader than liberalism's freedom of choice for autonomous individuals.[39]

To repeat a point made earlier, the very fact that many Catholics are unaware of this "Catholic" tradition, at least unaware that its vision of humanity is quite different from the one they imbibe from their culture, makes one wonder to what extent this "tradition" is an intellectual construct, or simply a potential vision whose ultimate worth could be known if it made a difference in actual societies, that is, if it could provide the inspiration for both a new vision of human rights and energies for their enhancement.

Having reviewed some recent discussion, especially among Catholics, at this point I wish to essay a statement of human rights of Central Americans. In doing so I am simply attempting to articulate the rights for which people there have struggled. Because it is the violation of human rights that makes them a topic for discussion, the stress here is on precisely those rights that have been most violated. In spirit this exercise is simply a restatement, with a particular accent and some added sharpness of the rights as enumerated in *Pacem in Terris*. I shall state some assumptions, make a brief catalogue of human rights, and then add some comments about the situations of struggle and initial reconstruction.

Assumptions

1. All human beings are the subjects of human rights. Particular attention, however, should be paid to the rights of the oppressed, namely, those whose rights have been violated.
2. Groups, communities, peoples, nations, as well as individuals, may be subjects of human rights.
3. Economic wealth is produced by human beings in concert and not simply as isolated units; the resources of the earth belong to all, prior to any rights acquired by individuals.
4. Economic, political, and social systems are the product of human creation and can be changed by human decision and action. They are not infinitely plastic, nor do human beings enjoy a Promethean power over nature or over social institutions; nevertheless, in principle human beings are responsible for the shape of their institutions.

A Catalogue

1. The most fundamental human right is the right to life and to the means necessary to sustain life. On a most basic level this includes the

right to physical integrity, the right not to be killed, abducted, raped, tortured, or threatened with such treatment.

2. Intimately flowing out of the right to life is the right to work and the right to a just share of the wealth produced by the labor of all and to the products of natural resources, which are the patrimony of all.

3. The peoples of Central America have a right to shape their economies and political systems in accordance with their own needs rather than in accordance with external forces (geopolitical or economic).

4. The right of the majorities to satisfy their basic needs is prior to the desire or aspiration of minorities to nonbasic needs.

5. People have a right to affirm their own culture and a right to those means giving access to cultural goods (for example, literacy and basic education).

6. Those groups discriminated against and oppressed (women, Indians, and others) have a right to equality in treatment and opportunity.

7. People have a right to meaningful political participation at all levels: They have a right to express themselves, a right to be organized, a right to have an influence in shaping policy, economic and political, domestic and foreign, and a right to mechanisms that will assure those rights.

Comments

The foregoing list is not meant to be an exhaustive catalogue but an attempt at synthesis; it is not meant to be utterly persuasive to all in its formulation, but to express succinctly in human rights terms the aspirations of Central Americans, and in a way that is in continuity and consonance with the "Catholic tradition."

It is clear that all the rights enumerated have been systematically violated by the dominant groups (oligarchy and military) and indeed by the dominant superpower, the United States, which has historically and at present supported such regimes (Somoza) and undermined those that presumed to make unauthorized changes (Arbenz). From the right to physical integrity to the right to "meaningful political participation" it can be said that people's rights have been violated.

An examination of this list may make it clear how the struggle in Central America is for human rights, even if the terminology is only occasionally used by opposition groups.

Apparently more problematic is the situation after a revolutionary movement, such as the FSLN in Nicaragua, has taken power. In its stated intentions the FSLN is quite in line with the rights outlined here. Moreover, human rights organizations and agencies that have examined conditions in Nicaragua (the Human Rights Commission of the Organization of American States, Amnesty International, Americas Watch, and the International Commission of Jurists)[40] have all credited the Sandinista government with an observance of human rights far better than that of the Somoza government and of other Latin American governments: they cite the absence of torture, the abolishment of the death penalty, and a functioning legal system with guarantees for citizens. Concern was expressed over the situation of political prisoners (both those from the time of Somoza and those accused of counter-revolutionary activities), the freedom of the press (specifically *La Prensa*) and of expression, particularly of political parties, and of the treatment of the Miskito Indians.

It must be admitted that it is difficult to come to a completely satisfactory answer on the question of human rights in Nicaragua—and in principle, to their observance in any regime attempting to make revolutionary changes. The question I raise here is one of the priority of rights. Those organizations evaluating human rights seem essentially to have been using the existing codifications, such as the United Nations Declaration, as checklists. Thus an essentially "liberal" bias seems to have been built into their method, since no hierarchical method was used, such as I attempted above, however inadequately.

The question of the priority of rights, nevertheless, must at least be taken into consideration. First, it is obvious that after the Sandinista victory Nicaragua was still a society of the privileged and the oppressed. To the extent that Sandinista policies set out to change structures, some people's privileges would be affected and those people would naturally resist. Among the means at their disposal were political parties and means for forming public opinion, particularly *La Prensa*. Moreover, before long there was not only an "opposition" but also an organized counter-revolutionary effort, supported and financed by the United States, which for its part had pointedly not ruled out the use of force against Nicaragua. It seemed entirely reasonable for the Sandinista government to take serious measures to safeguard the revolution.

The basic issue might be stated in this way: the Nicaraguan people have a right to their revolution, which is the means whereby the poor will achieve their rights to life and the basic means of life, to culture, to political participation, and so forth. Their rights are prior rights, both over the luxury consumption and further accumulation of wealth of the privileged and over the elites' right to "pluralism" or to certain political forms.

As stated, the point is clear. The difficulty arises to the extent one admits the possibility that the group in power (in this case the FSLN) might identify its own hegemony over the revolution with the revolution itself—that is, assume that any threat to itself was a threat to the revolutionary *proyecto*. There is further difficulty in that there seemed to be no independent entity to judge the issue; the FSLN itself made judgments and determined policies. Like any group in power, it could fall prey to the temptation of absolutism.

If such is the temptation of a revolutionary "vanguard," it seems clear that the revolution will best be served if there are critical independent forces. Certainly the "representatives" of "bourgeois" groups are ready to perform such a service, but behind their protests in the name of the people are clear class interests. If they could operate with autonomy, the mass organizations might fulfill such a role, but they must have some way of avoiding being simple "transmission belts" for the "vanguard" organization.

In short, the principle of "limited government" and the rights of citizens over against the government remain valid even within a revolution-in-process. What is less clear is how to embody this principle and these rights in institutional forms.

10

Becoming the Church of the Poor: Issues in Church Practice and Ecclesiology

> [The] radical truths of the faith
> become really truths
> and radical truths
> when the church involves itself
> in the life and death of its people.
> So the church,
> like every person,
> is faced with the most basic option for its faith,
> being for life or death.
> —Archbishop Romero

Unique in Central America is the fact that Christians and pastoral agents have played important roles in revolutionary struggles to take power and, at least in Nicaragua, to begin to build a new kind of society. This experience has presented new issues in pastoral practice, and as a consequence in ecclesiology. This chapter attempts a systematization of at least some of these issues.

The underlying question may be seen as: What does it mean to be the church of the poor in a situation of revolution? In an effort to indicate how this is articulated in Central America, I shall first seek to characterize the overall *pastoral* thrust (option for the historical *proyecto* of the poor) and its *theological* meaning (witness to life). Then I shall consider a cluster of issues around the general theme of "church and politics" (popular and revolutionary organizations, the "use" of the church and religious symbols, Marxism as a method, the challenge of living in a revolutionary regime). Finally I shall take up issues relating to church unity, hierarchical ministry, and the "popular church."

FROM "OPTION FOR THE POOR" TO COMMITMENT TO THE CAUSE OF THE POOR

Deepening Medellín's document on poverty, the Latin American bishops at Puebla affirmed "the need for conversion on the part of the whole church to a preferential option for the poor, an option aimed at their integral liberation" (Final Document, no. 1134). The document contained commitments to "denounce the mechanisms that generate . . . poverty" (no. 1160; cf. no. 1159) and to "uproot poverty and create a more just and fraternal world" (no. 1161; cf. no. 1154). The bishops also defended the peasants' right to organize (nos. 1162–63; cf. no. 1137).

Built into this language is a tension: it is not a church *of* the poor that is speaking but, rather, a church that feels itself to be outside the poor and hence must *opt for* them. The day the church—including its leadership—has its center of gravity in the poor there will be no need for an option for the poor. Strictly speaking, it is the hierarchy, the pastoral agents, and the privileged elites that wish to be Christian who need to "opt for" the poor.

This option for the poor is best understood as a process that takes place in individuals, groups, and the church as a whole. Contrary to stereotypes of guerrilla priests giving a Marxist interpretation of the Bible, the normal case is one of step-by-step radicalization (already sketched in general terms for Latin America in chapter 2, pp. 30–33). I would like here to describe this process once more, making reference to the histories of chapters 4–8 and seeking the overall direction of the movement.

The first step was simply "going to the poor," as many priests and sisters did in the late 1960s and early 1970s: for example, in El Salvador at the request of Archbishops Chávez and Romero, many sisters left their more usual work and went to do pastoral work in rural parishes.

Replacing "sacramentalization" as a pastoral focus was "evangelization," understood not as the traditional imparting of doctrine but a two-way dialogue in which the poor expressed their own experience. Themes emphasized in the "message" were those enhancing human dignity ("image of God"), God's concern to liberate his people (Exodus), the message of Jesus as a challenge to the existing (dis)order, equality as an exigency of Christian love, the kingdom as a final utopia to be striven for in (partial) realizations in the here-and-now.

Working for the kingdom was initially often translated into development projects (clinics, cooperatives, literacy training, agricultural improvement), which in themselves demanded some level of organization. Such evangelizing dialogues would also lead to a critique of the structural reasons for poverty (especially, land tenure) and to efforts on the part of the people to demand their rights.

Such efforts were always nonviolent at the outset but were frequently met with violence. In some cases the violence (or even the implied threat to use it) was enough to keep the people from organizing to exert pressure; in other cases the people became convinced of the need for organization and struggle. There were often sporadic confrontations with regimes, even at the national level (the occupations of the Catholic University and the cathedral in Managua in 1969–71, for example).

The use of violence by regimes made it increasingly clear that justice was not going to come about simply through specific struggles, such as that to raise wages, but that a whole reordering of society was called for—referred to as a new "historical *proyecto*."

To some extent this process has occurred throughout Latin America: there is a general conviction that basic changes have to be made, an awareness reflected even in official church documents. The critical point in Central America came when organizations embodying this historical *proyecto* appeared: the Frente Sandinista, and the various revolutionary groups in El Salvador and Guatemala.

Not all pastoral agents follow this dynamic all the way. Both American priests killed by the army in Guatemala—Bill Woods (Maryknoll) and Stanley Rother (Oklahoma City)—saw their role simply as helping the people in their development and did not support leftist organizations. Rutilio Grande in El Salvador, while he spoke clearly of the need for basic change, sought to maintain a clear distinction between the church and the popular organizations, which at that time (1977) were the bearers of the people's aspirations. The most common position of the priests and the sisters killed in Guatemala and El Salvador was that of sympathizing with the organizations and defending the people's right to belong to them, but not of being members or active collaborators themselves.

A small but important number have indeed become active collaborators or members of popular and even revolutionary organizations. Having made that step they then had to undergo a difficult apprenticeship learning how to practice and live by group discipline, how to take security measures for themselves and others, how to deal with what can be rough-and-tumble politics between groups and organizations. This radicalization process can be traced in groups as well as individuals and, as the polarization increased, the process here traced out might often be quite accelerated. Thus it can be seen that the overall pastoral tendency is not simply toward an option for the poor but toward a commitment to the historical *proyecto* of the poor, embodied in movements capable of bringing it to reality.

Can the poor "opt for the poor"? In the sense that they become actively committed to struggling for a basic change, and are willing to sacrifice themselves for it, the poor certainly opt for themselves as a class. To the extent they do this as Christians, the church is not only opting for the poor, but becoming a church *of* the poor.

THE CORE OF THE CHURCH'S SERVICE: WITNESS TO LIFE

In their pastoral practice church people and the church institution have engaged in a variety of activities in response to the particular circumstances of Central America:

1. Denouncing sin and announcing hope. In its official teaching, in small communities and large churches, in writing and in prayer, the church has at least denounced the worst repression and supported people's aspirations.
2. Formation of basic Christian communities. In villages and neighborhoods, people understand their life in the light of God's Word, and form among themselves bonds of support and experience a unity that is the germ of a future united community. Politically these communities form a network of trained and motivated people with experience in working together and a sense of how their community functions.
3. Leadership formation. In a phrase that does not translate well into English, Puebla called the basic Christian communities *escuelas de forjadores de la historia*, "schools for those who will forge history." A Sandinista leader said the basic Christian communities had served as "quarries" for the FSLN as it looked for cadres.[1] People who began as Delegates of the Word frequently became militants in popular or revolutionary organizations.
4. Pastoral contact with revolutionary organizations. In addition to contacts at the local community level, there were contacts of priests and sisters with leaders of revolutionary organizations; some pastoral agents have collaborated directly with these organizations.
5. Documentation and interpretation. Church groups have documented repression in a systematic way and have provided interpretation in writing (*ECA* magazine in El Salvador, for example), in briefing journalists and visiting delegations, and in speaking and preaching. Such interpretation may critically question conventional ways of framing issues; for example, Archbishop Romero spoke of the three *proyectos* facing El Salvador: the "oligarchical," the "military/ Christian Democratic," and the popular, indicating his rejection of the first, his criticism of the second, and his sympathy for the third.
6. Humanitarian aid. Churches provided food and medicine during the anti-Somoza struggle, and although it is under much greater harassment, the church in El Salvador has sought to take care of refugees. Repression has made humanitarian aid a clandestine activity in Guatemala.

What is the unifying point of all these activities? What is the core of the church's service in the midst of revolution? Jon Sobrino, in a remarkably penetrating essay, says: "Witness on behalf of life . . . constitutes the deep-est root of the church's activity in Latin America." For Sobrino, Christians are to bear witness "to the divine mediation that Jesus himself proclaims or expresses" (the "Kingdom," "resurrection," "life"). However, "the con-tent of that mediation is not some compartmentalized section of human life or some strictly 'religious' sphere; it is what we can call life in its totality." In Latin America "life is being threatened and annihilated by structural injustice and institutionalized violence." Sobrino continues:

> Witness in favor of the primacy of life thus becomes witness in favor of justice, and this entails involvement in the struggle against injustice. Witness to God the creator necessarily becomes witness to God the liber-ator.
>
> The relationship between experience of God and witness to a life of justice is all the more clear in Latin America because structural injustice is given implicit or explicit theological sanction. The reigning structures —capitalism and national security in their many forms—operate as true deities with divine characteristics and their own cult. They are deities because they claim characteristics that belong to God also: ultimateness, definitiveness, and untouchability. They have their own cult because they demand the daily sacrificing of the majority and the violent sacrificing of those who oppose them.
>
> . . . Since the reality of our continent makes it abundantly clear that there is no middle ground between life and death, grace and sin, justice and injustice, it is clear that in this matter the objective witness of the church cannot be any sort of third-way compromise.[2]

Sobrino is attempting to get at the theological core of the church's activity. It means that various activities, such as those mentioned above, far from being simply an ethical stand or unwarranted or questionable straying into politics are an exigency for the church at the deepest level of faith, because what is at stake is something ultimate.

In asking how this service is given, Sobrino asserts as a "basic thesis" that "the service of the church on behalf of the fullness of life consists in the ongoing humanization of the human realm at every level and in every situa-tion." The Christian faith has its own specific way of humanizing ("Chris-tianization"), which takes place on three levels: (1) historical (the human being as material/spiritual, personal/social, and in history); (2) transcen-dental (fulfillment in something greater); (3) symbolic or liturgical (express-ing the inner depths of the historic in terms of the transcendent). Sobrino emphasizes that the church must "explicitly cultivate each of the three levels."

Stated in an abstract manner, this formulation at first glance may not seem remarkable. It may help therefore to compare this position with com-mon positions in European and North American ecclesiology. Sobrino's emphasis on the "historical level" implies that the church is an actor even in conflictive situations. About these he says:

> [The] church's role is not just to pass judgment on the conflict and decide which side is right; its role is also to humanize the conflict from within so that life-fostering values are generated and more life results from the resolution of the conflict. Witness on behalf of the fullness of historical life must take on history as it is; such witness cannot be realized from outside history.[3]

As recently as the 1950s one of the starting points of Catholic ecclesiology was the dictum "Outside the church, no salvation." Salvation, in practice conceived as "dying in the state of grace," was considered the church's mission. The church was the "normal means" of salvation, although God's grace could find ways of saving (from damnation) non-Catholics of good will. With the theology of Vatican II, this theology of salvation was turned inside out: God's grace was everywhere and the Catholic church became an "extraordinary" means of salvation in the sense that most people were saved (presumably) without being members, even as "anonymous Christians." What, then, did being a Catholic (or a Christian) add? The answer frequently came as a "knowledge of the depth of meaning" of human life and destiny and their grateful celebration in liturgy.

Such a broad-stroke treatment could seem a caricature but it should be sufficient to indicate that much operative ecclesiology would focus on what Sobrino calls the transcendent and symbolic levels, ignoring his historic level. He speaks of the temptation to remain on those levels, especially in certain circumstances, as when one says that the church cannot give its witness in a conflict-ridden or a socialist society.

There is another kind of contrast also. North Atlantic theology tends to invoke the "eschatological reserve," namely, the conviction that no human order can be identified with the kingdom and that the Christian will always point beyond any given sociopolitical and economic order. As radical as this might seem in principle—Christians as permanent prophets—in fact it might tend to limit commitment to the here and now. While not disputing the validity of what is intended by the eschatological reserve, people in Latin America would stress that the "cause of the poor" has a quality of absoluteness that requires commitment now to the *proyecto* that best embodies it. In other words, the commitment to what Sobrino calls the historical level has a certain primacy.

The contrast in emphasis may derive from very different experiences. In North Atlantic countries many people despair of even adequately understanding the totality of the society they live in and have no real sense of how it could be changed in a fundamental way; in other words, there is no revolutionary *proyecto* on the horizon. Moreover, the inevitable ambiguity of action tends to make it much harder to see issues as a clash of life and death;

consequently, even activists work for more proximate goals. In Central America, on the other hand, both the problem and the path to its solution seem clearer and even necessary: a continuation of the present order will perpetuate hunger and violence.

In contrasting these two angles of vision on ecclesiology, I do not intend to propose Sobrino's as superior. Each is to a great extent a reflection of the practice out of which it arises. My main object has been to offer a formulation of what unifies a vision of the church's mission, before passing to a number of disparate topics, generally related to the area of "church and politics."

THE CHURCH AND POPULAR, OR REVOLUTIONARY, ORGANIZATIONS

As usually posed, the question of "church and politics," although expressed in terms of principles, refers primarily to hierarchy and clergy making public pronouncements about political matters. While logic might incline to beginning with principles, here I prefer to begin with what is most proper to the Central American experience, the close connection between significant church groups and opposition political organizations. These connections were traced out in some detail in earlier chapters. In brief summary:

1. El Salvador: the peasant organizations FECCAS and UTC, the core of the BPR, the largest popular organization, both emerged from church pastoral work and continued to have strong church connections, so much so, in fact, that on the village level there was often a symbiosis.
2. Nicaragua: CEPA, which began as a training center for peasant Christian leadership, gradually became an increasingly clandestine network of leaders, which was a main root of the ATC, the Sandinista organization for agricultural laborers.
3. Guatemala: CUC, the peasant organization, emerged mainly from the work of church groups and continued to maintain strong church ties; Justice and Peace Committee came to resemble popular organizations somewhat in its way of operation.
4. Basic Christian communities under some circumstances became something like popular organizations; for example, in the Quiché region of Guatemala Acción Católica (Catholic Action) was forced by circumstances to act like a resistance network.

Participation in revolutionary (that is, armed) organizations is a related, although not identical, question: people in Central America insist that the struggle takes place on different levels and that these differences should be respected. I would simply repeat that some church people have been active in the politico-military groups (as the guerrilla groups call themselves) as combatants (Gaspar García and José Antonio Sanjinés in Nicaragua, Neto Barrera and Sister Silvia Arriola in El Salvador, Donald McKenna in Guatemala), but more usually in some other role; Father Rogelio Poncelle, for example, was working pastorally with the ERP in Morazán in El Salvador, and a number of sisters and priests were discreetly doing humanitarian and pastoral work.

Archbishop Romero's 1978 pastoral letter, "The Church and the Popular Organizations," was an attempt to respond to the new issues arising from the popular organizations. The overall context is described in chapter 5; here it should simply be recalled that peasant organization in El Salvador was illegal and that these organizations were portrayed in public opinion as "terrorist" or as front organizations for the guerrillas. Since 1976 the oligarchy had been linking priests (and some bishops) with these groups in the propaganda campaigns in the newspapers, and persecution of the church followed in early 1977.

Before stating principles, Archbishop Romero devoted considerable attention to the people's right to organize and how it was violated in El Salvador; he lamented the sad spectacle of government-formed peasant groups (ORDEN, although the name was not used) participating in the repression of other peasants; and he reiterated the Vatican II teaching about the church's role and its relation to politics. This latter point was significant inasmuch as he was implicitly treating the popular organizations as at least as legitimate as traditional political parties, a position that undoubtedly infuriated those who saw them as "communist hordes."

After laying down basic ecclesiological criteria, Archbishop Romero applied them to the specific case of the popular organizations. His observations may be summarized as follows:

1. It is normal and natural that there be a relationship between the church and organizations that spring from it (meaning, presumably, FECCAS and UTC).
2. Faith and politics are united in the Christian, but they are not identified; there should be a synthesis, but particular programs of political organizations should not replace the content of the faith.
3. The autonomy of both the church and the organizations should be respected; no one should expect the church or its symbols to be used on behalf of an organization.
4. There may be tensions between loyalty to the faith and to an organization.
5. Christians in the organizations should keep their faith explicit. It should be their "ultimate frame of reference"; those who have lost their faith should not use the faith for political purposes.
6. Not all Christians have a political vocation and no one should be compelled to join an organization.

7. It is natural that priests should feel sympathies for popular organizations and be asked to work with them; their role, however, should be
that of "stimulators and guides in the faith and in the justice that
faith demands." Only in exceptional cases, in consultation with the
bishop, and after practicing discernment, should a priest become
involved in political tasks.

These applications closed with some references to other organizations
that did not have close relations with the church (presumably FAPU and
LP-28), and a recognition that "many questions are still in the air."[4]

What should be most apparent from Romero's commentary is that for
him the pastoral problem was not showing that there is a relationship between the church and the organizations. For the peasants, and the pastoral
agents with them, this was obvious. His pastoral problem was, rather, to
insist that the two not be utterly fused: hence his insistence on the "autonomy" of the church. That he should have to warn people not to use the
church's symbols for specific organizations indicates that this must have
been rather common. One imagines that the progression from general principles about human dignity, to a critique of the present order, to a vision of
a new order, to the specific organizations with programs embodying political proposals must have seemed to be all of a piece. In addition it would be
natural for Delegates of the Word to serve as FECCAS-UTC leaders as
well. The basic Christian community and the local peasant organization
could appear largely indistinguishable if they met in the same place (the
village chapel or community center) and perhaps did the organization's
business after a worship service.

There would be pastoral problems: individuals might feel a tension between loyalties to the faith and to an organization (or simply have to budget
their energies among different tasks). Some might be convinced that the
only consistent way to be a Christian would be to make a given political
option. Finally, some might begin as committed Christians but gradually
become so absorbed in working with the popular organization that it would
become the frame of reference for their life, the thing that gave life
meaning—and perhaps the explicit expression of Christian faith would no
longer be paramount.

Although it is not the only issue, the question of the participation of
priests (and sisters) in popular organizations is obviously important. At this
point I would like to move beyond the particular case of El Salvador and
consider it in more general terms. Although from a certain theological angle
all church members are equal (and priests, religious, and lay people simply
have different roles), nevertheless priests or sisters are a special personifica-
tion of the church and their lives and example do have a peculiar weight.

There are different levels of contact or belonging to a popular movement:
some people might be known "sympathizers," viewed as working for the
same cause; others "collaborators," people who consciously carry out some

tasks for the organizations; while still others would be "members" and thereby subject to the full discipline of an organization. In this latter case, one is at the total disposition of the organization, participating in planning, evaluating, criticism/self-criticism, working together, supporting one another, and practicing the vigilance necessary for security. Being a member of a popular or revolutionary organization at this level demands a commitment that is analogous to belonging to a religious order, and in practice is more demanding.

There seem to be three kinds of reasons for a priest or a sister to make such an option:

1. One view sees that, in such a life-or-death struggle, the tasks involved in liberation take precedence over normal pastoral work (rather like in the case of a flood or earthquake). Thus one simply becomes "another soldier"—not necessarily in combat, but one would see it as an emergency interrupting normal pastoral activity.

2. Another type of thinking accepts the fact that sisters and priests are visible symbols of the church. Hence their option for the revolu ionary project (as concretely embodied in a particular organization) may help many others to see it not only as compatible with their faith but even as an expression of love for neighbor.

3. A third motivation is a recognition that the world cannot be evangelized from outside, and that the popular and revolutionary organizations are in fact a special "world" with their own intense experience and new values, their own searching and unanswered questions. Although they are numerically a minority, in a qualitative sense they are very important and may well be the germ of a new society. Only those who share their danger, their anguish, their vision, and their hopes can adequately evangelize them. Hence there is a pastoral reason not only for supporting such organizations but for becoming members.

This last sentence is not intended to convey the impression that a priest or a sister would make such a decision as part of a logically preconceived pastoral strategy. Any such option would be the result of a process of collaboration with such organizations usually resulting from years of pastoral work. It would be more a question of the pastoral agents following the people as, under the pressure of events, the people became more radicalized.

This seems to be the case that Archbishop Romero had in mind in his last pastoral letter when he spoke of a *pastoral de acompañamiento* (pastoral work of accompanying), which he distinguished not only from a traditional mass-oriented pastoral work but also from work with basic Christian communities. In explanation he said that he did not intend this as "a politicized pastoral work, but a pastoral work that has to give Christian guidance to consciences in a politicized milieu." As a justification he quoted the Puebla Final Document on the church's need to be present in the political sphere (nos. 515–16). Among the qualities that he said this particular kind of work needed were discernment, spirit of sacrifice and commitment (to face risks and even false accusations), respect for other options, and a team spirit. There is a studied vagueness in Romero's words—he does not say explicitly that he is speaking about priests as members of popular organizations, for example—but the overall thrust is clear.

One ecclesiological basis for this pastoral option may be found in Romero's 1978 pastoral letter on the popular organizations. He says there is a fundamental relationship between the church and those organizations that did not arise from its work, since the church believes the work of the spirit who resurrects Christ in human beings is broader than itself:

> Beyond the limits of the church there is a great deal of the power of Christ's redemption; and efforts toward freedom by people and groups, even when they do not call themselves Christian, receive their impulse from the Spirit of Jesus; and the church will try to comprehend them, to purify, encourage, and incorporate them—along with the efforts of Christians—in the overall project of Christian redemption.[5]

To put it in plainer terms: the church should be present in the popular organizations because the Spirit is present in their struggle for liberation. (As noted in chapter 5, the other bishops arrived at entirely different conclusions. They forbade priests and religious to participate in popular organizations because they were political and leftist, and they strongly implied that such Marxist organizations were simply using the church.)

In his own practice Archbishop Romero exemplified the attitude toward the popular organizations that he laid down in his formal statements. He came to know some of the main leaders and wept when some were killed (among them, Apolinario Serrano, whom he referred to by his nickname "Polín"), and he was encouraged by the growing unity shown during the last weeks of his life, and which a month after his murder became the FDR. At the same time he felt free to criticize some of the uses of violence (especially kidnappings) and some tactics such as occupying churches when it would alienate potential supporters.

CHURCH AND POLITICS

This particularly Central American experience, and especially the relationship between the church and popular organizations, may help to shed light on the more general question of the relationship between the church and politics. A glance at recent developments in church teaching can serve to introduce the topic.

It has always been clear to outsiders that the Roman Catholic church was involved in politics, and until recent times it tended to identify with conservative regimes. Only during the early 1960s was this de facto alliance broken (at least in principle), first by Pope John XXIII's recognition of a distinction between false philosophies and the historical movements embodying them (a gingerly recognition that there might be some good in socialism), and then by Vatican II's Constitution on the Church in the Modern World (*Gaudium et Spes*), which explicitly recognized political pluralism and declared that the church did not have direct answers for political questions. A further step came when Paul VI in *Octogesima Adveniens* took note of the growing interest in socialism among Christians and called for a great deal of "discernment" (and gave warnings about Marxism rather than simple condemnations). Nevertheless, all these statements seem to have in view a fundamentally harmonious society with a high degree of consensus in which secondary matters are resolved in the political sphere.

One might have expected the Puebla Conference—held during the final phases of the anti-Somoza struggle—to have dealt more explicitly with highly conflictive societies, but the bishops seem to have preferred the high road of principle. On the one hand, they declared that "the church must examine the conditions, systems, ideologies, and political life of our continent—shedding light on them from the standpoint of the Gospel and its own social teaching" (Final Document, no. 511); "Christianity is supposed to evangelize the whole of human life, including the political dimension" (no. 515), although this is to be done according to the church's religious mission. On the other hand, the bishops sought to make a clear distinction between politics in the broad sense, the seeking of the common good, which "is of interest to the Church and hence to its pastors, who are ministers of unity," and "party politics," which is "properly the realm of lay people" (nos. 521–24).

While such a statement seems clear enough and may indeed offer pastoral guidelines for many situations, upon closer examination it shows inadequacies. It may easily serve to mask a de facto alliance with groups in power, since it seems more clearly aimed at priests who might identify themselves with opposition groups than at priests or bishops who might routinely attend state fuctions, for example, ostensibly serving the "common good" but in fact lending their symbolic support to narrow elites maintained by force. In a broader sense the seeming conceptual clarity evaporates when one asks who is to draw the line between what is partisan and what contributes toward the common good; for example, in Nicaragua priests working with the government saw the revolutionary *proyecto* as the concrete way in which the common good must be realized, while those opposed charged them with supporting a political party, the FSLN.

In this section I shall sketch a different approach to the question of the church's involvement in political matters. As an introduction to the topic let me briefly recall some examples of church practice. First, at the grassroots level there is the pastoral work of the formation of basic Christian communities, which served for consciousness-raising and leadership training. In addition church people have been important in documenting repression, in providing interpretation of events, and in humanitarian service.

Turning to the activity of the bishops, it can be said that in Nicaragua, El Salvador, and Guatemala the bishops conferences have at least sometimes condemned the worst human rights abuses and to that extent delegitimized repressive regimes. During the 1970s it was the Nicaraguan bishops who were the most insistent and clearest in their teaching. To my mind this was due to the existence of an anti-Somoza, middle-class group whose views the bishops tended to reflect; in Guatemala and El Salvador the bishops may have been more reluctant to denounce the groups in power, since to do so would objectively aid the only alternative, the leftist opposition. Finally, the Nicaraguan bishops both showed their approval of the insurrection (by invoking the doctrine of the just insurrection during the first few days of the Sandinista offensive) and made an early, highly positive evaluation of the Nicaraguan revolution—and subsequently came to take positions again similar to those of the middle-class opposition.

Archbishop Romero's approach was rather different. Particularly in his Sunday sermons, but also in pastoral letters, he was much more inclined to deal with ongoing conflictive issues and to make more explicit the analysis behind his statement of principles. Increasingly his sermons contained a running commentary on the political life of El Salvador, as seen from the viewpoint of the poor (and their organizations).

Other kinds of hierarchical involvement in politics should be mentioned. Although he very rarely made directly political statements in public, Cardinal Casariego spent much of his time with government and even military figures. Bishop Álvarez of El Salvador was an army chaplain with the rank of colonel and liked to appear in uniform, while Bishop Revelo was photographed blessing American weapons sent to El Salvador. Nicaraguans recalled that the apostolic nuncio was photographed drinking a toast with Somoza, whose planes were bombing Estelí at that very moment.

Conceivably in all these cases, the bishops might have seen themselves as simply pursuing the "common good" and not engaging in partisan activity: even publicly urging Somoza's resignation or endorsing the insurrection might be viewed as expressing the will of the people (the Somoza coterie not being really of "the people").

Nevertheless it seems that the teaching articulated at Puebla is not an adequate guide to practice—nor even a good description of what the bishops try to do. It does not explain the notable differences from country to country or even from diocese to diocese. For instance, many of the activities that the Justice and Peace Committee had to do in a semiclandestine manner in Guatemala (documenting repression, producing catechetical materials based on the Guatemalan experience) were done in El Salvador right in the chancery office. At the very least the Puebla principles seem too generic to serve as guides for practice.

In what follows I am suggesting another approach to the involvement of the church in politics. I am thinking mainly of hierarchical pronouncements on public matters; nevertheless the principles could be applied to other groups in the church. At first glance these appear to be guidelines for action, but in fact they imply an ecclesiology.

1. *The bishops should abandon the illusion of providing timeless principles and see their intervention as part of a process.* Bishops make statements on particular dates in particular places and in response to particular events. Yet there is a deep-seated tendency to see themselves as simply reiterating universal principles. Thus the endorsement of the Sandinista-led insurrection was made in the medieval language of the just insurrection. There may be prudential reasons for doing so rather than stating, for example, "We Nicaraguan bishops endorse this struggle." My essential concern here, however, is simply to draw attention to the unconscious striving for timelessness (at least partially due to a philosophical/theological training in "Greek" categories, which pitted the eternal and "real" against the temporal and "apparent") and to urge that the bishops' interventions be seen as part of an ongoing process.

2. *The bishops should see themselves as one set of actors on a stage in which there are other actors.* Consequently they should see their statements as elements in an ongoing dialogue and not as the end of the discussion. Sometimes, of course, they do this explicitly, as the Nicaraguan bishops did in the introduction to their November 1979 pastoral letter. *By themselves the bishops are not the church but one element in the church, the group charged with "oversight."* Their statements are therefore not ipso facto statements of the church but of the overseers. To the extent they are the product of a real process of dialogue and listening, whether systematic (as in Archbishop Romero's questionnaire, which fed into his fourth pastoral letter) or unsystematic, episcopal statements may be said to be the voice of the church. However, most often they will represent the viewpoint of the bishops themselves and as such will invite response, both from groups within the church and from others.

As is clear from the experience of Central America, the bishops, as a group, tend to reflect their own class perceptions rather than those of the majority in the church, who are the poor. The tendency to view their own statements as necessarily expressing the church obscures this fact. I am not saying the bishops' statements are nothing but expressions of one class but, rather, that their class (family origins, life experience, and normal contacts) inevitably colors their view of social reality. Eventually the Roman Catholic church may have formal structures and processes for arriving at the position of "the church" (consulting processes and assemblies with strong lay representation and open discussion, for example). Until such time it would be well to insist that the hierarchy not be identified with the church.

3. *Underlying any church pronouncement by the bishops on political matters should be a clear analysis (structural and conjunctural) of the context and causes.* Any such statement implies some analysis; if the bishops issued a statement warning of the dangers of Marxism, for example, ordinarily they would have concluded that some Marxist groups posed a concrete threat. Sometimes the bishops themselves explicitly include some of

their analysis, as in the 1976 pastoral letter in Guatemala, which began with references to the earthquake but then proceeded to describe the behavior of social classes and the use of violence. At other times the statement may presume the analysis. Again, the Nicaraguan bishops' invoking of the "just insurrection" comes to mind.

I am suggesting here that the analysis be as systematic as possible, at least in the deliberations prior to any public stand. Latin Americans frequently use two kinds of analysis, structural and conjunctural. Structural analysis considers the more permanent elements, such as the mode of production, classes, and longer-range tendencies. Conjunctural analysis examines a particular *coyuntura*, or period, and systematically reviews economic and political developments by focusing on the interplay of various classes or sectors (bourgeoisie, perhaps divided into "fractions"; military; government; political parties; church; popular organizations; revolutionary movements). The methodology is usually, but not necessarily, employed by Marxists (businesspeople also speak of *coyunturas*). This method provides a disciplined and systematic way of understanding the forces at work in society. People who do not employ some such methodology are simply left with more impressionistic approaches. These methods do not provide the answers, but they do offer a framework for integrating data and grasping a sense of the whole. In the present case they enable actors in the church to understand their role in context.

To illustrate by an example: in May 1980, less than a month after the resignation of Alfonso Robelo from the Junta signaled the end of the "honeymoon" and the beginnings of public anti-Sandinista opposition, the Nicaraguan bishops declared that the "emergency" was over and that therefore the priests in government posts should return to pastoral duties and make way for lay people. In the first place, they did not make clear on what basis they declared the emergency to be over; such was certainly not the impression of those working to recover from the damage of the war. A structural/conjunctural analysis might have led them to another conclusion; at the very least, they should have given their reasons for their own interpretation. They made no reference to Robelo, although by discounting in advance any political intentions on their part they seemed to be sensitive to a political interpretation. Had they made an explicit analysis along the lines I am suggesting, they might have concluded that, independent of their intentions, their action would objectively aid the anti-Sandinista groups. (At this point, of course, they could have consciously chosen to proceed, judging that these groups were worthy of support; or they could have waited for another moment to make clear that their own criteria were strictly pastoral.) To some degree, what I am suggesting is already practiced. Archbishop Romero, for example, accompanied his third pastoral letter with a document giving statistical data on El Salvador, and as early as the 1960s Archbishop Chávez asked Catholic University professors to present position papers to help him prepare a pastoral letter.

In some cases the analysis could be left implicit but in many cases it would be good to make it clearly available. To the extent the bishops were to make their analysis explicit they would invite response; some might disagree or urge other aspects to complement the analysis.

4. *What is proper to the church itself, however, is not analysis, but a clear pronouncement from the viewpoint of the gospel, the criteria for which should be clearly articulated*, first among the bishops themselves and then in their statements. That this point is not so obvious as might appear at first glance may be illustrated by the case of the almost simultaneous statements on the popular organizations by Archbishop Romero (and Bishop Rivera y Damas) and the other four bishops (see above, and also chapter 5). The main objection of these latter bishops to the organizations was simply that they were Marxist. For them Marxism seemed to be inevitably atheistic, whatever transitory tactics it might employ, and was hence incompatible with Christianity. The poverty of the Salvadoran peasants was clearly not their starting point, although they did abstractly recognize the right to organize. Possibly their underlying criterion was the church's freedom to carry out its mission, which they were convinced would be impaired under a Marxist regime.

Romero's letter is much more structured and coherent. Not only is its judgment on the organizations themselves radically different from that of the other bishops (see previous section of this chapter), but its criteria are quite different: for example, he insists upon the church's mission to denounce injustice and defend the cause of the weak and needy, and especially a sense that the church is not itself the kingdom, but is to serve the kingdom, which is broader.

Similarly, an examination of the Nicaraguan hierarchy's statements starting in 1980 would raise questions about its underlying criteria: to what extent were they an articulation of the needs of the poor majority and to what extent might stressing certain "values" reflect the criteria of the anti-Sandinista elites?

I would suggest (following Sobrino's language above) that in Central America it should be a basic criterion of the church's activity "to serve the life of the poor." In some ways this is simply a refinement of the notion of the "common good" (a term that by itself might serve to mask the objective divisions in society).

5. *Prior to any public position, there should be an effort to weigh its probable impact.* This recommendation is to some extent implicit in what was said above, but an example may make it clearer. Prior to issuing a statement on "Christian Civic Responsibility" in a pre-electoral period, the bishops should examine whether such a statement might not seem to legitimize elections, which a significant group of people regard as simply a device of the narrow elites to maintain themselves in power.

Many groups in the church already use a process similar to the one I have been describing as part of their pastoral work. It is normal procedure for them to seek to "contextualize" their own actions by using the discipline of structural/conjunctural analysis. Some bishops and bishops conferences do so to a certain extent. My suggestion is that it become normal procedure, in order to make the process explicit, conscious, self-critical, and, in the church as a whole, self-correcting.

THE "USE" OF THE CHURCH AND RELIGIOUS SYMBOLS

From the accounts in chapters 4 through 8, it is evident that all contending sides tended to invoke God and religion to support their particular options. From the phantom right-wing groups in El Salvador taking out newspaper ads to attack the Jesuits and the archbishop, to fundamentalist preachers working hand-in-glove with the Guatemalan army's "beans-and-bullets" counterinsurgency campaign, the groups in power invoked religion. For their part, those Christians committed to the revolution saw it as a logical consequence of their commitment in faith and they expressed it in many ways, such as Carlos Mejía Godoy's "Nicaraguan Mass," "*Misa Campesina,*" and other music, or in many catechetical materials produced, such as a mimeographed pamphlet with a picture of Gaspar García (the priest who fell in combat) with the words "I have to give my life for my people as Christ did," or posters showing Archbishop Romero holding his staff in his right hand and raising his left hand with a clenched fist.

In the United States the Institute for Religion and Democracy put out two pamphlets, "The Catholic Church in El Salvador" (an attempt to minimize expressions of grassroots sectors together with a selective reading of statements from Archbishop Rivera y Damas) and: "Nicaragua: A Revolution against the Church?"[6] The United States State Department on occasion made its own reading of the position of "the church" in Central American countries.

Within these countries each side accused the other of "using" religion in the service of its own ideology. In itself the debate is not new; it began around 1970 when some leftist Christians spoke of the necessity of a *desbloqueo ideológico* (literally "ideological unblocking," something like breaking the ideological bottleneck). Vatican II had in principle meant that the church had broken its ties with conservative regimes and had accepted the "pluralism" inherent in the modern world. This step was a recognition that the era of Christendom was past: the church would no longer ally itself with particular (usually conservative) governments and in return for its support receive special favors from such regimes. (Practice, of course, lagged behind the Vatican Council's declaration of principle.) According to critics, although the church now seemed independent vis-à-vis particular political parties and regimes, the church was seen as supporting, at least tacitly, the existing capitalist system. Hence there was a need for a *desbloqueo ideológico* to expose this more subtle alliance with dominant powers, even after the liberalizing effects of the council.

The debates of the early 1970s, as much as they may have pointed the way conceptually, were not related to any viable revolutionary *proyecto*. Central America revived the earlier discussion, now in a more pointed way. It became most controversial in Nicaragua after the Sandinista victory, where the main struggle was now precisely on the ideological level. It was present in El Salvador and Guatemala, but conditions of repression there meant that there was little public space for ideological issues as such.

Some accused Christian supporters of the revolution of practicing "clericalism of the left," a mirror-image of the conservative clericalism supposedly done away with by Vatican II. Chapter 8 mentioned how the priests in government service were described as having received "flattery and pay."

How did such Christians answer these charges? How did they explain the relationship between their commitment to the revolution and their faith, and yet avoid aiming at a new kind of "Christendom," this time from the left?

Some people it seems had a fairly straightforward answer. For example, some Nicaraguan peasants saw the priests in government as simply doing what Jesus had done, serving the poor. Others would argue that political neutrality was impossible and that the church should make a clear and conscious option to support the revolution, and do so with its preaching, liturgy, and symbols, infusing them with a revolutionary content. This would in effect be a relevant evangelization. To take one symbolic example: on the cover of *Fe Cristiana y Revolución Sandinista en Nicaragua* (the proceedings of a UCA seminar) [7] is a double image: Jesus, head down, arms outstretched as though on the cross (line drawing) and, standing in back, larger, as though arising out of the dead Jesus, a guerrilla fighter (in two colors), also with arms outstretched, one holding an automatic rifle.

Nevertheless, I find that these people in general do not contend that there is a straight line between Christian faith, as revealed in Jesus Christ, and particular movements in history. To express their position they have employed the notion of "mediations," a term to which they give three meanings: [8]

1. *Mediations in history*: the notion is that God's plan of salvation or liberation is embodied in specific realities in human history which "mediate" it. Another way to express the idea is to say that God's kingdom appears in history through partial realizations (or mediations)—it is not identified with them but they are a means to the realization of the kingdom, or steps toward it.
2. *The mediation of social-science analysis*: neither the Gospels nor the Christian tradition in themselves provide answers for choices that must be made; for this purpose social analysis is needed and, although at a certain level the people may respond to what seems obvious (for example, that an economy aimed at satisfying basic needs is preferable to one serving an oligarchy), nevertheless an adequate understanding of social reality (which is not transparent) requires the best instruments of analysis available.

3. *The mediation of practice*: faith itself must be acted out in a specific practice and not simply on the level of interiority. Thus, having determined (through the mediation of social analysis) that a given movement, for example, this present revolution, represents a significant liberation for the poor (and hence is a mediation of kingdom), one commits oneself to participate in it as an expression of faith (mediation of practice).

Such a conceptualization does not solve all problems. Obviously what some see as social-science analysis others might dismiss as "Marxist ideology" (Marxism as such is dealt with in the next section). So far I am only pointing out that these Christians do not see their political options as a straight-line deduction from their faith, but see "mediation" (in the senses outlined) as a crucial step.

The role of faith is not seen as simply passive (accepting and opting for what social analysis has determined) but as active. An IHCA-CAV publication says:

Our faith does not substitute for mediations in history; it demands them as it demands that we live this historic process in the midst of the people. But vis-à-vis any mediation, faith acts within us, clarifying, motivating, making demands, and respecting that motivation. And this unending activity of faith enters into and energizes our love, making it militant and efficacious in the historic work of hope with which we begin the building of the kingdom in the revolutionary process of this poor and believing people.[9]

The question remains, however: How does the involvement of Christians in present revolutions, and especially a revolution in power in Nicaragua, differ from the historical alliance of the church and existing regimes? In Nicaragua there is a strong insistence that the revolution does not ask the church or Christians for legitimation—it has its own internal legitimation and does not need any added "sacralization." This is repeatedly stated by Christians who support the "process," and it seems to be implied in the official FSLN statement on religion published in October 1980.

Pablo Richard has sought to explain the present position of the church by comparing it with the situation of Christendom, where the church came to rely on the political power with which it was allied, rather than its own resources of faith, hope, and love, to accomplish its mission. He argues that such an alliance began to enter into crisis especially in the 1960s and 1970s when the church, by defending people's right to basic needs, implicitly found itself beginning to delegitimize the existing capitalist system. He further argues that the church will find its true identity to the extent that it enters into the revolutionary process (and not, as some might expect, by keeping its distance). He makes a distinction between "civil society," quoting Gramsci's definition ("the ethical and intellectual movement of the masses") and "political society" (the state's power to coerce). In a revolutionary society, civil society is structured in the mass organizations and their activities:

> In the capitalist system the church has a privileged place in civil society. In it the church is integrated as a force that legitimizes political power, and it utilizes this integration as a mediation (instrument) for its missionary project. . . . It is evident that in present revolutionary Nicaragua, the church is not integrated into civil society, fulfilling that legitimating function. The revolution offers the church all the space it needs in civil society, but it does not ask the church to legitimate popular power or revolutionary political power, since this power has in itself its own legitimacy.

Conceptually, at least, that much is not difficult. Whether it is consistently carried out in practice is another question, to which I shall return. Richard's next point is more difficult, but important:

> The revolution cannot allow the church to utilize its presence within civil society for proselytizing purposes, if they are foreign to the structures and objectives of this civil society.

(This would seem to mean that the church cannot be allowed to carry out activities that would undermine the revolution.)

> Summing up, Christendom is incompatible with a popular and revolutionary civil society, but a church that breaks with the framework of Christendom and defines its identity as one of evangelization . . . in Nicaragua today is not incompatible [with such a civil society].

According to Richard "the *integration* of the church in civil society demands a radical *conversion* of the church to its own original identity." He sees a specific role for the church in the education of popular religiosity:

> The point is not to manipulate Chrisitanity to make it functional for the revolution, but to live as authentic Christians within the revolution. We should not respond to reactionary manipulation with another manipulation, but with a conversion that is Christian and ultimately revolutionary.[10]

I must confess that at times I have found this discussion to be somewhat obscure, and I have been tempted to take a more straightforward line: real neutrality is impossible and therefore the church should consider political options, including that of explicit support for a revolution. Nevertheless the point being made by Richard and others is important to understand, since, if it is correct, it indicates a fundamental shift in the kind of presence the church has in society.

Some of the difficulty may come from what is unstated: that there is a presumed discernment of the ethical legitimacy of the revolutionary *proyecto*. If it should happen that the revolutionary group in power should indeed become "totalitarian," then it would be the church's obligation to take an opposition stand in the name of life.

This whole point may be clarified by looking more specifically at what in fact has happened in Nicaragua. Juan Hernández Pico noted that the Nicaraguan hierarchy was disconcerted because the new Sandinista political power did not seek legitimation from the church; moreover, fearing that the revolution might turn antireligious, the hierarchy was already to some extent in opposition and even saw its posture as "an exercise of Christian prophetism and of courage in the face of a supposedly tyrannical power." He pointed out that the hierarchy was thereby giving "bourgeois freedoms" a priority over the cause of the poor, and he suggested that there was a real distinction between totalitarianism and the "hegemony" that the FSLN enjoyed.

A further aid to understanding what is being proposed is to recognize that the import of what Richard and others were arguing might become clear only after some time: that the church was taking a new position in society more in accord with its original identity and was not legitimizing the revolution as it historically had legitimized previous regimes. However, in the initial emergency period of consolidation, with Christians (some quite identified with the church) working in the revolutionary government, and with a need to counter the use of religion to undermine the revolution, it might at times seem as though revolutionary Christians were simply providing the revolution (and indeed the FSLN and government) with religious symbolism. Only in time would the newness of the relation become clear.

MARXIST ANALYSIS

In examining the question of the use of Marxism by Christians I would like to take a somewhat oblique approach. At the root is a question of how we know social reality at all.

I would suggest an experiment to my readers. Suppose you were asked to prepare, for a group of Egyptians, an overview of what is happening in the United States. What would be the main lines of your presentation? How would you organize them? (A pause here to make the experiment might be useful.)

Most of us, I imagine, would prepare a patchwork presentation made up largely of topics current in magazines and the media. We would probably feel overwhelmed by the complexity of the United States. We admire what appear to be penetrating insights into the American experience when we run across them, but we then simply incorporate them into the flotsam and jetsam that constitute our stock of ideas. We lack an overall framework of interpretation.

On the other hand, an educated Central American with a similar request would probably be able to improvise a quite coherent and structured account of the history of his or her country, its economic system, class structure, recent developments, and possible future courses. Part of the reason this person would find it easy to give such an account is the size and relative uncomplexity of Central American countries, which are smaller than some United States metropolitan areas. However, another reason might be that the person would have a habitual framework of analysis, including a sense of the historical evolution of his or her country, with emphasis on its changing economic role, an analysis that is both structural and conjunctural, as described above. Thus, for example, politics would be seen not as mainly the succession of personalities into the presidential office, but as a reflection of changing circumstances and the elites' responses to them.

With such a framework of analysis it is difficult to avoid being a Marxist to some extent—since it is Marxist categories that best help to identify the forces at work in such a society, most particularly social classes. "Bourgeois" social science tends to be less specific. Marxism sees social classes in terms of their role in the economy: the bourgeoisie (owners of the means of production) and the proletariat (those who must sell their labor), plus intermediate strata. Other kinds of analysis tend to see classes simply as they see themselves or are seen or according to their level of consumption (high, middle, lower). Even anti-Marxists find themselves using Marxist concepts—businessmen or officers speaking of the "correlation of forces," for example. Certain basic Marxist categories seem indispensable.

Marxism in this sense is more heuristic than doctrinal, more a questionnaire than a set of ready-made answers. It is a way of looking at a society. In itself it does not guarantee a clear and accurate vision. As a set of instruments or tools it can be used badly or well.

In my observation Central Americans have not made any notable contributions to Marxist theory as such, and indeed seem not to have studied it with any great thoroughness. What they have studied, rather, are their own countries, using in their study concepts taken from Marxism. Moreover, such study has not been aimed at knowledge for its own sake but, rather, to make changes. Regis Debray remarks that Latin Americans have received their Marx through Lenin, meaning, one assumes, that they have been more interested in how to struggle to take power than in arriving at a total analysis of how the capitalist system functions. As far as I can determine, Marxist movements in Nicaragua, El Salvador, and Guatemala for the most part have not become divided over the disputes involved in rival international "lines": such splits as have occurred have been over their strategic conceptions, such as a long-range "prolonged people's war" vs. a shorter-range "insurrectional" approach. In Guatemala they have had to get beyond narrow Marxist categories to deal with the "Indian question." In short, Central American Marxism is homegrown.

What has been said here may be applied to Christians using Marxism, namely, they have not become embroiled in elaborate theoretical discussions; their effort has been directed at understanding how their own societies work, and on organizing for, and struggling toward, the taking of power. There has been no "Christian-Marxist dialogue" with representatives of either side facing each other across the table, since in fact the encounter takes place within people who are at once Christians and (to some degree) Marxists.

Christians using Marxism in the sense described are clear that they do not subscribe to Marxism as a complete world-vision or philosophical system. They would see it as an ideology but in the sense that it is "a system of means and ends to meet a particular historical era in its different and changing situations [*coyunturas*]; at the same time it tries to lead this era along toward goals that are partial and subject to revision."[11]

Official Catholic teaching, on the other hand, continues to see Marxism as an ideology in the sense of being a total world-view. Thus Puebla examines three such ideologies: capitalist liberalism, Marxist collectivism, and national security. Its common definition of "ideology" is that of a conception which offers a view of the various aspects of life as seen from the standpoint of a particular group, representing its aspirations and summoning it to struggle. Although an ideology is therefore partial, it tends to absolutize the interests it upholds and so become a lay religion or a new idol (Final Document, nos. 535–36). While acknowledging that some people believe that aspects of Marxism may be separated, "its doctrine and method of analysis in particular," Puebla simply repeats a warning of Pope Paul VI that these elements are "closely linked to each other" and adds:

> We must also note the risk of ideologization run by theological reflection when it is based on a praxis that has recourse to Marxist analysis. The consequences are the total politicization of Christian existence, the disintegration of the language of faith into that of the social sciences, and the draining away of the transcendental dimension of Christian salvation [no. 545].

The bishops at Puebla seemed to take a position that the church was somehow above ideologies, quoting Pope John Paul II saying that the church "does not need to have recourse to ideological systems in order to love, defend, and collaborate in the liberation of the human being" (no. 552). They fear that the church may be manipulated by those who "look for the Kingdom to come from a strategic alliance between the Church and Marxism. . . . For these people it is not simply a matter of being Marxists, but of being Marxists in the name of the faith" (no. 561). Such a definition is highly polemical and even a caricature.

I would submit that those Christians who are using elements of Marxism do not see the kingdom coming in this way. They are simply convinced that they must search for those instruments of analysis most apt for making love efficacious and at the service of life. They find that conventional analysis, both economic and political, tends to hide rather than reveal the real mechanisms of power, for example, the myth that with economic growth there will eventually be a "trickle-down" effect to the poor. They see any use of Marxist analysis as part of a process of "discernment" to be carried out in a process of personal and collective searching to find out "which systems, which forces, which programs and which groups may be considered to be historic and concrete bearers of liberation." In this search there is no other way but to take sides (as God takes the side of the poor) and to give up the idea of never making a mistake (something which can be done only by remaining on the most general level).[12]

Social reality is not known directly; a society cannot be "seen" like a landscape; it must be known through concepts that are to some extent abstract. Those who believe that they are above ideologies (and this includes the bishops) in fact end up with an uncritical and unconscious use of the elements of analysis presented by the ideology of the dominant group in their society; in other words, willy-nilly, in a capitalist society, they will be using elements from capitalist ideology, even if they are criticizing some manifestations of it. One of the bishops at Puebla told the assembly, "Let him who is without an ideology throw the first stone." The alternative is not between being above ideologies or being absorbed by them, but rather, between using them critically and consciously or not.

There is another question involved in the use of Marxism, which is less susceptible to rational analysis and is more a question of one's belief in the possibilities of history. Some are convinced that any group using Marxism, once it is in power, inevitably ends up imposing a system of totalitarian control over the population. Such is the lesson of history for them: the roots of totalitarianism are present in Leninist theory if not in Marx himself.

Those using Marxism in Central America are not unaware of history. However, they would first argue that the historical record of socialism is not simply negative but mixed, particularly when seen from the angle of the poor; that the deformations of those societies calling themselves socialist must be seen in terms of their particular histories; and most important, that the future is open. Implied here is an act of faith in the creativity of the people of Central America, that out of their own resources, and learning from other experiences, they may be able to form a new kind of society, in which the needs of the poor will be better served and there will be a greater measure of real freedom for all. Those who are Christians are confident that faith itself will be part of this process, criticizing error and helping to avoid dehumanizing tendencies.

Part of the difference, then, between those who make use of Marxism and those who condemn its use a priori is that the former feel there may indeed be something new under the sun.

BEING THE CHURCH IN A REVOLUTIONARY REGIME

Although the church had endured revolutions before and has recognized Marxist regimes as a fact of life and adjusted to them, the Nicaraguan revolution represents something new, a revolutionary process in which Christians played important roles during the struggle to take power and in which they are participating at all levels. Similar developments may well occur in El Salvador and Guatemala. This situation presents new pastoral challenges, some of which are mentioned elsewhere in this chapter. In chapter 8 I have described what in fact happened during the first three years in Nicaragua. At this point I would like to move to a slightly higher level of generality, hoping to clarify, at least in outline, some of the questions.

The basic underlying question can be formulated as: How is the church to have an evangelizing presence in a revolutionary society? (The question assumes that the church's mission is evangelization; "evangelizing presence" is used to indicate that the concept is wider than simply communicating a message.)

A simple answer would be that there is little or no real difference between evangelizing in nonrevolutionary and revolutionary regimes. In each case the church would simply require a minimum of "space" within society for carrying out its activity. It is my sense that this is in fact the position of many Protestant churches, particularly of the sect variety. Some Catholic movements implicitly have a similar posture when they seek to continue their normal series of activities as though there were no convulsive social revolution all around them.

However, such a position is incompatible with evangelization, understood in a fuller sense, for at least two reasons: (*a*) evangelization must reach people and shed the light of the gospel on what is important in their lives; a revolution profoundly affects attitudes, values, and behavior (the issues are so fundamental they may divide families or split marriages); hence evangelization must engage people in terms of what is happening in their lives as a result of the revolution; (*b*) in some sense, the revolution itself as a collective process calls for evangelization.

As was seen in the case of Nicaragua (and there is every reason to anticipate something similar in other cases) the interpretation of the revolution tends to produce a radical split between those who see it as Marxist and therefore implicitly totalitarian and antireligious, and others who see it as the historical *proyecto*, which is the concrete mediation of life for the poor at this moment in history.

As is evident, I see the latter interpretation as essentially correct (at least in the case of Nicaragua at the time of writing). What I am concerned about at this point, however, is not the particular interpretation accepted, but the process of discernment leading to it.

There are several difficulties impeding church leaders from accepting a revolutionary process. To begin with, even those who might accept abstractly the need for changes are faced not with an "ideal" revolution, which unites all possible desirable qualities, but with *this* revolution, with all its deficiencies, some resulting from external limitations and some from real errors or moral failings.

One might prefer to pick and choose, supporting what seemed good and criticizing what seemed wrong: applaud the Literacy Crusade and question its use as a Sandinista organizing tool; praise the land reform and criticize restrictions on the private sector; support the extension of health services to rural areas and oppose curbs on *La Prensa*. The foregoing are not necessarily examples I agree with but are hypothetical examples of a pick-and-choose approach to interpreting the Nicaraguan revolution. One could even have in mind a "perfect" revolution, which would "square the circle" and pursue development for the poor, while not seriously cutting into the consumption of the privileged; encourage widespread organization and place no curbs on freedom of expression; show solidarity with the struggles of other peoples and yet maintain good relations with the United States.

However, there are no ideal revolutions. The church will always be faced with *this* revolution. What is demanded is a basic stance toward an existing revolution as a whole. I do not mean to imply that support must be uncritical. Some might believe that the best position is to "support the good and criticize the bad." As stated this sounds unobjectionable, but there are further considerations. In a period in which a revolution is still fragile and vulnerable and is facing many threats, internal and external, it is possible that consistent criticism, even of real faults, that does not come from a position of clear support will in fact serve to undermine the revolution. If the real alternatives are *this* revolution and a counter-revolution analogous, say, to Pinochet's Chile, the effects of criticism must be calculated.

The point I wish to emphasize is not the role of criticism in itself—I shall return to that below—but the harsh though undeniable fact that the church is not in a position to create its own ideal revolution or to wait until an ideal society comes along. Revolutions will always be particular and nonideal, led by particular groups—and the real alternatives will be specific and linked to particular (counter-revolutionary) groups.

There are further, related difficulties. It is difficult for many of the hierarchy and clergy to feel "at home" in a revolutionary atmosphere.

The hierarchy may well feel it has been somewhat downgraded. The revolutionary "vanguard" has a great deal of moral leadership, is proposing new values, and indeed often seems to be preaching a message which is more appealing and energizing than the church's. Thus there is a subtle temptation to sense a competition for moral leadership.

A further cultural difficulty may appear. Priests or sisters may find some of the forms of expression of a revolution, such as mass rallies and demonstrations with chanted slogans, alienating, and may see them as creating a "mass" mentality. At the local level, former guerrilla leaders now directing policies may seem militaristic or overbearing.

The net result of these cultural reactions may be that the church institutionally finds it hard to focus on the revolution in a clear way and so formulate its pastoral criteria properly. It may find an affinity with those classes that see their privileges eroded, whether gradually or rapidly, but rationalize their opposition as resistance to the "totalitarian" direction of the revolution or the faults of its leadership.

To illustrate with an example: in February 1981 the Nicaraguan bishops criticized the government for alleged human rights violations when it transferred several thousand Miskito Indians away from the area near the Honduran border. The bishops had made no on-site investigation and in their criticism made no analysis of the context of attacks from Somocista bands in Honduras, much less a criticism of those attacks. They echoed the criticism of the Sandinistas made by the opposition parties and the United States embassy. The Sandinistas responded to the bishops' statement with a vigorous defense. While this controversy was still fresh I attended a charismatic Mass in Managua. During the homily the celebrant spoke of the priesthood, saying that some refused to give it respect; at the communion time his version of the "Lamb of God" was to hold up the host and declare, "This is the *only Lord* of the Nicaraguans" three times with increasing emphasis. In his hands the Eucharist was an ideological weapon.

When faced with a revolution it would seem that ideally the church should engage in a process of collective discernment with the participation of all, from grassroots to leadership, and if it determines that this revolution, on balance, offers a real opportunity for meeting the basic needs of the majority in dignity and growing freedom, to support it, not basically as one more social force but by fulfilling its mission of evangelization—from within the revolutionary process. If it should be clear in the discernment that, despite its professed intentions, a given revolution was going to bring only oppression, the decision should be for resistance.

If the Nicaraguan experience is typical, the likely result of a revolution will be one of sharp division among pastoral agents: one group that supports the revolution, judging it to be a "mediation" of the kingdom; another group clearly in opposition; and another group, which while less clearly opposed may tend to line up on the opposition side. Again, if the Nicaraguan case indicates anything it is that these lines tend to harden rather than shift as the process itself advances. It may be recalled that when ACLEN (Nicaraguan Clergy Association) drew up a list of its pastoral problems, what predominated were various kinds of division (among the bishops themselves, between the diocese of Estelí, which was more supportive of the revolution, and others, division provoked by CELAM's involvement in Nicaragua, as well as the more obvious kinds of divisions along lines related to social classes).[13]

The following guidelines suggest how the church might face the problem of internal divisions within a revolutionary situation:

1. Church people might be well advised to take a "Gamaliel attitude": in advising the Sanhedrin to leave the apostles alone, Gamaliel said that if their activity were merely human it would come to nought, and that if it were from God "you will not be able to destroy them without fighting

God himself'' (cf. Acts 5:34–39). While it is only an analogy, it suggests an attitude of not prejudging God's way of acting.

2. Similarly there should be a recognition that a revolution is a new situation, one for which there are no ready-made answers. (Of course, the answer might be that the course of past revolutions tells us all we need to know. Here the difference comes down to a basic difference over the openness of history.)

3. The revolution should be seen as a process, whose course may be modified and affected by the conscious participation of Christians.

4. There should be an ongoing process of study, reflection, prayer, and a continual effort at discernment. Part of the study should be an effort to clarify what the pastoral issues are (and if there is no agreement, at least a clarification of the lines of disagreement); in addition, sufficient materials of historical, economic, and political analysis (structural and conjunctural) should be provided to enable pastoral agents to see their role within the overall social context. (Again, if agreement on what the facts are is lacking, there could be clarification through comparing alternate analyses.)

5. Laity should be thoroughly involved in this process of study and reflection. There should be an effort at proportionate participation by the poor—through basic Christian communities, for example.

6. Every effort should be made to keep disputes "in the family" of the church, recognizing and humbly accepting division among Christians as a reflection of division in society. Put another way, even if the hierarchy as a group tends to oppose the revolution, it should not place "the church" in conflict with the revolutionary leadership, if there is a significant group of Christians and pastoral agents who support the revolution. Rather, Christians on both sides should seek ways of achieving a modus vivendi in the church and engaging in an ongoing process of discernment.

During the priests-in-government controversy in Nicaragua, it was suggested that the "Council of Jerusalem" (cf. Acts 15) should serve as some kind of model. In that early dispute there was a process of both dialogue and confrontation over issues that each side felt to be important (the obligation of Christians to continue with Jewish ritual customs), and in which the apostles themselves were initially at odds. The council's solution, while favoring Gentile converts, showed some sensitivity to Jewish Christians' concerns. In Nicaragua the settlement of the priests-in-government controversy indicated some willingness on the part of the bishops to be responsive to sectors in the church with whom they disagreed. One aspect of the challenge of a revolutionary regime for the church is thus finding ways to endure a division that is painful and seemingly unresolvable within a foreseeable future.

From another angle it may be asked: What are the challenges for those Christians who consciously opt for the revolution as an expression of Christian commitment arising out of faith? To clarify: they do not intend to say, for instance, that God endorses the FSLN; rather, their reasoning is that God is on the side of the poor, and that, all things considered, this particular revolution (de facto with such-and-such characteristics) is a "mediation" in history of the kingdom, since it is the concrete way by which the poor will be able to live more fully. This latter is a political judgment, provisional, subject to critical revision—but nonetheless one on which a commitment can and must be made to something absolute—God's love for the poor.

From that starting point, Christians committed to the revolution ask themselves how they can have an evangelizing presence in it. A number of issues or issue clusters may be discerned (not all of which are limited to Christians).

1. *One of the basic challenges is maintaining a support for the revolution that is at the same time critical.* Christians supporting the revolution, and institutions such as the Valdivieso Center, the IHCA, and CEPA, have frequently been accused of simply uncritically serving as mouthpieces for the FSLN. They are said to be unwilling to recognize the errors, mistakes, and arrogance of the Sandinistas and are sometimes accused of having "sold out." There is even a tendency for those making such criticism to see themselves as exercising "Christian prophecy" in opposition to an established power.

For Christians who see the revolution as objectively embodying the aspirations of the poor, there is no doubt that their support should be critical. Criticism is needed, and is in fact a part of revolutionary discipline. The hard question is how to make it in a form that furthers the overall goals. There are genuine injustices done by people in Sandinista uniform and there are debatable points (and probably serious errors) in overall Sandinista policy. Constant public criticism, however, may objectively serve the counter-revolutionary forces.

One example of how some have dealt with these tensions was a document called "Christian Fidelity in the Revolutionary Process in Nicaragua" (already described in chapter 8), which was structured around the "challenges" to faith. Within an overall call to conversion and using the example and teaching of Archbishop Romero as a leitmotif, the document criticized a number of faults, or tendencies, in the revolution: a tendency to unjustified bureaucracy and expansion in the state, a temptation for the FSLN to think that its past heroism would justify arrogance toward the people, excesses in the mass organizations (understood as unjustified, if understandable, attacks on bourgeois political rallies). At times the criticism was made indirectly, as when it was insisted that the state is meant to serve, or that the FSLN document on religion could have more explicitly declared that government and party structures should not be used for antireligious propaganda, and especially when it pointed to the Atlantic coast as an area requiring special sensitivity and treatment.

In substance the document made serious criticisms, but it showed a sympathetic understanding of the context of difficulty and hostility facing the revolution and its fundamental thrust in favor of the poor. The overall framework was one of Christian discernment. In a panel discussion following several weeks of grassroots discussion of the document, a number of speakers were more explicit in their criticism; Tomás Borge, for one, admitted that there was not enough austerity among government employees. Many of the points of the document found their way into public discussion of the revolution. Such an effort may offer one model of an evangelizing presence.[14]

2. *Christians wishing to maintain a critical support have to face many tensions inherent in the revolutionary process.* (Some of these have been mentioned in chapter 8.) In economic policy there is a tension between placing resources into meeting immediate needs and laying the groundwork for a new economy that will satisfy those needs, and a tension between increasing personal income and increasing social income; politically there are tensions between what technicians may determine as the exigencies of production, or political leaders as the need for organization, and what grassroots people perceive; there is a tension between the need for a strong state to carry out programs of basic change, and respect for the opinions and freedoms of individuals and local groups. It should be pointed out that not all the tension with the revolutionary government comes from the privileged who fear radicalization; there are also pressures from the popular organizations which are impatient for basic changes and see the elites as still excessively rewarded (for example, with very high pay differentials).

Are there specifically "Christian" criteria for confronting these tensions? While abstractly one might think that the church should be on the side of the poor, over against the pretensions of party, state, or experts, a simpleminded "grassrootsism" could weaken the overall coherence of a revolutionary program and in the end be self-defeating. Thus while there may be an inclination deriving from the option for the poor, it would not supply ready answers for all circumstances.

3. *Christians may find a particular challenge coming from Marxism in the period after power has been taken.* As noted above, the Marxism of Central American organizations has been largely indigenous and has been mainly used as an instrument of analysis and a guide for struggle. When a revolutionary group suddenly assumes responsibility for a government and seeks to extend its organizing efforts among the population, it finds that it needs many cadres. At this point, pressured by the needs of the moment, it may find itself reaching for "ready-made" Marxism in the forms of manuals imported from elsewhere rather than continuing to elaborate its own characteristic vision with a creative application of Marxism. In this context it is conceivable that Christians might be able to play a useful role by themselves participating in the effort to elaborate the kinds of materials needed: ongoing theoretical studies and pedagogical materials, always with the pur-

pose of providing tools that will enable the people increasingly to become protagonists in shaping their own destiny. An indispensable prior step is competence among Christians in understanding Marxism itself, both in Marx and in its various historical embodiments in theory and realization, and in understanding other social-science currents and relevant history in general, as well as skill in preparing suitable pedagogical materials. To take one field: a revolution must confront the task of adapting educational curricula to make them apt for a society in revolutionary transformation. For such an enormous task there is an obvious temptation to borrow something elaborated elsewhere rather than to be creative. Christians may be able to help Marxist movements maintain their original creativity.

4. *Similarly, a revolution inevitably throws many aspects of life into question, and part of the church's pedagogical role should be to help people understand the changes taking place from a perspective of faith.* There is accordingly a need for new pedagogical and catechetical materials. The diocese of Estelí, for example, developed a catechetical manual called "Paths of Liberation," using the exodus as a unifying motif, but incorporating into its ten lessons around the biblical events a series of statements and examples not only from episcopal documents and individual bishops but from Nicaraguan history and from the FSLN. While there might be a danger of syncretism or of seeking to give the revolution a religious legitimation that it does not require, in principle such a catechetical program is simply seeking to be incarnate in the process of the history that the people are experiencing.

5. *The "education of popular religiosity" is a way in which the church might affirm its identity within a revolutionary process* (as has been suggested above). In Nicaragua the vast majority of the people have participated in the revolution motivated partly, if implicitly, by their Christian faith: the Nicaraguan people are "Christian and Sandinista." Thus the church and revolutionary Christians have a responsibility not only to the relatively small groups who participate in basic Christian communities, but to the "masses" whose relationship to the institutional church may be distant. There is a pastoral responsibility to help these "masses" reinterpret their inherited Christianity in the new context of the revolution; for example to understand Jesus not simply as defeated by human cruelty on the cross (something the poor traditionally saw from their own condition), but also as raised by God in vindication of his message and rising in human history (and not only promising a reward for poverty faithfully endured). Such a pedagogical process would require developing means suitable for reaching these "masses": traditional celebrations with a different orientation and even with a different style perhaps appropriating some of the style or feeling of a mass rally. (Readers should note that in Spanish *masas*, "masses," does not have an inherently pejorative cast, particularly in a revolutionary context—it simply means "majority").

6. *The basic Christian communities should be encouraged and they*

should increasingly become the basic pastoral unit. As they develop their own voice, and to the extent the church institution recognizes them they will help the whole church move toward becoming a church of the poor.

7. *Although the church should make a basic option for the poor, some pastoral attention should be given to the middle classes in order to help them make the conversion that the revolution demands.* These people have received a disproportionate attention from the church (through Catholic schools, parishes with a much higher ratio of clergy to people, middle-class apostolic movements) than the poor. Precisely for that reason these people may have internalized their relationship to the church institution more than the poor, who saw it as more remote. If the "revolutionary" pastoral agents all devote their exclusive attention to the poor, the middle classes will be left with those who are in opposition, who will then simply reinforce their own reaction to the revolution. What is required, therefore, is some pastoral attention that would provide a pedagogical process whereby those people open to conversion might be accompanied and aided. Such a pastoral effort might be justified both out of concern for middle-class people who sincerely want to grow in their faith, and in the interests of the poor, to avoid making the church a refuge of the disgruntled bourgeoisie and the source of ideological ammunition for their attacks on the revolution.

8. *There are signs that the revolution brings a "secularization."* For example, many of those who were deeply involved in the communities of Solentiname and barrio Rigueiro went on to occupy important posts in the FSLN. Almost all of them seemed to arrive at a point where they no longer saw themselves as Christians. Curiously, however, when pressed they seemed to have second thoughts, to doubt their doubting, so to speak. While the usual case might be that of university graduates, there were also indications that some people from the popular classes were beginning to drop some of their traditional practices (for example, a sergeant in the Sandinista army who decided not to have his child baptized).

It would seem that these people went through a process in which first they reinterpreted their inherited faith in terms of commitment to the poor, to the "people." In this connection it might be useful to recall some of the expressions from the Solentiname dialogues of chapter 1, where in a sense the "people" was God, or Jesus was giving an "atheistic" interpretation of the Bible. If people were convinced that Christianity was simply love of neighbor, expressed in an efficacious way, and then if their whole energies were devoted to political and military struggle, and in fact they were less and less concerned with expressions of liturgy, prayer, and Scripture discussion, they might put their belief in Jesus or even God in brackets, since it would seem to have little direct bearing on their all-absorbing activity; little by little they might conclude that it made no difference whether they believed or not, and they might no longer consider themselves Christian believers. Seeing the official church as in fact serving the counter-revolution might accelerate this process. At the same time they might see the whole question of belief/disbelief as more suspended than completely decided.

If this is a fair description of a common process, does it constitute a challenge to believing Christians? It would be well to define precisely what the challenge is.

First, the problem is not simply one of "keeping" people "in the church." The underlying theology that the church is to serve the kingdom remains valid. This does not mean that it is a matter of indifference whether people believe or not—for politically committed Christians the gospel should not only reveal the "hidden meaning" and depth of life, but also give energies for the demanding tasks of the present. Nevertheless, it is possible that the "secularization" accompanying revolutionary change may in itself signify that faith will be more of a free and personal act. This should not lead to a defeatist attitude that the church is destined to become a tiny diaspora community.

Second, one task would be that of helping people not to be driven to abandon their faith because they identify sectors of the church with the counter-revolution; hence the pastoral importance of other communities in the church. Even if basic Christian communities remain a minority phenomenon, they may be a "sign" to many others, who independently may see in them some motivation for interpreting their own life in a Christian way.

Third, and most fundamental, the aim should be neither to "keep" people in the church nor to launch them onto the sea of secularity, but to maintain an evangelizing presence, that is, to help individuals and groups hear the message of the gospel in a form adapted to their experience. It is quite possible that if there is a serious effort at evangelization within the revolutionary process, the final result will be something different both from the traditional forms of faith tied to Latin American culture, and from the secularization associated with the North Atlantic experience (whatever be the exact sociological and theological interpretation of the phenomenon and the importance attached to it).

9. *The possibility of a revolution becoming a new oppression is not utterly discounted* (even though the stress here has been on a critical support for the revolution). Christians should be vigilant not only about that ultimate possibility, but also particular developments that could eventually turn out to be steps in that direction.

THE UNITY OF THE CHURCH

In the final section of this treatment of issues in church practice and ecclesiology, I shall be dealing with the "hierarchical ministry" and the "popular church." As an introduction to this section a brief reflection on church unity, and criteria for it, may be useful.

Problems of unity, both in ecumenism between churches and over divisive issues within the church, have been characteristic of our time, especially since Vatican II. Such problems have spurred renewed research into ecclesiology, which has reflected on questions of pluralism and confict in the church going back to apostolic times.

Today's questions, however, are not simply repetitions of historical controversies. In Latin America especially, divisions arise (or become manifest) not over doctrine but over practice. Moreover—and here Latin America is clearly different from North America and Europe—the issues are fundamentally not over internal church matters but about society. Issues that in the United States have aroused passion (church authority, contraception, celibacy, women's ordination) are largely not issues of concern in Latin America, at least when compared to the response to be made to oppressive conditions and repressive governments.

In Central America, as amply evidenced in chapters 4 through 8, the issue of what stance to take has provoked clear divisions between groups "below" and those "above." The divisions have been so sharp that there have been public divisions in the episcopacies: in El Salvador, Archbishop Romero's third pastoral letter, countered by the "Declaration" of the other four bishops; and in Guatemala, disputes between Cardinal Casariego and other bishops over the unauthorized changes made in a pastoral letter from the Bishops Conference, and later, Bishop Manresa's attempt to force the Vatican to choose between this group and Casariego (by accepting Manresa's resignation, the Vatican favored Casariego).

Bishops may attempt to achieve unity simply by invoking their authority, although it may be clothed in biblical or postconciliar language (as when they described their authority as a "service of unity"). However, there are serious limitations, both pragmatic and theological, to making episcopal authority the main source of unity. On a practical level, bishops can effectively use their own authority only over those whom they can sanction (they can order a priest to move, or put pressure on the superior of a religious order to move its personnel, but can have little direct power over lay people). Their power can only control externals and public behavior (they may be able to curb what seem to be unorthodox statements in sermons, but they cannot control thinking or private expression).

Besides these practical limits, there are theological limits on the episcopal role. Bishops are, as stated previously, one particular element in the church, the group charged with oversight. It is normal, and in practice inevitable, that inspiration for how the church should respond to particular challenges in history will come not primarily from the bishops but from those most in contact with society and its problems. A proper role for bishops is to "oversee" the process of discernment but not to predetermine it by invoking episcopal authority for their own particular perceptions. For the specific case at hand: the bishops in themselves have no particular authority for judging the basic ethical legitimacy of a revolutionary *proyecto*; it is the people, and especially the poor, who should weigh its merits and decide, in a process that will inevitably take time. The bishops should promote a process of dialogue and might sometimes serve as the voice of the people, but they should not prematurely close the process of discernment.

It is helpful to keep in mind three theological criteria in striving for church unity:

1. *The church is not the kingdom but is to serve the kingdom*. This principle, frequently cited in Latin American theology, means that God's grace is wider than the church, that God's purpose is being fulfilled in history wherever people are growing in love and justice, and that the church should seek to discern where partial realizations of the kingdom may be found and encourage their growth. While such a perspective has been part of official church teaching since Vatican II, it is still tempting to confuse the advance of the church with the advance of God's purposes.

As applied to the question of unity, this principle means that the unity God wants is not simply harmony in the church under hierarchical authority but, rather, a much more difficult unity among humankind, which demands the ending of gross extremes of wealth and poverty maintained by force. Only in striving for that unity of the human family will the church find the deep kind of unity to which it is called.

2. *The road to church unity passes through an option for the poor*. If this option produces symptoms of disunity in the form of conflicts within the church, it is mainly a sign of the need for conversion. The church will also be judged on what it did "for the least of my brothers and sisters" (cf. Matthew 25).

3. *In a divided society it is likely that the church will also be divided, if it is incarnate in that society*. The unity of the church must then be seen as a process (unless of course it were totally identified with one side), something to be achieved in the course of achieving a greater unity in society.

These considerations are not meant to minimize the deep roots of unity found in the Bible: unity in the Spirit and in the body of Christ, but rather, to indicate the kinds of "mediations" this unification process must pass through.

Clearly the foregoing notes would not prove convincing to anyone who had a different perspective on church unity. They are meant more as an articulation of some of the underlying notions of unity from the theological-pastoral point of view held by many committed Central American Christians.

Episcopal Ministry

Although the activity of the bishops has been treated in connection with particular issues, at this point I would like to examine it as a whole. As a method, I propose to summarize the actions of the bishops in Nicaragua, El Salvador, and Guatemala, and then to examine the special case of Archbishop Romero, not primarily to judge the particular individuals occupying Central American episcopacies but to see what may be learned from this recent experience.

To introduce the discussion I find it useful to recall the portrait of a bishop sketched by the bishops themselves at Vatican II, the theology of the episcopacy being one of the themes most developed at the council. Bishops are united to their flocks by "the gospel and the Eucharist" and should be "witnesses of Christ before all men" and should "expound the whole mystery of Christ," which includes showing "that earthly goods and human institutions, structured according to the plan of God the Creator are also related to man's salvation. . . ." They list these realities, starting with the human person and freedom, and ending with "the very grave questions concerning the ownership, increase and just distribution of material goods, peace and war, and brotherly relations among all peoples." Episcopal teaching should be presented in a "manner adapted to the needs of the times." The bishop should "stand in the midst of his people as one who serves, . . . a good shepherd who knows his sheep and whose sheep know him." He should be concerned about gathering the whole flock and should have a particularly close relationship with his priests.[15]

What Vatican II did not envision, of course, was a conflictive situation emerging from structural injustice and the violence used against organized protest. In passing, I would note that I find no substantial progress in Puebla's treatment of bishops and, what is more revealing, little hint that bishops might have a special role in such conflictive situations.[16]

The question to be asked here is how the bishops, individually and in their conferences, have carried out their role in the conflictive circumstances of Central America, more specifically, how they have carried out the "preferential option for the poor," and more pointedly yet, what posture they have taken toward those "revolutionary *proyectos*" possibly promising liberation for the poor.

The Nicaraguan bishops both before and after the fall of Somoza took positions quite similar to the anti-Somoza (and later anti-Sandinista) bourgeoisie (see chapters 4 and 8, above). As far back as the early 1970s they began to abandon the traditional support for (or at least acquiescence to) the dictatorship; in 1974, for example, at almost the same period as an opposition group made a slogan of "There's no one to vote for," the bishops produced a pastoral letter on politics, one of whose statements was a somewhat more obscure formulation of the same position. They did in effect "endorse" the insurrection by speaking of a just insurrection at the time that the Sandinista final offensive was getting underway, and they produced a pastoral letter in November 1979 with a profound theological and pastoral reflection on the revolution. However, within a month after the first clear break of the bourgeoisie with the Sandinista government (Alfonso Robelo's resignation from the Junta), the bishops gave a sign of a similar "break" (ordering the priests in the government to return to pastoral duties). It may be that such parallels were unconscious on the part of the bishops, but they were perceived and utilized by anti-Sandinista sectors (particularly *La Prensa*), and it seemed clear that the United States government saw the bishops as an ally, mentioning them in the same breath as the private sector and *La Prensa*.[17]

It should be mentioned that individually some of the bishops differed from the Bishops Conference. Bishop Rubén López Ardón of Estelí clearly followed his own line, and his clergy and pastoral agents were as a group more integrated into the revolution. Similarly, one or two of the other bishops had more nuanced positions, but the conference as such took a line distinguishable from the middle-class opposition parties only by its use of scriptural and ecclesiastical language.

What most distinguishes the case of El Salvador—the ministry of Archbishop Romero—will receive special treatment. His example and influence radiated to the whole country and partly offset the clearly opposite position taken by the episcopacy as a whole. After his death some of the other bishops became even more active and vocal in their public support for the government, for United States military aid, and for the United States-imposed elections. Archbishop Rivera y Damas, for his part, sought to maintain a somewhat distinct line, which he regarded as in the middle, by criticizing the abuses of the Salvadoran official forces, opposing outside involvement, and favoring a negotiated solution. He was hampered by being isolated (40 percent of his clergy, by one count, had either been killed or were in exile), by his own temperament (which was not suited for tension-filled conflicts), and by his nonconfirmation by the Vatican, a permanent sword of Damocles, so to speak. The net result was that, after the death of Archbishop Romero, the hierarchy took no clear position, and as a whole had to be judged a party to the government's policies of repression in defense of the interests of the elites and of United States policy.

Guatemala presented a reverse image of El Salvador: rather than one archbishop defending the poor in contrast to the episcopacy as a body, one archbishop, Cardinal Casariego, was able to neutralize the efforts of roughly half the episcopacy to take a clearer stand in defense of human rights. Murder and terrorism as routine government instruments began in Guatemala during the 1960s, but the hierarchy was largely silent, and Casariego managed to neutralize efforts at a unified pastoral response and movements for unity among the clergy. There was one strong pastoral letter in 1976, a frustrated attempt at a statement in 1978, but only in 1980–82 did the Bishops Conference make clear statements, starting with the killing of priests and pastoral agents, but coming to denounce the massacres of Indians as "genocide." Some bishops in their individual dioceses were supportive of their clergy, and largely for this reason Bishop Gerardi was forced to leave Guatemala after an attempt on his life failed.

Given the extreme and indiscriminate use of violence in Guatemala, one should be reserved in passing judgment on the bishops. I would only assert that the combination of violence and the persistent neutralizing efforts of Cardinal Casariego were effective in reducing the witness of the bishops to a relatively low level.

While much of the story must remain unknown, it would seem that the Vatican must share the responsibility for the absence of a clear-cut witness in favor of the poor in El Salvador and Guatemala. Since the advent of the Sandinista government, Vatican policy toward Nicaragua seems to be tempered by the pragmatic recognition that the Sandinista government is in power and is not likely to be dislodged; hence, while not supporting the revolutionary aims out of principle, and while some forces in the Vatican oppose the revolutionary regime, an important current in the Vatican seems to favor realistic accommodation.

This overall judgment is not meant to be a condemnation of the bishops either individually or collectively. It is not meant to say they have consistently acted badly. They have at times made statements and taken actions, as we have seen. But it does seem clear that they have not made a consistent defense of the poor in defiance of those forces exploiting and ultimately attacking them. To a great extent they have acted as a result of their previous formation and experience; they have been conditioned by the kinds of elite contacts that bishops tend to have and partly motivated by a fear that was indeed realistic. This is simply another way of saying that the bishops taken as a group have not overcome their conditioning and practiced heroic virtue.

Against this background the example of Archbishop Oscar Romero assumes greater relevance. Already known to some extent through news accounts and books, he will no doubt continue to grow in stature. His words were chosen as a leitmotiv for these reflections, not only for their own value but because Romero preeminently embodied what has happened in the Central American church. Several ways of analyzing Romero's work come to mind: his evolution and growth, shifts in pastoral emphasis, his application and extension of the church's social teaching, the theological structure present, explicitly and implicitly, in his thought. Here I would like to focus on his episcopal ministry in the conflictive circumstances of El Salvador.

Although he had been designated in part because he was considered "safe" (as opposed to Bishop Rivera y Damas, then considered the most "progressive" Salvadoran bishop), Romero was thrust into the major crisis of 1977. He was consecrated bishop between the fraudulent election and the February 28 massacre, shortly before the killing of Rutilio Grande and Alfonso Navarro, the expulsion of many priests, the first military operation against the people of Aguilares, and the repeated threats from the oligarchy and right-wing groups. His own conceptual training and background did not prepare him for dealing with such a crisis, but he had a basic openness, honesty, simplicity, and faith, which overcame the shortcomings of his inherited ideas.

Romero did not work alone and was in no sense an isolated "prophet." From his first days in office he emphasized consultation with people, starting with his clergy. Plácido Erdozaín points to the significance of the archdiocesan cafeteria, set up in the chancery office, to encourage clergy and others to come together. The fact that the chancery office was located in the seminary complex made it easy for large groups to assemble there.

Peasants and other poor people found it easy to gain access to Archbishop Romero, and groups of them were always arriving to recount their experiences. It was this direct access to people's pain and anguish that gave his statements their authority. At the same time he used the documentation and analysis prepared by the Legal Aid Office as well as by the Secretariat of Social Communications and other sources (the archdiocesan Human Rights Commission, made up of prominent lay people, which antedated the Salvadoran Human Rights Commission).

Occasional voices have been raised seeking to minimize Romero's place by pointing out that his decisions and his sermons were not his but those of a whole group. This was indeed so: his Sunday sermons were painstakingly prepared the day before with the collaboration of a team of priests and sisters and lay people, who discussed the overall message; theologians, who helped to prepare the biblical commentary; and others, who helped with social analysis and factual documentation. However, despite the fact that some of the statements may have been drafted by other individuals or a group, Romero assumed those statements, and in doing so he was exemplifying the episcopal ministry as much as a bishop who composes his own texts.

From the first days of his episcopate Romero sought to put church institutions at the service of the people: he suspended his first pastoral meeting, in the midst of the 1977 election crisis, suggesting that the priests return and be ready to receive in their houses those who might be fleeing for their lives. Later on archdiocesan institutions such as *Orientación* (the weekly paper), the Legal Aid Office, and the church buildings themselves were increasingly seen as at the service of the poor and of those who were struggling for justice. During Romero's final days, the first refugees—a product of the military actions in the countryside accompanying the beginning of the "land reform"—were taken under the roof of the seminary/chancery office and other church institutions.

Romero did not seek controversy and his manner was almost always reconciliatory. Although he must have been pained by the attitude of the other bishops, he refrained from even a veiled criticism of them in public and simply sought to assure his own good standing with the pope. Similarly, he repeatedly sought to find ways of urging some peaceful path to the solution of the country's problems and he tried to find points on which to commend the government.

Inevitably Archbishop Romero was seen as meddling in politics. Although he was specific and clear in his judgments and condemnations, I find that he always spoke from an evangelizing viewpoint. To take only the most dramatic example, his exhortation to the soldiers not to shoot the peasants, their brothers and sisters, had a political resonance—but it was at the same time simply a reiteration of the Fifth Commandment.

In the most formal statement of his final weeks, his speech at Louvain, Romero stressed that the way to maintain the church's "transcendence" and "identity" was precisely by being involved with the poor, in their world, and from there to promote "those movements of liberation that really lead to justice . . . and peace for the majority." Modifying the ancient formula *Gloria Dei, vivens homo* to *Gloria Dei vivens pauper* ("The glory of God is the poor person alive"), he said:

> We believe that it is from the transcendence of the gospel that we can judge what life for the poor really means; and we also believe that by placing ourselves on the side of the poor person and trying to give him or her life, we may know what the eternal truth of the gospel means.[18]

In a long essay Jon Sobrino has systematically developed the notion that Romero was a prophet, by drawing up the biblical description of a prophet and verifying those characteristics in Romero. A prophet "directly proclaims God's will on what happens in history in all its cultural, social, economic, and political complexity." Prophecy is about the "life and death of human beings." He makes a detailed comparison between Romero's life activity and that of the Old Testament prophets.[19]

This notion of "prophet" may offer another way of seeing why Romero is an exception. Prophecy is not incompatible with the episcopacy, but it is in no sense connected with the office. While it may be traditional to speak of the roles of priest, king, and prophet, the latter is used in the sense of teaching, which is quite at variance with the biblical notion of prophet as the one who brings surprises, and often unwelcome news.

Archbishop Oscar Romero's episcopal ministry was not "normal" either in the demands it made or in his responses. It offers nevertheless powerful suggestions of how such a ministry can indeed serve a church of the poor.

Summing up: the bishops have varied from tacit and open support for the groups in power to a sporadic and sometimes courageous condemnation of official repression. Some bishops at the local level have been quietly supportive of their committed clergy and sisters. In Guatemala even this level of activity has brought them persecution. It seems to be most difficult for the bishops to take the step from an abstract advocacy of the poor and a condemnation of abuses to an acceptance of a given *proyecto* as embodying liberation for the poor and therefore being a logical consequence of the option for the poor. This difficulty seems to derive both from an ingrained repugnance for Marxism in any of its forms and a tendency to see themselves (being "ministers of unity") as somehow above the conflict in society, and from the conditioning of their own social background and a not unreasonable fear. In my judgment the net effect is an inadequate evangelizing presence from the bishops. Archbishop Romero was the one bishop willing to accompany the people pastorally, not by endorsing particular organizations, but by encouraging the "popular alternative" in the conflictive circumstances of El Salvador toward the end of his life. He was much more in contact both with his pastoral agents and with the poor than the other bishops were, and he clearly put the whole church, including its institutions and material resources, at the service of the poor and their organizations. At the same time, Romero's presence was the most evangelizing both in his words (right up to his ringing command, "Thou shalt not kill") and his attitude and actions, being willing to die, and at the end pardoning his murderers.

Iglesia Popular—*"People's Church"*

Yves Congar's *Lay People in the Church* was first published in 1953. His theology of the laity was in fact an ecclesiology aimed at overcoming the prevailing "hierarchology." Some of Congar's own positions may have been surpassed in the meantime, but his was a major contribution toward what became a renewed ecclesiology at Vatican II. Although clericalism is alive and well in Catholic church practice, there is at least a doctrinal foundation for a basic equality of Christians, with differing charisms, of which one is that of leadership. The problem is not so much of theology as of ingrained clericalism and the slowness of institutional change. It is doubtful that anyone would now write a "theology of the laity."

Such an analogy comes to mind when considering the term *iglesia popular*, which has been used widely in Latin America. Understanding the term requires an understanding of the Spanish *el pueblo*: literally it means "the people," but with two connotations not usual in English: (1) *el pueblo* has much more the sense of a collective reality, as an actor in history, and (2) *el pueblo* means especially the poor majority: the poor are the purest form of "the people." The notion can, of course, be used demagogically. In any case, *iglesia popular* denotes a "people's church," with the association understood as reaching out to the broad masses of the poor.

Just as Congar wrote his theology of the laity, inspired by a sense of what the actual church was not and should aim at being, the term *iglesia popular* is symptomatic, first, of a sense of something missing—that the existing Catholic church is not a church of the broad masses of the poor.

Yet there are significant beginnings, especially in the basic Christian communities throughout Latin America. The term "popular church" itself seems to have emerged from a national conference of such communities in Brazil in 1976, out of a process of discussion and a discovery that the people meeting there constituted a new kind of "church of the people." In March 1978 a small group of theologians and pastoralists meeting in Caracas, Venezuela, produced two documents on the topic: one with something of a manifesto tone, "A Good News: The Church Is Being Born from within the

Latin American People,'' and a second, more reflective, "The Church Being Born from the People: Reflections and Problems.''[20]

Both these documents were aimed partly at the Puebla Conference. Even prior to the meeting, the proponents of the term *iglesia popular* had been accused of denying or ignoring that the church is born "from above," from the Spirit, and not from any particular class, and also of seeking to oppose the "popular" to the official church. Prior to Puebla, Pope John Paul II warned of the dangers of the term (probably taking his cue from the dominant conservative sector of CELAM). Thus it was not surprising when the conference itself saw the term as "unfortunate" and echoed the criticisms, while stopping short of condemning the term itself.

Terminologically, then, *iglesia popular*, "people's church," has some disadvantages. For this reason, Christian groups in Nicaragua, at one time at least, preferred not to use the words. By contrast, in El Salvador after the killing of Archbishop Romero, a network of basic Christian communities called itself the National Council of the People's Church (CONIP), although Romero himself did not use the term. More important than the term itself is what it represents: a conviction that the church should be rooted in the poor, or find its center of gravity there; that the existing church is not so rooted; and that there are important beginnings of such a church.

One might think that "popular church" simply designates basic Christian communities, but this is not the case. Certainly they are a manifestation of what is meant, but there is a clear sense that the "people's church" includes more than these communities. One of the documents mentioned above speaks of a "new way of living the church in Latin America":

> It is something that is there, small and humble, still weak and newborn. Basic Christian communities in Brazil, popular communities in Peru, Christian reflection groups in Chile and Uruguay, peasant movements in Mexico, Paraguay, Central America, and Ecuador, Christian groups in the barrios of Argentina, Venezuela, and Colombia, youth groups in Bolivia . . . . And so many others in other countries.
>
> These groups are formed among the poor and among those who have allowed themselves to be evangelized by the poor. They have arisen in different ways and have taken different paths. And they have taken form as church, a concrete way of being church in our situation.[21]

From this passage and others it is clear that the authors see a vast movement taking place throughout the continent, and they see it as all in some sense the popular church. They elaborate their sense more theologically when they speak of a "first ecclesiality," namely, the real life of Christian men and women who in solidarity with the people find their ultimate Christian identity in becoming a church of the poor. From this fundamental ecclesiality stems a second ecclesiality, "the organic configuration of this church of the poor in doctrinal, sacramental, administrative, and hierarchical structures,'' which take their meaning from the basic ecclesiality.

These documents reflect a certain shift in how the poor are seen pastorally and theologically. During the 1960s, roughly speaking, there was a tendency among some of those seeking new pastoral forms to take the position that despite the fact that almost everyone was baptized and all regarded themselves as Catholics, in a real sense the church did not exist in Latin America because there was little adult conversion and because the church did not exist in the form of a community along the lines laid down in the New Testament. Hence the task was not simply to ''improve'' or ''renew'' the church's pastoral work but, more radically, to set up the church: to call people to form the church as a small community, which could be a ''sign'' over against the larger community.

Implied in the notion of a popular church is a critique of such a pastoral approach and particularly its assumptions. First, that earlier attitude is seen as ''blaming the victim,'' that is, blaming the people for not being the church, when it would be more valid to blame the church for not being of the poor. Second, there is now a recognition that some pastoral agents were bringing to the people a preconceived model of what the church ought to be (even if it was a basic Christian community and derived from the New Testament) and were requiring people to conform to that particular model or not be the church. Third, and in a more positive sense, the critique recognized that there is a good deal of the reality of the church in the actual life of the poor, their openness and generosity, their solidarity, their poverty itself— which is what the church is to be—and that this is not simply ''anonymous Christianity'' but often had explicitly Christian motivation. As was said in Nicaragua, ''The Nicaraguan people are Christian and Sandinista.''

Summing up thus far I would say that there are three main intuitions: (1) that already in the Latin American people there is a good deal of the substance of the church; (2) that today this is increasingly taking on organic form in a variety of ways, not only in basic Christian communities but even in popular movements, and (3) that those who wish to be Christian (and this includes the official church) must find their center of gravity in this church of the poor, or popular church, which is still being born, and consequently that much of what the popular church means has yet to appear.

Jon Sobrino, in an essay titled ''Resurrection of a Popular Church,'' ranges over a number of themes that actually constitute an overview of an ecclesiology of such a church. Here I would like to single out his reflection on the traditional ''notes'' of the church from this new perspective. He sees unity as being achieved around the poor. At the same time the church of the poor brings about division, not between hierarchy and laity (as in some other perspectives), but between the church of the powerful and the church of the poor. Sanctity for the church of the poor means being a servant and seeking justice, and from that perspective the sin of the church is revealed. Catholicity is being achieved as the Latin American church discovers its identity as a church of the poor in communion with the poor elsewhere in the third world: a universal church of the poor. Ecumenism cannot mean simply linking confessions but must pass through service to the poor. Regarding apostolicity there is something new in that evangelization is seen as mutual: the poor also evangelize the church.[22]

If, within a generation, the Latin American church becomes centered in the poor, today's sketches of a theology of the popular church may come to resemble Congar's *Jalons* of the 1950s.

11

The God of Life

. . . either we believe in a God of life or we serve the idols of death.
—Archbishop Romero

I here propose to look at a few themes of theology in Central America. They will not be an utterly new topic but an effort to find an expression of what is ultimately at stake from a Christian point of view. If my own efforts to get at this theological core prove superficial or anticlimatic I would encourage others to make up the deficiency.

Its detractors sometimes claim that Latin American liberation theology is not theology at all but an infiltration of Marxism using theological symbols. In so doing they prove that they have not read Gutiérrez, Segundo, Boff, Sobrino, and others with any attention, for whatever else may be said about their work they are concerned with the traditional themes of sin and grace, the church, Jesus Christ, and the ultimate mystery of God. The strength of liberation theology derives precisely from its quality as theology—reflection on God and God's ways with humankind—as seen from a context of struggle to overcome oppression. What launched the broad peasant movement in El Salvador was largely the pastoral work of basic Christian communities. Even under conditions of war, peasants were still drawing inspiration from the Bible in Guatemala and El Salvador. The underlying religious vision was not created by the theologians, nor was it entirely the work of peasants and their pastors; rather, theologians have been stimulated by pastoral problems arising from pastoral practice and they have made their contribution to the religious vision itself.

As a way of characterizing this theology I would like briefly to compare its overall *proyecto* with that of Karl Rahner's theology because his whole theology is a continual combination and variation of a few basic themes. From his earliest philosophical works, through his hundreds (even thousands) of essays and up to their recapitulation, after a fashion, in *Foundations of Christian Faith*, Rahner's work is of a piece. A few basic notions of philosophical anthropology form a core to which he always returns: the human being as subject, in freedom, open to ultimate mystery;

375

God who is present offering his own self-communication. Any particular human act of knowledge or love already involves a "prethematic" grasp of being, and hence of the ultimate mystery of God. Any particular theological issue—from humanity's "obediential potency" for the hypostatic union, to the meaning of Christ in an evolutionary framework, to the meaning of the eschatological images in Scripture, to the sacraments, to the meaning of death—tends to bring Rahner back to this theological-philosophical core, which in his usage proves extraordinarily fruitful.[1]

His enterprise seems to derive from several basic sources, or inspirations.

1. As a "revisioning" of St. Thomas Aquinas through the prism of modern philosophy (Heidegger), Rahner's theology is "transitional" for the Catholic church, helping it to move to modernity without jettisoning its tradition (for example, *Spirit in the World* originates in a detailed commentary on one question in the *Summa*).
2. Rahner has continually responded to pastoral questions, showing an uncanny ability to root them in his original philosophical matrix (from genetic manipulation to the frequency with which Mass should be celebrated).
3. His work can be seen as an effort to make Christianity intelligible to people today, not in the sense that his meaning is simple, but rather, that methodologically he has sought to point to what is essential in Christianity, not through a "demythologizing" style of "peeling away" what might seem outdated but by refocusing on the essence of Christianity.
4. Evidently besides being an intellectual endeavor, Rahner's work is the elaboration of a religious, even mystical, vision, which also accounts for its power and simplicity.

Although part of Rahner's anthropology is that the human being is social and historical and these dimensions sometimes enter into his "a priori" considerations, the root religious experience tends to be that of the individual human being, before God, confronting absolute mystery in silence.

This suggests a starting point for a comparison with Latin American theology. First, the reference point is much more clearly a group, and in a sense, a people—in the full sense given *pueblo* in Spanish—rather than simply an individual before God. The originating religious experience is collective. Its reference points are more immediately biblical: the Exodus and the historical Jesus, as well as his paschal mystery. Like Rahner, this theology tends to return to a few basic themes, such as the mission of the church to serve the kingdom.

Some of the following points of comparison can be made:

1. Latin American theology is primarily concerned with what is to be *done* and to this end seeks to illuminate the pastoral and political options of individuals, communities, and the church.

2. Latin American theology seeks not so much to make Christian faith intelligible but to help the church evangelize and itself be evangelized by the poor.
3. Latin American theology is biblical, finding its center in the historical Jesus and his death/resurrection, as well as motifs of exodus, creation, the prophets, and so forth. This rooting in the Bible may be seen as naive (some have said neo-orthodox). Neither defending the literal truth, nor demythologizing, nor remythologizing has in itself been a central concern.
4. Much of this theology is occasional and a response to urgent pastoral questions, for example, the hundreds of articles and position papers generated prior to the Puebla Conference.
5. This theology may be "transitional" if it prepares the church to move into noncapitalist societies.

This not entirely symmetrical comparison is meant only to illustrate the nature of the Latin American theological enterprise by comparing it to the work of the most outstanding North Atlantic Catholic theologian.

Central America, starting from the mid-1970s, has been a focal point for the development of Latin American theology.[2] Much of the writing has appeared in scattered articles. In what follows I would like to develop some of its major themes, in some cases with elaborations of my own.

DIVINITIES IN CONFLICT

In Central America the "problem of God" is not atheism (the question of how to make God "intelligible" in a secularized world), or even how to deal with the element of unbelief inside oneself (the doubt deep down: Does it make a difference whether I believe in God or not?). Certainly there are occasional unbelievers, and especially among those committed to revolutionary struggle. But normally belief in God is assumed. Even more, those groups in power believe they are defending "Western *Christian* civilization" against (atheistic) communism. Although the oligarchy and the military feel somewhat betrayed by the church in recent years, they can still find bishops and clergy to support them, and they themselves invoke the name of God freely. In Guatemala General Ríos Montt gave weekly talks on television in which he intermingled elements of preaching, prayer, and threats to annihilate the guerrilla opposition; there was a similar admixture at the local level in the counterinsurgency campaign.

Both sides in the struggle see their involvement in religious terms. One might be inclined to see it as simply a case of drawing opposite conclusions from the same premises or starting point: people believing in the same Christian God but differing in their ethical perceptions. Central American theologians, however, insist that the issue goes deeper, to the very conception of God. God as conceived by those in power is incompatible with the vision of a God of the poor. If God hears the cry of the poor, the God invoked by those bringing death to the poor is an idol, even if he is invoked in Christian terms. Although the point is most evident when God is specifically invoked, there is a quality of idolatry even when no specific Christian justification is given: something (the wealth of the oligarchy, or military rule, or United States policy) is being treated as an absolute—over the life of the poor.

The problem of God, then, is seen not as a struggle between belief and unbelief but as a struggle between rival divinities, between the "Living God" and idols. Central American (and Latin American) theologians are seeing idolatry as a *theological* category. Used metaphorically in preaching, we are familiar with idolatry in this sense, for example, the idolatry implicit in building nuclear arsenals. However, idolatry does not seem to be a category of analysis in serious North Atlantic theology. In standard theological and scriptural reference books, idolatry is seen to be a phenomenon of the ancient world or is even treated apologetically in defending the legitimacy of "venerating" saints' images.[3]

It would seem that idolatry is viewed as representing a stage of "primitive" religion, which has been long since outgrown. Even in the Bible there is a progression from an earlier phase when the Israelites see "Yahweh" as *their* God (not disputing the existence of other gods) to a postexilic awareness that the gods of other people are "nothing," the product of human hands.

Nevertheless the gods were very much present in the New Testament world, and idolatry rather than nontheism forms the background of the early church. Paul not only mentions idolatry among the catalogues of sins (1 Corinthians 5:9–13; 6:9–11; Galatians 4:19–21) but understands it as a root of sin when he sees avarice as idolatry (Ephesians 5:5; Colossians 3:5),[4] and the idolatry of political power is clear in Revelation (chapters 13 and 17).

A renewed sensitivity to the possibility of idolatry may sharpen a vision of the New Testament. Sobrino has taken such a look in "The Appearance of the God of Life in Jesus of Nazareth."[5] Compressing too much, I would say that Sobrino's argument is that for Jesus, God's original plan is that human beings have life, in its full sense, and that the "eschatological horizon of his mission" is the kingdom, a kingdom of life for all and especially for those who have been excluded by certain groups of the privileged, the rich (Luke 6:24; 12:13–21), scribes and Pharisees (Luke 11:46ff.; 11:39–44), priests (Mark 11:15–39), and those who hold political power (Mark 10:42)—this last case is not so well developed as the others. While some of these passages seem to be focused on interior disposition (hypocrisy, for instance), Sobrino finds a common thread in that some are depriving others of life by oppressing them. Jesus condemns not only the fact that these things are done in the name of God, but the underlying oppression, diminishing the life of others, which is incompatible with the God of Jesus.

For example, regarding the Sabbath curing (Luke 13:10-17; 14:1-6; Mark 2:27; Matthew 12:8): although some people might think nothing should interfere with the Sabbath celebration, Jesus insists that "Any supposed manifestation of God's will which goes against the real life of people is the automatic negation of the deepest reality of God." What is at stake, accordingly, in the controversies is not differing legal or ethical conceptions but the understanding of the very reality of God. In his treatment of the chief commandment (Matthew 22:34-40; cf. Luke 10:25-28), Jesus makes it clear that the "professionals of the first commandment, priests and Levites," are not to use it as an excuse for not loving the neighbor.

For his defense of "the life of human beings as the fundamental mediation of the reality of God," Jesus is persecuted by those who "objectively invoke other divinities," namely, the leaders of the Jewish people. This is the origin of the either/or alternatives that Jesus pronounces: *(a)* on the human level, the "beatitudes and woes," (Luke 6), gaining or losing life; *(b)* on the Christological level, people with or against Jesus (Matthew 12:20); *(c)* on the theological level, God or mammon (Matthew 6:24). Sobrino says:

> The basic problem is that divinities are at odds. Their differing mediations are at odds. So their mediators are at odds. If Jesus' controversies show the alternatives, the persecution of Jesus shows that the alternatives are mutually exclusive. The false divinities and their mediators want to exclude and eliminate the mediator of the true divinity.[6]

Jesus was killed "in the name of God" because his vision of the kingdom conflicted both with the Jewish theocracy and with the Pax Romana (although the Gospel texts tend to lay all the responsibility on the Jewish leaders). Sobrino quotes Jürgen Moltmann:

> The history of Jesus which led to his crucifixion was rather a *theological history* in itself and was dominated by the conflict between God and the gods; that is, between the God whom Jesus preached as his Father, and the God of the law as he was understood by the guardians of the law, together with the political gods of the Roman occupying power.[7]

To summarize, the basic conflict in Jesus' life, which is at the center of the Gospel narrative, was not simply over the "ethical implications" of belief in the same God, but went to the very vision of God: on the one side a God of life and on the other a god for whom the life of the poor could be subordinated to the law, or to religious or civil authority.

Although his study is primarily theological, Sobrino clearly has in mind the situation of Latin America, where the efforts of the poor reach the desperation of life-or-death struggle and where the ruling groups are willing to use systematic killings of civilians as an instrument of policy. He is seeking a theological rooting for understanding what is happening.

Some might find all this highly disquieting. They might see it as having all the earmarks of "wars of religion," both sides claiming God was with them, and both killing others in the name of God, even a God of life. They might feel that the greatest dangers are those of absolutism and seeing any human situation in black-or-white terms, and hence be convinced that what is needed is not theologizing but "detheologizing."

I concede that any application of such life-or-death categories depends on whether it is accurate to say that (1) the oligarchical/military economies and political regimes systematically deprive the poor of life, (2) the nonviolent efforts of the poor to press for change have been met with systematic violence, so that (3) they have chosen to struggle for a new revolutionary *proyecto,* which will seek to place the life of the poor majority as its first priority, and (4) there is a very clear qualitative difference in the use of violence by both sides: the groups in power systematically kill all judged to be in opposition, and especially noncombatants, while the opposition groups target their violence at the official troops and at those who are directly responsible for violence to others (informers, for instance). If the foregoing is a fair description of the overall direction of events, it may be reasonable to say that one side embodies death and idolatry (even in name of the Christian God), and the other represents life and the God of life. If the previous statement is an inaccurate description (if the opposition groups have opted for violence when there were other reasonable possibilities for change or if their use of violence is little different from that of the official forces), then I would agree that it clearly runs the risk of all the vices associated with "wars of religion."

In any case, the point is not that God is on the side of the guerrilla groups, but that God is on the side of the poor and that what is at stake in the life of the poor is not simply an ethical exigency but the very nature of God.

SIN, CONVERSION, AND GRACE

Since the time of the Medellín Conference it has been common in Latin America to speak of "structures of sin" or "social sin"—and to a lesser extent, by a similar kind of logic, to speak of a "structural conversion." As Christians for the Revolution, a group in Nicaragua, put it: ". . . according to the faith of the church, the grace of Jesus Christ, his liberating and saving action, is not only something that happens inside the heart. Just as there is a sin that is structural and not simply personal, there are also times, processes, and situations of grace that affect the structures of society."[8]

I cannot find any conceptual elaboration of this intuition, which is nevertheless basic to a theological view of what has happened. Here I intend to offer some reflections on the social, or structural, aspects of sin, conversion, and grace, conscious that they are merely the beginning of what is required (which, at root, I suspect is a view of human nature, wherein the social is as integral as the personal, and not added on).

"Somocismo is sin" wrote Father Gaspar García as he explained his reasons for joining the FSLN as a combatant. García's lapidary statement may serve as a starting point for considering the social dimension of sin. Somocismo was a whole system maintained by four kinds of power: the National Guard, the Liberal party (which provided legitimacy and acted as a national patronage mechanism), enormous wealth (since the Somozas owned an ever increasing share of the economy), and the backing of the United States. Somoza's Nicaragua was a personal dictatorship: even relatively unimportant matters, such as minor appointments, went to the "Chief"; (it should be remembered that the population was about two million people and the political machinery was less complex than that of a major American city). Yet the "Chief" had many associates who shared in the administration and thereby in the spoils. The National Guard was a good example, since young men could rise from poor circumstances, become officers, and even enjoy a comfortable life, especially through the rampant corruption (some officers got a rakeoff from the collection of fines, others controlled vice).

Anyone living in Nicaragua found it impossible to ignore the Somoza system: Somoza was "omnipresent." Some, considering themselves realists, opted to work with the system, others sought to keep some distance, and a few openly opposed it.

From the outside during the late 1970s the Somoza dictatorship was seen as especially opprobrious, more so than the oligarchical/military regimes in Guatemala and El Salvador, which in fact have been more ruthless in their treatment of their populations than Somoza was. The difference seems to have been the appearance of some democracy, through a periodic rotation of presidents, assembly representatives, and so forth. Nevertheless there is a *system* of violence and corruption just as surely in these countries as in Nicaragua.

Such systems have always needed to employ some violence, and violence was always present as a threat (Salvadorans, for example, carried the memory of the 1932 massacre). During much of the 1950s and 1960s, and even the early 1970s, there were relatively low levels of violence. As the level of confrontation and of violence increased, as abduction, torture, mutilation, terrorism, bombing, and massacres became instruments of policy, these regimes were simply revealing what had been there all along—a willingness to resort to the most gross kinds of killing in order to maintain the overall system. A further component of such systems is a national network of informers and sometimes of paramilitary death squads (ORDEN and others in El Salvador, *comisionados militares* in Guatemala).

The most visible manifestations of violence are the uniformed troops or the gangs of thugs who carry out killings or intimidate the population. However, civilian politicians who either appoint or accede to the appointment of top military officers, business executives who give lists of union leaders to the police, "counterinsurgency advisers" who collaborate with governments, or the United States government that provides backing for such regimes (and in exceptional circumstances works to overthrow others, as in Guatemala in 1954)—all make up a vast network.

Some might see what I have been describing as simply manifesting a "culture of violence." A conventional political scientist might seek to explain it in terms of "authoritarianism" (rather like explaining the effects of opium by its "dormitive properties"). Marxist-influenced social scientists provide an analysis in terms of class and of the constraints put on vulnerable "peripheral" economies by imperialism.

Without discounting systematic social analysis, a Christian must see such regimes as embodying "systems of sin." In fact, a good analysis should help an understanding of how sin works, in the way that a scientific understanding of the cosmos enhances appreciation for the religious doctrine of creation.

To examine how such social sin "works," let us consider the case of a young Guatemalan Indian forcibly recruited, virtually kidnapped, into the army. He is trained to chant slogans like "Students are communists" and is taught that it would be his duty to turn in his mother if she were a "subversive." At the same time, he is given certain "benefits": regular pay (including $25 a month sent directly to his parents), a limited assimilation into the dominant culture, possibly literacy classes. He may also learn off-duty "soldierly" ways, such as drinking and frequenting prostitutes. After such training (or conditioning) he is sent to battle subversives and, since for every armed guerrilla there may be ten sympathizers or supporters, he is frequently told that all are subversives; soon he is participating in actions against the population, and may bully, rape, or kill people, or burn villages and fields in obedience to orders and in the name of counterinsurgency.

For traditional theology, the question of sin, if raised, would focus on this young man's subjective culpability for his actions: Are the conditions for a "human act" present? To what degree does he have sufficient freedom?

Elaborated largely with the confessional in mind, the theology of sin was focused on the action of an individual. It scarcely considered the kind of situation I have been describing: and, in fact, implicitly it would be viewed as simply a total sum of individual sins and their consequences—if the question were raised at all.

Certainly from the 1950s on, in Catholic theology there has been a movement away from analyzing single acts of sin toward a notion of a "basic option" in life, and in general a perspective much more oriented toward growth and process; and also a movement away from an extrinsic concept of sin (law) and toward one that is more intrinsic (love). (One of the by-products of post-Vatican II "Christian humanism" may be a lessened sense of sin; or, more accurately, while a somewhat infantile and inadequate concept of sin has been abandoned, no adequate new vision of sin in Christian theology has appeared.)

The rethinking of "original sin," seeing it as the "sin of the world" rather than as something transmitted physically through generation, undoubtedly offers further help. What the concept of "social sin" adds, I would suggest, is a willingness to identify the manifestations of the "sin of the world."

Nevertheless there seems to be some resistance to the notion, a feeling that social sin is sin only by "analogy" with sin in the most proper sense, the free action of an individual against a conscience declaring that the action is ethically wrong and ultimately an offense against God. The question that must be raised, however, is whether such an atomistic image of human behavior should not be replaced with one that is more social from the outset.

The notion of social sin suggests that the starting point for a theological (and pastoral) understanding of sin might be found in its social manifestation. Somocismo was sin because it corrupted, it made people dishonest, and it killed. Its power was such that to stand up to this sin required a rare heroism.

Although it may be desirable to develop a conceptual framework adequate to account for structural sin, a more urgent theological and pastoral task is that of identifying how social sin operates in particular circumstances.

It might be objected that the notion of "social sin" risks distorting the biblical message, because more important than defining sin is being aware of one's own sin and being converted. To the extent that the notion of "social sin" passed the onus of responsibility onto another group, the exploiters, it might seem to abandon a Christian notion of sin in the sense that overcoming structural sin would seem to mean overcoming oppression, namely, throwing off the oppressors (for example, Gaspar García's becoming a guerrilla in order to overcome the "sin" of Somocismo).

I would first point out that the notion of structural sin does not eliminate personal sin but, in the end, brings a more subtle notion, since such sin is in a way all-pervasive. If I wish to combat the "sin of Somocismo" I must first begin to root it out of myself, that is, examine my own complicities, which might be in collaboration (voting in Somoza-managed elections), or simply in omission (trying to stay uninvolved, out of trouble, which is like walking past the wounded Samaritan). Thus, correctly understood, the notion in no sense exonerates individuals but, rather, deepens a sense of how sin works in the world and in oneself.

The question of combating sin offers a natural transition to the consideration of conversion. The biblical renewal of the twentieth century has made "conversion" once more a central category. Where at one time the word may have conjured up experiences as dramatic as those of Paul or Ignatius Loyola, the stress is now on *metanoia* (change of mind and heart) as a permanent dimension of Christian life.

The Latin American bishops at Medellín seemed to say that personal conversion must precede structural change (Justice, no. 3). At Puebla conversion was not a major theme, but at one point the bishops said, "We affirm the need for conversion on the part of the whole Church to a preferential option for the poor, an option aimed at their integral liberation" (Final Document, no. 1134). In Central America and elsewhere it became common to specify that an option for the poor should mean an option for the *cause* of the poor and for that historical *proyecto* that will bring life to the poor.

There is then a kind of extension of the notion of conversion to one that is a collective "conversion of the church," and not simply to God but to an option for the poor. How is this notion of conversion similar to conversion in the classical sense?

One approach might be along the following lines. Conversion is never "purely interior": it always requires some "matter" in which it is expressed or embodied. It may be in changing a kind of behavior, such as giving up drinking or renouncing marital infidelity. Or a change might be more positive, such as deepening an existing marital relationship. Even in those cases where the conversion seems purely "religious" there is always some "matter"; for instance, joining a monastic order implies a whole structured way of life.

In the present case, an "option for the poor" then might be seen as the "matter" of a conversion to God. In chapter 5 there was an account of the basic Christian communities in El Salvador in the early 1970s, which described how people would leave meetings of the Christian communities and go to destroy a clandestine liquor still, or help a widow repair her house, or visit a sick neighbor and leave some gift. Participation in revolutionary organizations demands a degree of austerity, discipline, and willingness to accept criticism and hardships, which for pastoral agents has meant a conversion more demanding than their original entry into the religious life. Again, in Nicaragua those members of privileged classes who willingly accept the consequences of the revolution know their own privileges will be eroded, and in effect they must be converted. These are simply examples of the "matter" in which a conversion might be expressed (of course, many people might make an option for the poor, without it being a conscious religious conversion).

From another viewpoint, this view of conversion may involve and represent more of a novelty vis-à-vis tradition: a collective conversion ("conversion of the church"). At first glance the term "collective conversion" seems to be a contradiction: conversion seems to be quintessentially an act by which an individual person takes a stand over against the environment

(Luther's "Here I stand"). If many people are taking the same course, how can it have the radical quality of *metanoia*?

Let us illustrate with the example of a nation beginning a process of revolutionary structural change, which implies a whole shift in values (from competition toward cooperation, for example). In a real sense it must reflect a collective decision by the "people." There may be support in the form of official ideology (speeches, slogans, billboards) and policies (reducing differentials in pay scales). Nevertheless, the change itself requires myriad individual acts, which are personal as well as collective (one example: doctors who consider the alternative of leaving the country and encourage each other to stay, not for material incentives but to serve and to create a new kind of medical system). That there is an overall movement in a particular direction does not make it any less the product of many individual efforts.

To consider the question from another angle: What were the possibilities of a "conversion to the poor" under Somoza? Since the overall thrust of society went to serve the dictatorial system, there were few avenues for real service. Certainly some sisters or priests could go to live with the poor, some foreign development-workers might promote local projects, a few individuals in the interstices of the government bureaucracy might be able to do some good (a health worker or schoolteacher, for instance). All would be struggling against the current in isolation.

Under the Sandinista government the whole society at the official level is committed to working out an economic system according to "the logic of the majorities," which might be understood as another expression of a "preferential option for the poor." Such a change, however, will not come from decrees, laws, or policies alone, but necessarily involves changes in attitude and behavior of such a magnitude that they are, in Christian terms, "conversion."

Such a revolutionary situation not only permits more people to make an option, it challenges them to do so. Although there is a favorable climate—it is not the case of an isolated individual opting against a whole system—the personal element is by no means excluded.

This example suggests a rereading of the Medellín passage on conversion in an attempt to get beyond a sterile opposition between conversion of the heart and structural change:

> The originality of the Christian message does not consist directly in the affirmation of the need for a change in structures, but in its insistence on conversion of the individual, which then demands such change. We will not have a new continent without new and renewed structures; above all, there will be no new continent without new people, who know how to be truly free and responsible in the light of the gospel [Peace, no. 3].

Read superficially the text seems to insist on the logical and even sequential priority of personal conversion over structural change. It is perhaps more clear today than in 1968 that the change of structures will require the taking of power by movements representing the majority of the people and with their participation. (In itself such a taking of power need not be by violence, but experience thus far does not indicate a clear nonviolent course.) Such a taking of power cannot be postponed until all hearts are converted (whatever that might mean); and the taking of power, far from diminishing the importance of conversion, makes it more urgent, since such a change of attitude is an essential condition for carrying out a truly innovative revolution. Without conversion (whatever be the name given to it) a revolution would indeed degenerate into the advent of a ''new class'' to power.

This whole discussion has but one point, to explore the relationship between personal and collective conversion. Certainly the Bible presents God as exhorting the ''people'' to conversion throughout the Old Testament. Even in the New Testament, there is a collective dimension, as, for example, in the letters to the churches of Asia (Revelation, chapters 1-3). Here, as elsewhere, the Bible reflects a ''corporate'' sense of human life and action. In church history, conversion has often been embodied in reform movements.

The new element here is the consequence of an awareness that social organization is not simply a ''given,'' but is the creation of human beings and can be modified by human reason and organization. If human beings can change the shape of society they become responsible for it in a new way. And if a deep moral change is needed—one like that traditionally seen as requiring conversion—something like a ''social conversion'' must be possible.

Initially the intuition of a ''social grace'' is a priori: if sin is ''structural/ social,'' so also must grace be and indeed, following the Adam/Christ reasoning of Romans 5, grace must ultimately ''abound'' more. The Nicaraguan group quoted at the beginning of this section goes on to say:

> For some time we have wondered whether the present process, which aims at leading to a new Nicaragua, might not be one of these historic opportunities of grace; the presence of so many Christians along with so many other Nicaraguans hungry for justice, in a struggle that has been carried out with what many have seen as remarkable generosity and political skill—may this not be a sign of the times, the breaking in of something new in history, which the whole church, and hence the hierarchy as well, should discern in a climate of careful dialogue and fruitful listening for the Spirit?[9]

The question is not simply whether a revolutionary time might not be a time of grace (which could be understood in a negative sense, in that such times demand grace to face the *dangers* of revolution), but whether such a movement is not a *bearer* or embodiment of grace. There is perhaps some immediate reservation: carried to an extreme it might seem that the gospel was being identified with the program of a revolutionary group and could provoke a reaction like that of the writer in *La Prensa* who sarcastically said that God the Father had made a mistake in sending his Son and should have sent Marx and Lenin.

Part of such resistance may come from the connotation of grace as being strictly a religious and interior reality. After centuries of controversies and a rather elaborate conceptualization in the categories of Scholastic philosophy, contemporary theology has sought a more simplified and unified notion of grace, for example, "God's free self-communication to human beings" (Rahner). Previously it seemed as though the church had been entrusted with the main "means of grace," and grace itself seemed to be a "scarce commodity"; the thrust of modern theology had been to show that "grace is everywhere," to quote Georges Bernanos. Leonardo Boff writes: "God, Christ, and grace are always free. They manifest themselves in the world through many mediations. The Church is one such manifestation— an explicit, conscious, and communitarian one—but it is not the only one."[10]

Boff's statement is a logical extension of the position of Vatican II, which while it did not speak directly of grace in this connection, saw an interpenetration of the church and the world and expressed a positive relationship between human progress and the kingdom of God:

> . . . the expectation of a new earth must not weaken but rather stimulate our concern for cultivating this one. For here grows the body of a new human family, a body which even now is able to give some kind of foreshadowing of the new age.
>
> Earthly progress must be carefully distinguished from the growth of Christ's kingdom. Nevertheless, to the extent that the former can contribute to the better ordering of human society, it is of vital concern to the kingdom of God.[11]

Vatican Council II said that the church "labors to decipher authentic signs of God's presence and purpose in the happenings, needs, and desires" which it shares with other people. Since the church "acknowledges and greatly esteems the dynamic movements" by which human rights are fostered,[12] it would seem that, in principle at least, a revolution could be discerned as such a movement, and recognized as embodying God's grace.

At this point the question might be likened to the question of whether or not grace can be "experienced." A particular understanding of the distinction between natural and supernatural seemed to indicate that grace (as super natural) could not be experienced. While not rejecting what was gained intellectually by the natural/supernatural distinction, contemporary theology has sought to recover the possibility of experiencing grace (which seems clearly in accord with the sense of the Scriptures).

Again Rahner deals with the question by reverting to his usual categories:

If God's self-communication is an ultimate and radicalizing modification of that very transcendentality of ours by which we are subjects, and if we are such subjects of unlimited transcendentality in the most ordinary affairs of our everyday existence, in our secular dealings with any and every individual reality, then this means in principle that the original experience of God even in his self-communication can be so universal, so unthematic, and so "unreligious" that it takes place, unnamed but really, wherever we are living out our existence.[13]

What this adds to the previous statements is that not only is God's grace "everywhere" but that God's self-communication is indeed experienced in the midst of human life.

However, human beings cannot sort out what is of grace and what is simply human in their own experience (including their own orientation to transcendence). So much so, in fact, that they can never know with total assurance to what extent they have accepted or rejected God's offer. Rahner only suggests that the experience of grace has "its more prominent moments: in the experience of death, of radical authenticity, of love, and so forth."[14] He is interested in establishing the principle that grace is indeed experienced but never in a pure, unambiguous state.

Leonardo Boff takes the question further in a discussion of "the law of the Incarnation and the constant presence of the Holy Spirit." We must suffer the pain of "God's relative absence" and see God mediated through the world: "when we embrace the world, we know that we are also embracing God." Theology "will always be a process of deciphering the presence of God's love and learning from one experience to the next":

> . . . the law of the Incarnation tells us that the experience of grace is never pure grace; it is also the world. And our experience of the world is never mere world; it is also grace. . . . It is always a diaphany of grace rather than an epiphany: grace shines through some experience of the world and life. The realities of this world are mediations or sacraments of grace. Grace comes to us in them and through them.
>
> . . . Even more than the Son, the Spirit has hidden himself behind the movement of history and the world with which he is so closely associated. The Spirit was experienced as a nameless force, an imperceptible vitality, and an invisible wind that made his presence felt. After the event of Pentecost we know his name. He is the Spirit of God, he is the Spirit of Christ, the Holy Spirit. This presence is manifested in the human experience of faith, grace, and salvation. He lies buried in these experiences, not diminishing human personalities but arousing them to free activity. He nourishes their creative imagination, helping them to move forward in history or to change its direction. So when we talk about the experience of grace, we should always remember it is an experience of the Holy Spirit and his activity in the world.[15]

To state it briefly, the signs of grace in a revolutionary *proyecto* would be that the life of the poor is enhanced, their dignity respected; that there is an overall movement toward equality, a willingness to accept austerity in the interests of all, a conscious effort to build a society on cooperation and common effort—all qualities that have their analogues in the ideal vision of the church and Christian life in the New Testament (Acts, chapters 2 and 4; Philippians 2:5–11; Matthew, chapter 25; and the many exhortations in the epistles). Hence a revolution could be regarded as a bearer, or mediation, of grace—and to make such a discernment would be a responsibility for the church in such a situation.

However, no movement in history would be an unambiguous mediation, and a consistent Christian view would require seeing these movements as at the same time affected by sin. A revolution would not instantly do away with all "structures of sin." Some aspects of social sin, such as men's oppression of women, or discrimination by race, are not done away with by structural changes in the economy.

More fundamentally, sin is more than structural. Individuals even in movements with a high ethical purpose will be prey to personal weaknesses and pride. Movements truly embodying the people's aspirations may nonetheless come to identify their interests as a party with the good they pretend to be serving; for example, they may eventually act as though holding onto power were the ultimate priority.

The aim here has not been to exercise such discernment. In fact the position taken throughout this book implies a basic sense that these movements (not directly the organizations leading them) are such a mediation and that this is an opportunity of grace. Here the purpose has been to sketch the theological justification implicit in such a view.

EXISTENCE IN CHRIST

From the beginning Latin American liberation theologians insisted on the need for an appropriate Christology. Possibly part of their concern came from a sense that, at first glance, the Old Testament with its image of God hearing the cry of his people and leading them out of bondage into a new land offered a more useful paradigm for liberation than the New Testament: the movement led by Moses was collective, material, and political.

Before long well-developed Christologies came from the pens of Leonardo Boff (1972) and Jon Sobrino (1975).[16] However, more important than such works in themselves is a general deepening awareness of the paschal mystery of Christ in its historical dimension.

The return to the sources associated with Vatican II brought a rediscovery of the paschal mystery as the key to the Scriptures: exodus, the central event of the Old Testament, was seen as taken up into Jesus' "exodus," his paschal journey embracing all salvation-history and so providing the pattern for the church and all Christian life.

However, there could be a "spiritualization" in such a reading: Jesus' paschal mystery could be seen as a key to understanding human life, but its operation would take place solely in the interior of individuals, a hidden mystery that would be symbolized in the sacraments. The paschal mystery of death/resurrection would reveal the "hidden mystery" of God's grace and motivate people to live and carry out their lives with a Christic pattern (dying to self and living for others and God) but would have no direct consequences in history.

Latin American theologians have sought to carry the paschal mystery further by insisting on "historicizing" the life, death, and resurrection of Jesus in two senses: (1) taking seriously the specific history of Jesus of Nazareth; (2) seeing it as Jesus' purpose to stimulate further history.

These theologians are convinced that Christology is not an idle or purely academic question, but has practical consequences. We may consider, for example, the Christology of the Puebla Conference. In treating Jesus' life and message, Puebla says that "the forces of evil, however, rejected this service of love" and mentions together the incredulity of the people and Jesus' family, the incomprehension of the disciples, and the actions of the authorities. Puebla sees Jesus setting out on the "road of self-sacrifice and self-giving," gathering a small group of disciples, and freely surrendering himself on the cross, "the goal of his life's journey." Because he is the "High Priest," the "Paschal Victim," and the "obedient Son," God raises him up (nos. 192, 194, 195).

Such a view does not see Jesus as really engaged in struggle in his life; the entire thrust of the passage seems to present him as moving through life, almost as though he were reading a prewritten script, knowing that he must die in "sacrifice" rather than as a human being acting in history.

Thus in Latin America attention has been turned to the message of Jesus (the kingdom) and the controversy it created—ultimately leading to his execution. Direct experience of persecution and oppression has heightened an awareness of certain aspects of Jesus' life (cf. dialogues in Solentiname, quoted in chapter 1, above). Archbishop Romero told the people that Jesus could "be here in the Cathedral and not be distinguishable from you [the poor of El Salvador]." The child Jesus should not be sought in pretty crib-scenes, he continued, but among undernourished children or poor newspaper vendors or bootblacks; when Jesus said "my soul is troubled" he was not insensitive, but felt like someone who is "picked up by the National Guard and taken to a place of torture."[17] However, there has been no effort to find the most "revolutionary" reading of Jesus' life, making him a crypto-Zealot and anachronistically likening the Zealots to modern revolutionaries. Jesus is seen as revealing a God of life—and being killed as a consequence.

Moreover, God's raising of Jesus from the dead is seen not only as a demonstration of power, but as a vindication of the kingdom, which had been rejected by the powerful. Thus Jesus' message (Blessed are the poor . . . be

as those who serve . . . whatever you do for the least of my little ones . . .)
is not simply moral exhortation but enters directly into the paschal mystery:
it is what provoked his death and what God vindicated in the resurrection.

It seems to me that perhaps the most powerul element in the motivation
of Christians in their struggle in Central America is a paschal sense of life:
what Archbishop Romero meant when he said, "If they kill me, I will rise in
the Salvadoran people."[18] This statement was not a "secularized" or
"purely horizontal" view of the resurrection; on the contrary, it came from
one whose belief in final resurrection was utterly orthodox. But it expressed
his view that the ultimate meaning of present struggle is revealed in the
death/resurrection of Jesus. Romero was able to combine the most traditional view of "offering up" sacrifice with that of struggle.

> Our paschal hope gives meaning to the outcast, to the illiterate, to those
> dying of malnutrition. It not only shouts that things should not be like
> this but says to the one suffering, "You will perhaps die like this. Offer it
> in redemption." That is why I said in my pastoral call in this new situa-
> tion for the country that all those who have offered up their life, their
> heroism, their sacrifice—if they have really offered it with a sincere de-
> sire to give true liberty and dignity to our people—that they are incor-
> porating themselves into the great sacrifice of Christ.

Romero then urged the sick and the poor to offer their sufferings to the
Lord, but not passively.

> And you will see my beloved poor . . . oppressed . . . outcasts . . . sick,
> that the dawn of the resurrection is now beginning to shine. The hour is
> coming for our people. And we should wait for it, as Christians, not only
> in its particular political dimensions, but in its dimensions of faith and
> hope.[19]

In these words, in a sermon of November 1979 (a month after the coup),
Romero was not only alluding to the paschal dimension of suffering and
struggle, but strongly hinted a "resurrection" within history soon to arrive,
which would include (but should go beyond) political changes.

One of the factors impelling toward such a basic Christological centering
has been the experience of martyrdom. Prior to the Puebla Conference
there was some discussion of the "persecution of the church" and the use of
the term "martyrdom." Some objected that theologically martyrdom
means dying for the faith and certainly not for a political cause. Puebla
itself produced no statement on martyrdom. However, there was a growing
conviction that Christians today in Latin America, when they are persecuted and killed for the cause of the poor, are indeed dying for the faith—
not over a doctrinal formulation, or simply for maintaining adherence to
Christ—but that they are indeeed dying for the substance of the faith, par-

ticularly love for neighbor. Thus it was legitimate to extend the meaning of the term "martyrdom."

Such a discussion was secondary. Many Christians were being killed and their death was widely regarded as martyrdom—following the path of Jesus the great Witness (martyr)—and this closeness to martyrdom tended to give a sense of ultimacy to people's actions and options.

In my observations a paschal sense of life is at the center of the religious vision of the "popular church" in Central America. One revealing indication is that the main liturgical celebrations have often been funerals for those who have "fallen" (usually not in armed combat). On these occasions there is a sense of shared community, commitment, risk, and joy, and a certitude that this death is not in vain.

I would describe this paschal sense of life as having at least these characteristics: (1) a willingness to give one's life and a recognition that this is quite possible; (2) a sense that giving life is necessary in order that others may have life; (3) a grounding of life in the example of Jesus; (4) ultimate trust in the God who resurrected Jesus; and (5) a strong hope that there will soon be a resurrection in present history in the form of a new society, founded on new principles, starting out with a basic respect for the life of all.

Ignacio Ellacuría takes this all a step further in his essay "The Crucified People: An Essay in Historical Soteriology." The reference to Moltmann (*The Crucified God*) is conscious, but not intended polemically. "People" is the *pueblo*, which is seen as rather more of a collective subject than is normally indicated in English usage.

It is Ellacuría's intention to propose that the poor and oppressed are "historical salvation" for the world. In aiming at a *historical* soteriology, he is concerned that it relate to the unfolding of history and not be "purely mystical and sacramental." Certainly there is a "transhistorical dimension" in Jesus' life "but it will be real only if it is in fact transhistorical, that is, if it goes through history." Hence the question: Who carries out in history Jesus' life and death?

When Christian faith recognizes that there is a "crucified people," it will begin to suspect that "besides being the people at whom this salvific effort is aimed in the first place, it will also be in its situation of crucifixion a principle of salvation for the whole world." It is a "scandal" to see the poor and outcast as saviors of the world just as Jesus himself was a "scandal." The poor are not only those to be saved but they participate in a special way in the realization of salvation.

Ellacuría's focus is on the death of both Jesus and the people: "The crucifixion of the people avoids the danger of mystifying the death of Jesus, and the death of Jesus avoids the danger of exaggerating salvifically the mere fact of the crucifixion of the people, as if the simple fact of being crucified would thereby bring resurrection and life." He makes an extended meditation on the servant figure in Isaiah as applied to both Jesus and the crucified people.[20]

In his treatment Ellacuría steers away from a precise definition of who belongs to the crucified people. He expressly states that it is not to be identified with any particular organization of the people. Earlier in the essay he had quoted a long passage on the "proletariat" from Marx, noting its "deep religious inspiration." The implication, not clearly stated, is that the crucified people is the bearer of salvation for the world, something like the proletariat for Marxists. However, Ellacuría differs from Marx's judgment on the *Lumpenproletariat*. Presumably what he means is that membership in the crucified people is not limited to those who are immediately efficacious politically.

In all I find the essay highly suggestive, but not entirely clear to my (irremediably Anglo-Saxon) mind. As I read it, Ellacuría is suggesting that Jesus and the crucified people form a unity (suggested by the individual/ corporate Servant figure) and that salvation, as mediated by Jesus and the people, is to be seen as salvation in the unfolding of history. Ellacuría does not spell out how this salvation takes place. I would hazard that it takes place in historical movements for liberation, which involve a real suffering among the poor—a crucifixion that is redemptive in that it brings a new kind of life in the form of a society more closely approximating the kingdom. All will eventually benefit from the new society, which is brought in through the suffering of the poor, who are therefore the bearers of salvation for the whole. In principle this would refer not only to what happens within the confines of a country but to humankind as a whole. The poor of today's struggles, in our case in Central America, are accordingly the Servant in today's world, taking on their shoulders the sins of all, and leading the way to a redemption whose effects will eventually extend to all.

There is a danger in my brief presentation of such an idea that it may seem to be simply a theological fancy, suitable perhaps for a sermon or a retreat meditation. I would emphasize, then, that this idea is proposed as serious theology—as an attempt to fathom and express God's ways with humankind. If it is valid it should modify our understanding of salvation. In this presentation I can only point to this interpretation and insist on its seriousness.

THE PENULTIMATE AND THE ULTIMATE

Throughout this treatment the accent has been on God's activity in the present situation of Central America. There has been nothing about the "inner life" of God, nor even about many classical theological questions. Some might readily call it a "horizontal" theology.

This brings up what will be a final point. Although it is conventional to speak of transcendence and immanence as though they were at opposite poles, always in tension, this may not be the most appropriate kind of formulation. Jon Sobrino offers another perhaps more fruitful view.

His thinking starts with an approach to Jesus' own life. In contrast to classical Christologies, he sees Jesus' ignorance of God's design, his temptations, and his prayer of seeking as an essential part of Jesus' life: Jesus did not possess God but had to seek him through a process of conversion, through a genuine living-through of a history. He thus had to accept the mystery of God. He even had to accept death without having seen the realization of the kingdom he had preached—and this he did in fidelity to God. Sobrino here cites several passages from Hebrews. In his life, but especially in his death, Jesus had to "let God be God":

> [The] radicalness of the life and praxis of Jesus is based on his radical conviction that at the root of reality there is something ultimate, which is for human beings, and this must be maintained at any price. In this sense, for Jesus, God is not something added on to life in history and even less something opposed to life in history. Jesus invokes God to radicalize what is in history and maintain what can be seen through history of the inexhaustible and unmanipulable mystery.

Jesus does not define God for himself or for us; he is concerned that God not be manipulated. "The ultimate mystery is the guarantee for the seriousness of the penultimate."[21]

On another occasion Sobrino takes up some of these same themes and accents, now applied to the question of "God in revolutionary processes." He points to certain experiences, within the revolution itself, that confront people with the challenge of "letting God be God"—not in the sense of simple resignation, but in bringing one to the mystery of God. First, he points to the fact that *history moves on*, and that even revolutions pass on. What is required is an ever new effort at incarnation into reality, of fidelity to the process of history as it unfolds. He then recalls a classically disputed question on whether people could avoid sin without the grace of God, to which the answer was: yes, but not over the long run. Applying this to the present, Sobrino concludes that without the grace of God, people cannot avoid the "sin" of not being incarnate, that is, they will not be faithful to the process without the grace of God. In order for people to be faithful to the impulse of the revolution, God's grace is needed.

A second experience is that of *human limitation*. There is simply the persistence of sin in individuals. But even more, there is the "structural difficulty, not simply ethical, of uniting justice and compassion, firmness and mercy, freedom and efficacy, enthusiasm and realism." Another facet of limitation Sobrino calls "anonymity," the fact that the sacrifice and death of many people will simply be forgotten.

A third experience mentioned by Sobrino introduces the *eschatological reserve* (which was treated briefly in the previous chapter). Its purpose is not to relativize every achievement in history as though all were equally distant from the kingdom, but to hierarchize them. In this sense the eschatological reserve may be seen not as relativizing human efforts in history—and thus in possibly making people's strivings less intense—but as being a principle of tension that will in fact bring out the best in human effort. To put it another way: the awareness of the ultimate mystery of God and the distance of any human realization from the kingdom should not make it a matter of indifference whether people live in a society of extreme inequality or of relative equality. The eschatological reserve should provide the kind of tension that draws human efforts forward, conscious both that any realizations are provisional, and yet that they should be steps toward the ultimate.

In this sketch (chapter 9–11) of the issues (ethical, pastoral, and theological) that I see emerging from the experience of Central America, there are many blurred lines, for much is *terra incognita*. It is my conviction, however, that these issues are of utmost importance for the church. I hope this sketch enables readers to appreciate the theological seriousness of developments in Central America and stimulates further reflection.

Epilogue

This book has been concerned to give an account of how the church has become involved in struggle in Central America and to reflect on the issues arising therefrom. While the issues might be of wider interest, the focus has been on the region itself and how people there have formulated them.

In closing I would like to offer a few observations on the relevance of this experience for the Christian churches in the United States. The first point scarcely needs stating. The United States government's policy of supporting the ruling groups (despite a professed concern to support or even to create a political "center") has been ethically wrong and, in opposing it, the churches have been faithful to their mission. In both their liberal (Jimmy Carter) and their conservative (Ronald Reagan) forms, United States policies have ignored the real roots of the struggle and have supported the brutal tactics of the military and oligarchy used against the unarmed population.

Following the lead of Archbishop Romero and affected by his murder, as well as by the rape/killing of American church women in El Salvador and American missionaries in Guatemala, the churches have taken a lead in the anti-intervention movement. It seems probable that without church opposition, United States intervention in Central America would be much deeper. In all this, the church has been faithful to its mission. This book may serve as a modest contribution to Christians exercising that ministry.

My main concern here, however, is of another nature: the relevance of the Central American experience of Christians for the church in the United States.

What leaps to the mind immediately are the enormous differences between the two situations. Central American countries are tiny in population and relatively uncomplex socially and economically: the notion of a revolution to set in motion basic changes, while difficult to execute, is not hard to formulate conceptually. The United States, by contrast, has 10 times the population of all Central America; its per-capita income is roughly 10 times as great and its economy produces something on the order of 100 times what Central America produces in value, and is of a proportionate level of complexity. While one might daydream of a revolution, it is much harder even to formulate comprehensively and clearly the root problems of United States society (everyone will have his or her own list). Central American countries are poor and on the periphery, while the United States is a superpower with a worldwide economic empire.

The position of the church on both sides is different. In Central America the Roman Catholic church has a public role and is willy-nilly a main protagonist in events; in the United States, the relationship between the churches and public life is more complex and subtle.

Despite such obvious differences, some church people in North America have looked to Latin America for inspiration: Latin American theology is taken seriously in the theological community, and basic Christian communities have provided a model for some pastoral work, particularly among Hispanics.

Nevertheless I would suggest that rather than start with liberation theology or basic Christian communities, one must start further back with the process that generated them. Latin American Christians and the church institutionally sensed the crisis in their society, the failure of "development" and the need for "liberation," and began to express this and so to find their own identity. As the question was being articulated theologically, pastoral agents were beginning a long apprenticeship at the grassroots level, a process that may still be in its early stages for the continent as a whole.

If we look at the United States, it is apparent that no similar crisis has been felt on a widespread level. Although church people have been active in the civil-rights and antiwar movements since the 1960s and in a host of public issues, much energy during the postconciliar period has gone into internal church issues. This lack of a clear sense of crisis in society is probably the most important reason why the United States church has not developed its own equivalent to liberation theology. Certainly there are any number of books that might offer proposals, but missing is the overall atmosphere of crisis to which such proposals could be a response.

To my mind the crisis issue for the United States church is the manufacture, possession, and preparation for use of nuclear weapons. Certainly it is a question of death-or-life for many millions of people, possibly of the human race. On any ethical calculation the only thing to be done is strong, concerted action toward reversing the arms race.

I would suggest that the question is more than ethical: it is theological in that the arms race is idolatry and a denial of the God of life. Therefore the church's very identity is at stake, since the question is: What God is the church to give witness to?

Just as "liberation" became a generative theme for the Latin American church at Medellín, I would suggest that some notion relating to "life" and the God of life could become a focal point for a new vision of what it means to be Christian in our context. Just as the original intuitions of liberation theology had to find appropriate pastoral forms, a commitment to human life would have to find a suitable pedagogy and process. Papal documents are fine, episcopal statements are useful, petitions inserted into the Prayer of the Faithful have their place—but none of these will stop the doomsday preparations. There must be a broad mobilization of the American people, and the churches have a clear responsibility.

One can imagine a systematic effort to organize study/action groups at parish and neighborhood levels, with, for example, a scripturally based course examining the reality of nuclear war, the current state of preparations for it, and increasingly dangerous commitments—all challenged with the biblical Word.

Just as "liberation" has been a rich notion, with different dimensions and relating to a whole complex of issues, so an approach to the problem of nuclear war as seen in a Christian way would tend to extend to other, related issue areas: (1) *the "enemy"*: raising the question of whether or not Christians can designate a whole nation for obliteration on grounds of their own security; examining the whole East-West confrontation framework; seeking to understand these people and regimes defined as the enemy, and perhaps making gestures of peace; (2) *militarism*: questioning the use of military power for policy objectives and the impact of military spending on human life in the United States; studying the power of the military-industrial complex; (3) *economic effects*: studying the role of corporations in United States policy; examining alternatives; (4) *politics*: studying the political mechanisms that permit and perpetuate the arms race; examining possibilities for citizen involvement now; raising basic questions about political systems and alternatives; (5) *international relations*: studying ways of checking the pretensions of nation-states, and seeking possible kinds of transnational politics for the sake of the human race; (6) *sexist culture*: examining the connections between male domination and militarism.

The foregoing are no more than improvised examples: they illustrate that taking seriously the challenge of nuclear war tends to raise other large questions, of which these are representative. To the extent such an effort began to show its effects, the church would be accused of meddling in politics, of abandoning its "spiritual" mission, of being taken over by leftist (or pacifist) ideologues. Such charges would probably be a good sign.

In Latin America the renewal of "evangelization" went hand in hand with the focus on liberation, that is, the effort was not simply to preach a biblically correct "message" but to evangelize particular societies. A message of hope and a challenge to be converted to life might be the "good news" that the church in the United States should be preaching now, its form of evangelization.

Finally, I strongly suspect that taking seriously the "fate of the earth" will be fruitful for theology. It may be the way to a deeper understanding of the cross and of sin. Moral theologians over the years have made studies, and theologians in their own lives have taken their stand, but it is difficult to see how it has affected their theology. The intuition here is that if theologians allowed themselves to be penetrated with the reality of the impending holocaust, they would begin to elaborate a more fruitful theology, as well as to serve the ongoing practice of the church.

Notes

1: PRELUDE IN SOLENTINAME

1. Ernesto Cardenal, *The Gospel in Solentiname*, 4 vols., trans. Donald Walsh (Maryknoll, N.Y.: Orbis Books, 1976–82). Citations, in parentheses, follow quotations; e.g., 3:40 refers to vol. 3, p. 40.

2. Basic information from interview with William Agudelo, July 1981.

3. Cf. Phillip Berryman, "Latin America: 'Iglesia que Nace del Pueblo,' " *Christianity and Crisis* 41, no. 14 (Sept. 21, 1981): 238–42.

4. Some of these characterizations are from Cardenal's introduction, pp. ix–x, in each volume.

2: LAYING THE GROUNDWORK: THE LATIN AMERICAN CHURCH

1. John Cobb's Introduction to Delwin Brown, *To Set at Liberty* (Maryknoll, N.Y.: Orbis Books, 1981), p. xi.

2. Ivan Illich, "The Vanishing Clergyman," *The Critic*, June–July 1967.

3. Walter J. Broderick, *Camilo Torres: A Biography of the Priest-Guerrillero* (Garden City, N.Y.: Doubleday, 1975); Phillip Berryman, "Camilo Torres, Revolutionary-Theologian," *Commonweal* 96, no. 7 (Apr. 21, 1972):164–67; for Torres's writings, see Camilo Torres, *Cristianismo y revolución*, ed. Oscar Maldonado, Guitemie Olivieri, and Germán Zabala (Mexico, D.F.: ERA, 1970).

4. "Mensaje de Obispos del Tercer Mundo (15 de agosto de 1967)," in José Marins et al., eds., *Praxis de los padres de América Latina* (Bogotá: Ediciones Paulinas, 1978), pp. 42–47.

5. CELAM, *La Iglesia en la transformación de América Latina a la luz del Concilio*, vol. 2, *Conclusiones* (Bogotá: CELAM, 1969). English edition: *The Church in the Present-Day Transformation of Latin America in the Light of the Council*, vol. 2, *Conclusions*, published in 1970 by the Latin American Bureau of the United States Catholic Conference and the General Secretariat of CELAM. References to Medellín *Conclusions* will be by name of document and paragraph number.

6. *Elites*, no. 9; *Paz*, no. 16; *Elites*, no. 5–12; *Pastoral de Conjunto*, no. 10–12; *Educación*, no. 3; cf. "liberación" in Indice Alfabético.

7. Gustavo Gutiérrez, *A Theology of Liberation* (Maryknoll, N.Y.: Orbis Books, 1973); Hugo Assmann, *Theology for a Nomad Church* (Maryknoll, N.Y.: Orbis Books, 1976).

8. For overviews of liberation theology up to the mid-1970s, see Phillip E. Berryman, "Latin American Liberation Theology," in *Theology in the Americas*,

ed. Sergio Torres and John Eagleson (Maryknoll, N.Y.: Orbis Books, 1976), pp. 20–83; Roberto Oliveros, *Liberación y teología: Génesis y crecimiento de una reflexión (1966–1976)* (Lima: CEP, 1977). For a good sampling from most of the major writers, see Rosino Gibellini, *Frontiers of Theology in Latin America* (Maryknoll, N.Y.: Orbis Books, 1979).

9. An analogy heard from Fr. Dan Driscoll, M.M.

10. *Octogesima Adveniens*, nos. 31–34, in Joseph Gremillion, ed., *The Gospel of Peace and Justice: Catholic Social Teaching since Pope John* (Maryknoll, N.Y.: Orbis Books, 1976), pp. 499–501.

11. "Option for Struggle: Three Documents of Christians for Socialism" (New York: Church Research and Information Projects, 1974).

12. For a detailed account, see Enrique Dussel, *De Medellín a Puebla: Una década de sangre y esperanza (1968–1979)* (Mexico: Edicol, 1979), pp. 268–96.

13. A major conference of theologians held in Mexico City, focusing on methodology, published its proceedings with the title *Liberación y cautiverio* (Mexico City, 1976).

14. See lists and tables prepared by DIAL (Bureau of Information on Latin America), in Penny Lernoux, *Cry of the People: The Struggle for Human Rights in Latin America—The Catholic Church in Conflict with U.S. Policy* (New York: Penguin, 1982), pp. 463–70.

15. See the untitled bibliography drawn up by CRIE and distributed at the Puebla Conference, January 1979.

16. Cf. Phillip Berryman, "What Happened at Puebla," in Daniel Levine, ed., *Churches and Politics in Latin America* (Beverly Hills: Sage Publications, 1980), pp. 55–86.

3: CENTRAL AMERICA: WHY THE CRISIS?

1. Population and gross domestic product figures from Inter-American Development Bank, *Economic and Social Progress in Latin America* (Washington, D.C., 1979), cited in "Informe de la O.E.A. sobre la situación de los derechos humanos en Guatemala" (Washington, D.C., 1981), reprinted in *Polémica*, no. 2, November–December 1981, p. 62; comparisons of countries to U.S. states have been made using area statistics in Hammond, *The Whole Earth Atlas* (1975).

2. U.S. trade figure taken from presentation of Mike Conroy, Ph.D., at conference on Central America, in Austin, Texas, 1981.

3. *Nuevo Diario* (Guatemalan daily paper), Oct. 24 and Dec. 12, 1978: figures for these five commodities comprised 66.3% of exports; eliminating trade between Central American countries gave the 85% figure.

4. Emile McAnany, "Television and Crisis: Ten Years of Network News Coverage of Central America," January 1982 (mimeo), p. 10.

5. Data in this section based largely on Ralph Lee Woodward, Jr., *Central America: A Nation Divided* (New York: Oxford University Press, 1976). Woodward combines a great deal of material in a readable account; and also includes an extensive annotated bibliography. Woodward's seems to be the only relatively up-to-date historical survey of the region in English. For an economic interpretation of Central American history, see Edelberto Torres Rivas, *Interpretación del desarrollo social centroamericano* (3rd ed.; San José, Costa Rica: EDUCA, 1973).

6. Woodward, *Central America*, pp. 21–22.

7. Declaración de Iximché, in "Guatemala: Documentos y testimonios de un pueblo en lucha" (Mexico City: Coordinadora Cristiana de Solidaridad con la Lucha del Pueblo de Guatemala, 1980; mimeo).

8. David Browning, *El Salvador: Landscape and Society* (London: Oxford University Press, 1971), pp. 111–12, 84, cited in Eduardo Colindres, *Fundamentos económicos de la burguesía salvadoreña* (San Salvador: UCA Editores, 1977), pp. 23–24. The map is in the Spanish translation of Browning, *El Salvador: La tierra y el hombre* (San Salvador: Ministerio de Educación, 1975), p. 172. Browning's work, a history of land use, is highly regarded .

9. Woodward, *Central America*, pp. 39–41.

10. Robert Armstrong and Janet Shenk, *El Salvador: The Face of Revolution* (Boston: South End Press, 1982), p. 6.

11. Woodward, *Central America*, p. 169.

12. Armstrong and Shenk, *Face*, p. 22.

13. Cf. Susanne Jonas, "La ayuda externa no ayuda a la integración centroamericana," *Estudios Sociales Centroamericanos*, January–April, 1974, pp. 34–74.

14. *Nuevo Diario* (Guatemala), Dec. 13, 1978.

15. James F. Petras and Morris H. Manley, "Economic Expansion, Political Crisis and U.S. Policy in Central America," *Contemporary Marxism*, no. 3, Summer 1981, p. 78.

16. SIECA, *El desarrollo integrado de centroamérica en la presente década*, vol. 7, table II-3, p. 47; cited in César Jerez, "El contexto socioeconómico de las decisiones políticas en el proceso de integración centroamericana," *ECA*, 339/340, January–February 1977, p. 19. To my knowledge there are no more recent income figures covering all five countries. Incomes have risen with inflation but remain skewed.

17. Organization of American States Human Rights Commission, "Informe de la OEA sobre la situación de los derechos humanos en Guatemala" (Washington, D.C.: OAS, 1981) reprinted in *Polémica*, no. 2, November–December 1981, pp. 63–64. Cited in Armstrong and Shenk, *Face*, pp. 6–7.

18. Instituto de Investigaciones Económicas y Sociales, University of San Carlos (Guatemala), 1979; cited in *Central America Report* 6 (1979):139.

19. By some accounts income distribution has improved in El Salvador in recent years. This conclusion seems to run counter to the experience of people and the presumed consequences of increasing landlessness. Caution should be taken with any statistics from Central America, especially when gathered on different occasions.

20. Melvin Burke, "El sistema de plantación y la proletarización del trabajo agrícola en El Salvador," *ECA*, nos. 335/336, September–October 1976, p. 80.

21. Shelton H. Davis and Julie Hodson, *Witnesses to Political Violence in Guatemala: The Suppression of a Rural Development Movement* (Boston: Oxfam-America, 1982), p. 46.

22. U.S.A.I.D., "Small Farmer Improvement" (loan 520-11-190-233, 520: 26), December 1975, p. 12.

23. U.S. Embassy (Guatemala) "Quarterly Economic Report: Guatemala," June 1980, p. 4.

24. Coffee figures from Banco de Guatemala cited by U.S. Embassy Economic Report and from ANACAFE (Asociación Nacional del Café). I have seen both reports but no longer have them and cite from memory.

25. Burke, "El Sistema," pp. 173–75. See also article by Eduardo Colindres in the same issue.

26. For the case of Guatemala, see Richard N. Adams, *Crucifixion by Power: Essays on Guatemalan National Social Structure, 1944-1966* (Austin: University of Texas Press, 1970).

27. Shelton H. Davis, "State Violence and Agrarian Crisis in Guatemala," p. 11 (mimeo).

4: "FREE COUNTRY OR DEATH!"

1. Ralph Lee Woodward, Jr., *Central America: A Nation Divided* (New York: Oxford University Press, 1976), pp. 136–46; Universidad Nacional Autónoma de Nicaragua, Departamento de Ciencias Sociales, Sección de Historia, *Apuntes de historia de Nicaragua (Selecciones de textos)*, 2 vols. (Managua: UNAN, 1980), vol. 1, pp. 14–23 (hereafter cited as *Apuntes*, with vol. no.); Richard Millett, *Guardians of the Dynasty* (Maryknoll, N.Y.: Orbis Books, 1977), pp. 18f.; Thomas W. Walker, *Nicaragua: The Land of Sandino* (Boulder, Colo.: Westview Press, 1981), pp. 13–15.

2. Jorge Eduardo Arellano, *Breve historia de la iglesia en Nicaragua (1523-1979)* (Managua: n.p., 1980), p. 57. This is a separate publication of material that will appear in the volume on Central America in *Historia de la Iglesia en América Latina* being produced by CEHILA (Centro de Estudios de la Historia de la Iglesia en América Latina) under the direction of Enrique Dussel.

3. Thomas Walker, *Nicaragua: The Land of Sandino*, p. 16.

4. Millett, *Guardians*, p. 33.

5. The U.S. also acquired rights to lease the Corn Islands in the Caribbean and the option to establish a naval base in the Bay of Fonseca. This latter right was contested by Costa Rica and El Salvador, and when the Central American Court of Justice decided in their favor the U.S. ignored the decision, thereby contributing to the court's demise. T. Walker, *Nicaragua*, pp. 20f.

6. Arellano, *Breve historia*, pp. 69–74, 77.

7. Ibid., p. 80. When Pope John Paul II landed in Nicaragua during his March 1983 trip through Central America, Daniel Ortega quoted extensively from Pereira y Castrellón's letter. Media accounts missed the quotation and simply called Ortega's welcome a "tirade."

8. The possible direct involvement of the American ambassador, Arthur Bliss Lane, is not clear. Accounts of how Somoza decided to kill Sandino vary. Cf. Millett, *Guardians*, pp. 156–58. For a circumstantial account implicating the ambassador, cf. Carlos Fonseca Amador, "Crónica secreta: Augusto César Sandino ante sus verdugos," in *Bajo la bandera del sandinismo (Textos políticos)* (Managua: Editorial Nueva Nicaragua, 1981), pp. 281–98.

9. On Sandino: *Apuntes*, pp. 81–165; Sergio Ramírez, "Un muchacho de Niquinohomo" (Managua: FSLN, 1981); Sergio Ramírez, ed., *El pensamiento vivo de Sandino* (5th ed., San José: EDUCA, 1980); Gregorio Selser, *Sandino, General de hombres libres* (2nd ed.; San José: EDUCA, 1979); Woodward, *Central America*, pp. 199f., 219.

10. *Apuntes*, vol. 1, pp. 132, 130, 138, 114.

11. Arellano, *Breve historia*, pp. 79, 86.

12. Ibid., p. 90.

13. Ibid., p. 85.

14. Ibid., p. 90f.

15. Ibid., p. 98.

16. Cf. Arellano, *Breve historia*, chap. 3, pt. 1, which treats of the church's relation to governments and the rise of Catholic Action.

17. Thomas Walker, *Nicaragua: The Land of Sandino*, p. 28; Millett, *Guardians*, pp. 214f. Eisenhower quotation from Carlos Fonseca, *Crónica secreta*, p. 289, quoting Associated Press cable from Washington, Sept. 29, 1956.

18. Thomas Walker, *Nicaragua: The Land of Sandino*, pp. 30f.; Millett, *Guardians*, p. 235.

19. Walker, *Nicaragua: The Land of Sandino*, p. 86.

20. Millett, *Guardians*, p. 229, gives the figure of 40; Jacinto Suárez, in Pilar Arias, ed., *Nicaragua: Revolución* (Mexico City: Siglo XXI, 1980), p. 40, gives the figure as 200; *Un pueblo alumbra su historia* (Managua: Departamento de Propaganda y Educación Política del FSLN, 1981), p. 16, gives a figure of 400. These latter works will henceforth be cited as Arias, ed., *Nic. Rev.*; and *Un pueblo*.

21. See list of Somoza companies in NACLA (North American Congress on Latin America), *Latin America and Empire Report*, February 1976. An American businessman, in an interview in Managua in 1977, told me of Somoza's practice of asking for shares.

22. Thomas Walker, *Nicaragua: The Land of Sandino*, p. 56. Walker sees Luis Somoza as having been more open, democratic, development-minded, and intelligent than Anastasio, his brother, who succeeded him.

23. Anastasio Somoza and Jack Cox, *Nicaragua Betrayed* (Belmont, Mass.: Western Islands, 1980); for a conservative view, see James R. Whelan, *Through the American Looking Glass: Central America's Crisis* (Washington, D.C.: Council for Inter-American Security, 1980); also, see other publications of the council. For the Sandinista view, see Humberto Ortega Saavedra, *50 años de lucha sandinista* (Havana, Cuba: Editorial de Ciencias Sociales, 1980); see also Arias, ed., *Nic. Rev.*; and also *Apuntes*.

24. For the formation of the FSLN I have used Arias, ed., *Nic. Rev.*; *Un pueblo*; Fonseca, *Crónica secreta*, pp. 353–76 and passim; Humberto Ortega Saavedra, *50 años*; *Apuntes*, vol. 2; Millett, *Guardians,* and Thomas Walker, *Nicaragua: The Land of Sandino*.

25. Ortega Saavedra, *50 años*.

26. John Booth, "Celebrating the Demise of Somocismo: Fifty Recent Spanish Sources on the Nicaraguan Revolution," *Latin American Research Review* 17, no. 1 (1982), p. 178. He adds that Fonseca and Borge came upon Marxism in different ways, presumably meaning that Fonseca Amador was first a member of the Nicaraguan Socialist party.

27. Arias, *Nic. Rev.*, p. 34.

28. Interview with Félix Jiménez, Managua, Nicaragua, July 1981.

29. Gregorio Smutko, "Cristianos de la costa atlántica en la revolución," *Nicarauac*, 2, no. 5 (April–June 1981), pp. 51f. (this issue henceforth cited as *Nicarauac*).

30. Arellano, *Breve historia*, pp. 101–6.

31. José Miguel Torres, "El cristianismo protestante en la revolución sandinista," *Nicarauac*, p. 43.

32. Arellano, *Breve historia*, pp. 98ff., 118.

33. Ibid., p. 100. Michael Dodson and T. S. Montgomery, "The Churches in the Nicaraguan Revolution," in Thomas Walker, ed., *Nicaragua in Revolution* (Boulder, Colo.: Westview Press, 1982).

34. Quote from Arellano, *Breve historia*, p. 113. For other incidents, see pp. 100, 113.

35. Ibid., p. 113.

36. Ibid., pp. 116f.

37. Ibid., pp. 123f. It is not completely clear whether Obando sold the Mercedes that was given to him, or whether he simply refused to accept it. All see the event as an important symbol.

38. Ibid., p. 124.

39. Text in José Marins et al., *Praxis de los padres de América Latina: Documentos de las conferencias episcopales de Medellín a Puebla (1968-1978)* (Bogotá: Ediciones Paulinas, 1978), pp. 383-94; quotations from pp. 385, 387, 388, 390, 392 (henceforth cited as Marins, *Praxis*).

40. Arellano, *Breve historia*, p. 127.

41. Ibid., p. 124.

42. Uriel Molina, "El sendero de una experiencia," *Nicarauac*, pp. 17-25, quotation from p. 22.

43. Ibid., p. 24. For an oral history of the community, Margaret Randall, *Del testimonio a la lucha* (forthcoming in Spanish and in translation).

44. Fernando Cardenal, "Como cristiano revolucionario encontré un nuevo camino," *Nicarauac*, pp. 99-108; quotation from p. 103.

45. Fernando Cardenal, "Como cristiano revolucionario," p. 103.

46. Millett, *Guardians*, p. 237; Thomas Walker, *Nicaragua: The Land of Sandino*, p. 31.

47. Penny Lernoux, *Cry of the People* (New York: Penguin, 1982), pp. 103f., citing Alan Riding story in *New York Times*, Mar. 23, 1977.

48. Walker, *Nicaragua: The Land of Sandino*, pp. 31, 110; Lernoux, *Cry of the People*, p. 82.

49. Arias, ed., *Nic. Rev.*, pp. 85-105.

50. Margaret Randall, ed., *Todas estamos despiertas: Testimonios de la mujer nicaragüense de hoy* (Mexico City: Siglo XXI, 1980), chap. 3; see pp. 120-37 for her own version.

51. "Mensaje y comunicado al pueblo católico," in Marins, *Praxis*, pp. 584-88 (where it is mistakenly dated 1974).

52. Molina, "El sendero," p. 25.

53. Arias, ed., *Nic. Rev.*, p. 87.

54. Smutko, *Cristianos*, p. 52; Arias, ed., *Nic. Rev.*, p. 87.

55. Interviews and personal observation, 1973-1977. See also Dodson and Montgomery, "The Churches in the Nicaraguan Revolution," pp. 166ff. The 70,000 figure was given the author by members of the CEPAD staff. Some estimate the number of Protestants at over 250,000 (10 percent). The low figure might include only enrolled members; the higher number might include all members of households.

56. Dodson and Montgromery, "The Churches in the Nicaraguan Revolution," p. 168.

57. *Encuentro* (UCA journal), July–December 1978, pp. 87ff. This issue hereafter cited as *Encuentro*. Marins, *Praxis*, pp. 589–97; quotation from p. 595.

58. Millett, *Guardians*, p. 241.

59. Arias, ed., *Nic. Rev.*, pp. 106–13; Millett, *Guardians*, p. 242; *Apuntes*, vol. 2, pp. 243–55.

60. Arias, ed., *Nic. Rev.*, pp. 119–23.

61. *Nicarauac*, p. 52. Smutko says that some did take up arms, some supported the guerrillas with food, and some tried not to become involved.

62. Lernoux, *Cry of the People*, p. 83, citing Amnesty International report on Nicaragua (1976) and her interviews and letters from Capuchins.

63. "Statement of Father Fernando Cardenal, S.J." and documents submitted by Cardenal, in *Human Rights in Nicaragua, Guatemala, and El Salvador: Implications for U.S. Policy*, Hearings before the Subcommittee on International Organizations of the Committee on International Relations, House of Representatives, Ninety-Fourth Congress, Second Session, June 8 and 9, 1976 (Washington, D.C.: U.S. Government Printing Office, 1976), pp. 10–30.

64. Interview with Felix Jiménez, July 1981.

65. Uriel Molina, "El sendero," pp. 25–27.

66. Ibid., p. 27.

67. Interview with priest in Managua, Nicaragua, July 1981.

68. Dodson and Montgomery, "The Churches in the Nicaraguan Revolution," pp. 100–102. Some Protestants see CEPAD as having been very slow to take an antidictatorial stance.

69. Marins, *Praxis*, p. 980.

70. Molina, "El sendero," p. 28; *Encuentro*, p. 132.

71. "Sucesos nacionales," *Encuentro*, p. 8. Amando López and Juan B. Arrién, "El papel de la iglesia en la coyuntura nacional," *Encuentro*, p. 133.

72. Arias, ed., *Nic. Rev.*, pp. 128ff.; Humberto Ortega Saavedra, *50 años*, esp. pp. 60ff.

73. Arias, ed., *Nic. Rev.*, chap. 6; *Apuntes*, vol. 2, pp. 259ff.; *Un pueblo*, pp. 45–47. Again these sources vary slightly regarding dates.

74. *Apuntes*, vol. 2, p. 277; Arias, ed., *Nic. Rev.*, pp. 147, 212. *Un pueblo*, p. 47. Note that there is slight variation in dates in these accounts.

75. "Sucesos nacionales," *Encuentro*, pp. 10f.

76. Ibid., p. 12.

77. Gaspar García Laviana, in *Nicarauac*, p. 67.

78. Interview with priest, Managua, Nicaragua, July 1981. José Antonio Sanjinés, a Jesuit, also served as an FSLN combatant in 1978, subsequently leaving the priesthood.

79. Marins, *Praxis*, pp. 1005f. (whole document, pp. 1000ff.).

80. Arias, ed., *Nic. Rev.*, pp. 152f.

81. Julio Suñol, *Insurrección en Nicaragua: La historia no contada* (San José, Costa Rica: Editorial Costa Rica, 1981), pp. 65–75; *Apuntes*, vol. 2, pp. 284ff.; Thomas Walker, *Nicaragua: The Land of Sandino*, pp. 34f.; "Sucesos nacionales," *Encuentro*, pp. 15ff.

82. "Sucesos nacionales," *Encuentro*, p. 115.

83. McAnany, "Television and Crisis," pp. 36–37.

84. Lea Guido, in Randall, ed., *Todos estamos despiertas*, pp. 49ff.; cf. "Sucesos nacionales," *Encuentro*, pp. 19, 21.

85. "Sucesos nacionales," *Encuentro*, pp. 20, 23, 25.

86. Marins, *Praxis*, p. 1007.

87. *Encuentro*, pp. 105–7.

88. Ibid., p. 104.

89. "Sucesos nacionales," *Encuentro*, pp. 21f.

90. Ibid., p. 23.

91. In Arias, ed., *Nic. Rev.*; *Apuntes*, vol. 2; and Ortega Saavedra, *50 años*, the killing of Chamorro is treated simply as one event in a continuous chain of events. On the other hand, people at *La Prensa* told me in November 1980 that the killing of Chamorro "started the revolution."

92. "Sucesos nacionales," *Encuentro*, p. 23.

93. Ibid.

94. Arias, ed., *Nic. Rev.*, pp. 153–56.

95. "Sucesos nacionales," *Encuentro*, pp. 25ff. Note that the Indians on the Atlantic side (Miskitos, Sumos, and Ramas) preserve more features of a traditional way of life but have been on the margins of Nicaraguan national life. There was little combat in their region.

96. "Un ocho de marzo: Nora Astorga," chap. 5, in Randall, *Todas estamos despiertas*, pp. 167–80. Nora Astorga led four squadrons on the southern front and after victory was made special prosecutor in charge of trying Somocistas accused of crimes. (Her participation in the killing of Pérez Vega happened to take place on International Women's Day.)

97. "Sucesos nacionales," *Encuentro*, p. 27.

98. Ibid., p. 28.

99. Smutko, *Cristianos*, p. 55.

100. Thomas Walker, *Nicaragua: The Land of Sandino*, p. 36.

101. *Encuentro*, pp. 108–11.

102. Ibid., pp. 112–14.

103. Suñol, *Insurrección*, p. 114; see whole narration, chap. 8.

104. *Apuntes*, vol. II, pp. 298ff.; Arias, ed., *Nic. Rev.*, pp. 160ff.; T. Walker, pp. 36f.

105. Arias, ed., *Nic. Rev.*, p. 172; *Apuntes*, vol. 2, pp. 302ff.; T. Walker, pp. 37ff.

106. *Encuentro*, pp. 118–21.

107. The nuncio, Gabriel Montalvo, was declared persona non grata after the victory, and Ernesto Cardenal said that if the Vatican wished to send a representative it should send a Christian—the previous one had been a Somocista.

108. Walker, *Nicaragua: The Land of Sandino*, p. 36; Washington *Post*, Sept. 3, 1978.

109. The three "tendencies" were still so divided in November 1978 that they could not meet together with a fact-finding delegation led by the author but, instead, held three separate appointments.

110. Arias, ed., *Nic. Rev.*, pp. 176–81.

111. Smutko, *Cristianos*, p. 59.

5: "NO LAW HIGHER THAN GOD'S: THOU SHALT NOT KILL!"

1. On the Salvadoran economy see Eduardo Colindres, *Fundamentos económicos de la burguesía salvadoreña* (San Salvador: UCA Editores, 1977). Colindres's summary in chapter 1 is largely based on the work of David Browning, *El Salvador: Landscape and Society* (London: Oxford University Press, 1971).

2. Thomas Anderson, *Matanza: El Salvador's Communist Revolt of 1932* (Lincoln: University of Nebraska Press, 1971), pp. 16f.

3. Ignacio González Janzen, *La batalla de El Salvador* (Mexico City: Prolibro, 1981), pp. 21f.

4. Letter to Uruguayan poet Blanca Luz Brum, quoted in Anderson, *Matanza*, p. 38.

5. For Martí, see Anderson, *Matanza*, chaps. 2 and 5; Robert Armstrong and Janet Shenk, *El Salvador: The Face of Revolution* (Boston: South End Press, 1982), pp. 21ff. (hereafter cited as *Face*); González Janzen, *La batalla*, pp. 21ff.

6. Anderson, *Matanza*, p. 17.

7. There is disagreement over the date of Martí's capture, Anderson claiming it was Jan. 18. Cf. *Matanza*, pp. 93–94.

8. González Janzen, *La batalla*, p. 25.

9. Armstrong and Shenk, *Face*, pp. 29f., quoting Lilian Jiménez, *El Salvador: Sus problemas socio-economicos* (Havana: Casa de las Américas, 1980), p. 121.

10. Anderson, *Matanza*, pp. 134–36, discusses the different calculations of the numbers of people killed in 1932. His own estimate of 8,000 to 10,000 is based on an estimate of the capability of the known number of troops to kill people in a given period of time.

11. González Janzen, *La batalla*, p. 26; Anderson, *Matanza*, pp. 124–25, 141–43.

12. E.g., in 1977 I read an ad from a coffee growers' association, which referred back to a "ruler [Hernández Martínez] who knew how to put the needs of the nation first." I am quoting from memory, but despite the subtlety of the allusion, there was no doubt of its meaning for Salvadorans.

13. Gabriel García Márquez, *The Autumn of the Patriarch*, trans. Gregory Rabasa (New York: Harper and Row, 1976).

14. From Roque Dalton, *Las historias prohibidas del pulgarcito* (Mexico: Siglo XXI, 1974), quoted in Armstrong and Shenk, *Face*, p. 26.

15. Armstrong and Shenk, *Face*, p. 33.

16. Ibid., pp. 40–42; quotation from p. 42.

17. For this whole period, see Vicente Serrano, "Génesis y consolidación del Movimiento Revolucionario en El Salvador (1930–1980)," in *Cuadernos Farabundo Martí*, no. 1 (November 1980), pp. 19–27; Armstrong and Shenk, *Face*, pp. 33–42; Horacio Trujillo and Oscar Menjivar, "Economía y política en la Revolución del 48: Algunos elementos para su análisis," *Estudios centroamericanos*, no. 361/362 (November–December 1978), pp. 877–88 (*Estudios Centroamericanos* henceforth cited as *ECA*).

18. Information on Archbishop Chávez from interviews with José Inocencio Alas (January 1982) and Héctor Dada (February 1982).

19. "El Salvador: The Search for Peace," United States Department of State, Bureau of Public Affairs, September 1981.

20. Armstrong and Shenk, *Face*, p. 43.

21. Ibid., p. 47.

22. Ibid., p. 50.

23. Testimony of Dr. Fabio Castillo, *Human Rights in Nicaragua, Guatemala, and El Salvador: Implications for U.S. Policy,* Hearings before the Subcommittee on International Organizations of the Committee on International Relations, House of Representatives, Ninety-Fourth Congress, Second Session, June 8 and 9, 1976 (Washington, D.C.: U.S. Government Printing Office, 1976), p. 38.

24. Tomás Guerra, *El Salvador en la hora de la liberación* (San José, Costa Rica: Editorial Farabundo Martí, 1980), pp. 34–46. See the quotations from Medrano and Sánchez Hernández on the purposes of ORDEN.

25. It has frequently been pointed out that the American Institute for Free Labor Development exists not so much to promote unions as to combat communism. AIFLD strategy has been to develop an alternative to those unions that look beyond the company to structures in society and are therefore deemed too "political." AIFLD leaders are taught to stick to "bread-and-butter" issues. Typically a Latin American country will have Marxist, Christian Democratic (at least in origins), "gringo" (AIFLD), and independent unions.

26. Interviews with José Inocencio Alas (January 1982) and Héctor Dada (February 1982).

27. Carolyn Forché and Philip Wheaton, "History and Motivations of U.S. Involvement in the Control of the Peasant Movement in El Salvador: The Role of AIFLD in the Agrarian Reform Process, 1970–1980" (Washington, D.C.: EPICA, 1980), p. 5; Philip Wheaton, "Agrarian Reform in El Salvador: A Program of Rural Pacification" (Washington, D.C.: EPICA, 1980), pp. 2f.

28. Héctor Dada interview, February 1982.

29. José Inocencio Alas interview, January 1982.

30. For the 1969 war and its effects, see Marco Virgilio Carías and Daniel Slutsky, *La guerra inútil: Análisis socio-económico del conflicto entre Honduras y El Salvador* (San José, Costa Rica: EDUCA, 1971); Woodward, *Central America,* pp. 252–55; Armstrong and Shenk, *Face,* pp. 53ff.; Serrano, "Génesis y consolidación," p. 32.

31. Serrano, "Génesis y consolidación," Carías and Slutsky, *La guerra inútil,* pp. 19–27 passim.

32. Eduardo Colindres, "La tenencia de la tierra en El Salvador," *ECA,* nos. 335/336, pp. 469f. I have changed figures in colones to dollars.

33. Carpio quotation from González Janzen, *La batalla,* p. 51; see extensive interview in Mario Menéndez Rodríguez, *El Salvador: Una auténtica guerra civil* (San José, Costa Rica: EDUCA, 1980), pp. 23–102. Although this book, consisting largely of edited interviews with guerrilla leaders, was published in July 1980, the guerrillas remained "shadowy" and "elusive" for the U.S. media until spring 1982, when *Time* and other magazines began to publish some information on them. Since at least January 1981 Mexicans could find full-page interviews with them in their daily papers.

34. Marins, *Praxis,* pp. 116–19.

35. Text of conclusions of Pastoral Week in LADOC, vol. 1 (April 1971):65 (mimeo).

36. Benito Tobar, "Origen y peculiaridades de la iglesia que nace del pueblo en El Salvador"; Astor Ruiz, "Fe cristiana y guerra popular a partir de la experiencia centroamericana," both photocopied from CENCOS (Centro Nacional de Comunicación Social) *Iglesias* (documentation and news bulletin), November 1980.

37. Armstrong and Shenk, *Face*, pp. 59–64, say 200 were killed in the bombing and several hundred were killed in the subsequent repression, but do not give a source. Fabio Castillo in his testimony (see n. 23, above) did not give similar figures. For the most thorough study of the election, see Juan Hernández-Pico et al., *El Salvador, Año político 1972* (San Salvador: UCA, 1973).

38. Fabio Castillo in his testimony, p. 39 (see n. 23, above), describes the case of Fr. Nicolas Rodríguez, abducted by National Guardsmen in plainclothes in January 1972 and subsequently killed. In my inquiries it was not clear whether this killing was for political reasons or not.

39. UCA, *Rutilio Grande: Mártir de la evangelización rural en El Salvador* (San Salvador: UCA, 1978); documents in *ECA* nos. 348/349 (October-November 1977): 832-62; thesis of Carlos Cabarrús, "Génesis de una revolución: Análisis del surgimiento y desarrollo de la organización campesina en El Salvador" (forthcoming); also William J. O'Malley, S.J., *The Voice of Blood: Five Christian Martyrs of Our Time* (Maryknoll: Orbis Books, 1980), pp. 1–63.

40. Salvador Carranza, "Aguilares, Una experiencia de evangelización rural parroquial," *ECA*, nos. 348/349 (October-November 1977): 842.

41. Interview with Roberto Cuellar, July 1981. See also interview with Cuellar, in *Brecha* (Mexico City), May-June 1981, p. 4.

42. Armstrong and Shenk, *Face*, p. 68; José Inocencio Alas interview, January 1982.

43. Fabio Castillo testimony (see n. 23, above). Interviews with Roberto Cuellar (July 1981) and José Alas (January 1982). Bishop Aparicio's reaction to the attack was not clear from my interviews. I was told that he condemned the organizations and the attack. Both of these statements could be true.

44. Text of letter in DEI, *Centroamérica: Cristianismo y revolución* (San José, Costa Rica: DEI, 1980), pp. 15–24. On a priest being involved in writing the letter, see Benito Tobar, in prologue to Plácido Erdozaín, *Monseñor Romero: Mártir de la Iglesia Popular* (San José, Costa Rica: DEI-EDUCA, 1980), p. 12.

45. Fabio Castillo testimony (see n. 23, above), pp. 40f.; Armstrong and Shenk, *Face*, pp. 68ff.: interviews with Alas (1982), Cuellar (1981), Dada, Erdozaín (1981).

46. Armstrong and Shenk, *Face*, pp. 70ff.

47. See Gabriel Zaid, "Enemy Colleagues," *Dissent*, Winter 1982.

48. Melvin Burke, "El sistema de plantación y la proletarización del trabajo agrícola en El Salvador," *ECA*, nos. 335/336 (September-October 1976), chart p. 476.

49. Ibid., p. 480.

50. UCA, *Rutilio Grande: Mártir*, p. 50.

51. Ibid., p. 88.

52. Referring to the "Galilean crisis" discerned by Scripture scholars in the Gospel accounts: Jesus carrying out his ministry in Galilee sees his popularity diminish and opposition grow, and prepares to go up to Jerusalem to meet his destiny.

53. See tables listing holdings of the twenty leading Salvadoran families, in Colindres, *Fundamentos económicos,* table 67, pp. 399–428.

54. See *ECA* special issue nos. 335/336 (September-October 1976).

55. Impressions of the 1976 land reform attempt based on author's visits to El Salvador during and after the period; see also Wheaton, "Agrarian Reform in El Salvador"; and Armstrong and Shenk, *Face,* passim.

56. Cabarrús, "Génesis de una revolución," pp. 291–93.

57. Much of what appears here is based on my own recollection of events. For details I have found useful the day-by-day chronology in "Alfonso Navarro: Evangelio vs. opresión," *Búsqueda* (San Salvador) 5, no. 15 (March-June 1977): 23–29 (hereafter cited as "Alfonso Navarro"). This whole issue of *Búsqueda* deals with the events of the first half of 1977 and contains valuable documentation.

58. UCA, *Rutilio Grande: Mártir,* p. 92.

59. Personal observation in El Salvador.

60. First-person accounts in Ana Guadalupe Martínez, *Las cárceles clandestinas de El Salvador* (El Salvador (?): n.p., 1978), pp. 378–456. This book gives a valuable inside look at a guerrilla operation and an account of the treatment of a hostage.

61. Erdozaín, *Monseñor Romero,* passim.

62. Rutilio Grande, "Homilía con motivo de la expulsión del padre Mario Bernal," *ECA,* nos. 348/349 (October-November 1977): 858–62.

63. "Alfonso Navarro," p. 25; Erdozaín, *Monseñor Romero,* p. 31 f.; Lernoux, *Cry of the People,* p. 73; O'Malley, *The Voice of Blood,* p. 44.

64. Armstrong and Shenk, *Face,* p. 85.

65. The accounts of the attack on the postelection vigil are confusing. The account here is a composite of what I heard in El Salvador shortly afterward, and Armstrong and Shenk, *Face,* pp. 87ff. (they give the Geyer quotation, citing the *Washington Post,* Sept. 10, 1978), Lernoux, *Cry of the People,* p. 73 (she bases her account on subsequent hearings in the U.S. Congress and press accounts). Note that UCA, *Rutilio Grande: Mártir,* p. 93, says that the figure of 100 people killed cannot be confirmed.

66. Marins, *Praxis,* pp. 967–72; quotations from pp. 968, 970.

67. O'Malley, *The Voice of Blood,* p. 52.

68. O'Malley, *The Voice of Blood,* has a vivid description of the assassination but it is not clear how much is imaginative reconstruction and how much is the product of information from witnesses.

69. Erdozaín, *Monseñor Romero,* pp. 38–43; see also UCA, *Rutilio Grande: Mártir;* "Alfonso Navarro"; and O'Malley, *The Voice of Blood.*

70. Astor Ruiz, "Fe cristiana y guerra," p. 10.

71. "Alfonso Navarro," p. 27.

72. Ibid.

73. Archdiocesan bulletin no. 9 (Apr. 21, 1977) gives a detailed summary of this meeting; see *Búsqueda,* March-June 1977, pp. 78–81.

74. Archdiocesan bulletin no. 14, *Búsqueda,* March-June 1977, pp. 84–88; "Alfonso Navarro," pp. 27ff.; O'Malley, *The Voice of Blood,* pp. 52f.

75. "Alfonso Navarro," pp. 19, 23.

76. O'Malley, *The Voice of Blood,* pp. 53f.; Lernoux, *Cry of the People,* p. 76; my visits to El Salvador in 1976.

77. Oscar Romero, *La voz de los sin voz: La palabra viva de Monseñor Romero* (San Salvador: UCA Editores, 1980), pp. 201–5 (henceforth cited as Romero, *Voz*).

78. Armstrong and Shenk, *Face,* pp. 93ff.; Lernoux, *Cry of the People,* pp. 61ff. (and the whole chap.); O'Malley, *The Voice of Blood,* pp. 54ff.; Erdozaín, *Monseñor Romero,* pp. 49ff.; and author's visit to El Salvador, May 1977.

79. Romero, *Voz,* pp. 208–12.

80. O'Malley, *The Voice of Blood,* pp. 56f.

81. Armstrong and Shenk, *Face,* p. 92. *Búsqueda,* March-June 1977 (pp. 108–10), gives a list of incidents.

82. *ECA*, No. 345, July 1977 (pp. 515–19), gives text of President Carlos Romero's inaugural address; see also editorial, pp. 453–57.

83. My visits to El Salvador in 1977, including interviews in U.S. embassy.

84. Erdozaín, *Monseñor Romero,* pp. 54ff.; letter in Romero, *Voz,* pp. 67–79.

85. Armstrong and Shenk, *Face,* pp. 97f. For an analysis of the law, see report of the International Commission of Jurists, prepared by Donald Fox: translation in *ECA,* no. 359 (September 1978): 779–86.

86. O'Malley, The Voice of Blood, p. 60.

87. *ECA*, no. 354 (April 1978): 245f. My impressions of human-rights work in the Archdiocese of San Salvador and of the Human Rights Commission of El Salvador, gathered on frequent visits, 1977–80.

88. *ECA*, no. 353 (March 1978), pp. 109ff.

89. *ECA*, no. 355 (May 1978), pp. 330–32.

90. Text in Romero, *Voz,* pp. 91–121.

91. *ECA*, no. 359 (September 1978), pp. 774f.

92. Romero, *Voz,* pp. 113–19.

93. Erdozaín, *Monseñor Romero,* pp. 83–97; Romero, *Voz,* p. 332.

94. Social Communication Secretariat, Archdiocese of San Salvador "Informe sobre la represión en El Salvador," bulletin no. 10, Dec. 12, 1979, cited in Ignacio Martín-Baró, "Monseñor Romero: Una voz para un pueblo pisoteado," in Romero, *Voz,* p. 22.

95. *ECA*, nos. 361/362 (November-December 1978), pp. 865–76; quotations from p. 870.

96. Commission on Human Rights, *Informe sobre derechos humanos en El Salvador* (San José, Costa Rica: CIDH, 1979).

97. Oscar Romero, sermon of Jan. 21, 1979, *Voz,* p. 222.

98. Ibid., p. 221.

99. Ibid., p. 222.

100. Erdozaín, *Monseñor Romero,* p. 114, says 380 priests and 600 sisters marched; but Ivan D. Paredes, "La situación de la iglesia católica en El Salvador y su influjo social," *ECA* (photocopy, issue number unclear, some time in late 1979), p. 604, puts the total number of priests in the country at 330 (192 religious and 138 diocesan), of whom 189 were in San Salvador.

101. Remark of a UCA professor. Speech from American Chamber of Commerce in San Salvador (mimeo no longer in author's possession).

102. E. C. Anaya, "Crónica del mes: Mayo 1979," *ECA*, no. 368, pp. 450–52, cited in Martín- Baró, "Monseñor Romero," p. 26.

103. Armstrong and Shenk, *Face,* p. 113, Erdozaín, *Monseñor Romero,* pp. 114–17; E. C. Anaya, "Crónica del mes: Junio-Julio 1979," *ECA*, no. 369, p. 712.

104. Ibid., p. 712.

105. My visits to El Salvador, 1979; Anaya, "Crónica del mes: Junio-Julio 1979," *ECA* 369, p. 712.

106. Whole text in Romero, *Voz,* pp. 123–72 (quotation on coffee growers, etc., p. 133; on violence, pp. 156–59).

107. Romero, *Voz:* on Marxism, pp. 159–60; on national dialogue, pp. 160–62.

108. Romero, *Voz,* pp. 168–70.

109. My visits to El Salvador, 1979. See E. C. Anaya, "Crónica del mes: Septiembre-Octubre 1979," in *ECA* (mimeo). Figures on arrests and people killed from Martín-Baró, "Monseñor Romero," p. 25.

110. "Communist Interference in El Salvador," Special Report No. 80, Feb. 23, 1981. A second White Paper was prepared (September 1981; see n. 19, above), apparently to counter the criticism of the February paper that it had ignored internal Salvadoran history, but the September 1981 paper was superficial and ignored important events. One evidence of the essential ignorance of those who compiled it was the assertion that Rutilio Grande may have been killed in retaliation for the killing of Foreign Minister Mauricio Borgonovo—who was in fact kidnapped after Grande's death. Borgonovo was probably confused with Roberto Poma. However, the fact that the error was not detected shows the paper to be essentially the work of library researchers and State Department polemicists rather than of people with any direct knowledge of El Salvador.

111. "Proclama de la fuerza armada emitida a raíz del golpe," in Rafael Menjivar, *El Salvador: El eslabón mas débil* (San José, Costa Rica: EDUCA, 1981), pp. 143–47.

112. For a description of the coup process, see Armstrong and Shenk, *Face,* pp. 116ff. The "three-coup" theory was heard in El Salvador during my visits from October 1979 to March 1980.

113. Erdozaín, *Monseñor Romero,* pp. 118ff., assumes the coup to have been directed from Washington and lines up a sequence of events and meetings to illustrate; on the U.S. embassy having been advised, cf. E. C. Anaya, "Crónica del mes: Septiembre-Octubre 1979," *ECA* (1979; photocopy, issue number not clear), p. 1005; alternate view given by former Christian Democratic leader.

114. Interviews in U.S. embassy and U.S.A.I.D., San Salvador, October 1979, including interview with Ambassador Devine. U.S. officials did not speak of a "Taiwan model," but did speak of "industrialization" in similar terms.

115. Anaya, "Crónica del mes: Septiembre-Octubre 1979," p. 1007.

116. Ibid., p. 1007.

117. Archbishop Romero, sermon (Oct. 21, 1979), *Voz,* pp. 379–81. Author present at meeting with family members of "disappeared."

118. Romero, sermon (Nov. 4, 1979), *Voz,* p. 382.

119. Ibid., pp. 417ff.

120. Ibid. (Nov. 11, 1979), *Voz,* p. 418.

121. Erdozaín, *Monseñor Romero,* pp. 121ff.

122. Armstrong and Shenk, *Face,* p. 140.

123. Ibid., pp. 126f.; Romero, *Voz,* p. 389.

124. Armstrong and Shenk, *Face,* pp. 127f.

125. Legal Aid Office, Archdiocese of San Salvador, *El Salvador: Del genocidio de la junta militar a la esperanza de la lucha insurreccional,* p. 36; Armstrong and Shenk, *Face,* p. 129.

126. Statement reprinted in Menjivar, *El Salvador: El eslabón mas débil,* pp. 177–84.

127. Statement in Menjivar, ibid. pp. 185ff. (quotations on pp. 187, 188).

128. Romero (Jan. 6, 1980), *Voz,* pp. 382–84.

129. Ibid. (Jan. 13, 1980), *Voz,* pp. 385f.

130. For a very detailed report, see Francisco Andrés Escobar, "En la linea de la

muerte (La manifestación del 22 de enero de 1980)," *ECA,* Nos. 375/376 (January-February 1980), pp. 21–35 (photocopy).

131. James Cheek, interview in State Department, Washington, D.C., fall 1980.

132. Interview in Romero, *Voz,* p. 444; see also, pp. 419f.

133. Archbishop Romero, sermon (Jan. 20, 1980), *Voz,* pp. 237ff.

134. Guerra, *El Salvador,* pp. 93ff.; Romero, *Voz,* p. 262.

135. Ibid., pp. 263f.

136. Visits to El Salvador, March 1980. Also Armstrong and Shenk, *Face,* p. 141.

137. Author made three visits to El Salvador in March 1980 and was present when the land reform began.

138. Romero, sermon (Mar. 23, 1980), *Voz,* pp. 269–91 (quotation from p. 291).

139. Paul Heath Hoeffel, "The Eclipse of the Oligarchs," *New York Times Magazine,* Sept. 6, 1981, p. 26.

140. My view differs from what I understood to be the analysis of the popular organizations at the time. They saw the assassination as a "provocation" intended to spark a premature uprising; I saw it as an extremely calculated move by people who had weighed the pros and cons carefully and decided they could afford the risk of killing Archbishop Romero. To me it is not idle to recall that in early 1979 it was reported that the CIA had been ordered by President Carter to study church movements in Latin America so as not to be caught "unprepared" as in Iran. (See account in Lernoux, *Cry of the People,* p. 445, and Lernoux and Mark Winiarski, "CIA Ordered to Survey Latin American Church," *National Catholic Reporter,* Feb. 16, 1979). If such an order were given it seems reasonable to conclude that the CIA (or other intelligence agencies) had come to understand something of church politics and could have "hypothesized" the probable effects of the elimination of Romero—such calculations would have been implicit in the assignment, one assumes. Hence one is led to wonder whether any U.S. intelligence operatives (or "independent assets" moving at some distance for plausible deniability) were privy to the assassination plans at any point. The future may bring revelations—for the moment the point remains speculative.

141. Interview in *Excelsior* (Mexico City), and in Romero, *Voz,* p. 62.

142. Hoeffel, "The Eclipse of the Oligarchs," *New York Times Magazine,* Sept. 6, 1981, p. 26. On land reform, see Forsché and Wheaton, "History and Motivations of U.S."; Wheaton, "Agrarian Reform in El Salvador"; Leonel Gómez "Prepared Statement of Leonel Gómez before the Sub-Committee on Inter-American Affairs, March 11, 1981 (mimeo); Armstrong and Shenk, *Face,* pp. 142ff. and passim; Laurence R. Simon and James Stephens, Jr., *El Salvador Land Reform 1980–1981* (revised 1982 with supplement by Martin Diskin; Boston: Oxfam-America); Washington Office on Latin America, *Conference on Land Tenure in Central America* (proceedings of conference held March 23, 1981, Johns Hopkins University, School of Advanced International Studies), pp. 45–53; Raymond Bonner, *New York Times,* Apr. 19, 1982.

143. *ECA,* nos. 377/378 (March-April 1980), special issue.

144. Events reported in Guatemalan papers, May 1980. Armstrong and Shenk, *Face,* pp. 159–61.

145. Armstrong and Shenk, *Face,* pp. 164–67.

146. Legal Aid Office, *El Salvador: Del genocidio de la junta,* pp. 21–29 (quotations from pp. 28, 29.)

147. CUDI (Centro Universitario de Documentación e Información San Salva-

dor) *Balance Estadístico*, Year 1, No. 2, August 1980, pp. 40, 42. Also FPL bulletins nos. 6–8.

148. For a thorough critique of the White Paper, see Warner Poelchau, ed., *White Paper Whitewash: Interviews with Philip Agee on the CIA and El Salvador* (New York: Deep Cover Books, 1981).

149. For the controversy over the possibility of an inflated vote count, see *New York Times*, June 3, 4, 6, 14, 17, 1982.

150. James Petras, "Behind the Salvador Vote Turnout," *The Guardian*, Apr. 28, 1982.

151. *Brecha* (Mexico City), May-June 1981, p. 15, carries a facsimile of a letter of Arriola committing herself to virginity in the service of Christ and the people.

152. Interview in *Brecha*, May-June 1981, p. 12.

153. See also Clifford Krause, "The Religious Roots of Rebellion in El Salvador," *The Nation*, July 3, 1982, pp. 7–10.

6: "THE COLOR OF BLOOD IS NEVER FORGOTTEN!"

1. Susanne Jonas and David Tobis, *Guatemala* (Berkeley, Calif.: North American Congress on Latin America, 1974), p. 30 (henceforth cited as NACLA, *Guatemala*).

2. Official figures are low: according to the 1950 census Indians were more than 53%, whereas by the 1964 census they were only 43.3% of the population (John Dombrowski et al., *Area Handbook for Guatemala* [Washington, D.C.: U.S. Government Printing Office, 1970]). Such official figures, based on signs of acculturation to the dominant culture, are generally considered to carry a bias, e.g., people may speak Spanish and wear some non-Indian clothes and still be Indian. Hence, while there are no precise figures, Indians constitute at least half of the population, and some people estimate them at up to 60%.

3. Richard Newbold Adams, *Crucifixion by Power: Essays on Guatemalan National Social Structure, 1944–1966* (Austin: University of Texas Press, 1970), p. 278.

4. NACLA, *Guatemala*, p. 45.

5. For the first version: Ronald M. Schneider, *Communism in Guatemala: 1944–1954* (New York: Frederick A. Praeger, 1958); and more recently, L. Francis Bouchey and Alberto M. Piedra, *Guatemala: A Promise in Peril* (Washington, D.C.: Council for Inter-American Security, 1980), with bibliography. A recent study with many new details, especially of the U.S. role, is Stephen Schlesinger and Stephen Kinzer, *Bitter Fruit: The Untold Story of the American Coup in Guatemala* (Garden City, N.Y.: Doubleday, 1982).

6. *The Economic Development of Guatemala* (Washington, D.C.: International Bank for Reconstruction and Development, 1951). This report is interesting inasmuch as it provides evidence that the IBRD (World Bank) accepted as normal the development aims of the Arévalo-Arbenz governments. Although Arbenz rejected the report, a superficial reading indicates that subsequent governments have carried out its recommendations in general lines.

7. NACLA, *Guatemala*, p. 48.

8. Ibid., pp. 49f.

9. Guatemalans old enough to remember this period, even those today identi-

fied with the left, do not always see the period as clearly as it is presented by the left outside the country. It is possible, of course, that they were affected by the "psychological war" used against the Arbenz government.

10. NACLA, *Guatemala*, p. 56.

11. Incident recalled by a priest working in Guatemala at the time.

12. NACLA, *Guatemala*, pp. 57–73; also pp. 50f.; Schlesinger and Kinzer, *Bitter Fruit*.

13. Schlesinger and Kinzer, *Bitter Fruit*, pp. 155, 174, 214, 198; Gregorio Selser, "La Iglesia en Guatemala," *Cuadernos de Marcha*, 11th year, no. 10 (November-December 1980), p. 62; Pablo Richard and Guillermo Meléndez, eds., *La Iglesia de los pobres en centroamérica* (San José, Costa Rica: DEI, 1982), pp. 197–99.

14. NACLA, *Guatemala*, pp. 74–81 (Nixon quotation from p. 74).

15. Adams, *Crucifixion by Power*, pp. 282ff.; Dombrowski et al., *Area Handbook for Guatemala*, p. 118; Selser, "La Iglesia en Guatemala," says a half-million people attended the Eucharistic Congress, but gives no source. The figure seems exaggerated.

16. Shelton H. Davis, "State Violence and Agrarian Crisis in Guatemala," paper presented at the Latin American Studies Association (LASA) Conference, Washington, D.C., March 1982 (mimeo), p. 8. Davis's sources are the Inter-American Development Bank and several monographs.

17. On the development associated with the Central American Common Market, see NACLA, *Guatemala*, pp. 132–50.

18. The most detailed account of the guerrilla movement of the 1960s is to be found in Regis Debray, *Las pruebas de fuego: La crítica de las armas/2* (Mexico City: Siglo XXI, 1975), pp. 249–339, co-written with Ricardo Ramírez, a participant in the struggle. NACLA, *Guatemala*, pp. 176–208, gives a very good account of the guerrilla struggle and the U.S.-directed "counterinsurgency." Eduardo Galeano, *Guatemala: Occupied Country* (New York: Monthly Review Press, 1967), gives an up-close journalistic look. Concerned Guatemalan Scholars, "Dare to Struggle, Dare to Win" (New York: Concerned Guatemalan Scholars, 1981) gives a good short summary and links the 1960s movement with present developments.

19. On EXMIBAL, see NACLA, *Guatemala*, pp. 151–69; on the Northern Transversal Strip, see U.S.A.I.D., "Small Farmer Improvement, Project Number 520-11-190-/233/520-L-026" (December 1975; mimeo, title page missing), and "Subprograma de desarrollo integral de la Franja Transversal Norte," from the Secretariat of Planning, Guatemalan government.

20. Roger Plant, *Guatemala: Unnatural Disaster* (London: Latin America Bureau, 1978), p. 22; Instituto de Investigaciones Políticas y Sociales (Institute for Political and Social Research—University of San Carlos—i.e., national university), "Los partidos políticos en Guatemala," *ECA*, no. 356 (June 1978): 478, and whole article; also in the same issue, José M. Rivas, "Elecciones presidenciales en Guatemala: Ilegitimidad progresiva del gobierno," pp. 429–36.

21. Data from charts photocopied from CELAM Ecclesiastical Directory of the late 1960s.

22. Dombrowski et al., *Area Handbook for Guatemala*, p. 119; Adams, *Crucifixion by Power*, pp. 305ff.

23. Figures on cooperatives from Davis, "State Violence," p. 11; Plant, *Guatemala*, p. 87.

24. Thomas and Marjorie Melville, *Whose Heaven, Whose Earth?* (New York: Alfred A. Knopf, 1971); statement by Thomas Melville in *National Catholic Reporter*, Jan. 31, 1968, reprinted in Galeano, *Guatemala*, pp. 149–59.

25. Galeano, Guatemala, pp. 34f.

26. Selser, "La Iglesia en Guatemala," p. 68, and interviews by author.

27. Interviews with priests who worked in Guatemala during the 1960s; Richard and Meléndez, *La Iglesia de los pobres*, p. 210.

28. Text in José Marins et al., *Praxis de los padres de América Latina* (Bogotá: Ediciones Paulinas, 1978), pp. 110ff. (cited hereafter as Marins, *Praxis*).

29. Ibid., pp. 324ff.

30. Marins, in *Praxis*, lists hundreds of documents from Latin American episcopates during the 1968–78 period. Between 1971 and 1976 there is only one from the Guatemalan bishops (Mar. 20, 1974, period of electoral fraud against General Ríos Montt). That it was simply listed and not included in this 1,000-page collection would indicate that it was not viewed as significant. For the expulsion of Frey, etc., see Richard and Meléndez, *La Iglesia de los pobres*, pp. 215f.

31. These observations are based on interviews with priests who worked in Guatemala during this period and on the chapter on the church in Adams, *Crucifixion by Power*.

32. Interviews with Anna and Donald Sibley; Kenneth G. Grubb, *Religion in Central America* (New York: World Dominion Press, 1937). Statistics also from *The Christian Ministry in Latin America and the Caribbean* (tables photocopied, publisher unknown, date probably mid-1960s). Information on "Pascual" from Debray, *Las pruebas del fuego*, p. 267.

33. Plant, *Guatemala*, p. 7; Miguel Ángel Albizurez, "Luchas y experiencias del movimiento sindical, Período 1976–Junio 1978," *ECA*, no. 356 (June 1978): 478–89.

34. Albizurez, "Luchas and experiencias," pp. 478–83.

35. Text in Marins, *Praxis*, pp. 791–817; quotations from pp. 795, 799, 804.

36. Mario Payeras, *Los días de la selva* (Mexico City: Escuela Nacional de Antropología e Historia, 1981); on the killing of Arenas, pp. 97–106. The whole book gives a remarkable glimpse into the early days of the EGP struggle.

37. Interviews with priests who worked in the area; also Plant, *Guatemala*, p. 91.

38. Talk with Woods two weeks before his crash; interviews with his colleagues and with relatives of other passengers on the plane who investigated the crash; also cf. Ron Chernow, "The Strange Death of Bill Woods," *Mother Jones*, May 1979, pp. 32–41. (In some details Chernow is in error, e.g., painting Woods as leftist ideologically.)

39. Figures from Instituto de Investigaciones Económicas y Sociales, USAC (San Carlos, National University), cited in *Dare to Struggle, Dare to Win*.

40. Carlos Felipe Castro Torres, "Crecimiento de las luchas campesinas en Guatemala, Febrero 1976–Mayo 1978," *ECA*, no. 356 (June 1978): 462–77, brings together a great deal of information.

41. Author's personal recollection. On the bishops' statement and its emendation, see Ignacio López Amezcua, "Una conferencia episcopal para la galería," *ECA*, no. 354 (April 1978): 250–58.

42. On CNT split from CLAT and founding of CUC, see Castro Torres, "Crecimiento de las luchas campesinas," pp. 475–77.

43. None of the major U.S. media carried accounts of the Panzos massacre

except the wire services, which gave the government version, and *Newsweek*, which allowed a reporter to go to Guatemala and then published a half-page story. One is left with the impression that the mass killing of nonwhites in out-of-the-way places is not considered a major news event.

44. I am here following a mimeographed document, "Repressive Violence in Guatemala, January 1978–March 1979: Overview and Background," which has extensive documentation as it is largely based on two documents, titled "Violencia política en Guatemala," covering the periods January-June and July-December 1978. These are summaries of newspaper accounts.

45. Cf. "Notes on Guatemala: 1979," pp. 17–26, a document similar to the one referred to in n. 44.

46. "Notes on Guatemala: 1979," pp. 17ff.

47. Personal recollections of author; on resignation of Manresa, see Richard and Meléndez, *La Iglesia de los pobres*, p. 234.

48. "Genocide in El Quiché: A Testimonial of the Persecuted Church," Popular History No. 1, Guatemala Information Center. This is a first-person account by a priest from Quiché (hereafter cited as "Genocide").

49. The author interviewed four of the peasants who subsequently occupied the embassy (including Vicente Menchu), was present at the funeral march and demonstration, and studied the many media accounts of the attack in Guatemala. A friend of the author attended the funeral of the two Guatemalan dignataries. There he met a relative of ex-Vice President Caceres Lenhoff and remarked how terrible the incident was. "Yes," came the reply, "but it had to be done." This member of the Guatemalan upper class refused to blame the police or the government for the death of his own relative.

50. "Declaración de Iximché," reprinted in "Guatemala: Documentos y testimonios de un pueblo en lucha" (Mexico City: Coordinadora Cristiana de Solidaridad con la Lucha del Pueblo de Guatemala, n.d.) (mimeo), pp. 10–16.

51. Personal recollection; "Genocide."

52. "Message of the Bishops Conference of Guatemala, May 15, 1980," in *The Church Martyred: Guatemala* (Minneapolis: Guatemala Solidarity Committee of Minnesota, 1981) pp. 24f. See statement of Jesuits in ibid., pp. 12f. (hereafter cited as *Church Martyred*).

53. *Church Martyred*, pp. 22f., translation slightly emended.

54. Ibid., pp. 31–34.

55. See documents of FDCR in "Guatemala: Documentos y testimonios de un pueblo en lucha."

56. *Noticias de Guatemala*, 2nd year, no. 44 (June 16, 1980), p. 15 (hereafter cited as *Not. de G.*).

57. For this period, see *Not. de G.*, 2nd year, no. 45 (June 30, 1980).

58. *Not. de G.*, 2nd year, no. 46 (July 14, 1980), pp. 2ff. and passim; no. 45, p. 17.

59. Second National Conference of Religious, in *Church Martyred*, p. 35.

60. "Genocide," p. 8.

61. Ibid., pp. 9–10.

62. *Not. de G.*, 2nd year, no. 47 (July 28, 1980), p. 3.

63. *Church Martyred*, pp. 23–24.

64. *Not. de G.*, 2nd year, no. 56 (Dec. 1, 1980), pp. 4–6.

65. *News from Guatemala* (Toronto), vol. 2, no. 11 (December 1980), pp. 7–8.

66. American Chamber of Commerce, bulletin (Guatemala City) no. 162, May 23, 1980.

67. One measure of how little influence Villagrán had: in April 1979 he had not talked to Lucas more than two times so far that year, according to a journalist who spoke with the author after interviewing Villagrán.

68. Elías Barahona, extensive interview in *La República* (Panama), Sept. 4, 1980. Lucas's chief-of-staff told American investigative reporter Alan Nairn that the interior minister, Donaldo Ruiz, had taken Barahona into his confidence after getting good information from him about the guerrillas. Alan Nairn, "Controversial Reagan Campaign Links with Guatemalan Government and Private Sector Leaders," Council on Hemispheric Affairs press statement, Oct. 30, 1980. An added reason for Barahona's credibility is that the government initially claimed he had been its agent—rather than simply denying his story.

69. Interviews with Coca-Cola union leaders, 1976–80; Walker Simon, "After Global Pressure, Things Go Better with Coke," *Food Monitor*, no. 19 (November-December 1980): 5ff.

70. Barahona interview.

71. Nairn, "Controversial Reagan Campaign Links."

72. Amnesty International, "A Government Program of Political Murder,"

73. ORPA, "One Year of War," *Erupción*, no. 8 (1981); EGP bulletin, Oct. 5, 1980.

74. *Not. de G.*, no. 60 (Feb. 9, 1981): 1; no. 65 (May 4, 1981): 11; bulletin of FP-31.

75. Documentation in "Guatemala, Centroamérica, testimonios: Exodo de campesinos a México," and "Recortes de prensa: Refugiados guatemaltecos en México, Junio-Julio 1981." Documentation reprinted in San José, Costa Rica.

76. FP-31 documents.

77. "Religious Only a Fraction," *National Catholic Reporter*, Mar. 5, 1982, pp. 22f.

78. "Foreigners Threatened," *National Catholic Reporter*, July 3, 1981, p. 21.

79. *National Catholic Reporter*, Aug. 14, 1981, and Oct. 9, 1981; Frankie Williams's statement in *Human Rights in Guatemala*, hearings July 30, 1981, pp. 53–63.

80. *Prensa Libre* (Guatemala), Aug. 4 and 5, 1981; on McKenna, see Mario Menéndez Rodríguez, "La Iglesia de Cristo en armas," *Por Esto* (Mexico City) no. 5 (July 30, 1981): 6–13, with photographs.

81. *Church Martyred*, pp. 26–28.

82. "Declaraciones del P. Luis Pellecer" (transcript of statement and question period).

83. URNG statement (mimeo).

84. Justice and Peace Committee, "Informe de los principales hechos represivos atribuidos al gobierno de Guatemala, bandas paramilitares y otros."

85. *New York Times*, July 18, 1982.

86. Gráfico quoted in CRIE, no. 96, Apr. 12, 1982.

87. Bishops statement and Confregua.

8: CHRISTIANS IN SANDINISTA NICARAGUA

1. Leslie Dewart, *Christianity and Revolution: The Lesson of Cuba* (New York: Herder and Herder, 1963).

2. Quotation from mimeo document summarizing news events, January-August 1979: original source, Guatemalan daily papers.

3. Thomas Walker, *Nicaragua: Land of Sandino* (Boulder, Colo.: Westview Press, 1981), p. 42.

4. Ibid., p. 43.

5. Mimeographed document summarizing news events: original source, Guatemalan daily papers.

6. Meeting of *MDN* in October 1979, witnessed by the author.

7. *Noticias Aliadás*, Sept. 6, 1979; *CRIE*, no. 76-77 (July 1981): 5. This special issue of *CRIE*, on the second anniversary of the Sandinista victory, is a valuable collection of documents on the church and the revolution. (Hereafter cited as *CRIE*, no. 76-77.)

8. *El Diario de Honduras*, Aug. 13, 1979; *Noticias Aliadas*, Sept. 6, 1979, and Sept. 20, 1979; all in *CRIE*, no. 76-77, pp. 5ff.

9. *Fe cristiana y revolución sandinista en Nicaragua* (IHCA Conference proceedings) (Managua: IHCA, 1980), pp. 81-102 (quotation from p. 98).

10. Ibid., pp. 352, 116ff.

11. *Compañero* literally means "companion"; although it may be translated as "comrade" it is distinguished from *camarada*, which has a distinctly communist-party tone.

12. *Fe cristiana y revolución sandinista en Nicaragua*, p. 358. The introduction to the book develops the idea.

13. RIPEN II, "Declaración de los 500" (mimeo). Meeting reported also in *La Prensa*, Oct. 6, 1979.

14. Sergio Ramírez, when asked what he thought of the bishops' letter, said (approximately): "We think it's fine—but it puts us in a bit of a problem: we're not speaking about socialism!"

15. "Los cristianos están con la Revolución: Carta pastoral de los obispos nicaragüenses" (San José, Costa Rica: DEI, n.d.), pp. 15-30 (quotations from pp. 20, 21-22, 23-24, 26).

16. *Barricada*, December 9, 1979.

17. Ministry of Planning, *Programa de reactivación económica en beneficio del pueblo* (Managua: Secretaría Nacional de Propaganda y Educación Política del FSLN, 1980). Jaime Wheelock called the Sandinista approach to the economy a "creative application of Marxism" (*Central America Report* [Guatemala] 7, no. 16, [Apr. 28, 1980]: 124f.; *Central America Report* hereafter cited as *CAR*).

18. *CAR* 7, no. 16 (April 28, 1980): 125.

19. *CAR* 7, no. 13 (Mar. 31, 1980): 99; no. 48 (Dec. 6, 1980): 382.

20. *CAR* 7, no. 43 (Nov. 8, 1980): 347-48.

21. *CAR* 7, no. 16 (Apr. 28, 1980): 123; no. 17 (May 5, 1980): 129ff.; no. 18 (May 12, 1980): 144.

22. *CAR* 7, no. 6 (Feb. 11, 1980): 44; no. 8 (Feb. 25, 1980): 61; no. 9 (Mar. 3, 1980): 60; no. 10 (Mar. 10, 1980): 79; no. 12 (Mar. 24, 1980): 91; no. 25 (June 30, 1980): 195; no. 36 (Sept. 13, 1980): 284; no. 38 (Sept. 27, 1980): 299.

23. Newspapers in early 1980: on Obando in Cuba, *La Prensa* and *Barricada*, both Mar. 13; bishops' Lenten message, *La Prensa*, Mar. 2; on Archbishop Romero, *Barricada* Mar. 25 and 26.

24. Bishops' statement quoted in *CRIE*, nos. 76-77, p. 13; CEPAD statement in CRIE, nos. 76-77, p. 12.

25. *La Prensa*, Aug. 28, 30, 1980; *Barricada* and *La Prensa*, both Aug. 31, 1980.

26. *CRIE* (Centro Regional de Información Ecuménica) bulletin, July 1981, nos. 76–77, p. 14, reprinting *Proceso* (Mexico City), May 5, 1980; *Barricada*, Apr. 24, 1980.

27. Bishops' text in *Barricada*, May 16, 1980; for Hassán, see *Barricada*, May 23, 1980; for Cardenal, see *Barricada*, May 17, 1980.

28. *La Prensa*, May 28, 1980.

29. *Barricada*, June 1, 1980.

30. These impressions of Protestant churches are based on my frequent visits to Nicaragua as well as on formal interviews; nevertheless, I have been unable to assess adequately the role of these churches and the exact role of the Ecumenical Axis.

31. *La Prensa*, August 12, 1980. The Christian Businessmen group returned to Nicaragua later even after relations with the Reagan administration had become tense.

32. *CRIE*, nos. 76–77, p. 26; *El Nuevo Diario*, Aug. 20, 1980; *La Prensa*, Sept. 16, 1980.

33. *El Nuevo Diario*, Aug. 27, 1980.

34. On CELAM, see *CRIE*, nos. 76–77, which reprints articles from *Noticias Aliadas* and *El Nuevo Diario*; see also *El Nuevo Diario*, Sept. 21–22, 1980, for extensive two-part article.

35. Cf. *Apuntes para una teología nicaragüense: Encuentro de teología, Managua, Nicaragua, 8–14 de Septiembre de 1980* (San José, Costa Rica: DEI, 1981), especially "Problemas que plantea a la fe eclesial el proceso revolucionario" and the Conclusions.

36. Author present at Borge speech.

37. Note that all three dailies in Managua are managed by members of the Chamorro family: Pedro Joaquín Chamorro (*La Prensa*), Xavier Chamorro (*Nuevo Diario*), Carlos F. Chamorro (*Barricada*).

38. *La Prensa*, Aug. 28, Sept. 8, Sept. 9, Sept. 17, Oct. 1, 1980.

39. *La Prensa*, Aug. 4, 1980.

40. "Comunicado oficial de la Dirección Nacional del FSLN sobre la Religión," *Barricada*, Oct. 7, 1980. For an overview and discussion of the relationship between Marxism and Christianity as a basis for appreciating the innovative aspect of the FSLN communiqué, see Arthur McGovern, *Marxism: An American Christian Perspective* (Maryknoll, N.Y.: Orbis Books, 1981), esp. chaps. 2 and 8; on the Latin American background, chaps. 5 and 6.

41. The Spanish is *halagos y prebendas*, the word *prebendas* being a reference to clerical benefices; in other words, the priests are accused of being at the service of the Sandinista government like clerics of an earlier age who supported feudal power arrangements.

42. *CRIE*, no. 61.

43. Ibid.

44. *CAR* 7, no. 15 (Apr. 11, 1981): 114; *New York Times*, March 17, 1981; *CAR* 7, no. 12 (Mar. 21, 1981); no. 9 (Feb. 28, 1981): 68; no. 19 (May 16, 1981): 147.

45. *CAR* 7, no. 2 (Jan. 10, 1981): 10; no. 15 (Apr. 11, 1981): 114f.; no. 24 (June 20, 1981): 185f.; no. 26 (July 4, 1981): 206; no. 12 (Mar. 21, 1981): 92; no. 13 (Mar. 28, 1981): 98.

46. *CAR* 7, no. 16 (Apr. 25, 1981): 124; no. 29 (July 25, 1981): 225ff.; no. 32 (Aug. 15, 1981): 253.

47. *CAR* 8, no. 48 (Dec. 5, 1981): 379f.; *CAR* 9, no. 3 (Jan. 23, 1982): 17f.; no. 9 (Mar. 6, 1982): 70–71.

48. "Jesucristo y la unidad de su Iglesia en Nicaragua," printed in *La Prensa*, Jan. 11, 1981.

49. Christians for the Revolution, "Los cristianos interpelan a la Revolución: Fidelidad crítica en el proceso de Nicaragua" (Managua: IHCA-CAV, 1981), booklet containing text of the document, introduction, and panel discussions.

50. Bishops' decree in *Barricada*, June 5, 1981.

51. These reasons are taken from the decree and from interviews, esp. interview with Fr. Bismarck Carballo, diocesan press secretary, who strongly insisted on the church's maintaining its own identity (February 1982 interview), not only regarding this controversy but in its overall posture.

52. Wire service stories on Obando reported in *El Nuevo Diario*, June 7 and 21, 1981; *La Prensa*, June 21 and 24, 1981; *Barricada*, June 18 and 21, 1981.

53. Sandinista television station's letter, in *Barricada*, July 7, 1981; controversy continued for several days in the papers; statement of Priests' Council of Managua, in *La Prensa*, July 12, 1981.

54. *El Nuevo Diario*, June 11, 1981; *Barricada*, June 8 and 9, 1981.

55. Internal document of Christian groups supporting priests in government (photocopy).

56. One indication of the controversy: the author has over 100 pages of material photocopied from Managua papers during June and the first half of July 1981, all reflecting the priests-in-government controversy and the controversy around Obando. On the Vatican: *El Nuevo Diario*, June 20 and 23, 1981; on secrecy and use of authority, and on Bishop López Ardon: *El Nuevo Diario*, June 6, 1981.

57. *Barricada*, June 8, 1981.

58. Ibid.

59. *Barricada*, June 7, 1981; *El Nuevo Diario*, June 9, 1981; column by Raúl Orozco, *El Nuevo Diario*, June 12, 1981.

60. *El Nuevo Diario*, June 19, 1981; cf. June 12, 1981.

61. "Carta abierta de las comunidades cristianas de base," p. 2.

62. Christians for the Revolution, "Tiempos de crisis, tiempo de discernimiento y de gracia: Reflexión pastoral ante el comunicado pastoral de los obispos del 1 de junio de 1981."

63. "Carta abierta," p. 3.

64. Opinion expressed by people in Managua during priest controversy, June-July 1981.

PART THREE:
ISSUES IN ETHICS, CHURCH PRACTICE, AND THEOLOGY

1. Archbishop Romero, speech at Louvain, Belgium, February 1980, "La Dimensión política de la fe desde la óptica de los pobres," *Voz*, pp. 190–91.

9: ETHICS OF THE REVOLUTIONARY *PROYECTO*

1. In *Freedom Made Flesh* Ignacio Ellacuría devotes the three final chapters to the theme of violence. However, his considerations are theoretical and are not a

reflection on the specific struggle of El Salvador, since the work was written in the early 1970s.

2. Some further remarks on these figures are in order. They reflect approximately the situation in 1977–78. At that time ANACAFE, the Guatemalan coffee growers association, showed me its calculation that put production costs of coffee at about $55 a bag. However, coffee growers would have reasons to exaggerate their costs (e.g., in dealing with the government about taxes). A Salvadoran coffee grower told me he calculated his production costs to be $35 a bag. The tax rate is more complicated than indicated here, but 45% of the price above $50 is accurate enough. The legal minimum wage was $1.04 a day and there were reports of some laborers who lived on farms in feudal arrangements (especially in Alta Verapaz) being paid only 50 cents a day. According to my memory, ANACAFE documents showed some 79 plantations in Guatemala producing more than 6,000 bags (about one-third of the crop); about 300 plantations producing from 200 to 6,000 bags (another third); and over 30,000 small producers, who made up the other third. Finally, I am fully cognizant that there are lean years in which agroexporters do not make large profits and that to present an accurate picture of the relative share of capital and labor, profits would have to be averaged over a long period of time. Nevertheless, it is not irrelevant to point out that, according to the political attaché in the U.S. embassy in San Salvador in early 1977, there were families who were making $4 million extra that year because of the coffee boom—and none of the bonanza was going to the workers.

3. American Embassy (Guatemala), "Foreign Economic Trends and Their Implications for the United States," Guatemala, June 1980.

4. Oscar Romero, *La voz de los sin voz* (San Salvador: UCA Editores, 1980), pp. 157, 440; Guatemalan bishops: in Marins et al., *Praxis de los padres de América Latina* (Bogotá: Ediciones Paulinas, 1978), p. 804; Puebla Final Document, nos. 28, 30; cf. nos. 1160, 1207–9, 1260–64. Cf. many episcopal letters in Marins, *Praxis*.

5. The figure of 96% is perhaps too precise, since GNP fluctuated with the war and accurate figures on capital flight are impossible. Jaime Wheelock estimated that $800 million had left the country (*Habla la dirección de la vanguardia* (Managua: Departamento de Propaganda y Educación Política del FSLN, 1981), p. 253.

6. In direct quotations the sexist use of "man" is (regrettably) retained here.

7. FDR, "Plataforma programática del Gobierno Democrático Revolucionario," in Ricardo Sol, *Para entender El Salvador* (San José, Costa Rica: DEI, 1980), p. 146.

8. *Theological Investigations*, vol.14 (New York: Seabury, 1976), pp. 320, 324.

9. Ronald H. Chilcote, *Theories of Comparative Politics: The Search for a Paradigm* (Boulder, Colo.: Westview Press, 1981).

10. The Hinton remark was quoted on National Public Radio program "All Things Considered" during week of June 13, 1982. Hinton was referring specifically to the judicial system, but the overall sense seemed clear. In the same vein, Assistant Secretary of State for Human Rights and Humanitarian Affairs Elliott Abrams repeatedly said that the U.S. had to "remake the political culture of El Salvador" (*Philadelphia Inquirer*, July 27, 1982).

11. Researchers at UCA speculated that it was impossible for all the voters who were claimed to have voted to have been able to do so (1.5 million, although final figures were never released) if it took them two and a half minutes to proceed

through the lines. Although the basis for the calculation was discounted in strong language by Hinton and other U.S. spokespersons, it was little noticed that a legislative aide of Senator Jesse Helms, John Carbaugh, also calculated the necessary time to be three minutes (Thomas P. Anderson and Enrique Baloyra, "Opinion: El Salvador: The Elections of 28 March 1982," *LASA* (Latin American Studies Association) *Newsletter* 13, no. 2 [Summer 1982]: 10).

12. John Peeler has borrowed Robert Dahl's concept of "polyarchy" in examining the "democracies" of Colombia, Costa Rica, and Venezuela; but he says that the polyarchy is a "mode of domination, founded on elitism, inequality, institutionalized inertia and unconcern for the human development of citizens" ("La poliarquía en América Latina: Un estudio comparado de Colombia, Costa Rica y Venezuela" [mimeo], July 1981, p. 32).

13. FDR, Plataforma programática, in Sol, *Para Entender*, pp. 146–47.

14. Marta Harnecker, *Cuba: Los protagonistas de un nuevo poder* (Havana: Editorial de Ciencias Sociales, 1979).

15. IRD, "Christianity and Democracy" (Washington, D.C.: Institute on Religion and Democracy, 1981).

16. IRD brochure, "Religion and Politics: Is There a Problem in Your Denomination?"

17. Guatemala Solidarity Committee of Minnesota, *The Church Martyred: Guatemala* (Minn.: GSCM, 1981), pp. 2–6.

18. Joseph Gremillion, *The Gospel of Peace and Justice* (Maryknoll, N.Y.: Orbis Books, 1976), p. 497.

19. See Joseph Comblin, *Théologie de la révolution*, vol. 1 (Paris: Editions Universitaires, 1970), and *Théologie de la pratique révolutionaire* (Paris: Editions Universitaires, 1974); J.G. Davies, *Christians, Politics, and Violent Revolution* (Maryknoll, N.Y.: Orbis Books, 1976), and their ample bibliographies.

20. Gene Sharp, *The Politics of Nonviolent Action* (Boston: Porter Sargeant Publishers, 1973), 3 vols.

21. Phillip Berryman, "Non-Violence in Central America," *WIN Magazine* 17, no.5 (Mar. 15, 1981). Since attending a seminar led by Hildegarde and Jean Goss-Mayr, Glenn Smiley, and others in Medellín, Colombia, in 1968, the author has followed the development of a network of Latin Americans concerned to find viable forms of nonviolent action.

22. From Gremillion, *The Gospel of Peace and Justice*, p. 396.

23. Puebla Final Document, no. 532, trans. John Drury. In *Puebla and Beyond*, ed. John Eagleson and Philip Scharper (Maryknoll, N.Y.: Orbis Books, 1979), p. 198.

24. Romero, *Voz*, pp. 113–19.

25. Ibid., pp. 156–59 (quotations from p. 157).

26. Ibid., pp. 443, 444.

27. Ibid., p. 441

28. E.g., screenplay on the action by Gabriel García Márquez, *Viva Sandino* (Managua: Editorial Nueva Nicaragua, 1982).

29. Romero, *Voz*, p. 438.

30. Note the subtitle of the Penguin edition of Lernoux's *Cry of the People*: "*The Struggle for Human Rights in Latin America—The Catholic Church in Conflict with U.S. Policy.*"

31. Cf. Hugo Assmann, ed., *Carter y la lógica del imperialismo*, 2 vols. (San

José, Costa Rica: EDUCA, 1978); and Elsa Tamez and Saul Trinidad, *Capitalismo: Violencia y anti-vida*, 2 vols. (San José, Costa Rica: EDUCA, 1978).

32. Segundo, "Derechos humanos, evangelización e ideología," in Assmann, ed., *Carter y la lógica del imperialismo*, vol. 2, p. 348 and passim.

33. *Philadelphia Inquirer*, July 27, 1982.

34. Medellín, Peace, no. 22. Gustavo Gutiérrez, *La fuerza histórica de los pobres, Selección de Trabajos* (Lima, Peru: Centro de Estudios y Publicaciones, 1979), esp. pp. 150-52. Eng. trans.: *The Power of the Poor in History* (Maryknoll, N.Y.: Orbis Books, 1983).

35. See Adamantia Pollis and Peter Schwab, eds., *Human Rights: Cultural and Ideological Perspectives* (New York: Praeger Publishers, 1979), esp. the bibliograpy by John T. Wright. One measure of interest in human rights is the ongoing bibliographical information provided by Internet in Washington D.C. From a specifically Christian viewpoint, see Alfred Hennelly, S.J., and John Langan, S.J., eds., *Human Rights in the Americas: The Struggle for Consensus* (Washington, D.C.: Georgetown University Press, 1982). Margaret E. Crahan, ed., *Human Rights and Basic Needs in the Americas* (Washington, D.C.: Georgetown University Press, 1982), is a companion piece, growing out of the same extensive research and consultation, and addresses policy issues.

36. Pollis and Schwab, "Human Rights: A Western Construct with Limited Applicability," in Pollis and Schwab, eds., *Human Rights* (quotation from p. 14). This whole book is useful in that it brings together examples of other important perspectives.

37. *Pacem in Terris*, nos. 12-27, passim, in Gremillion, *The Gospel of Peace and Justice*, pp. 203-6.

38. See Max Stackhouse, "A Protestant Perspective on the Woodstock Human Rights Project" and Monika Hellwig, "The Quest for Common Ground in Human Rights—A Catholic Reflection," in Hennelly and Langan, *Human Rights*.

39. Philip Rossi, S.J., "Moral Community, Imagination, and Human Rights: Philosophical Considerations on Uniting Traditions," in Hennelly and Langan, *Human Rights*.

40. "Human Rights in Nicaragua," an Americas Watch report, May 1982, lists other reports by the International Commision of Jurists, the Organization of American States, Amnesty International, and the U.S. State Department.

10: BECOMING THE CHURCH OF THE POOR: ISSUES IN CHURCH PRACTICE AND ECCLESIOLOGY

1. On basic Christian communities as "quarries": Luis Carrión, one of the nine Sandinista commanders in the FSLN Directorate, describing the experience of the university community in barrio Rigueiro, quoted in Margaret Randall, *"Del testimonio a la lucha: Cristianos en la revolución Nicaragüense"* (manuscript), p. 234.

2. Jon Sobrino, "The Witness of the Church in Latin America," in Sergio Torres and John Eagleson, eds., *The Challenge of Basic Christian Communities* (Maryknoll, N.Y.: Orbis Books, 1981), pp. 163, 166.

3. Ibid, pp. 181-84 (quotation from 184).

4. Romero, *Voz*, pp. 91-121, esp. pp. 97-112.

5. Ibid., p. 113.

6. Booklets by Kerry Ptacek, Institute for Religion and Democracy, 1981.

7. *Fe cristiana y revolución sandinista en Nicaragua*, proceedings of a UCA seminar held in September 1979.

8. This division into three related meanings is my own.

9. "Los cristianos interpelan a la revolución" (Managua: IHCA-CAV, 1981), p. 9.

10. Pablo Richard, "Identidad eclesial en el proceso revolucionario," in CAV-IHCA, *Apuntes para una teología nicaragüense* (San José: DEI, 1981), pp. 91-104 (quotations from p. 100).

11. From "Iglesia que nace del pueblo—Reflexiones y problemas," by various Latin American theologians (Mexico City: Centro de Reflexión Teológica, 1978), p. 32.

12. Ibid., pp. 35-41, for discussion of the subject.

13. CAV-IHCA, *Apuntes para una teología nicaragüense*, pp. 74-75.

14. "Los cristianos interpelan a la Revolución," passim, esp. pp. 48-71.

15. Decree on Bishops in the Church, nos. 13-16, in Walter Abbott, S.J., ed., *The Documents of Vatican II* (New York: America Press, 1966), pp. 403-8.

16. See index of John Eagleson and Philip Sharper, eds., *Puebla and Beyond: Documentation and Commentary* (Maryknoll, N.Y.: Orbis Books, 1979); among the many entries there is only one about defending justice and human rights (No. 707).

17. Author's interviews in U.S. embassy, Managua, Nicaragua, 1981.

18. *Voz*, p. 193.

19. "Monseñor Romero: Verdadero profeta" (Managua: IHCA-CAV, 1981). See also "Monseñor Romero: Mártir de la liberación. Análisis teológico de su figura y obra," in Romero, *Voz*, pp. 35-62.

20. "Una buena noticia: La Iglesia nace del pueblo latinoamericano," reprinted in *ECA*, no. 353, pp. 161-73. "Iglesia que Nace del Pueblo: Problemas y Perspectivas" (Mexico City: CRT, 1978). Jesús García told the author that the term *iglesia popular* was born in a meeting in Vitoria in Brazil. For other statements see n. 11, above.

21. "Una buena noticia," p. 161.

22. Jon Sobrino, "Resurrección de una iglesia popular," in CRT, *Cruz y Resurrección: Presencia y anuncio de una iglesia nueva* (Mexico City: CRT-Servir, 1978), pp. 83-159, esp. pp. 102-59.

11: THE GOD OF LIFE

1. For Rahner, see the many volumes of *Theological Investigations* (New York, Seabury) articles in *Lexikon für Theologie und Kirche* (Freiburg: Verlag Herder, 1957-65); monographs in the *Quaestiones Disputatae* series; and particularly *Foundations of Christian Faith: An Introduction to the Idea of Christianity* (New York: Seabury, 1978).

2. As examples: Ignacio Ellacuría, *Freedom Made Flesh* (Maryknoll, N.Y.: Orbis Books, 1976); Jon Sobrino, *Christology at the Crossroads* (Maryknoll, N.Y.: Orbis Books, 1978); Hugo Assman, ed., *Carter y la lógica del imperialismo* (San José, Costa Rica: EDUCA, 1978); Tamez and Trinidad, eds., *Capitalismo: Violencia y anti-vida* (San José, Costa Rica: EDUCA, 1978)—both the Assmann and Tamez-Trinidad volumes contain theological contributions; Franz Hinkelammert, *Las armas ideológicas de la muerte;* DEI-CAV, *La lucha de los dioses;* CRT, *Cruz y*

resurrección: Presencia y anuncio de una iglesia nueva; IHCA-CAV, *Fe cristiana y revolución sandinista, y Apuntes para una teología nicaragüense.* In addition other publications of DEI (Departamento Ecuménico de Investigaciones) in Costa Rica might be mentioned as well as a number of articles appearing in *ECA* and other magazines (full data on these titles in bibliography).

3. No theological entries on idolatry were found in Rahner und Höfer, *Lexikon für Theologie und Kirche; Handbuch Theologischer Grundbegriffe;* Leon-Dufour, ed., *Vocabulaire de Théologie Biblique.*

4. Pablo Richard, "Nuestra lucha es contra los ídolos—Teología bíblica," in DEI-CAV, *La lucha de los dioses: Los ídolos de la opresión y la búsqueda del Dios liberador* (San José, Costa Rica: DEI, 1980), pp. 25–32.

5. Jon Sobrino, "La aparición del Dios de Vida en Jesús de Nazaret," in DEI-CAV, *La lucha de los dioses.*

6. Ibid., p. 104.

7. Quoted by Sobrino, from Moltmann, *The Crucified God: The Cross of Christ as the Foundation and Criticism of Christian Theology* (New York: Harper & Row, 1974), p. 127.

8. Christians for the Revolution, "Tiempo de crisis: Tiempo de discernimiento y de gracia—Reflexión pastoral ante el comunicado pastoral de los obispos del 1 de Junio de 1981."

9. Ibid.

10. Leonardo Boff, *Liberating Grace* (Maryknoll, N.Y.: Orbis Books, 1979), p. 6.

11. *Gaudium et Spes*, no. 39, in Abbott, ed., *The Documents of Vatican II*, p. 237.

12. Ibid., nos. 11, 41, in Abbott, ed., *The Documents of Vatican II*, p. 209.

13. Rahner, *Foundations of Christian Faith*, p. 132.

14. Ibid.

15. Boff, *Liberating Grace*, pp. 50, 51.

16. Leonardo Boff, *Jesus Christ Liberator: A Critical Christology for Our Time* (Maryknoll, N.Y.: Orbis Books, 1978); Jon Sobrino, *Christology at the Crossroads: A Latin American Approach* (Maryknoll, N.Y.: Orbis Books, 1978).

17. Romero, *La voz de los sin voz* (San Salvador: UCA Editores, 1980), pp. 362, 363, 364.

18. Ibid., p. 461.

19. Ibid., p. 367.

20. Ellacuría "El pueblo crucificado," in CRT, *Cruz y resurrección* (Mexico City: CRT-Servir, 1978), pp. 49–82.

21. Sobrino, "La aparición del Dios de Vida en Jesús de Nazaret," in DEI-CAV, *La lucha de los dioses*, p. 114.

Bibliography

ARTICLES, DOCUMENTS, REPORTS

Albizúrez, Miguel Ángel. "Luchas y experiencias del movimiento sindical: Período 1976–Junio 1978." *ECA*, no. 356 (June 1978):478–89.

"Alfonso Navarro: Evangelio vrs. opresión." *Búsqueda* 5, no. 15 (March-June 1977):19–34.

American Chamber of Commerce of Guatemala. Bulletin no. 162, May 23, 1980.

American Embassy (Guatemala). "Foreign Economic Trends and Their Implications for the United States: Guatemala," June 1980.

Americas Watch. "Human Rights in Nicaragua." Report, May 1982.

Amnesty International. "A Government Program of Political Murder." Washington, D.C.: Amnesty International, 1981.

———. "Testimony on Guatemala, Submitted to the Subcommittee on International Development Institutions and Finance of the Banking Committee of the U.S. House of Representatives." August 5, 1982.

Anaya, Eugenio C. "Crónica del mes: Mayo 1979." *ECA*, no. 368 (June 1979): 450–52.

———. "Crónica del mes: Junio–Julio 1979." *ECA*, no. 369 (July-August 1979): 711–14.

———. "Crónica del mes: Septiembre–Octubre 1979." *ECA*, no. 371 (October-November 1979): 1001–8.

Anderson, Thomas P., and Enrique Baloyra. "Opinion: El Salvador: The Elections of 28 March 1982," *LASA [Latin American Studies Association] Newsletter* 13, no. 2 (Summer 1982):10–14.

Arriola, Sister Silvia Maribel. Letter in *Brecha* (Mexico), May-June 1981.

Barahona, Elías. "El gobierno monta en Guatemala la ola de crímenes y secuestros, Denuncia un alto funcionario infiltrado." *La República* (Panama), September 4, 1980.

Basic Christian Communities (Comunidades Cristianas de Base), Nicaragua. "Carta abierta de las comunidades cristianas de base." June 1982.

Berryman, Angela. "Guatemalan Refugees: The Terror Continues." Testimony by Angela Berryman, representing the American Friends Service Committee, presented to the Subcommittee on International Development Institutions and Finance, Committee on Banking, Finance, and Urban Affairs of the U.S. House of Representatives, August 5, 1982.

Berryman, Phillip. "Camilo Torres, Revolutionary-Theologian." *Commonweal* 96, no. 7 (April 21, 1972):164–67.

———. "Latin America: 'Iglesia Que Nace del Pueblo.' " *Christianity and Crisis* 41, no. 14 (September 21, 1981).

———. "Latin American Liberation Theology." In *Theology in the Americas*, edited by Sergio Torres and John Eagleson. Maryknoll, N.Y.: Orbis Books, 1981.

———. "Non-Violence in Central America." *WIN Magazine* 17, no. 5 (March 15, 1981): pp. 10–15.

———. "What Happened at Puebla." In *Churches and Politics in Latin America*, edited by Daniel H. Levine. Beverly Hills, Calif.: Sage Publications, 1980.

Booth, John. "Celebrating the Demise of Somocismo: Fifty Recent Spanish Sources on the Nicaraguan Revolution." *Latin American Research Review* 17, no. 1 (1982):173–89.

Burke, Melvin. "El sistema de plantación y la proletarización del trabajo agrícola en El Salvador." *ECA*, nos. 335/336 (September-October 1976):473–86.

Campos, Tómas R. "La iglesia y las organizaciones populares en El Salvador." *ECA*, no. 359 (September 1978):692–702.

Cardenal, Fernando. "Como cristiano revolucionario encontré un nuevo camino." *Nicarauac*, 2nd year, no. 5 (April-June 1981):99–108.

Carranza, Salvador. "Aguilares: Una experiencia de evangelización rural (Septiembre de 1972-Agosto de 1974)." *ECA*, nos. 348/349 (October-November 1977):838–54.

Castro Torres, Carlos Felipe. "Crecimiento de las luchas campesinas en Guatemala: Febrero 1976-Mayo 1978." *ECA*, no. 356 (June 1978):462–77.

Chernow, Ron. "The Strange Death of Bill Woods." *Mother Jones*, May 1979, pp. 32ff.

Christian Coordinating Body in Solidarity with the Struggle of the Guatemalan People (Coordinadora Cristiana de Solidaridad con las Luchas del Pueblo de Guatemala). "Guatemala: Documentos y testimonios de un pueblo en lucha." Mexico: n.p., n.d.

Christians for the Revolution (Cristianos por la Revolución). "Los cristianos interpelan a la Revolución." Managua: IHCA-CAV, 1981.

———. "Tiempo de crisis, Tiempo de discernimiento y de gracia: Reflexión pastoral ante el comunicado pastoral de los obispos del 1 de Junio de 1981."

Church Research and Information Project. "Option for Struggle: Three Documents of Christians for Socialism." New York: Church Research and Information Project, 1974.

Colindres, Eduardo. "La tenencia de la tierra en El Salvador." *ECA*, nos. 335/336 (September-October 1976):463–72.

Committee for Justice and Peace (Comité Pro-Justicia y Paz). "Informe de los principales hechos represivos atribuidos al gobierno de Guatemala, bandas paramilitares y otros." 1982 (mimeo).

Concerned Guatemalan Scholars. "Guatemala: Dare to Struggle, Dare to Win." New York: Concerned Guatemalan Scholars, 1981.

CRIE (Centro Regional de Informaciones Ecuménicas). Mexico City, 1979, "Bibliografía—Puebla."

CUDI (Centro Universitario de Documentación e Información—San Salvador), "Balance Estadístico," year 1, no. 2, August 1980.

Cuellar, Roberto. "Entrevista." *Brecha* (Mexico), May-June 1981, pp. 4ff.

Davis, Shelton. "State Violence and Agrarian Crisis in Guatemala." Paper presented at LASA (Latin American Studies Association) meeting, March 1982, Washington, D.C.

——, and Julie Hodson. "Witness to Political Violence in Guatemala: The Suppression of a Rural Development Program." Boston: Oxfam-America, 1982.

Department of Government Planning, Guatemala (Departamento de Planificación Gobierno de Guatemala). "Plan nacional de desarrollo 1979-1982." Guatemala City: Departamento de Planificación del Gobierno, 1978.

Dodson, Michael, and T. S. Montgomery. "The Churches in the Nicaraguan Revolution." In *Nicaragua in Revolution*, edited by Thomas W. Walker. New York: Praeger Publishers, 1982.

Dougherty, William C., Jr. "U.S. Labor's Role in El Salvador." *AFL-CIO Free Trade Union News* 36, no. 2 (February 1981).

ECA (*Estudios Centroamericanos*). "Amnistía para el Salvador." *ECA*, no. 353 (March 1978):109-12.

——. "División y conflicto en el episcopado Salvadoreño." *ECA*, no. 359 (September 1978):687-89.

——. "El Salvador, Juicio sobre el año 1978." *ECA*, nos. 361/362 (November-December, 1978):865-76.

——. "En busca de un nuevo proyecto nacional." *ECA*, nos. 377/378 (March-April 1980):155-80.

Ellacuría, Ignacio. "El pueblo crucificado: Ensayo de soteriología histórica." In *Cruz y resurrección*, edited by Centro de Reflexión Teológica. Mexico City: CRT-Servir, 1978.

Escobar, Franciso Andrés. "En la linea de la muerte (La manifestación del 22 de Enero de 1980). *ECA*, nos. 375/376 (January-February 1980): 21-35.

FECCAS-UTC. "FECCAS-UTC a los cristianos de El Salvador y Centroamérica." *ECA*, no. 359 (September 1978):776-78.

Forché, Carolyn, and Philip Wheaton. "History and Motivations of U.S. Involvement in the Control of the Peasant Movement in El Salvador: The Role of AIFLD in the Agrarian Reform Process." Washington, D.C.: EPICA, n.d.

Fox, Donald T. "Reporte de la Comisión Internacional de Juristas sobre la Ley de Defensa y Garantía del Orden Público." *ECA*, no. 359 (September 1978): 779-86.

FPL (Fuerzas Populares de Liberación). *Boletín Farabundo Martí*. (International Information Weekly). Nos. 5, 6, 7, 8, 9, 14/15.

García Laviana, Gaspar. "Carta de Navidad." *Nicarauac*, 2nd year, no. 5 (April-June 1981):67ff.

Gómez, Leonel. "Prepared Statement of Leonel Gómez before the Subcommittee on Inter-American Affairs." March 11, 1981 (mimeo).

Grande, Rutilio. "Escritos del Padre Grande." *ECA*, nos. 348/349 (October-November 1977):833-62.

——. "Homilía con motivo de la expulsión del Padre Bernal." *ECA*, nos. 348/349 (October-November 1977).

Guatemala Information Center. "Genocide in El Quiché: A Testimonial of the Persecuted Church." Popular Histories, no. 1.

Hoeffel, Paul Heath. "The Eclipse of the Oligarchs." *New York Times Magazine*, September 6, 1981, pp. 21ff.

IHCA (Instituto Histórico Centroamericano). "Sucesos nacionales." *Encuentro* (UCA review), no. 14, July-December 1978, pp. 7-29.

Illich, Ivan. "The Vanishing Clergyman." *The Critic*, June-July 1967.

Institute for Religion and Democracy. "Christianity and Democracy." Washington, D.C.: IRD, 1981.

Iribarrén, Javier. "La CONIP y el proceso salvadoreño." *Brecha* (Mexico City) May-June 1981, pp. 10-13.

Jerez, César. "El contexto socioeconómico de las decisiónes políticas en el proceso de integración centroamericana." *ECA*, nos. 339/340 (January-February 1977): pp. 5-32.

Jonas, Susanne. "La ayuda externa no ayuda a la integración centroamericana." *Estudios Sociales Centroamericanos,* no. 7 (January-April 1974):34-74.

Krause, Clifford. "Religious Roots of Rebellion in El Salvador." *The Nation*, July 3, 1982, pp. 7-10.

Legal Aid Office (Socorro Jurídico), Archbishopric of San Salvador. "El Salvador: Del genocidio de la junta militar a la esperanza de la lucha insurreccional." Place and date not given; about 1981.

López, Amando, S.J., and Juan B. Arrién, S.J. "El papel de la Iglesia en la coyuntura nacional: 1978." *Encuentro,* no. 14, July-December 1978, pp. 125-38.

López Amezcua, Ignacio. "Una comunión episcopal para la galería." *ECA*, no. 354 (April 1978):250-58.

López Vallecillos, Italo, and Victor Antonio Orellana. "La Unidad Popular y el surgimiento del Frente Democrático Revolucionario." *ECA*, nos. 377/378 (March-April 1980):183-206.

McAnany, Emile. "Television and Crisis: Ten Years of Network News Coverage of Central America." January 1982 (mimeo).

Menéndez Rodríguez, Mario. "La Iglesia de Cristo en armas." *Por Esto* (Mexico City), no. 5 (July 30, 1981):6-13.

Menjivar, Oscar, and Santiago Ruiz. "La transformación agraria en el marco de la transformación nacional." *ECA*, nos. 335/336 (September-October 1976): 487-96.

Molina, Uriel. "El sendero de una experiencia." *Nicarauac*, 2nd year, no. 5 (April-June 1981):17-37.

Nairn, Alan. "Controversial Reagan Campaign Links with Guatemalan Government and Private Sector Leaders." Washington, D.C.: COHA (Council on Hemispheric Affairs), October 30, 1980.

Nicaraguan Bishops Conference. "Jesucristo y la unidad de su Iglesia en Nicaragua." *La Prensa*, January 11, 1981.

———. Pastoral Letter: "Los cristianos están con la Revolución: Carta pastoral de los obispos Nicaragüenses." San José, Costa Rica: DEI, n.d.

———. "Respuesta al FSLN." Dated October 20, 1980. *CRIE*, no. 61 (November 11, 1980):2-6.

"Notes on Guatemala—1979" (mimeo).

Organization of American States, Human Rights Commission (Organización de Estados Americanos, Comisión de Derechos Humanos). "Informe de la OEA Sobre la situación de los derechos humanos en Guatemala." Washington, D.C.: OAS, 1981. Reprinted in *Polémica*, no. 2, November-December 1981.

———. "Informe sobre los derechos humanos en El Salvador." San José, Costa Rica: CIDH, 1979.

Parades, Ivan D. "La situación de la iglesia católica en El Salvador y su influjo social." *ECA*, 1979 (photocopy, number and date not given), pp. 601-14.

Peeler, John. "La poliarquía en América Latina: Un estudio comparado de Colombia, Costa Rica y Venezuela." July 1981 (mimeo).

Pellecer, Luis. "Declaraciónes del P. Luis E. Pellecer" (transcript of television interview).

Petras, James, and Morris H. Manley. "Economic Expansion, Political Crisis and U.S. Policy in Central America." *Contemporary Marxism*, no. 3.

Pollis, Adamantia, and Peter Schwab. "Human Rights: A Western Construct with Limited Applicability." In *Human Rights: Cultural and Ideological Perspectives*, edited by Pollis and Schwab (New York: Praeger Publishers, 1979).

Ptacek, Kerry. "The Catholic Church in El Salvador." Washington, D.C.: Institute for Religion and Democracy, 1981.

———. "Nicaragua: A Revolution against the Church?" Washington, D.C.: Institute for Religion and Democracy, 1981.

Ramírez, Sergio. "El muchacho de Niquinohomo." Managua: Unidad Editorial Departamento de Propaganda y Educación Política del FSLN, 1981.

"Repressive Violence in Guatemala, January 1978-March 1979: Overview and Background" (mimeo).

Retiro Interdenominacional de Pastores Evangélicos de Nicaragua, II. "Declaración de los 500" (mimeo).

Rivas, José M. "Elecciónes presidenciales en Guatemala: 1966-78: Ilegitimidad progresiva del gobierno." *ECA*, no. 356 (June 1978):429-36.

Romero, General Carlos Humberto. "Mensaje al pueblo salvadoreño." *ECA*, no. 345 (July 1977):515-19.

Ruiz, Astor. "Fe cristiana y guerra popular a partir de la experiencia centroamericana." CENCOS (Centro Nacional de Comunicación Social), *Iglesias*, November 1980.

Salvadoran Bishops Conference. "Declaración de cuatro obispos de la Conferencia Episcopal de El Salvador." *ECA*, no. 359 (September 1978):774-75.

Sebastián, Luis de. "Algunas directrices para organizar una economía popular." *ECA*, nos. 377/378 (March-April 1980):207-18.

Secretariat of Social Communication (Secretaría de Comunicación Social), San Salvador. "Los sucesos de San Pedro Perulapán." *ECA*, no. 354 (April 1978): 223-47.

Segundo, Juan Luis, S.J. "Derechos humanos, evangelización e ideología." In *Carter y la lógica del imperialismo*, edited by Hugo Assmann. San José, Costa Rica: EDUCA, 1978.

Selser, Gregorio. "La Iglesia en Guatemala." *Cuadernos de Marcha*, 2nd year, second series, no. 10 (November-December 1980):59-71.

Seminar on the National Reality. "Hacia una economía de transición (Análisis crítico e interpretativo de la Plataforma Programática del Gobierno Democrático Revolucionario en sus aspectos económicos y sociales)." *ECA*, nos. 377/378 (March-April 1980):293-328.

Serrano, Vicente. "Génesis y consolidación del movimiento revolucionario en El Salvador (1930-1980)." *Cuadernos Farabundo Martí*, no. 1 (November 1980): 13-40.

Simon, Walker. "After Global Pressure, Things Go Better with Coke." *Food Monitor*, no. 19 (November-December 1980):5ff.

Smutko, Gregorio. "Cristianos de la costa atlántica en la Revolución." *Nicarauac*, 2nd year, no. 5 (April-June 1981):49-65.

Sobrino, Jon. "La aparición del Dios de Vida en Jesús de Nazaret." In *La lucha de los Dioses*, edited by DEI-CAV. San José, Costa Rica: DEI, 1980.

———. "Evangelización e Iglesia en América Latina." *ECA*, nos. 348/349 (October-November 1977):723-48.

———. "Monseñor Romero: Verdadero profeta." Managua: IHCA-CAV, 1981.

————. "Resurrección de una iglesia popular." In *Cruz y Resurrección*, edited by Centro de Reflexión Teológica. Mexico City: CRT-Servir, 1978.

————. "La unidad y el conflicto dentro de la Iglesia." *ECA*, nos. 348/349 (October-November 1977):787–804.

————. "The Witness of the Church in Latin America." In *The Challenge of Basic Christian Communities*, edited by Sergio Torres and John Eagleson. Maryknoll, N.Y.: Orbis Books, 1981.

Third World Bishops. "Mensaje de los obispos del Tercer Mundo." In *Praxis de los padres de América Latina*, edited by José Marins, et al. (Bogotá: Ediciones Paulinas, 1978), pp. 42–47.

Tobar, Padre Benito. "Origen y peculiaridades de la iglesia que nace del pueblo en El Salvador." CENCOS, Iglesia, November 1980.

Torres, José Miguel. "El cristianismo protestante en la revolución sandinista." *Nicarauac*, 2nd year, no. 5 (April-June 1981):39–47.

Torres-Rivas, Edelberto. "Seven Keys to Understanding the Central American Crisis." *Contemporary Marxism*, no. 3 (Summer 1981), pp. 49–61.

Trujillo, Horacio, and Oscar Menjivar. "Economía y política en la Revolución del 48: Algúnos elementos para su análisis." *ECA*, 361/362 (November-December 1978):877–88.

U.S.A.I.D. (United States Agency for International Development). "Small Farmer Improvement Loan 520-11-190-233, 520:26" (photocopy).

U.S. House of Representatives. "Audiencia del Subcomité de Organizaciónes Internacionales de la Camara (USA) sobre la persecución a la Iglesia en El Salvador, 21 de julio de 1977." *ECA*, no. 345 (July 1977):520–27.

U.S. State Department. "Communist Interference in El Salvador: Special Report No. 80," Feb. 23, 1981. Washington, D.C.: U.S. Government Printing Office, 1981.

————. "El Salvador: The Search for Peace," September 1981. Washington, D.C.: U.S. Government Printing Office, 1981.

Various Theologians. "Iglesia que nace del pueblo: Problemas y perspectivas." Mexico City: CRT, 1978.

————. Una buena noticia: La iglesia nace del pueblo latinoamericano (Contribución a Puebla '78)." *ECA*, no. 353 (March 1978):161–73.

Wheaton, Philip. "Agrarian Reform in El Salvador: A Program of Rural Pacification." Washington, D.C.: EPICA, n.d.

Zaid, Gabriel. "Enemy Colleagues." *Dissent*. Winter 1982.

Zamora, Rubén. "Seguro de vida o despojo?: Análisis político de la transformación Agraria." *ECA*, nos. 335/336 (September-October 1976):511–34.

BOOKS

Abbott, Walter M., S.J., ed. *The Documents of Vatican II*. New York: America Press, 1966.

Adams, Richard Newbold. *Crucifixion by Power: Essays on Guatemalan National Social Structure, 1944–1966*. Austin: University of Texas Press, 1970.

Anderson, Thomas. *Matanza: El Salvador's Communist Revolt of 1932*. Lincoln: University of Nebraska Press, 1971. (Spanish edition: *El Salvador, 1932: Los sucesos políticos*. San José, Costa Rica: EDUCA, 1976.)

Arellano, Jorge Eduardo. *Breve historia de la Iglesia en Nicaragua (1523-1979)*. Managua: n.p., 1980. (This will appear in *Historia de la Iglesia en América Latina*, which is being prepared by CEHILA [Centro de Estudios de la Iglesia en América Latina].)

Arias, Pilar, ed., *Nicaragua: Revolución—Relatos de combatientes del Frente Sandinista*. Mexico City: Siglo XXI, 1980.

Armstrong, Robert, and Janet Shenk. *El Salvador: The Face of Revolution*. Boston: South End Press, 1982.

Assmann, Hugo. *Theology for a Nomad Church*. Translated by Paul Burns. Maryknoll, N.Y.: Orbis Books, 1976. (Spanish edition: *Opresión-Liberación: Desafío a los Cristianos*. Montevideo: Tierra Nueva, 1971.)

————, ed. *Carter y la Lógica del Imperialismo*. 2 vols. San José, Costa Rica: EDUCA, 1978.

Boff, Leonardo. *Jesus Christ Liberator*. Maryknoll, N.Y.: Orbis Books, 1978.

————. *Liberating Grace*. Maryknoll, N.Y.: Orbis Books, 1979.

Bouchey, L. Francis, and Alberto M. Piedra. *Guatemala: A Promise in Peril*. Washington, D.C.: Council for Inter-American Security, 1980.

Broderick, Walter J. *Camilo Torres: A Biography of the Priest-Guerrillero*. Garden City, N.Y.: Doubleday, 1975.

Brown, Delwin. *To Set at Liberty: Christian Faith and Human Freedom*. Maryknoll, N.Y.: Orbis Books, 1981.

Browning, David. *El Salvador: Landscape and Society*. London: Oxford University Press, 1971. (Spanish edition: *El Salvador: La tierra y el hombre*. San Salvador: Ministerio de Educación, 1975.)

Cabarrús, Carlos. *Génesis de una Revolución: Análisis de la organización campesina en El Salvador*. Thesis, 1981. To be published. Mimeo.

Cardenal, Ernesto. *The Gospel in Solentiname*. 4 vols. Translated by Donald Walsh. Maryknoll, N.Y.: Orbis Books, 1976-82. (Spanish edition: *El evangelio en Solentiname*. 2 vols. Salamanca, Spain: Ediciones Sígueme, 1975, 1977.)

Carías, Marco Virgilio, and Daniel Slutsky. *La guerra inútil. Análisis socioeconómico del conflicto entre Honduras y El Salvador*. San José, Costa Rica: EDUCA, 1971.

CELAM (Consejo Episcopal Latinoamericana). *La Iglesia en la actual transformación de América Latina a la luz del Concilio*. Vol. II, *Conclusiones*. Bogotá: CELAM, 1969.

Chilcote, Ronald H. *Theories of Comparative Politics. The Search for a Paradigm*. Boulder, Colo.: Westview Press, 1981.

Colindres, Eduardo. *Fundamentos económicos de la burguesía salvadoreña*. San Salvador: UCA Editores, 1977.

Comblin, Joseph. *Théologie de la pratique révolutionaire*. Paris: Editions Universitaires, 1974.

————. *Théologie de la révolution: Theorie*. Paris: Editions Universitaires, 1970.

CRT (Centro de Reflexión Teológica). *Cruz y resurrección: Presencia y anuncio de una iglesia nueva*. Mexico City: CRT-Servir, 1978.

Davies, J. G. *Christians, Politics, and Violent Revolution*. Maryknoll, N.Y.: Orbis Books, 1976.

Debray, Regis. *Las pruebas de fuego: La crítica de las armas*. Vol. 2. Mexico City: Siglo XXI, 1975. (Translated from French by Felix Blanco from *Les epreuves du feu, La critique des armes*, vol. 2. Paris: Editions du Seuil, 1974.)

DEI (Departamento Ecuménico de Investigaciones). *Centroamérica: Cristianismo y revolución: Documentos de algunas organizaciones populares centroamericanas acerca de la participación de los cristianos en la revolución.* San José, Costa Rica: DEI, 1980.

DEI-CAV (Departamento Ecuménico de Investigaciones-Centro Antonio Valdivieso). *La lucha de los dioses: Los ídolos de la opresión y la búsqueda del Dios Liberador.* San José, Costa Rica: DEI, 1980; Eng. trans.: *The Idols of Death and the God of Life: A Theology.* Maryknoll, N.Y.: Orbis Books, 1983.

Dewart, Leslie. *Christianity and Revolution: The Lesson of Cuba.* New York: Herder and Herder, 1963.

Dombrowski, John et al. *Area Handbook for Guatemala.* Washington, D.C.: U.S. Government Printing Office, 1970.

Dussel, Enrique. *De Medellín a Puebla: Una década de sangre y esperanza (1968–1979).* Mexico City: Edicol, 1979.

Eagleson, John, and Philip Scharper, eds. *Puebla and Beyond: Documentation and Commentary.* Translated by John Drury. Maryknoll, N.Y.: Orbis Books, 1979.

Ellacuría, Ignacio. *Freedom Made Flesh.* Maryknoll, N.Y.: Orbis Books, 1976.

Erdozaín, Plácido. *Archbishop Romero: Martyr of Salvador.* Translated by John McFadden and Ruth Warner. Maryknoll, N.Y.: Orbis Books, 1981. (Spanish edition: *Monseñor Romero: Mártir de la iglesia popular.* San José, Costa Rica: DEI-EDUCA, 1980.)

Fonseca, Carlos. *Bajo la bandera del sandinismo (Textos políticos).* Managua: Editorial Nueva Nicaragua, 1981.

FSLN (Frente Sandinista de Liberación Nacional), Department of Propaganda and Political Education. *Un pueblo alumbra su historia.* Managua: FSLN, 1981.

Galeano, Eduardo. *Guatemala: Occupied Country.* New York: Monthly Review Press, 1967.

García Márquez, Gabriel. *The Autumn of the Patriarch.* Translated by Gregory Rabasa. New York: Harper & Row, 1976.

———. *Viva Sandino* (screenplay). Managua: Editorial Nueva Nicaragua, 1982.

Gibellini, Rosino. *Frontiers of Theology in Latin America.* Maryknoll, N.Y.: Orbis Books, 1979.

González Janzen, Ignacio. *La batalla de El Salvador.* Mexico City: Prolibro, 1981.

Gremillion, Joseph, ed. *The Gospel of Peace and Justice: Catholic Social Teaching since Pope John.* Maryknoll, N.Y.: Orbis Books, 1976.

Grubb, Kenneth G. *Religion in Central America.* London: World Dominion Press, 1937.

Guatemala Solidarity Committee of Minnesota. *The Church Martyred: Guatemala.* GSCM, 1981.

Guerra, Tómas. *El Salvador en la hora de la liberación.* San José, Costa Rica: Editorial Farabundo Martí, 1980.

Gutiérrez, Gustavo. *The Power of the Poor in History.* Translated by Robert Barr. Maryknoll, N.Y.: Orbis Books, 1983. (Spanish edition: *La fuerza histórica de los pobres: Selección de trabajos.* Lima, Peru: CEP [Centro de Estudios y Publaciónes], 1979.)

———. *A Theology of Liberation.* Translated and edited by Sister Caridad Inda and John Eagleson. Maryknoll, N.Y.: Orbis Books, 1973. (Spanish edition: *Teología de la liberación: Perspectivas.* Lima, Peru: CEP, 1971.)

Harnecker, Marta. *Cuba: Los protagonistas de un nuevo poder.* Havana: Editorial de Ciencias Sociales, 1979.

Hennelly, Alfred, S.J., and John Langan, S.J. *Human Rights in the Americas: The Struggle for Consensus.* Washington, D.C.: Georgetown University Press, 1982.

Hinkelammert, Franz. *Las armas ideológicas de la muerte.* 2d ed., rev. San José, Costa Rica: DEI, 1982.

IHCA (Instituto Histórico Centroamericano). *Fe cristiana y revolución sandinista en Nicaragua.* Managua: IHCA, 1979.

IHCA-CAV (Instituto Histórico Centroamericano-Centro Antonio Valdivieso). *Apuntes para una teología nicaragüense: Encuentro de teología, Managua, Nicaragua, 8–14 Septiembre de 1980.* San José, Costa Rica: DEI, 1981.

Institute of Faith and Secularity (Instituto Fe y Secularidad). *Fe cristiana y cambio social en América Latina: Encuentro de El Escorial, 1972.* Salamanca, Spain: Ediciones Sígueme, 1973.

International Bank for Reconstruction and Development (IBRD [World Bank]). *The Economic Development of Guatemala: Report of a Mission Sponsored by the International Bank for Reconstruction and Development in Collaboration with the Government of Guatemala.* Washington, D.C.: IBRD, 1951.

Jonas, Susanne, and David Tobis. *Guatemala.* Berkeley, Calif.: NACLA (North American Congress on Latin America), 1974.

Lernoux, Penny. *Cry of the People: The Struggle for Human Rights in Latin America—The Catholic Church in Conflict with U.S. Policy.* New York: Penguin Books, 1982.

Levine, Daniel H., ed. *Churches and Politics in Latin America.* Beverly Hills, Calif.: Sage Publications, 1980.

Marins, José; Teolide M. Trevisán; Carolee Chanona. *Praxis de los padres de América Latina: Documentos de las conferencias episcopales de Medellín a Puebla (1968–1978).* Bogotá: Ediciones Paulinas, 1978.

Martínez, Ana Guadalupe. *Las cárceles clandestinas de El Salvador. Libertad por el secuestro de un oligarca.* N.p. [El Salvador (?)]: n.p., 1978.

McGovern, Arthur. *Marxism: An American Christian Perspective.* Maryknoll, N.Y.: Orbis Books, 1981.

Melville, Thomas, and Marjorie Melville. *Whose Heaven, Whose Earth?* New York: Alfred A. Knopf, 1971.

Menéndez, Rodríguez, Mario. *El Salvador: Una auténtica guerra civil.* San José, Costa Rica: EDUCA, 1980.

Menjivar, Rafael. *El Salvador: El eslabón mas débil.* San José, Costa Rica: EDUCA, 1981.

Millett, Richard. *Guardians of the Dynasty: A History of the U.S. Created Guardia Nacional de Nicaragua and the Somoza Family.* Maryknoll, N.Y.: Orbis Books, 1977.

Ministry of Planning (Ministerio de Planificación), Nicaragua. *Programa de reactivación económica en beneficio del pueblo.* Secretaría Nacional de Propaganda y Educación Política del FSLN, 1980.

Moltmann, Jürgen. *The Crucified God: The Cross of Christ as the Foundation and Criticism of Christian Theology.* New York: Harper & Row, 1974.

National University of Nicaragua, Social Sciences Department, History Section (Universidad Nacional Autónoma de Nicaragua, Departamento de Ciencias Sociales, Sección de Historia. *Apuntes de historia de nicaragua: Selección de textos.* 2 vols. Managua: UNAN, 1980.

Oliveros, Roberto. *Liberación y teología: Génesis y crecimiento de una reflexión (1966–1976).* Lima, Peru: CEP, 1977.

436   BIBLIOGRAPHY

O'Malley, William J., S.J. *The Voice of Blood: Five Christian Martyrs of Our Time*. Maryknoll, N.Y.: Orbis Books, 1980.

Ortega Saavedra, Humberto. *50 años de lucha sandinista*. Havana: Editorial de Ciencias Sociales, 1980.

Payeras, Mario. *Los días de la selva*. Mexico City: Escuela Nacional de Antropología e Historia, 1981.

Plant, Roger. *Guatemala: Unnatural Disaster*. London: Latin America Bureau, 1978.

Poelchau, Warner, ed. *White Paper Whitewash: Interviews with Philip Agee on the CIA and El Salvador*. New York: Deep Cover Books, 1981.

Pollis, Adamantia, and Peter Schwab, eds. *Human Rights: Cultural and Ideological Perspectives*. New York: Praeger Publishers, 1979.

Rahner, Karl. *Foundations of Christian Faith: An Introduction to the Idea of Christianity*. New York: Seabury Press, 1978.

———. *Theological Investigations*. Vol. XIV. New York: Seabury Press, 1976.

——— and Josef Höfer. *Lexikon für Theologie und Kirche*. Freiburg: Verlag Herder, 10 vols., 1957–65.

Randall, Margaret. "Del testimonio a la lucha. Los cristianos en la revolución nicaragüense" (manuscript).

———, ed. *Todas estamos despiertas: Testimonios de la mujer nicaragüense de hoy*. Mexico City: Siglo XXI, 1980.

Richard, Pablo, and Guillermo Meléndez. *La iglesia de los pobres en América Central: Un análisis socio-político y teológico de la iglesia centroamericana (1960–1982)*. San José, Costa Rica: DEI, 1982.

Romero, Oscar. *La voz de los sin voz: La palabra viva de Monseñor Oscar Arnulfo Romero* (introductions, commentaries, and selection of text by R. Cardenal, I. Martin-Baró, and J. Sobrino). San Salvador: UCA Editores, 1980.

Schlesinger, Stephen, and Stephen Kinzer. *Bitter Fruit: The Untold Story of the American Coup in Guatemala*. Garden City, N.Y.: Doubleday, 1982.

Selser, Gregorio. *Sandino, General de hombres libres*. 2nd edition. San José, Costa Rica: EDUCA, 1979.

Sharp, Gene. *The Politics of Nonviolent Action*. 3 vols. Boston: Porter Sargent Publishers, 1973.

Simon, Laurence R., and James C. Stephens, Jr. *El Salvador Land Reform 1980–1981: Impact Audit* (with 1982 Supplement by Martin Diskin). Boston: Oxfam-America, 1982.

Sobrino, Jon, S.J. *Christology at the Crossroads*. Translated by John Drury. Maryknoll, N.Y.: Orbis Books, 1978. (Spanish edition: *Cristología desde América Latina*. Mexico City: Centro de Reflexión Teológica, 1976.)

Sol, Ricardo. *Para entender El Salvador*. San José, Costa Rica: EDUCA, 1980.

Somoza, Anastasio, and Jack Cox. *Nicaragua Betrayed*. Belmont, Mass.: Western Islands, 1980.

Suñol, Julio. *Insurrección en Nicaragua: La historia no contada*. San José, Costa Rica: Editorial Costa Rica, 1981.

Tamez, Elsa, and Saul Trinidad. *Capitalismo: Violencia y anti-vida*. 2 vols. San José, Costa Rica: EDUCA, 1978.

Torres, Sergio, and John Eagleson, eds. *The Challenge of Basic Christian Communities*. Maryknoll, N.Y.: Orbis Books, 1981.

———. *Theology in the Americas*. Maryknoll, N.Y.: Orbis Books, 1976.

Torres-Rivas, Edelberto. *Interpretación del desarrollo socioeconómico centroamericano*. 3rd edition. San José, Costa Rica: EDUCA, 1973.

UCA (Universidad Centroamericana José Simeón Cañas). *Rutilio Grande: Mártir de la evangelización rural*. San Salvador: UCA Editores, 1978.

U.S. House of Representatives. *Human Rights in Guatemala* (Hearing before the Subcommittees on Human Rights and International Organizations and on Inter-American Affairs of the Committee on Foreign Affairs, House of Representatives, Ninety-seventh Congress, First Session, July 30, 1981. Washington, D.C.: U.S. Government Printing Office, 1981.

————. *Human Rights in Nicaragua, Guatemala and El Salvador: Implications for U.S. Policy* (Hearings before the Subcommittee on International Organizations of the Committee on International Relations, House of Representatives, Ninety-fourth Congress, Second Session, June 8 and 9, 1976). Washington, D.C.: U.S. Government Printing Office, 1976.

Walker, Thomas W. *Nicaragua: The Land of Sandino*. Boulder, Colo.: Westview Press, 1981.

————, ed. *Nicaragua in Revolution*. New York: Praeger Publishers, 1982.

Washington Office on Latin America. *Conference on Land Tenure in Central America*. Washington, D.C.: WOLA, 1981.

Whelan, James R. *Through the Looking Glass: Central America's Crisis*. Washington, D.C.: Council for Inter-American Security, 1980.

Woodward, Ralph Lee, Jr. *Central America: A Nation Divided*. New York: Oxford University Press, 1976.

INTERVIEWS

The following people were formally interviewed by the author for this book. In addition to those listed below, many others were consulted and much of the material in this book is based on information acquired during the author's work in Central America (1976–80). Interviewers are grouped by country. When interviews were held in another country, the site is noted.

Nicaragua

Agudelo, William (founding member of the Solentiname community), July 1981.

Aguirre, Luis (lay leader of the parish in OPEN 3 barrio), July 1981.

Aragón, Rafael (Spanish Dominican priest, doing pastoral work), February 1982.

Arellano, Luz Beatriz (sister, working at Centro Antonio Valdivieso), July 1981.

Bravo, José Ernesto (priest and diocesan official, diocese of Estelí), July 1981.

Carvallo, Bismarck (priest and press secretary for Archbishop Obando and archdiocese of Managua), February 1982.

Cortés, Benjamín (program director, CEPAD), July 1981.

Iacomelli, Mario (Franciscan priest in parish of Fatima, subsequently transferred), July 1981.

Jiménez, Félix (Spanish parish priest in 14 de Septiembre barrio), July 1981.

Macías, Edgard (leader of Social Christian party; vice-minister of labor; subsequently left office and left Nicaragua), July 1981.

Quintanilla, Felix (pastor of Jinotega; president of ACLEN), July 1981.

Sambola, Agustín (priest doing pastoral work on Atlantic coast, the region of his birth), July 1981.

Virgil, Miguel Ernesto (minister of housing; layman active in Christians for the Revolution), July 1981.

El Salvador

Alas, José Inocencio (formerly pastor in Suchitoto; prominent in pastoral renewal), January 1982, Washington, D.C.

Bracamonte, Ricardo (organizer in ANDES), 1981, Philadelphia.

Cuellar, Roberto (director of Socorro Jurídico, Legal Aid Office, Archbishopric of San Salvador), July 1981, Mexico City.

Dada, Héctor (economist; Christian Democratic leader; Junta member), January 1982, Mexico City.

Ellacuría, Ignacio (Jesuit theologian; dean and rector of UCA; editor of ECA), July 1981, Managua, Nicaragua.

Erdozaín, Plácido (priest: leader in CONIP), July 1981, Managua, Nicaragua.

García, Marianela (director of Salvadoran Human Rights Commission; killed in Suchitoto, El Salvador, March 1983), July 1981, Mexico City.

Hernández, Luz (sister in pastoral work; subsequently working with popular organizations), July 1981, Mexico City.

Moreno, Rafael (Jesuit; Director of Social Communications Office, Archdiocese of San Salvador, under Archbishop Romero), June 1981, New York City.

Sánchez, Carlos (Baptist pastor in San Salvador), July 1981, Mexico City.

Guatemala

Calel, Antonio (CUC leader and organizer), July 1981, Mexico City.

Curtin, James (Maryknoll priest in Guatemala since the 1940s, working with highlands Indians), January 1982, Maryknoll, New York.

Esquivel, Julia (laywoman; editor of *Diálogo*), Summer 1981, Philadelphia.

Falla, Ricardo (Jesuit anthropologist), July 1981, Managua.

Gurriarán, Javier (pastor in Nebaj, Quiché), July 1981, Managua.

Gurriarán, Luis (priest who worked in Ixcán and Quiché), July 1981, Managua.

LaRue, Frank Rafael (labor lawyer; leader of Justice and Peace Committee), Summer 1981, Washington, D.C.

Pérez, Alicia (CUC organizer), July 1981, Mexico City.

Reilly, Charles (political scientist; Maryknoll priest in Guatemala during the 1960s), Summer 1981, Washington, D.C.

Rondo, Margaret (field representative of Catholic Institute for International Relations, London), 1982, Philadelphia.

Schmidt, Siena (sister in pastoral work from mid-1960s to late 1970s), Spring 1981, Austin, Texas.

Sibley, Anna and Don (Presbyterians doing agricultural development and pastoral work in Guatemala from early 1960s to 1981), Spring 1982, Philadelphia.

Theologians and Social Scientists

Cabestrero, Teófilo (Spanish theologian working at Centro Antonio Valdivieso, Managua), February 1982.

Dussel, Enrique (Argentine philosopher, theologian, historian), February 1982, Mexico City.

García, Jesús (Mexican leader in social apostolate), January 1982.

Gorostiaga, Xabier (Panamanian economist, Ministry of Planning and INIES), July 1981 and February 1982, Managua.

Hernández Pico, Juan (sociologist and theologian; director of Jesuit seminarians in Central America, with broad experience in the region), July 1981, Managua.

Richard, Pablo (Chilean biblical scholar and theologian; director of DEI, San José, Costa Rica), February 1982, Managua.

Vidales, Raul (Mexican theologian), January 1982, Mexico City.

Index

441